ECONOMIC DEMOCRACY

ECONOMIC DEMOCRACY

The Political Struggle of the Twenty-first Century

J.W. Smith

M.E. Sharpe
Armonk, New York
London, England

Library of Congress Cataloging-in-Publication Data

Smith, J. W., 1930–
Economic democracy : the political struggle of the twenty-first century /
J.W. Smith.
p.   cm.
Includes bibliographical references and index.
ISBN 0-7656-0468-X (alk. paper)
1. Free enterprise—History.   2. Free trade—History.
3. Capitalism—History.   4. Democracy—History.   5. International
economic relations—History.   I. Title.
HB95.S587   2000
330.12'2—dc21   99-16254
CIP

Printed in the United States of America

The paper used in this publication meets the minimum requirements of
American National Standard for Information Sciences—
Permanence of Paper for Printed Library Materials,
ANSI Z 39.48-1984.

∞

BM (c)   10   9   8   7   6   5   4   3   2   1

Contents

Foreword   ix
Acknowledgments   xi
Introduction   3

PART I. EXTERNAL TRADE: WORLD TRADE STRUCTURED FOR SECURITY OF POWERFUL NATIONS ENTAILS INSECURITY FOR WEAK NATIONS

1   The Secret of Free Enterprise Capital Accumulation   23

2   The Violent Accumulation of Capital Is Firmly Rooted in History:
     Establishing the Underlying Principles of Twentieth-Century ''Free Trade''   33

3   Imposing a Belief System Under Which the Unwitting Willingly Hand
     Their Wealth to the Cunning   41

4   The Defeat of Napoleon at Waterloo Eliminated France as a Major Threat
     to British Trade   51

5   World Wars, Trade Wars: Battles Over Who Decides the Rules of
     Unequal Trade   57

6   The World Breaking Free Frightened the Security Councils of Every
     Western Nation   63

7   Suppressing the Former Colonial World's Break for Economic Freedom   94

8   Creating Enemies for the Masses: The Inquisitions of the Middle Ages Were,
     and the Inquisitions of Today Still Are, to Prevent Democratic Choice   114

9   Suppressing the Freedom of Others under the Flag of Freedom:
     Twentieth-century Inquisitions   125

PART II. EXTERNAL TRADE: CAPITAL DESTROYING CAPITAL

10   The IMF/World Bank/GATT/NAFTA/WTO/MAI/Military Colossus:
     The Enforcers of Structural Adjustments and Unequal Trades   143

11   The IMF/World Bank/GATT/NAFTA/WTO/MAI/Military Colossus:
     Emerging Corporate Mercantilism   150

12   IMF/World Bank/GATT/NAFTA/WTO/MAI Structural Adjustments:
     Impoverishing Labor and Eventually Capital   158

13   Unequal Trades in Agriculture   166

14   Developing World Loans, Capital Flight, Debt Traps, and Forgiveness of
     Unjust Debt   174

15   Multiplier Factor: Accumulating Capital Through Capitalizing Values of
     Externally Produced Wealth   181

16   Japan's Post–World War II Defensive Economic Warfare Plan   188

17   Japanese/Chinese/Southeast Asian Post–World War II Development:
     An Accident of History and a Crisis for Western Imperial Centers of Capital 192

18   Capital Destroying Capital   195

19   A New Hope for the World   201

**PART III. EXTERNAL TRADE: SHARING TECHNOLOGY WITH THE WORLD
THROUGH COOPERATIVE CAPITALISM: THE ROUTE TO WORLD PEACE
AND PROSPERITY**

20   The Earth's Capacity to Sustain Developed Economies   207

21   The Political Structure of Sustainable World Development   213

22   Sustainable World Development: Equal Free Trade as Opposed to Unequal
     Free Trade   221

23   Sharing Technology with the World Through Cooperative Capitalism:
     A Grand Strategy for World Peace and Prosperity   235

PART IV. INTERNAL TRADE: ECONOMIC RIGHTS FOR ALL PEOPLE THROUGH ELIMINATION OF SUBTLE MONOPOLIES

24   Subtly Monopolizing Land   245

25   Subtly Monopolizing Society's Tools (Technology) Through Stock Markets and
     Patents   265

26   Subtly Monopolizing Money   290

27   Subtly Monopolizing Information   314

28   Media to Empower the Powerless   337

Conclusion: A Grand Strategy for Cooperative Capitalism in the Twenty-first Century   343
Bibliography   349
Index   367
About the Author   381

Foreword

At the pivotal point of each age, scholarship comes forward that becomes the defining template of the age to come. This is such a work of scholarship. It is a work that explains the creation of today's world, both its marvels and its violence and misery. Fortunately, it does not leave us with that analysis; it goes on to define what must be done in the future so we all may enjoy the fruits and comforts provided by the social productive capacity that is the property of us all.

History is written by the conquerors but there have always been the intellectual dissenters who have shaken the edifice erected by power and wealth. Jean Jacques Rousseau, Friedrich List, and Karl Marx were such voices, as were America's Thorstein Veblen and Henry George. At times these voices were muffled by the drumbeat of the cheerleaders for the dominant ideological explanation of reality. But, as Dr. Smith demonstrates, these unapproved philosophies are reexamined as each crisis returns to shatter our security and faith in the orthodox explanations.

Smith examines the economic basis of the history of Imperial Civilization. His examination of the precursor configuration of society just prior to the advent of the Industrial Revolution reveals the configuration that is with us even now. Cities of the Middle Ages monopo-

lized the means of production to themselves and conquered and controlled the source of raw materials and the markets in the countryside. Through financial, technological, and military power, allied imperial centers of capital control the present world, their countryside, by the same methods and for the same reasons. Smith laboriously outlines the changing verbal coloration of this chameleon through each age and documents that its configuration has not changed.

This serious academic study documents in detail the strategies and techniques whereby a small part of the world's population consumes the majority of the world's resources.

Fewer than 500 people now have more wealth than more than half of the earth's population. This is an astounding condition. That this is only known by scholars who study obscure statistics of economics attests to what Smith documents: the intense monopolization of all structures of modern society, especially information, by those who own the bulk of it.

The masses of society have struggled for centuries to establish the rights that some of us now enjoy. Labor rights, political rights, women's rights, and human rights are now a popular item of interest in all countries, even though control of society by the masses is waning. Instructively, in the United States, through the sleight of hand of the money that finances politics, political control has incrementally moved toward the one-half of one percent of the population whose wealth in 1995 roughly equaled that of the lower 90 percent of society.

Those same people have guided the removal of political control from the level of the voters to more and more rarefied levels, ultimately to what Smith refers to as the IMF/World Bank/GATT/NAFTA/WTO/MAI/military colossus. As he describes, this is the legal and policing framework of a functioning, worldwide, corporate-controlled empire.

The value of Smith's scholarship is that he not only reveals the heretofore unrecognized forces that have created the present world, but he goes beyond that to paint a clear and concise picture of the future world. In a world in which we are told there is scarcity and therefore poverty, Smith documents the fact that only part of the money spent on military and economic warfare since the close of World War II could have developed the entire presently "underdeveloped world." In a time in which those who inhale the world's wealth for speculation, military

hardware, and economic warfare tell us there is no money for human needs, Smith documents there is an abundance of money and lays out specific and reasonable plans for providing for the world's human needs. Simply stated, one of the great values of this work is that it demonstrates in reasonable terms that there are real and legitimate solutions to the problems of housing, food, environment, and peace.

All students who read this work will understand that the world does have a future. There are reasonable solutions. The way that those solutions will be achieved is that the people of the earth will take control of their collective destiny and that the activities of society will be directed toward our common goal of the care of all of human society and the earth. Thus, Smith brings into focus the urgent fact that economic democracy must be the next claim of the world's masses, in order to create full human rights and to institute policies beneficial to the collective destiny rather than profit and power for a few.

William H. Kötke
Author, *The Final Empire*

Acknowledgments

This treatise, like all knowledge and accomplishments, is the result of many people's thoughts and efforts. My special thanks go to the hundreds of authors and reporters who each had a special window on the world, knew that what they viewed was of importance, and had the talent and courage to express it. Their work was the hard part, and, in comparison, synthesizing their clear views of reality into a broad picture of the world economic and political landscape was easy.

Special thanks go to M.E. Sharpe, their senior editor Sean M. Culhane, his assistant Esther Clark, and copy editor Barbara Chamberlain. William H. Kotke, author of the impressive *Final Empire*, took the pressure off the final manuscript preparation and his forthcoming books are something we will be watching for. Ralph McGehee and his twelve-megabyte database on sources were indispensable. The support of the many friends at the San Luis Obispo Unitarian Church, especially William and Ann Furtick, is greatly appreciated. Mr. Petru Dumitriu, United Nations Permanent Mission for Romania, provided important support.*

Crucial statistics were provided by Professor Seymour Melman of Columbia University (*Prof-its Without Production*), Greg Bishak of the National Commission for Economic Conversion and Disarmament, Professor David Gordon (Bowles, Gordon, and Weisskopf), Professor Robert Blain of Southern Illinois University, and Arjun Makhijani of the Institute for Energy and Environmental Research.

The faith and advice of my doctoral committee (Professors Marvin Surkin, Stanley Aronowitz, and Tom O'Connell; Dr. Colin Greer; Mr. Richard Barnet; and Ms. Ingrid Lehmann) were greatly appreciated and this project would never have been completed without the credits and support of The Union Institute. Professors Ekema Manga, Nancy Owens, Sylvia Hill, and Rhoda Linton of The Union were especially helpful as was Bill Elison, social science librarian at the University of Montana's Mansfield Library.

The support of *Earth Island Journal* Senior Editor Gar Smith is sincerely appreciated as is the encouragement of Frances Moore Lappé and Professor Ismail Sharriff, Economics Chair at the University of Wisconsin. I thank Professor Richard Hienberg for suggesting this book's name. The support of Fred Rice will always be remembered. Bill Ellis, founding editor of TRANET, provided encouragement. The support of my friend Professor William Alexander of California Polytechnic (retired) is appreciated

*Professor Hillar D. Newman Jr. offered crucial advice while the manuscript was being finalized.

and the advice of author Michael Parenti was followed.

Bob Swann of The Schumacher Society, William F. Hixson, William Krehm, Cliff Cobb of Redefining Progress, and freelancer Robert Carroll provided crucial advice on money. Professor Tom Arysman, Joe Yarkin, and Clark Branch of Antioch College gave enormous support and advice.

Before they took off for a new life in Australia, Jay and Sue McCadden were crucial in helping me understand the complexities of my computer. Ray Miklas and Pete Gannon (*www.stuffguys.com*) now do that job and do it well. Susan and Mark Coward and their Slonet group and Bob Banner of *Hopedance Magazine* were more helpful than they realize. Emanuel Wongibe of Cameroon and my longtime friend Jack Ferguson have been consistent friends and supporters, as has Franz Nahrada, of Vienna, Austria.

The talents of editors Priscilla Pichè and Terri Dunivant were greatly appreciated. My first editor Michael Kriesberg was possibly the most crucial support of all.

Last, and most important, I wish to dedicate this book to my children, Betty, Ada, Patti, and Cynthia, and grandchildren Sam C., Will, Stephan, and Sam O. I hope that this work will contribute to their understanding of the world.

ECONOMIC DEMOCRACY

Introduction

Eliminating poverty is not philosophically complicated: Eliminate the monopolization of land, technology, and finance capital and equalize pay for equally productive work, both within internal economies and between trading nations. Once all nations and all people have access to technology and their labor is paid equally for equally productive work, the buying power of labor in different nations, and within nations, will equalize.

So long as all have access to land and technology as outlined herein, those monopolies cannot reconstitute themselves and the huge overcharges which lay claim to the wealth produced by others will disappear. The managers of capital will be under such intense competition that the incompetent will quickly disappear, economic efficiency will rise steeply, and the competent will be held to a fair profit. That fair profit will then be recognizable for what it really is, their fair wages.

It is those inequalities of pay for equal work which create the poles of an extremely wealthy few and an impoverished many. Following the currency collapses of the several once-robust Asian and Latin American economies in 1997–98, equally productive labor's pay in the developing world dropped to 10 percent that of workers in the developed world. This is not just a tenfold difference in buying power. As will be seen in our opening chapter, wealth accumulates exponentially with the wage differential between equally productive labor. That tenfold differential in wage rates translates into a one hundred-fold differential in potential wealth accumulation power, and accumulated wealth (capital) is the engine of capitalism. Indeed, if unequal pay for the equally productive work of weak nations were reduced to a 50 percent pay differential, the potential wealth accumulated by the high-paid nations in direct trades with low-paid labor nations would be reduced from the current wealth accumulation potential of one hundred times to a potential of only four times.

Suppression of the Freedom of Others Through Denial of Their Economic Rights Is the Untold Secret of "National Security" and the "National Interest"

Early capital formation began with European city-states monopolizing technology through militarily destroying the primitive industries of the countryside and forcing those villagers to sell their raw produce to the city and purchase back from them the manufactured products. The Europeans battled for nearly 800 years over who would own industrial capital, who would have the right to labor with those tools of production, and who would control trade. Each

3

center of capital required a "countryside" to provide it with raw materials and markets. Each center of capital controlled its "countryside" as best it could to maintain a low price for raw material "imports" and a high price for manufactured "exports."

This control of trade developed during the pre-industrial era and was not only essential for the security of city-states, states, nations, and finally empires, but was the foundation for the accumulation of great wealth and power. The loss of freedom, both political and economic, in the dependent colonial nations in the eighteenth and nineteenth centuries was specifically the result of the need for imperial centers of capital to control resources crucial for their survival, wealth, and power.

This is the meaning of the terms "national security" and "national interest" which we hear so much; economic security is normally the subject, not military security. Thus, the true meaning of "national security" of powerful nations is the control of an economic empire of subject states. The strategies through which this is carried out become "national security secrets." It is the trumpeting of peace, freedom, justice, rights, democracy, and majority rule that requires that those Grand Strategies for controlling other people and their resources be kept secret. What is practiced is the total antithesis of what is preached.

All of us have known all our life that the Managers of State have "secrets" and we all accept this as normal and right. The "we" includes the lower echelons of government, the media, the university system, and even members of Congress not privy to these secrets who have not taken an oath of secrecy. Only the inner sanctums of the national government (the National Security Council, the State Department, the Joint Chiefs of Staff, the intelligence agencies, and members of congress with security clearances [the primarily nameless and faceless "they" deciding our destiny]) know what those secrets are and they are sworn to secrecy. Those employed in the diplomatic corps, intelligence agencies, and the military carrying out those secret tasks are also sworn to secrecy and face severe penalties for violating that oath.

We all understand that dictatorships have secrets because they do vile and unjust things that they do not want known. But what could be so secret in democratic societies where governments are supposed to be employees of the people? Quite simply, most wealthy societies have very few resources and even the resource-wealthy American consumer society is dependent upon resources and markets throughout the world. The secret that cannot be told is that the wealth of an imperial center requires controlling the "countryside" to provide cheap resources: the minerals, timber, fuel, and fibers necessary for a comfortable society. Increasingly, that dependency extends to products manufactured with cheap labor on the periphery. Thus the terms "national security" and "national interest" we hear so much about, and we accept those spoken words as all we are entitled to know.

There is only one reason "we the people" are not entitled to know what those policies "for our national security" and "in our national interest" are: if known, they would create greater *insecurity* for they are against the best interests of, and they lay claim to, what are properly the rights of people in the "countryside" providing those crucial resources and cheap labor. Such claims seem normal and right only when considering the rights of those within a nation or alliance of nations whose well-being depends upon the resources and cheap labor of their "countryside." As soon as one steps outside the borders of an alliance and into the world of those being dispossessed of their resources and production of their labors, it becomes obvious that these dispossessions are neither just nor right.

The secret of the more powerful nations is that their Managers of State do not practice what they preach. Instead of permitting democracy to function on the periphery of empire (their countryside), they must subtly and secretly control those weaker nations in order to control those crucial resources and markets. We will be addressing in depth this simple secret of the inner sanctums of governments. It is the reason for the great wealth of resource-poor, but powerful, nations and the impoverishment of resource-rich, but weak, nations. No wonder it has to be kept secret even from most members of Congress, academics, and the media.

Control of other nations has functioned for so many centuries under so many excuses that most, even in the inner sanctums of government, are unaware of this fundamental secret: the imperial centers of capital are claiming a large share of what rightfully belongs to the impoverished on the periphery. This truth has been hidden all these centuries through the demonization of other leaders and other nations to justify the violence required to maintain the wealth of the world moving towards the imperial centers. Other nations have been demonized so much, and for so long, that we take it as a given that they are inherently bad and we do not look beyond those created belief systems to the struggles of those peripheral countries for their own freedom to control their own destiny.

Why should we? The struggles of those nations to gain, or maintain, their independence is described to us as the violence of dictators slaughtering their own people, the most threatening political consolidations as plans to rule the world. Those struggles for control of their own destiny, democratic revolutions (misnamed as insurgencies), thus become the very proof that other leaders and other nations are those demons. After all, we are taught that it is they who depend upon us and it is they who should emulate us, not that it is we who are dependent upon their resources and markets.

There is a germ of truth in all we are told. Historically, the resources of the losers of these wars enriched the lives of those who won and *realists* recognize how crucial those resources are. But social scientists recognize the enormous waste of the systems of production and distribution, and that the wars they engender are wasting a large share of those precious resources as well as causing rapid destruction and pollution of the waters, soils, and ecosystems. Although believing it is always other nations that are the aggressor, not their nation, most people understand that, if this continues, powerful nations battling— or the wastes of mass production and mass consumption—may eventually destroy the world. To avoid that, we need only restructure from the violence of neomercantilism (metamorphosed to corporate imperialism) monopolizing the world's resources into all the world's people sharing those resources through cooperative capitalism. Once that choice is made, all need for national secrets disappears and the goals of all— world peace, sustainable development, and elimination of poverty—can be attained, and all while rebuilding and protecting the world's soils and ecosystems.

Professors and Intellectuals Are Conscientious and Sincere

Professors are conscientious and sincerely want to teach true history, honest economics, and honest political science. However, when a society is under extreme threat, such as the Managers of State of the imperial centers of capital were all through the Cold War, honest expressions of threatening thoughts are not permitted in the mainstream of these soft sciences. Honest analysis can be found at the margins but those are effectively "voices in the wilderness." Quality professors and intellectuals who could, and did, challenge the Cold War belief systems being imposed upon the world as a cover for those suppressions of economic freedom were stripped out of the universities and the media or were silenced.[1]

Now that the Cold War is over, opposing thought is surfacing, but those thoughts are only a whisper against the thunder of Social Control belief systems that have been carefully cultivated by the Managers of State of powerful nations for forty years. Biased and compliant historians of the winners of the hot wars—wars over who will set the rules of unequal trade and thus who will be wealthy and powerful—wrote this history and left out the real causes of those wars. We will be addressing in depth how these were battles over who will have the advantage of unequal trades.

The CIA's "Mighty Wurlitzer" Creating Reality for America and Much of the World

Through the expansion of empires in the nineteenth century, the world had become the "countryside" for the European centers of capital. The old imperial centers of capital broke themselves in World Wars I and II, battling over the world's wealth. America, the newest imperial center of capital, was at that time the only intact center of capital. The frightened leaders of the old imperial nations ultimately handed the baton to the United States to keep the entire world from gaining its *economic freedom*, and America has done that job well.

The risk to the imperial world was primarily the loss of the former colonial world and its precious resources, but to maintain control of those economies it was essential that the influence of the once rapidly developing former Soviet Union be contained. If the Soviet Union successfully developed, that success would be a beacon for historians, social scientists, and intellectuals worldwide—that history would be written, those economic and political philosophies would be followed—and controlling the rest of the world would be impossible.

As the Cold War was being won, Peter Coleman, author of *Liberal Conspiracy*, gained complete access to the archives of the Congress for Cultural Freedom, an American and European writers' support group that had been covertly established by the Central Intelligence Agency (CIA). The path to easy publication of books and articles throughout the "free" world was through this worldwide, CIA-orchestrated and -funded network:

> Five years after their victory in 1945, the Western democracies were about to lose the battle for Europe, but this time to Stalinist totalitarianism instead of Nazis. To combat this prospect, an intellectual guerrilla group was formed: over one hundred European and American writers and intellectuals met in Berlin to establish the Congress for Cultural Freedom to resist the Kremlin's sustained assault on Western and liberal values. During the 1950s the Congress spread throughout the world, creating a network of affiliated national committees, a worldwide community of liberal intellectuals fiercely committed to democratic governance, but supported by grants which, unknown to *most* of them, originated in the Central Intelligence Agency. Through the Congress's influential publications, conferences, and inter-

national protests, it kept the issues of Soviet to- talitarianism and liberal anti-Communism alive in a largely hostile environment. . . . It was finally dissolved in 1967 amid the revelations of its funding by the CIA.[2]

Coordination of the writings of Western authors was only one of the many ''black ops'' and covert actions, occasionally breaking out into overt actions, which became the hidden history of the Cold War. That hidden history was first exposed by the Church and Pike Congressional Committees in 1975 and 1976 and by many good researchers and reporters since. The CIA had its own wire service and its own publishing companies. It set up and supported magazines, newspapers, and radio stations. It established the largest news conglomerate in West Ger- many and other major media in many countries. Canned Cold War editorials were prepared and sent to large and small newspapers all over the world. These editorials were available for any editor to restructure as his or her own creation. Large independent think tanks were established, funded, and staffed with ideological supporters, as were think tanks within universities.

CIA-established and -funded foundations were only one of the many financial conduits that provided the funds for this immense oper- ation. The CIA's covert propaganda budget throughout the Cold War exceeded that of UPI, AP, and Reuters even as those news services were the unwitting primary carriers of its care- fully crafted views of the world. That the CIA offered reporters news scoops in exchange for publication of fraudulent articles tells us some of the leading columnists in the world were planting this nonsense. If they were not already successful, their scoops would be so sensational they would rise quickly to the top. In fact, some well-known Washington reporters social- ized with the Managers of State, knew well

that the ''Grand Strategy'' was to massively misinform the nation, cooperated with spread- ing that misinformation, and never breathed a word.

The powerful were writing history to main- tain control of the thoughts of the masses well into the future (the intention was, and still is, forever). Unless the process is fully exposed, sincere researchers will forever be using these published accounts as sources to write history. In addition, intelligence agencies of most major nations were simultaneously producing support- ing propaganda. In fact, the OSS and CIA learned from Britain's MI6. This orchestrated propaganda machine was eventually described by the CIA itself as its ''Mighty Wurlitzer.''[3]

The route to being well-published and well- known was through parroting this intelligence service created view of the world. Certainly most writers and reporters had no contact with the Congress for Cultural Freedom, but the Cold War hysteria created by the intelligence serv- ices—and government press releases—left them no options but parroting the same line. Thus, almost every political or economic writer and columnist was busy creating the literature/ historical base to contain the Soviet Union and protect the current power structure.

These gross fabrications and crafted propa- ganda provided a firm foundation for the social- control belief systems of the Cold War and are now not only a major part of Western literature and history, *they are Western literature and his- tory.* It is to the credit of conscientious academ- ics that they attempted to stand up and tell the American people the truth, but they were quickly silenced by McCarthyism and the House Un-American Activities Committee.

The destruction of the careers of 300-plus blacklisted Hollywood stars and writers—as was pointed out during the March 21, 1999,

Academy Awards when the recipient of an Oscar was acknowledged by all major media as having testified against his friends to the House Un-American Activities Committee—provides just a hint of the thousands of professors and intellectuals whose careers were destroyed, badly damaged, or severely restricted. As these conscientious voices were silenced, the careers of academics, reporters, and writers parroting the misinformation of the CIA's "Mighty Wurlitzer" soared. Little did they know that, just like the hard right (Aryan Nations, Posse Comitatus, John Birch Society, etc.), which all respectable academics know better than to source, they were, unwittingly, creating their own reality and then referencing each other.

Control of the masses required control of governments through control of information. Ralph McGehee was a career CIA agent who spent the last few years of his career studying CIA archives. He concluded:

> The CIA is not now nor has it ever been a central intelligence agency. It is the covert action arm of the President's foreign policy advisers. In that capacity it overthrows or supports foreign governments while reporting "intelligence" justifying those activities. It shapes its intelligence . . . to support presidential policy. Disinformation is a large part of its covert responsibility, and the American people are the primary target of its lies.[4]

To target the American people, American intelligence services must simultaneously target those the masses look up to for designing and interpreting our world, Congress and academics. McGehee claimed that, "He has never once seen a CIA official tell the truth to Congress. Instead comes a steady stream of lies."[5] Even the information going to those with security clearances is controlled. This solves the mystery, as addressed in part above, of why good people in the American government approve such violence and then deny any knowledge of U.S. involvement. It also explains why academics and other intellectuals are so misled and, in turn, mislead the masses. The "Mighty Wurlitzer" was established to write history to protect power brokers as they imposed enormous violence upon the world to protect their wealth and power, those outright lies and distorted histories are recorded as real history, and there is little else in the historical record. Perhaps this is true of all empires but, if that pattern of social control is ever to be broken, we must recognize and analyze this process.

For the first stage of that analysis, study a globe. Note the enormous expanse of the world which is undeveloped, impoverished, consuming fourteen percent of the world's resources, and the small area of the world which is developed, wealthy, powerful and consuming eighty-six percent of the world's resources.[6] Note that the resources which produce the wealth and power of the imperial centers are primarily in, and thus properly owned by, the impoverished undeveloped world. The secret that can never be acknowledged is that if the impoverished countries had access to finance capital, technology, and markets, it is they who would be wealthy.

Controlling the Flow of Information Worldwide Required Control of Nations on the Periphery of Empire

After World War II, colonial nations were declaring their full independence. Many were electing democratic governments and hoping to emulate the United States, economic successes and freedoms. The loss of the resources in their former colonies meant impoverishment for the war-shattered historic imperial centers of capital. For the American-led coalition of empires to regain control it was crucial that the educational institutions and media of emerging countries not be permitted unbiased observation and critiques of the battle between the superpowers or their own continued suppression. This meant that newly free democracies had to be covertly overthrown and puppet governments put in place (Indonesia, Iran, Chile, Guatemala, Nicaragua, etc.).

Even though many of the colonial oppressed fought hard and suffered tens of thousands or even hundreds of thousands of casualties, most were unable to break free. Massive military and financial support was put behind puppet dictators to prevent loss of those countries by the vote. All this was accepted by the citizens of the imperial centers because the information reaching them through the CIA's "Mighty Wurlitzer" essentially reversed reality: dictators were described as "authoritarian governments" while fledgling democracies, defending themselves against overthrow by CIA covert destabilizations, were portrayed as "dictatorships."

Freedom and democracy are taught, preached, and believed in fully throughout the world. So suppression of these breaks for freedom could only be accomplished under a cover of "free" elections. As the progressive leaders of the impoverished of those countries could easily explain true freedom to their followers, controlling the elections required funding the campaigns of current dictators and even establishing reactionary newspapers.

But not even these massive efforts could fool the people into voting against their own best interests. No matter how idealistic these second- and third-tier planners were, it was obvious to them that those standing up and preaching freedom for their countries had to be eliminated. Because they were so thoroughly indoctrinated into the enemy belief system, idealistic people— no different than you and I—established and orchestrated death squads which—counting their family members and closest confidants— assassinated 150,000 to 300,000 teachers, professors, labor leaders, cooperative leaders, and church leaders, the budding Washingtons, Jeffersons, Madisons, Lenins, Gandhis, Churchills, and Martin Luther Kings of those countries.

Then, to protect this exceptionally violent suppression of freedom and democracy by imperial centers of capital, the "Mighty Wurlitzer" of the imperial nations created the image to the world that these primarily nonviolent, patriotic, and courageous people were terrorists and a threat to the world. The real terrorists, armed insurgents battling for freedom who would be praised as heroes if they were fighting for our side, were dealt with by U.S.-supported military forces. Civilians, whose only threat was a potential win at the ballot box, were dealt with by CIA-orchestrated death squads. One marvels at the courage of these people to keep standing up for the freedom and rights of their country and their people when they knew their name would go on a death squad list. One cannot help but notice that those on the periphery of trading empires are fighting for freedom just as the suppressed on the periphery of empire have fought for freedom from the imperial centers throughout all history.

With U.S. military forces in over 100 countries around the world, even though the Cold War is theoretically over, it is impossible for America to deny it is an empire or that, with its military and trading allies, it forms an allied empire. The evidence is indisputable. Where America was originally only one of the smaller colonial empires, today—along with the allied centers of capital—it is, although somewhat fragile due to internal contradictions, the largest and most powerful empire in history. Of course, "trading empires" is a commonly used term but these trading empires, expanded and protected by military might so as to lay claim to the wealth of the periphery, are true empires in the deepest and most original meaning of the word. Today's empires are only hiding under the cover of new names (free trade) and new slogans (peace, freedom, justice, rights, and majority rule). We address in depth the evolution of modern world trade and how inequalities of trade are just as fundamental to today's trade as they were when the secret of "plunder by trade" was learned centuries ago.

The Breaks for Freedom Were Coming Too Fast: The Cold War Required a Master Plan

The Maoist-led revolution in China in 1949 triggered an intense study by the U.S. State Department that culminated in National Security Council Directive 68 (NSC-68) being presented to President Truman on April 16, 1950. Although it was not signed until September 30, 1950 (as NSC-68/2), that document's master plan for the containment of those breaks for economic freedom officially became America's secret policy of covert and overt financial, economic, political, and military warfare.

Although the world was theoretically at peace, this directive called for increasing the U.S. arms budget by 350 percent ($13.5 billion to $46.5 billion). This was just under the $300 billion annual budget (1990 dollars) with which the United States fought the Cold War. U.S. economic and military power was being mustered to support the collapsed power structure of the former colonial empires and suppress those breaks for economic freedom.[7]

While admitting there was no military threat to the West, Dean Acheson's memoir, *Present at the Creation*, unwittingly exposes NSC-68 as the master plan for the Cold War. It was a Grand Strategy for increasing the military budget of the United States by 350 percent to wage a worldwide covert war (or overt when necessary—Korea, Vietnam, the Gulf War, and the containment of Cuba, Iran, Iraq, Libya, and now Kosovo) to suppress the rising tide of social and economic revolutions which were intent on breaking the dependency imposed upon them and turning their resources to the care of their own people.[8]

Office of Strategic Studies (OSS) officers, the primary designers of post–World War II covert actions, had been carrying out major covert operations well before the CIA was officially established. Very large military support to reinstall or maintain the old ruling elite was undertaken in Greece and China before World War II ended. Tens of thousands of valiant patriots who had held two-thirds of Greece out of Hitler's control were slaughtered. At the same time, with U.S. support, Vietnam was being reclaimed by the French, who killed 20,000 in Haiphong harbor alone and killed another million Indochinese before America took over the suppression of that break for economic freedom to slaughter another 3 million in the 1960s and 1970s. Britain retained her claim to Malaysia by slaughtering thousands. With American and British support, the Dutch slaughtered 150,000 Indonesians in an unsuccessful attempt to reclaim those resource-rich islands (using Dutch SS battalions which had been fighting for Hitler just weeks earlier). In one bombardment alone, over 90,000 were killed in the suppression of Madagascar's bid for freedom. There were many more, even if smaller, suppressions of the wordwide break for economic freedom.

Those OSS Cold Warriors were the primary staffers of the CIA when it was first established in 1947 to carry out future covert operations.[9] It was the experiences of these Cold Warriors in suppressing breaks for economic freedom (called insurgencies) between 1945 and 1950 that were codified into NSC-68. All earlier Security Council directives were on a learning curve leading to that April 1950 master plan to suppress these breaks for economic freedom and all later directives were supplemental to it. Most "insurgency" suppressions succeeded in maintaining the dependent status of the crucial "countryside" with its precious resources. But China, with one-fifth of the world's people, was a big loss that reverberated in the boardrooms of major corporations, and protective government policies were called for. Managers of State knew well that if other revolutions were successful, the imperial center would lose those cheap resources and profitable markets.

To maintain control, it was necessary to suppress and/or contain both the rising socialist centers of capital to the East and the emerging countries that might take the rhetoric of democracy and freedom seriously and either form an independent trading bloc of nonaligned nations or tie their economies to other emerging centers of capital. But with the world at peace the planners admitted there was no way to get even $1 billion a year out of either Congress or the American people, and NSC-68 called for an additional $33 billion per year ($200 billion in 1990 dollars).[10]

Note these simultaneous occurrences of major events: (1) The Korean War, proving communists were aggressors bent on world conquest; (2) the Congress for Cultural Freedom, along with other black ops of the CIA and other intelligence agencies, designed to control the information flow to the world; (3) and McCarthy-

ism's silencing of any with the credentials and authority to tell the people anything different. All these mutually supporting events made their debut in the first half of 1950 and all within two months of the finalization of NSC-68, the master plan for the Cold War.[11] None of this was accidental or incidental—it was all part of the Grand Strategy of Managers of State.

While McCarthyism—painting any remotely progressive person or philosophy as communist—was in full swing, it was political, social, and career suicide to be objective and intellectually balanced. During those forty years of suppression of dissenting opinion, the CIA paid compliant professors to write twenty-five to thirty fraudulent books a year. Right-wing think tanks were set up to produce thousands of books based on those original planted stories. Tens of thousands of CIA articles based on, and in turn supporting, the fraudulent books were planted in the media around the world (700 CIA articles were planted worldwide during the overthrow and assassination of Allende in Chile, and the fact that reporters were being provided news scoops in exchange for publication of fraudulent articles tells us that some of the leading columnists in the world were planting this nonsense).

For almost two generations social scientists have used, and are still using, those fraudulent books and articles as the foundation of their research. Such books have been the official textbooks for forty years. And the intelligence agencies, corporate think tanks, and state departments of all powerful nations were busy writing the same distorted history. With intellectual figures and skillful writers throughout the Western world supported and coordinated in this massive falsification of history, as the above quote on the Congress for Cultural Freedom demonstrates, only academics and intellectuals on the fringe knew the difference and even they could only be very unsure of what was real and what was not real. When it was learned that the CIA had supported the printing of these thousands of books, sincere academics sued for the titles of those fraudulent books to be revealed. But the Supreme Court ruled that this would expose CIA methods and endanger the national security.[12]

But the imperial nations of Europe also had to worry about the loss of their heartland by the vote. Post–World War II France and Italy were especially vulnerable to ballot box revolutions. Massive CIA funds were only barely able to avert that loss. In Italy it required more than money. As the partisans were the only effective political force left in Italy and many were communist, Allied troops released Mafia leaders from Mussolini's prisons, armed them, and placed them in charge of the cities as they marched up the Italian peninsula.[13]

Control of the Italian elections was still in question and, besides other methods of funding conservative Italian politicians, the CIA was deeply involved in the super-secret P2 lodge, the primary group trying to prevent that election disaster for the Western world's Managers of State. The only way to obtain a seat of power in the Italian government was through that secret lodge. The risk of an overthrow by the vote was still high. For further belief system protection, the Bologna railway bombing, which killed 84 people and injured 150, and other fatal bombings in Italy were planned and carried out by the CIA-connected P2 lodge and blamed on the "Red Guards." The explosives from that bombing and others were traced to some of the 139 buried weapons and explosives caches for the CIA's "Operation Gladio."[14]

Operation Gladio was the Italian segment of the CIA's "Operation Statewatch" operating, with the support of other intelligence services, throughout Western Europe. Though the cover story when exposed in September 1990 was that these were "stay behind forces" in case the Soviet Union overran those countries, they were really there to take back by force (through assassinations, black ops, and military coups) any government lost by the vote. Their permanent in-place numbers ranged from 400 operatives in Belgium to 2,000 in Italy. The super-secret covert operation's bombings and blaming of the Red Guards in other countries within the Western alliance were done more sensibly, where and when no one would be hurt. The Red Guards, of course, either never existed or what they actually stood for, or what they did, was severely distorted by intelligence services.

In 1997–98, there were exposures of South Africa's secret service using and planting Soviet weapons on its own covert missions to blame the massacres of blacks on the African National Congress. Such framing of opponents is an old political trick and planting counterfeit letters, documents, and weapons (black ops) is standard operating procedure for intelligence services. The CIA's Mighty Wurlitzer had this all down to a science. Those bombings and other violence blamed on the left within Europe were to provide a base for many of the planted articles but throughout most of the world the intent was to destroy and/or kill.[15]

Control of Information Within the Imperial Centers Required Destabilizing Internal Political Groups

Preventing other political voices from being heard required destabilizing internal political groups in all allied countries. In the United States, this was the purpose first of the House

Un-American Activities Committee and Mc-Carthyism and then of the FBI's Operation COINTELPRO (a replay of the post–World War I shattering of the forming solid labor front; the destruction of the Wobblies [International Workers of the World, IWW]). Chaos, Cable Splicer, and Garden Plot were internal destabilization exercises carried out in cooperation with military intelligence services.[16] Through *agents provocateurs, counterfeited letters, planted narcotics, false arrests, poison-pen letters, malicious articles planted in the press, blacklisting from jobs, harassment, electronic surveillance, burglary, mail tampering,* and *other forms of terrorism,* hundreds of budding political groupings were destabilized. In March 1998, the Socialist Workers Party (SWP) and Young Socialist Alliance (YSA) won a fifteen-year legal battle against the FBI for decades of spying, harassment, and disruption. During that trial, these two groups—out of hundreds that were spied upon and/or destabilized—proved that the FBI had conducted 20,000 days of wiretaps and 12,000 days of listening "bugs" between 1943 and 1963 as well as 208 burglaries of offices and homes of their members with the photographing or theft of 9,864 private documents.[17] This is only two groups out of hundreds and only the events that were proven.

If the largest and most politically motivated of these hundreds of groups had been allowed to form and grow, some of their leaders would eventually have been elected to local, state, and national governments. From that position, they would have had platforms to speak to the masses. Belief systems not in their best interest, as had been accepted in the past when there were no other choices, are much harder to impose upon a population under conditions of true freedom. The independent views on national

and international events that would have been carried by the media when addressed by those new leaders, as opposed to the desired view of Managers of State as they suppressed both internal dissent and the world's break for freedom, were the real threat. For exercising their democratic rights, these innocent people were systematically monitored, systematically destabilized, some were sent to prison, and their voices were never heard except by a few on the margins. Silencing those who stood up on the periphery of empire was a much harder job than silencing dissenting voices within the imperial center but—at least until the financial and economic meltdowns on the periphery—this too was, to a large extent, accomplished.

No profound thought which ran counter to the mainstream was permitted on either side of the opposing Cold War blocs, rhetoric about a free, open, and unbiased educational system in the "democratic" West notwithstanding. Classics of alternative thought were taught in the universities, but the massive propaganda of the CIA's "Mighty Wurlitzer", the weeding out of professors with independent thought through loyalty oaths and the threat of—or even actual—job loss, and the pressure of propagandized peers assured these philosophies would only be taught as dictatorial, violent, and/or impractical. The violence of the Cold War was to suppress the implementation of any competing philosophies so that no such example could exist to gain the allegiance of intellectuals, opinion makers, and voters.

The fact that the masses had attained voting rights dictated that their perception of the world must be controlled. These gross fabrications and crafted propaganda provided a firm foundation for the Social Control belief systems of the Cold War and are now not only a major part of Western literature and history; *they are Western lit-*

erature and history. After the Cold War was won, major universities officially restored the good name of those who were forced out of academia and had their careers destroyed. This proved—of course—that the innocence of these accused and shattered people was well understood all along by the information gatekeepers. The organs of social power (academia, politics, and the media) are only now recovering from that suppression of free speech and free thought.

Understanding the suppressions and oppressions of the Cold War is essential to understanding this book's primary theses: inequalities in world trade impoverish naturally wealthy regions, and imperial centers impose belief systems that allow them to lay claim to the impoverished nations' wealth. Wealth and power are based on inequalities of both external and internal trade, the rules of which have been fine-tuned for centuries. For the powerful to permit the establishment of equality in trades would be to immediately lose their massive accumulations of unearned wealth and their power. Thus, the suppressions and oppressions of the Cold War are not an aberration. Whenever the threat to wealth and power is high, such suppressions and oppressions are the norm.

With all political, economic, financial, and military options blocked, the defeated, dependent, and impoverished world has no options outside of what the imperial centers have to offer. All plans of the developing world fail (the specific purpose of the covert actions of the Cold War), the imposed (reimposed) belief system takes hold, and the old order is restored. This is an exact description of the Cold War and the *reimposition* of Adam Smith free trade philosophies and neoclassical economics upon the world that we will be addressing in depth.

That Monopolization Has Been Eliminated Is a Myth

That monopolization has been eliminated and the world is functioning under free trade is a myth. Mason Gaffney and Fred Harrison alert us as to how, through massive efforts to impose neoclassical economics upon the world, land had been taken out of the land/labor/capital wealth creation formula after Henry George's exposure of that primary monopoly as the cause of most poverty.[18] Even before the dawn of the Industrial Revolution and free thought, the true meaning of monopolies had been suppressed. Focusing on corporate monopolies, and avoiding analysis of monopolization through the structure of property, labor, and trading rights, continues to hide that embarrassment. We will be addressing how the simple example of one huge corporation monopolizing a market, as taught in economics, is only a subsidiary monopoly within the framework of overarching subtle monopolies.[19]

Never Did a Nation Develop Under Adam Smith: They All Developed Under the Principles of Friedrich List

To understand how the world's wealth is controlled and distributed, we must study centuries of suppressed history. Eight hundred years ago, the powerful of the cities of Europe learned to control the resources and markets of the countryside by destroying others' primitive industrial capital, thus monopolizing that capital and establishing and maintaining extreme inequality of pay, which, as described in our first chapter, siphoned the wealth of the countryside to the imperial centers of capital. They had learned to "plunder by trade" and have been refining those skills ever since.[20]

Two hundred years ago, Britain's William Pitt (1759–1806), building on the unspoken concept of unequal trade that the First Earl of Shaftesbury (1621–83) had established over a century earlier as the base for the British Empire, realized that Adam Smith's *Wealth of Nations* (if interpreted carefully and parts of it ignored), would be a great philosophy under which England could consolidate those unequal trades into customary practice and maintain dominance in world trade. As a cover under which England could maintain that dominance, British government, British intelligence, and British industry supported lecturers throughout the world promoting their interpretation of Adam Smith's philosophy. That imposed belief system successfully protected powerful nations' access to resources and markets and, for the same purpose, continues as the world's dominant belief system yet today.[21]

We will be analyzing how virtually every nation that developed did so following the protectionist philosophy of German economist and naturalized American citizen Friedrich List (1789–1846) even as they were mouthing the free-trade philosophy of Adam Smith. This includes Britain, America, Germany, Japan, and the Asian tigers who were so essential for philosophically containing the rapid expansion of socialism.

Friedrich List observed the collapse of European industry when Napoleon's continental system was dismantled after Napoleon's defeat at Waterloo in 1815. From those observations, and after watching firsthand America's rapid development through ignoring Britain's imposition of Smith's philosophy, List published his protectionist classic, *The National System of Political Economy,* in 1841. When British power was shattered by World Wars I and II, America was the only remaining wealthy imperial nation.

To protect herself and her historic allies, and against the interests of the economic liberation of the colonial world from the weakened imperial powers, America took over the job of maintaining the imposition of the neomercantilist/neoclassical interpretation of Adam Smith upon the world.[22]

Establishing the Legal Structure to Assure Access to the World's Resources

Denial of technology to the periphery by the cosmopolitan centers in the early centuries of capitalism is the cause of wealth concentration in the resource-poor, but powerful, regions of the world and impoverishment in the resource-rich, but weak, regions.

The powerful, developed world established the International Monetary Fund (IMF), World Bank, General Agreement on Trades and Tariffs (GATT), North American Free Trade Agreement (NAFTA), and World Trade Organization (WTO), and is in the process of establishing the Multilateral Agreement on Investments (MAI), as the financial and legal structure under which it retains access to the world's cheap resources.

The wealthy world both creates and protects its wealth through processing those cheap resources into valuable products and powerful military weapons. Thus, a part of the natural wealth of the impoverished regions finances the military that protects the unequal trade structure maintaining the status quo. This wealth confiscation process, ostensibly to accumulate capital, is not the efficient developer of the world we are taught to believe. That worldwide battle to maintain the dominance of imperial nations in world trade adds up to nothing less than "capital destroying capital"[23] in which far more wealth is destroyed than is accumulated as capital (one of several fundamental theses in this book).

What Can the World's Dispossessed Do?

Accumulated capital and consumer purchasing power are both derived from title to natural resources, title to industrial capital, title to distribution mechanisms, and adequately paid labor, as well as efficient industries. High capitalized values require mass markets, and mass markets develop only from adequately paid labor. Therefore, whenever possible, developing nations should be trading with each other. If wages paid for production of the products traded are equal, neither appropriates the wealth of the other and trade functions efficiently and honestly. Because much more wealth is retained when nations with low-paid labor trade with each other, they can develop their economies much more rapidly than when trading with a high-paid labor nation. As we will be addressing in depth, capital accumulation is not the limiting factor. Capital can be accumulated more easily, more equitably, and far more rapidly than through the current monopolization of the world's technology, resources, and markets.[24]

The monopolization of world trade and internal commerce, having been hidden under imposed belief systems so long, makes it hard to conceptualize a world with true equality, freedom, and rights. All this thesis is saying is, "Be who we say we are. Do what we say we do. Have honest free trade and honest free enterprise." This requires equalizing wages worldwide for equally productive work and thus eliminating the system of subtle monopolization of the world's resources, industry, and trade under which those inequalities of trade are maintained.

Freedom and rights cannot be obtained until there is equal sharing of the money creation process. We suggest accomplishing this through tying currencies to the value of a basket of commodities. There are only three foundations to production: resources (land), labor, and industrial capital. Under conditions of full equality of rights for money creation, any region may create the money to combine surplus resources and labor to produce industrial capital to produce needed consumer products or services.

The World Bank Says It Is Moving Toward These Suggestions

The underlying discussions at the 1999 World Bank meeting in Tokyo on the 1997–98 financial meltdowns of former healthy economies were: "American style free-market policies are seen as finished . . . government should guide development, . . . if necessary protecting key industries from competition and rely on bureaucratic wisdom instead rather than market forces, . . . and expanding political rights and freedoms are the best means to development."[25] There is much more to do but that is a major shift by the World Bank, at least in words, towards what this book is recommending.

Even if the full extent of the injustice of inequalities of trade were realized by enough people and change forced upon the world, adjusting to equal trade will be a slow and traumatic process. The world's arteries of commerce are built upon inequalities of trade, and severing those arteries will create extreme political crises. Whenever those arteries of commerce are threatened, the historic response has been to activate political, financial, economic, and military resources to reimpose the belief system that has protected the beneficiaries of those unequal trades.

Progressive philosophies that would equalize rights and wealth for all have been around for at least the last 120 years. However, the powerful have been able to avoid such threats to the status quo by cosmetic change, imposition of Social Control belief systems, and suppression of all efforts to utilize those progressive philosophies. If we eliminate the waste of resources and capital battling over the world's wealth, extreme poverty can be eliminated in one generation and the world can be industrialized to a sustainable level and poverty largely eliminated in two generations.[26]

It is impossible for the developing world to accumulate its own capital without owning its own resources, owning and running its own factories, being paid equally for equally productive labor, and selling through established markets. It cannot develop a healthy economy without broad-based local buying power. It is, after all, consumer purchasing power—adequate wages, adequate commodity prices, and profits from efficient industry and efficient traders—that determines who ends up with the world's wealth.[27] This book is an effort to show how simple it would be to restructure from the current subtle-monopoly capitalism (corporate imperialism) with all its violence and poverty to a caring cooperative capitalism with a minimum level of violence and poverty.

Notes

1. Ellen Schrecker, *No Ivory Tower* (New York: Oxford University Press, 1986).

2. Peter Coleman, *Liberal Conspiracy* (London: Collier Macmillan, 1989), dustjacket.

3. Ralph W. McGehee, *CIABASE* (12-megabyte database on this history), http://come.to/CIABASE/, Box 5022, Herndon, VA 22070; Coleman, *Liberal Conspiracy;* John Prados, *The Presidents' Secret Wars* (New York: William Morrow, 1986 and *The Presidents Secret Wars: CIA and Pentagon Covert Operations From World War II Through the Persian Gulf War* Warwick: Elephant Paperbacks, 1996); William Blum, *The CIA: A Forgotten History* (London: Zed Books, 1986), pp. 127–28, 131, 185; Victor Marchetti and John D. Marks, *The CIA and the Cult of Intelligence* (New York: Dell, 1980), chapter 6, especially pp. 152–56, also pp. 53–54, 62–63, 541–42; John Stockwell, *The Praetorian Guard* (Boston: South End Press, 1991), pp. 100–101; Ralph W. McGehee, *Deadly Deceits* (New York: Sheridan Square Press, 1983), especially pp. 30, 58, 62, 189; Philip Agee and Louis Wolf, *Dirty Work* (London: Zed Books, 1978), especially p. 262; David Wise and Thomas B. Ross, *The Espionage Establishment* (New York: Bantam Books, 1978), pp. 256, 257; Frank J. Donner, *The Age of Surveillance: The Aims and Methods of America's Political Intelligence System* (New York: Random House, 1981); John Prados, *Keepers of the Keys: A History of the National Security Council from Truman to Bush* (New York: William Morrow, 1991); Loch K. Johnson, *America's Secret Power* (New York: Oxford University Press, 1989); C.D. Ameringer, *U.S. Foreign Intelligence* (Lexington, MA: Lexington Books, 1990); H.B. Westerfield. *Inside CIA's Private World: Declassified Articles from the Agency's Internal Journal 1955–1992* (New Haven: Yale University Press, 1995); J. Adams, *Secret Armies* (New York: Atlantic Monthly Press, 1987); P.V. Parakal, *Secret Wars of the CIA* (New Delhi: Sterling, 1984); Christopher Simpson, *Blowback* (New York: Weidenfeld and Nicolson, 1988); Ernest Volkman and Blaine Baggett, *Secret Intelligence* (New York: Doubleday, 1989); John Ranelagh, *The Agency: The Rise and Decline of the CIA* (New York: Simon and Schuster, 1987); Dan Jacobs, *The Brutality of Nations* (New York: Alfred A. Knopf, 1987); Darrell Garwood, *Under Cover: Thirty-Five Years of CIA Deception* (New York: Grove Press, 1985); Philip Agee, *Inside the Company: CIA Diary* (New York: Bantam Books, 1975); B. Hersh, *The Old Boys: The American Elite and the Origins of the CIA* (New York: Charles Scribner's Sons, 1992); H. Rositzke, *The CIA's Secret Operations* (New York: Thomas Y. Crowell, 1977); T. Powers, *The Man Who Kept the Secrets* (New York: Alfred A. Knopf, 1979); P. Willan, *Puppetmasters: The Political Use of Terrorism in Italy* (London: Constable, 1991); E. Thomas, *The Very Best Men: Four Who Dared: The Early Years of the CIA* (New York: Simon and Schuster, 1995); K. Nair, *Devil and His Dart: How the CIA Is*

Plotting in the Third World (New Delhi: Sterling, 1986); D.S. Blaufarb, *The Counterinsurgency Era: U.S. Doctrine and Performance 1950 to Present* (New York: The Free Press, 1977); Michael T. Klare and P. Kornbluh, *Low Intensity Warfare* (New York: Pantheon Books, 1988); S.E. Ambrose, *Ike's Spies* (Garden City, NY: Doubleday, 1981); Susanne Jonas, *The Battle for Guatemala: Rebels, Death Squads, and U.S. Power* (San Francisco: Westview Press, 1991); C. Andrew, *For the President's Eyes Only: Secret Intelligence and the American Presidency from Washington to Bush* (New York: HarperCollins, 1995); William Blum, *Killing Hope: U.S. Military Interventions Since World War II* (Monroe, ME: Common Courage Press, 1995); H. Frazier, ed., *Uncloaking the CIA* (New York: The Free Press, 1978); *Covert Action Information Bulletin,* all issues; *Counterspy,* all issues. See also, Wendell Minnick, *Spies and Provocateurs: A Worldwide Encyclopedia of Persons Conducting Espionage and Covert Action, 1946–1991* (Jefferson, NC: McFarland, 1992); I.F. Stone, *The Hidden History of the Korean War* (Boston: Little Brown, 1952); John Loftus, *Belarus Secret* (New York: Alfred A. Knopf, 1982); Robin W. Winks, *Cloak & Gown: Scholars in the Secret War, 1939–1961* (New York: Quill, 1987); D.F. Fleming, *The Cold War and Its Origins* (New York: Doubleday, 1961); Milton Mayer, *They Thought They Were Free,* (Chicago: University of Chicago Press, 1955; Michel Chossudovsky, *The Globalization of Poverty: Impacts of IMF and World Bank Reforms* (London: Zed Books, 1997).

To understand why powerful nations resort to state terrorism as covered in the above books, one must understand policies of State. The following books on diplomacy further outline those policies: John R. Commons, *Legal Foundations of Capitalism* (New Brunswick/London: Transaction Publishers. 1995): John R. Commons, *Institutional Economics* (New Brunswick/London: Transaction Publishers, 1995); Carey B. Joynt and Percy E. Corbett, *Theory and Reality in World Politics* (Pittsburgh: University of Pittsburgh Press, 1978); Richard L. Rubenstein, *The Age of Triage* (Boston: Beacon Press. 1983); Peter Rodman, *More Precious Than Peace* (New York: Charles Scribner & Sons, 1994); Angelo Codevilla, *Informing Statecraft* (New York: The Free Press, 1992); Arie E. David, *The Strategy of Treaty Termination* (New Haven: Yale University Press, 1975); Francis Neilson,

How Diplomats Make War (San Francisco: Cobden Press, 1984).

4. McGehee, *Deadly Deceits*, p. 192.

5. Check Wade Frazier's review of *Deadly Deceits* in Ralph McGehee's *http://come.to/CIABASE/*.

6. United Nations Human Development Report, 1998.

7. Dean Acheson, *Present at the Creation* (New York: W. W. Norton, 1987), pp. 373–79; the complete NSC-68 document can be found in Thomas H. Etzold and John Lewis Gaddis, *Containment: Documents on American Policy and Strategy, 1945–50* (New York: Columbia University Press, 1978), chapter 7. See also note three above.

8. Acheson, *Present at the Creation*, p. 377; Etzold and Gaddis, *Containment*, chapter 7.

9. See note three, especially Hersh, *Old Boys;* Winks, *Cloak & Gown;* Willan, *Puppetmasters;* Thomas, *Very Best Men.*

10. Acheson, *Present at the Creation,* p. 377. See also Stone, *Hidden History*, and Etzold and Gaddis, *Containment.*

11. Stone, *Hidden History;* Coleman, *Liberal Conspiracy;* Schrecker, *No Ivory Tower;* Etzold and Gaddis, *Containment,* chapter 7.

12. See note three (Coleman's *Liberal Conspiracy,* especially Appendix D, lists almost 200 of these thought control books); see Chapters Six and Nine of this work.

13. See note three.

14. Willan, *Puppetmasters,* pp. 146–59; Thomas, *Very Best Men,* pp. 65–66; David A. Yallop, *In God's Name* (New York: Bantam Books, 1984); see note three. Gladio was not uncovered until November 1990, too late for most books listed here, so one must go to McGehee's *CIABASE* for articles and later sources.

15. Ibid.

16. Ibid; Holly Sklar, *Washington's War on Nicaragua* (Boston: South End Press, 1988), p. 359; Rositzke, *CIA's Secret Operations,* pp. 218–20; Powers, *Man Who Kept the Secrets,* pp. 246–70, 364.

17. Angus MacKenzie and David Weir, *Secrets: The CIA's War at Home* (Berkeley: University of California Press, 1997); M. Wesley Swearingen, *FBI Secrets: An Agent's Exposé* (Boston: South End Press, 1995); Ward Churchhill, *Cointelpro Papers: Documents from the FBI's Secret Wars Against Domestic Dissent* (Boston: South End Press, 1990); Mar-

garet Jayko, *FBI on Trial: The Victory in the Socialist Workers Party Suit against Government Spying* (New York: Pathfinder Press, 1989); Nelson Blackstock, *Cointelpro: The FBI's Secret War on Political Freedom* (New York: Anchor Foundation, 1988); Ward Churchill, *Agents of Repression: The FBI's Secret Wars Against the Black Panther Party and the American Indian Movement* (Boston: South End Press, 1989); Martin Luther King Jr., *The Black Panthers Speak* (New York: Da Capo Press, 1995); Hugh Pearson, *The Shadow of the Panther: Huey Newton and the Price of Black Power in America* (Reading, MA: Perseus Press, 1995); also see note three.

18. Mason Gaffney and Fred Harrison, *The Corruption of Economics* (London: Shepheard-Walwyn, 1994).

19. See Part IV.

20. See Chapter Two.

21. Friedrich List, *The National System of Political Economy* (Fairfield, NJ: Augustus M. Kelley, 1977), in *Memoirs and Extracts.*

22. See Chapters Six through Eleven.

23. See Chapter Eighteen.

24. See subchapters "Accumulation of Capital through Cooperative Capitalism" in Chapter Twenty-Six, "Investment" in Chapter Twenty-Seven, and Chapter Twenty-Three.

25. Cameron W. Barr, "Making the Financial Architecture More Crisis Proof," *The Christian Science Monitor,* March 3, 1999, pp. 1, 7. See also William H. Hatal and Richard J. Verey, "Recognizing the 'Third Way,'" *The Christian Science Monitor,* March 3, 1999, p. 9.

26. See Chapter Twenty-Three.

27. See Chapters Twenty-Two and Twenty-Three.

Part I

External Trade: World Trade Structured for Security of Powerful Nations Entails Insecurity for Weak Nations

1

The Secret of Free Enterprise Capital Accumulation

Capitalism's capital accumulation has some secrets that are studiously ignored. That capital is properly owned and employed by labor is recognized by no less an authority than Adam Smith: "Produce is the natural wages of labor. Originally the whole belonged to the labourer. If this had continued all things would have become cheaper, though in appearance many things might have become dearer."[1] Of course, the production once claimed by labor and now lost is the ever-increasing share that is going to profits of monopoly landrent and monopoly patents.

What Smith means by all things being cheaper, though they appear dearer, is that if workers had been fully paid they would have retained full title to the value of what they produced. Things would be cheaper because fully paid workers would be able to buy more from other fully paid workers, who in turn would both produce more and purchase more. Quite simply, not only would purchasing power have been advancing in step with productive capacity, but those who lived off the labors of others would instead have to work productively.

Instead of workers being paid full value for their labor, much of history has been a case of capital—through control of the law-making process—transferring a part of labor's rights to itself. As Adam Smith goes on to explain, this is a centuries-long process of the wealth produced by labor becoming a right of capital through monopoly title to land and technology.[2] The wealth produced by the increased efficiencies of labor thereby accrues to capital.

The Simple Math Not Addressed by Free Trade Philosophers: Wealth Accumulation Potential Expands or Contracts Exponentially With the Differential in Pay

> Technology and skill gaps, if initially large, tend to grow under free trade. This is an old Mercantilist insight that the modern economic analysis of innovation has reaffirmed and renamed the "learning-by-doing" requirement—that is, experience with the productive process is a *sine qua non* for building up productive skills and innovative prowess.
> —David Felix, "Latin America's Debt Crisis," *World Policy Journal*

The secret to siphoning away others' wealth is the low-paid labor in the poor nations and high profits and high wages in the rich societies that have dominated global trade for centuries. Arjun Makhijani calculates that, through an imbalance of currency values, equally productive labor in the world's defeated, dependent nations were paid 20 percent that of the developed world.[3] Currency collapses in the developing world increased that differential to 10 to one.

23

Capital accumulation advantage increases or decreases exponentially with the differential in pay for equally productive labor. Follow this example carefully: The equally productive worker in the poorly paid Third World produces a unique model car, is paid $1 an hour, and is producing one model car an hour. The equally productive worker in the developed world produces another unique model car, is paid $10 an hour, and also produces one car per hour. Each equally productive worker likes, and purchases, the other's model cars. All true costs are labor costs so we ignore monopoly capital costs, which go to the developed world and only increases the advantage anyway, and calculate the cost of those model cars at the labor cost of production, $1 an hour and $10 an hour. The $1 an hour worker must work 10 hours to buy one of the model cars of the $10 an hour worker but, with the money earned in the same 10 hours, the $10 an hour worker can buy 100 of the model cars of the $1 an hour worker. While in a homogenized market of many producers there is a 10 times differential in buying power, *in direct trades between each other there is an exponential 100 times differential in retained wealth.*

The wealth accumulation advantage of the higher-paid nation over the lower-paid nation is equal to the high pay divided by the low pay squared: $(Wr/Wp)^2 = A$ (Wr is the wages paid to equally productive labor in the rich country [$10 earned for every 1 hour time unit of production]; Wp is the wages paid to equally productive labor in the poor country [$1 earned for every 1 hour time unit of production]; A is the capital accumulation advantage of the well-paid nation [*100 to 1* in this example]).

The scenario above is expressed *a priori* (assuming the labor cost to build industries in each country and the resources harvested in each country, and thus the value of those industries and resources, and the profits produced, at the same differential). In reality, only a part of the workers in world trade are equally productive but all could be relatively so if they had equal access to technology, training, and markets. Even now, grape pickers, strawberry pickers, janitors, guards, etc.—any work which is not mechanized anywhere else in the world, and a share of the industrial labor of the developing world—are just as productive as other workers anywhere in the world. It has been thoroughly proven that labor everywhere can be trained to run industries just as efficiently, and at times more efficiently, than developed world labor. Whenever the difference in pay is greater than the difference in productivity, a part of the production of the low-paid worker or nation is transferred to the high-paid country. It has been the Grand Strategy of imperial nations for centuries to monopolize the production processes through denying other nations the use of technology, and access to markets. Thus, it has been imperial policies that have kept poor countries from learning industrial skills and building productive, affluent, economies, not their incapacity to learn.

To clarify the exponential increase or decrease in wealth accumulation *potential* between nations as the differential in pay for equally productive work increases or decreases, we will compare the above twenty-five to one capital accumulation *advantage example* with today's most extreme example, twenty-three cents an hour for equally productive Russian industrial labor against $23 an hour for equally productive German industrial labor (1997), which is a 10,000 to one advantage in wealth (capital) accumulation.[4] Obviously the Russian workers' factory is essentially shut down, they are still being paid their twenty-three cents an hour, at times even nothing is produced, and, on that basis, the formula appears inaccurate. But it is the basis that is inaccurate, not the formula. Before its collapse, the Soviet Union was calculated to be within eight years of equaling the West in technology. With its huge resources and its highly skilled workforce operating factories utilizing the latest technology, and assuming it had access to markets, Russia could theoretically produce just as efficiently as anyone else. But the billions of dollars poured into Russia since its collapse were not building any *manufacturing* industry at all, let alone modern industries. The problem is not the productivity of labor in the developing world per se. The problem is denial of technology and denial of access to markets. Immense sums flowing into a country or region are meaningless if there is no access to technology and markets. In fact, a massive inflow of funds used for almost anything else except building a technologically modern industrial capacity becomes a debt trap that lays claim to ever more of a dependent nation's wealth. The fundamental problem is that finance capital to build modern industry is automatically denied when patent monopolies and unacknowledged trade restrictions (monopolization), which we will also be addressing, deny equality in trade.

Equal Pay for Equal Work Is an Essential Part of the Answer to World Poverty

In direct trades between individuals or countries, wealth accumulation potential compounds in step with the pay differential for equally productive labor. If the pay differential is five, the difference in wealth accumulation potential is twenty-five to one. If the pay differential is ten, the wealth accumulation advantage is one-

hundred to one. If the pay differential is twenty, the wealth accumulation advantage is 400 to one. If the pay differential is forty, the wealth accumulation advantage is 1,600 to one. If the pay differential is sixty (the pay differential between the defeated Russia and the victorious America [twenty-three cents an hour against $14 an hour]), the wealth accumulation advantage is 3,600 to one. And if the pay differential is 100, the pay differential between the collapsed Russia and the victorious Germany addressed above, the wealth accumulation advantage is 10,000 to one.* Place a trader between those two unequally-paid nations to claim all surplus value both through outright underpaying in hard currency or through paying in soft currency and selling in hard currency, capitalize those profits by ten to twenty times, and you have accumulated capital through capitalized value.

Lowering the pay differential for equally productive labor demonstrates equality of pay as the simple way to alleviate world poverty. If unequal pay for equally productive work were raised to only a 50 percent pay differential (a

---

*The only way to avoid the claiming of the wealth produced by the lower paid nation so rapidly and unjustly through unequal currency values is to contract resources, production, and labor at values established in the hard currency regions. Weak currency nations using another nation's hard currency as a trading medium within their own economy and between weak currency nations create another dimension of claiming others' wealth. People and nations all over the world hoard hard currency. Until those hoarded dollars, pounds, marks, euros, or yen are spent in their country of origin, they are interest-free loans to the powerful imperial centers. Money spent to purchase outside the imperial center may be a debit to the person purchasing, but so long as that money circulates outside the imperial center the only cost of the money-creating nation is the cost of printing and accounting. An interest-free loan properly invested would accumulate that value to the imperial center every five to fifteen years.

$5-an-hour nation trading with a $10-an-hour nation), the wealth accumulation advantage of the high-paid nation in direct trades with low-paid labor nations would be reduced to a four-fold wealth accumulation potential. When a $3-an-hour equally productive labor nation trades with a $4-an-hour labor nation, there is still almost a doubling (1.77 times) of wealth potentially accumulated (or consumed) by the better-paid nation. When all have access to technology and markets and pay is equal for equally productive work, the wealth retained (and available for accumulation or consumption) by each nation is equal.

Because we propose restructuring to an efficient economy with wasted labor time converted to free time and do not allow for the appropriation of wealth by monopolies and then the waste of that wealth through the financing of wars, trade wars, covert wars, cold wars, hot wars, and internal battles over wealth,[5] this formula will be challenged. But once the world economy equalizes, both in internal and external trades, those monopolies will disappear and wealth will equalize. A properly designed trading system, both internal and external, will eliminate the waste, and this capital accumulation formula will work as outlined. Just reinstate those extreme unequal wages upon a world of equal wages and equal wealth distribution and shortly all the wealth will, through laying claim to others' wealth through unequal trades, again be back in the monopolists' hands.

Underpay for Both Resources and Labor in World Trade Is Primarily Through Unequal Currency Values

A currency valued below equal labor value means that the Grand Strategy of an opposing imperial center of capital has been successful, the collapsing society has lost the trade war, is weak, is dependent upon other societies, and cannot defend itself from powerful societies confiscating its wealth through unequal trades. Witness the hemorrhaging of the natural resource wealth from Latin America, Africa, and now the fifteen former republics of the collapsed Soviet Union.

When the IMF/World Bank/GATT/NAFTA/WTO/MAI/military colossus forces other countries to devalue their currencies and reduce consumption to increase sales of their valuable resources to the developed world, this lowers the value of their labor and commodities, and raises the relative value of manufactured products from the developed world. The claim is made that this is due to the inefficiencies of developing world industry and labor, but this is hardly so:

> The low level of wages is intimately linked not to low productivity of labor-time, as classical economic theory would suggest, but to the undervalued exchange rates and the workings of the international monetary system.... The world's monetary system does not set values of the currencies on the basis of relative productivity of workers.... The present system is based on balance of payments considerations and on capital flows.... *[T]he Mexican currency is valued much lower than the relative productivity of Mexican workers collectively....* [W]hile the average amount produced per unit of time by workers in Mexico, Brazil or Bangladesh is lower than in France, the United States or Japan, the *difference in wages at present exchange rates is much bigger than the difference in productivity.* This explains why the purchasing power of American dollars, French francs or Japanese yen is much bigger in Mexico, Bangladesh or Brazil than it is in their countries of origin.[6]

Arjun Makhijani explains further:

> The product that export platform countries in the developing world are selling is not merely cheap

labor, but highly productive labor. In Singapore ... McGraw Hill produces in one year an encyclopedia that takes five years to produce in the U.S. ... Mexican metal workers are 40 percent more productive than U.S. workers, electronics workers 10 to 15 percent more productive, and seamstresses produce 30 percent more sewing per hour than their U.S. counterparts.[7]

The fact that there are millions of dispossessed, unemployed, and impoverished in the defeated developing world ensures that they will accept a very low wage. The more than sixty sweatshop exploited women from Thailand—sewing garments sixteen hours a day for seven years in an El Monte, California, housing complex, complete with a barbed wire-topped fence— paid pennies per hour (typically 56 cents alongside the U.S. average of $7.31), and the millions of children in the developing world producing shoes and toys for developed world markets for even less, are also effectively slave labor. One study concluded these workers were paid as little as eight-tenths of 1 percent of the product sales price in the industrial world and in all cases they were paid under 2 percent of the final sales price.[8] That study was before the currency collapse on the periphery of empire reduced those essentially slave wages by half and increased dollar-denominated imports and debt service by 100 percent.

During the 1997–98 economic and currency collapses on the periphery of empire, externally contracted wage costs in Indonesia dropped 75 percent in one catastrophic year and its import and debt servicing costs doubled and tripled even as its per capita income dropped from $1,200 a year to $300. When Indonesia reached that level, South Korea was still laying off 10,000 workers a day and orphanages were filling up with children of distraught parents who could not feed them while, through a sharp drop in commodity prices, importers' profits in the

still intact world received a boost (at least in the short term).

Paying equally productive developing world labor 20 percent the rate of developed world labor (since the currency collapses, under ten percent), and the former Eastern bloc only a fraction of that, is surely a wealth confiscation rate far greater than that at the origin of the monopolization of the tools of production and protomercantilist control of trade (plunder by trade) in the city-states and emerging nations of Europe centuries ago.

There is "a continuing South-to-North resource flow on a scale far outstripping any the colonial period could command."[9] In fact, that wealth confiscation is picking up speed. During Kennedy's presidency there were three dollars flowing north for every dollar going south; in 1998 the ratio was seven to one; and assuming the financial meltdown of the imperial centers is avoided it will pick up speed. With their enormous reserves of wealth in the developed world, corporations and speculators are buying up properties in the financially collapsed world for three cents to thirty cents on the dollar. Those titles to others' industries and resources will demand profits and those profits will flow to the imperial centers.

Purchasing Power Parity, Another Strategy of Deception

The farther one goes east from the borders of Western Europe, the lower the value of local currencies and thus the higher the rate of wealth confiscation. In each case, if labor values were calculated by the Purchasing Power Parity (PPP) system, one would find greater wealth in those countries.

Simply stated, PPP calculates commodity values in countries with undervalued currencies at their values in the imperial centers of capital.

Those values may have been calculated in all sincerity. But the low wages and prices received by the already impoverished when calculated in "hard" currency gave substantial moral power to impoverished countries when negotiating with the IMF and World Bank. The IMF and World Bank chose PPP to offset such embarrassment. What was not addressed was that these low currency values denied full value to the soft currency nations when purchasing from the imperial center, while simultaneously they were required to make their sales to the imperial center below value.

If the IMF, World Bank, and traders used these PPP equal values in purchase of commodities and payment of debts, the world's currently suppressed and oppressed people would be fully paid for their labors and would thus have gained their economic freedom. Of course, such calculations would immediately expose how powerful societies lay claim to others' wealth through unequal wages and low-priced commodities by imposed "soft" currency values.

Equalize Currency Values to Equally Productive Labor Values and Third World Deficits Become Large Surpluses

By conceptually reversing the process, the mystery of wealthy, resource-poor nations and impoverished resource-wealthy nations is solved. Historically, inequality of pay has been justified as due to greater productivity. But the studies addressed above document that equally productive labor is paid extremely unequally.

Throughout this treatise we will be documenting that a large share of the inequalities in pay are due to inequalities in financial, economic, and military power. Documented also is how, after massive trade struggles and wars, powerful nations developed a rough equality in

trades, but still in place was a massive inequality in trades between powerful nations and weak nations.

At each point we address these inequalities of trade and the huge deficits and debts they impose on the weak impoverished world, we ask the reader to note how those deficits and debts will quickly disappear by matching currency values to equally productive labor values. Equal currency values and equal pay for equally productive labor eliminate one nation's laying claim to another's wealth.

The Periphery of Empire Finances the Imperial Centers of Capital

Developed countries claim to be financing the developing world, but actually the poor countries are financing the rich through the wealthy world underpaying equally productive developing world labor, paying far less than full value for natural resources, and through primarily investing in commodity production for the wealthy world. In this process, between 1980 and 1990—when measured against the dollar (not internal [PPP] relative values)—"wage levels in Mexico declined by sixty percent [another forty percent in 1994–95], . . . in Argentina by fifty percent and in Peru by seventy percent" and again that was before the 1997–98 collapse of developing world currencies reduced wages on the periphery of empire by half.[10] The above appears to list IMF/World Bank/GATT/NAFTA/WTO/MAI failures. However, they are not failures—they are the successes of financial and economic warfare. The prices of developing world commodities are lowered while the prices of developed world products are retained, siphoning ever more wealth to corporate imperialists:

Capital that has extended its influence over these new territories knows its own interests, works together in its common interests even while individual capitals compete, [and] coordinates its goals and its strategies in its common interest. . . . There will always be social inequality, because that increases profits; winners win more because losers lose more. Keeping the Third World in dependence and poverty is not an accident or a failure of the world capitalist system, but part of its formula for success.[11]

It is this simple. Holland consumes fourteen times the natural resources within its borders as calculated in monetary units, which far undervalues Third World labor. Other European countries are more or less comparable, and the United States, with under 5 percent of the world's population, consumes almost 30 percent of the world's natural resources.[12] That there is any intention of developing the Third World under a philosophy that siphons such enormous wealth from the impoverished to the wealthy is an oxymoron. For the impoverished people to gain control of their destiny means the wealthy world must pay them equally for equal work, must pay full value for their resources, and must permit them equal access to finance capital, technology, and markets.

Though the IMF/World Bank/GATT/NAFTA/WTO/MAI purport to practice equal and honest trade, this is so only between developed imperial centers of capital and then only partially so. Labor on the periphery of empire is being asked to take severe reductions in pay; the original advantages granted to Japan, South Korea and Taiwan (upon those established advantages China and other Southeast Asian nations were also riding) are being scaled back; and the needs of most impoverished nations for industrialization support (equal pay for equal work, access to technology, protection of home industry and markets, and access to world markets) are not even being addressed. Except for the currently emerging China and Southeast Asian countries (and their 1997–98 financial meltdown highlights that their success is not yet assured), the former colonial world is still the countryside providing cheap resources to an imperial center of capital.

Trumpeting Partial Rights as Full Rights

The following scene is repeated over and over throughout history: Rights are taken away from the weak through violence and cunning. The excessive rights of power become excessive rights of capital formalized into law. Those excessive rights accumulate wealth. The greater share of that confiscated wealth is wasted (trade wars, cold wars, covert wars, hot wars, and high living) and a smaller share becomes accumulated capital.

A society becomes accustomed to whatever structure of rights through which it obtains food, clothes, and shelter. A change in the structure of rights will feel abnormal. If a gain of rights for the masses—and thus a loss of rights for the powerful—is imminent, political power (supported by true believers in academia, the media, and among the masses) will immediately be deployed to suppress it and reimpose the belief system which protects that power.

After the initial appropriation of rights through violence or cunning, the further claiming or suppressing of rights is done by good people (it could be you or me) maximizing the gains to themselves within the law and customs of society. There is no conspiracy. It is Adam Smith's hidden hand—each looking after his or her self-interest. That self-interest typically takes the form of supporting the reimposition of belief systems.[13] This process may have been the only way to break out of the iron grip of the excessive rights of aristocracy in Adam Smith's time but it is not a process in everybody's best interest once aristocracy's iron grip was broken.

Each partial gain of rights as society comes out from under that iron grip is trumpeted as full rights (a Social Control belief system); that incomplete gain in rights becomes customary; technology continues to gain in efficiency, producing ever more wealth; the masses receive the smaller share, or none, of that increased wealth; the powerful receive the larger share or even a part of what once went to labor; the rich get richer, the poor get poorer; and eventually another revolution is born.

After a gain in rights through a successful revolution, new power brokers, or a coalition of old and new power brokers, continue the structuring of rights to lay claim to the greater share of the wealth produced by the ever-increasing efficiencies of technology. This cycle keeps repeating itself, normally giving more rights to more people each time. But full political rights cannot be won without full economic rights. If full rights were given to all through equal pay for equal work, the wealth produced and accumulated by society would be far greater than under today's monopolized rights, which translate into monopolized wealth.

Former Colonies Do Not Have Their Economic Freedom

The former colonial societies furnishing those resources were defeated centuries ago. We are taught that they are now free but that is not so, rhetoric that they are notwithstanding. Labor is too poorly paid in defeated, weak, and dependent nations to create buying power and those cheap resources are processed into useful products that become the wealth of the industrialized powerful countries. A small share of those manufactured products is returned to the weak defeated nations to pay for the raw material from which those manufactured products (created wealth) were made.

To purchase a small share of manufactured products from the industrialized countries produced with their resources, defeated societies must sell even more of their resources. Manufactured product sales above the needs of payment for resources and money wasted on arms and corruption continually increase the debts of the dependent nations, and servicing that continually increasing debt requires the sale of even more resources.

Heavy investment in extraction of the natural wealth of weak resource-wealthy nations while paying local labor subsistence wages assures a surplus of production and low prices for those natural resources while simultaneously denying both the accumulation of capital and buying power in the dependent nation. Of course, those debts cannot be paid off and that is the much spoken of, but little understood, debt trap.

Summary

Control of trade, and thus control of who becomes wealthy, has for centuries been through monopolization of technology and unequal currency values. The cooperative approach to Germany, Japan, and Southeast Asia we witnessed for forty years as technology was shared and currency values equalized with allies was only a cover for the battle to suppress the breaks for freedom worldwide that we will be addressing in depth. But those battles have been won by the imperial centers of capital and the rules are changing.

If developing centers of capital were permitted to mature and true free trade developed, this would be a crisis of the first order for the imperial centers of capital. The high price of technology is a function of monopolies. Honest capital is but stored labor and the proper cost of virtually every manufactured product, including industrial capital, is the price of labor to produce it. This includes a fair wage (not monopoly wage) for management and reasonable interest on capital (stored labor) for owners.

The fact that almost every region of the world has more natural resources than Japan suggests that, once it has industrial capital, an efficient internal transportation system, and access to markets, the developing world can, on the average, produce more cheaply than Japan. Where are Hong Kong's resources? Where are South Korea's resources? Where are Taiwan's resources? Where are the resources of most of Europe? The answer, of course, is that those resources are primarily in the impoverished world and that natural wealth has been confiscated through inequalities of trade to become the wealth of the imperial centers of capital.

The centuries-long process of embedding excessive rights in property and taking rights away from labor and those on the periphery of empire has created an economic monster. We grow up within that monster, no other system for comparison is permitted to evolve, everything looks normal to us, and people are instinctively threatened by thoughts of major changes. After all, their livelihoods are tied to those same horrendously wasteful arteries of commerce.

But consider this: The greater share of low-paid labor we have been describing is essential work while over half the labor in the high-paid *services* in the industrialized world is, except as a method of distribution, totally unnecessary. The rights of property are so excessive and the rights of labor so inadequate that throughout the Industrial Revolution distribution through unnecessary labor has evolved to pull some of the unearned wealth back from property. Of course it is the buying power of the masses from the wages of that unnecessary labor that created more demand, that created more industry, and that created today's developed world economy of income (wealth) distribution through unnecessary labor.[14]

Wasted labor within what appeared to be an efficient economy has been outlined in classics by Benjamin Franklin 200 years ago, Charles Fourier 180 years ago, and Thorstein Veblen, Bertrand Russell, Lewis Mumford, Stuart Chase, Upton Sinclair, and Ralph Borsodi in the first half of the twentieth century. Late twentieth-century writers describing the same phenomenon are Juliet Schor, Seymour Melman, Samuel Bowles, David Gordon, Thomas Weiskopf, Jeremy Rifkin, Andre Gorz, numerous European authors, and this author in *The World's Wasted Wealth 2*.

A reading of those authors will convince one that well over 50 percent and possibly even 70 percent of all labor expended in the developed world produces nothing essential or even desirable. It is only a method of wealth distribution. This means technology is far more efficient than we realize and if we eliminated the waste of resources and capital that accompanies that wasted labor, the entire world could be quickly developed to a sustainable level.

Notes

1. Adam Smith, *The Wealth of Nations* (New York: Random House, 1965), p. 64.

2. Ibid, pp. 64–67.

3. Makhijani, *Economic Justice*.

4. Doug Henwood, ''Clinton and the Austerity Cops,'' *The Nation*, November 23, 1992, p. 628. Colin Hines, Tim Lang, Jerry Mander, and Edward Goldsmith, eds., *The Case Against the Global Economy and For a Turn Toward the Local* (San Francisco: Sierra Club, 1996), p. 487, say $24.90 an hour for Germany and $16.40 for the U.S.

5. For those internal struggles see J.W. Smith, *The*

World's Wasted Wealth 2 (San Luis Obispo, CA: The Institute for Economic Democracy, 1994).

6. Makhijani, *Economic Justice*, pp. xv, 80–81, 121–22, 162–65; see also pp. 159, 167–70.

7. Ibid, p. 163.

8. Jack Epstein, "Dickens Revisited," *The Christian Science Monitor*, August 24, 1995, pp. 1, 8; Amy Kaslow, "The Price of Low-Cost Clothes: U.S. Jobs," *The Christian Science Monitor*, August 20, 1995, p. 4; Christopher Scheer, "Illegals Made Slaves to Fashion," *The Nation*, September 11, 1995, pp. 237–38.

9. Susan George, *The Debt Boomerang* (San Francisco: Westview Press, 1992), p. xvii.

10. Susan George and Fabrizio Sabelli, *Faith and Credit* (San Francisco: Westview Press, 1994); Duncan Green, *Silent Revolution* (London: Cassel, 1995), especially pp. 95–96; Graham Hancock, *Lords of Poverty* (New York: Atlantic Monthly Press, 1989); James Petras, "Latin America's Free Market Paves the Road to Recession," *In These Times*, February 13–19, 1991, p. 17.

11. Peter Marcuse, "Letter from the German Democratic Republic," *Monthly Review* (July/August 1990), p. 61.

12. David C. Korten, *When Corporations Rule the World* (West Hartford, CT: Kumarian Press, 1995), p. 33.

13. Chapter Nine.

14. J.W. Smith, *World's Wasted Wealth 2.*

2

The Violent Accumulation of Capital Is Firmly Rooted in History

Establishing the Underlying Principles of Twentieth-Century "Free Trade"

The economic system [neomercantilism] we are now creating in [Adam] Smith's name bears a far greater resemblance to the monopolistic market system he condemned ... [and] opposed as inefficient and contrary to the public's interest ... than it does to the theoretical competitive market system he hypothesized would result in optimal allocation of a society's resources.
— David C. Korten, *When Corporations Rule the World*

That unique historian of the Middle Ages, Petr Kropotkin, also recognized a "*resemblance*" in societies as they evolved towards modern times. At first glance, cities of different cultures may appear different and quaint but the basic structure was the same:

The medieval cities ... [were] a natural growth in the full sense of the word. ... Each one, taken separately, varies from century to century. And yet, when we cast a broad glance upon all the cities of Europe, the local and national unlikenesses disappear, and we are struck to find among them a wonderful resemblance, although each has developed for itself, independently from the others, and in different conditions. ... The leading lines of their organization, and the spirit which animates them, are imbued with a strong family likeness. Everywhere we see the same federations of small communities and guilds, the same "sub-

towns" round the mother city, the same folkmote, and the same insigns of its independence. ... Food supplies, labour and commerce are organized on closely similar lines [and] inner and outer struggles are fought with the same ambitions.[1]

The "wonderful resemblance" Kropotkin spotted as such a social positive had a dark side that went on to become the "resemblance to the monopolistic system" that David C. Korten spotted in today's world economy. Monopolization through violence and economic warfare is with us today just as in the early history of commerce in the Middle Ages. We will be following that common thread of plunder by trade through history, demonstrating that it is the foundation of today's world trade and the cause of immense wealth for the few and impoverishment for the many.

The Evolution of the City States and Plunder by Trade

Just as their predecessors fought to appropriate their neighbors' wealth through raids, the cities of the Middle Ages used their military superiority to monopolize the tools of production, control trade, and make the outlying societies dependent upon their commerce. They were learning to "plunder by trade." Henri Pirenne and Eli F. Heckscher in their classics on the Middle Ages describe the birth of the modern market economy through the monopolization of the tools of production and protomercantilist trade imposed and controlled through violence:

> Up to and during the course of the fifteenth century the towns were the sole centers of commerce and industry to such an extent that none of it was allowed to escape into the open country.... The struggle against rural trading and against rural handicrafts lasted at least seven or eight hundred years.... The severity of these measures increased with the growth of "democratic government."... All through the fourteenth century regular armed expeditions were sent out against all the villages in the neighborhood and looms and fulling-vats were broken or carried away.[2]

Immanuel Wallerstein in *The Origin of The Modern World System* describes the same process: The problem of the towns collectively was to control their own markets, that is, be able to reduce the cost of items purchased from the countryside and to minimize the role of stranger merchants. Two techniques were used. On the one hand, towns sought to obtain not only legal rights to tax market operations but also the right to regulate the trading operation (who should trade, when it should take place, what should be traded). Furthermore, they sought to restrict the possibilities of their countryside engaging in trade other than via their town. Over time, these various mechanisms shifted their terms of trade in favor of the townsmen, in favor thus of the urban commercial classes against both the land-owning and peasant classes.[3]

Those simple looms and fulling vats were primitive industrial capital. With this primitive technology, the cities could produce cheaper and better cloth and trade these commodities to the countryside for wool and food. But when the serfs came to town and looked at the simple looms and fulling vats, it did not take them long to build their own tools and produce their own cloth.

The loss of the city's markets for both raw material and manufactured products due to the comparative advantage of the countryside meant impoverishment and possibly even starvation for those in the city who formerly produced that cloth. The same loss of monopoly through increased technological knowledge of the countryside and its natural comparative advantage held true for other products and other cities. The wealth-producing process had to be protected. The comparative advantages of the outlying villages were eliminated by force to maintain dependency upon the city and lay claim to both the natural wealth of the countryside and the wealth produced by technology.

Obtaining their raw material from the countryside cheap and selling their manufactured products high—through a legal system of "entitlements" of their own creation—the powerful and crafty of the city transferred manufactured, monetized, and capitalized wealth within their trading region to themselves. Those same powerful and crafty groups throughout history continually restructured laws to protect property rights because these property rights "entitled" them to all wealth (above labor costs and other production costs) produced on, or with, that property. As an assured producer of wealth, privately owned, income-producing property developed capitalized value.

Immanuel Wallerstein's phrase describing the problems of the towns in controlling commerce—"they sought to restrict the possibilities of their countryside engaging in trade other than via their town"[4]—describes the same problem facing the powerful today. To maintain their wealth and power, and the standard of living their citizens now feel is normal, the powerful must maintain both the inequalities of world trade and a monopoly on trade.

To permit the countryside to utilize its natural comparative advantage would mean a drastic drop in living standards for the forming imperial centers of capital and open revolt of their citizenry as they faced starvation and impoverishment. Thus, the emergence of conscientious leaders in powerful imperial centers of capital, with a sincere interest in the well-being of people in dependent societies providing their crucial resources, is a rare occurrence. Right by the philosophical books on diplomacy and statecraft, reality requires leaders to care for their own even as millions—or even billions—of people on the periphery are impoverished by the leaders' "grand strategies" (financial, economic, legal, and military), "realpolitiks," "containments," "economic warfare," and "financial warfare."[5]

To protect their access to crucial resources, powerful imperial cities of the Middle Ages used military power to eliminate the comparative advantage of the countryside and that of other cities. Power struggles between city-states had intrigues, alliances, balance of power, and preponderance of power foreign policies identical to, and for the same purpose as, modern nations and empires—control of resources and trade to maintain their security:

> The leading mercantile cities [of Europe] resorted to armed force in order to destroy rival economic power in other cities and to establish a [more complete] economic monopoly. These conflicts were more costly, destructive, and ultimately even more futile than those between the merchant classes and the feudal orders. Cities like Flor-

ence, which wantonly attacked other prosperous communities like Lucca and Siena, undermined both their productivity and their own relative freedom from such atrocious attacks. When capitalism spread overseas, its agents treated the natives they encountered in the same savage fashion that it treated their own nearer rivals.[6]

Title to industrial capital (the tools of production) and control of trade were the primary mechanisms for claiming the wealth of the countryside, another city, the weak within an empire, or the weak on the periphery of empire. The destruction of another society's capital to protect markets substituted "plunder by trade" for "plunder by raids." Instead of appropriating another's wealth directly, societies learned to accomplish this through the protomercantilist policies of making others dependent and laying claim to their wealth through unequal trades.

Thus evolved the foundation philosophy of mercantilism. The quote below describing British mercantilism is from Adam Smith's *The Wealth of Nations* but the origin of that trade philosophy in modern nations in the twentieth century can be traced to the cities of Europe several hundred years earlier. Adam Smith's philosophical work was the result of studying world trade patterns that had been in force for centuries:

> [Mercantilism's] ultimate object . . . is always the same, to enrich the country [city] by an advantageous balance of trade. It discourages the exportation of the materials of manufacture [tools and raw material], and the instruments of trade, in order to give our own workmen an advantage, and to enable them to undersell those of other nations [cities] in all foreign markets: and by restraining, in this manner, the exportation of a few commodities of no great price, it proposes to occasion a much greater and more valuable expor-

tation of others. It encourages the importation of the materials of manufacture, in order that our own people may be enabled to work them up more cheaply, and thereby prevent a greater and more valuable importation of the manufactured commodities.[7]

Evolving from Imperial Cities to Nascent Imperial Nations: The Origin of Today's Clichés of "Secrecy," "National Security," and "The National Interest"

With the cities battling over the wealth of the countryside, aristocracy and the church reorganized and, while consolidating the first modern states, one by one defeated the free cities of Europe. As those people's livelihoods were dependent upon control of their coveted wealth-producing resources, convincing them that their well-being should be entrusted to others controlling these resources went against all instinct and common sense. The masses wished to maintain control of their resources and retain their community support structures. "Only wholesale massacres by the thousand could put a stop to this widely spread popular movement, and it was by the sword, the fire, and the rack that the young states secured their first and decisive victory over the masses of the people."[8]

As the formation of the states overwhelmed the free cities of Europe and their communal ways, the fourteenth century saw the beginning of a 300-year effort to erase all trace of community support structures and community ownership of social wealth. The process to individualize the masses to limit their power had begun:

> For the next three centuries the states . . . systematically weeded out all institutions in which the mutual-aid tendency had formerly found its ex-

pression. The village communities were bereft of their folkmotes [community meetings], their courts and independent administration; their lands were confiscated. The guilds were spoliated of their possessions and liberties, and placed under the control, the fancy, and the bribery of the State's official. The cities were divested of their sovereignty, and the very springs of their inner life—the folkmote, the elected justices and administration, the sovereign parish and the sovereign guild—were annihilated; the State's functionary took possession of every link of what formerly was an organic whole. Under that fatal policy and the wars it engendered, whole regions, once populous and wealthy, were laid bare; rich cities became insignificant boroughs; the very roads which connected them with other cities became impracticable. Industry, art, and knowledge fell into decay. . . . For the next three centuries the states, both on the Continent and in these islands [Great Britain], systematically weeded out all institutions in which the mutual-aid tendency had formerly found its expression. It was taught in the universities and from the pulpit that the institutions in which men formerly used to embody their needs of mutual support could not be tolerated in a properly organized State.[9]

Having gained control of the masses through the power of the state, those with power could safely concentrate on gaining control of the wealth-producing mechanisms of world trade:

> The problem of the towns collectively was to control their market, that is, be able to reduce the cost of items purchased from the countryside and to minimize the role of stranger merchants. . . . But the profits in [controlling the trade of the countryside], while important, were small by what might be earned in long-distance trade, especially colonial or semicolonial trade. Henri Sée estimates the profit margins of the *early* commercial operations as being very high: "Sometimes in excess of 200 or 300 percent from dealings that were little more than piracy."[10]

The raiders of the Middle Ages did not need to keep what they were doing secret; that it was for their survival was obvious. But, as soon as imperial cities evolved into imperial states, the connection between the traders who would lose business and those who would have to fight was broken. Here is where the secrecy of policies of state as it relates to world trade in the twentieth century was born. Managers of State cannot teach their citizens to be kind and just and then arm them and send them out to destroy the industries of peaceful neighbors. The excuses used are those we read in history and those excuses have became so ingrained we accept them as the biological imperative of humankind. They are not biological imperatives. Humans are far more peaceful and cooperative than they are aggressive. Expose the real reason for these wars and suppressions, provide the world with a peaceful option for its ''national interest'' and ''national security,'' establish a modest security force whose mission is everybody's security, and the world will become peaceful. Security is the key to peace.

The Enormous Advantage of Cheap Water Transportation

While cities fought back and forth, those with access to the sea and with seafaring skills had a unique advantage. So long as they could maintain dominance on the seas, they could move commodities much more cheaply than their competitors. Thus, the great trading and seafaring city state of Amalfi was destroyed by the sea power of Pisa. Pisa was then defeated by Genoa only to be later overwhelmed by Venice. Through naval power, Venice was able to enforce the rules of trade for centuries. However, along with the loss of the silk and spice trade through Muslim control of those routes, the Venetians slowly succumbed to the combined power of competing sister states and European powers.[11]

With the battles between Italian city-states preventing a consolidation of wealth and power, it was now the turn of Western European cities. The Hanseatic League formed in the late thirteenth century and, within a hundred years, eighty-five to one hundred cities were cooperating on quelling pirates, fostering safe navigation with lighthouses and trained pilots, importing raw material and exporting manufactured goods (by agreement only in Hanseatic boats), and had established navigation laws and custom duties with trading enclaves on foreign soil—the forerunner of today's duty-free ports and industrial enclaves.

Having copied the principles of monopolization of trade practiced by the Venetian Empire, the Hansa dominated the trade of Western and Middle Europe for 300 years. With treaties between sister cities, this powerful league avoided most, but not all, of the pitched battles typical of Southeastern and Eastern European city-states. However, identical to those sister city-states, it was weakened by principalities and ruling families within its geographical area demanding tributes within its jurisdiction; it lacked the power, cohesiveness, and coordination of a unified nation; and it was overwhelmed by unified national powers (Denmark, Sweden and Norway; Lithuania and Poland; the principality of Moscow; and the Dutch) in a replay of the unified coalitions which defeated Venice.[12] As the Hanseatic League's trade declined, nations with unique advantages of coastline, timber for building ships, and skilled seamen (Spain, Portugal, France, England, and Holland) spread across the world, overwhelmed primitive cultures, and created their colonial trading empires.

With the development of ships that carried many more tons of cargo, thus greatly reducing shipping costs, tiny Holland's trade blossomed. Out of 20,000 ships in world trade in the middle of the seventeenth century, 16,000 were Dutch. But other imperial nations were continually studying the process of gaining wealth and power through control of trade and Holland's expanding trade monopoly would soon be overwhelmed by the English, who were slowly building a base for economic and military power.

The Foundation of the British Empire Was Control of Technology and Trade

The shortage of labor created by the Black Death of the fourteenth century and the wool market created by Hanseatic traders provided the impetus for English sheep farming (in the fifteenth century, ninety percent of English exports were wool), and the greater profits of wool triggered the English Enclosure Acts of the fifteenth, sixteenth, and seventeenth centuries.

Skilled artisans were encouraged to emigrate from countries where they suffered religious persecution and declining economic fortunes, such as in France after the revocation of the Edict of Nantes. This was quite the opposite of today's industry fleeing high-priced skilled labor and moving to cheap labor. During Britain's early industrial development, from virtually every country in Europe and as far away as Persia, India, and China, the technology and skilled labor to produce almost every product in world commerce were brought to England. English labor was trained in those productive skills, custom duties were enacted to protect those new

industries, and bounties were given to promote exports of manufactures.[13]

The cornerstone of British control of trade was the Navigation Acts (1651–1847), copying Hanseatic and Venetian trade rules, which required British trade to be handled on British ships with British sailors. England and Scotland peacefully forming into one nation in 1707 provided a cohesive government under which all industry could be nurtured and protected.

The Navigation Acts were economic warfare aimed directly at Dutch dominance of commercial trade, which triggered war. English warships attacked Dutch shipping, and English exports and imports—now produced and transported largely by English fishermen, manufacturers, and shippers—increased rapidly. The Methuen treaty of 1703 with Portugal, shutting the Dutch off from trade with the Portuguese empire, was a deadly blow to Holland's trade; and suddenly idled Dutch capital and skilled labor emigrated to the *protective* trade structure of England.

Take note that Britain developed under the protection principles as outlined by Friedrich List, not under the principles of Adam Smith free trade as interpreted by neomercantilists. Britain becoming the wealthiest nation in the world for over one hundred years is powerful evidence for Friedrich List's philosophy of protecting a nation's industry and markets. Past error has been, and still is, that protection is always for one selfish nation or bloc. Weaker nations—which need even more protection—are at its mercy.

> [Britain's Navigation Acts] became the fundamental basis for the Old Colonial System. According to this Act the colonies could send their most important products, the so-called Enumerated Commodities, only to the mother country.

By an important law passed three years later, actually called the Staple Act, the same was ordered with regard to the export of European goods to the colonies, with the express purpose of "making this Kingdom a staple not only of the commodities of those plantations but also of the commodities of other countries and places for the supplying of them."[14]

Starting out more industrially and culturally advanced, the Spanish concentrated their labors on confiscating shiploads of gold and silver booty from their Latin American colonies. They ignored the production of consumer products for the elite and imported them instead.[15] In 1593, an advisor explained the problem to King Philip II:

> The Cortes of Valladolid in the year 1586 petitioned Your Majesty not to allow the further importation into the kingdom of candles, glassware, jewelry, knives and similar articles; these things useless to human life come from abroad to be exchanged for gold, as though Spaniards were Indians . . . the general remote cause of our want of money is the great excess of this Kingdom in consuming the commodities of foreign countries, which prove to us discommodities, in hindering us of so much treasure, which otherwise would be brought in, in lieu of those toys.[16]

Holland, Britain and France supplied these "toys" and Spain's wealth ended up in their vaults. Britain's First Earl of Shaftesbury (1621–83) was the primary promoter of the mercantilist plan to lay claim to Spain's wealth through trade. To his critics Shaftesbury explained, "If you will therein follow our directions we shall lay a way open to you to get all the Spanish riches in that country with their consent and without any hazard to yourselves."[17]

The wealth accumulated by Britain and the simultaneous impoverishment of Spain (its major enemy and rival), the eventual dominance of Britain in world trade for over one hundred years, and the immense wealth this produced for the small nation of Britain proved the validity of Shaftesbury's economic warfare plans. Although Spain was immensely wealthy, its riches and power were sapped by unnecessary purchases of other societies' labor, and that same economic warfare, backed and enforced by superior sea power as in the defeat of Spain, overwhelmed other nations.

Notes

1. Petr Kropotkin, *Mutual Aid* (Boston: Porter Sargent, 1914), pp. 187–88.

2. Karl Polanyi, *The Great Transformation* (Boston: Beacon Press, 1957), p. 277, quoting the classics Henri Pirenne's *Economic and Social History of Medieval Europe* and Eli F. Heckscher's *Mercantilism.*

3. Immanuel Wallerstein, *The Origin of The Modern World System,* vol. 1 (New York: Academic Press, 1974), pp. 119–20. For "plunder by trade," see William H. McNeill, *The Pursuit of Power* (Chicago: University of Chicago Press, 1982).

4. Wallerstein, *Modern World System,* nd.1, pp. 119–20

5. Christopher Layne, "Rethinking American Grand Strategy," *World Policy Journal* (Summer 1998), pp. 8–28.

6. Lewis Mumford, *Technics and Human Development* (New York: Harcourt Brace Jovanovich, 1967), p. 279; see also George Renard, *Guilds of the Middle Ages* (New York: Augustus M. Kelley, 1968), p. 35; Petr Kropotkin, *The State* (London: Freedom Press, 1987), p. 41; Kropotkin, *Mutual Aid,* chapters 6 and 7; Dan Nadudere, *The Political Economy of Imperialism* (London: Zed Books, 1977), p. 186.

7. Adam Smith, *The Wealth of Nations* (New York: Random House, 1965), p. 607.

8. Kropotkin, *Mutual Aid*, chapters 6–8, especially p. 225.

9. Ibid, especially p. 226. See also Renard, *Guilds of the Middle Ages*, p. 66 and chapters 7–8; A. Smith,

The Wealth of Nations, pp. 523–626, 713; Wallerstein, *Modern World System,* vol. 2, pp. 5, 37, 245, vol. 3, p. 137.

10. Wallerstein, *Modern World System*, vol. 1, pp. 119–20, emphasis added.

11. Friedrich List, *The National System of Political Economy* (Fairfield, NJ: Augustus M. Kelley, 1977), pp. 5–10.

12. List, *National System,* pp. 9–10, 12–33, 40–45, 78–79.

13. Ibid., pp. 71, 56, 345, chapters 26, 27.

14. Heckscher, *Mercantilism*, 1955, vol. 2, pp. 70–71; see also A. Smith, *The Wealth of Nations*, pp. 429–31, 544–65, 580.

15. Michel Beaud, *A History of Capitalism, 1500 to 1980* (New York: Monthly Review Press, 1983), p. 19.

16. Eric Williams, *From Columbus to Castro* (New York: Vintage Books, 1984), pp. 46–47. See also Paul Kennedy, *The Rise and Fall of The Great Powers* (New York: Random House, 1987), p. 54, and Kevin Phillips, *Boiling Point* (New York: Random House, 1993), especially chapter 8.

17. List, *National System*, pp. 57–59, 66–68; William Appleman Williams, *The Contours of American History* (New York: W. W. Norton, 1988), pp. 50–77, especially pp. 57, 77. See also Heckscher, *Mercantilism*, 2 vols.

3

Imposing a Belief System Under Which the Unwitting Willingly Hand Their Wealth to the Cunning

Adam Smith wrote his bible of capitalism, *The Wealth of Nations,* to expose mercantilism and to promote free trade. However, his description of eighteenth-century mercantilist trade describes well the protomercantilist trade between the cities and countryside 600 years earlier and mirrors the neomercantilist trade between developed and undeveloped nations for the next 223 years when the world was supposedly operating under his philosophy. For neomercantilists to restructure their overt plunder of weak societies into covert plunder through inequalities of trade, it was necessary to ignore statements in *The Wealth of Nations* that contradicted neoclassical trade philosophy. Free Trade was diplomatic code for continued mercantilist unequal trade:

> A small quantity of manufactured produce purchases a great quantity of rude produce. A trading and manufacturing country, therefore, naturally purchases with a small part of its manufactured produce a great part of the rude produce of other countries; while, on the contrary, a country without trade and manufactures is generally obliged to purchase, at the expense of a great part of its rude produce, a very small part of the manufactured produce of other countries. The one exports what can subsist and accommodate but a very few, and imports the subsistence and accommodation of a great number. The other exports the accommodation and subsistence of a great number, and imports that of a very few only. The inhabitants of the one must always enjoy a much greater quantity of subsistence than what their own lands, in the actual state of their cultivation, could afford. The inhabitants of the other must always enjoy a much smaller quantity. . . . Few countries . . . produce much more rude produce than what is sufficient for the subsistence of their own inhabitants. To send abroad any great quantity of it, therefore, would be to send abroad a part of the necessary subsistence of the people. It is otherwise with the exportation of manufactures. The maintenance of the people employed in them is kept at home, and only the surplus part of their work is exported. . . . the commodities of Europe were almost all new to America, and many of those of America were new to Europe. A new set of exchanges, therefore, began to take place which had never been thought of before, and which should naturally have proved as advantageous to the new, as it certainly did to the old continent. The savage injustice of the Europeans rendered an event, which ought to have been beneficial to all, ruinous and destructive to several [most] of those unfortunate countries.[1]

Before Britain's near defeat by Napoleon and his Continental System, these protectionist maxims, later to be so vehemently denied under Adam Smith, were plainly professed by all English ministers and parliamentary speakers: [1] Always to favour the importation of productive power, in preference to the importation of goods. [2] Carefully to cherish and to protect the development of the productive power. [3] To import only raw materials and agricultural products, and to export nothing but manufactured goods. [4] To direct any surplus of productive power to colonization, and to the subjection of barbarous nations. [5] To reserve exclusively to the mother country the supply of the colonies and subject countries with manufactured goods, but in return to receive on preferential terms their raw materials and especially their colonial produce. [6] To devote especial care to the coast navigation; to the trade between the mother country and the colonies; to encourage sea fisheries by means of bounties; and to take as active a part as possible in international navigation. [7] By these means to found a naval supremacy, and by means of it to extend foreign commerce, and continually increase her colonial possessions. [8] To grant freedom in trade with the colonies and in navigation only so far as she can gain more by it than she loses. [9] To grant reciprocal navigation privileges only if the advantage is on the side of England, or if foreign nations can by that means be restrained from introducing restrictions on navigation in their favour. [10] To grant concessions to foreign independent nations in respect of the import of agricultural products, only in case concessions in respect of her manufactured products can be gained thereby. [11] In cases where such concessions cannot be obtained by treaty, to attain the object of them by means of contraband trade. [12] To make wars and to contract alliances with exclusive regard to her manufacturing, commercial, maritime, and colonial interests. To gain by these alike from friends and foes; from the latter by interrupting their commerce at sea; from the former by ruining their manufactures through subsidies which are paid in the shape of English manufactured goods.[2]

Listening to later rhetoric as William Pitt refined the First Earl of Shaftesbury's formula for British trading supremacy, Britain seems to have decided that the protectionist policies through which she had become immensely wealthy had all been a mistake. In his classic, *The National System of Political Economy* (1977 edition), Friedrich List outlines how Britain, under the guidance of William Pitt, for the first time eulogized Adam Smith's doctrine of free trade. While secretly maintaining the old maxim of becoming wealthy through selling expensive manufactured goods and buying cheap commodities from weak dependent societies as outlined in the above twelve protectionist maxims, the British state department, British intelligence, and British industry were funding think tanks, correspondents, writers, and lecturers to impose their interpretation of Adam Smith's free-trade philosophy on the world.[3]

In short, Friedrich List alerts us that capitalism's foundation philosophy, Adam Smith free trade—as interpreted, designed, and managed by neomercantilists—is a brer rabbit/don't throw me in the brier patch scam designed to prevent the rest of the world from industrializing, thus maintaining its dependence and maintaining the flow of the world's resources to imperial centers of capital at a fraction of their true value.

Friedrich List points out that the forces of production are the tree on which wealth grows and that an individual may be better off purchasing something cheaper from another society but collectively everybody is better off if a society produces its own basic commodities, machine tools, and finished products.[4] For those who understand the multiplier factor, this is obvious. However, note the relative equality that must be assumed; it is specifically that equality which is missing.

With a quote, List tells us Napoleon knew well that any nation would be impoverished if its industry and trade were dominated by another: "Under the existing circumstances . . . any state which adopted the principles of free trade must come to the ground . . . [and] a nation which combines in itself the power of manufacturers with that of agriculture is an immeasurably more perfect and more wealthy nation than a purely agriculture one."[5]

And he tells us that both "Adam Smith and J.B. Say had laid it down that . . . nature herself had singled out the people of the United States [and most of the rest of the world] exclusively for agriculture." *The Wealth of Nations* had no allowance for industrial development beyond a few select nations; and Friedrich List, who challenged the philosophy of Adam Smith because his native Germany could not develop under a philosophy designed to maintain the supremacy of Britain, allowed only for the industrialization of the temperate zones.[6] Even List's staunchest supporters criticized his philosophy for not considering the rights of all people throughout the world. An honest philosophy for world development, such as we are laying out, must put rights for all as a first consideration.

Adam Smith recognized that by protection an undeveloped nation could "raise up artificers, manufacturers and merchants of its own" but claimed this would lower the price of its agriculture products.[7] This was a difficult logic, considering that agricultural production would be marketed to those employed in the new local industries and that engineering the dependency of others on British commodities markets and manufactures was the centerpiece for maintaining the wealth of his native Britain. This tells us that Adam Smith was considering only the rights of an imperial center and had relegated the periphery to providers of resources for that center.

For other major nations planning on industrializing (the newly free American colonies,

France, and later Germany), William Pitt's promotion of a philosophy for their dependency was easy to see through. "Such arguments did not obtain currency for very long [in France]. England's free trade wrought such havoc amongst the manufacturing industries, which had prospered and grown strong under the Continental blockade system, that a prohibitive *régime* was speedily resorted to under the protecting aegis of which, according to Dupin's testimony, the producing power of French manufactories was doubled between the years 1815 and 1827."[8]

List's insights into the "distinction between the *theory of values* and the *theory of the powers of production*" and the "difference between *manufacturing power* and *agricultural power*" were gained through observing firsthand both the rapid development of the newly free United States as they ignored Britain's promotion of Adam Smith [unequal] free trade and "the wonderfully favourable effects [to the continent] of Napoleon's Continental system and the destructive results of its abolition."[9]

Adam Smith pointed out that "England had founded a great empire for the sole purpose of raising up a people of customers. . . . The maintenance of this monopoly has hitherto been the principal, or more properly perhaps the sole end and purpose of the dominion which Great Britain assumes over her colonies."[10] Historian Barbara Tuchman concurs:

> Trade was felt to be the bloodstream of British prosperity. To an island nation it represented the wealth of the world, the factor that made the difference between rich and poor nations. The economic philosophy of the time (later to be termed mercantilism) held that the colonial role in trade was to serve as the source of raw materials and the market for British manufacture, and *never* to usurp the manufacturing function.[11]

The Much Respected Freedoms in America Are Based on Economic Freedom

The Grand Strategy of Britain to control the industry and markets of the American colonies, acutely restricting their wealth accumulation, was the primary reason for the American war of independence. America's founding fathers recognized that the "consumption of foreign luxuries, [and] manufactured stuffs, was one of the chief causes of [the colonies'] economic distress":[12]

> In the harbor of New York there are now 60 ships of which 55 are British. The produce of South Carolina was shipped in 170 ships of which 150 were British. . . . Surely there is not any American who regards the interest of his country but must see the immediate necessity of an efficient federal government; without it the Northern states will soon be depopulated and dwindle into poverty, while the Southern ones will become silk worms to toil and labour for Europe. . . . In the present state of disunion the profits of trade are snatched from us; our commerce languishes; and poverty threatens to overspread a country which might outrival the world in riches.[13]

The famous Boston Tea Party, touted as one cause of the revolution, was only a particularly theatrical protest over a rather minor example of this systematic injustice. To maintain colonial dependency, not even a horseshoe nail was to be produced in America, and under no circumstances were manufactured products to be exported to countries within Britain's trade empire. The colonialists

> could import only goods produced in England or goods sent to the colonies by way of England. They were not allowed to export wool, yarn, and woolen cloth from one colony to another, "or to any place whatsoever," nor could they export

hats and iron products. They could not erect slitting or rolling mills or forges and furnaces. After 1763, they were forbidden to settle west of the Appalachian Mountains. By the Currency Act of 1764, they were deprived of the right to use legal tender paper money and to establish colonial mints and land banks.[14]

After American independence, still attempting to maintain that dependency, England's Lord Brougham proposed destroying America's infant industries by selling manufactured goods to America below cost. "He thought it 'well worthwhile to incur a loss upon the first exportation [of English manufactures], in order, by the glut, TO STIFLE IN THE CRADLE THOSE RISING MANUFACTURES IN THE UNITED STATES.' " This experience (and the fact that Spain and France now blocked America's expansion) caused Americans to lay the foundation for their own Grand Strategy, copying Britain's neomercantilist trade policy. This required military might and led to establishing the Naval War College and a powerful navy.[15]

Americans understood well that Britain was attempting to control their trade through a philosophy of unequal free trade. U.S. statesman Henry Clay quotes a British leader: "[N]ations knew, as well as [ourselves], what we meant by 'free trade' was nothing more nor less than, by means of the great advantage we enjoyed, to get a monopoly of all their markets for our manufactures, and to prevent them, one and all, from ever becoming manufacturing nations."[16]

Lord Brougham's economic warfare plan was thwarted when, thirty-six years after gaining their political freedom and theoretical rights in the Revolutionary War, and while Britain was busy battling Napoleon on the Continent, Americans fought the War of 1812 to remove Britain's iron grip from America's commerce. America was now both politically and economically free. It was through winning the War of 1812 that America truly gained its independence. Until then, the American economy, and thus the fundamental rights of Americans, were dependent upon the whims of British neomercantilists backed by British naval power.

America, Canada, and Australia were the only former colonies that eventually gained both their political and economic freedoms. There is more to independence than the right to vote, free speech, and choice of religion, the political freedoms first gained by the American Revolution. For example, the states could trade between themselves, but they could not trade freely with the rest of the world due to the British navy's denial of that basic right, which thus maintained colonial dependence upon British industry and shipping. A humiliating treaty (Peace of Versailles, 1783) had been forced on the colonies that "permitted only the smallest American vessels to call at the island ports and prohibited all American vessels from carrying molasses, sugar, coffee, cocoa, and cotton to any port in the world outside the continental United States," and Britain's navy was there to ensure compliance.[17] But when Britain was fighting Napoleon on the Continent, the War of 1812 broke those trade barriers and gave the United States economic freedom.

And, of course, with its great natural wealth, rapid industrialization, and rich gold and silver discoveries, America was able to break free from Britain's monopolization of finance capital.

Friedrich List Wrote His Classic on Successfully Industrializing Nations from Observations of America's Industrialization

Friedrich List, the German diplomat, writer, and promoter of a German state with no internal tar-

iffs, observed "the wonderful favourable effects of Napoleon's Continental System, and the destructive effects of its abolition" when Napoleon was defeated at Waterloo.[18]

Thirteen years after the American/British war of 1812, Friedrich List arrived in America, became an American citizen, and studied America's protectionist break for economic freedom. This American Grand Strategy, designed by America's founders and promoted through List's German language newspaper *Outlines of Political Economy,* provided the foundation for his 1841 protectionist classic, *The National System of Political Economy.*[19] Virtually every nation which has ever industrialized did so under the principles outlined by Friedrich List.

List simply analyzed how the British had industrialized; analyzed their strategy of technological monopolization and control of trade; noticed the collapse of European industry when sales of English products penetrated Europe after Napoleon's defeat at Waterloo; analyzed how America ignored British free trade propaganda, protected its industry and markets, and became wealthy; and designed a philosophy under which his beloved native Germany or any other nation could industrialize and become powerful.

The prosperity Americans enjoyed once they had gained both their political and economic freedom exposes the Grand Strategy of the original promoters of Adam Smith to keep America's, and the world's, wealth going to British vaults. America's treasured *independence* is little more than its breaking of the chains of financial *dependence*. Financial independence depends on gaining control of industrial technology, access to raw material and fuel to process it into more industrial tools and useful products, and access to markets to sell enough products to pay for necessary imports.

Gaining their economic freedom to manufacture and trade is what most colonial nations were unable to do.

Adam Smith's philosophy, although quite just between equally developed nations and quite valuable as an analysis of trade between nations of equal power, is the industrial world's self-protective philosophy being forced upon the rest of the world under the guise of it being for their own good.

America Allies with the Imperial Nations

America's two Grand Strategy choices (championing the economic freedom of other colonized nations or joining the imperial nations in neomercantilist siphoning of their wealth) were complicated by its being forced to take sides in the battles between the old imperial nations (the two world wars) and by the almost certain post–World War II collapse of the American and European imperial centers of capital if the entire world became nonaligned or allied with the emerging socialist centers of capital.

The enormous industrial success of Bismarck and the Third Reich following List's precepts again proved the sound logic of List's philosophy, as did America's support (protection) for European industrial development under the Marshall Plan. That support was protection, even if it came from without. Under threat of the entire world gaining its economic freedom, and thus the loss of crucial resources and markets, the old imperial nations allied, informally, under one protective bloc.

Protection of the old imperial nations required bringing Japan, Taiwan, and South Korea under that protection. Their success not only again proved the soundness of List's philosophy, it proved the Managers of State knew exactly what they were doing. They were pro-

tecting crucial allies and maintaining—frequently imposing—the dependency status of others. When the threat to the old imperial nations disappeared with the collapse of the Soviet Union and those protections were withdrawn, the financial meltdown of those once allied nations again proved the validity of protecting tender emerging economies.

Those nations still had full rights to sell their production but their industrial capacity, developed to feed the imperial center, was far overbuilt; their population was far underpaid and thus unable to purchase its own production; and their rights to capital to make that adjustment disappeared with the flight of capital in the 1997–98 financial meltdown. The IMF/World Bank was imposing structural adjustments which reduced regional development and buying power. Private capital analyzed that overcapacity, knew that much of that industry must close down, and fled.

Economies of former allies can be subtly controlled from any point: finance capital, technology, resources, or markets. (Additional control methods—puppet governments, covert activities, or overt military action—are reserved for those not deemed necessary as allies.) Some leaders of the nations that underwent financial meltdowns complain that Federal Reserve Chairman Alan Greenspan, Secretary of the Treasury Robert Rubin, then-Deputy Secretary of the Treasury Larry Summers, and "their henchmen at the International Monetary Fund—have turned countries like Malaysia and Russia into leper colonies by isolating them from global capital and making life hellish in order to protect U.S. growth. The three admitted they had made hard choices—and they will even cop to some mistakes."[20] These same "usual suspects"—as Professor Stephen Gill, Professor of Political Science at York University in Toronto calls those always paraded forward to justify such policies—derailed Japan's plan for an Asian Monetary Fund (AMF) which would not have required the massive structural adjustments which a growing number are satisfied collapsed those tiger economies.[21] The "hard choices" faced by these "usual suspects" can only be taking care of one's own and letting others take care of themselves when it all falls apart. We must remember that historically all rising centers of capital are a threat to established centers of capital. Such financial and economic warfare has been the latter's policy when threatened, and very well could be the policy in this case even if this remains unrealized by the second and third echelons of power.

Forty Years of Successful Post–World War II American Protection of the "Free" World Validates Friedrich List

> Throughout the century the flood of "foreign aid" grew and grew until in the half century preceding 1914 Western Europe, led by Great Britain, "had invested abroad almost as much as the entire national wealth of Great Britain. . . . If the same proportion of American resources were devoted to foreign investment as Britain devoted . . . in 1913, the flow of investment would require to be thirty times as great. The entire Marshall Plan would have to be carried out twice a year.[22]

The economic miracle after World War II was rebuilding Europe in five years under the Marshall Plan. However, if the entire industrialized world today provided industry to the developing world at the relative rate that Britain exported capital at the height of the empire's expansion, the annual "*donation*" of capital from the currently developed world to the developing world would total over four times that given Europe during the five-year period of the Marshall Plan.

Note that is "donation," not "export," of capital. If control of world trade is to be maintained as capital is "exported," Third World labor must remain underpaid and overcharged. This prevents development of purchasing power in the undeveloped world, and wealth will continue to flow from the impoverished world to the wealthy world.

Although Adam Smith free trade was being preached, Friedrich List protection was provided to Japan, Taiwan, and South Korea, and later, until the Soviet Union collapsed, Southeast Asia and China were allowed under that umbrella. Within that bloc, capital was provided on easy terms, access to markets was provided, equality of trade was maintained, and labor was continually being better paid. Under that protection, buying power and prosperous economies were developing.

As the rest of the undeveloped world was not really included (its share of world trade dropped from 28 percent to 13 percent as its commodity prices dipped to values of twenty-one years earlier), that is Friedrich List protection of tender industries within a block of nations with need for group protection, not Adam Smith free trade as designed, preached, and managed by neo-mercantilists. Southeast Asia and China had only moved in under the protection provided Japan, Taiwan, and South Korea at the height of the Cold War and the rest of the undeveloped world remained the providers of raw material and markets.

The clincher that the imperial centers of capital are practicing Friedrich List protection philosophy under the cover of Adam Smith free trade philosophy is the current (1997 to 1999) collapse on the periphery of empire while the center holds firm. With the exception that China is still reasonably intact as this book goes to press, this is a perfect model of a successful neomercantilist policy under the cover of free trade as we are describing. The economic vigor of those collapsed nations can return only if a reasonable level of protection is reinstated either by the still intact powerful nations or by their collective actions. If those collapsed nations do not recover, promoting Adam Smith unequal free trade to them as true free trade will be quite difficult.

To maintain credibility and thus protect the center, almost certainly structural adjustment rules—which are little more than the withdrawal, and forced elimination, of protections that brought on those collapses—will be relaxed. That event will also be an acknowledgment that Adam Smith (as interpreted and applied) was wrong and Friedrich List was right.

In a World Economic Collapse, Secondary Industrial Powers Are at Greatest Risk

Even the center collapsing will prove List and disprove Adam Smith. If there is another worldwide collapse such as that of the 1930s, we must remember that world trade was in British pounds and Britain—with its ability to print and allocate the currency of world trade—suffered the least of all industrialized nations, that the undeveloped nations on the periphery of empire defaulted on their debts and actually found life easier during the Depression than before, and that it was the newly emerging industrial nations, especially the United States, that suffered the most.

In the current collapse of the periphery, we can analyze why. Money flees the periphery of empire for the safety of the center. That money is available both to push up the stock markets of the center and to invest in the real economy. IMF loans to the financially troubled countries are made under the condition that those funds repay investors from the center. Those IMF funds never leave the center of empire. The worried investors of the center are credited, the IMF funds debited, and the collapsed nation now has the identical debt as before, only owed to the IMF. While the center is still holding and with money seeking safety stuffing its financial institutions, speculators and stock market "bottom fishers" borrow those funds and purchase equities and property on the collapsed periphery. Resources, labor, and production costs in the peripheral nations dropping by half—due to the currency collapses—while prices and sales in the center hold, transfers enormous wealth from the periphery to the center. So long as that center holds, that wealth is now (1998–99) being transferred at a rate unheard of in modern times.

If the world economy collapses, the weakest and most impoverished nations can repudiate their debts and, just as they were in the Great Depression, be better off than before the crash. The emerging nations will be at greatest risk but, with the substantial technology and skilled labor they now have, they too have the option of repudiating unjust debts, creating their own trading currency, and reorganizing their economies to trade with the weaker nations now at least partially free of the old imperial centers of capital.

The Dilemma of the Old Imperial Centers of Capital

Choosing to support its ethnic, religious, and cultural European cousins, America took the helm of the imperial nations and led the battle to suppress the world's break for economic freedom. But, now that the Cold War is won, four possibilities remain:

Do the developed nations develop the world and establish equality of trades?

Do they include only China and Southeast Asia and form a subtle bloc of forty percent of the world trading unequally with the other sixty percent (a trading empire feeding upon the remaining sixty percent of the world)?

Will the corporate mercantilists decide (state department policies are, as is much domestic law, corporate decisions) to "contain" the once fast-emerging Chinese and Southeast Asians and return to the old standard of white, Western Christian, European-cultured, wealthy nations— fifteen percent of the world's people—covertly and militarily controlling the world?

Or will the world break into three competing trading blocs—the newly expanded and allied Europe, a Western hemisphere bloc, and an Asian bloc (three trading empires)?

This is a bigger dilemma than it first appears. Previous capital accumulations were little more than the world's wealth siphoned from defeated people of color to the winners of colonial wars, the white, Western Christian, European cultures. The need for allies to defeat fast-expanding socialism and the nonaligned movement for the first time brought non-white nations (Japan, Taiwan, and South Korea) into the fold. Idealistic planners' sincere desire to develop the world and the inability of the more selfish to exclude the non-white nations was, until the financial meltdowns on the periphery of empire, bringing all China and Southeast Asia (25 percent of the world's people) into the club of wealthy nations. Since over 60% of the developed world (40 percent of the total world) will then be people of color, many whites will disclaim any problem with this percentage, although many of the powerful behind closed doors will consider it the primary problem. But if these racial jealousies can be overcome, if the financial meltdown of the developing world is reversed, and if the waste of the world's wealth can be eliminated, there would be substantial capital to develop the remaining 60 percent of the world.

Notes

1. Adam Smith, *The Wealth of Nations* (New York: Random House, 1937), pp. 413, 426, 642.

2. Friedrich List, *The National System of Political Economy* (Fairfield, NJ: Augustus M. Kelley, 1977), pp. 366–370.

3. Ibid., pp. xxvii–xxviii, 368–69.

4. List, *The National System*, summarized.

5. Ibid., p. 73.

6. List, *The National System*, Memoirs of p. 99.

7. Smith, *Wealth of Nations,* pp. 66–67, 636–37; see especially List, *National System*, pp. xxvi, xxvii, 11, 73–75, 150–55, 99–100, 351.

8. List, *National System,* pp. 73–75.

9. Ibid, p. xxv.

10. Quoted by Herbert Aptheker, *The Colonial Era* (New York: International, 1966), pp. 23–24; taken from Smith, *Wealth of Nations,* pp. 579–80, 626.

11. Barbara Tuchman, *The March of Folly* (New York: Alfred A. Knopf, 1984), pp. 130–31 (emphasis added).

12. Charles A. Beard, *An Economic Interpretation of the Constitution* (New York: Macmillan, 1941), p. 46. See also Michael Barratt Brown, *Fair Trade* (London: Zed Books, 1993), p. 20.

13. Beard, *Economic Interpretation,* pp. 46–47, 171, 173.

14. Philip S. Foner, *From Colonial Times to the Founding of the American Federation of Labor* (New York: International, 1982), p. 32. See also William Appleman Williams, *Contours of American History* (New York: W.W. Norton, 1988), pp. 105–17; Smith, *Wealth of Nations,* pp. 548–49, Book IV, chapters 7, 8; James Fallows, "How the World Works," *The Atlantic*

Monthly, December 1993, p. 42; Frederic F. Clairmont, *The Rise and Fall of Economic Liberalism* (Goa, India: The Other India Press, 1996), p. 100.

15. Williams, *Contours of American History,* pp. 192–97, emphasis in original. See also Aptheker, *Colonial Era,* pp. 23–24; List, *National System,* especially pp. 59–65, 71–89, 92, 342, 421–22, chapter 9; 339–40; Dean Acheson, *Present at the Creation* (New York: W.W. Norton, 1987), p. 7; Richard Barnet, *The Rockets' Red Glare: War, Politics and the American Presidency* (New York: Simon and Schuster, 1983), pp. 34, 40, 60, 68.

16. Williams, *Contours of American History,* p. 221.

17. Barnet, *Rockets' Red Glare,* p. 40.

18. List, *National System, Economy,* pp. xxv–xxvi.

19. List, Memoirs, in *National System.*

20. "The Three Marketeers," *Time,* February 15, 1999, pp. 34–42.

21. Stephen Gill, "The Geopolitics of the Asian Crisis," *Monthly Review* (March 1999), pp. 1–9.

22. Acheson, *Present at the Creation,* p. 7.

4

The Defeat of Napoleon at Waterloo Eliminated France as a Major Threat to British Trade

With the discovery of the sea route to the East and America, the maximum control of natural resources and markets for manufactured products could be attained through claiming title to the lands of primitive and weak cultures. Title to the land and control of trade meant title to the wealth-producing process and the race was on for nations with imperial ambitions to colonize the world. "By 1900 Great Britain had grabbed 4,500,000 square miles; . . . France had gobbled up 3,500,000; Germany, 1,000,000; Belgium 900,000; Russia, 500,000; Italy, 185,000; and the United States, 125,000."[1]

The language of British law demonstrates the recognition that an imperial center must be careful about importation of manufactured products from either its colonies or other great powers:

> "So it is now," explained the Protectionist Act of 1562, "that by reason of the abundance of foreign wares brought into this realm from the parts of beyond the seas, the said artificers are not only less occupied, and thereby utterly impoverished . . . [but] divers cities and towns within this realm greatly endangered, and other countries notably enriched."[2]

In the late seventeenth century, Jean Baptiste Colbert, French Naval Secretary of State and Finance Minister, recognized the threat if France became dependent upon British mercantilism as was being established by Lord Shaftesbury. Therefore, Colbert duplicated Britain's industrial development efforts. France's purchase of the latest technology, encouragement of skilled workers, protection of the home markets, elimination of internal tariffs, and construction of canals and roads produced for France flourishing industries, a profitable shipping industry, and a powerful navy. However, wars, spendthrift governments, the revocation of the Edict of Nantes (which again encouraged blatant persecution of Protestants and forced 500,000 of France's most productive workers to flee) and the 1786 Eden Treaty with Britain (a replay of the Methuen Treaty's monopoly agreements which severely damaged Portugal, Holland, and Germany) impoverished the French economy through the same unequal trades.[3]

Napoleon understood Britain's economic warfare and, in 1807, issued his Continental Decrees to establish manufacturing on the Continent to protect France's market from Britain and prevent the loss of continental wealth:

> Napoleon was forced to devise a new tactic to deal with his perpetual enemy [Britain]: the Continental System. Developed during 1806/1807, this policy called for economic warfare against

the "nation of shopkeepers," whereby France, either through the cooperation of friends or by the use of force against enemies, would close the entire European continent to British trade and commerce. By weakening Britain's economy, Napoleon would destroy her ability to wage war, and also make it impossible for Great Britain to provide the huge subsidies to Continental allies which had characterized all the previous coalitions against France.[4]

Resurrecting Colbert's protective system, Napoleon's Continental System started the rapid industrialization of Europe. As this immense trading bloc meant the end of Britain's dominance of world trade, a "Holy Alliance" of Britain, the threatened monarchies on the continent, and the Church defeated Napoleon at Waterloo. With the elimination of Napoleon's Continental System, the markets of Europe were breached and industries throughout the continent collapsed.[5] This is the European collapse that first alerted Friedrich List to the necessity of protecting regional industries and markets. One cannot miss the similarity between the industrial collapse on the Continent and its *dependency* upon Britain after the French defeat, and the current (1991–1999) collapse of the Russian economy and its *dependency* upon the West.

At the peak of Britain's power, 54 percent of manufactured products in world trade were manufactured there. The British "exulted at their *unique* state, being now (as the economist Jevons put it in 1865) the trading center of the universe." The world was Britain's "countryside," a huge plantation system feeding its developed imperial center of capital:

> The plains of North America and Russia are our corn fields; Chicago and Odessa our granaries; Canada and the Baltic our timber forests; Australia contains our sheep farms, and in Argentina and on the Western prairies of North America are our herds of oxen; Peru sends her silver, and the gold of South Africa and Australia flows to London; the Hindus and the Chinese grow our tea for us, and our coffee, sugar and spice plantations are all in the Indies. Spain and France are our vineyards and the Mediterranean our fruit garden; and our cotton grounds, which for long have occupied the Southern United States, are being extended everywhere in the warm regions of the earth.[6]

If ever there was a statement that outlined a nation ruling the world as it monetized its natural wealth in the production and distribution process, funneled the world's resources and production to itself, made the world dependent upon its commodity markets, and capitalized those values into its hands, this is it. To funnel this wealth to the mother countries, exclusive trading companies—East India Company (English, Dutch, and French), Africa Company, Hudson Bay Company, etc.—were established. These exclusive companies had most of the rights of governments.

At this point, the famous bottom line of corporate accounting imposed its logic. If the natives could be forced to work for nothing while providing their own subsistence, the profits would be enormous. Thus Indians were enslaved in Spanish mines and Africans were enslaved to replace the Indians when over 95 percent of their population died off under such oppression. Wealth on the periphery—American, African, and Asian colonies—was claimed by Europe in trade for trinkets, knives, and guns.

The wealth accumulation power of imperialists was bounded only by the limits of their naval and military power, which were used to prevent other societies from infringing on their control of trade and accumulation of capital and wealth.

India: Her Vast Wealth Siphoned to Britain

In 1897, Britain's statesman Neville Chamberlain wrote a Colonial Office report: "During the present century . . . you will find that every war, great or small, in which we have engaged, has had at bottom a colonial interest, that is to say, either of a colony or else of a great dependency like India." The impoverishment of India is a classic example of "plunder by trade" backed by military might. Before being subdued, colonized, and enforced to become *dependent* upon British industry,

> India was relatively advanced economically. Its methods of production and its industrial and commercial organization could definitely be compared with those prevailing in western Europe. In fact, India had been manufacturing and exporting the finest muslins and luxurious fabrics since the time when most western Europeans were backward primitive peoples.[7]

Hand weaving was tedious and paid little, so the British purchased much of its cloth from India rather than producing its own. India had no need or desire for British products, so imports had to be paid for with gold. However, Britain did not make the same mistake as Spain; Indian textiles were embargoed and British cloth was produced with the evolving technology of weaving machinery. After India was conquered, its import and export policies were controlled by Britain, which not only banned Indian textiles from British markets but also taxed them to a disadvantage within India so that British cloth dominated the Indian market. Not only was India's internal production of cloth excluded from its own internal market so as to be undersold by Britain's inferior cloth, Britain excluded those beautiful and much

higher quality fabrics from England while marketing them all over Europe. Controlling India and the seas "entitled" British merchants to buy for a pittance and sell at a high price. Friedrich List points out that the purpose of this control of trade was building Britain's "productive power":

> Was England a fool in so acting? Most assuredly according to the theories of Adam Smith and J.B Say, the Theory of Values. For, according to them, England should have bought what she required where she could buy them cheapest and best; it was an act of folly to manufacture for herself goods at a greater cost than she could buy them elsewhere, and at the same time give away that advantage to the Continent. The case is quite contrary according to our theory, which we term the Theory of the Powers of Production, and which English Ministry . . . adopted when enforcing their maxim of *importing produce* and *exporting fabrics. . . .* The English ministers cared not for the acquisition of low-priced and perishable articles of manufacture, but for that of a more costly but enduring *manufacturing power.* . . . They have attained their objective to a brilliant degree. At this day [1841] England produces seventy million pounds' worth of cotton and silk goods, and supplies all of Europe, the entire world, India itself included, with British Manufactures. Her home production exceeds by fifty or a hundred times the value of her former trade in Indian Manufactured goods. What would it have profited her had she been buying for a century the cheap goods of Indian manufacture? And what have they gained who purchased those goods so cheaply of her? The English have gained power, incalculable power, while the others have gained the reverse of power.[8]

Through the forced sales of British products and the simultaneous embargoing of, or high tariffs on, the cheaper and higher quality Indian cloths, India's wealth started flowing toward Britain. "It was [only] by destroying [the] Indian textile industry that [the British textile industry of] Lancaster ever came up at all."[9] Other Indian industries were similarly devastated. In the words of historian Lewis Mumford:

> In the name of progress, the limited but balanced economy of the Hindu village, with its local potter, its local spinners and weavers, its local smith, was overthrown for the sake of providing a market for the potteries of the Five Towns and the textiles of Manchester and the superfluous hardware of Birmingham. The result was impoverished villages in India, hideous and destitute towns in England, and a great wastage in tonnage and man-power in plying the oceans between.[10]

One exceptionally rich sector of India was East Bengal (Bangladesh). When the British first arrived,

> [they] found a thriving industry and a prosperous agriculture. It was, in the optimistic words of one Englishman, "a wonderful land, whose richness and abundance neither war, pestilence nor oppression could destroy." But by 1947, when the sun finally set on the British Empire in India, Eastern Bengal had been reduced to an agricultural hinterland. In the words of an English merchant, "Various and innumerable are the methods of oppressing the poor weavers . . . such as by fines, imprisonment, floggings, forcing bonds from them, etc." By means of every conceivable form of roguery, the company's merchants acquired the weaver's cloth for a fraction of its value.[11]

Later, still under British control and ignoring the fact that the East Bengalis were being impoverished through dispossession of the land which produced their food and cotton, Bengal produced raw materials (indigo and jute) for world commerce, and poppies for the large, externally imposed Chinese opium market. As Adam Smith commented, money was lent to farmers "at forty, fifty, and sixty percent" and this, and other profits of trade, would confiscate all wealth except that paid in wages. Of course, Bengali labor was paid almost nothing, which meant Bengal's wealth was rapidly transferred to Britain. Foreign control—which enforced its dependency upon British industry and siphoned its wealth away through unequal trades in everyday commerce—devastated the once-balanced, prosperous Bengali economy and created the extreme poverty of Bangladesh today. "[O]nce it was the center of the finest textile manufactures in the world . . . [with] a third of its people . . . employed in non-agricultural occupations, . . . today, 90 percent of its workers are in agriculture or unemployed."[12] The destruction of the once-thriving economy of East Bengal (Bangladesh) was so thorough that even the long-staple, finely textured local cotton became extinct.[13]

Those who saw the movie *Gandhi* will remember that Indian citizens were denied the right even to collect salt from the ocean and were required by law to buy their salt and other everyday staples from British monopolies. Such enforced dependencies were little more than a tax upon defeated societies under the guise of production and distribution. Much work was being done, but it could have been done just as well or better by those being dispossessed of their land, denied the right to produce for themselves, and overcharged for monopolized products.

Japan, because it had no valuable resources, was the only country not culturally, racially, and religiously tied to Europe that escaped domination during this period in history. Until Taiwan and South Korea (and now China and Southeast Asia) were industrialized, all under the same protectionist barrier to contain fast expanding socialism, Japan was the only nonwhite society to industrialize and join the club of wealthy nations.[14]

In *The Discovery of India,* Prime Minister Jawaharlal Nehru wrote, "If you trace British influence and control in each region of India, and then compare that with poverty in the region, they correlate. The longer the British have been in a region, the poorer it is."[15] What applies to British colonialism applies to all colonialism and, as bad as it was, as we have just outlined, India and China were the least damaged by Europe's mercantilist policies. In other parts of the world, such havoc was created that ancient and culturally advanced civilizations completely disappeared, as in Peru and West Africa. Major primitive nations that did not have immunity to diseases common to Europe and Asia were simply erased off the map, populations collapsed to a fraction of their previous levels, and entire tribal subdivisions in these regions disappeared. Over 95 percent of the native population of the Americas disappeared in what was undoubtedly the greatest genocide in history.

These genocides are recorded only in little-known archives. Military commanders would record their assaults on native populations as defensive battles of an ongoing war, not an offensive that slaughtered innocent women and children. Death from disease is frequently addressed; even the distribution of blankets infected with smallpox is occasionally mentioned. But the destruction of a culture's food supply and economic structure which provided food, clothing, and shelter, the resultant sickness and deaths, and the fact that populations not having some immunity to smallpox (the world's greatest killer) suffered a 75 percent mortality rate—and thus the giving of those infected blankets was mass genocide—are not mentioned in polite history.

The little studied process of the collapse of the civilizations of the losers in these "clashes of cultures" can be seen today as the population of the collapsed Russian economy shrinks by 800,000 per year. As Russians "theoretically" still have control of their land and resources and they have not been subject to germ warfare, their defeat was not nearly as total as that of the native populations of the Americas and Africa.[16]

Controlling China Was Always a Much More Difficult Problem

In 1800, the per capita standard of living in China exceeded that of Europe.[17] Like India, China did not need or want Britain's products. However, Britain consumed large quantities of Chinese teas and, to avoid the loss of Britain's gold, it was imperative that something else be traded. Though it was done covertly and not acknowledged by the British government, it became official policy for British merchants to peddle opium to China. "Opium [sold to China] was no hole-in-the-corner petty smuggling trade but *probably the largest commerce of the time in any single commodity.*"[18] This injustice was challenged by Chinese authorities (the Boxer Rebellion); but their attempt to maintain sovereignty was put down by a combined force of 20,000 British, French, Japanese, German, and United States troops (5,000 were Americans) led by a German general.[19] This was a blatant attempt to carve up China among those imperial centers of capital.

With the sales of opium exceeding the purchases of tea, Britain lost neither gold nor currency. There were capital and labor costs; but these involved an internal circulation of money. No wealth was lost to another society, which is the essence of a successful mercantilist policy. This appears productive only because the wealth gained or protected by Britain was considered; the much greater losses suffered by China, India, and much of the world were conveniently left uncalculated.

While the imperial centers of capital were battling each other in World War II, China was laying its base for economic freedom. Although it is little known to Americans, United States troops were guarding key rail lines and ports for the collapsing Chinese government; and the OSS, precursor to the CIA, was busy ferrying Chiang Kai-shek's troops back and forth across China to suppress that revolution. However, China did break free in 1949, was marginalized for years by the imperial nations, yet still built a modest industrial capacity, and—by moving under the same protectionist umbrella as Japan, Taiwan, and South Korea—eventually averaged production gains of well over 10 percent a year.

Notes

1. E.K. Hunt and Howard J. Sherman, *Economics* (New York: Harper and Row, 1990), p. 144.

2. William Appleman Williams, *Contours of American History* (New York: W.W. Norton, 1988), introduction, especially p. 43.

3. Friedrich List, *The National System of Political Economy* (Fairfield, NJ: Augustus M. Kelley, 1977), pp. 33, 41–60, 72, 323, 342, 357, 369, 391.

4. Gordon C. Bond, *The Grand Expedition* (Athens: University of Georgia Press, 1979), pp. 1–2, 8.

5. List, *National System,* Chapter 6, Chapter 25, pp. 39, 72–73, 85–87, 323, 343–45, 357, 421–22.

6. Paul Kennedy, *Rise and Fall of Great Powers* (New York: Random House, 1987), pp. 151–52, quoted from R. Hyam, *Britain's Imperial Century 1815–1914* (London: B.T. Batsford, 1975), p. 47. See also these subchapters in Chapter Thirteen: "Conceptually Reversing the Process of Impoverishing Other Nations Through Selling Cheap Commodities" and "The Periphery of Empire Functions as One Huge Plantation System Providing Food and Resources to the Imperial Center."

7. Hunt and Sherman, *Economics,* p. 142.

8. List, *National System,* pp. 43–44.

9. Dan Nadudere, *The Political Economy of Imperialism* (London: Zed Books, 1977), p. 35, 68, especially 86. See also Betsy Hartmann and James Boyce, *Needless Hunger: Voices from a Bangladesh Village* (San Francisco: Institute for Food and Development Policy, 1982).

10. Lewis Mumford, *Technics and Civilization* (New York: Harcourt Brace Jovanovich, 1963), pp. 184–85.

11. Hartmann and Boyce, *Needless Hunger,* pp. 10, 12.

12. Arjun Makhijani, *From Global Capitalism to Economic Justice* (New York: Apex Press, 1992), p. 79.

13. Adam Smith, *Wealth of Nations* (New York: Random House, 1937, 1965), pp. 94, 97; Hartmann and Boyce, *Needless Hunger,* describes this devastation.

14. Hunt and Sherman, *Economics,* 1990, pp. 142–47, 624.

15. Noam Chomsky, *The Prosperous Few and the Restless Many* (Berkeley: Odonian Press, 1993), p. 56.

16. *60 Minutes,* May, 19, 1996; Frederic F. Clairmont, *The Rise and Fall of Economic Liberalism* (Goa, India: The Other India Press, 1996), dissects the colonizing and impoverishment of India and provides many other sources.

17. Anthony Sampson, *The Midas Touch* (New York: Truman Talley Books/Plume, 1991), p. 108.

18. Samuel Flagg Bemis, *A Diplomatic History of the United States* (New York: Henry Holt, 1936), pp. 1027–1142; Michael Greenberg, *British Trade and the Opening of China 1800–1842* (New York: Monthly Review Press), p. 104; Eric R. Wolf, *Europe and the People Without History* (Berkeley: University of California Press, 1982), pp. 255–58. (Emphasis added.)

19. Jack Beeching, *The Chinese Opium Wars* (New York: Harcourt Brace Jovanovich, 1975). See also Michael Bentley, *Politics Without Democracy* (London: Fontana Paperbacks, 1984), p. 154.

5

World Wars, Trade Wars

Battles Over Who Decides the Rules of Unequal Trade

Spain, Holland, Portugal, and France had been overwhelmed by British sea power and cunning control of markets. Otto von Bismarck, the unifier of the German nation, deduced that "free trade is the weapon of the dominant economy anxious to prevent others from following in its path."[1] Studying the development philosophy of Friedrich List, he consolidated the German nation in the late 1800s and industrialized: "factories, machinery, and techniques were bought wholesale, usually from England."[2]

At first German manufactures were of inferior quality, just as Japan's products were later when it first industrialized. However, it did not take the Germans long to learn. By 1913, Germany had 60,000 university students to Britain's 9,000, and 3,000 engineers to Britain's 350. Its industries were not only outproducing Britain, they were producing superior products.[3]

Earlier, in 1888, philosopher T.H. Huxley outlined the disaster that would befall Britain if it should ever lose its dominance in trade:

> We not only are, but, under penalty of starvation, we are bound to be, a nation of shopkeepers. But other nations also lie under the same necessity of keeping shop, and some of them deal in the same goods as ourselves. Our customers naturally seek to get the most and the best in exchange for their produce. If our goods are inferior to those of our competitors, there is no ground, compatible with

> the sanity of the buyers, which can be alleged, why they should not prefer the latter. And if the result should ever take place on a large and general scale, five or six millions of us would soon have nothing to eat.[4] [Twenty-six years later, when Britain was threatened with just such a loss, World War I began.]

Outlining that the concern was Germany's threat to British trade, in 1897 the publication *Saturday Review* wrote: "If Germany were extinguished tomorrow, the day after tomorrow there is not an Englishman in the world who would not be richer. Nations have fought for years over a city or right of succession; must they not fight for two hundred fifty million pounds sterling of yearly commerce?"[5]

Britain's survival depended upon selling overpriced manufactured products, and losing those markets would collapse her economy. As Britain's "national interest" was at stake, she had signed agreements with France, Austria-Hungary, Italy, and eventually Russia, all designed to contain Germany. The clash of interests in the Balkans between these competing imperial centers of capital led directly to World Wars I and II.[6] Before World War I, Europe

was "stifling" within her boundaries, with production everywhere outstripping the European demand for manufactured products. All Europe was therefore "driven by necessity to seek new markets far away," and "what more secure markets" could a nation possess than "countries placed under its influence?".... The rapid growth of German trade and the far-flung extension of German interests first encouraged in Germany a demand for a larger merchant marine, and then for a larger and more effective navy.... Without a strong fleet, Germany would find herself at the mercy of Britain, a "grasping and unscrupulous nation which, in the course of history, had taken opportunity after opportunity to destroy the trade of its commercial rivals."[7]

As Germany tried hard to break Britain's control of world commerce, Britain was

> reinforcing her position by making a hard and fast alliance with Austria-Hungary and Italy.... In 1904, Britain made a sweeping deal with France over Morocco and Egypt; a couple of years later she compromised with Russia over Persia, that loose federation of powers was finally replaced by two hostile power groupings; the balance of power as a system had now come to an end.... About the same time the symptoms of the dissolution of the existing forms of world economy—colonial rivalry and competition for exotic markets—became acute.[8]

Those "two hostile power groupings" were the old imperial centers of capital, Britain and her allies, and the emerging imperial centers of capital, Germany and her allies. Restrictive trade practices were strangling potentially wealthy countries and "everyone knew it would start but no one knew how or when ... until Archduke Ferdinand was shot."[9]

Except for religious conflicts and the petty wars of feudal lords, wars are primarily fought over resources and trade. President Woodrow Wilson recognized that this was the cause of World War I: "Is there any man, is there any woman, let me say any child here that does not know that the seed of war in the modern world is industrial and commercial rivalry?"[10]

> The real war, of which this sudden outburst of death and destruction is only an incident, began long ago. It has been raging for tens of years, but its battles have been so little advertised that they have hardly been noted. It is a clash of traders. ... All these great German fleets of ocean liners and merchantmen have sprung into being since 1870. In steel manufacture, in textile work, in mining and trading, in every branch of modern industrial and commercial life, and also in population, German development has been equally amazing. But geographically all fields of development were closed.... Great Britain took South Africa. And pretended to endless surprise and grief that the Germans did not applaud this closing of another market.[11]

Financial warfare is a powerful weapon in trade wars:

> It should be recalled that the practically universal use of sterling in international trade was a principal component of Britain's financial sway, and it was precisely into this strategic sphere that Germany began to penetrate, with the mark evolving as an alternative to the pound. The Deutsche Bank conducted "a stubborn fight for the introduction of acceptance [of the German mark] in overseas trade in place of the hitherto universal sterling bill ... this fight lasted for decades and when the war came, a point had been reached at which the mark acceptance in direct transactions with German firms had partially established itself alongside the pound sterling." ... "It seems probable that if war had not come in 1914, London would have had to share with Germany the regulatory power over world trade and economic development which it had exercised so markedly in the nineteenth century."[12]

Take special note how serious researchers recognize that a dominant currency has "regulatory power over world trade and development."

Almost fifty years after the American dollar replaced the British pound as the world's trading currency, the *Washington Post* noted: "Under the Bretton Woods system, the Federal Reserve acted as the world's central bank. This gave America enormous leverage over economic policies of its principal trading partners."[13] Control of a trading currency is a powerful tool and the primary mechanism through which imperial centers of capital maintain unequal currency values, which in turn maintain unequal trading values, which keeps the wealth of the periphery flowing to the imperial center as per the formula outlined in Chapter One.

The British were afraid of both German economic power and the loss of their central bank operating as the world's central bank and were not about to openly compete under the principles of Adam Smith free trade they were preaching. After that war, Britain thought that

> placing a ring of new nations around Germany (supported by proper guarantees) would do away with the immediate danger of a German-led economic union. . . . Once Germany's threat to British economic supremacy had abated the prewar crisis inside British politics would resolve itself.[14]

Germany and World War II

German leaders were still angry over their humiliating defeat in World War I, a war fought over trade, and trade was a large component of this second struggle. "The peace conference of 1919, held in Versailles, marked not the end of the war but rather its continuation by other means."[15] The injustice of controlled markets under the guise of free trade was never rectified. A resentful Germany prepared, at first secretly, then more and more openly, to employ military might to break those trade barriers and eliminate the humiliation and restrictions of Versailles:

The late 1920s and early 1930s began with a series of worldwide financial crashes that ultimately spiraled downward into the Great Depression. As GNPs fell, the dominant countries each created trading blocks (the Japanese [East Asia] Co-Prosperity Sphere, the British Empire, the French Union, Germany plus Eastern Europe, America with its Monroe Doctrine) to minimize imports and preserve jobs. If only one country had kept imports out, limiting imports would have helped it avoid the Great Depression, but with everyone restricting trade, the downward pressures were simply magnified. In the aggregate, fewer imports must equal fewer exports. Eventually, those economic blocks evolved into military blocks, and World War II began.[16]

This is not a defense of Germany's racist motives or conduct in World War II. The supporters and goals of fascism represent the antithesis of this treatise. Fascism would severely restrict rights for the masses; this treatise would expand them to full rights. However, the injustice to Germany in denying her equality in world trade was extreme and injustice breeds extremism. As we have shown, World Wars I and II were caused by the attempt to economically strangle (contain) Germany.[17]

William Appleman Williams, in *The Tragedy of American Diplomacy,* identified control of markets as the cause of both World Wars I and II. He notes that free trade was then called the "Open Door Policy" and "It was conceived and designed to win the victories without the wars. . . . It does not prove that any nation that resisted (or resists) those objectives was (or is) evil, and therefore to blame for [the] following conflicts or violence."[18]

Both Presidents McKinley and Wilson "unequivocally pointed to Germany as the most dangerous rival of the United States in that economic struggle" and President Franklin Roosevelt and his advisors "explicitly noted as early as 1935 . . . that Germany, Italy and Japan were defined as dangers to the well-being of the United States.''[19] In fact, on April 10, 1935 (four years before World War II and six years before America entered that war), Roosevelt ''wrote a letter to [Britain's] Colonel House telling him he was considering American participation in a joint military and naval blockade to seal off Germany's borders.''[20]

Because Germany was bypassing Britain's monopolization of finance capital through barter agreements, that blockade was intended to reimpose neomercantilist ''free'' trade and contain German economic power as well as its Aryan supremacist philosophy. After the war, Secretary of State Cordell Hull reaffirmed that trade was the primary cause of World War II:

> Yes, war did come, despite the trade agreements. But it is a fact that war did not break out between the United States and any country with which we had been able to negotiate a trade agreement. It is also a fact that, with very few exceptions, the countries with which we signed trade agreements joined together in resisting the Axis. *The political line-up followed the economic line-up.*[21]

Walter Russell Mead, a senior fellow of the World Policy Institute and the Foreign Policy Institute, concurred that wars are extensions of trade wars. He warned: ''The last time the world deprived two major industrial countries, Germany and Japan, of what each considered its rightful 'place in the sun' the result was World War II.''[22]

Japan's Greater East Asia Co-Prosperity Sphere and World War II

Under the guns of Admiral Perry's naval task force in 1854, Japan's markets were forced open. Japan was forced to sign a trade agreement with a tariff limit of 5 percent while the average tariff on imports into America of almost 30 percent was immediately raised even higher.[23] Learning the mechanics of becoming wealthy through this experience with neomercantilist unequal trade (and on the advice of Herbert Spencer), the Japanese studied Western economic theories carefully and in 1872 formed their trade policies.

Japan copied and improved upon Germany's industrial cartels, and followed the European model of establishing colonial empires, in creating the pre–World War II Greater East Asia Co-Prosperity Sphere. Both Germany and Japan were following Friedrich List's philosophy of consolidating nations and developing industrial power.

The post-Meiji Japanese government had built the most up-to-date factories and sold them to industrialists for 15 to 30 percent of building costs, the origin of many of today's Japanese corporations.[24] Take specific note of how Germany and Japan could create money to combine resources and labor to produce industrial capital. They could not have built those basic industries so quickly while remaining dependent upon the British pound as their trading currency. A nation without resources need only create the money, build the industry, barter production from that industry for more resources, and pay for it all with the goods produced.

After World War II, under United States protection as a buffer against fast-expanding socialism, Japan reestablished her centrally planned cartels (Germany reestablished hers at the same time) to maintain low import prices for raw materials, high prices for Japanese citizens, and lower export prices of high-quality consumer goods to penetrate world markets.

Japan's industrialization was a strengthened

and fine-tuned copy of Germany's cartel industrialization that was such a threat to England and it has been equally successful: "America is no longer such a rich country. And Japan is no longer poor. Much of America's wealth has been transferred to the Japanese through the medium of exports and imports. Their exports and our imports."[25]

Japan's pre–World War II conquests cut powerful European traders off from what was once their private domain. This was the common bond between Germany and Japan in World War II and virtually any respectable history of the origin of the war in the Pacific outlines the embargoes against Japan and the trade negotiations carried out right up to the bombing of Pearl Harbor. The total embargo of oil against Japan just before war broke out in 1941 was squeezing its economy even more effectively than a Middle East embargo of the Western world would squeeze Western economies today.

After World War II, America Picks Up the Baton to Protect the Historic Imperial Centers of Capital

As nations started breaking free from the chains of neomercantilist imperialism and exercising their rights as free people, the words spoken by Western security councils demonstrated they clearly realized their dilemma: "China is moving towards an economy and a type of trade in which there is no place for the foreign manufacturer, the foreign banker, or the foreign trader."[26] "We cannot expect domestic prosperity under our system without a constantly expanding trade with other nations. The capitalist system is essentially an international system; if it cannot function internationally, it will break down completely."[27]

The threat of the governments of half of Europe being no longer allied with the West and the loss of China after that war led to the inclusion of Germany and Japan, as well as Taiwan and South Korea, right on the border of China, as allies. The strategy of allowing those once threatening imperial centers of capital access to finance capital, technology, resources, and markets rapidly rebuilt Germany and Japan and eventually developed much of Southeast Asia.

The Friedrich List protection once provided post–World War II Japan, Taiwan, and South Korea would be a great model to develop the entire world. The rest of the colonial world—which was forming its own nonaligned bloc and gaining control of its destiny—was not only denied all those protections, but was covertly destabilized and the rules of Adam Smith free trade, as interpreted by neomercantilists, applied. True free trade was nonexistent, all the free trade rhetoric notwithstanding.

America allied with Britain to defeat Germany in World War I, allied with both Britain and the Soviet Union to defeat Germany again, and defeated Japan almost alone in World War II. The United States then allied with the old hostile imperial centers of capital to defeat the rising center of capital to the East, the Soviet Union, and suppress the many breaks for economic freedom of the former colonial nations. European nations were prostrate after bankrupting each other battling over the world's wealth and America picked up the baton as protector of the imperial centers of capital.

Notes

1. Steven Schlosstein, *Trade War* (New York: Congdon and Weed, 1984), p. 9.
2. Kurt Rudolph Mirow and Harry Maurer, *Webs of Power* (Boston: Houghton Mifflin, 1982), p. 16.

3. D.J. Goodspeed, *The German Wars* (New York: Bonanza Books, 1985), p. 71.

4. Petr Kropotkin, *Mutual Aid* (Boston: Porter Sargent, 1914), p. 334.

5. Frederic F. Clairmont, *The Rise and Fall of Economic Liberalism* (Goa, India: The Other India Press, 1996), pp. 195, 197; and books by William Appleman Williams: *The Contours of American History* (New York: W.W. Norton, 1988), *Empire as a Way of Life* (Oxford: Oxford University Press, 1980), and *The Tragedy of American Diplomacy* (New York: W. W. Norton, 1972); Eli F. Heckscher, *Mercantilism* (New York: Macmillan, 1955); Fritz Fisher, *Germany's Aims in the First World War* (New York: W.W. Norton, 1967), pp. 38–49; Dwight E. Lee, *Europe's Crucial Years* (Hanover, NH: Clark University Press, 1974).

6. Williams, *Contours of American History,* pp. 54, 66, 122–23, 128–29, 144–45, 168–70, 221–22, 272, 319, 338–40, 363, 349, 368–69, 383, 411, 417–23, 429, 434–37, 452, 455–58, 461–64; other books by Williams: *Empire as a Way of Life* and *Tragedy of American Diplomacy;* Heckscher, *Mercantilism,* especially vol. 2, pp. 70–71.

7. Nazli Choucri and Robert C. North, *Nations in Conflict* (San Francisco: W.H. Freeman, 1974), in part quoting other authors, pp. 58–59, 106–07. See also Samuel Williamson Jr., *The Politics of Grand Strategy* (London: Ashfield Press, 1969).

8. Karl Polanyi, *The Great Transformation* (Boston: Beacon Press, 1957), p. 19.

9. Lawrence Malkin, *The National Debt* (New York: Henry Holt, 1988), p. 11; W.A. Williams, *Contours of American History;* Heckscher, *Mercantilism;* Lloyd C. Gardner, *Safe for Democracy* (New York: Oxford University Press, 1984).

10. Terry Allen, "In GATT They Trust," *Covert Action Information Bulletin* (Spring 1992), p. 63; George Seldes, *Never Tire of Protesting* (New York: Lyle Stuart, 1968), p. 45; Gardner, *Safe for Democracy,* chapters 1 and 2. See also W.A. Williams, *Contours of American History,* p. 412; Heckscher, *Mercantilism,* vol. 2.

11. John Reed, *The Education of John Reed* (New York: International, 1955), pp. 74–75.

12. Harry Magdoff and Paul M. Sweezy, *Stagnation and the Financial Explosion* (New York: Monthly Review Press, 1987) p. 167. Quotes are from H. Parker Willis and B. H. Beckhart's *Foreign Banking Systems* and from J. B. Condliffe's *The Commerce of Nations.*

13. Bookworld, *Washington Post,* April 14, 1994, p. 14 (from McGehee's database).

14. Gardner, *Safe for Democracy,* p. 98.

15. Goodspeed, *German Wars,* pp. 267–68.

16. Lester Thurow, *Head to Head: The Coming Economic Battle Among Japan, Europe, and America* (New York: William Morrow, 1992), pp. 55–56.

17. James and Suzanne Pool, *Who Financed Hitler* (New York: Dial Press, 1978), p. 41.

18. Williams, *Tragedy of American Diplomacy,* pp. 128–29.

19. Ibid., pp. 73, 128–29, 172–73; see also pp. 72–73, 134–35, 142; also *Contours of American History,* pp. 412, 451–57, 462–64.

20. Richard Barnet, *The Rockets' Red Glare: War, Politics and the American Presidency* (New York: Simon and Schuster, 1990), p. 194.

21. Williams, *Tragedy of American Diplomacy,* pp. 163–64, emphasis added.

22. Walter Russell Mead, "American Economic Policy in the Antemillenial Era," *World Policy Journal* (Summer 1989), p. 422.

23. James Fallows, "How the World Works," *The Atlantic Monthly,* December 1993, p. 82.

24. Clairmont, *Rise and Fall of Economic Liberalism,* pp. 169, 268.

25. Schlosstein, *Trade War,* pp. 9, 13, 55, 99. Fallows, "World Works," pp. 73, 82. See also J.M. Roberts, *The Triumph of the West* (London: British Broadcasting Company, 1985), p. 33.

26. Noam Chomsky, "Enduring Truths: Changing Markets," *Covert Action Quarterly* (Spring 1996), p. 49.

27. Eric R. Wolf, *Europe and the People Without History* (Berkeley: University of California Press, 1982), p. 9.

6

The World Breaking Free Frightened the Security Councils of Every Western Nation

The security councils of the historical colonial empires were horrified to observe that not only were populations on the periphery of empire who provided their cheap resources taking the rhetoric of democracy seriously and breaking free, but the empires were losing traditional allies. After World War II, when Hitler's armies were driven from Eastern Europe, a Soviet system of government was installed in all but Hungary and Czechoslovakia. The security councils of all major Western nations were traumatized as:

1. Hungary and Czechoslovakia, with diplomatic pressure from the Soviet Union but still of their own choice, quickly slipped into the Soviet orbit and labor now governed half of Europe.
2. In Greece, only an alliance with Hitler's puppets, massive repression, and massacres of the partisans who had kept two-thirds of the country out of Hitler's control throughout World War II kept the Greek nation in the Western orbit (the first battle of the Cold War, started before World War II ended, and fought strictly against our former allies, the awakened workers of Greece).[1]

3. Through nonviolent protest, Gandhi freed India from Britain.
4. In spite of large expenditures of money and arms, military advisors, and the United States transporting Chiang Kai-shek's troops back and forth across China, a fifth of the world's population was lost to the West; China was suddenly free to chart her own destiny.
5. World opinion forced the dictation of the U.S. presidential "white paper" that returned Taiwan (Formosa) to China.[2]
6. South Korea was having massive riots (over 100,000 killed), the followers of the United States–installed dictator Syngman Rhee (who had spent twenty years in exile in Hawaii) were overwhelmingly voted out of parliament, "several crack South Korean military units [had] defected to leftist forces," and South and North Korea were rejoining as one nation outside the control of imperial capital.[3]
7. Japan, Germany, and Italy—being far from friends with their recent conquerors—made it uncertain that the facade of democratic control of those populations would hold, and France was equally insecure.[4]

8. Workers in all nations of Europe were developing a political consciousness and Western economies were not only not picking up as planned, they were moribund. The beacon of capitalism—the receptacle of power for the descendants of the old First and Second Estates and philosophical foundation for their Social Control belief systems—was not shining brightly enough to claim the loyalties of the world's intellectuals or that of the stirring masses. The Marshall Plan to rebuild Europe and retain its loyalty went forward at full speed and only by expenditure of tens of millions of dollars in the Italian and French elections (a practice that lasted two decades in France and four decades in Italy) were those two countries kept within the system of allied imperial centers of capital.

9. Virtually the entire colonial world was breaking free; its resources would be turned to the care of its own people and no longer could be siphoned to the old imperial centers of capital for a fraction of their value.

10. China and Eastern Europe were now allied with the Soviet Union.

If India and the rest of the world's former colonies continued to take the rhetoric of democracy seriously and form the nonaligned bloc as they were planning, over 80 percent of the world's population would be independent or on the other side of the ideological battle. And, if Japan, Germany, Italy, and France could not be held (it was far from sure they could be), that would leave only the United States, Britain, Canada, and Australia, about 10 percent of the world's population, still under the old belief system, and even there the ideological hold would be tenuous at best. After all, if there were no countryside under the firm control of an imperial center, the entire neoclassical/neomercantilist belief system would have to be totally restructured.

What Western nations were observing, of course, was the same potential loss of the resources and markets of their ''countryside'' as the cities of Europe had experienced centuries earlier. ''National security'' and ''security interests,'' which citizens were coached (propagandized) to believe meant fear of a military attack, really meant maintaining access to the weak, impoverished world's valuable resources. The ''domestic prosperity'' worried about was only their own and the ''constantly expanding trade'' was unequal trades maintaining the prosperity of the developed world and the impoverishment of the undeveloped world as the imperial centers of capital siphoned the natural wealth of their ''countryside'' to themselves.

The Grand Strategy of Western Security Councils: Containing Rising Centers of Capital

The countryside was breaking free. If those newly free nations allied with the developing socialist centers of capital in the East (the Soviet Union and China), restructured their laws to protect their natural resources and the labor power of their citizens, developed their own industry and commerce, and sold their cheaper manufactured products on world markets, the imperial centers of capital faced an economic disaster of the first order. The economic structure of the West would have collapsed just as effectively as Russia did when the West breached its trade defenses and an official 50 percent (estimated 60 percent, see below) of

Russian consumer needs was provided by the West.

Those crucial natural resources are in the Third World and developed world capital could never compete if those people had their own industrial capital and processed their own resources into consumer products. With their own industrial capital, and assuming political and economic freedom as opposed to world neoclassical/neomercantilist law dictated by military power, they could demand full value for their resources while simultaneously underselling the current developed world on manufactured product markets. The Managers of State had to avert that crisis. The world's break for freedom must be contained.

A Crisis of Overproduction Also Had to Be Averted

With industrial capacity having increased 50 percent during World War II, U.S. industry was calculated to be twice what was necessary for America's needs and almost enough to produce for the entire world at its pre-war level of consumption.[5] One of the primary tenets of a capitalist market economy is that surplus production at much smaller levels than that spells an economic depression.

The eighth conclusion of NSC-68, the master plan for the Cold War, states: "There are grounds for predicting that the United States and other free nations will within a period of a few years at most experience a decline in economic activity of serious proportions unless more positive government programs are developed than are now available." In a democracy, the legitimacy of both ideology and leaders is judged at the ballot box by how well its citizens are cared for. Every leader in the developed world still remembered how near the world was to a ballot box revolution during the Great Depression; a market for that excess productive capacity was crucial. In short, the waste utilized in building arms and covert and overt wars was both to protect the existing trade structure and to be a Keynesian infusion of money into the economy to prevent a replay of the Great Depression and the threat of a voter's revolution.

But the post–World War II stirring of the masses worldwide was a more immediate concern. Noting the threat to their commerce and wealth as the entire world was taking the rhetoric of freedom and democracy seriously, corporations, through control of policy of the one remaining wealthy nation (America) and the devastated nations of Europe and Japan, made the same decision as the free cities of Europe centuries earlier. Threatened with loss of their cheap, but valuable, resources and profitable markets, they had to reclaim control of their countryside.

> Fostering a world environment in which the American system can flourish . . . embraces two subsidiary policies. One is a policy which we would probably pursue even if there was no Soviet threat. It is a policy of attempting to create a healthy international community. The other is a policy of "containing" the Soviet system. These two policies are closely interrelated and interact with one another.[6]

Of course, the "healthy international community" Secretary of State Dean Acheson, one of the primary architects of the Cold War, had in mind as he was justifying NSC-68 was only from the perspective of those who watch the wealth of others roll into their vaults. A healthy community as enforced by the free cities of Europe 800 years ago meant wealth to them and poverty for the defeated neighboring cities. A healthy international community, from the perspective of corporate imperialism, means wealth for the developed corporate world and poverty for the formerly colonized, still defeated, and recolonized undeveloped world.

Control had to be reestablished. Although done in the name of peace, freedom, justice, rights, and majority rule (a part of the Social Control belief system, especially when girding for war), the fundamental goal of the forming IMF/WorldBank/GATT/NAFTA/WTO/MAI/military colossus and the covert actions authorized by NSC-68, and many lesser Security Council directives both before and after that master plan, was the reclamation and maintenance of control over valuable resources and profitable markets, and the very negation of the principles so loudly touted as their rationale. The real fear was people taking democracy seriously, deciding their own destiny, and corporations losing access to those cheap resources and valuable markets.

National Security Council Directive 68: The Master Plan for the Cold War

A study of NSC-68 will conclude that, besides being a master plan for the Cold War, as discussed in the Introduction, this directive was also a propaganda instrument to stampede government officials into accepting that military posture. That analysis and the crisis facing the developed Western world are confirmed. Secretary of State Dean Acheson, one of the primary architects of NSC-68, sums it up for us:

> Western Europe . . . shattered by its civil war, was disintegrating politically, economically, socially, and psychologically. Every effort to bestir itself was paralyzed by two devastating winters and the overshadowing fear of the Soviet Union

no longer contained by the stoppers on the east, west, and south—Japan, Germany, and British India. . . . It was in this period [the first three years after the beginning of the Cold War] that we awakened fully to the facts of the surrounding world and to the scope and kind of action required by the interests of the United States; the second period, that of President Truman's second administration, became the time for full action upon those conclusions and for meeting the whole gamut of reactions—favorable, hostile, and merely recalcitrant foreign and domestic—that they produced. In the first period, the main lines of policy were set and begun; in the second, they were put into full effect amid the smoke and confusion of battle. . . . *The purpose of NSC-68 [the master plan for the Cold War] was to so bludgeon the mass mind of "top government" that not only could the president make a decision but that the decision could be carried out.*[7]

Although President Truman may have been fully aware, the fact that the finalized NSC-68 was presented to him on April 16, 1950, but not signed until September 30, 1950 (as NSC-68/2), three months after the start of the Korean War, demonstrates the likelihood that the American president was one of the "top government officials" the designers of the Cold War were stampeding into a war posture.

The Korean War: The Most Important Political Event since World War II

The political instrument to put NSC-68 into effect was the Korean War, that started seventy-two days after that directive was finalized and presented to President Truman. When I.F. Stone wrote *The Hidden History of the Korean War* in 1952, NSC-68 was still classified. However, in that book, Stone demonstrated the Korean War was little more than a political instrument to impose the policies of America's Managers of State upon the world.

No empire (or nation) instigates a war on the periphery that is already politically won and most empires instigate actual wars on the periphery only if loss of a political or trade war is imminent. But this planned war was not only to save an outpost on the periphery of empire, this was a war to save the empire. There was nothing to lose in Korea, it was going to be lost anyway, and there was an entire world to gain by mobilizing the population of the industrialized world for a war to suppress the renewed breaks for economic freedom of the emerging world. Though the plans were made in State, an analysis of our sources will conclude the excuse for the Korean War was obviously staged by General Douglas MacArthur, South Korean President Syngman Rhee, and Chiang Kai-shek of Formosa under the political cover of the American hard right (called the China Lobby), McCarthyism, and the CIA's "Mighty Wurlitzer."

Highlights from Stone's book outline a war created by those threatened with the loss of their power and wealth. Massive riots were breaking out all over South Korea with the goal of North and South Korea reuniting, and over 100,000 were killed. Crack military units were defecting to the so-called left and the CIA and South Korean government were unable to control the elections. Syngman Rhee's puppet government was voted out wholesale and the next to go would be Syngman Rhee.

North and South Korea were going to rejoin outside Western control; South Korean troops pulled back from the 38th parallel the day before the war started; South Korean government press releases were saying a North Korean attack was imminent; the UN inspected the 38th parallel—just hours before the war started—and concluded there was no imminent attack; and intelligence briefings concluded that North Korea was not prepared for war yet ships were in place to evacuate American families. Everything was set to fabricate an excuse for war.

But the clincher that the invasion of South Korea was a much more elaborately staged war than Hitler's staged invasion of Poland was North Korea's announcement that South Korea had invaded North Korea in three places and had been hurled back. Author John Gunther, General Douglas MacArthur's personal biographer, just happened to be in MacArthur's personal railroad car when a high occupation official returned from being called to a phone, saying, "A big story has just broken. The South Koreans have attacked North Korea."[8]

That statement which accidentally slipped into history and Stone's cold political analysis verify the North Korean claim that South Korea, under American guidance and promise of protection by America's full military might, started that war. (A third verification was the couple of days it took to dislodge South Korea from Heiju, three miles above the 38th parallel.) I.F. Stone describes how many of the massive battles with hordes of Koreans and Chinese attacking were nothing more than military press releases (Social Control belief systems manufactured by intelligence service wordsmiths and passed out through military and government channels). Stone would quote the headlines built from those press releases and then print the communiqués from ground commanders who were essentially searching for enemies they could not find.

Certainly four million were killed but they were primarily killed by an unopposed air force that napalmed North Korea to the ground, an unopposed navy that shelled North Korean coastal cities to rubble, and massive artillery that extracted a horrendous price in lives when a real attack was faced. This accounts for the small number of Americans killed. Only 35,000 Americans were among the four million who died. Half those numbers were women and children who died in this carnage when defenseless and totally undefended North Korean cities and villages were napalmed and bombarded to the ground.

Neither China nor the Soviet Union provided any great support to North Korea until that tiny impoverished nation was essentially destroyed. Couple that war by press release with the documented efforts of the North Koreans, Chinese, and Soviets to bring that war to an end—every such effort unreported in Western media and thwarted by either a massive air attack or ground offensive—and it is clearly marked as a political event.

Fabricating Incidents to Start Wars

Fabricating incidents to start wars empires feel they can win—such as Hitler faking an attack by Poland on a German radio station and America's creation of the Gulf of Tonkin incident in order for President Johnson to get congressional backing to widen the war in Vietnam to justify a heavier assault on North Korea—is a standard practice. This is the careful writing of history by the powerful. United States documents on the destabilization of Cuba, titled "Pretexts to Justify U.S. Military Intervention in Cuba" and declassified in 1998, demonstrate how it is done. Phrases used in those in-depth deception plans include:

> Fake an attack on the U.S. naval base in Guantanamo, Cuba, with friendly Cubans masquerading as attackers. . . . Arrange for an unmanned vessel to be blown up near a major Cuban city. . . . Stage a "Communist Cuban terror campaign" in the Miami area. . . . Plant arms in a Caribbean country and send jets painted to look like Cuban MiGs, creating the appearance of a "Cuban based, Castro supported" subversion. . . . Blow up an unmanned U.S. plane that would surreptitiously replace a charter flight of civilians.[9]

Peace in Korea Could Not Be Permitted Until the Enemy Belief System Was Fully Implanted in the Minds of Western Citizens

When it appeared the Chinese were willing to see a cessation of hostilities at the 38th parallel where it all began, three defenseless North Korean port cities were subjected to forty-one straight days and nights of bombardment by the navies of three nations and America's Air Force.

That most intense naval and air bombardment of any city in history, against totally defenseless women and children, went totally unreported in the Western press.[10] Instead of dictatorial powers planning to overwhelm the West militarily, those we were told were a dreaded dictatorial enemy were making every effort to return to peace and were being bombed and shelled to rubble to prevent a peace settlement.

Those attacks on defenseless civilians were specifically to create anger and prevent negotiation. For a government to sign a peace treaty under such conditions is essentially unconditional surrender. During two years of negotiations at Panmunjom, every time it appeared a peace settlement was near there would be a massive air raid, a ground offensive, a naval bombardment, or all three.

The Korean War could not be permitted to end until the West's war machine was fully rebuilt, until treaties were signed with Japan and

Germany that fully committed them to the West, and until the entire Western world believed that it was at high risk of being attacked. The Korean War was necessary to gain full support from governments and the masses so that other overt and covert wars to suppress the world's break for economic freedom could be successfully fought.

To understand that the deciding factor in imposition of belief systems to control people is military power, read this book on how inequalities of trade are militarily imposed, then read NSC-68 while noting Acheson's statement quoted above that the purpose of NSC-68 was to *"bludgeon the mass mind of 'top government' that not only could the president make a decision but that the decision could be carried out,"* and then read I.F. Stone's *The Hidden History of the Korean War*.

We are not exaggerating. These wars, in which we were told we were in such imminent danger of being attacked, were only wars to maintain control of the developed world's countryside with their immense natural resources and markets so crucial to those corporate industries. Since voters would quickly change leaders if they knew what the Grand Strategy really was—to maintain control of the countryside through such violence—it was necessary to maintain control of the beliefs of the masses through a secretly functioning national security state.

The decisions had been made. America's Managers of State were accepting the reality that only they had the economic and military power to reimpose control upon the world, and, though most of the planning (such as NSC-68) had yet to be done, most of world history since British Prime Minister Winston Churchill's famous 1946 Iron Curtain speech has been efforts to reimpose that control and the efforts of others to resist that imposition of control. We know this struggle as the Cold War and it was fought far more fiercely around the world than it was against the Soviet Union.

Thanks to the hysteria of the Korean War, which legitimized the West's primary Social Control belief system (that the West was under imminent threat of attack), South Korea and Taiwan were kept within the sphere of Western influence; the influence of so-called "leftist" dissidents in Germany, Italy, France, and Japan was totally suppressed (by a Social Control paradigm identical to American McCarthyism); the military budget did increase 350 percent as planned in NSC-68; the Cold War was on full force; and—after an intense forty-year battle—that struggle to regain control worldwide to protect those cheap resources, those markets, and the very right to govern the imperial center was won.

That four million people were killed (half women and children), millions more wounded, that the entire Korean peninsula was scorched earth, that another ten million would be violently killed as other breaks for economic freedom were suppressed all over the world, that tens of millions more would be wounded, that hundreds of millions would die from starvation and disease as the economies of impoverished countries struggling for freedom were shattered, that billions would remain impoverished as their governments were covertly overthrown, or that trillions of dollars of the world's resources would be wasted could not deflect the Managers of State from their decisions. They, like imperial centers of capital for centuries, felt they had no other choices. To lose those natural resources, that cheap labor, and those markets was to lose their power and their wealth. As we will be addressing below, other choices are not only available today, they are imperative.

The security councils of all the Western European nations had long since realized that they could not rebuild their devastated societies if they lost control of the resources of the world, nor could they rebuild if their industry, money, and labor were expended on arms. Churchill had earlier made it clear that, even though Britain was damaged less than ten percent as much as Eastern Europe and Western Europe was damaged, possibly only twenty percent as much as Eastern Europe and the Soviet Union, "If rearmament is not spread out over a longer time the nations of Western Europe [far wealthier and far less damaged than Eastern Europe] will be rushing to bankruptcy and starvation."[11]

The Grand Strategy paid off. Except for China and all Southeast Asia slipping in under the umbrella of protection provided to Japan, Taiwan, and South Korea, the natural-resource-wealthy Third World remained poor, leaving those resources available for the use of the imperial centers, and the resource-depleted developed world rebuilt its wealth to a level far higher than before.

Though it ended up a close race militarily and technologically as the Soviets fought for survival, the enormously expensive arms race imposed by the enormously wealthy and undamaged United States precluded the development of a Soviet consumer economy and eventually bankrupted the severely damaged and impoverished Soviet Union, just as the Managers of State knew it would. Wasting the resources of the entire world building arms has been very profitable for corporate imperialists in a system that, as acknowledged by America's President Eisenhower, in the final analysis is paid for by the world's poor, but processing their own resources into arms is always an enormous loss for socialist economies.

The First Efforts to Contain the Soviet Union

To understand how even powerful, threatening rising centers of capital can be destroyed, we will encapsulate the short seventy-three-year history of the former Soviet Union.[12] The Soviet reorganization to unwieldy community ownership, equally inefficient direct distribution, yet very sensible community mutual support principles, had barely begun when fourteen countries sent in 180,000 troops and armed 300,000 dissidents within Russia to overthrow that revolution.[13] Reclaiming this breakaway nation for capitalism's Managers of States almost succeeded; nearly two-thirds of the Soviet Union came under interventionist and counterrevolutionary control before the Soviets defeated the allied invaders.

The effort was more successful than the history books acknowledge—Finland, Latvia, Lithuania, Estonia (these four countries having been a part of the old Russian empire for over one hundred years), the Eastern half of Poland, and Bessarabia were carved from the forming Soviet nation by that intervention.[14] Except for Leningrad, this barred the Soviet Union from Atlantic ports and restricted its access to world trade. Note the similarity of the carving off of these historic sectors of Russia from 1917 to 1921 to the later carving up of the Soviet Union and the continued moving East of the line between Eastern Orthodox Christianity and Western Christianity after the collapse of the Soviet Union in 1990. The shattering of empires has a long and repetitive history.

Where only a few thousand died in the Bolshevik revolution, possibly fifteen million Soviets died of disease, starvation, and the interventionist battles between 1918 and the withdrawal of the last foreign forces in 1922.[15] We hear of the millions who then died from famine in the decade of the 1930s in the wake of social disruptions caused by putting farms under collective or state ownership. But we are now alert to how intelligence services, furthering the policies of Managers of State, expand or even create these images of threatening centers of capital as terrorist states. The truth is that the citizens of the former Soviet Union were fiercely loyal to, and worked hard for, their revolution and one should be very skeptical of those figures. The real threat was their potential for success.

Russian pre–World War I industrial capacity, three percent that of America, was not replaced until 1928. But once the people were educated and the political and industrial base was laid, the successes came quickly. In the next twelve years the Soviets soared well past France, Japan, and Italy, matched Britain, and their industrial capacity was now twenty-five percent that of the United States.[16]

The Soviet Union's rapid development was matched by that of Germany. The plans of the Managers of State are too well hidden to document but the similarities between the wars against these emerging centers of capital and previous such threats to imperial centers of capital are high. Germany's second-in-command, Rudolf Hess,[17] fled to England forty-three days before Germany's attack on the Soviet Union. His lifetime incarceration at Spandau prison, where he was essentially denied the right to speak on any except the most mundane subjects, allows only a glimpse of the hopes of Fascists in Germany and Britain for an alliance against the Soviet Union and a reallocation of the world's industries, resources, and markets among Western powers. The nations already

overrun were of Aryan descent and many had already accepted Fascist governments during the recent Great Depression. So a restructured European alliance would have been easily organized if Britain had agreed. Except that German sympathizers were automatically kept out of the British government both before and during the war, a defecting Hess would have been welcomed by the Fascist element in Britain. There are no other logical reasons for his flight except to form an alliance against the rapidly developing Soviets. Hitler and Hess were simply taking a gamble on Britain accepting a realignment of power to avoid a long war and they lost.

There were elements in Britain amenable to such alliance plans but Germany's Fascist violence, Britain's treaty commitments with countries invaded by Germany, the impossibility of restructuring the belief systems of the masses of Britain in that short a time, and the almost certain eclipse of Britain's economic, financial, and military power as Germany drew on a defeated Soviet Union's vast resources and sold the products manufactured from those resources on Britain's historic markets precluded any such alliance.

While the Germans felt for a political settlement in the West, their June 22, 1941, offensive against the Soviet Union, Operation Barbarossa, took the invading troops to the outskirts of Stalingrad and within sight of Moscow. In desperation, the Soviets moved their industrial machinery ahead of the invading army and rebuilt beyond the Ural Mountains. Industrial technology is the key not only to a wealthy economy, but also to modern warfare, and the Soviets, who only thirteen years earlier were a minor industrial power, produced far more weapons than Germany for the remainder of the war. By the beginning of 1945, ''on the Byelorussian and Ukrainian fronts alone, Soviet superiority was both absolute and awesome, fivefold in manpower, fivefold in armor, over sevenfold in artillery and seventeen times the German strength in the air."[18]

Essentially unrecorded in Western history is what the West owes the Soviets in that war. The estimation that 85 percent of Germany's firepower was expended against the Soviet Union alerts the serious researcher. Simple history and battlefield statistics tell the story well: Once the Germans were stopped, the massive seventeen-month battle for Stalingrad (liberated on February 2, 1943) ended with the death or capture of 1.5 million Germans, the death of 800,000 Soviets and wounding of hundreds of thousands more. That victory was followed by the greatest tank and artillery battle in all history at Kursk and the almost simultaneous immense battles at Kharkov and Orel, all of which the Soviets decisively won. The Soviet Union had been holding off the Germans for three years and had cleared the Germans from half the occupied area six months before the Allies landed at Normandy on June 6, 1994. As the Allies fought inland the last year of the war, over two German or Axis soldiers out of every three were still on the Soviet front. In a replay of their 1944 offensive to take the pressure off the West's Normandy beachhead, the Soviets launched an all-out attack on January 11, 1945, to take the pressure off the West in the Battle of the Bulge. The German counterattack collapsed five days later as German troops rushed to the Eastern front to stem that Soviet offensive. By the end of March, six weeks before the German surrender, there were seven German soldiers on the Eastern front for every one in the West and the Soviets would still reach Berlin first.[19]

World War II's Huge Costs for the Soviet Union

But a huge price was paid for that victory. The Soviets destroyed industries, railroads, and bridges as they were pushed East and the Germans destroyed what basic infrastructure the Soviets missed (oil wells, coal mines, dams, etc.) as they were forced back West. The Germans burned the cities and villages to the ground and hauled 7 million horses, 17 million cattle, 20 million hogs, 27 million sheep and goats and 110 million poultry away to feed Germany.[20]

That the Soviet Union was scorched earth, there can be no doubt. The destruction was there for all to see: twenty-five million Soviets were eating sunflower seeds and living in holes in the ground. By comparison, the United States had only 12.3 million men and women under arms, lost 405,399, its homeland was untouched, and its industrial capacity had increased 50 percent.[21] The creation of belief systems to control people is neverending. The first figure for the total number of Soviet citizens killed, 20.6 million, was quickly upgraded to 27 million. But Stalin's response to Churchill's 1946 Iron Curtain speech in Fulton, Missouri, stated the losses at seven million. Possibly the Soviets embellished their human losses and the West's intelligence services went along with the deception. Possibly those high losses were right and Stalin was hiding how badly the Soviet Union was hurt. Though a few may know the true figure, no one knows whom to believe and it is unlikely that the world will ever know the true number killed.

World War II was over and the Soviet Union was again reduced to under 20 percent of the industrial capacity of the U.S., a much smaller percent of all Western industrial capacity. More important, social infrastructure is much more expensive to build than industrial, and the Soviets not only had to build anew, they had to remove all the rubble first.

In 1947, U.S. Secretary of State General George C. Marshall made a trip across Western Europe and Eastern Europe all the way to Moscow. Western Europe, damaged possibly 20 percent as much as Eastern Europe and Russia, was prostrate under capitalism's laissez-faire principles while the shattered Eastern Europeans and even more badly damaged Soviets with their community support structures were rapidly rebuilding. Marshall rushed back to Washington to report that obviously capitalism's security interests were at stake. His comments mirrored the concerns of all Managers of State:

> "All the way back to Washington," [fellow diplomat] Bohlen wrote, "Marshall talked of the importance of finding some initiative to prevent the complete breakdown of Western Europe." . . . [In a speech to the nation, Marshall gave a bleak report.] We cannot ignore the factor of time. The recovery of Europe has been far slower than had been anticipated. Disintegrating forces are becoming evident. The patient is sinking while the doctors deliberate. So I believe that action cannot [a]wait compromise through exhaustion. New issues arise daily. Whatever action is possible to meet these pressing problems must be taken without delay.[22]

The Managers of State placed the Marshall Plan into effect in 1948 and, under those Friedrich List protection principles, Europe was rebuilt in about five years. The race for industrial and technological supremacy that had triggered the recent world war and many other wars was on again. The containment of the Soviet Union and the simultaneous suppression of the world's break for economic freedom was going to require an enormous amount of expensive arms and, again as addressed above, the Korean War and the CIA's "Mighty Wurlitzer" provided the belief system—the West was under imminent threat of attack from the East—under which the citizens of the West would support the expensive arms race and violence that would be required.

Fictional Missile Gaps: The West Was Far in the Lead in the Arms Race

Professor George Kistiakowsky's impeccable credentials include a position as head of the explosives division for the Manhattan Project that built the atomic bomb, professor of chemistry at Harvard University, and later science advisor to Presidents Eisenhower, Kennedy, and Johnson. Professor Kistiakowsky had a rude awakening as he observed the workings of the "defense" planners from the inside.

> I attended all the National Security Council meetings, by order of the President. I began to realize that policy was being formed in a way which really was quite questionable. It was being formed by people who didn't really know the facts and didn't have time to learn them because of bureaucratic preoccupation. . . . But it took time for all this to sink in. And then I began to see all of the lies, such as the so-called missile gap. I knew there was no missile gap, because our U-2 reconnaissance flights over the Soviet Union could not find any missile deployment. This was 1958—after the U-2's began flying. We put a lot of effort into detecting possible deployment sites. And we could find only one, north of Moscow. This was really a test site. It wasn't really an operational site. Those first ICBMs were so huge that you couldn't hide them.[23]

With full knowledge that the Soviets had no missiles pointed at anyone, the Managers of State requested that the CIA crank up its

"Mighty Wurlitzer" and propagandize American citizens that the Soviets had them targeted with fifty intercontinental ballistic missiles (ICBM). Fear was instilled in the population by having school children crawl under desks in simulated attacks and encouraging the building of bomb shelters.

The truth of the arms race was that the West led the Soviets by five to ten years in the development of every weapon and that the devastated Soviets, who both desperately wanted and desperately needed peace, were encircled with immense firepower by the very nations that had invaded them in 1918 in an attempt to overthrow their government and who still loudly proclaimed they were evil and should be destroyed.

The Soviet Union had paid an enormous price and was owed an enormous debt for saving the world from Fascism. The imperial centers of capital repaid that debt by encircling the Soviets with steel, embargoing them from technology and trade, and vilifying them throughout the world through the CIA's "Mighty Wurlitzer" and the work of other Western intelligence services. The basic principles of world trade had not changed. Any rising center of capital may take over scarce resources and markets—that is, the base of wealth and power of established imperial centers of capital. The proof is that the West's military shrank very little when the Soviet Union collapsed. Seven years after that collapse, America alone spent more for arms than the next ten top military powers and most of those are America's friends. The combined military power of the now allied imperial centers of capital is truly immense, and in the eighth year after the Cold War ended (1999) military expenditures are rising significantly as the struggle for control of crucial resources and markets continues.

The Massive, But Very Expensive, Resources of the Soviet Union and the More Massive, and Cheap, Resources of the West

Soviet successes under extremely harsh conditions were what was worrying Western Managers of State. Covering one-sixth of the world's land surface, the Soviet Union had massive natural resources. However, its citizens lived primarily in Europe while its major resources were in Asia, 3,000 miles away, and much of them under frozen tundra. To mine and process those resources, entire cities had to be built in a cold and hostile climate. Shipping those raw materials to the Soviet industries in the West and supplies from the West to those new cities in the tundra required construction of expensive roads and railroads. The Soviets estimated their costs of production at 1.8 times those in America.

When the Industrial Revolution dawned, Britain had a heretofore unrealized advantage: she had rich coal and iron ore deposits, those necessary resources for making iron and steel were only fifteen miles apart, and she had cheap water transportation to anywhere in the world. These largely unspoken-of advantages allowed Britain to produce more and sell more cheaply, and thus industrialize more quickly, than other nations. The West had the same advantage over the Soviet Union after World War II and that advantage continues to this day. Not only were the resources of America closer to population centers and cheaper to mine and process, its roads and railroads were already in place.

And the West has advantages far beyond that. Paying equally productive developing world labor 20 percent of the wages of developed world labor denies buying power to the periphery of empire, effectively leaving the undeveloped world in debt to the developed world. This leaves the only market for resources and products in the developed world, which gives the West effective title to the richest resources all over the world. Maintaining that effective title requires the suppressions of economic freedom worldwide that we have been describing.

Not only was the harvesting of Soviet resources, and thus the production of Soviet wealth, far more labor-intensive than in the West, the Soviets provided those resources and industrial technology to the periphery of their sphere of influence (Eastern Europe, China, Cuba, etc.) at far below world prices. Thus the Soviets denied themselves a large share of the wealth produced by their own labors. With adequate resources within their borders, the Soviets were taxing their center to build their periphery, exactly the opposite of Western empires.

Errors in Soviet Planning

Thirty percent of Soviet industrial capacity and a large share of Soviet infrastructure and social wealth were destroyed in World War II. As soon as Germany was defeated, the Soviets started rebuilding. By the 1980s the Soviets' basic industrial production was approaching that of the United States. They even pulled ahead in steel, oil, coal, and a few other industries. In only seventy years the Soviets had moved from the bottom among industrial nations to number two, accomplishing this while fighting off the four-year effort of fourteen nations to overthrow them, after the massive losses of World War II, and while being forced to arm to offset the ring of steel being placed around them by the West.

One can only wonder what the Soviet Union could have done if left in peace.

But a serious error was being made in Soviet planning. Some 77 percent of manufactured products was being produced by only one or two huge factories.[24] If the technology were equal, these huge factories could initially produce consumer products more cheaply than many competing companies, each with separate production, publicity, and distribution networks. But they could not keep up with ongoing technological developments.

Retooling factories is expensive. When there is no competition, managers simply will not retool a huge factory, while market capitalism, with its virtually hundreds of initial producers, will typically shake out to three competing producers of roughly equal economic strength, each with several factories. The others disappear from the scene. But those three or more remaining competing producers innovate, develop, retool, produce, distribute, train repair people, and receive feedback from all elements of society for further innovation and retooling, and the cycle keeps repeating itself. Thus, in a competitive society, both factories and the products produced become ever better and ever more efficient.

Soviet industry did not have that technological innovation and retooling cycle. Without getting feedback from society, innovating, retooling, and thus producing and distributing better products, the Soviet civilian economy became moribund.

Containing the Soviet Union Through Forcing It to Waste Its Industrial Production

But there were far greater costs to the Soviet Union than its errors. The rubble of World

War II had to be cleared away and homes, stores, and the complete economic infrastructure had to be rebuilt to the level of a modern nation. The Soviets had made the decision to sacrifice the present to build for the future.

But the arms race short-circuited those plans. We must remember British Prime Minister Churchill's warning that Britain and Western Europe could not rearm quickly without facing poverty and starvation. The result of offsetting the ring of steel being placed around the Soviet Union while simultaneously cleaning up the rubble, building homes (twenty-five million were homeless), repairing the damaged infrastructure, and then building new dams, highways, railroads, and industry was an economic nightmare.

"The estimate of a Soviet economist [is] that 51.4 percent of total Soviet industrial investment between 1950 and 1985 went into military production." A large share of the rest—roughly 43 percent—was going into building and rebuilding basic infrastructure (roads, steel mills, etc.) and providing industry and resources to the embattled periphery (China, Eastern Europe, Cuba, etc.), and a minuscule 5 percent was left for producing consumer durables.[25]

Before they collapsed in 1990, the Soviets were able to raise their technology to about 1982–83 U.S. levels.[26] But their expenditure of labor and resources toward rebuilding from the rubble of World War II, their building of infrastructure, and their transfer of a share of their production to the periphery, as well as errors in Soviet planning, denied them the opportunity to apply that technology to consumer production. The mining of resources and land transportation in the arctic tundra thousands of miles away from their population centers were simply too expensive.

Destabilizing Eastern Europe and the Soviet Union

Peter Gowan, senior lecturer in European politics at the Polytechnic of North London, describes the neomercantilist policy towards the East which eventually shattered the Soviet Bloc:

[I]n the closing decades of the Cold War, the Atlantic Alliance had combined a formidable economic blockade against Eastern Europe.... The West possessed two principal means of control. Through the IMF, it exerted political control over international finance and currency matters. Furthermore, it could restrict commercial access to Western markets through bilateral export policy, through the Coordinating Committee for Multilateral Export Controls (Cocom) on high technology, and through import duties—largely imposed by the European Community (EC)—on ECE goods.... It is scarcely an exaggeration, therefore, to say that following the upheaval of 1989 the West had the capacity to shape events in ECE to an extent comparable to that enjoyed by the Soviet government in the region after 1945. In field after field the ability of governments to deliver to their people depended on the intervening decisions of the G7 [the seven leading Western countries]. Employing this power, Western policy makers could shape the destiny of the region according to a very particular, and very political, agenda. The Western powers did not respond to the challenge of 1989 in a piecemeal fashion. Although the form and speed of the collapse took most policy makers by surprise, the G7 had, by the summer of 1989, established new machinery for handling the political transformation of Poland and Hungary and had worked out both the goals and the means of policy. Even before the region's first noncommunist government ... took power in Poland in September 1989, the G7 framework was in place.... Coercive diplomacy, not persuasion, became the tool by which the West established market economies in the East.[27]

Peter Gowan explains further how coercion was practiced by outside powers:

> The EC, the G7, and the IMF treated each country separately according to its domestic program, setting off a race among the governments of the region to achieve the closest relations with, and best terms from, the West. . . . The economic "liberalization" measures urged upon the new governments of ECE by Western agencies were bound to push these economies into serious recession, a situation only made worse by the disruption of regional economic links and the collapse of the Soviet Union. The result has been less a move to the market than a large-scale market destruction. . . . G7 experts were well aware that the drive for social system change would thoroughly destabilize ECE economies.[28]

The East was destabilized, those countries did not just collapse. The above destabilizations were the policy decisions of America's 1982 National Security Council Directive 54 (NSD-54) to destabilize all East European countries except Yugoslavia, which throughout the Cold War was provided financial aid and some access to markets so as to wean it away from the Soviet Union.

The opening guns of financial warfare for the destabilization of Yugoslavia were the IMF's 1980–84 demands for a currency devaluation and an increase in the Yugoslavian Central Bank's discount rate. That currency devaluation immediately increased the debt, the interest rate hike slowed the Yugoslav economy, and, as per the wealth accumulation formula in Chapter One, Yugoslav wealth started moving towards the historic imperial centers of capital. The drop in living standards created by those structural adjustments led to economic and political turmoil.

Then U.S. National Security Council Directive 133 (NSD-133), issued in 1984, titled "United States Policy towards Yugoslavia" and labeled "SECRET SENSITIVE," contained the marching orders for the final fragmentation of that nation: Further IMF-imposed structural adjustments denied the Yugoslav government the right to credit (money creation) from its own central bank, thus losing the ability to fund crucial economic and social programs (industry and health care). Those structural adjustment policies included imposing a freeze on all transfer payments from the central governments to the outlying provinces. The results were planned and predictable: A growth rate of 7.1 percent from 1966 to 1979 "plummeted to 2.8 percent in the 1980–87 period, plunging to zero in 1987–88 and to—10.6 percent in 1990." Another currency devaluation (30 percent) accelerated the 140 percent inflation to 937 percent in 1992 and 1,134 percent in 1993, with GDP dropping 50 percent in four years. Imported commodities flooded in to further disrupt domestic production and drain Yugoslavia's hard currency reserves. It was calculated that, under those policies, 1.9 million workers—out of a total workforce of 2.7 million—were headed for unemployment.[29]

Simultaneous with the denial of Yugoslavia's right to fund her outlying regions were offers to those provinces for funds and trade if they declared their independence. German foreign minister Hans Dietrich Genscher was in almost daily contact with his Croatian counterpart, promoting independence. The 1990–91 U.S. Foreign Operations Appropriations Bill (an annual event funding destabilizations) demanded separate elections in each of the six Yugoslav provinces with State Department approval of their conduct and outcome and, again, all aid to go to independent republics and none to the central government. A total embargo imposed in 1991 was still in effect in June 1999 during the final breakup of Yugoslavia. Independence meant funding and trade for the provinces, while continued federation with Yugoslavia meant continued embargoes and no funds. A country that had been peaceful and relatively prosperous since World War II, with 30 percent of the marriages interethnic, erupted into civil war and, with continued overt and covert support from Germany and America, Macedonia, Slovenia, and Croatia were torn away from the Yugoslav federation. The Serbian populations of the seceding provinces, who had forgiven the Western Christians for the slaughter of possibly one-third of the Serbian men during Hitler's holocaust and formed the multiethnic nation of Yugoslavia after World War II, were again facing second-class citizenship.

Now it was Bosnia-Herzegovina's turn. Western Christians allied with Muslims to give that secession the necessary majority voice. The November 1995 Dayton Accords, established under the threat of NATO intervention to suppress the ensuing struggle over who should govern, established a virtual colonial government which allowed the United States and the European Union to appoint a high representative (HR) with full executive powers in civilian matters. A constitution for the Bosnian Federation was written at those peace talks stipulating that the HR could overrule the government. That façade of democracy (the Parliamentary Assembly) simply rubber-stamped the decisions of the HR and his expatriate advisors. Those dictates (called "Accords") actually stipulated that "the first governor of the Central Bank of Bosnia and Herzegovina is to be appointed by the IMF and 'shall not be a citizen of Bosnia and Herzegovina or a neighboring state.'" The elected president of the Serbian segment of Bosnia—who objected to forcibly selling off banks, water, energy, telecommunications, transportation, and metal industries at firesale prices—was forcibly removed by NATO.[30] Of course, these dictates were all carried out under the flag of "democracy."

As Bosnia-Herzegovina was being digested by the NATO alliance, the foundation for the breaking away of Kosovo was being laid. Due to fear of secession, the autonomous status of Kosovo had been revoked by Yugoslavia as ethnic Albanians increased from 40 percent at the end of World War II to 80 percent. That political stalemate became violent when German and American intelligence armed the Kosovo Liberation Army (KLA). Before that arming of the KLA by outside powers, the Kosovar rebellion had been a peaceful one similar to Gandhi's peaceful rebellion in India fifty years earlier. The newly armed KLA surfaced in 1997 and started assassinating Serbian police officers and ethnic Albanian collaborators. Yugoslavia sent in the army to suppress that armed insurrection. In February 1998, as a sure sign that America's CIA, Germany's BND, and the Military Professional Resources (MPRI, retired U.S. generals under Pentagon contract) were still orchestrating this destabilization, the Croatian General, Agim Ceku—who had been in command of the ethnic cleansing of Serbs from the Krajina region of Croatia—took over command of the KLA.[31]

In a replay of the Dayton Accords, an assembly was convened in Rambouillet, France, to decide the fate of Kosovo. The prepared accords allowed for 50,000 NATO troops overseeing that autonomous republic: NATO was to be granted the use of airports, roads, rail, and ports free of any charges, NATO troops were not to be subject to Yugoslav law, they were to be given the right to inspect any part of not just

Kosovo but Serbia itself, and the Kosovo economy was to be structurally adjusted as per the Bosnian-Herzegovenan economy described above. NATO gave Yugoslavia only two choices: sign the accords (dictates) or be bombed. Virtually every serious diplomat of good conscience agreed that these were articles of surrender that no sovereign nation could sign. In short, those accords were little more than a disguised declaration of war. The world, of course, heard only the prepared press releases about intransigent Yugoslavia, and NATO proceeded, with the support of the majority of their citizens, to bomb the regional Orthodox Christians back to the eighteenth century.[32]

Here we must comment that the destabilization of Yugoslavia is a chance to study a classic case of how propaganda works in what are called democracies with "freedom of the press." Before the bombing, Yugoslavia had opposition radio stations, dissident publications, and over twenty political parties, each with its own newspaper. Milosovic had been elected three times, twice as president of Serbia and later as president of Yugoslavia. The Yugoslav president had a cabinet to discuss and decide policy and an elected parliament that approved all decisions, both of which had even been shown occasionally on Western television. Yet Milosovic was labeled a dictator in almost every news report, while Croatian descendants of Hitler's Ustashe, who ethnically cleansed Jews, Gypsies, and Serbs during World War II, who had just imposed a one-party press, and who had just ethnically cleansed several hundred thousand Serbs from Croatia, were simultaneously labeled democratic.

There will be analysis of this propaganda process after the fact but, as every social system protects itself and its own, those books will not become part of assigned, well-read history.

Thus it will remain largely unknown to most that this was a civil war covertly organized and supported by the same governments militarily imposing the Rambouillet accords. The Serbs knew the KLA had been armed and coached by U.S. and German intelligence to carve Kosovo off from Yugoslavia, refused to sign the Rambouillet Accords, and—when the bombing began with the purpose of forcing Yugoslavians to sign away their sovereignty—reacted by expelling the Albanian Kosovo population. The excuse for bombing Yugoslavia was the ethnic cleansing and genocide of Kosovar Albanians from Kosovo. The "free" press should be called to account for not alerting the public to this fiction and that it was NATO members acting and Yugoslavia reacting just as any student of foreign policy would expect them to react. Yugoslavia was not threatening anyone outside its borders, the Kosovar Albanians were not threatened with violence before the external orchestration of the KLA for a civil war (over 1,100 attacks on Serb police and Kosovar Albanian collaborationists), and the holocaust within their borders was only a reaction to this destabilization and forthcoming loss of a province Serbians consider the cradle of their civilization. Villages were destroyed as the KLA were rooted out of the houses from which they were firing on Serb soldiers, but no ethnic cleansing occurred until after NATO started bombing Yugoslavia. That will make no difference. Knowing the bombing was Western pressure that Serbs accept the loss of the heart of their culture, the atrocities required to demonize the Serbs occurred and will be kept in the world news through war crimes trials even as the far greater violence against the Serbs (the total shattering of their country with the deaths of tens of thousands) disappears from all except the most deeply researched history. Researchers should note that original propaganda figures of 100,000 to 250,000 Albanian men missing and thought to be slaughtered were reduced to a still sensationalized 10,000 expected to be found in mass graves when NATO first entered Kosovo. If that figure holds, it will be a testimonial to slaughter induced by the externally planned destabilization of Yugoslavia. If the final Kosovar Albanian body count drops to the low thousands, that will be a testimonial to successful NATO propaganda that will never be covered in depth by the media of record. When to the above disinformation we add the Pentagon wordsmiths' claim of the destruction of one-third of the Serbian military (122 tanks, 454 artillery pieces, and 222 armored personnel carriers) and the postwar audit that fewer than ''20 tanks, a similar number of artillery pieces, and fewer than 10 armored personnel carriers'' were destroyed, the outline of a planned propaganda campaign becomes visible.[33]

Powerbrokers within NATO are concerned with Yugoslavia only as a small battle within one or more of four centuries-long struggles: (1) The splitting of the Roman Empire into Eastern Orthodox Christianity and Western Christianity starting in the fourth century. This created the East and West that are fighting over territory on the boundaries between those religions yet today, and it is obvious that, without the support of Western Christian nations, Yugoslavia's Western Christians would not have had the political strength to shatter that once peaceful federation. (2) The 1,300-year struggle between both Eastern and Western Christians and Muslims, a battle between a different East and the same West. The current alliance of the West with Balkan Muslims is only a strategic decision of Managers of State. (3) The seventy-year battle between communism and capitalism, the Cold War. Most, but not all, communists are

Eastern Orthodox and most, but not all, capitalists are Western Christian. This is the historic in-step march of religion and governments as empires expand and contract. (4) And the centuries of battles over who will control world trade and thus who will lay claim to wealth, the primary subject of this book. This battle over the world's wealth is between the fragmented periphery of empire and the same allied, coordinated, powerful West.

That last struggle, Managers of State utilizing religious and political loyalties to control the wealth-producing process, is the one that counts. At any one moment, what is motivating any one person depends upon that person's position and loyalties within those four struggles. For those deeply committed to religion, or moderately religious and not interested in politics, which covers most of the masses, religious loyalties will determine their opinions. Those committed politically will be on one side or the other of the battle between capitalism and any form of cooperative society. If one is a corporate strategist, a Manager of State, or aware that one's livelihood is deeply affected—either positively or negatively—by the inequalities of trade, then some subdivision of the battle over world trade will be a primary consideration.

The breakup of Yugoslavia is little more than Western Christianity's continuation of pushing the line between Western Christianity and Eastern Orthodox Christianity (or capitalism and communism if politics is one's motivation) further East to build a coalition of friendly nations between Europe and the world's last great pool of oil in the Caspian Basin. The policies of state here are obvious, isolating Russia politically, excluding her from the oil and gas deposits in the Caspian Basin, and piping those hydrocarbons to Europe. Germany reached an agreement with Croatia (announced in the UN) for a pipeline through its territory and—even as the bombs were falling on Yugoslavia—officials of Georgia, Ukraine, Uzbekistan, Azerbaijan, and Moldova were in Washington, DC, signing a regional alliance (GUUAM) that included discussions of oil pipeline export routes to the West. There was also high interest in turning the rich minerals of Kosovo (the Stari Trg mining/manufacturing complex, which was too valuable to bomb), the suspected oil and gas deposits within the Dinarides Thrust, and other mineral wealth of Yugoslavia (coal, bauxite) towards Europe, which—through the breakup of Yugoslavia—will deprive Eastern Orthodox Christians of that wealth, will weaken that tiny enclave of communism, and all while simultaneously increasing the wealth of Western Europe.[34]

Check a map and note that the world's great oil-bearing sands go from the Middle East, through the Caspian Basin, and end at Romania. The straightest route to Europe for that oil is through Yugoslavia. Both Iraq and Yugoslavia were working hard to break their dependence upon the West, but the economic infrastructure and reputation of both nations are being destroyed by propaganda and bombing so they will not be able to break out of dependency in the foreseeable future. Though the human cost is greater today (1.5 million Iraqi civilian deaths due to the embargoes plus a few tens of thousand in the Gulf War and 2,000 Yugoslavian civilians and 5,000 military personnel killed by NATO bombs), the destruction of the economic infrastructure of those two nations is a replay of the raiding parties of the cities in the Middle Ages destroying the industrial capital of the countryside to maintain its dependency upon the city.[35]

Estimate the cost of rebuilding the economies of that shattered region: Croatia, $23 billion;

Bosnia $47 billion; Kosovo, $30 billion; and Yugoslavia itself, $100 billion (in the West's estimation; Yugoslavia estimates $40 billion). The only source of funds to rebuild those economies is in the West (who told us the problem was monopolization of capital?), so resources must be sold to the West to generate those funds. Considering that a large share of the industries of the newly ''independent'' provinces have been sold to Western investors, as described above, the planned shattering of Yugoslavia has delivered her natural wealth, her industrial wealth, and her future wealth—lock, stock, and barrel—to predatory Western finance capital.[36]

One need only analyze how deeply far worse human slaughters affected past strategic decisions to convince one that the death of 2,000 people in Kosovo's externally supported civil war was not the reason for NATO's bombing of Yugoslavia. Over 1.5 million people, largely children, have died in Iraq, due to the ongoing, American-led sanctions. One-third of the East Timorese (200,000) have died in the ongoing Indonesian suppression of their independence (utilizing American-supplied weapons). The estimated number killed in five years of ethnic cleansing in Rwanda is 500,000. Fifty thousand have perished in the still on-going, twenty-year conflict between Ethiopia and Eritrea (which was originally covertly supported by America). Two million have perished in the sixteen-year struggle in neighboring Sudan. The estimated number killed in Russia's Chechnya suppression is 80,000. And of course thousands were killed—with the backing of the United States and Germany—when Croatia ''ethnically-cleansed'' her territory when breaking from Yugoslavia.

In the next chapter, we will learn that most wars around the world are just such destabilizations by major outside powers as that which shattered Yugoslavia. Those listed slaughters (12 million to 15 million, of which 150,000 to 300,000 were the victims of death squads orchestrated by Western intelligence services) from just such destabilizations are to be added to the above list of shattered people whose terror and impoverishment were of no concern to the managers of state carrying out "strategic" decisions within the "Grand Strategies" of imperial centers of capital. Managers of state were taking care of their national interests through destabilizing already impoverished emerging nations attempting to gain control of their destiny.

Note how, after the fragmentation of Yugoslavia, the Eastern Orthodox Serbs are surrounded by the Western Christian nations of Romania, Bulgaria, Hungary, Slovenia and Croatia, most of which are anticipated to be brought within NATO soon or are already members. One must remember that the West had Yugoslavia embargoed throughout the decade of the 1990s as she was being destabilized and the Serbs simply refused to collapse. Until its destabilization, Yugoslavia was quite prosperous relative to the surrounding nations before the total shattering of her industry by NATO bombs and her subsequent loss of access to resources. Just as Cuba is still under economic and financial assault to prevent the world from observing the higher standard of living obtained by her citizens, Eastern Europe could not be totally restructured along Western political and economic lines so long as Yugoslavia remained intact and her citizens well cared for. Nor could NATO permit an opposing ideology with an intact military west of the planned new line of defense, Romania, Bulgaria, and Greece. It is for this reason that the Serbian economic infrastructure was pulverized by NATO bombs and missiles.

Serbia is now shattered, her citizens cannot be properly cared for, she cannot rise as an example for other dependent countries for generations, and she cannot afford to maintain a powerful military.

If Western capital dominates the economies of the fragmented former Yugoslavia, if oil pipelines from the Caspian Sea oil basin (according to the U.S. Energy Information Association, possibly nine times more oil reserves than in the U.S.) and the Middle East are built across Turkey and the former Yugoslavia to reach Europe, if Montenegro also breaks away, and if the natural resources of the Balkans feed Europe's industries, we will know what today's "Grand Strategy" of the breakup and impoverishment of Yugoslavia was all about. It is nothing less than Germany's dream of gaining control of Eastern Europe to obtain its resources for the thousand-year Reich. The only difference as addressed earlier, is that the imperial nations have given up on battling between themselves over the world's resources and have allied together to maintain control of the wealth-producing process. The struggle in the Balkans at the close of the twentieth century is only one of the battles of that Grand Strategy.

The Final Destabilization: Making a Deal with the Corrupt of Russia

The majority of the Russian people wanted change, but only slowly and carefully. They were not so foolish as to throw away their very means of living and the natural wealth of their nation. But Russian power brokers were given the opportunity to immediately own the "crown jewels of Russian industry" and the possibility of eventually owning the vast natural wealth of that nation. While a few of these corrupted managers of the Russian state were gaining enormous wealth, Western financiers would be gaining title to whatever wealth of the defeated nation they could through purchasing at bargain basement prices or buying off corrupt Managers of State. When the Soviet borders crumbled, subversive funds flowed in (much of them from the National Endowment for Democracy, NED), political allies were organized, those heavily funded politicians won enough control to pass the necessary laws, corrupt Managers of State (universally from the old communist elite) gained title to valuable properties by various subterfuges, and predatory capital came across the border to buy up technology and resources at a fraction of their value.

Western Managers of State made the same alliance with power brokers of the defeated former Soviet Union as they have with corrupt leaders throughout the former colonial world. The wealth and power of those corrupt leaders are protected so long as the West has access to their nation's resources at a fraction of their value and so long as there is access to their markets for the wealthy world's manufactured goods. As outlined by professors Alexander Buzgalin and Andrei Kolganov in *Bloody October in Moscow: Political Repression in the Name of Reform* and Boris Kagarlitsky in *Square Wheels: How Russian Democracy Got Derailed,* shock therapy in the former Soviet Union was an attempt to compress the seventy years of America's age of the robber barons into a few short years.[37] It is unlikely those aspirations of the West will hold as they are applied to Russia, Belarus, and Ukraine. To survive, those countries will have to limit that access. When that happens, Western money will be withdrawn and those countries will have to rebuild without access to finance capital, technology, or markets. But the corrupt elite of some of the remaining twelve provinces of the shat-

tered former Soviet Union will accept being paid off and a part of their resources, primarily oil, will continue to flow to the West. The East will be weaker and the West will be stronger and this, of course, is what the battles are all about. The math is quite simple: Western traders and the corrupt of those provinces share the difference between the market price in the West and the pennies per hour paid labor in those collapsed provinces to harvest, mine, and ship those resources.

On an evening news show, Harvard economist Jeffrey Sachs, who was in charge of the U.S. economic team coaching the Soviets in their shock therapy economic collapse, said that the problem with the former Soviets is they do not yet have enough free enterprise. Having just cut economic arteries in the former Soviets with abandon, this same economist, in a later statement, had deep concerns over the fragility of the world economic system and expressed fears about U.S. efforts to penetrate the Japanese market, which he described as ''reckless.''

Sachs was in charge of the Harvard Institute for International Development that oversaw Russia's destabilization. We do not know if there is a connection between the CIA hiring economists during the middle and late 1980s and the Soviet collapse, and we do not know if that institute was one established by the CIA as addressed above. But consider these points:

The wholesale shutdown of Soviet industry was done following the advice of that institute.

These same economists would surely not offer the same advice to an allied nation, as the above comment on opening Japan's markets demonstrates.

Any student of mercantilism would have recognized these suggestions as creating a dependency.

Any economist could analyze that there was

virtually nothing anywhere to replace the industry that was being defunded and shut down except imports from the West. We know that imposing belief systems to protect a nation's "national interest" (the way Adam Smith free trade was imposed upon the world, as addressed above) is a highly used tactic of Managers of State.

So, how else can that be interpreted? As would be expected, the Soviet collapse rapidly worsened as industries were shut down, the Russians figured that out after it was too late, and those advisors were expelled from Russia.[38]

A quick changeover from a centralized economy to a market economy means nothing less than massive decapitalization of the society, purchase of modern manufactured goods from the West by the few who have money, sale of valuable resources to the West cheaply (which is where those fortunate few will, through corrupt deals selling off their nation's natural wealth, obtain the money to buy those products from the West), and impoverishment for the majority. In short, any nation which tried such a thoughtless plan would revert to developing world status with its wealth essentially confiscated by intact imperial centers of capital.

Which is exactly what happened. When the Soviets collapsed in 1990 there were few consumer imports. But these luxuries quickly rose to an unsustainable officially acknowledged 39 percent of Russian consumer products as imported in 1996 and climbed to an official 50 percent (and an estimated 60 percent) by 1998 with no compensating manufactured exports. Meanwhile, 30 percent of America's consumer products are imported against large compensating manufactured exports, and many economists, including the "Harvard boys" mentioned above, are concerned. Couple that impoverishing 50 percent to 60 percent consumer product

import statistic with the fact that Russia has a $35 billion per year trade surplus (touted as a Russian success but really an enormous success for the West's Grand Strategy) while its industrial production has fallen 80 percent and capital investment nearly 90 percent. This all tells us that Russia's massive natural resources are being turned to the West to produce consumer needs for Western citizens and a small share of those manufactured products are returned to Russia to pay for those resources.[39] Massive natural resources exported to pay for a small amount of manufactured wealth—this is an exact replay of centuries ago when raiders from the cities of Europe controlled the resources of the countryside, when the science of laying claim to others' wealth through inequalities of trade all began.

To really understand the immensity of the inequalities of trade between the imperial centers of capital and Russia, we return to the math on wealth accumulation through unequal pay for equally productive labor in Chapter One. There we learned that the pay differential between the defeated Russia and the victorious America (twenty-three cents an hour against fourteen dollars an hour) was a wealth accumulation potential in favor of America of 3,600 to one while Germany's higher wages (twenty-three dollars per hour) gave her a wealth accumulation advantage of 10,000 to one.[40] We will quote from Chapter One where that formula is addressed:

> Obviously the Russian workers' factory is essentially shut down, they are still being paid their twenty-three cents an hour, at times even nothing is produced, and, on that basis, the formula appears inaccurate. But it is the basis that is inaccurate, not the formula. Before its collapse, the Soviet Union was calculated to be within eight years of equaling the West in technology. With

its huge resources and its highly skilled work-force operating factories utilizing the latest tech-nology, and assuming it had access to markets, Russia could theoretically produce just as effi-ciently as anyone else. But the billions of dollars poured into Russia since its collapse were not building any *manufacturing* industry at all, let alone modern industries. The problem is not the productivity of labor in the developing world per se. The problem is denial of technology and de-nial of access to markets. Immense sums flowing into a country or region are meaningless if there is no access to technology and markets.

The immense sums then loaned to Russia and the former provinces of the former Soviet Union, ostensibly to help them rebuild their economy, are used for everything except build-ing efficient modern industry. That debt trap can be escaped only through massive sales of re-sources, and their fire-sale prices dictate many years of a depressed economy for those belea-guered souls.

The Decision to Restructure to a Market Economy Was Made by Soviet Intellectuals

Soviet intellectuals studied both their economy and that of the West closely and made a con-scious decision for change. It is interesting to note that once the decision to change to a mar-ket economy was made, these same intellectuals had little to say about the actual restructuring. As in the West, important economic decisions will be made by those who own (or in this case the corrupt who anticipate owning) the wealth.

When I [Fred Weir] came here seven years ago at the outset of perestroika, there was very little belief in socialism among the generation dubbed the golden children. These sons and daughters of the Communist party elite had received excellent

educations, had the best that the society could give them, and only aspired to live like their Western counterparts. Many had high positions in the Communist Party, but were absolutely ex-uberant Westernizers, pro-capitalists, and from very early in the perestroika period, this was their agenda. . . . People who thought they were going to be the governing strata in a new society are [now] losing their jobs, being impoverished and becoming bitter. The intellectuals, for instance—whose themes during the Cold War were intel-lectual freedom, human rights, and so on—had a very idealized view of Western capitalism. They have been among the groups to suffer the most from the early stages of marketization as their huge network of institutes and universities are de-funded.[41]

Those golden children of the communist elite are undoubtedly quite silent as they gaze at their once proud country lying prostrate at the feet of imperial capital. The population of Russia is falling at the astounding rate of 800,000 a year; birth rates have plummeted to the lowest in the world; only one in four children are born healthy. There are dramatic increases in the number of children born with physical and men-tal impairment and the average lifespan of Rus-sian men has fallen from sixty-five years to fifty-eight, below that of Ghana.[42]

To the Soviets It Could Only Have Looked as if War Were Imminent

From the Soviet side it certainly looked as if war were coming. From 1945, and up to at least 1956 when the U-2 spy flights started, thousands of U.S. "ferret" spy flights photo-graphed Soviet territory and raced back before they could be identified and attacked. In 1946 and 1947 alone (note this was before the Cold War officially started), thirty such planes were shot down, and at least twenty U.S. airmen were captured alive; never acknowledged by their government, they finished out their lives in Soviet prisons, and their families were told they died in various accidents. As acknowledged by the highly respected *U.S. News and World Report,* between 1950 and 1970 (after the Cold War officially started) there were over 10,000 and possibly over 20,000 such overflights deep into Soviet and Chinese territory by military aircraft. There was a lot more going on than just the acknowledged photographing of Soviet territory. Sabotage and assassination teams were being dropped in to hide among their relatives and ethnic brothers. Almost universally their operations failed, with large losses among the agents and their relatives who were to hide them.[43]

These acts of war did not all succeed. In June 1992, when Russian President Boris Yeltsin met with President Bush and said, "We may have American prisoners yet," quite a stir was created. News commentator Tom Brokaw reported this disturbing news and the congressional uproar over these possible prisoners. The next night Brokaw said, "These were American airmen shot down during the Cold War. This is the first time Americans have been apprised of this." Then for weeks, except for an occasional, highly sanitized statement, all went silent on that explosive subject. A few months later, the headlines read, "Yeltsin: POWs 'Summarily Executed.'" But the last line of that front-page article depicting these execution horrors told the real story: "The largest group of Americans imprisoned in the Soviet Union included more than 730 pilots and other airmen who either made forced landings on Soviet territory or were shot down on Cold War spy flights."[44]

The intelligence agencies of Britain, France, and Germany were running similar, but smaller, covert operations against the Soviet Union and other nations of the Eastern bloc. This was a massive assault on Soviet sovereignty, actually outright acts of war, by essentially the same powers that had invaded them twenty-five years earlier and also the same powers that owed an enormous debt to the Soviets for saving them from Fascism in World War II.

The fact that there were no Soviet spy planes, or any carrying assassination and sabotage teams, overflying Western territory during this period is something scholars should note. Nor should the presence of U.S. pilots in the Soviet Union have been news to U.S. newscasters. With the Soviets complaining to Washington, DC, and to the United Nations and holding many trials, for the American people not to be informed of these assaults on Soviet territory can be due only to cooperation by the major media of record in the misinforming of America. These illegal flights being a secret only to the citizens of the West testifies to how Social Control belief systems require suppression of information about acts of war by Managers of State simultaneously with depictions of imminent attack from the targeted society. That is, of course, the creation of enemies to protect a power structure.

As in any society after any revolution, there were those within the Soviet Union who were sympathetic to, and subject to manipulation by, outside forces. Thus, when Germany invaded the Soviet Union, whole communities of ethnic Germans and other communities that still had ties and loyalties to the West joined the invading army.

When that war was over, those entire communities were resettled in Siberia where they could not link up with outside powers still threatening to overthrow the Soviet government. Millions of innocent people (even many dedicated and loyal communists) were rounded up for resettlement; many were executed. But many were far from innocent. Many executed were harboring trained saboteurs who had been parachuted into the Eastern European countries (or infiltrated across the border) all the way to Byelorussia.[45] Struggles for power became mixed with the legitimate battle to defend the revolution, and many within the power structure were swallowed up in that holocaust.

But note! It was protecting their country from being overthrown by external powers manipulating internal ethnic groups that created these suppressions. Where America faced no such threat after its revolution, the cooperative efforts of many nations to overthrow the Soviets had been ongoing for seventy years. These included direct intervention in their revolution, the World War II effort to exterminate them, years of covert actions such as training and flying in assassins and saboteurs, being embargoed from world trade, and their post–World War II military encirclement.

Ignoring the background behind the forced migrations to Siberia, the Western press in its constant search for drama, openly pushed the governing Social Control belief system, giving the death toll as sixty million. But then it became forty million, then twenty million, then ten million, and the figures are still coming down towards the true number killed under "Stalinism"—certainly under 100,000 and most likely under 50,000.[46]

These are the same principles that peddlers of crisis have been using for thousands of years. The greater the lie, the more surely it will be believed by their followers. Even if it is done only verbally and the accuser is in no personal physical danger, the surest way to be recognized as a leader is to lead an attack against an enemy.

There has been so much fabrication that it is impossible to know what is true. We are satis-fied that, of the citizens of those Soviet communities who welcomed the German armies and were the contacts for the saboteurs the West was infiltrating into those countries, and thus were a threat to the security of this new nation, a minimum of six to seven million were relocated to Siberia. This was a full-fledged war, the Soviets knew it, and many innocent people died from the paranoia created by seventy years of intense destabilization efforts and outright wars.

Propaganda Was the Essence of the Cold War: Be Cautious of All Clichés and All Statistics

Former attaché to the Soviet Embassy George Kennan, undoubtedly the U.S. citizen most knowledgeable about the Soviet Union (one of the prime promoters of the Cold War, and one who had a change of heart about the morality of that deception), is quoted as saying that those executed in the Soviet Union were in the tens of thousands, meaning the total is under 100,000, as addressed above.[47] Tens of thousands is still a large number, to be sure, but, even though many—even possibly most—were innocent, a large number were attempting to overthrow that new government, and that is a capital offense in any country. (For a balanced perspective, compare the under 100,000 killed within the former Soviet Union as they searched for those being supported by the West to overthrow the government with the numbers killed on the periphery of empire by the West as documented in the next chapter.)

Many innocent people within the Soviet Union were swallowed up in this mass hysteria. The Soviets are now opening their records and restoring the good names of these people. Historians are tracing what happened to each individual so their families can know their fates. Perhaps the world may someday know the true numbers of those unjustly persecuted souls.

Lately, whenever the subject comes up in the news we notice phrasing such as, "had their lives damaged by Stalinism." This is entirely different than "sixty million executed" and suggests the media are well aware they were deceived and, in turn, deceived the public. If "damaged lives" are the criterion, then that damage must be compared with the damage other countries inflict on minorities within their own societies and on other societies, including that done by financial warfare, covert wars, and overt wars—all trade wars—which are the policies of Managers of State of imperial centers of capital.

We caution the reader on the statistics that will be published. The slaughters of defeated centers of capital and others threatening to break free will be exaggerated, while the suppressions and oppressions of the dominant centers of capital will be camouflaged as defensive actions and the statistics of slaughter of innocents will be essentially nonexistent.

When Hitler was planning World War II, Reinhard Heydrich, deputy chief of Hitler's SS, operated a covert operation that counterfeited letters from top Soviet military officers to falsely indicate a counterrevolution by these officers.[48] Possibly 35,000 highly loyal officers were executed. We say possibly because again we must remember how intelligence services create and exaggerate facts to demonize an enemy; these exaggerated figures then tend to become recorded history.

After World War II, copying Heydrich's successful destabilization efforts, Western secret services counterfeited papers and letters that caused massive arrests of innocent people in Eastern Europe and the Soviet Union. Citizens of the West heard all about the repressions but nothing about the cause or that, when the Soviets caught on to the scam, they released those imprisoned and even paid compensation to an innocent American couple who were caught up in that intrigue and imprisoned for several years.[49]

Even as the Russian revolution succeeded, the British were attempting to destroy Lenin's reputation to the world. By the same methods that placed Napoleon in history books as a megalomaniac, the leaders of the Bolshevik Revolution will be in future history books as mass terrorists.[50] That creation of history will be accomplished through financing already highly biased historians to research executions and point out the total innocence of those executed, and will simultaneously totally ignore the counterfeit papers fingering innocent people, the destabilization teams inserted, the many who were guilty, or the massive amounts of money spent to overthrow the government as a ring of steel was placed around the Soviet Union.

The alert can watch this writing of history unfold. Alternative views typically find little financing and, due to the already programmed masses, no audience. A created enemy continues to control a population even after the defeat of that enemy. Major publishers publish only books they think can make a profit, the masses read only books which support the Social Control belief system that has been imposed upon them, and thus books based on this fraudulent history are best sellers while there is little audience for a book that documents honest history.

Thus, when a society is under dire threat, even in a free enterprise society, honest histories are published only on the fringes. With the collapses of the economic firewalls on the periphery of empire, this, of course, may change.

People want answers and books of in-depth exposés can now be published in the mainstream press. However, entrenched beliefs create a skeptical publishing community and a limited market so those books even then will not typically be mainstream.

Conceptually Reversing the Process

America was protected by wide oceans, has never been seriously threatened for the 200 years of its existence, and had received massive investments from Europe; its industrial development was accelerated to produce for European wars; Americans were on friendly terms with almost all countries except the Soviet Union; and their 50 percent increase in industrial capacity during World War II was thought to be enough to produce for the entire Western world at expected levels of consumption. Most economists know well that such an excess of industrial capacity means economic collapses such as the Great Depression.

However, once America was restocked with cars and other consumer needs, that excess industrial capacity was turned to producing arms for the Cold War. Roughly 30 percent of America's post–World War II jobs were created as an economic multiplier from those Cold War arms expenditures. Thus, the Cold War can be credited with keeping factories humming and creating an America wealthier than ever. In fact, when the Soviet Union collapsed and the Cold War was officially over, none of the Managers of State in the Western world dared shut down their war industries. Industrial overcapacity was so huge and their economies so dependent upon the economic multiplier from those arms expenditures that shutting down the huge military machine would collapse their economies just as it did in the Soviet Union. (Economic studies

on investment in social infrastructure being more efficient in wealth distribution than military production notwithstanding. Such massive social investment could be done only by central planning or massive guarantees and, under the then-current, and still current, economic philosophies, those were not options.)

In comparison to America's 200 years of peace and wars that actually strengthened its industrial base, the Soviet Union had only nineteen years of real peace (1922 to 1941), was devastated by both the intervention and World War II, and war production subtracted from rather than added to the wealth available to Soviet citizens. The Soviet Union went from being an agrarian nation powered by horsepower to the second or third largest industrial producer in only thirteen years, 1928 to 1941, the year their Great Patriotic War began. Soviets were building infrastructure rapidly, were still largely horse-powered, and thus were only approaching their industrial takeoff point. One can only wonder what they could have done if World War II had not been forced upon them.

The Soviets pulled abreast of America in industrial capacity, even as they armed to offset the ring of steel they were encircled with. They had developed their technology to within eight years of that in the West, even as they were embargoed from technology and access to world markets. But, as addressed above, that industrial production was all going into infrastructure, arms, and to the periphery and only a minuscule 5 percent was for consumer production.

But let's go one step further. Remembering how close the Soviets came to winning the arms race and thus winning the Cold War, does anyone doubt what would have happened if the Soviet Union were untouched and America were the one that had been invaded, the nation that lost 30 percent of its prime labor, and the nation in which everything above the Mason-Dixon line and east of the Mississippi River had been blown up or burned to the ground? The conclusions are obvious. The expensive arms race imposed upon it broke the Soviet Union and, because there was no other mechanism in place to distribute the wealth, the same wasteful expenditures in the West actually strengthened the economies of the West.

Their cooperative ways explain why the Soviets developed so fast under such adverse conditions and our research demonstrates that development could even be much faster yet under cooperative capitalism. Thus, the chapter Sharing Technology with the World through Cooperative Capitalism conceptually reverses the process of subtle-monopoly imperialism (monopoly capitalism) and replaces it with cooperative capitalism. Under cooperative principles with competitive equality as opposed to competition between unequals, the world can be developed to a sustainable level and poverty eliminated in forty-five years.

Competence Was the Problem, Not Incompetence: If the Soviets Had Been Incompetent, There Would Have Been No Threat

If the Soviets had been incompetent, as we hear so often, they would have been no threat and there would have been no Cold War. They would have simply been quietly overwhelmed by capitalism. It was their competency that was the problem. To have advanced as far as they did under such adverse conditions before finally collapsing under the weight of the entire Western world testifies to a fiercely loyal population working hard for their country. They were not a terrorized and sullen population.

If the Soviets had been given the time and support for a slow transition to capitalism, as most citizens wanted, they would have likely adopted a two-track economy—a steadily decreasing public sector and a steadily increasing private sector—such as is working so successfully in China. But the danger of a powerful center of capital with a strong sense of egalitarianism and justice and enormous resources of its own was simply too big a threat to the imperial centers of capital. That proud nation of cooperative soviets, to which those same imperial nations owed their very salvation from fascism, had to be shattered.

Forces in the former Soviet Union to take back their country are rapidly rebuilding. This means the property titles of those who bought Russia's wealth for pennies on the dollar are at risk. But for a quick lesson on what Marx meant by "monopoly capital," and what "debt traps" mean, look at what those shattered economies face. If they repudiate or default on any external debts, any assets outside their borders can be, and will be, attached. This means businesses, property titles, bank accounts, goods in transit, ships, or planes. Those beleaguered societies would be in one of the tightest containment traps that any imperial center of capital ever devised.

Notes

1. Lawrence Wittner, *American Intervention in Greece* (New York: Columbia University Press, 1982), especially pp. 162, 283; Kati Marton, *The Polk Conspiracy: Murder and Cover-up in the Case of CBS* (New York: Farrar, Straus, and Giroux, 1990); C.M. Woodhouse, *The Rise and Fall of the Greek Colonels* (New York: Franklin Watts, 1985); Stephan Rosskamm Shalom, *Imperial Alibis* (Boston: South End Press, 1993) p. 26; William Blum, *CIA: A Forgotten History* (London: Zed Books, 1986), pp. 31–36; David Leigh,

The Wilson Plot (New York: Pantheon, 1988), pp. 17–18; William Manchester, *The Glory and the Dream* (New York: Bantam Books, 1990), pp. 433–43; Michael McClintock, *Instruments of Statecraft* (New York: Pantheon, 1992), pp. 11–17. See Introduction, note three, for many more.

2. Eric R. Wolf, *Europe and the People Without History* (Berkeley: University of California Press, 1982), pp. 99–100.

3. Wolf, *People Without History,* pp. 99–100.

4. Ibid., chapter 3, pp. 43, 61, 97, 108, 110, 119; Gabriel Kolko, *The Politics of War* (New York: Pantheon, 1990), chapters 3 and 4; I. F. Stone, *The Hidden History of the Korean War* (Boston: Little Brown, 1952).

5. Sidney Lens, *Permanent War* (New York: Schocken Books, 1987), pp. 20–21; William Appleman Williams, *The Tragedy of American Diplomacy* (New York: W.W. Norton, 1972), pp. 208, 235.

6. Arjun Makhijani, *From Global Capitalism to Economic Justice* (New York: Apex Press, 1992), pp. 25–26, quoting a memorandum on NSC-68.

7. Dean Acheson, *Present at the Creation* (New York: W.W. Norton, 1987), pp. 374, 726; see also p. 377; emphasis added.

8. Stone, *Hidden History,* pp. 1–3.

9. Linda Robinson, "What Didn't We Do to Get Rid of Castro," *U.S. News & World Report,* October 26, 1998, p. 41.

10. Stone, *Hidden History,* pp. 263–64.

11. John Ranelagh, *The Agency: The Rise and Decline of the CIA* (New York: Simon and Schuster, 1987), p. 257.

12. For a fuller study read J.W. Smith, *The World's Wasted Wealth 2* (San Luis Obispo, CA: The Institute for Economic Democracy, 1994).

13. Lloyd C. Gardner, *Safe for Democracy* (New York: Oxford University Press, 1984), pp. 197–98; Philip Knightley, *The First Casualty* (New York: Harcourt Brace Jovanovich, 1975), chapter 7; Mikhail Gorbachev, *Perestroika* (New York: Harper and Row, 1987), p. 33, endnote 2; Edmond Taylor, *The Fall of the Dynasties* (New York: Dorset Press, 1989), p. 359; Ernest Volkman and Blaine Baggett, *Secret Intelligence* (New York: Doubleday, 1989), chapter 1.

14. Walter Isaacson and Evan Thomas, *The Wise Men* (New York: Simon and Schuster, 1986), p. 150; Michael Kettle, *The Allies and the Russian Collapse* (Minneapolis: University of Minnesota Press, 1981), p. 15; Taylor, *Fall of the Dynasties,* p. 381.

15. Knightley, *First Casualty,* p. 138; D.F. Fleming, *The Cold War and Its Origins* (New York: Doubleday, 1961), pp. 26, 1038.

16. Paul Kennedy, *The Rise and Fall of the Great Powers* (New York: Random House, 1987), pp. 321, 323.

17. James Douglas-Hamilton, *Motive for a Mission: The Story Behind Rudolf Hess's Flight to Britain* (New York: Paragon House, 1979). As it does not even mention the "Clivedon Set" of Britain, this book's analysis is far too soft. There is a serious school of thought on the pre–World War II worldwide alliance of Fascists but that history is too well hidden and unsure for us to address.

18. Vilnis Sipols, *The Road to Great Victory* (Moscow: Progress Publishers, 1985), pp. 109, 132, 179–80; Kennedy, *Rise and Fall,* especially pp. 321, 323, 352.

19. Jeffrey Jukes, *Stalingrad at the Turning Point* (New York: Ballantine Books, 1968), p. 154; *National Geographic* (TV), August 23, 1987; Fleming, *Cold War and its Origins,* p. 157; Kolko, *Politics of War,* pp. 19, 351, 372.

20. Kennedy, *Rise and Fall,* pp. 357–58; David Mayers, *George Kennan* (New York: Oxford University Press, 1988), pp. 190–91; Oleg Rzheshevsky, *World War II: Myths and the Realities* (Moscow: Progress Publishers, 1984), p. 175.

21. Lens, *Permanent War,* pp. 20–21; Williams, *Tragedy of American Diplomacy,* pp. 208, 235.

22. Don Cook, *Forging the Alliance* (London: Secker and Warburg, 1989), pp. 78–79.

23. E. P. Thompson and Dan Smith, *Protest and Survive* (New York: Monthly Review Press, 1981), p. 123. See J.W. Smith, *World's Wasted Wealth 2.*

24. Lester Thurow, *Head to Head: The Coming Economic Battle Among Japan, Europe, and America* (New York: William Morrow, 1992), pp. 92, 95; David Kotz, "Russia in Shock: How Capitalist 'Shock Therapy' Is Destroying Russia's Economy," *Dollars and Sense,* June 1993, p. 9.

25. Patrick Flaherty, "Behind Shatalinomics: Politics of Privatization," *Guardian,* October 10, 1990, p. 11.

26. Rich Thomas, "From Russia, with Chips," *Newsweek,* August 6, 1990.

27. Peter Gowan, "Old Medicine in New Bottles," *World Policy Journal* (Winter 1991–92), pp. 3–5.

28. Ibid., pp. 6–8, 13.

29. Michel Chossudovsky, *The Globalization of Poverty: Impacts of IMF and World Bank Reforms* (London: Zed Books, 1997), Chapter Thirteen; Michel Chossudovsky, "Dismantling Yugoslavia, Colonizing Bosnia," *Covert Action Quarterly* (Spring, 1996), pp. 31–37; Sean Gervasi, "Germany, U.S., and the Yugoslavian Crisis," *Covert Action Quarterly* (Winter 1992–93), pp. 41–45, 64–66; David Lorge Parnas, "Con: Dayton's a Step Back—Way Back," *Peace* (March/April 1996): pp. 17–22; McClintock, *Instruments of Statecraft,* pp. 71–82; Catherine Samaray, *Yugoslavia Dismembered* (New York: Monthly Review Press, 1995; Charles Lane, Theodore Sranger and Tom Post, "The Ghosts of Serbia," *Newsweek* (April 19, 1993), pp. 30–31; Dusko Doder. "Yugoslavia: New War, Old Hatreds," *Foreign Policy* (Summer 1993), pp. 4, 9–11, 18–19: Thomas Kielinger and Max Otte, "Germany: The Presumed Power," *Foreign Policy* (Summer 1993), p. 55. German support was essentially acknowledged by former Acting Secretary of State Lawrence Eagleburger on *The McNeil/Lehrer Report* (May 6, 1993) and many other talk shows and news programs, pointing out that there were those who pushed for the collapse of Yugoslavia, specifically pointing to Germany. On that same show, Michael Elliot of the respected British publication *The Economist* agreed.

30. Ibid.

31. Ibid. Check *Jane's Defense Weekly*, especially the May 10, 1999, issue.

32. See note 29. See also later articles and books by those same authors.

33. See note 29. For reduced Serbian losses: Richard J. Newman, "A Kosovo Numbers Game," *U.S. News & World Report* (July 12, 1999), p. 36.

34. See note 29.

35. Ibid.

36. Ibid.

37. Alexander Buzgalin and Andrei Kolganov, *Bloody October in Moscow: Political Repression in the Name of Reform* (New York: Monthly Review Press, 1994); Boris Kagarlitsky, *Square Wheels: How Russian Democracy Got Derailed* (New York: Monthly Review Press, 1994). The tables of contents of most good magazines, both mainstream and alternative news, will have many good articles on the legal theft of the wealth of the Soviet Union through privatization.

38. Janine R. Wedel, "The Harvard Boys Do Russia," *The Nation,* June 1, 1998, pp. 11–16.

39. "Proud Russia on Its Knees," *U.S. News & World Report,* February 8, 1999, pp. 30–36; David R. Francis, "Debt-riddled Russia to Ask for Forgiveness," *The Christian Science Monitor,* April 5, 1999, p. 17; Katrina vanden Heuvel, editorial, *The Nation,* August 10–17, 1998, pp. 4–6. See also Julie Corwin, Douglas Stranglin, Suzanne Possehl, and Jeff Trimble, "The Looting of Russia," *U.S. News & World Report,* March 7, 1994; John Feffer, "The Browning of Russia," *Covert Action Quarterly* (Spring 1996).

40. Doug Henwood, "Clinton and the Austerity Cops," *The Nation,* November 23, 1992, p. 628. Colin Hines, Tim Lang, Jerry Mander, and Edward Goldsmith, eds., *The Case Against the Global Economy and For a Turn Toward the Local* (San Francisco: Sierra Club, 1996), p. 487, say $24.90 an hour for Germany, $16.40 for the U.S.

41. Fred Weir, "Interview: Fred Weir in Russia," *Covert Action Quarterly* (Summer 1993), pp. 54–55.

42. *60 Minutes,* May 19, 1996.

43. Michael Ross, "Yeltsin: POWs 'Summarily Executed,' " *The Spokesman Review,* November 12, 1992, pp. B1, A10; Volkman and Baggett, *Secret Intelligence,* p. 187; John Loftus, *Belarus Secret* (New York: Alfred A. Knopf, 1982), especially chapters 5–8, pp. 109–10; Blum, *The CIA,* chapters 6, 7, 8, 15, 17, especially p. 124; see Introduction, note three.

44. Ross, "POWs Summarily Executed," pp. B1, A10. Later TV documentaries on this episode claimed 130 airmen lost, the above referenced *U.S. News* article claimed 252, but all pointed out the losses may have been much higher.

45. Besides those with ethnic ties to the West who betrayed their new country by joining forces with the Nazi invaders (such as Vlasov's army and Byelorussian, Ukrainian, Croatian, and Polish volunteers for the mobile death squads; twenty thousand were volunteers; the rest were conscripts who were granted amnesty). John Prados, *The Presidents' Secret Wars* (New York: William Morrow, 1986), chapters 2 and 3; Loftus, *Belarus Secret,* chapters 1–3, pp. 51–53, 49, 102–03, especially p. 43; Ranelagh, *Agency,* p. 156.

46. Blum, *The CIA,* pp. 127–28, 131, 185; Victor Marchetti and John D. Marks, *The CIA and the Cult of Intelligence* (New York: Dell, 1980), chapter 6, especially pp. 152–56; Philip Agee, *Inside the Company*

(New York: Bantam Books, 1975), especially pp. 53–54, 62–63, 541–42; John Stockwell, *The Praetorian Guard* (Boston: South End Press, 1991), pp. 100–101; Ralph W. McGehee, *Deadly Deceits* (New York: Sheridan Square Press, 1983), especially pp. 30, 58, 62, 189; Philip Agee and Louis Wolf, *Dirty Work* (London: Zed Press, 1978), especially p. 262; David Wise and Thomas B. Ross, *The Espionage Establishment* (New York: Bantam Books, 1978), pp. 256, 257; Ellen Schrecker, *No Ivory Tower: McCarthyism and the Universities* (New York: Oxford University Press, 1986); Frank J. Donner, *The Age of Surveillance: The Aims and Methods of America's Political Intelligence System* (New York: Random House, 1981). See also Introduction, note three.

47. Alexander Cockburn, "Beat the Devil," *The Nation,* March 6, 1989, p. 294; David Corn and Jefferson Morley, "Beltway Bandits," *The Nation,* April 9, 1988, p. 488. An interesting appraisal of Stalinist terror is made by Soviet dissident Roy Medvedev, "Parallels Inappropriate," *New Times* (July 1989), pp. 46–47. See also Volkman and Baggett, *Secret Intelligence,* p. 187; Loftus, *Belarus Secret,* especially chapters 5–8, pp. 109–10; Blum, *The CIA,* Chapters 6, 7, 8, 15, 17.

48. Donald Cameron Watt, *How War Came: The Immediate Origins of the Second World War* (New York: Pantheon Books, 1989), p. 45.

49. Blum, *The CIA,* Chapter 7.

50. Volkman and Baggett, *Secret Intelligence,* p. 9, and check the sources in the Introduction and Chapter Seven.

7

Suppressing the Former Colonial World's Break for Economic Freedom

The titles of this and other chapters and sub-chapters are so antithetical to everything we have heard or read since childhood that it requires deep study and overwhelming hard evidence to gain an understanding of the Grand Strategy controlling societies on the periphery of empire in the twentieth century. For a short-cut to understanding this history, and thus a broad understanding of the political economy of the world, one should read this treatise on the 800-year history of imposed inequalities of world trade, browse through books we have referenced, browse through Ralph McGehee's database of thousands of sources on post–World War II CIA covert operations, and then browse his referenced key articles and books (especially John Prados' 1996 updated *Presidents' Secret Wars*) which document this history.[1] There one will find the underlying truth we are all searching for, the hidden history of the imperial centers' Grand Strategies, known fully only to the senior Managers of State. Searching in that database for Third World nations that have had severe postwar internal conflicts will bring to light the many covert actions against those nations that denied them the right to control their destinies. Through both covert and overt wars, the imperial centers of capital of the twentieth century were denying those former colonial nations the very rights and freedoms loudly

championed by the very people, and the nation, destabilizing them.

A careful study of those books and articles will alert one to how a society's official history is created, since these covert suppressions of other people's rights are recorded only as insurgencies, civil wars, and internal conflicts. The real history, as we will be outlining below, seldom surfaces in official history. The public is conditioned to believe that they were battling communism all over the world but of the major governments overthrown only Afghanistan was communist. Most of the rest wished to emulate America's freedom and prosperity. Not a word will one find in our histories about those violent events being financed and orchestrated by imperial centers of capital. Control of other nations' media and elections is ignored and not a hint will one find that death squads on the periphery of empire are orchestrated from the imperial center to decapitate popular movements that stand to win elections and threaten the imperial centers with democratic leadership on the periphery.

For example: During the seven years William Casey was CIA director (1981 to 1987), fifty major CIA covert operations were initiated throughout the world and thousands of minor ones.[2] Those major destabilizations caused massive deaths and destruction while the minor operations destabilized small democratic groups before they could gain a following, and controlled the media on both the periphery and in the imperial center. As Casey was director for only seven of the CIA's forty-two years, one starts to get a sense of the massive covert destabilizations it took to suppress these breaks for freedom.

Only after one understands how freedom and rights are being suppressed by the managers of imperial states—even as they preach peace, freedom, justice, rights, and majority rule to their citizens to maintain their beliefs in the morality of their society, and thus assure the continued support of the masses for inflicting such violence upon the world—can one write honest history. If one does not understand that process, one is almost certain to write a history in which, unbeknownst to the author, the background and documentation have been carefully created to give Managers of State the freedom to suppress other people's rights and transfer their wealth to the imperial center through unequal trades.

America as an Empire and Colonial Power Predates the Cold War

America's march across the continent in the nineteenth century through broken treaties with the Indians was made easier by the Louisiana purchase from France in 1803 and the purchase of Florida from Spain in 1819. Besides the various battles with Britain for freedom and territory, Mexico was the only nation the United States went to war with over territory on the American continent. Texas became independent from Mexico in 1836 and from the victory in the Mexican-American War of 1848 America gained the Southwestern states and California. The only territory gained after that acknowledged in history books was Alaska and Hawaii.

But that was only a matter of what was easy to absorb while declaring itself a defender of colonial nations. That America won the Spanish-American War in 1898 is recognized by all but even some encyclopedias typically do not inform the reader that Spain *ceded* Cuba, Puerto Rico, Guam, and the Philippines to the United States for $20 million. Similarly, but not totally, ignored, is that the Philippine patriots' struggle for freedom from America was violently suppressed from 1899 through 1903 in a manner very similar in tactics and level of violence to the Vietnam War in the twentieth century. In that break for freedom, an estimated 600,000 Filipinos died from combat and starvation. Control through a puppet government was substituted for outright colonial control as authorized by the ceding of these lands by Spain. Just as the rest of the colonial world was breaking free, the Filipinos again fought for their freedom after World War II. Tens of thousands of Filipinos have been killed, primarily by private death squads, as the elite fight to retain control of the government and their land, and that suppression of true independence through covert American support is still ongoing as we go into the twenty-first century.[3]

Before World War II, Marine Corps Major General Smedley Butler knew the U.S. military was essentially a weapon to force the Third World to accept its position as provider of wealth to the imperial centers of capital. Alternative history buffs are very familiar with General Butler's description of America as an imperial nation so this is no secret. But history as they know it, and as General Butler knew it while he was helping create it, does not get into high school, or even university, history books:

> I spent thirty-three years and four months in active service as a member of our country's most

agile military force—the US Marine Corps. . . . And during that period I spent most of my time being a high-class muscle man for big business, for Wall Street and for the bankers. In short, I was a racketeer for capitalism.

Thus I helped make Mexico and especially Tampico safe for American oil interests in 1914. I helped make Haiti and Cuba a decent place for the National City Bank boys to collect revenues in. I helped purify Nicaragua for the international banking house of Brown Brothers in 1909–12. I brought light to the Dominican Republic for American sugar interests in 1916. I helped make Honduras "right" for American fruit companies in 1913. In China in 1927 I helped see to it that Standard Oil went its way unmolested.[4]

The highly competent historians Gerard Colby and Charlotte Dennett researched the "conquest of the Amazon" and wrote *Thy Will Be Done: The Conquest of the Amazon: Nelson Rockefeller and Evangelism in the Age of Oil.* Although they were unaware when starting their research, they soon learned that corporate powers, working in part through missionary groups first to gain control of indigenous societies and then to gain control of their land, had been behind these destabilizations and genocides throughout the twentieth century. Since World War II the CIA had been deeply involved in the same process for the same purpose. Equally of interest is that key cloak-and-dagger figures involved in guiding the destiny of the natives to their impoverishment and destruction, as outlined in Colby's book, were assigned positions of power in the American government developing Latin America policy.[5]

Even as the primary Social Control belief system focused on the Soviet Union as a dictatorship and enemy, many Americans noticed that their country supported dictators all over the world, not democracies. What they did not know was that under the guidelines of NSC-68 (which Kennedy had planned to cut back before his assassination, and which were cut back drastically by President Carter), the CIA organized at least a hundred major covert operations to prevent these outbreaks of freedom and overthrow those that succeeded.[6] Serious commitment to democracy, and loss of those highly undervalued resources and profitable markets for the imperial centers of capital, were the threats.

As with every empire in history, there are three primary threads to the grand strategies of imperial centers of capital: (1) Economic interdependence of weaker nations is vital to their *security interests.* If a weak nation is *dependent* upon a powerful nation, it is much more amenable to control. So powerful nations leave weak nations few, or no, economic choices while maintaining their own *independence* through many economic choices. (2) Control of weak nations is necessary to prevent them from allying themselves with another center of capital and gaining independence. (3) Other rising centers of capital must be contained. This is, of course, the other side of the coin of controlling weak nations. Weak nations cannot be controlled if another center of capital emerges to provide them with military protection and other economic options (technology and markets).

As we outline examples of a few of the major destabilizations of post–World War II democratic governments that were breaking out from under the control of the imperial centers that had maintained them in poverty, remember that these destabilizations were done by good people just like you and me who believed fully in what they were doing. Quality people throughout the world were firmly locked within a Social Control paradigm carried by a political, academic, and media system from which conscientious scholars had been either purged or silenced.

Those carrying out the orders of Managers of State had never heard anything other than that they were battling the world's worst elements that were attempting to take away our democratic freedoms. A few eventually came into close contact with the people they were suppressing, saw the fraud that had been imposed upon them, resigned, wrote books, and actively fought against this massive state-sponsored terrorism. Their courageous efforts alerted Senator Frank Church and Representative Otis G. Pike, who held congressional hearings on these exposures. Those 1975–76 hearings alerted good reporters and provided the foundation for almost all that is known of the dark secrets of the Managers of State. Without those courageous defectors, the American people would have known no more about what their government was doing than would a society within a dictatorship. (We can be thankful that we do have more rights. In a dictatorship, any such defectors would be killed before they could damage the state.)

Iran Breaks Free

When Iran gained its freedom after World War II under the leadership of Dr. Mohammad Mossadeq, it was America's friend and wished to emulate both America's democratic government and economic success. Operation Ajax—with Kermit Roosevelt in charge of reinstalling the Shah and training SAVAK, the Iranian Secret Service—was the CIA's covert operation to stem that burst of democracy. Under the reinstalled Shah, Gulf Oil, Standard Oil of New Jersey, Texaco, and Socony-Mobil gained a 40 percent share of Iranian oil rights. Thousands of Iranians were tortured by SAVAK and a few thousand were killed.[7]

The Iranians were as angry as any American

or European would be if a foreign power overthrew their government. But government press releases (most news can be traced to press releases of governments or corporate-funded think tanks) and planted articles building the image of a great enemy (traceable to the CIA's "Mighty Wurlitzer") denied all knowledge of this suppression of democracy to the masses in Western nations. That enemy is, of course, then not hard to prove. The overthrow of its government to control its oil and its destiny had made Iran that enemy.

Whenever such brazen dictates to one society by another take place, the angry and violent come to the fore, and that is exactly what happened in Iran. The Muslim religion has been the bastion of defense (also offense) for Arabs against the Europeans for 1,300 years. On November 4, 1979, fundamentalist Muslims overthrew America's puppet dictator, overran the American Embassy, and held fifty Americans hostage for 444 days.[8] This was the greatest peacetime tweak of America's nose in its history. Considering the imperial nations were actively fomenting intrigues, overthrowing budding democracies with immense loss of life, and installing and supporting puppet dictators all over the world to control resources and markets, to think that America would peacefully take that nose tweaking as well as the loss of control of Iranian oil would be an exercise in extreme denial.

To our knowledge the true history has not been uncovered yet, and may never be, but by accident we do have a hint. The Iran-Iraq War started four months before those hostages were released. Through the CIA's "Mighty Wurlitzer," the American people were being told the Soviet Union was backing Iraq. The truth came out when the Iraqis gassed their own Kurdish population. A U.S. senator angrily fumed on national news, ''We have $800 million of arms in the pipeline to Iraq and we should cancel it all.'' The surfacing of that piece of hidden history (and other tidbits) and simple common sense tells us Iraq was likely coached into that invasion to lay claim to the oil fields right across its borders. With the strongest nation in the world behind it and Iran in turmoil, Iraq would have felt assured of success.

Economic Freedom for Indonesia, Large and Rich in Natural Resources, Was a Big Threat

Indonesia, rich in oil and other resources, was gaining its economic freedom and was designing its industrial future. Besides those massive resources, it were going to set up an honest democracy. Twenty-five percent of the nation's citizens were following the Communist Party so they were to be entitled to 25 percent representation in the government. But the CIA could not permit this. On the second try, the CIA overthrew Sukarno and installed Suharto. The managers of the American state were still not secure enough; their newly installed puppet was not actively pursuing that 25 percent of the voters who were such a threat. If they were left intact, control could quickly be lost in another election.

Arms were beached on the islands, papers were counterfeited to make it appear a revolution was imminent, and a list of over 4,000 political leaders and activists targeted for assassination was passed to the Indonesian military. By the lowest estimate, 500,000 Indonesians were slaughtered; by the highest, 1,000,000; and by the CIA's own estimate, 800,000.[9] These innocents were not slaughtered because they were going to overthrow anybody, as the citizens of the Western world were told, but because with their enormous resources a truly democratic Indonesian government had a high potential for both political and economic success and that success would catch the attention of other nations who would then insist on their freedom. That suppression of freedom was handled by such fine control of the news that it was almost unknown to the citizens in the Western world and what little was in the news seldom mentioned the immense slaughter. Of course, America's connection was totally ignored.

Nigeria Tried But Did Not Break Free

In Nigeria, 1966 to 1971, it was oil again and possibly 1.2 million Ibos, mostly children, starved as, during that nation's destabilization, relief was prevented from reaching the starving Ibo people. Dan Jacobs, a United Nations relief worker trying to help avert that tragedy who later researched its causes, was aghast to discover that British Managers of State, with the passive support of American Managers of State, were behind that disaster: ''I went to a National Security Council staff man and said: 'The British did this.' 'Oh, of course,' he responded. 'The British orchestrated the whole thing.' '' Newsreels were constantly showing footage of starving Nigerians but not a hint did one see that—to prevent a nation with huge natural resources and oil from gaining control of its own destiny—this civil war was externally orchestrated by Britain, with the passive diplomatic support of the United States.[10]

Vietnam Won the War But Did Not Gain Its Economic Freedom

During World War II, while working directly with American agents to rescue downed U.S. pilots, Ho Chi Minh sent six letters to the U.S. government asking for support and stating that the Vietnamese wished to pattern their constitution after America's. Only after America *refused* to recognize and support their freedom, and instead supported the French suppression of their freedom, were the Vietnamese forced to turn to China and the Soviet Union.[11] It is said that America lost in Vietnam but three million people were slaughtered (four million if one included the previous twenty years of French suppression), millions of acres of forest poisoned with herbicides were destroyed, rice fields were pockmarked with bomb craters, and after winning its freedom Vietnam was further decimated by embargoes.[12] That Vietnamese resources are now available to intact imperial centers of capital marks that war as a success. After all, control of resources to feed the industries of imperial centers is what these wars are all about.

If one has any doubts that the slogans "peace, freedom, justice, rights, and majority rule" are only rhetorical cover for imposition of belief systems to control resources and populations, consider this: A treaty was signed in Paris in 1973 for the future of Vietnam to be decided by free elections. The South Vietnamese puppet government and its American backers knew well that over 80 percent of the votes would be for rejoining with North Vietnam. So the treaty was ignored and that tiny country and its theoretically neutral neighbors, Laos and Cambodia, were pummeled with over 15.5 million tons of firepower. The total firepower expended throughout the Vietnam War exceeded all the firepower expended in World War II. The 6.3 million tons of bombs dropped were 50 percent more than dropped in World War II and created over 5,000 square miles of craters. At the officially acknowledged cost of $800 billion (1990 dollars) to conduct that war and another $800 billion for the cost and damage incurred by the Vietnamese, for a total of $1.6 trillion,

the world could have given every man, woman, and child in Vietnam (sixty-two million people) $13,000, or about $90,000 per family.[13]

Guatemala Broke Free Briefly

In 1951, the Communist Party was one of the smaller of four parties which supported the election of Jacobo Arbenz as president of Guatemala. Arbenz's goal was a quality life for Guatemalans. That better life required reorganization of land (resources), labor, and capital and/or higher pay for the exported production of labor and resources.

Knowing that foreign-owned land titles had been obtained under far from free market conditions, President Arbenz immediately started the legal process of reclaiming several hundred thousand acres of idle land from The American United Fruit Company. For the first block of 178,000 acres, United Fruit was offered a twenty-four-year bond valued at $525,000, its valuation on United Fruit's tax records.

But United Fruit had close connections to the old-boy network of the National Security Council and the CIA: The brothers John Foster Dulles (appointed Secretary of State one year before the overthrow of Arbenz) and Allen Dulles (appointed director of the CIA the year of that overthrow), General Walter Bedell Smith (director of the CIA when Arbenz was elected), and John J. McCloy (World Bank president who refused loans to Guatemala during their destabilizations). All four of these powerful men in American intelligence and the World Bank either had a longstanding connection to United Fruit before Arbenz's overthrow, or became directors of that company shortly afterwards.[14]

An earlier coup attempt with the CIA backing the remnant colonial elite with money and arms failed, so the CIA prepared more thoroughly for Arbenz's overthrow in 1954. A propaganda campaign was launched throughout Latin America claiming that Arbenz was a Communist. Russian-made arms were parachuted into Guatemala to be found and support the claim of a Communist takeover. The CIA and the United States Information Service (USIA, an integral part of the "Mighty Wurlitzer") cooperated in a media blitz. The USIA created over 200 articles on Guatemala and provided them to Latin American newspapers for anonymous use. Over 100,000 pamphlets titled "Chronology of Communism in Guatemala" and 27,000 copies of anti-communist cartoons and posters were distributed. The USIA produced three propaganda movies on Guatemala. Seven weeks before the successful coup, the CIA launched a clandestine radio misinformation campaign.[15]

When all was ready, powerful transmitters broadcasting messages of confusion overrode Guatemala's national radio while fighter aircraft bombed oil and ammunition dumps, strafed Guatemala City, and dropped smoke bombs to make it appear the attack was even larger. Although the CIA army of expatriate Guatemalans never numbered over 400 and were staying close to the Honduran border so they could escape if the Guatemalan army was activated, the bluff worked. Arbenz was overthrown.[16]

Undestroyed documents eventually forced out of the CIA under the Freedom of Information Act showed that fifty-eight of Guatemala's freely elected officials were targeted for assassination. A comparable number of elected officials and intellectuals targeted for assassination to control the American government would be 2,300. Only the CIA knows how many of those original fifty-eight leaders were assassinated, but with 200,000 killed and unaccounted for during the thirty-five years Guatemalans attempted to wrest back their government, and with Guatemala's U.S.-supported military and CIA-orchestrated death squads being responsible for a documented 93 percent of the slaughters, it is highly likely that most were.[17]

Chile Broke Free Very Briefly

Cold War Managers of State feared governments coming to power in free elections and taking control of the destiny of those peripheral countries, and the subsequent loss of control of their resources, not military attacks. Thinking there were no serious problems in Chile and spending only a modest amount of money to influence its 1972 election, those managers went into shock when Salvador Allende was freely elected president on a platform of control of Chilean resources for Chileans.

The CIA immediately financed ten economists, primarily from the Chicago School of Economics, to put together an alternative economic program for Chile to assure stability once that errant nation was brought back within the fold. To assure that they would return, the Managers of State embargoed Chile, and the CIA and America's military, primarily the Navy, coordinated plans for Allende's overthrow. This included picking Chilean military personnel for training at the School of the Americas (then in Panama and now in Fort Benning, Georgia, and properly nicknamed The School of the Assassins or School of Coups). Among those handpicked recruits would be dependable supporters for a coup when the time was ripe. Although the guns used to assassinate President Allende were proven to have been given to the assassins by the CIA, it, of course, must abide by the rules of plausible denial at all times and disclaimed any responsibility.[18]

Three thousand is the lowest number one

reads as slaughtered to overthrow Chile's demo-cratic election while other sources say thousands were killed during the suppression and 11,000 were killed the first year of Pin-ochet's regime, among them citizens of the United States, Spain, and a few other countries. The Chilean government's official figure of 3,197 killed by its security forces in the sup-pression can be ignored. Those who were a po-litical threat were still disappearing, being detained, and being jailed ten years later.[19]

As I write this (March 1999), the British House of Lords has ruled that Pinochet, under house arrest in Britain since October 16, 1998, can be extradited to Spain to stand trial for kill-ing Spanish citizens. Spain's initiative has many countries, especially America, holding their breath. If this legal strategy succeeds, a good many citizens of a good many countries who have been designing, financing, implementing, and supporting these violent destabilizations—in which hundreds of thousands were tortured for information before being killed and millions slaughtered—may not dare leave their home countries.

Chile since the overthrow of Allende is trum-peted as a great success story of Adam Smith free trade. But when all wealth is accounted for, it is a testimonial to Chilean resources and wealth going to the imperial centers of capital and their wealthy puppets now running Chile. In statistics, where you start and where you quit is typically everything. After Allende's over-throw, national output dropped 15 percent, the unemployment rate rose to 20 percent, wage re-ductions averaged 15 percent, and that low level provides the base for most statistics.

But a proper statistical base would start from Chile's production level under Allende. Chile's GDP sixteen years after Allende (1986) had only regained that 1970 level, real wages were

still below that year's level, per capita con-sumption was 15 percent lower (some calculate 23 percent lower). In the next five years (1985 to 1990) the income of the top 10 percent of Chileans rose 90 percent while the share of Chile's wealth for Chile's poorest 25 percent fell from 11 percent to 7 percent.[20]

Thousands of Chilean strikers have been fired, their leaders were jailed, and collective bargaining and labor courts have been elimi-nated. The result: the percentage share of na-tional income going to labor dropped from 47.7 percent in 1970 to 19 percent twenty years later. Likewise, Argentina's labor share dropped from 40.9 percent to 24.9 percent, Ecua-dor's from 34.4 percent to 15.8 percent, Mexi-co's from 37.5 percent to 27.3 percent, and Peru's from 40 percent to 16.8 percent.[21] The real story of Chile is that the earnings of labor-ers have declined significantly, their rights have declined precipitously, the earnings of the al-ready wealthy have climbed astronomically, and the natural wealth of Chile is being rapidly mined, harvested, and shipped to the imperial centers of capital. A beautiful example of a suc-cessful neomercantilist policy.

Such disregard for people and resources is the greatest risk to civilizations. It is just such policies of overharvesting of resources that have led to the collapse of civilizations for millennia. Greece once had rich topsoil, but now bedrock and rocky soil are the norm. The currently bar-ren North Africa once had lush forests with plentiful wildlife. The "fertile crescent" of the Middle East, the cradle of Western civilization due to its original high fertility, is now largely barren.

As William H. Kötke details in his study, *The Final Empire*, this pattern has continued histor-ically through the destruction of the vast forests of Europe and then has followed the march of empire with European emigration to its colonies. The United States, for example, has already lost one-third of its best topsoils and the loss is accelerating. Soil loss is also accelerating on all other continents. The most recent figure, quoted in *The Final Empire,* indicates world soil loss is on the order of twenty-five billion tons annually and growing.[22]

El Salvador Fought Hard But Did Not Gain Even Its Political Freedom

With the exception that a free election was never permitted, the 1980 through 1982 suppression of El Salvador's break for freedom paralleled that of Guatemala as described above. When several tortured bodies with their thumbs wired behind their backs show up outside the El Salvadoran capital almost daily, their numbers rise into the hundreds per month and thousands per year, and there is no serious effort by the officials to get to the bottom of those tortures, one can safely assume these are government assassinations of the political opposition. This was the conclusion of the United Nations El Salvador Truth Commission. Its 1993 report placed responsibility for 85 percent of the 70,000-plus deaths on security forces trained, armed, and advised by the American military and another 10 percent upon the El Salvadoran elite's private death squads, which, of course, could function only with the silent approval of the government. The suppression was successful and El Salvador remains a provider of cheap resources and labor. It is now "the eighth-largest exporter worldwide of apparel to the United States. This year it will send us 268 million garments." With the pattern well established, we are providing sources for any who wish to check deeper.[23]

Although a truce is signed in both El Salva-dor and Guatemala, it is far from certain that true democracy can develop. The elite are wary of elections and the managers of the imperial American state are unlikely to accept a government democratic enough to take control of its own destiny. If such a government were successfully elected and installed, the twelve-year El Salvadoran and thirty-six-year Guatemalan civil wars would likely be recorded in history much differently.

Nicaragua Gained Brief Political Freedom But Never Attained Economic Freedom

Nicaragua gained its freedom July 19, 1979, when the Sandinista liberation forces overthrew President Somoza. Under the guidelines of NSC-68, American Managers of State immediately made plans to reverse that revolution. The CIA armed, trained, and oversaw the sabotage and assassinations within Nicaragua by Nicaraguan defectors called Contras. While tens of thousands of people were killed under the oppressive Somoza dictatorship, only a few thousand died in the American-orchestrated overthrow of that burst of democracy. The Nicaraguan government was protecting its citizens as opposed to being the primary source of murderous assault upon its own people as in Chile, Guatemala, and El Salvador. The immediate improvement in education, health, and living standards under the Sandinistas was reversed by the destabilization process. The beleaguered Sandinistas eventually agreed to a free election, massive U.S. funds illegally financed the opposition, the people knew the war of attrition would continue if Daniel Ortega and the Sandinistas still governed, and the American-backed Violeta Chamorro became president of Nicaragua in February 1990.[24] Though the

Chammoro government was not the thief and oppressor the old guard Somoza government was, that suffering nation has not yet (1999) attained the standard of living of the early years of its revolution, and its resources again feed the industries and populations of the imperial centers of capital.

A Rapidly Advancing Afghanistan Is Shattered

In 1998, after the successful destabilization of Afghanistan, Zbigniew Brzezinski, President Carter's National Security Advisor at the time, admitted that covert U.S. intervention began long before the USSR sent in troops. "That secret operation [National Security Council Directive 166] was an excellent idea," he explained. "The effect was to draw the Russians into the Afghan trap."[25]

Take note of what was "an excellent idea": It was the peaceful, rapid successes of Afghanistan that were a problem for imperial America. To subvert those successes, a country rapidly developing and moving towards modernization was politically and economically shattered, 1.5 million Afghanistani were killed, millions more were refugees, and there is no end in sight to the violence fourteen years later. One of the many forces financed and armed by the CIA to suppress the progress of that impoverished nation now rules Afghanistan, and it is today one of America's most implacable enemies.

The destabilization of Afghanistan was only one of many covert actions undertaken with the primary goal of destabilizing the Soviet Union. If outside powers would stay out of them, the political conflicts of most countries would be settled peacefully and quickly. But when powerful outside powers offer to finance and arm radical groups to take over and govern, there are leaders in every society willing to take that offer. These impoverished people are given massive funds to fight proxy battles. Even the inexperienced can quickly make a value judgment that they are currently in poverty with little opportunity for a quality life, that the supporting nation has immense power, and that—through the patronage of the world's greatest power—they may end up as their nation's leaders.

What would happen in America if outside forces supported African Americans or any other political grouping with immense funds and arms and the promise of continued support for them to become America's leaders? What would happen in Europe if disaffected groups were funded and armed to sabotage and destabilize those countries?

Angola, Mozambique, and Southern Africa's Frontline States

As the Vietnam War wound down in 1976, the CIA, under the instructions of Secretary of State Henry Kissinger, was getting deeper into Angola and other regions of the world. John Stockwell, former CIA officer in Langley, Virginia, overseeing the destabilization of Angola, emphatically points out that America was supporting the National Union for Total Independence of Angola (UNITA) while the vast majority of Angolans supported the Popular Movement for the Liberation of Angola (MPLA). Moreover, it was well recognized that the MPLA was "best-qualified to run Angola; nor was it hostile to the United States," while the leader of UNITA, Jonas Savimbi, had taken training in the Soviet Union and was distinctly more ideologically tuned to the Soviet Union than MPLA.[26]

Facing the greatest threat from black Africans gaining their freedom, South Africa's white minority government orchestrated Renamo's terror campaign in Mozambique and, in conjunction with the remnant colonial power structures, ran similar covert destabilization campaigns in Zambia, Namibia, Zimbabwe, and Botswana.[27]

The CIA, with support from Belgium, destabilized the Congo and assassinated the charismatic and popular Patrice Lumumba (read sources) before he could be electorally legitimized as their leader. Control still could not be assured, so Zaire was created to remove those rich copper deposits from the uncontrollable Congolese and Joseph Mobutu was installed as the Belgian/American puppet. That it was business interests that were being protected in the Congo is just as obvious as in General Smedley Butler's overseas incursions by U.S. marines addressed above.[28]

Angola, Mozambique, the Congo (Zaire), and the other frontline southern African states fit the pattern of most destabilizations. Those nations were not going communist and the CIA was deeply involved long before the Soviets provided support to the MPLA. The problem was that those nations were gaining their independence and, with that freedom, they would gain control of their valuable resources and their destiny.

As they were breaking free after World War II, many countries of Africa were looking forward to cooperating, building their infrastructure, educating their citizens, building modern industry, and joining the world of developed nations. It must be noted that for those nations to bond into a cohesive productive economy would be identical to the countryside of the nascent imperial cities of Europe utilizing their comparative advantage to produce cloth and leather, fabricate metals, and grow food. In both cases the development of the countryside would impoverish the imperial center and in both cases

that organization of political and productive forces was prevented by military actions. The suppressions to prevent those breaks for freedom on the southern cone of Africa cost between 1.5 million and 2 million innocent lives and left those nations shattered, deeply in debt, and torn apart by factions fighting for political supremacy.

The Libyan Threat

Libyan, Iranian, and Iraqi economic freedom meant they, along with other newly developing oil-rich nations that would follow their lead, would build their own refineries and take over a significant share of the world's oil industry. With their cheap oil and massive reserves (pennies per barrel as both raw material and fuel for their refineries and factories against $17 to $30 a barrel for others to import), they would also control all the thousands of derivative products of oil (medicines, plastics, synthetic fibers, etc.).

With the immense profits that were sure to be earned utilizing those cheap resources and selling on the high-priced world market, other fuel-intensive industries—such as steel, copper, aluminum—were sure to be taken over by countries with both massive oil reserves and the freedom to control their own destiny. The comparative advantage of the "countryside" would monopolize those industries and the wealth generated would purchase other industries. The cash flow from title to the resources and those industries would establish these countries' currency as a world trading currency, which would complete the shattering of the historic monopolies. For all that to happen, the West's mighty military would have to stand idly by, which they are obviously not doing.

Study again how plunder through unequal trades began centuries ago as addressed in

Chapters One and Two. Every imperial center of capital must control the countryside from which it obtains the resources to operate its industries. Because all people are taught to be good (a society could survive no other way), maintaining that control requires designing a Social Control belief system, typically by creating an enemy that has little relevance to truth. Thus the imposed belief system of Libya being a terrorist nation, when what really threatens the imperial center is the potential of success of Libya's development plans and the loss not only of control of that oil but of the current monopolization of other industries through the Libyans' use of the immense profits they could generate.

Cuba: Almost Free and May Yet Succeed

In 1959 the American-backed Cuban dictator, Fulgencio Batista, fled as Fidel Castro's forces freed Cuba. The new Cuban government was not Communist and attempted to maintain friendly relations with America. But the redistribution of the wealth-producing processes in Cuba from foreign ownership to Cuban ownership and its recapture of control of its destiny was the very thing that threatened American Managers of State the most. Embargoes were put into effect to force a rescinding of those policies. Cuba promptly turned to the Soviet Union for technological and economic support and embraced the Communist ideology. The Cuban economy developed rapidly. Within twenty years, the Cuban people's education and health care equaled those of Americans. No Cubans were hungry, housing was being rapidly built, and a sign outside Havana read: "Millions of children in the world sleep in the street and not one is Cuban."

All this was accomplished even as Cuba was totally embargoed by the West. No ship trading with America dared dock in a Cuban port; if they did they could not dock in the United States. No corporation dared trade with Cuba, as to do so would result in fines or withdrawal of trading rights in the United States. Such rapid development of a nation breaking free was the great fear of Managers of State. Saboteurs trained, armed, financed, and managed by the CIA counterfeited Cuban money and ration books, burned cane fields and infected them with fungus, infected tobacco fields with mildew, and infected potato fields with the potato-ravaging insect thrips palmi. African swine fever, never before seen in the Western hemisphere, ravaged Cuba twice and 500,000 pigs had to be destroyed. Three hundred thousand Cubans were infected with dengue fever and over one hundred died. Enough operatives have acknowledged their part in this biological warfare that serious researchers accept the accuracy of the Cuban allegations. This author watched a news broadcast where one operative boasted of fifty forays into Cuba creating such havoc, including blowing up a Cuban railroad trestle and "watching the train go into the ravine just like in the movies."[29]

American people remained blissfully unaware that Cubans had attained a level of education and health care equal to America's and had eliminated hunger while the rest of Latin America remained in poverty. Many times this author would test his peers by bringing up the subject of Cuba. Their immediate angry response of casting Castro as a dictator and killer testifies to the effectiveness of the American propaganda machine. Any government that made such great progress in eliminating poverty and hunger would gain the very loyalty and respect the Cuban people give their government. Far fewer people died in the Cuban revolution than in most and those who were killed were killing Cubans, attempting to overthrow the government, and otherwise cooperating with the American government in the suppression of Cuban freedom.

That Cuba was ever a military threat is totally silly. No serious diplomat of state thought the Soviets, China, or anyone else was going to invade anyone in the powerful Western bloc. It was Cuba's rapid, exemplary successes in bettering the living standards of her people, which made it impossible to control the governments and resources of other impoverished nations, that were the threat.

When the Soviet Union collapsed, one of the conditions for financial help was that it withdraw its support of Cuba. This effectively totally isolated Cuba's economy. Building cranes went silent for lack of building materials, machinery was idled for lack of spare parts, and the once prosperous Cuban economy rapidly regressed. As this book goes to press, the Cubans have found a few countries to trade with and have turned their economy back up. But it appears that they will stay embargoed until they abandon control of their destiny and accept control by the imperial center.

Orchestration of Death Squads by the Imperial Nations

It is understandable that the United States is using its immense power to prevent the establishment of an international criminal court with auhority to judge the planners and perpetrators of these atrocities. If such a court were ever established and given investigative authority and funds, true history might be recorded. The powerful, currently protected because their acts are unrecorded in history and thus unknown, would be immediately weakened as their illegal acts were put on record,

and the power of the suppressed masses would be simultaneously strengthened.

When U.S.-trained covert operatives are caught in criminal acts that are extensions of these operations, typically they are not charged in U.S. courts. To do so would require opening those CIA records, so—since every operation is the total antithesis of law, justice, honesty, and right—these charges are dismissed or never brought in the first place. As we write this, we are watching this scene play out with four long-term CIA agents set for trial in Puerto Rico for plotting to kill Fidel Castro of Cuba. They are threatening to expose the fact that their assassination project was only an extension of the spreading of exotic livestock diseases and exotic human diseases in Cuba, burning Cuban cane fields, blowing an airliner with a champion Cuban fencing team (and other innocent people aboard) out of the sky, and many other covert operations they were trained to do by the CIA, including the now well-known thirty-year CIA effort to assassinate Castro.[30]

Typically, in such cases, judges rule that those records stay sealed because of national security; but this case is quite different. In those other cases, national security was only tangentially connected to the crime. In this case these assassins were doing exactly what they were trained—and previously financed—to do: assassinate Castro. How does a court of law convict people for doing exactly what their government had once armed, trained, financed, and ordered them to do?

An attempt was made to assassinate Zhou En Lai of China, second in power only to Mao Zedong. The plane was successfully sabotaged when it landed to refuel outside of China and all aboard were killed. However, Chou En Lai had taken another plane. This was a precursor to sabotaging the plane with the Cuban athletes, and these were far from the only such Western state-sponsored assassinations of fundamentally nonviolent and peaceful leaders and potential leaders.[31] Those death squads were killing teachers, professors, labor leaders, cooperative leaders, and church leaders. They were not the terrorists and killers that we are told. They were the budding Washingtons, Jeffersons, Madisons, Churchills, Gandhis, and Martin Luther Kings of those countries.

It is possible that U.S.-sponsored state terrorism was greater than all other world terrorism combined, state and private, and it is a certainty that all Western nations together supported and guided several times more terrorism than the entire rest of the world. And remember, much, if not most, private world terrorism is in reaction to these assaults (overt, covert, financial, and economic) that subvert the governments and economies of defenseless societies.

Future Leaders of Nations on the Periphery of Empire Must Be Picked And Trained

The CIA picks candidates in Third World countries for an all-expense-paid education at Milton Friedman's Chicago School of [neoclassical] Economics and other conservative institutions, and these students go back to teach and run governments. To regain control of Chile, the CIA handpicked several hundred Chilean students for training at the Chicago School. These graduates returned to Chile, and are—along with the graduates of the School of the Americas (School of Coups/School of Assassins) addressed above—the professors and political leaders of Chile today. So it goes with military officers and students from all over the world. Money is always available for the "right students" to take the "right classes" under the

"right professors" in America; others must fend for themselves. This is a continuation of William Pitt's imposition of Adam Smith free trade philosophy (as interpreted by neomercantilists) upon the defeated world to maintain its dependency, as addressed in depth earlier. History is then written through the lens of that imposed belief system.

Writing History Through Erasing the Records

CIA agents are trained on how to keep records to protect themselves, and purging the records of damaging information is standard practice. When Congress was questioning the covert actions in Angola, John Stockwell, in charge of that operation, explained that the CIA director, George Bush, sent a young lawyer to his office to purge his files of any such records. Bush then testified to Congress "that no files in the Agency corroborated any of the Congressional allegations." The CIA and other intelligence agencies are going even further. They are finishing their writing of this history by destroying their covert action records, which, of course, then leaves only the record of the tens of thousands of fraudulent articles and thousands of fraudulent books, and no record of their destabilizations.[32] Argentina has also destroyed its records on assassinating 30,000 essentially peaceful people (among them nuns and teenagers, about 500 of them pregnant women who, after caesarian sections, went straight to the plane that dropped these drugged people into the Atlantic Ocean[33]), and it is a safe bet that other allied imperial nations have destroyed their incriminating records.

Due to the perseverance of mothers, the violence that Argentina imposed on its own people is being recorded even if it is thirty years late. But the ironclad rule of all imperial nations is "plausible denial." These government-sponsored terrorist acts against other people, or their own people, are not to be traceable to those governments. The perpetrators have been very successful in keeping their violence secret. There were fifty major covert operations and thousands of minor ones undertaken in just the seven years William Casey was CIA director, yet only a few surface in the alternative news dedicated to uncovering such undemocratic acts. Only what is acknowledged or proven can be recorded in history. When someone does bring this government-imposed violence to light, the very people planning or carrying out this violence testify in front of Congress that it is not happening and the government denies to the people and the world that it is involved. So even if recorders of history (the media) know that their government is responsible for extreme violence against quite innocent people, it does not get recorded in the papers and magazines of record and thus does not get recorded in history.

South Africa's policy of amnesty for all who fully tell the story of their involvement in that country's state terrorism has exposed these practices. But the South African government's poisonings, tortures, and assassinations pale into insignificance alongside those carried out under Western destabilization policies. El Salvador's 1993 Truth Commission recorded that government's atrocities but, with the same government in power that imposed that violence upon its citizens, the truth was promptly swept under the rug. Guatemala's 1999 Truth Commission reports the same atrocities by that government. The Argentine search for the truth through the courts seems to be having some success. Chile's former violent and oppressive dictator, Pinochet, is scheduled to go on trial in Spain for his crimes against humanity. If that trial takes place, and there will be powerful political pres-

sure by powerful governments to prevent it, his atrocities will be recorded. But we must remember the title of George Seldes's book, *Even the Gods Can't Change History,* and his many examples of totally falsified events recorded as fact that simply cannot get changed in the history books. Quite simply, the winners of wars write history, claims of a free press and free thought notwithstanding. Those old history books become the source for new history books and the same errors are repeated.

When Peace Returns, the Battle for Technological and Trade Supremacy Continues

That these countries have neither their political nor economic freedom is outlined by L. Fletcher Prouty, who was in position to see the Cold War developing even before World War II ended. From 1955 to 1964, he was Chief of Special Operations for the U.S. Air Force, supporting clandestine CIA operations overthrowing governments that were declaring their economic independence. As a participant who helped write the training manuals and briefed presidents and Pentagon chiefs on these covert operations, Colonel Prouty points out:

> One of the least-known divisions of the CIA is that headed by the Deputy Director of Economics. This division moves into a country to work with a new regime and to begin the task of selecting and setting up new franchise holders for as many goods as possible to assure that they are imported from American companies and that those from other sources, formerly the Soviet sphere in particular, are excluded.... The CIA screens and selects these new "millionaires" and arranges for them to meet with various companies they will front for under the new regime. It might be said that this cleansing of the economic system is the real reason for most of the coups d'état and that political ideology has very little to

do with it. . . . Some of the more daring, in an attempt to escape the severe financial and profit-making controls placed upon them and their government by U.S. manufacturers and by the canopy of international banks that is spread over all imports and exports to their country, attempt to make deals with other countries. They believe they may be able to buy essential goods cheaper that way and to sell their labor and resources at better rates. . . . As such actions increase, the national leadership will be increasingly attacked by the United States on the grounds that it is turning toward communism and becoming a base for the infiltration of the communist ideology and military system into the hemisphere.[34]

Those assasinations of promising leaders of emerging nations continue even though the Cold War is over. Witness the trial in late July 1999 in Harare, Zimbabwe. Though one would never realize it reading the American news, the three CIA agents caught with dozens of assault rifles and machine guns were obviously intent on weighting the outcome for the leadership of the Congo and Zimbabwe towards a controllable puppet government.

There we have it. All intelligence agencies have been, and are still, in the business of destabilizing undeveloped countries to maintain their dependency. It is the dependency of weak nations that maintains the flow of the world's natural wealth to powerful nations' industries at a low price and provides markets for those industrial products at a high price. This is identical to those raiding parties centuries ago who raided the countryside to destroy its capital, maintain its dependency, and force it to sell its raw material to, and purchase manufactured products from, the city.

The defeated and impoverished former colonial world is the countryside for today's wealthy imperial centers of capital. The military forces of today's powerful nations have the same purpose as those raiding parties of the

Middle Ages. Thus, with per capita natural wealth many times that of Europe, those defeated nations remain impoverished as their wealth is continually siphoned to powerful imperial centers of capital.

The various repressions going on around the world today occur for the same reason governments have attacked citizenry throughout history; rich and powerful people are afraid that if the world's powerless gain democratic and economic rights, they will organize, collaborate together, and reclaim their rightful share of the world's wealth.

Notes

1. Ralph McGehee, http://come.to/CIABASE/ (CIABASE, Box 5022, Herndon, VA 22070).

2. *Covert Action Information Bulletin* (Summer 1987), p. 28.

3. Bernard Grun, *Timetables of American History* (New York: Simon and Schuster, 1979); W. Bello, *U.S. Sponsored Low Intensity Conflict in the Philippines* (San Francisco: Institute for Food and Development Policy, December 1987); S. Karnow, *In Our Image: America's Empire in the Philippines* (New York: Random House, 1989); Fred Poole and Max Vanzi, *Revolution in the Philippines: The United States in a Hall of Cracked Mirrors* (New York: McGraw-Hill, 1984); Daniel B. Schirmer and Stephen Rosskamm Shalom, *The Philippines Reader: A History of Colonialism, Dictatorship, and Resistance* (Boston: South End Press, 1987); William Blum, *The CIA: A Forgotten History* (London: Zed Books, 1986); C.B. Currey, *Edward Lansdale: The Unquiet American* (Boston: Houghton Mifflin, 1988); R. Constantino and L. R. Constantino, *The Philippines: The Continuing Past* (Quezon City, Philippines: The Foundation for Nationalist Studies, 1978); G. Porter, ''The Politics of Counterinsurgency in the Philippines: Military and Political Options.'' Philippine Studies Occasional Paper No. 9 (Honolulu: University of Hawaii, Center for Philippine Studies, 1987); R. Bonner, *Waltzing with a Dictator* (New York: Times Books 1987); J. Prados, *The Presidents' Secret Wars* (New York: William Morrow, 1986) Prados, rev ed Warwick: Elephant Paperbacks, 1996; K. Nair, *Devil and His Dart: How the CIA Is Plotting in the Third*

World (New Delhi: Sterling, 1986); *Bulletin of Concerned Asian Scholars*, Boulder, CO, many issues; E. G. Lansdale, *In the Midst of Wars* (New York: Harper and Row, 1972); D. S. Blaufarb, *The Counterinsurgency Era: U.S. Doctrine and Performance 1950 to Present* (New York: The Free Press, 1977); E. Thomas, *The Very Best Men: Four Who Dared: The Early Years of the CIA* (New York: Simon and Schuster, 1995); J. Ranelagh, *The Agency* (New York: Simon and Schuster, 1986); Michael T. Klare and P. Kornbluh, *Low Intensity Warfare* (New York: Pantheon Books, 1988); McGehee, CIABASE.

4. Frederic F. Clairmont, *The Rise and Fall of Economic Liberalism* (Goa, India: The Other India Press, 1996), p. 223.

5. Gerard Colby and Charlotte Dennett, *Thy Will Be Done: The Conquest of the Amazon: Nelson Rockefeller and Evangelism in the Age of Oil* (New York: Harper Collins, 1995). Conversation with the authors shortly after their book was published.

6. *Covert Action Information Bulletin* (Summer 1987), p. 28; Church and Pike Committee hearings, *Congressional Record*, 1975, 1976; John Stockwell, *The Praetorian Guard* (Boston: South End Press, 1991), especially pp. 70, 72, 81. Read also Dean Acheson, *Present at the Creation* (New York: W.W. Norton, 1987), p. 377; other sources listed throughout this chapter, and those in the Introduction, note three.

7. Amir Taheri, *Nest of Spies: America's Journey to Disaster in Iran* (New York: Pantheon Books, 1988); Burton Hersh, *The Old Boys: The American Elite and the Origins of the CIA* (New York: Charles Scribner's Sons, 1992), pp. 330–34; Kermit Roosevelt, *Countercoup: The Struggle for the Control of Iran* (New York: McGraw-Hill, 1979): C. Andrew, *For the President's Eyes Only: Secret Intelligence and the American Presidency from Washington to Bush* (New York: HarperCollins, 1995), pp. 203–05; McGehee, CIABASE

8. Taheri, *Nest of Spies,* pp. 122–126.

9. Philip Agee, *Inside the Company* (New York: Bantam Books, 1975), p. 9; Steve Weissman, *The Trojan Horse* (Palo Alto: Ramparts Press, 1975); McT. Kahin, *Subversion as Foreign Policy: The Secret Eisenhower and Dulles Debacle in Indonesia* (New York: New Press, 1995); Wendell Minnick, *Spies and Provocateurs: A Worldwide Encyclopedia of Persons Conducting Espionage and Covert Action, 1946–1991*

(Jefferson, NC: McFarland, 1992), especially pp. 183–84; S.E. Ambrose, *Ike's Spies* (Garden City, NY: Doubleday, 1981), p. 251; M. Caldwell, ed., *Ten Years Military Terror Indonesia* (Nottingham: Spokesmen Books, no date); Blum, *The CIA*, especially p. 221; search databases for articles or books by Kathy Kadane, reporter for *States News Service;* McGehee, CIABASE.

10. Dan Jacobs, *The Brutality of Nations* (New York: Alfred A. Knopf, 1987), especially p. 5.

11. Stockwell, *Praetorian Guard,* p. 78.

12. G.M. Kahin and J.W. Lewis, *United States in Vietnam* (New York: Dell, 1969); M. Gettleman, J. Franklin, M. Young, and B. Franklin, *Vietnam and America: The Most Comprehensive Documented History of the Vietnam War* (New York: Grove Press, 1995); *Pentagon Papers: The Defense Department History of United States Decision Making on Vietnam*, ed. Senator Mike Gravel (Boston: Beacon Press, 1971); L. Ackland, *Credibility Gap: A Digest of the Pentagon Papers* (Philadelphia: The National Literature Service, 1972); O. DeForest and D. Chanoff, *Slow Burn* (New York: Simon and Schuster, 1990); N. Sheehan, *A Bright Shining Lie* (New York: Random House, 1988); Currey, *Edward Lansdale;* F. Prouty, *JFK: The CIA, Vietnam, and the Plot to Assassinate John F. Kennedy* (New York: Birch Lane Press, 1992); Committee of Concerned Asian Scholars, *The Indochina Story: A Fully Documented Account* (New York: Pantheon Books, 1970); Frank Snepp, *Decent Interval* (New York: Random House, 1977); M. Young, *The Vietnam Wars 1945–1990* (New York: HarperCollins, 1991); Douglas Valentine, *The Phoenix Program* (New York: William Morrow, 1990); D. Kaplan, *Fires of the Dragon: Politics, Murder and the Kuomintang* (New York: Atheneum, 1992); K. Conboy and J. Morrison, *Shadow War: The CIA's Secret War in Laos* (Boulder, CO: Paladin Press, 1995); *Bulletin of Concerned Asian Scholars;* McGehee, CIABASE.

13. "The Costs of War," *The Nation,* December 24, 1990, p. 793; Matthew Cooper, "Give Trade a Chance," *U.S. News & World Report,* February 14, 1994, p. 20; C. Robbins, *The Ravens: The Men Who Flew in America's Secret War* (New York: Crown, 1987), p. 332; Prouty, *JFK,* p. 55; V. Levant, *Quiet Complicity: Canadian Involvement in the Vietnam War* (Toronto: Between the Lines, 1986), p. 46.

14. B. Cook, *The Declassified Eisenhower* (Garden City, NY: Doubleday, 1981), pp. 228–29; see also L.

Shoup and W. Minter, *Imperial Brain Trust: The Council on Foreign Relations & United States Foreign Policy* (New York: Monthly Review Press, 1977); Hersh, *Old Boys;* Robin Winks, *Cloak & Gown: Scholars in the Secret War, 1939–1961* (New York: Quill, 1987); McGehee, CIABASE; see Introduction, note three.

15. Stephen Schlesinger and Stephen Kinzer, *Bitter Fruit* (New York: Anchor Press/Doubleday, 1984); Peter Grose, *Gentleman Spy: The Life of Allen Dulles* (Boston: University of Massachusetts Press, 1996).

16. N. Miller, *Spying for America* (New York: Paragon House, 1989); P. Gleijeses, *Shattered Hope: The Guatemalan Revolution and the United States, 1944–1954* (Princeton: Princeton University Press, 1991); H.J. Hunt, *Undercover: Memoirs of an American Secret Agent* (New York: Berkeley, 1974).

17. United Nations Guatemalan Truth Commission Report carried on AP wires February 25, 1999; Beatriz Manz, *Refugees of a Hidden War: The Aftermath of Counterinsurgency in Guatemala* (New York: State University of New York, 1988); Jean-Marie Simon, *Guatemala: Eternal Spring Eternal Tyranny* (New York: W.W. Norton, 1988); Susanne Jonas, *The Battle for Guatemala: Rebels, Death Squads, and U.S. Power* (San Francisco: Westview Press, 1991); Michael McClintock, *The American Connection: State Terror and Popular Resistance in Guatemala* (London: Zed Books, 1985); B. Cook, *The Declassified Eisenhower;* Thomas, *Very Best Men;* D.A. Phillips, *The Night Watch* (New York: Atheneum 1977); T. McCann, *An American Company: The Tragedy of United Fruit* (New York: Crown, 1976); Andrew, *For the President's Eyes Only;* Eduardo Galeano, *Guatemala: Occupied Country* (New York: Monthly Review Press, 1969); J. Heidenry, *Theirs Was the Kingdom: Lila and Dewitt Wallace and the Story of the Reader's Digest* (New York: W.W. Norton, 1993), pp. 594–97; *Covert Action Quarterly; Counterspy;* run library database searches for anything written by Allen Nairn; Blum, *The CIA;* Blum, *Killing Hope: U.S. Military Interventions Since World War II* (Monroe, ME: Common Courage Press, 1995); McGehee, CIABASE.

18. Lucy Komisar, "Documented Complicity: Newly Released Files Set the Record Straight on U.S. Support for Pinochet," *The Progressive* (September, 1999), pp. 24–27; Samuel Chavkin, *The Murder of Chile* (New York: Everest House, 1982); John Dinges and Saul Landau, *Assassination on Embassy Row* (New York: Pantheon Books, 1980); Blum, *The CIA,* pp. 232–43; Blum, *Killing Hope;* R.L. Borosage and J. Marks, eds., *The CIA File* (New York: Grossman, 1976); *Church and Pike Committee Report* (1975–1976); William Colby, *Honorable Men* (New York: Simon and Schuster, 1978), pp. 302–306; M. Copeland, *Beyond Cloak and Dagger* (New York: Pinnacle Books, 1975), note 221; *Counterspy,* Spring/Summer 1975, pp. 43–47; Louis Wolf, review of *The American Federation of Teachers and the CIA,* by George N. Schmidt, *Covert Action Quarterly* 2 (October 1978), p. 23; Fred Landis, "CIA Media Operations in Chile, Jamaica and Nicaragua," *Covert Action Quarterly* 16 (March 1982), pp. 42–43; Fred Landis, "Opus Dei: Secret Order Vies for Power," *Covert Action Quarterly* 18 (Winter 1983), pp. 14–15; Louis Wolf, "Inaccuracy in Media; Accuracy in Media Rewrites the News and History," *Covert Action Quarterly* 21 (Spring 1984), pp. 31–32; Fred Landis, "Moscow Rules Moss's Mind," *Covert Action Quarterly* 4 (Summer 1985), pp. 37–38; Stella Calloni, "The Horror Archives of Operation Condor," *Covert Action Quarterly* 50 (Fall 1994), pp. 11, 13, 58–59; Darrin Wood, "Mexico Practices What School of the Americas Teaches," *Covert Action Quarterly* 59 (Winter 1996–97), pp. 38–43; Lisa Haugaard, "Textbook Repression: US Training Manuals Declassified," *Covert Action Quarterly* 61 (Summer 1997), pp. 29–38, 63; Saul Landau and Sarah Anderson, "Autumn of the Autocrat," *Covert Action Quarterly* 64 (Spring 1998), pp. 38–40; Michael Ratner, "The Pinochet Principle: Who's Next?," *Covert Action Quarterly* 66 (Winter 1999), pp. 46–48; H. Frazier, ed., *Uncloaking the CIA* (New York: The Free Press, 1978), pp. 34–54, 60–63; Darrell Garwood, *Under Cover* (New York: Grove Press, 1985), pp. 104, 127; F.S. Landis, "Psychological Warfare and Media Operations in Chile, 1970–1973" (Doctoral dissertation, University of Illinois, 1975), pp. 4, 14, 235, 254, 309–12; Victor Marchetti and J.D. Marks, *The CIA and the Cult of Intelligence* (New York: Alfred A. Knopf, 1974), especially p. 17; Nair, *Devil and His Dart;* Prados, *Presidents' Secret Wars* (1996 ed.), p. 319; Ranelagh, *Agency,* pp. 514–20; *Latin America Magazine,* August 1974, pp. 14, 37; J. Richelson, *American Espionage and the Soviet Target* (New York: William Morrow, 1987), pp. 232–33; R.R. Sandford, *The Murder of Allende,* trans. A. Conrad (New York: Harper and Row, 1975); F.F. Sergeyev, *Chile: CIA Big Business,* trans.

L. Bobrov (Moscow: Progress Publishers, 1981), pp. 52–53, 93, 98, 108, 114, 163; Stansfield Turner, *Secrecy and Democracy: The CIA in Transition* (Boston: Houghton Mifflin, 1985), pp. 80–81, 113, 191; A. Uribe, *The Black Book of American Intervention in Chile* (Boston: Beacon Press, 1975); Elton Rayack, *Not So Free to Choose: the Political Economy of Milton Friedman and Ronald Reagan* (Westport, CT: Praeger, 1986); Hersh, *Old Boys;* Winks, *Cloak & Gown;* Juan José Arévalo, *Anti-Kommunism in Latin America* (New York: Lyle Stuart, 1963); McGehee, CIABASE; see also Introduction, note 3.

19. P. Gunson, A. Thompson, and G. Chamberlain, *The Dictionary of Contemporary Politics of South America* (New York: Routledge, 1989), p. 228; Rayack, *Not So Free to Choose.* See also note 18 above and Introduction, note 3.

20. Duncan Green, *Silent Revolution* (London: Cassel, 1995), pp. 101, 108; Noam Chomsky, *Deterring Democracy* (New York: Verso, 1992), p. 231; Thomas Skidmore and Peter Smith, "The Pinochet Regime," in *Modern Latin America* (New York: Oxford University Press, 1989), pp. 137–38; Rayack, *Not So Free to Choose;* Silvia Bortzutzky, "The Chicago Boys, Social Security and Welfare in Chile," in *The Radical Right and the Welfare State*, ed. Howard Glennerster and James Midgley (Lanham, MD: Barnes and Noble, 1991), pp. 88, 91, 96; See also above two endnotes.

21. Rayack, *Not So Free to Choose*; Bortzutzky, "Chicago Boys," pp. 88, 91, 96. See also above three notes. Statistics on labor's share of income is from James Petras and Henry Veltmeyer, "Latin America at the End of the Millennium," *Monthly Review* (July/August 1999), p. 44.

22. William H. Kötke, *The Final Empire: The Collapse of Civilization and the Seed of the Future* (Portland, OR: Arrow Point Press, 1993).

23. United Nations Commission on the Truth in El Salvador, *From Madness to Hope: The 12-Year War in El Salvador* (U.N. Security Council, 1993); Charles Kernaghan, "Sweatshop Blues," *Dollars and Sense* (March/April, 1999); Michael McClintock, *The American Connection: State Terror and Popular Resistance in El Salvador* (London: Zed Books, 1985); Blum, *The CIA*, pp. 232–43; Blum, *Killing Hope*; Dennis Volman, "Salvador Death Squads: A CIA connection?" *The Christian Science Monitor,* May 8, 1984, p. 1; many issues of the *Covert Action Quarterly* and *Counterspy;*

Klare and Kornbluh, *Low Intensity Warfare;* Edward S. Herman and F. Broadhead, *Demonstration Elections: U.S. Staged Elections in the Dominican Republic, Vietnam, and El Salvador* (Boston: South End Press, 1984); Jonathan Kwitny, *Endless Enemies: The Making of an Unfriendly World* (New York: Congdon and Weed, 1984); McGehee, CIABASE.

24. William I. Robinson, *A Faustian Bargain: U.S. Intervention in the Nicaraguan Elections and American Foreign Policy in the Post–Cold War Era* (Boulder, CO: Westview Press, 1992); Peter Kornblush, *Nicaragua, The Price of Intervention: Reagan's War Against the Sandinistas* (Washington, DC: Institute for Policy Studies, 1987); Reed Brody, *Contra Terror in Nicaragua: Report of a Fact Finding Mission: September 1984–January 1985* (Boston: South End Press, 1985); *The Rise and Fall of the Nicaraguan Revolution* (New York: New International, 1994); G. Garvin, *Everybody Has His Own Gringo: The CIA and the Contras* (New York: Brassey's, 1992); Peter Kornbluth and M. Byrne, *The Iran-Contra Scandal: The Declassified History* (New York: The New Press, 1993); Twentieth Century Fund, *The Need to Know: The Report of the Twentieth Century Fund Task Force on Covert Action and American Democracy* (New York: The Twentieth Century Fund Press, 1992); E. Chamorro, "Packaging the Contras: A Case of CIA Disinformation," *Monograph Series Number 2* (New York: Institute for Media Analysis, 1987); Minnick, *Spies and Provocateurs;* John Prados, *Keepers of the Keys: A History of the National Security Council from Truman to Bush* (New York: William Morrow, 1991); Loch K. Johnson, *America's Secret Power* (New York: Oxford University Press, 1989); C.D. Ameringer, *U.S. Foreign Intelligence* (Lexington, MA: Lexington Books, 1990); H.B. Westerfield, ed., *Inside CIA's Private World: Declassified Articles from the Agency's Internal Journal 1955–1992* (New Haven: Yale University Press, 1995); J. Adams, *Secret Armies* (New York: Atlantic Monthly Press, 1987); Tony Avirgan and M. Honey, eds., *Lapenca: On Trial in Costa Rica* (San Jose, CA: Editorial Porvenir, 1987); J. Marshall, P.D. Scott, and J. Hunter, *The Iran-Contra Connection* (Boston: South End Press, 1987); P.V. Parakal, *Secret Wars of the CIA* (New Delhi: Sterling, 1984); Christopher Simpson, *Blowback* (New York: Weidenfeld and Nicolson, 1988); *National Endowment for Democracy, Annual Report*; McGehee, CIABASE.

25. Greg Guma, "Cracks in the Covert Iceberg,"

Toward Freedom (May 1998), p. 2; Yousai Mohammad and M. Adkin, *The Beartrap: Afghanistan's Untold Story* (London: Leo Cooper, 1992); K. Lohbeck, *Holy War, Unholy Victory: Eyewitness to the CIA's Secret War in Afghanistan* (Washington, DC: Regnery Gateway, 1993); J. Peterzell, *Reagan's Secret Wars,* CNSS Report 108 (Washington, DC: Center for National Security Studies, 1984); T. Weiner, *Blank Check: The Pentagon's Black Budget* (New York: Warner Books, 1990); E.T. Chester, *Covert Network: Progressives, the International Rescue Committee, and the CIA* (Armonk, NY: M.E. Sharpe, 1995); D. Cordovez and S.S. Harrison, *Out of Afghanistan: The Inside Story of the Soviet Withdrawal* (New York: Oxford University Press, 1995); S. Emerson, *Secret Warriors* (New York: G.P. Putnam, 1988); Westerfield, *Inside CIA's Private World;* L.K. Johnson, *America's Secret Power;* R. Kessler, *Inside the CIA: Revealing the Secrets of the World's Most Powerful Spy Agency* (New York: Pocket Books, 1992); Duane R. Clarridge, *A Spy for All Seasons: My Life in the CIA* (New York: Scribner, 1997); McGehee, CIABASE.

26. John Stockwell, *In Search of Enemies* (New York: W.W. Norton, 1978), especially pp. 43, 63–64, 272; Stockwell, *Praetorian Guard;* Jonathan Kwitny, *The Crimes of Patriots* (New York: W.W. Norton, 1987); Kwitny, *Endless Enemies;* Clarridge, *A Spy for All Seasons;* H. Rositzke, *The CIA's Secret Operations* (New York: Thomas Y. Crowell, 1977); S. Gervasi and S. Wong, "The Reagan Doctrine and the Destabilization of Southern Africa" (Unpublished paper from McGehee's CIABASE, April 1990); B. Freemantle, *CIA* (New York: Stein and Day, 1983), p. 68.

27. Gervasi and Wong, "Reagan Doctrine," pp. 56–57; W. Minter, *Apartheid's Contras: An Inquiry into the Roots of War in Angola and Mozambique* (London: Zed Books, 1994).

28. Stockwell, *In Search of Enemies,* pp. 10, 105, 137, 169, 172, 236–37; Sean Kelly, *America's Tyrant: The CIA and Mobutu of Zaire* (Washington, DC: American University Press, 1993); D. Gibbs, *The Political Economy of Third World Intervention: Mines, Money and U.S. Policy in the Congo Crisis* (Chicago: University of Chicago Press, 1991); R.L. Borosage and J. Marks, eds., *The CIA File* (New York: Grossman, 1976); Gervasi and Wong, "Reagan Doctrine"; Prados,

Presidents' Secret Wars; Kwitny, *Endless Enemies;* Blum, *Killing Hope;* McGehee, CIABASE.

29. Minnick, *Spies and Provocateurs,* especially p. 262; R. Ridenour, *Back Fire: The CIA's Biggest Burn* (Havana: José Martí, 1991), especially pp. 73, 77–78, 145–49; Prados, *Presidents' Secret Wars* (1996 ed.), pp. 333, 337, 349; Prados, *Keepers of the Keys,* especially pp. 142–44, 203–317; J.T. Richelson, *The U.S. Intelligence Community* (Cambridge, MA: Ballinger, 1985), especially p. 231; P.V. Parakal, *Secret Wars of the CIA;* R.S. Cline, *Secrets, Spies, and Scholars* (Washington, DC: Acropolis Books, 1976), especially p. 195; Garwood, *Under Cover,* especially p. 92; P. Wyden, *Bay of Pigs: The Untold Story* (New York: Simon and Schuster, 1979); D. Martin, *Wilderness of Mirrors* (New York: Harper and Row, 1980), especially pp. 151–53; Ranelagh, *Agency,* especially pp. 356–60; G. Treverton, *Covert Action: The Limits of Intervention in the Postwar World* (New York: Basic Books, 1987); D. Corn, *Blond Ghost: Ted Shackley and the CIA's Crusades* (New York: Simon and Schuster, 1994); L.F. Prouty, *The Secret Team* (Englewood Cliffs, NJ: Prentice-Hall, 1973); Borosage and Marks, *CIA File;* Hersh, *Old Boys;* Thomas, *Very Best Men;* Jeffreys-Jones, R., *The CIA & American Democracy* (New Haven: Yale University Press, 1989); B. Watson, S. Watson, and G. Hopple, *United States Intelligence: An Encyclopedia* (New York: Garland, 1990); *Covert Action Information Bulletin; Counterspy;* McGehee's CIABASE.

30. See note 29

31. Prados, *Presidents' Secret Wars* (1996 ed.), pp. 333, 337, 349; Garwood, *Under Cover,* pp. 60–64; Church Committee Report (1976), Congressional Record; Blum, *The CIA,* p. 108; check McGehee's CIABASE for other successful and unsuccessful attempts to assassinate leaders and potential leaders of other countries.

32. Stephen Schlesinger, "The CIA Censor's History," *The Nation,* July 14, 1997, pp. 20–22; Stockwell, *Praetorian Guard,* p. 21.

33. Jack Epstein, "Argentina's 'Dirty War' Laundry May Get a Public Airing," *The Christian Science Monitor,* December 4, 1997, p. 7.

34. Prouty, *JFK: The CIA, Vietnam,* pp. 236–37, 341.

8

Creating Enemies for the Masses

The Inquisitions of the Middle Ages Were, and the Inquisitions of Today Still Are, to Prevent Democratic Choice

When empires clash, each demonizes the competing culture. These are Social Control belief systems in action. Every social group, large or small, has its enemies and its friends, always portrays its friends with affection, and, at some level of intensity, always portray that enemy as a danger. Both portrayals are crucial for survival.

The Inquisitions of the Middle Ages

The Roman emperors Constantine and Theodosius I, in the fourth century AD, stopped the persecution of the Christian church and essentially made it the state religion. Just as the wealth of today migrates toward tax shelters, over the next 700 years aristocracy migrated toward the tax-sheltered positions of power in the higher offices of the church—those of bishops, cardinals, and pope. Where the church and its people were once one, the church hierarchy (First Estate) and aristocracy (Second Estate) were now one; there was now a distinct division between the church leaders and the common people. From their new power base running the church, the combined First and Second Estates sold indulgences and salvations. The common people were terrified of purgatory (Hell) and the

last bit of wealth could be extracted from those who hoped to be saved and go to heaven. Edward Burman, in *The Inquisition*, from which this chronology is taken, explains that with the returning Crusaders in the late eleventh and early twelfth centuries came many different Christian beliefs, others (called cults and heresies) were springing forth all over Europe, and various unorthodox Christian beliefs were filtering into Europe from Jerusalem.

Some of these sects permitted each person to find his or her own way to heaven and (primarily the well-organized and rapidly expanding Cathars and Waldensians) openly frowned on a wealthy, licentious church. Others were drawing away church members by competing claims of miraculous cures. All power brokers fear the expansion of the political powers of others while their own power shrinks.

Such was the Church's fear of these competing beliefs. The Albigensian Crusade (1209–1229) was organized by Pope Innocent III to destroy the Cathars of southern France with their threatening doctrines and parallel organization of dioceses headed by bishops. This was only the largest of various efforts to suppress heresies since the middle of the tenth century. As with all crusades (the crusade of the Cold

War is a very good example), this required a massive Social Control belief system (propaganda) portraying the Cathars as a dangerous enemy, in this case as infidels and heretics, to justify the slaughter of targeted people and theft of their wealth.

The burning of heretics at the stake for 200 years coalesced between 1123 and 1206 into the formal Inquisition. In 1206 and 1210 Pope Innocent III founded the Franciscan and Dominican Mendicant Orders to preach against heresy; and in 1215 the Lateran Council was held which listed "clause by clause" heretical interpretations of the faith, the removal from office of heretics, confiscation of their property, excommunication, and their referral to the feudal lords for punishment.

With the Cathars fleeing to other sections of Europe to escape certain death from zealous inquisitors and secular lords, between 1227 and 1252 Pope Gregory IX and Pope Innocent IV issued several bulls that further encoded and formalized the form of the Inquisition.

"The Inquisition was ready to start work on a grand scale shortly after the mid-point of the thirteenth century" and, as the Christian sects went underground, Popes Alexander IX, Urban IV, Clement IV, and Boniface VIII issued bulls to maintain that momentum and root out the last vestiges of threat to their power.

Franciscan and Dominican priests organized to lead heretics back to the fold evolved into a few zealous priests becoming inquisitors and torturers. They condemned hundreds of thousands of heretics to burn at the stake over a period of 700 years, the majority being Cathars, Waldensians, Jews, and Muslims; as they disappeared, Freemasons, alleged witches, midwives, and personal enemies were targeted.

"Only the fear of losing power acquired over a period of a thousand years can satisfactorily explain such violent reactions."[1] That it was political power that was at stake was evident in the Albigensian Crusade and in the Spanish Inquisition. "Wars are politics by other means" and the Cathar, Waldensian, Jewish, and Muslim communities were under assault by formal military forces led by Catholic secular powers.

Because they did not believe in buying one's way out of salvation and would draw people from the state church, the Cathars were headed for extinction. They, the Waldensians, and smaller sects in most of Europe were suppressed by 1270; but Jews and Muslims survived as a political force on an ever-shrinking part of the Iberian peninsula. Because of bureaucratic perpetuation and the immense profits from confiscated property, the Inquisition turned from burning heretics to searching out sorcery and witchcraft. The political underpinning of it all was again exposed when doctors and universities chose to increase their power by turning the force of the Inquisition against midwives.

The Spanish Inquisition

With the inquisitorial pattern well established, starting in 1478 the Christian secular powers of Spain proceeded to eradicate Jews and Muslims from their territory. The choice was between leaving Spain, converting to Christianity, or being burnt at the stake. It is only because the power of the Spanish empire was a threat to British and other empires that the world knows so much about the Spanish Inquisition and so little about the French, Italian, and British Inquisitions. Although all were equally violent, the history of each culture suppressed the exposure of its own inquisitorial violence and emphasized the violence in its archenemy Spain. This is the "creation of enemies" to protect a power structure as it has functioned throughout history.

Here is a Social Control belief system in action that is rather easy to dissect. A recent documentary took the stand that the Spanish Inquisition was largely a creation of historical revisionists and that actually there had been almost no tortures and only 4,000 to 5,000 burned at the stake. The similarity to those who are saying the World War II Jewish holocaust did not happen is striking. In order to draw in or maintain followers, the foundation of power—those with a vested interest in expansion of their power—must put out a positive image. This requires suppressing knowledge of violence and unjust acts perpetrated by a power structure and this was undoubtedly the purpose of that falsification of history.

To challenge that documentary, one need only recognize the power of religion and ask, "Where did all the other religions once dominant and flourishing in Spain go?" As many people will suffer the worst tortures and death before ever abandoning their faith, and other religions in that region disappeared, one can make the rational judgment that, just as the German holocaust (which was but the latest eruption of the thousand-year effort to eradicate Jewry), did take place, the Spanish Inquisition did happen and it was very violent.

The supposed scholarly documentation that this did not happen are only efforts to eradicate this horror from history and thus from social memory just as Italy and other European countries have successfully eliminated the true level of violence of their inquisitions from popular history. This, of course, is to gain and retain followers, which increases and maintains power. It was the creation of another Social Control paradigm among a long list of such previous, and later, creations.

Turning on Their Own: The Inquisitorial Suppression of the Templars

The eradication of the highly respected and powerful Templars in the Middle Ages was done through the Inquisition and is a classic example of the destruction of a competing group of people through accusations by political powers that they are immoral and a threat to the rest of society, when in reality they are only a political threat to those in power.

The Knights Templar were industrious and faithful servants of Christianity. Their history began in 1119 when nine knights formed an association to protect pilgrims in the Holy Land. They fought so valiantly that

> gifts in abundance flowed in on the Order, large possessions were bestowed on it in all countries of the west. . . . By the Bull, *Omne datum optimum,* granted by Pope Alexander III in 1162, the Order of the Templars acquired great importance, and from this time forth, it may be regarded as totally independent, acknowledging no authority but that . . . of the supreme pontiff.[2]

The Templars fought many battles for Christianity, and by 1302 they had spread over much of Europe and were enormously wealthy and powerful. Much of the land owned by the Templars had been given to their forebears by the grateful ancestors of local aristocracy (in trade for the slaughter of non-Christian or heretical Christian populations) and by a Church whose successors resented and feared the power of this great order. Local bishops and clergy made many complaints to the pope about the Templars' refusal to recognize local religious authority.

When a French pope was consecrated in 1305, he rewarded King Philip IV of France and other nobles by supporting an intrigue against the respected Templars. The French secret service established a Social Control belief system to protect the power structure as they proceeded to destroy the Templars and steal their wealth. They spread vicious rumors and

> on the night of the 13th of October, [1307], all the Templars in the French dominions were simultaneously arrested. . . . They were accused of worshipping an idol covered with an old skin, embalmed, having the appearance of a piece of polished oil-cloth. "In this idol," we are assured, "there were two carbuncles for eyes, bright as the brightness of heaven, and it is certain that all hope of the Templars was placed in it: it was their sovereign god, and they trusted in it with all their heart." They are accused of burning the bodies of the deceased brethren, and making the ashes into a powder, which they administered to the younger brethren in their food and drink, to make them hold fast their faith and idolatry; of cooking and roasting infants, and anointing their idols with the fat; of celebrating hidden rites and mysteries, to which the young and tender virgins were introduced, and of a variety of abominations too absurd and horrible to be named.[3]

Like all Inquisition charges, the fabrications of this Social Control belief system could not be defended against and confessions were obtained by torture. King Philip then sent the findings to other European countries. These preposterous accusations were at first rejected, but by 1314 the Templars were totally discredited and destroyed; over 2,000 of them confessed under torture and were quartered or burned at the stake. In only nine years the Templars, who had been perceived for centuries as elite warriors and builders of the Christian world, and who commanded both large resources and respect, were labeled enemies and cast into oblivion. The First and Second Estates had acted together to reclaim their wealth and power.[4]

Normally those targeted are not the enemies of the people. They are the enemies of the powerful leaders of institutions (religions, governments, and wealthy classes). The population is easily manipulated into providing protection for the powerful by warnings of threats to the foundations of society. Of course, the Managers of State warning that an enemy is trying to take over the world neglect to tell, and will always deny, that it is they, collectively, who exercise most control in this world. The creation of enemies is the dominant feature of that control.

The Winding Down of the Inquisitions of the Middle Ages

As the Inquisition wound down in Europe in the eighteenth century (except in Spain), its dying flame, now picked up by Protestant evangelists, reached America in the form of the Salem witch trials. Small inquisitorial flames in Peru and Columbia died out in the seventeenth century but in Spain and Mexico it was a primary political tool well into the nineteenth century.

Although under a different name (changed twice, in 1908 and 1965), the Inquisition still exists as "The Sacred Congregation for the Doctrine of the Faith," the conservative political arm that suppresses liberal elements within the Church.[5] It can only be ideological descendants of this political arm, if not they directly, who were behind the above noted documentary minimizing the Spanish Inquisition.

The world will never know the true number slaughtered. Some authors claim reliable estimates of between 200,000 and 1 million burned at the stake in the witchcraft craze of the sixteenth and seventeenth centuries alone. Others claim 500,000 burned at the stake over a period of 400 years before the witchcraft craze started.

There was almost certainly a greater number killed in the sweeps of military forces organized specifically to slaughter entire communities of Cathars, Waldensians, Jews, and Muslims. And Templar and Hospitaler knights gained much of their land through local Christian feudal lords giving them free rein to slaughter heretical populations and sharing with them the spoils.

So, when one includes those killed other than by burning at the stake—which is by far the greater number—the number of deaths at the hands of inquisitors to increase the power of the already powerful throughout the full 700-year Inquisition history is truly massive. Secular powers have not abandoned the ways of the Inquisition; they still ally with conservative evangelical Christian factions to maintain their power.

The Successful American and French Revolutions Required the Inquisitorial Suppression of the Illuminati

The twentieth-century rhetoric of fear engineered to gain the loyalty of populations for the protection of the powerful began much earlier in history than the rise of the Soviet Union as a world power; it went back to the American and French Revolutions and the declaration of rights for all men. It is the potential of others to attain economic rights through their newly attained democratic rights (the vote) that creates fear in the heart of those with wealth and power.

The battle to prevent a rekindling of democratic expression has a long history. After the defeat of the ''Free Cities of Europe'' as addressed above, the suppression of rights they had known, the erasure of those rights from social memory, and the suppressions of the Inquisitions, what little democratic expression that could function did so through secret societies.

Thus these secret societies were the constant enemies of the managers of the First and Second Estates.

In 1776, the American Revolution reclaimed many of those suppressed rights. In the same year, Professor Adam Weishaupt of the University of Ingolstadt in Bavaria (Germany) established the Bavarian Illuminati (''enlightened ones''), a secret group to expand the rights of the people. Thirteen years later, the French Revolution's promise of more extensive rights created even greater fear in the First and Second Estates.

The Third Estate, bourgeoisie with the support of the common people, now ruled France, and increased rights, or even the potential for full rights for everybody, could have become contagious. The Illuminati supported those increased rights. In a replay of earlier inquisitions, managers of the religious state immediately asserted their control by frightening the population into a witch hunt. A Social Control belief system of an imminent enemy was put into place. The war cry went out that in effect said, ''Look out for the Illuminati! Look out for the Illuminati! They want to take over your country! Your church! The world!''[6]

Note that no one today will dispute that it was the king, aristocracy, and church (those sounding the warning) who then controlled the so-called civilized world. Today's defense of the powerful through the creation of enemies that we have been describing is specifically to prevent the further expansion of common people's rights declared, but not fully gained, in the American and French revolutions.

That the Illuminati are active today and a threat to freedom is a fiction kept alive by the far right wing, whose politics are too extreme even for most of those who do hold the reins of power. It was the ruling powers who created these Social Control paradigms to control the masses to protect their own wealth and power. It is ironic to note that when people without sufficient education—or of radical bent—dig up those old writings about the Illuminati (the Social Control belief system at that time), they point to the current organizations of the powerful (such as the Trilateralists) as being the Illuminati attempting to rule the world. Poetic justice!

However, the forward march of history could not be stopped. The intense efforts of the aristocracy and church to overthrow the French Revolution resulted in Napoleon Bonaparte taking the reins of power in France. Through the conquest of many of the nations conspiring to overthrow the French Revolution, Napoleon spread throughout Europe the rights declared for all men by that revolution. Known as the Napoleonic Codes, "they are the basis for the law of thirty nations today."[7]

The twin threats of loss of trading rights in Europe (Napoleon's Continental System) and the threat of replacing aristocratic privilege with rights for all people led to a "Holy Alliance" (more often called a "Monarchical Alliance" but the church was always a crucial ally) between European monarchies and the church to reclaim their aristocratic rights.

Though Napoleon freed most of Europe, he was ultimately defeated at Waterloo in 1815. The aristocracy and European monarchies immediately convened the Congress of Vienna to abrogate the newly gained rights of the masses. However, "Napoleon's omelet couldn't be unscrambled. . . . It was a force destined to destroy the dynastic system."[8]

History teaches of Napoleon's desire to be a world dictator, when he was really destroying the power of the First and Second Estates who did rule the world. Because Napoleon was such a threat to the powerful, the secret services and state departments of the European monarchies guided the writing and publication of books depicting Napoleon as a megalomaniac and tyrannical dictator. These concepts saturated the literature of the time and still saturate the literature of today. In a replay of the Illuminati nonsense, once Napoleon was demonized as an enemy of the people, the masses remained, and still are, unaware that Napoleon really stood for reclaiming their rights.

The Czarist Secret Police Demonize the Jews

Another example of a Social Control belief system to justify assault on a specific people to destroy their power and steal their wealth was *The Protocols of The Learned Elders of Zion*. The czarist (Russian) secret police created this alleged Jewish/Zionist master plan for world domination out of thin air in 1903 to condition the population for pogroms (government-sponsored riots) against the created enemy, the Jews.

English and French translations appeared in 1920, but in 1921 a correspondent for the *Times,* Philip Graves, proved they were forgeries. With the cooperation of a Russian refugee who had helped create the deception, it was shown that the forgers "plagiarized paraphrases from a satire on Napoleon."[9] This satire was no doubt a previous creation intended, as explained above, to demonize Napoleon because his egalitarian concepts of justice were a threat to the privileged groups.

The primary job of an empire's intelligence

service is writing history to create Social Control belief systems that further the goals of, and protect, whoever is in power.[10] Though the fraud of the *Protocols of Zion* is well known, there are many instances of such hoaxes that are recorded in history and accepted as fact. Those thousands of CIA-created fraudulent articles and hundreds of fraudulent books put out by compliant professors and reporters addressed above are good examples. As intelligence services of all imperial centers do this, one society will have its created version of history and another society a different history favorable to its desired view of the world. The holocaust of World War II was just the climactic finale of over 2,000 years of hate rhetoric against the Jews, preached from the pulpit, supposedly for killing Jesus. Just as the power of right-wing extremists in U.S. society ebbs and flows, the power of church right-wing extremists ebbs and flows.

Where it was once common to persecute the Jews openly, the horrors of the holocaust made it no longer acceptable. All who would advocate such a thing are now outside the permitted parameters of political or religious debate. Today most Christians are supportive of the rights of Jewish people. This stems from the positive statements of church leaders, as opposed to the previous violent rhetoric of the right-wing minority.

Barnet Litvinoff, in his masterly work on 2,000 years of Jewish persecution, *The Burning Bush,* points out that the persecutors and supporters of the Jews have periodically changed sides.[11] Each of these changes required the targeted population to be programmed either as an enemy or a friend. That change is the necessary paradigm shift to gain a following that telegraphs the intentions of the Managers of State.

And Then the World Starts Breaking Free from Imperial Centers of Capital

Fear gripped the powerful when Russia broke free of control in the 1917 Bolshevik Revolution. The Third Estate, the bourgeoisie, with the support of the common people, had revolted and taken the reins of power from the First and Second Estates. As World War I ground to a halt, Communist revolutionaries were taking over railroads and factories as Germany collapsed. The disillusioned German navy and much of the army were hoisting the red flag. Only an alliance between Social Democrats and the Socialist wing of labor gave private armies called "free corps" enough time to wrestle those railroads, factories, and disaffected military from the Communists.[12] That Social Democrat/Socialist alliance was broken five years later when the old power brokers reclaimed control through the installation of Hitler and his Fascists.

The Managers of State of the old imperial nations knew how close the Bolshevik Revolution in Russia came to spilling over into Poland, Austria, Germany, and even Italy. They knew that, if those major nations were lost, the rest of Europe was sure to follow. A firewall to prevent that threatening philosophy from sweeping them from power had to be built. The scourge of Bolshevism (Communism) was created as the primary Social Control paradigm. Copied from the old Illuminati scare, the basic message was the same, "Communism! Communism! They want to take over your country! Your church! The world!" Under that call to arms, most of the governments of Europe were turned over to Fascists.[13]

In the United States, in 1920, this took the form of the Palmer Raids, in which, just as in the attacks on the Templars in the Middle Ages, thousands, mostly labor unionists suspected of Soviet sympathies, were arrested in the middle of the night. Hundreds were deported, and hundreds more were sent to prison.[14] Again take note that most of the world was still under the control of the Managers of State of those countries sounding the warning. The country that had broken away from capitalism's control was, by comparison, extremely weak.

What the Managers of State really feared was the failure of the fourteen-nation attempt to overthrow the Bolshevik Revolution, the governing of Russia by the common people, and how close Germany and Italy had come to succumbing to the same revolutionary forces. Lest the revolution would spread and destroy the power structure of the imperial nations, the masses of these "free" countries had to be inoculated against the ideology of that revolution through creation of the Bolshevik (Communist) "enemy."

But during the crisis of the Great Depression that soon followed, the inoculation was quickly wearing off. The Managers of State of European countries knew that the leaders of labor would govern if honest elections were permitted, so they turned the governments over to Fascists. Managers of State all over Europe acted to avoid a ballot-box revolution such as occurred in Spain. The Fascist takeovers of the governments of Europe were a sham to suppress the democratic voice of the people:

> Hitler was eventually put in power by the feudalist clique around President Hindenberg, just as Mussolini and Primo de Rivera were ushered into office by their respective sovereigns. . . . In no case was an actual revolution against constituted authority launched; fascist tactics were those of a sham rebellion arranged with the tacit approval of the authorities who pretended to have been overwhelmed by force.[15]

Note how the Fascists were put in power by back-room political deals, specifically for the protection of power and wealth and to avoid democratic solutions, yet are recorded in history as only Fascism. The preceding quotation was from economic historian Karl Polanyi, who recognized that desperate power brokers used the violence of Fascism to prevent democracy from functioning.

Hitler was a German intelligence officer throughout Germany's post–World War I crisis and it is highly likely his rise to power was orchestrated by German intelligence specifically to protect a power structure that was crumbling.[16] That these realities can be found only by in-depth reading, or by chance, is because much of history has been written, and is being written, to protect a power structure.

The famed march of the Black Shirts that supposedly put Mussolini in power took place three days *after* Italy had been effectively handed over to Fascist control. Germany's famous Reichstag fire was several months *after* Hitler had been given power in a secret January meeting of German power brokers.[17] That act was part of the campaign to depict the opposition as terrorists and enemies and weaken them before the national election that legitimized Hitler's rule.

Again it was democracy that was feared. Only in Spain were free elections permitted and, to the horror of the captains of capitalism, labor won the right to govern. The connection between the power brokers, Fascism, and the fear of ballot-box revolutions was evident when troops from Germany and Italy (with unspoken but real support from America, Britain, and France) supported Franco, and, in a bloody foreshadow of World War II, overthrew that election.[18]

The real target of the back-room political

deal in Germany was labor leaders who were poised to take over the reins of the German government by the vote. When Hitler seized power in 1933, police were ordered to shoot key labor leaders on sight and within a year 100,000 politically aware persons were in prison.[19] Witness the comments of a member of Hitler's cabinet, Colonel Walther von Reichenau. His analysis of the crisis in Germany could be used almost without changing a word to describe labor's position in America since 1980 and in the collapsed economies on the periphery of empire since 1997:

> The trade unions have been smashed, the communists driven into a corner and provisionally neutralized, the Reichstag has surrendered its rights with the Enabling Law. The workers are keeping their heads down and, after the previous slump, their wage packets will be more important to them than any politics.[20]

Although there had previously been much rhetoric against, and individual persecution of, the Jews within Germany, organized attacks against them did not start until November 9, 1938—*Kristallnacht* (The Night of Broken Glass).[21] The onslaught against the Jews by Fascists was undertaken to repay the super-secret Thule Society (surely now rebuilding in Europe and roughly similar to America's Aryan Nations) for their early financial support of Hitler. The Thule Society organized Hitler's German Workers' Party and supported it financially. Their symbol was the swastika, and this became the symbol of German Fascism. It is reasonable to assume that Hitler put these fanatics into positions of power because they were the power behind him.[22]

Throughout the world and throughout history, politicians have copied the religious practice of targeting the enemies of the powerful by labeling them as enemies of the people and accusing them of atrocities.[23]

To believe differently than a society's primary beliefs is heretical and heretics are easily targeted enemies. This is a primitive social survival mechanism practiced on a national and international scale.

The "witch hunts" of the post–World War II McCarthy era have a remarkable similarity to the Inquisitions. When the original targets of the Inquisition (Christian Cathars and Waldensians) were eliminated, the inquisitors turned towards searching for witches and satanic cults to justify their existence and maintain their power.[24] Those first accused of practicing the "black arts" and burned at the stake were rather defenseless people. However, as the hysteria continued, the accusatory finger pointed higher and higher and eventually pointed towards those in power. When these powerful became the target, the hysteria died down. After a respite, the witch hunts would start again.

In the same pattern, when McCarthy's "witch hunts" started destroying those in power, the powerful turned and destroyed him and the hysteria died down. Whenever the personal risk to leaders is high, they are motivated to defend themselves. This demonstrates that the process can be controlled and the public protected if the leaders ever decide they wish to do so.

Persecution of the Jews was primarily religious, with economic jealousy and theft of their property secondary. The Muslim/Christian standoff is religious, but control of resources follows religious control of populations. Witness the "Holy Alliance" formed by the monarchies and the church to defeat Napoleon; the later "Holy Alliance" against the Ottoman Empire that ended in the collapse of the Muslim economic world; the role of religion in the seventy-year battle that ended in the current collapse of the Soviet Union; and how religion marched hand in hand with armies of both the Muslims and Christians as they laid claim to most of the earth.[25] If a society cannot be subverted religiously or politically, typically the military is activated to remove that threat. In fact, religion and politics normally work in tandem (the restructured First and Second Estates) and the military is only an extension of these religious/political powers.

Notes

1. Edward Burman, *The Inquisition: Hammer of Heresy* (New York: Dorset Press, 1992), p. 39.

2. James Burnes, *The Knights Templar* (London: Paybe and Foss, 1840), pp. 12–14. See also Stephen Howarth's *Knights Templar* (New York: Dorset Press, 1982).

3. Charles G. Addison, *The Knights Templar* (London: Longman, Brown, Green, and Longman, 1842), pp. 194–203, especially p. 203. See also Burman, *Inquisition,* pp. 95–99.

4. Burman, *Inquisition,* pp. 95–99.

5 Ibid., pp. 213–14.

6. David Caute, *The Great Fear* (New York: Simon and Schuster, 1978), pp. 18–19; Richard Hofstadter, *The Paranoid Style in American Politics* (Chicago: University of Chicago Press, 1979), pp. 10–11; Arkon Daraul, *A History of Secret Societies* (Secaucus, NJ: Citadel Press, 1961); James and Suzanne Pool, *Who Financed Hitler?* (New York: Dial Press, 1978); Barnet Litvinoff, *The Burning Bush* (New York: E. P. Dutton, 1988); Heiko A. Oberman, *The Roots of Anti-Semitism* (Philadelphia: Fortress Press, 1984); David H. Bennet, *The Party of Fear* (Chapell Hill, NC: University of North Carolina Press, 1988), pp. 23–26, 205–06.

7. Daniel J. Boorstin, "History's Hidden Turning Points," *U.S. News & World Report,* April 22, 1991, cover story.

8. Ibid., p. 61.

9. David Fromkin, *A Peace to End All Peace* (New York: Avon Books, 1989), pp. 468–69; Michael Kettle, *The Allies and the Russian Collapse* (Minneapolis: University of Minnesota Press, 1981), p. 17. For how the *Protocols* evolved further to support Fascism in Europe read F. L. Carsten, *The Rise of Fascism* (Berkeley: University of California Press, 1982), pp. 24, 29, 118, 184. The Thule Society's efforts to promote anti-Semitism through Hitler would likely have not had much effect on the world except for Henry Ford, through his *Dearborn Independent* newspaper, spreading those *Protocols* to every corner of the world and imprinting anti-Semitism into the world's mind (Pool and Pool, *Who Financed Hitler,* pp. 3, 23, chapter 3).

10. G.J.A. O'Toole, *Honorable Treachery* (New York: Atlantic Monthly Press, 1991), pp. 402–71.

11. Litvinoff, *Burning Bush.*

12. Edmond Taylor, *The Fall of the Dynasties: The Collapse of the Old Order, 1905–1922* (New York: Dorset Press, 1989), chapters 17–19.

13. Caute, *Great Fear,* pp. 18–19.

14. Bennet, *Party of Fear,* pp. 191–98, 205–206.

15. Karl Polanyi, *The Great Transformation* (Boston: Beacon Press, 1957), pp. 237–241; see also F.L. Carsten, *Britain and the Weimar Republic* (New York: Schocken Books, 1984), especially chapter 8; Carsten, *Rise of Fascism.*

16. Taylor, *Fall of the Dynasties,* p. 366.

17. Carsten, *Rise of Fascism,* pp. 150–55.

18. The wrongly titled Spanish Civil War is a textbook study of how the battle cry of communism has been used to motivate populations to support the overthrow of some of the world's most democratic elections. The competing parties in Spain's election "consisted of two Republican parties with 126 representatives in the Cortez, ninety-nine socialists, thirty-five Catalan Separatists, and just seventeen Communists" (George Seldes, "The Roman Church and Franco," *The Human Quest,* March–April 1994, pp. 16–18. Also see George Seldes, *Even the Gods Can't Change History* (Secaucus, NJ: Lyle Stuart, 1976), part II, chapter 3. Very few Americans realized the 1984 Nicaraguan election that legitimized the Sandinista government was a replay of the overthrow of the Spanish dictatorship. There were fourteen political parties in the Nicaraguan election and the Communist Party was one of the smallest.

19. Carsten, *Weimar Republic,* especially chapter 8; also Michael N. Dobbowski and Isodor Wallimann, *Radical Perspectives on the Rise of Fascism in Germany* (New York: Monthly Review Press 1989), especially pp. 194–209.

20. J. Noakes and G. Pridham, eds., *Nazism 1919–1945,* vol. 2 (New York: Schocken Books, 1988), p. 626.

21. Ibid.

22. Pool and Pool, *Who Financed Hitler?* pp. 7–8, 19–21.

23. John 8: 42–44; Matthew 27: 24–25. See Litvinoff's *Burning Bush;* Richard L. Rubenstein, *Approaches to Auschwitz: The Holocaust and Its Legacy* (Atlanta: John Knox Press, 1987); Dennis Prager, *Why the Jews: The Reason for Antisemitism* (New York: Simon and Schuster, 1983); Rosemary Ruether, *Faith and Fratricide: The Theological Roots of Anti-Semitism* (New York: Seabury Press, 1974); Peter De Rosa, *Vicars of Christ: The Dark Side of the Papacy* (New York: Crown, 1988); Hal Lindsey, *The Road to the Holocaust* (New York: Bantam Books, 1989); Charles Patterson, *Anti-Semitism: The Road to the Holocaust and Beyond* (New York: Walker, 1982); Edward A. Synan, *The Pope and the Jews in the Middle Ages* (New York: Macmillan, 1965); Abram L. Sachar, *A History of the Jews* (New York: Knopf, 1965); Shlomo Hizak, *Building or Breaking: What Does a Jew Think When a Christian Says "I Love You"?* (San Diego: Jerusalem Center for Biblical Studies and Research, 1985); Lewis Browne, *Stranger Than Fiction: A Short History of the Jews* (New York: Macmillan, 1925); Oberman, *Roots of Anti-Semitism;* Paul E. Grosser and Edwin G. Halperin, *Anti-Semitism: Causes and Effects* (New York: Philosophical Library, 1983). See also Caute, *Great Fear;* Daraul, *A History of Secret Societies;* and Pool and Pool, *Who Financed Hitler,* p. 23, chapter 3; Immanuel Wallerstein, *The Modern World System,* vol. 1 (New York: Academic Press, 1974), pp. 147–56.

24. Burman, *Inquisition;* Henry Charles Lea, *The Inquisition of the Middle Ages* (New York: Citadel Press, 1954), a condensation of his 1887 three-volume monumental work, *A History of the Inquisition of the Middle Ages.*

25. Carl Bernstein, "The Holy Alliance," *Time,* February 24, 1992.

9

Suppressing the Freedom of Others Under the Flag of Freedom

Twentieth-century Inquisitions

A Social Paradigm is a constellation of concepts, values, perceptions and practices shared by a community, which forms a particular vision of reality that is the basis of the way a community organizes itself.

—Fritjof Capra

Three tenets of capitalism are: pay the lowest possible price, charge all the market will bear, and give nothing to anybody. That is great philosophy for power brokers with a monopoly on capital, technology, markets, and military might. It takes no deep thought to realize that these tenets of classical economic philosophy were implanted by an earlier power structure to maximize its claims to the wealth of others. Aristocracy and financial aristocracy, through control of all positions of power in the church and universities, had full control of what was taught. The Social Control belief systems taught were philosophical tenets chosen for the protection of that society and/or its power structure, not philosophical tenets chosen by free thought to maximize the well-being of all within that society— let alone the welfare of the rest of the world's citizens whose natural wealth and labors were confiscated to create the wealth of the imperial centers of capital. As the inequalities of world trade are now structured, caring for the imperial centers not only ignores the well-being of the

periphery but actually is the primary cause of its poverty.

Writing History to Protect Wealth and Power

History is written by the powerful to protect their wealth and power. (Those carefully crafted press releases and carefully crafted recordings of events are the writing of history.) Because all people are trained to be just (a society could survive no other way), destabilizing other societies so as to lay claim to, or retain claim to, their wealth requires creating the belief system of the imperial center that targeted and oppressed people are enemies and/or incompetents.

To justify colonizing the world, confiscating much of the world's wealth, enslaving entire populations to produce that wealth, and actually wiping entire civilizations off the face of the earth in the process, it was necessary to develop a belief system that those in these besieged societies were not really people (they had no soul). When it was no longer possible to ignore the fact that they were people, for continued control of their resources, it was necessary to create the belief system that the indigenous people were incompetent, that they could not run their own affairs (a belief system only now being slowly set aside), and that the technologically advanced and "civilized" society was there to help (a primary aspect of today's belief system).

When the blatant injustices of mercantilist imperialism became too embarrassing, a belief system was imposed that mercantilism had been abandoned and true free trade was in place. In reality the same wealth confiscation went on, deeply buried within complex systems of monopolies and unequal trade hiding under the cover of free trade. Many explanations were given for wars between the imperial nations when there was really one common thread: "Who will control resources and trade and the wealth produced through inequalities in trade?" All this is proven by the inequalities of trade siphoning the world's wealth to imperial centers of capital today just as they did when the secret of plunder by trade was learned centuries ago. The battles over the world's wealth have only kept hiding behind different belief systems each time the secrets of laying claim to the wealth of others have been exposed.

Thus it is that students of statecraft and foreign policy are openly taught that what the people believe is happening is only a control mechanism created through a public education campaign (a polite way of saying propaganda), and those planning the Grand Strategies of state are "defensive realists" or "offensive realists" dealing with the "realities" of the "real" world. Trained to be "realists," students of statecraft are taught to care for their nation's "national interest." Students with the right connections, along with many more who moved up through the corporate, political, and military world, move into the inner sanctums of government, take a pledge of secrecy, and become the Managers of State we have been discussing

throughout this treatise. None of the Managers of State are trained to care for interests of the impoverished world, while those who rose through the corporate, political, and military ranks are deeply ingrained with the need to care for the corporate world and the imperial center. For Managers of State to care for those on the periphery of empire when the confiscation of the natural wealth and labors of that periphery are creating the wealth and power of the imperial center is an oxymoron.

While powerful nations are controlling other people's resources or denying the use of those resources to competing centers of capital, it is necessary to create a belief system that people targeted for covert or overt attack, economically or militarily, are a serious threat to "national security." Of course, the ones under threat are the already impoverished, whose natural wealth and labor products are being siphoned to the powerful developed imperial centers of capital. The belief systems that imperial nations are under military and terrorist threat and these "good" nations are supporting "good" people on the periphery of empire is accomplished through loudly proclaiming this through the now lower-key, but still operational, "Mighty Wurlitzer." Those imposed belief systems establish the parameters of national and international debate and the real problem, monopolies and unequal trade, is not one of the "politically correct" or "economically correct" subjects of discussion.

The low-key approach is used only when there is no serious threat. "No serious threat" means the subject of injustices of imperial centers and unequal trades is far outside the permitted parameters of debate. However, when the threat of loss of power and wealth is high, meaning imperial injustices and unequal trades are being placed on the table for discussion on the periphery of empire, Western cultures engage in massive propaganda and covert destabilizations (both internally and externally), which is exactly what we are taught is done in dictatorships.

After the threat is past, only an occasional violent covert operation is necessary. Populations have been so thoroughly indoctrinated by the propaganda of the Cold War—and there is so little else recorded in articles, books, or history—that the imposed belief system is firmly in place in the social mind. As both the survival and wealth of most citizens of the imperial centers are based on the system as structured, most are firmly within the aura of a society's protective belief system. Extending that belief system to the periphery and maintaining it is what these covert and overt destabilizations are all about.

Whereas the elite and Managers of State know well the Social Control belief systems of the masses exist—after all, they created them—the masses (all institutions below the National Security Council, the State Department, the intelligence services, the few in Congress with security clearances, and other inner-sanctum Managers of State) are unaware they are being controlled so their governments can do throughout the world just what they are warning others wish to do to them: subvert their governments and steal their wealth.

Once a crisis is past and the powerful imperial centers of capital are in one of their relatively peaceful stages, the belief system of the masses requires only minor propaganda pushes to keep it rolling. However, it still requires considerable effort by the powerful nations to strengthen the belief system within the social institutions of dependent nations whose wealth is siphoned away through following that very philosophy. These people are looking for answers to their poverty and proving to them that their well-being depends upon accepting the current inequalities in trade is a neverending job.

It would be a difficult task for a professor or journalist to step back and realize that his or her entire education was a Social Control belief system that had been imposed upon society and had been in place for generations, that had been reimposed by extreme violence, and that these fundamental beliefs had little relevance to reality. Those professors and journalists would instinctively and instantly realize that all the rewards (money, career advancement, acceptance of one's work for publication, acceptance by one's peers, appointments to government posts) were stacked totally in favor of parroting the Social Control belief systems.

After observing those who did stand up being totally ostracized by their peers and denied any of the above described rewards for their achievements, only an insignificant few will stand up. However, after the crumbling of the tiger economies on the periphery, this is changing. Those who question those unjust and unequal policies and provide different answers are starting to find an audience. The threat that embarrassing subjects and philosophies that have been pushed to the margins will develop an audience is uppermost in the minds of Managers of State.

Libel Law: One Mechanism for Locking Journalists into Conduits for Propaganda

If a paper reports a statement made by an authority, it is not liable. A reporter friend was driving by the local airport and watched four people killed as their airplane crashed on landing. He reported the crash and the deaths and went home, where he received a phone call from the Associated Press, who asked "On whose authority?'' ''Mine,'' said the reporter. ''I saw it all.'' ''Not good enough,'' said AP. ''It must be a sheriff, the police department, the coroner, or someone else with authority.'' Media fear of libel suits was dramatically outlined again when *The Ecologist* of Britain shredded its October 1998 issue, which had an article railing against the giant Monsanto chemical corporation. Monsanto's reputation for suing the media effectively censured its critics.[1]

When an authority has said it, and thus the paper is not liable, governments are free to tell the people anything they want in their press releases and it will be printed, while the views of a credible witness who challenges that view will be ignored. Taking advantage of this, government intelligence agencies and information services manufacture reality, much of it pure creation—sometimes, but not always, built upon a small base of reality—but totally distorting the truth.

While ignoring all other claims as propaganda, Western news (and that of much of the rest of the world) comes directly from the CIA's ''Mighty Wurlitzer'' and other intelligence services' presentation of reality. Intelligence agencies' wordsmiths structure every world event to the desired reality. It is this reality that ambassadors and other government agencies hand to reporters. Lower-level officials have to parrot the same words they hear from higher officials. With the many years required to reach such a position of authority, every government official has been through this many times and knows what he or she is expected to say. To deviate from the proper script, no matter how much reality demands it, would incur immediate dismissal. Any accredited reporter who seriously challenges these creations at a presidential news conference or any other high-level news briefing would quickly lose accreditation to attend such briefings. To seriously address these creations as the propaganda they are would immediately place one outside the loop, cost most their jobs, and be instant political suicide. That peer pressure is at the heart of primary belief systems, so little else is heard or read. Thus, children can quickly understand what adults find incomprehensible. Children are honest and have nothing to lose while adults have everything to lose, and following the crowd can quickly quiet their consciences. No one challenges them there, but they would face big challenges if they tried to peel aside any major portion of the Social Control belief systems and expose the truth.

Impositions of Belief Systems Through Corporate-funded Think Tanks

We would do well to study the *Covert Action Quarterly,* put out by dissaffected CIA agents. They recognized that corporate America was imposing Social Control belief systems upon the world under the cloak of false scholarship, the same way America's enemy belief system during the Cold War had been manufactured and also the way Britain imposed the Adam Smith free trade beliefs 200 years ago. This is of such importance, we obtained permission to quote Sally Covington at length. Note how corporate control of information (creation of public opinion) is a close parallel to the post–World War II imposition by intelligence services of these same belief systems:

> Spearheading the assault has been a core group of 12 conservative foundations: the Lynde and Harry Bradley Foundation, the Carthage Foundation, the Charles G. Koch, David H. Koch, and Claude R. Lambe charitable foundations, the Phillip M. McKenna Foundation, The JM Foundation, The John M. Olin Foundation, the Henry

Salvatori Foundation, the Sarah Scaife Foundation, and the Smith Richardson Foundation. . . . From 1992–94, they awarded $300 million in grants, and targeted $210 million to support a wide array of projects and institutions. . . . The 12 have mounted an impressively coherent and concerted effort to shape public policy by undermining—and ultimately redirecting—what they regard as the institutional strongholds of modern American liberalism: academia, Congress, the judiciary, executive branch agencies, major media, religious institutions, and philanthropy itself. They channeled some $80 million to right-wing policy institutions actively promoting an anti-government unregulated market agenda. Another $80 million supported conservative scholars and academic programs, with $27 million targeted to recruit and train the next generation of right-wing leaders in conservative legal principles, free-market economics, political journalism and policy analysis. And $41.5 million was invested to build a conservative media apparatus, support pro-market legal organizations, fund state-level think tanks and advocacy organizations, and mobilize new philanthropic resources for conservative policy change. . . . Conservative foundations also provided $2,734,263 to four right-of-center magazines between 1990 and 1993, including *The National Interest, The Public Interest, The New Criterion,* and *The American Spectator.*[2]

With millions of dollars in funding at their fingertips, conservative institutions have taken

the political offensive on key social, economic, and regulatory policy issues. . . . These institutions have effectively repositioned the boundaries of national policy discussion, redefining key concepts, molding public opinion, and pushing for a variety of specific policy reforms. . . . These groups flood the media with hundreds of opinion editorials. Their top staff appears as political pundits and policy experts on dozens of television and radio shows across the country. And their lobbyists work the legislative arenas, distributing policy proposals, briefing papers, and position statements . . . [The American Enterprise Institute

has] ghost writers for scholars to produce op-ed articles that are sent to the one hundred and one cooperating newspapers—three pieces every two weeks. . . . The Hoover Institution's public affairs office . . . links to 900 media centers across the U.S. and abroad. The Reason Foundation . . . had 359 television and radio appearances in 1995 and more than 1,500 citations in national newspapers and magazines. The Manhattan Institute has held more than 600 forums or briefings for journalists and policy makers on multiple public policy issues and concerns, from tort reform to federal welfare policy. . . . The Free Congress Foundation, in addition to its National Empowerment Television, is publishing NetNewsNow, a broadcast fax letter sent around the country to more than 400 radio producers and news editors. [3]

As Karen Rothmyer wrote sixteen years ago:

"Layer upon layer of seminars, studies, conferences, and interviews [can] do much to push along, if not create, the issues, which then become the national agenda of debate . . . By multiplying the authorities to whom the media are prepared to give friendly hearing, [conservative donors] have helped to create an illusion of diversity where none exists. The result could be an increasing number of one-sided debates in which the challengers are far outnumbered, if indeed they are heard at all." . . . [The Heartland Institute] introduced *Policy Fax* . . . a revolutionary public policy fax-on-demand research service that enables you to receive, by fax, the full text of thousands of documents from more than one hundred of the nation's leading think tanks, publications, and trade associations. *Policy Fax* is easy to use and it's free for elected officials and journalists. . . . The American Legislative Exchange Council and the newer State Policy Network provide technical assistance, develop model legislation, and report about communications activities and conferences. ALEC, well funded by private foundations and corporate contributors, is a powerful and growing membership organization, with almost 26,000 state legislators—more than one-third of the nation's total.

The organization, which has a staff of 30, responds to 700 information requests each month, and has developed more than 150 pieces of model legislation ranging from education to tax policy. It maintains legislative task forces on every important state policy issue, including education, health care, tax and fiscal policy, and criminal justice.[4]

The above quote is describing today's refined methods of information control. Early histories of all developing democracies show power brokers buying up or establishing the major information systems, at that time primarily newspapers. That control has moved from one center of power to other centers of power as those media are sold or taken over, but they are never released to seriously inform the masses, the occasional, or even many, exposés notwithstanding. The foundation belief systems that maintain unequal internal and external trades are not only not challenged, they are heavily promoted.

The corporate-owned media is there to push the Social Control corporate belief systems. Scholars have easy access to the massive literature put out by corporate-funded think tanks. Everyone everywhere feels he or she has independence of thought, but when analyzed most stay safely inside the permitted parameters of debate. For those who dare to write or speak truly independent thought, the market is extremely limited. These heavily funded schools of thought become the belief systems of society (its economic religion) and, as both individuals and society can only function under one belief system, all other belief systems are crowded to the margins.

Those imposed belief systems protecting the powerful surface again and again. (As no society has yet become totally free, a deeper study will find it in all societies throughout history.) Except as a Social Control belief system, there

was no need to latch onto silly theories such as was done in the Great Depression: putting labor to work by digging holes and filling them back up again, shooting pigs and cattle to lower the supply of pork and beef and recreate that market, and protecting crop prices by paying farmers for not growing anything.

Having spent massive effort to suppress Henry George's philosophies, which were spreading rapidly when first introduced, the Managers of State knew well that this sensible economic philosophy was there.[5] However, this philosophy gave equality and rights to all, which meant that unearned wealth had to be given up, and the power brokers were not about to do that. For example: In the 1917 crisis that brought on the Bolshevik Revolution in Russia, in an attempt to avoid total overthrow, the Russian Managers of State (Kerensky in this case) offered to adopt the philosophies of America's Henry George. So they too knew this philosophy for full and equal rights was available and only reached for it in a last-ditch effort to avoid revolution. The Bolsheviks following the philosophy of Karl Marx were in no mood for compromise. They overthrew the provisional government and took over. Now Managers of State of the imperial centers of capital had a new threatening belief system to deal with.

The Residual Effects of McCarthyism in the Halls of Academia and the Media

After World War II, nations throughout the world were taking control of their destiny. The old imperial centers of capital had shattered each other's power, and the former colonial world was breaking free. The only wealth left in the world to suppress those breaks for freedom was in America.

The United States had two Grand Strategy

choices: join the newly emerging nations in their break for freedom or join the old imperial centers of capital in suppressing their freedom. The behind-the-scenes cultural and financial ties to Western, Christian, white Europe were too great; America chose the old imperial nations and the historical record shows that this choice was chiseled in stone decades before.

For 130 years, British intelligence services, the British Diplomatic Service, and British industry financed university systems and think tanks to teach neomercantilist free trade. U.S. intelligence services, the State Department, and multinational corporations took over that role as the British Empire crumbled. Thus most universities and opinion makers in Europe and America preached that Social Control belief system for the next fifty years (1945 to the present).

Within the old imperial centers of capital, for that 180-year period, it was not possible to remain in a position of influence in either government or academia if one promoted anything other than some form of the Social Control belief systems protecting that society. The crisis of the Great Depression created openings for other belief systems but World War II and the following Cold War reimposed those protective beliefs. While McCarthyism was in full swing—painting any progressive philosophy as Communist—it was political, social, and career suicide to be objective and intellectually balanced.

Where European professors had for centuries been the carriers of the Social Control paradigms of imperialism and there was little else taught, there were conscientious professors in the American universities who knew the history of Americans gaining their economic freedom, who knew that most other colonial nations were still under the sway of imperial centers of capital, and who recognized the potential of those former colonies joining the brotherhood of free nations. These idealistic and conscientious professors were recognized authorities whose views would be freely expressed through the media. To take over the imperial mantle and suppress the post–World War II breaks for freedom, it was necessary for the United States to strip these potential carriers of truth and reality out of the universities.

McCarthyism was no aberration of one individual, as recorded in history. Senator Joseph McCarthy was the chosen point man for the House Un-American Activities Committee (whose members themselves were point men for the wealthy and powerful and the first-echelon Managers of State) to strip those professors out of the universities and their thoughts out of the media. Hundreds of professors and thousands of others lost their jobs as both the lower-level Managers of State and the masses (most congresspersons without security clearances, the universities, the media, and the lay intellectuals) were being conditioned to keep their heads down, their mouths shut, and their typewriters silent.[6]

The major universities' rehabilitation of the reputation of these persecuted souls when the Cold War was won (most were dead then) proves even the power brokers of the universities—the very people sworn to provide an honest education to the nation and the world—knew that students, the masses, and the world were being fed a controlled and fraudulent picture of the world. Professors took leaves of absence and were paid to organize the CIA; they then returned to their ivory towers.[7] By not telling their students that they had established a massive propaganda organization that was to put all others to shame, which would have been an honest education, they, and all who knew but remained silent, became propagandists.

The 1975–76 Church Committee and Pike Committee hearings exposed many of these black ops. The thousands of fraudulent books financed by intelligence services (all imperial centers were doing it), the tens of thousands of articles planted all over the world (intelligence agencies of all imperial centers were also doing this, including making movies and newsreels), the massive literature put out by the subsidized think tanks and subsidized academics, the thousands of books written by sincere academics but sourcing all that fraudulent literature being passed off as honest scholarly work, as well as the massive fiction (novels and movies) written to take advantage of the created hysteria—these were the rhetorical thunder of the Cold War.

After thirty to forty years of this hysteria, when honest and sober works were dismissed as the works of radicals, misguided souls, and conspiracy theorists, only a few on the fringes of academia understood how deeply they were involved in suppressing truth through parroting these carefully created belief systems. The truth can be found only through intense research and dedication and few have the time, money, or desire to do that. Thus, although the claim is made that it is long dead, the legacy of McCarthyism and the orthodoxy thus created still rule the halls of academia, the media, and the masses.

By Not Fully Informing the Public, the News Media Eventually Trapped Themselves

In the Introduction, we documented how the CIA, with its worldwide ''Mighty Wurlitzer'' and with the support of other intelligence agencies, controlled the Western world's information systems. Those who were educated under those conditions so far from free thought eventually moved into positions of power and, within the limitations of their power and misinterpretation of free trade, were likely sincere in their efforts to develop the world through free trade. Those who would question free trade as practiced by neomercantilists were kept silenced, at first by McCarthyism's threat to their careers and later, as all such people were seen as allied with an enemy, by peer pressure and lack of financial or identity rewards. As opposed to the certainty of being cast into oblivion if one tried to stand up against the propaganda, those who staked their careers on promoting the cosmopolitan philosophy received high financial and career (identity) rewards.

Thus the Brer Rabbit/don't throw me in the brier patch, neomercantilist, free trade scam became firmly entrenched. To the extent we believe our own Social Control belief system and force these policies on the world, the scam will seriously retard world development, will continually ratchet down the wages of labor in the developed world, could collapse the world economy into a depression, and could again lay the foundations for war. (It does not have to either. If the financial monopolists and military are strong enough, it could freeze the world into the mold of extremely rich and extremely poor.)

While enjoying the followers and income they gained by publishing the Social Control belief system of Cold War hype created by the power structure, the media trapped themselves. Once the nation was fully propagandized, readers and advertisers now controlled the media. With the masses believing enemies were planning to attack them at any moment and intelligence services spending hundreds of millions of dollars continually reinforcing that belief, any media that would dare present a rationalization outside the Cold War belief system would lose both their readers and advertisers in droves.

The market then worked its magic. With the world programmed that there were enemies lurking behind every bush, the occasional scholarly and honest critique could not be sold, while paranoid and hysterical writings, and some total frauds, sold millions.

Providing a Beacon for Intellectuals Throughout the World

Though one would never know it listening to the belief system rhetoric, the efficiencies of centralized planning were crucial to the West's post–World War II success. The Cold War military buildup, the economic rebuilding of the old shattered imperial centers of capital (Japan and West Europe), and the rise of new allied centers of capital (Taiwan and South Korea) to prevent expansion of socialism were all the product of central planning nursing corporate capitalism.

The question of whether socialism and central planning will work or not has been thoroughly settled. The only two functioning economies during the Great Depression were Germany's and the Soviet Union's, both were centrally planned (Germany's only because it had to usurp the rhetoric of National Socialism or be forced by its politically aware labor movement to accept Soviet socialism), and both were building industrial capital faster than had ever been built before.

Because it is viable and thus threatening, socialism has always faced the full military might of capitalism's propaganda. If it were not viable, there would be no need to demonize it. Destabilizations have prevented socialist centers of capital from becoming established, and its efficiencies have been utilized only by dictators attacking socialism (Hitler) and by socialism

defending against not only those attacks but against the ring of steel put around it by the entire allied developed world.

While the well-funded think tanks were pouring out the rhetoric against central planning, covert—and occasionally overt—destabilizations (and the enormous military expenditures of emerging nations defending against the threat of military overthrow) were preventing the Soviet Union, Cuba, and many other nations from putting their economies together. (The hoped-for coopting of China as she develops is still ongoing.) The reason for these destabilizations is obvious: an efficient social system providing a better standard of living for its people becomes a beacon drawing the loyalty of intellectuals and the impoverished worldwide.

The rapid restructuring of the German economy, which successfully cared for its citizens during the depths of the Great Depression even as they were being denied equality in world trade, caught the attention of the world. In every corner of the globe during the crisis of the Great Depression, German "Bunds" were forming. Both the rapidly developing Soviet form of socialism and Germany's rapidly developing Fascist (corporate) socialism were drawing intellectual followers away from neoliberal capitalism that was collapsing under the weight of the Great Depression.

German Fascist National Socialism was little more than Social Darwinist white supremacist ideology protecting the power of German corporate wealth, primarily against British corporate wealth and power. The success of German Fascism would have meant the loss to Britain of a large part of its all-important countryside and the cheap resources that were the foundation for British wealth and power.

The successful rule of labor in the Soviet Union would have meant the industrialization of other nations by that new socialist center of capital and the loss of the countryside for corporate imperialism. As neoliberal capitalism shrank—or even collapsed as the countryside shrank—either capitalism would have had to become efficient, such as we demonstrate cooperative capitalism can, or socialism would have assumed power worldwide.

Maintaining both power and wealth required that both socialism and Fascist National Socialism be contained, and both were contained by military force: World War II contained Germany and the Cold War (on top of the severe Soviet losses in World War II) both contained the Soviet Union and suppressed others' break for freedom worldwide.

Even though most of those attempting breaks for freedom in the former colonial world looked to the United States as their political and economic model, they had the universal danger of popular leaders who were not puppets, leaders who would turn those resources to sustaining their own people. Empires whose economies depended upon the resources of those countries for raw material for their industries would be faced with a disaster of the first order if their countryside gained its economic freedom. Those breaks for freedom had to be suppressed.

Suppressing True Democratic Social Structures

Belief systems are designed to marginalize dangerous thoughts. Indonesia's decision to allow equal representation of all political parties, which led to the overthrow of Sukarno by the CIA, as addressed above, is a leading example. The common people throughout the world had no idea that a democracy was overthrown or, for that matter, that an external power had overthrown it.

The Soviet Union's citizens voting on the issues, not for candidates, and the recall of many representatives who did not vote in the Soviet parliament as instructed by the voters, is another good example.

Many newly free and potentially democratic governments have been backed into a corner through covert activities by the major powers and forced to use repressive violence in attempting to avoid destabilization. This has made the emergence of true democratic governments extremely difficult. All such governments are a threat to neomercantilist (corporate imperialist) governments posing as democracies so they must accept the latters' belief system or they will be covertly destabilized and overthrown.

A battle between an emerging democratic government and some of its own people is assured if an outside power decides to destabilize it. Using both these real examples of suppression and created ones, intelligence agency wordsmiths then paint idealistic leaders of emerging societies as dictators and murderers, the media parrot these press releases and planted news articles, historians are unaware of the origins of those created distorted facts, and created and distorted history becomes recorded history. There have been many violent dictators in history but not as many as history has recorded. Much, if not most, of that violence was externally imposed and those governments were battling both for their survival and for the removal of external control of their economies.

Who Are the Powerful?

So who are the powerful? It could, unwittingly, be you or me. We all have some power. Only it is, through the imposition of belief systems, turned to the protection of what we would never tolerate if we ever knew: the suppression of other peoples' freedom and confiscation of their wealth. After all, most of us unwittingly supported the system as corporate imperialism suppressed breaks for freedom all over the world.

The CIA could not have suppressed those worldwide breaks for freedom without the support of American citizens. The fact that most did not know their government was avoiding democratic choice worldwide through an offensive policy only outlines the imposed belief systems which protect this system of claiming the wealth of others through inequalities of trade. Fully believing they live in a true democracy with a free press and educational institutions of free thought, most Americans find incomprehensible any suggestion that a belief system has been imposed upon them.

Only a small number of the wealthy or moderately wealthy pay any attention to imposing belief systems on the masses but they do provide generous financial support to those who do. The wealthy recognize that it is this belief system that is the source of, and the protection of, their wealth. It is likewise with the middle class. They recognize their living is tied to the current arteries of commerce and thus easily believe their security is under threat. They are totally unaware that much of this wealth comes from their society imposing inequalities of trade on weaker societies and perpetuating others' impoverishment. Thus, a propagandized population provides the power base for Managers of State to inflict such violence upon defenseless people.

Who Are the Violent and Powerful?

A study of CIA power brokers and others deeply involved in leadership positions pushing the Cold War will expose that they all either are powerful corporate lawyers, have close ties to the powerful developed while being in elite educational institutions, have other close ties to wealth, or are themselves extremely wealthy, with substantial investments in the developing world. Thus when Guatemala's elected government was overthrown and a dictator imposed to protect United Fruit, "the head of the CIA, General Walter Bedell Smith, joined the board of the United Fruit Company, while United Fruit's president, Allen Dulles, became CIA director."[8]

John F. and Allen Dulles, both long-term power brokers in the State Department and CIA, came from entrenched wealth and were also corporate lawyers for others of the world's wealthy. Probably no one else except William Casey, another CIA director and leading corporate lawyer coming from old wealth, was in on the planning for the covert actions of the Cold War throughout the CIA's first forty-five years more than they were.

After being pushed into the disastrous Cuban Bay of Pigs invasion in 1961, President John F. Kennedy fired CIA director Allen Dulles, who he felt had misled him into that debacle. President Kennedy was learning fast, and over the next two years it appeared he was going to shut down the Vietnam War and instead lead America to be the peaceful nation it claimed to be. Military power is always the final arbiter between competitive societies and ever since World War II only America's military power protected the imperial centers of capital from the loss of control of world resources and trade, the source of their wealth and power. There did not have to be any rocket scientists among the Managers of State and the corporate powers behind them to know that Kennedy's altruism would cost them dearly. President Kennedy was assassinated and a member of the old-boy CIA network, the recently fired Allen Dulles, decided what evidence was to be presented to the Warren Commission in what most of the world is satisfied was a cover-up of the assassination of an American president by the hard right of American government and intelligence services. America's social fabric would have been shredded by such revelations so those disturbing facts were not addressed by the mainstream media, were never pursued by any law enforcement or legal institution, and remain essentially unknown to the American people.[9] If the truth about this assassination had been vigorously pursued by either major authorities or the mainstream media, America could have become what it claims to be, a government of, for, and by the people.

Where most presidents are firmly under the control of a power structure, Kennedy was not. He was so popular and was so thoroughly trusted by the American people he would have had their full support if he had embarked on a policy of peace. The hundreds of corporate think tanks would not have dared to continue trumpeting for war. A policy of peace would have been so eminently sensible that their followers would have defected en masse if such a peaceful policy by such a popular president were attacked.

If peace had been permitted to break out through such a courageous act by a popular American president, the massive suppressions all over the world would have come to an end. Once a policy of true peace had been put into effect, a president would not even have the option of changing his mind if he wanted to. The cat would have been out of the bag, too many think tanks would be cranking out supporting literature, and a return to a Cold War could be accomplished only by the same method this Cold War was established, by instigating a real war.

Without the covert wars and overt wars of imperial centers of capital, the world would have broken free, the world's resources would no longer have been available to the industrialized world for a fraction of their value, and that would be a loss to corporate imperialists that could not be permitted. The CIA is only an arm of presidential policy when presidential policy is corporate policy. When presidential policy threatens corporate policy, a rare event, a president must figure out how to control the corporate-connected old-boy network of the CIA.

The violent and powerful who carry out corporate policies, such as the above we just described, are good citizens, good neighbors, good husbands, and good parents who kiss their children when they put them to bed. But their loyalty is to their wealth or the wealthy who put them in power. Even when considering what is right for the weaker in their country, they do not expand their view of rights to include all people, as when, to justify their oppression, they expounded a philosophy that colonial natives had no souls and thus were really not people. The rights of others cannot be acknowledged, much less sincerely promoted and enforced. To redefine rights in the broadest sense and act accordingly would not only shatter everything the power brokers have believed in and everything they have done, it would mean a total repudiation of the philosophies the imperial nations have been, and are, functioning under.

Damage Control

If one has any doubts as to how thorough propaganda and thought control are, consider the more than 730 American airmen shot down or crashed as they were flying sabotage and assassination teams into Byelorussia and the Ukraine in the heart of the Soviet Union and photographing Soviet territory, as addressed in Chapter Six.[10]

Much effort went into "damage control" to tone down that explosive story. In later documentaries and feature articles the admission of over 730 airmen lost over the Soviet Union was downgraded to 130, but, knowing they had been deceived once, each documentary noted the story might be much bigger. A few years after the exposure of the covert air assaults on the Soviet Union, a military spokesman said in an interview that "Americans would be surprised if they knew how many airmen had been lost over the Soviet Union and China."

A documentary on the subject of the downed pilots showed their routes over the Baltic Sea and claimed that all planes veered off before going over Soviet territory. That falsification of history—telling a part of the story as the full story and ignoring the major story of the thousands of flights into the heart of the Soviet Union—required both a careful selection of facts by the Pentagon and a cooperative producer. Even as Western citizens were being brought to near hysteria that they were under dire threat of attack, there were no planes from either Eastern Europe or the Soviet Union flying towards the West with teams trained for sabotage and assassination, or any other kind of destabilization.

Imprinted in everyone's mind is that these flights were necessary because the Soviet Union was a military threat and the intelligence to be gathered was crucial. But the facts—that the Soviet Union was devastated by World War II, that it wanted—and desperately sought—peace, and that sabotage teams were being trained and dropped deep into the Soviet Union to hide among their ethnic and religious cousins and sabotage the economy—all discredit that cover story.

The story is even less credible because the real threat was to the Soviet Union, not from it. The massive destruction of the Soviet Union's infrastructure and slaughter of 20 million people (adjusted later to 27 million but announced by Stalin in 1946 as 7 million) in World War II was well known. The West knew that not only was the Soviet Union's infrastructure and economy in no shape to be a military threat, but the necessary propaganda campaign to condition the long-suffering Soviet people to undertake a military offensive against their recent allies, who were militarily far superior, would be impossible. (The Soviets could not legally propagandize for war. Most Americans will be surprised to learn it was against Soviet law to demonize another society.)

Damage control was exercised again when CNN and *Time* magazine spent two years documenting over twenty instances of the use of nerve gas by Americans in Vietnam. The story (Operation Tailwind)—aired and printed in July 1998—was withdrawn, senior editors who stood by their story were fired, others demoted or chastised, and the story was successfully suppressed. Note how that surfacing of true history was quickly erased from history. Such revelations are so damaging to the imposed belief system that protects corporate imperialism, they cannot be permitted to stand.

The CIA's intelligence game is "demonize one's enemies." For that demonization to succeed, it is crucial that all analysis of moral transgressions and arrogant ignoring of international law (actually thousands of acts of war) by the imperial centers of capital be suppressed. That such acts of war could be carried out with relative impunity highlights the immense power of the imperial centers and the weakness of those nations the masses of the West were being told were going to militarily attack them.

Whenever the powerful are challenged, the longstanding tradition of the owners of newspapers backing their editors and editors backing their reporters (at least we have always been told it is so) is blown out the window. Witness reporter Ray Bonner's banishment to obscurity by the *New York Times* for exposing the El Mozote massacre by U.S.-trained soldiers in El Salvador; Robert Parry's departure from *Newsweek* after "path-breaking work on the Iran-Contra scandal"; *The San Jose Mercury News*'s retraction of its exposure of CIA involvement in drug trafficking and subsequent resignation of its star reporter, Gary Webb; and James Fallows' firing from *U.S. News & World Report* for trying to insert a little reality into that publication. This author was especially appreciative of James Fallows' writings and had wondered how his broad and sensible view of the world could ever be tolerated at *U.S. News*. It wasn't.

And if all we have documented to this point is not enough to prove that the West was never under threat of a military attack, that the Managers of State knew this well, and that there was no need for intelligence agencies to alert the West about any such attack, consider this: Immediately after World War II, U.S. intelligence coopted Switzerland's Crypto-Ag (and other encryption companies) to get the codes to supposedly the most secure encryption machines sold to nations all over the world. U.S. intelligence officers read the most secret messages of most nations, friend and foe, as easily as they might read the morning newspapers.[11] American intelligence services not only knew well there was no attack imminent, they knew how weak and defenseless these besieged people really were.

Assassinations and covert actions were the least of what interested the Western powers (they were responsible for most of them anyway) as they read other nations' mail. The economic plans of those nations were their primary interest. Playing the high-stakes diplomatic poker game of international trade with a mirror behind everyone else's back gave the United States an insurmountable advantage in trade negotiations. They knew the most intimate secrets of nonaligned nations attempting to ally together to develop their industries and internal economies.

Few of those nations had any intention of allying their economies with the Soviet Union. Although a nation embargoed by the West would be forced to trade with the Soviet Union, their goal was freedom to control their resources and economies and trade with any nation they chose. (By 1998, seventy countries—66 percent of the people on earth—were under some form of American embargo or sanction.[12] Control of trade hides behind a rhetorical cover of human rights abuses. If a nation is recalcitrant, those human rights abuses provide the legitimacy for sanctions.)

Though hundreds of billions of dollars were spent to destabilize emerging nations, funds can no longer be found to rebuild these shattered nations. Without development funds and without access to technology and markets, the weak are again relegated to providing cheap commodities and labor to imperial centers of capital. However, if the threat of loss of the countryside to imperial centers of capital returns, massive funds will again be available for development of those nations who are crucial as allies and equally massive funds for destabilization of all others.

The current collapsed periphery countries (as of 1999) present a unique problem. If they do not regain their financial and economic health, Adam Smith free trade will be in serious question. Expect modest adjustments of past policies of imperial centers of capital to bring back some health to the periphery, but do not expect the robust growth rates that once were common.

Notes

1. Ben Lilliston, "Shredding 'the Ecologist,'" *The Progressive* (February 1999), p. 39.

2. Sally Covington, "Right Thinking, Big Grants, and Long Term Strategy: How Conservative Philanthropies and Think Tanks Transform U.S. Policy," *Covert Action Quarterly* (Winter 1998), pp. 6–16.

3. Ibid.

4. Ibid.

5. Mason Gaffney and Fred Harrison, *The Corruption of Economics* (London: Shepheard-Walwyn, 1994).

6. Ellen Schrecker, *No Ivory Tower: McCarthyism and the Universities* (New York: Oxford University Press, 1986).

7. Robin W. Winks, *Cloak and Gown: Scholars in the Secret War, 1939–1961* (New York: Quill, 1987).

8. Frederic F. Clairmont, *The Rise and Fall of Economic Liberalism* (Goa, India: The Other India Press, 1996), pp. 7, 18; See also Gerard Colby, *Du Pont: Behind the Nylon Curtain* (Englewood Cliffs, NJ: Prentice-Hall, 1974).

9. B. Hersh, *The Old Boys: The American Elite and the Origins of the CIA* (New York: Charles Scribner's Sons, 1992); Winks, *Cloak & Gown.*

10. Michael Ross, "Yeltsin: POWs 'Summarily Executed,'" *The Spokesman Review,* November 12, 1992, pp. B1, A10; Ernest Volkman and Blaine Baggett, *Secret Intelligence* (New York: Doubleday, 1989), p. 187; John Loftus, *The Belarus Secret* (New York: Alfred A. Knopf, 1982), chapters 5–8, pp. 109–10; William Blum, *The CIA: A Forgotten History* (London: Zed Books, 1986), chapters 6, 7, 8, 15, 17, especially p. 124; see Introduction, note 3.

11. Wayne Madsen, "Crypto Ag: The NSA's Trojan Whore?" *Covert Action Quarterly* (Winter 1998), pp. 36–42.

12. Thomas Omestat, "Addicted to Sanctions," *U.S. News & World Report,* June 15, 1998, pp. 30–31.

Part II

External Trade: Capital Destroying Capital

10

The IMF/World Bank/GATT/NAFTA/ WTO/MAI/Military Colossus

The Enforcers of Structural Adjustments and Unequal Trades

Susan George, author of *A Fate Worse Than Debt,* points out that debt is an excellent mechanism for ensuring that developing world countries will continue to export cheap natural resources to corporate mercantilists.

Debt is an efficient tool. It ensures access to other peoples' raw materials and infrastructure on the cheapest possible terms. Dozens of countries must compete for shrinking export markets and can export only a limited range of products because of Northern protectionism and their lack of cash to invest in diversification. Market saturation ensues, reducing exporters' income to a bare minimum while the North enjoys huge savings. . . . The IMF cannot seem to understand that investing in . . . [a] healthy, well-fed, literate population . . . is the most intelligent economic choice a country can make.[1]

An IMF managing director claimed, "An international institution such as the fund cannot take upon itself the role of dictating social policy and political objectives to sovereign governments." That this, "politely put, is rubbish" is obvious, given the control exerted by the IMF/World Bank/GATT/NAFTA/WTO/MAI/military colossus[2]:

When the WTO replaced GATT on January 1, 1995, all of the GATT rules and its 47 years of

precedents were folded into the WTO. . . . The WTO is an organization of some 500 highly paid professionals, mostly lawyers . . . [which] make significant decisions about international trade out of the public's view. It has no written bylaws, makes decisions by consensus, and has never taken a vote on any issue. It holds no public hearings, and in fact has never opened its processes to the public. . . . Its court-like rulings are not made by U.S.-style due process. Yet WTO today [because it has a dispute settlement mechanism with enforcement powers] rivals the World Bank and International Monetary Fund in global importance. . . . Three minimalist GATT principles continue to operate through the WTO. The first is the famous most-favored-nation status (MFN): Products traded among GATT members must receive the best terms that exist in any bilateral trading agreement. . . . [The second:] Goods produced domestically and abroad must receive the same "national treatment"—equal access to markets. . . . [The third] is "transparency," which requires that any trade protection be obvious and quantifiable—like a tariff. . . . The WTO has the authority to resolve disputes and to issue penalties and sanctions.[3]

IMF/World Bank/GATT/NAFTA/WTO/MAI structural adjustment rules strictly forbid government support of developing world industry. Yet Japan's industry pays possibly only 30 percent for its industrial capital (the public pays the rest). U.S. states and cities pay ransoms (in the form of tax breaks) for industries to be built in their region. High tariffs are placed on imported manufactured products, low or no tariffs on raw materials. An established infrastructure (roads, airports, harbors) is already in place in the developed world, built and maintained with public funds. Agriculture and industry receive enormous support. Germany subsidizes her mining industries to the tune of $85,000 per miner and all Western nations provide tens of billions of dollars in subsidies annually in dozens of different ways to major corporations and farmers. Not only are there massive subsidies and protections for the imperial centers of capital, the United States has some level of embargo against seventy countries, 66 percent of the people on earth.[4] Yet all these advantages for the wealthy world are denied the developing world.

Society is a machine and the well-developed, highly subsidized transportation, education, and research systems of the developed world mean it can produce much more efficiently and cheaply than the undeveloped world. This gives insight into why structural adjustments insisted on by the IMF/World Bank/GATT/NAFTA/WTO/MAI reduce supports in these crucial areas. So long as a belief system can be imposed upon developing nations that is the opposite of how every successful nation developed, they can never be a serious industrial threat to the imperial centers of capital and their resources will always be available to the imperial nations for far less than full value.

The Greatest Peacetime Transfer of Wealth in History

Most Americans are aware of the "Contract with America," the Republican assault on spending (the behind-the-scenes corporate pol-

icy nicknamed Reaganism/Thatcherism) that was intended to cut government spending for environmental care, pollution cleanup, health care, education, welfare, and other essential social services. This corporate assault on labor started in earnest in 1972 and gained substantially more momentum under Reagan in the early 1980s. Even as "the real per capita gross domestic product . . . climbed by a third," before the 1997–99 increase in labor pay, that policy had reduced wages for 80 percent of Americans, with the poor losing the most. Simultaneous with that loss, the share of the national income and national wealth held by the wealthy climbed to levels normally seen only before collapse of economic bubbles or revolutions. The income share of America's richest 20 percent and poorest 20 percent stood at 30: 1 in 1970 and at 78:1 in 1999. "Probably no country has ever had as large a shift in the distribution of earnings without having gone through a revolution or losing a major war."[5]

Gone unnoticed by most in the developed world but felt crucially in the developing countries were the same assaults ongoing against the developing world. The Reagan/Bush team had, through their monopolization of finance capital (financial warfare), imposed a far more severe Reaganism/Thatcherism on the world. During their twelve years at the helm of government, IMF/World Bank loans came with structural adjustment conditions: all who take their loans to devalue their currency, lower their import barriers, remove restrictions on foreign investments, remove subsidies for local industry, lower their social welfare funding, pay lower wages, reduce government in general, and expand production and export of their timber, minerals, and agriculture. The result was almost universally the same: wages went down, hunger increased, health care decreased, education decreased and, most important because this is the primary purpose of it all, the price of Third World export commodities went down.[6]

Meanwhile, these same Managers of State did precisely the opposite for poorer nations within their trading bloc. They easily agreed that West Germany must put $1.5 trillion into the former East Germany to simultaneously build industry, social infrastructure, and buying power.[7] And when Greece, Portugal, and Spain, relatively poorer than the rest of Europe, wanted to join the Common Market, these leaders implemented a fifteen-year plan that reads as if it came right out of Friedrich List's protectionist classic. This included "massive transfers of direct aid . . . to accelerate development, raise wages, regularize safety and environmental standards, and improve living conditions in the poorer nations."[8] Emerging former colonies receive no such care for developing consumer buying power and protection of tender industries so their economies can become viable.

This is a pure mercantilist policy of enforced dependency guiding the wealth of the countryside to current imperial centers of capital. It worked just as intended. In 1970, the poorest 20 percent of the world's people received 2.2 percent of the world's income while the richest 20 percent received 70 percent. By 1990, the poorest 20 percent received only 1.4 percent while the richest 20 percent received 83.4 percent.[9] When the universal result is low resource export prices and increased poverty in the Third World, the IMF/World Bank/GATT/NAFTA/WTO/MAI/military colossus can hardly claim its intent was to develop those countries:

> Structural Adjustment [demanded by the IMF] is best summed up in four words: earn more, spend less. While such advice might be valid if it were given to only a few countries at once, dozens of debtors are now attempting to earn more by ex-

porting whatever they have at hand; particularly natural resources including minerals, tropical crops, timber, meat and fish. With so many jostling for a share of limited world markets, prices plummet, forcing governments to seek everhigher levels of exports in a desperate attempt to keep their hard currency revenues stable. The "export-led growth" model on which the fund and the World Bank insist is a purely extractive one involving more the "mining" than the management—much less conservation—of resources.[10]

Susan George's "earn more, spend less" is nothing less than a quick snapshot of futile attempts to break out of debt traps. These efforts are futile because trades are so unequal that the weak and impoverished just go deeper into debt as their irreplaceable resources flow to the imperial centers of capital to service their everincreasing debt with its compounding interest.

Producing for Local Consumption Is Not the Purpose of IMF/World Bank Loans to the Periphery of Empire

"The IMF has repeatedly stated that it is not, and was never intended to be, a *development* institution." Neither was the World Bank: "The fundamental goal of creating markets for industrialized countries' exports was written into [their] charter."[11] That means that debt traps and mercantilist dependency were the goals all along. Most investment in the developing world has been geared toward producing low-priced commodities for corporate industries to fabricate into products for the developed world. Investing in development of resources to produce the same product in various parts of the world ensures a surplus of those commodities at low, or very low, prices. The need to service its debts compels the dependent developing world to produce more and more of the commodities desired by the developed world. Through simultaneous investments in various parts of the world in commodities desired by the developed world, surpluses develop and, as those low wages ensure there is little buying power and thus no markets in the developing world, prices are kept low for the imperial centers of capital. It is really the old colonial plantation system that once produced for Europe, restructured on a massive scale to produce for the industrialized world.[12] (Please consider the subchapter "The Periphery of Empire Functions as a Huge Plantation System Providing Food and Resources to the Imperial Center" of Chapter Thirteen as an integral part of this subchapter.)

The IMF/World Bank/GATT/NAFTA/WTO/MAI colossus lays down the rules of unequal trade and the military forces of the imperial nations are there, as a last resort, to enforce the rules. The developing world is expected to lower its living standards and export more minerals, lumber, and food, all to pay debts that did little for its economic development. Typically those debts were incurred for investments to extract resources, produce agricultural exports, and build the infrastructure to ship these commodities to the developed world. From the late nineteenth century to shortly before World War II, when empires had absolute control of their colonies, the price of primary commodities dropped 60 percent relative to manufactured commodities prices.[13] That nineteenth-century success of low import prices and high export prices for the imperial centers of capital has been far exceeded under the flag of free trade in the twentieth century.

Investment in the same primary-export commodities throughout the developing world competes for markets, creating surpluses and low export prices. As those export commodity surpluses build, there is little investment in local industry for local consumers. As wages are too low to provide buying power, the products and services needed for the local population's everyday use are not produced within that society and thus there is no balance of industry, social capital, local purchasing power, commerce, and markets for a prosperous market economy. The dependent countries end up "producing too much of what [they do not] consume, and consuming too much of what [they do not] produce." This denies these people their natural comparative advantage and creates dependent economies. Then, while the prices of developing world commodities plummet because of excessive investments in export products (as opposed to balanced investments in a regional economy to create buying power), the prices of developed world products soar, the very signature of a successful mercantilist dependency policy.[14]

In only seven years, the price of a tractor for Tanzania, measured by the export value of Tanzanian sisal, doubled. The relative value for rubber exporters dropped 300 percent between 1960 and 1975. Cotton exporters lost 60 percent of their buying power in the same time span.[15] In 1996, prices for primary commodities exported by the developing world were the same price as twenty-one years earlier while prices for its imported manufactured products had soared, forcing the developing world to export more and more while importing less and less. The IMF/World Bank/GATT/NAFTA/WTO/MAI imposes these austerity measures but seldom restricts the purchase of arms, toys for the elite, or consumer purchases from the developed world.

To become prosperous or maintain prosperity, the developed nations know they must educate their citizens, they must provide them with health care, they must build transportation systems so people and goods can be moved, they must support the building of efficient industries to process their natural resources, they must pay their labor well to produce consumer buying power, they must maintain a healthy economic multiplier through a proper balance between manufacture of their own consumer products and their imports and exports, and they must not permit their wealth to be claimed by another center of capital through unequal trades.

However, Managers of State of the imperial centers of capital simply do not stand up and acknowledge that what is right for the wealthy nations is even more right for the impoverished world whose resources and labor are exploited for the benefit of imperial centers of capital. Their slogans of peace and rights are not only meaningless, they are actually covers for financial, economic, diplomatic, covert, and overt warfare. After all, these Managers of State have spent centuries perfecting the political, legal, and military mechanisms that maintain the rules of trade in their favor. These Managers of State are highly intelligent, they have massive resources, they are not working in a vacuum, and they are not reacting to oppression upon the imperial center. They are only reacting to others' efforts to break out from under their oppressions. We have provided only a broad outline of the Grand Strategies of corporate imperialists. Author Robin Hahnel explains what happens when the financial warfare plans, the economic warfare plans, and the diplomatic warfare plans succeed and all the ducks are lined up in a row for the corporate imperialists to slaughter:

> Multinational corporations and banks will soon have reacquired the most attractive economic assets the third world has to offer, at bargain base-ment prices. They may succeed in doing this in a fraction of the time—the next 3 to 5 years—it took progressive and nationalist third world movements and governments to [regain] control of their natural resources from colonial powers— 50 to 100 years. . . . All of the gains of the great anti-imperialist movements of the 20th century may soon be wiped out by the policies of neoliberalism [corporate imperialism] and its ensuing global crisis. What may become the greatest asset swindle of all time works like this: International investors lose confidence in a third world economy, dumping its currency, bonds, and stocks. At the insistence of the IMF, the central bank in the third world country tightens the money supply to boost domestic interest rates to prevent further capital outflow in an unsuccessful attempt to protect the currency. Even healthy domestic companies can no longer obtain or afford loans so they join the ranks of bankrupted domestic businesses available for purchase. As a precondition for receiving the IMF bailout the government abolishes any remaining restrictions on foreign ownership of corporations, banks, and land. With a depreciated currency and a long list of bankrupt local businesses, the economy is ready for the acquisition experts from Western multinational corporations and banks who come to the fire sale with a thick wad of almighty dollars in their pockets. . . . [In Thailand alone,] ''foreign investors have gone on a $6.5 billion shopping spree this year [1999], snapping up bargain basement steel mills, securities companies, supermarket chains, and other assets.''[16]

Security of the state has required control of resources and markets ever since social wealth started being produced by simple industrial technology centuries ago. That control of resources has been transferred to private ownership. Corporations have the same need for control of resources and markets that states once had. They exercise that control through controlling the rules of trade and thereby governments and military forces, which impose *their* unequal rules of trade upon others. In a final analysis, if control cannot be maintained by financial, economic, and diplomatic means, then the covert forces are called upon. If those combined efforts cannot stem a break for freedom on the periphery of empire, the navy, marines, and army are called out.

Providing Friedrich List Supports for the Developed World While Imposing Adam Smith Structural Adjustments upon the Developing World

"The developing world has a simple answer to the question of primitive accumulation [of capital]: the West stole it."[17] The wars over resources and markets, the poverty within the underdeveloped world, and the poverty remaining in the "wealthy" countries all testify to the bankruptcy of this residual neomercantilist, corporate mercantilist policy as a route to a truly free and prosperous world.

The IMF/World Bank/GATT/NAFTA/WTO/MAI/military colossus insists that nations on the periphery of empire reduce their education, reduce their health care, eliminate supports for industry, reduce the wages of an already impoverished labor force, and enforce the developed world's monopoly on industrial technology. The entire process imposes unequal trades upon the periphery of empire.

The funds to purchase industries, when weak nations are forced to privatize publicly owned businesses, are primarily in the developed world. Thus, the same powerful people who impose these harsh conditions upon the weak are the ones who buy up their resources and industries at a fraction of true value when those harsh conditions trigger a collapse. Not only does privatizing the world's industries and resources under corporate imperialism provide opportu-

nities for the investment of monopolized capital and control of industries, resources, and markets, but a portion of that monopolized capital (a small portion) owned by the emerging "robber barons" of the dependent nations gives the appearance of equality and makes it difficult to identify and target a nation, or block of nations, as an enemy imposing the harsh conditions of financial warfare.

That the structural adjustments forced upon the developing world are exactly opposite the policies under which every wealthy nation developed tells us the Managers of State of the imperial centers of capital know exactly what they are doing. Their Grand Strategy is to impose mercantilist unequal trades, that formula of the high pay divided by the low pay squared, as outlined in Chapter One, to lay claim to the natural wealth and the labors of weak nations.

Notes

1. Susan George, *A Fate Worse Than Debt* (New York: Grove Weidenfeld, 1990), pp. 143, 187, 235.

2. Ibid., chapter 3, especially pp. 53, 93.

3. Howard Wachtel, "Labor's Stake in WTO," *The American Prospect* (March/April 1998), pp. 34–38.

4. Laura Karmatz, Alisha Labi, and Joan Levinstein, Special Report, "States at War," *Time,* November 9, 1998, pp. 40–54; Donald L. Bartlett and James B. Steele, "Fantasy Island and Other Perfectly Legal Ways That Big Companies Manage to Avoid Billions in Federal Taxes," *Time,* November 16, 1998, pp. 79–93; Donald L. Bartlett and James B. Steele, "Paying a Price for Polluters," *Time,* November 23, 1998, pp. 72–82; *The Banneker Center's Corporate Welfare Shame Links,* http://www.progress.org/banneker/cw.html, Thomas Omestat, "Addicted to Sanctions," *U.S. News & World Report,* June 15, 1998, pp. 30–31.

5. Richard Douthwaite, "Community Money," *Yes* (Spring 1999), pp. 35–37; "In Fact," *The Nation,* March 25, 1996, p. 7.

6. Duncan Green, *Silent Revolution* (London: Cas-

sel, 1995), pp. 22–57, especially pp. 44, 50, 100–111, 131–36, 200–22; Susan George and Fabrizio Sabelli, *Faith and Credit* (San Francisco: Westview Press, 1994), pp. 18–19, 31–33, 65–72, 126–25, especially 130–34, 161, 216–22; Graham Hancock, *Lords of Poverty* (New York: Atlantic Monthly Press, 1989).

7. Lester Thurow, *Head to Head: The Coming Economic Battle Between Japan, Europe, and America* (New York: William Morrow, 1992), p. 89.

8. AFL-CIO Task Force on Trade bulletin (1992).

9. Harry Magdoff, ''A Note on the Communist Manifesto,'' *Monthly Review* (May 1998), p. 12.

10. Susan George, *The Debt Boomerang* (San Francisco: Westview Press, 1992), pp. 2–3.

11. Arnold J. Chien, ''Tanzanian Tales,'' *Lies of Our Times* (January 1991), p. 9. See also Michael Barratt Brown, *Fair Trade* (London: Zed Books, 1993), p. 108.

12. See the subchapters ''Conceptually Reversing the Process of Impoverishing Other Nations Through Selling Cheap Commodities'' and ''The Periphery of Empire Functions as a Huge Plantation System Providing Food and Resources to the Imperial Center'' in Chapter 13; also Duncan Green, *Silent Revolution,* especially chapter 4; Hancock, *Lords of Poverty;* George and Sabelli, *Faith and Credit;* Philip Agee and Louis Wolf, *Dirty Work* (London: Zed Books, 1978), chapter 11.

13. Frederic F. Clairmont, *The Rise and Fall of Economic Liberalism* (Goa, India: The Other India Press, 1996), p. 308.

14. Hancock, *Lords of Poverty,* pp. 47–75, especially p. 65; George, *Fate Worse Than Debt,* especially pp. 62, 78.

15. Susan George, *How the Other Half Dies* (Montclair, NJ: Allen Osmun, 1977), p. 17. The developing world exports sugar and imports candy, exports iron and imports machinery, exports timber and imports paper, exports oil and imports fuel and petroleum products, etc.

16. Robin Hahnel, ''Capitalist Globalism in Crisis,'' *Z Magazine* (March 1999), pp. 52–57.

17. Walter Russell Mead, *Mortal Splendor* (Boston: Houghton Mifflin, 1987), p. 197.

11

The IMF/World Bank/GATT/NAFTA/ WTO/MAI/Military Colossus

Emerging Corporate Mercantilism

With technology and access to markets already broadly dispersed among Cold War allies and even China being wooed away from the Soviet Union by promised access to markets and technology, corporations stood to lose their monopoly on technology if they remained within national borders behind a neomercantilist free trade shield. Even if a developed world factory were far ahead in technology, market share could be lost to a corporation in a developing nation using older technology but paying extremely cheap wages.

With corporate fronts already established in thirty-nine tax havens around the world and firm neomercantilist control of the national policies of both strong and weak nations (a reversible condition), corporate industries began moving offshore, essentially becoming stateless, and laying the foundation for corporate mercantilism.

To avoid sharing those quasi-aristocratic privileges with labor, control of the economies of other countries from the bastion of protective laws of another nation is the norm. Different forms of this process have constituted proto-mercantilism, mercantilism, and neomercantilism for over 800 years. Today it is taking the form of corporate mercantilists moving their wealth offshore where they can avoid paying their share of taxes, avoid environmental laws,

extort subsidies from desperate communities, pay subsistence wages to extract and process rich natural resources, and sell their manufactured products in any market. Mercantilist unequal trades enforced by the military power of the state are the very signature of mercantilist colonial empires.

Fifty years after the Bretton Woods agreement established the rules for post–World War II banking, the respected *U.S. News and World Report* commented: "Under the Bretton Woods system, the Federal Reserve acted as the world's central bank. This gave America enormous leverage over economic policies of its principal trading partners." Richard Douthwaite outlines how retaining the central bank's right to create the world's trading currency appropriated essential rights of other trading nations:

> Currencies produced by one group for use by another have been instruments of exploitation and control. For example, whenever Britain, France, or one of the other colonial powers took over a territory during the "scramble for Africa" towards the end of the [eighteenth] century, one of their first actions was to introduce a tax on every household that had to be paid in a currency that the conquerors had developed for the purpose. The only way the Africans could get the money to pay the tax was to work for their new rulers or supply them with crops. In other words, the

tax destroyed local self-reliance, exactly as it was designed to do. . . . Very little has changed. Over 95 percent of the money supply in an industrialized country is created by banks lending it into existence. These banks are usually owned outside of our areas, with the result that we have to supply goods and services to outsiders even to earn the account entries we need to trade among ourselves. Our district's self-reliance has been destroyed just as effectively as it was in Africa, and whatever local economy we've been able to keep going is always at the mercy of events elsewhere, as the current world economic crisis is making too clear.[1]

The rules of modern world trade (the IMF/ World Bank/GATT/NAFTA/WTO/MAI) defined by corporations, and those rules enforced by the financial and military might of powerful nations essentially governed by those same corporations, define today's world trade as corporate imperialism.

Besides the military, which is the final arbiter, the power of the imperial centers of capital to lay claim to the wealth of the developing world rests in their monopolization of finance capital. No bank in the world will loan to a country blacklisted by the World Bank. To obtain funding from any bank, developing world governments must adjust their policies (called structural adjustments) to the dictates of the ''corporate utopian'' IMF/World Bank/ NAFTA/GATT/WTO/MAI/military colossus. It is specifically under the imposed structural adjustment rules of that colossus that protections for the fast developing nations were withdrawn.

Not only is the developing world locked within the parameters of the decisions of international capital, if any developed world government veers from the prescribed path, enough capital will flee to turn the economy downward, the politicians (not the finance monopolists) will be blamed and—to maintain themselves within

the good graces of the voters—the politicians will bend to the wishes of capital, even if it is to the detriment in the long run of the nation of their birth or of the world.

The Cold War was only an instrument of interim control as the world was guided towards the acceptance of rule by corporations with the IMF/World Bank/NAFTA/GATT/WTO/MAI colossus backed by their financial and economic power and allied nations' military power in which corporations have the dominant voice on the priority for foreign policy—enforcing its laws.

We must remember that the pre–World War II power structure of both Germany and Japan was a corporate-dominated alliance of wealth and government to protect and expand their empires. This alliance and the violence of those empires are the defining attributes of Fascism. Transnational corporations have applied the principles of Fascism to their attempt at world rule. As they effectively run the major governments of the Western world, the above described banking/trade agreement/military colossus effectively rules the world. Under the umbrella of the Cold War, that colossus established an unseen (except when the military is activated) world government ruled by stateless multinational corporations superseding the laws of the most powerful countries. As it is ruled dictatorially and not democratically (weak nations are essentially voiceless), that is a corporate-ruled empire.

The Legal Structure for Corporate Imperialism

Averell Harriman, Dean Acheson, and George Marshall, three of America's leading post–World War II State Department Cold War planners, ''devoted a great deal of time and energy formulating the legal structure for the transition to corporate imperialism. The General Agreement on Tariffs and Trade (GATT), signed by twenty-eight nations in Geneva on October 30, 1947 (later to become the World Trade Organization, [WTO] and to be strengthened further by the Multilateral Agreement on Investments, MAI [yet to be approved but sure to be even if under another name]), was to be the cornerstone of this new world."[2]

> [A]ny member can challenge, through the WTO, any law of another member country that it believes deprives it of benefits it is expected to receive from the new trade rules. This includes virtually any law that requires import goods to meet local or national health, safety, labor, or environmental standards that exceed WTO accepted international standards. . . . [Both national and local government] must bring its laws into line with the lower international standard or be subject to perpetual fines or trade sanctions. . . . Conservation practices that restrict the export of a country's own resources—such as forestry products, minerals, and fish products—could be ruled unfair trade practices, as could requirements that locally harvested timber and other resources be processed locally to provide local employment.[3]

With the intention of imposing a fait accompli upon an unaware world, negotiations on the Multilateral Agreement on Investment (MAI) were held in secret for two years and were still under negotiation in late 1998. This agreement is designed to grant transnational investors the unrestricted "right" to buy, sell, and move businesses and other assets wherever they want, whenever they want. It would ban regulatory laws now in effect around the globe and preempt future efforts to hold transnational corporations and investors accountable to the public. The intent of the backers (the United States and the European Union) is to seek assent from the twenty-nine countries that comprise the OECD (Organization for Economic Cooperation and Development) and then push the new accord on the rest of the world.

GATT/NAFTA/WTO guidelines for food purity standards would be those of the heavily corporate-influenced Codex Alimentarius Commission, an obscure agency in Rome that issues advisory food standards often much weaker than those of the United States.[4] Labor leaders are essentially excluded from designing and negotiating GATT/NAFTA/WTO/MAI agreements and their rights are only addressed in the breach.[5] World banking and trade rules are designed for corporations by corporate lawyers to obscure the real meaning, leaving affected parties all over the world to decipher what those agreements really say. For example, it was a requirement of the 1974 Trade Act that labor be included in trade negotiations but the Labor Advisory Committee was given a text of the NAFTA agreement only twenty-four hours before its comments were due to be filed (September 9, 1992). Those several hundred pages would have required weeks of study by the world's best minds to be fully understood.[6] The current plan under negotiation, known as the Dunkel Plan,

> if approved, would give GATT a "legal personality," known as the Multilateral Trading Organization (MTO) [later organized as the World Trade Organization or WTO], that could strictly enforce global trading laws . . . MTO [now WTO] will have the power to pry open markets throughout the world. . . . The proposed agreement would also extend GATT oversight from "goods" (machinery for instance) to "services" (insurance, banking). In order to protect trade in services, GATT would guarantee intellectual property rights—granting protection for patents and copyrights . . . MTO would have the authority to restrict a developing nation's trade in natu-

ral resources (goods) if it didn't allow a first world country's financial service company sufficient access to its markets . . . GATT panels may some day rule on the trade consequences of municipal recycling laws or state and local minority set-aside programs. In any trade dispute, the nation whose law is challenged must prove its law is not a trade barrier in secret hearings. The new GATT says plainly, "Panel deliberations shall be secret." Under this system, newly elected federal executives could allow the trade or environmental laws of their predecessors to be overturned by mounting a lackluster defense of the laws. And since the defense would occur in secret, without transcripts, interest groups and the public would never know the quality and vigor of the defense. Environmental or health and safety laws (and possibly labor rights and human rights laws) affecting another nation's commerce, no matter how well intended, will be more easily challenged. Again, the executive branch from the challenged nation would defend the law in star-chamber proceedings in Geneva—out of view of media and interest groups back home.[7]

David C. Korten titled his book *When Corporations Rule the World,* pointing out,

> the burden of proof is on the defendant to prove the law in question is not a restriction of trade as defined by the GATT. . . . Countries that fail to make the recommended change within a prescribed period face financial penalties, trade sanctions, or both. . . . The WTO is, in effect, a global parliament composed of unelected bureaucrats with the power to amend its own charter without referral to legislative bodies. . . . [It] will become the highest court and most powerful legislative body, to which the judgments and authority of all other courts and legislatures will be subordinated.[8]

Through the above-described colossus, multinational corporations have gained control of other countries' internal policies, a reestablished colonialism that has colonized both the developed and undeveloped worlds. These laws, essentially created by corpoations, can bypass national laws protecting environments and economies throughout the world. Legal challenges are now starting to come in (1998), and the rulings—all made behind closed doors and not subject to challenge or appeal—have sided with the corporations. Early examples are the Canadian government being prevented from protecting its Pacific salmon runs; forced to abandon strengthening pesticide laws; blocked from enacting laws to reduce emissions of lead, zinc, and copper from smelters; blocked from banning dangerous chemicals in fuels; and prevented from setting up a single-payer automobile insurance plan modeled on Canada's national health insurance system, which, as the insurance chapter of this author's *The World's Wasted Wealth 2* demonstrates, could have saved consumers 50 percent in insurance costs.[9] Nations' laws denying the right to market fish catches by trawlers who use netting methods that fail to protect turtles, dolphins, and other endangered species and thousands of other environmental protection laws can be overruled by what amounts to a court system established, run, and the decisions made, by corporations.

The legal changes necessary to break the multinational corporations' control of valuable world resources and profitable markets, and their control over labor, are not permitted under corporate utopian world banking and trade agreement guidelines. Those guidelines, backed by financial and military power (exercised through control of foreign policy of governments), lock the world into the corporate mercantilist system of siphoning the world's wealth to these enormous blocks of international corporate capital that have no loyalty to any country, or anyone, except themselves.

The siphoning of the wealth of weak nations

to wealthy citizens domiciled in mother countries and subject to the laws of that country is being replaced by a legal system to siphon the wealth of both the developed and developing world to stateless corporations domiciled in offshore tax havens and subject to no law but their own. For example, suppose: (1) country A has wage rates averaging ten dollars an hour, environmental laws that prevent pollution and increase the cost of production, and equal property and income taxes on corporations; (2) country B's wage rates are one dollar an hour, it has no environmental laws, and low taxes for corporations.

The corporate boardroom response, and the foundation which gives corporate mercantilists more power than nations, would be transfer pricing: (1) on paper, move their headquarters to, or establish a subsidiary in, a third country tax haven; (2) build their factory in a low-wage developing country with a low unit cost of production, say ten dollars; (3) invoice (bill) their production to the offshore tax haven at a price that leaves no profit, that same ten-dollar production cost; (4) invoice that production from the tax haven to a high-wage country at a price that will show a profit in the paper corporation in the tax haven and none in the real corporation in the high-wage country, let's say thirty dollars per unit; (5) ship their products directly from the low-wage developing country to the high-wage developed country; and (6) bank those tax-free profits in the tax haven which is nothing more than a mailing address and a plaque on a door.

No products touch that offshore entity; even the paperwork is done in corporate home offices. In 1980, there were 11,000 such corporations registered in the Cayman Islands alone, which has a population of only ten thousand. William Walker, whose firm held the record for the number of fictitious corporations, says, "We are directors of about 500 of them. . . . We funnel a lot of money out of Central and South America." Corporate mercantilists are doubly insulated from accountability. "Of the thousand American holding companies that control U.S. firms and their subsidiaries throughout the world, *six hundred have their registered offices in Switzerland.*"[10] With thirty-nine tax havens worldwide, this is a conservative analysis.[11]

Between the price contracted in the emerging world and the sales price in the developed world, there is room for huge profits. Studies have shown developing world labor is paid less than 2 percent the value of clothes and toys sold on the U.S. market and, through underpaying labor (go deep enough and most costs are labor—labor builds industrial capital and harvests those resources), the total production costs of those imported products are 5 percent those of production costs in the United States.[12]

As the laws now stand, a corporation practicing this "transfer pricing" (and almost all transnationals do) could pocket the greater share of the wholesale value of production. The wealth of the low-wage country would continue to be siphoned to those imperial centers of capital, and the high-wage country would have its wealth siphoned to the powerful company's bank account in the offshore tax haven. This, of course, is neomercantilism restructured into corporate mercantilism functioning to perfection, siphoning the wealth of both the impoverished periphery and the imperial center.

Those corporate owners will abandon any country that restricts what they view as their rights and move their wealth to a country that has few, or no, financial scruples. The reason is greed. "Transnational entities [are] loyal only to themselves. To continue making exaggerated profits, they are quite willing to sell the U.S.

economy [or any other economy] down the drain.''[13] Corporations would have no such powers of extortion if the world were relatively equally developed and labor relatively equally paid. But with legal protections stripped from labor and communities, only the logic of capital functions. The inequalities of world development and labor pay, combined with the vastly increased mobility of capital, provide the framework for siphoning the wealth of both the developed world and developing world to stateless corporations. If capital maintains control of the world's legislative bodies, labor's earnings will continue their rapid decline and capital will extract ever more of the world's surplus wealth to itself.

Here is where the logic of capital, as currently structured and taught, falls apart and exposes this massive accumulation of the world's wealth as only a cover for the same greed that has collapsed societies since time immemorial.[14] As the buying power of the middle class declines, capital will continue to destroy capital battling for that limited or even shrinking market. The world will continue its equalization march towards the lowest common denominator, which is the subsistence wages of the steadily declining labor requirements necessary to operate the steadily declining economic system.

So long as capital sets it own rules, and so long as current developed world labor remains at a higher level and developing world labor remains at a lower level, the logic of capital grasping for every surplus in every niche in the economy will reach into the mass of unemployed humanity for lower-paid labor and the march towards the lowest common denominator will continue.

The flaw is in capitalism's foundation philosophy. Surplus, by Adam Smith's law of wages, is nothing more than wealth produced above subsistence. If we are to follow the philosophy that labor is to be paid only a subsistence wage, we are following a philosophy of no middle class; there will only be the impoverished masses, the enormously wealthy, and a few well-to-do managing the wealth confiscation (surplus appropriation) system.

Thinking in Terms of Units of Production Exposes the Errors of Adam Smith and Affirms the Need for Cooperative Capitalism

The key is to design a social policy to maintain, rather than abandon, efficient ''production units.'' Corporate mercantilists moving to areas with cheap labor, tax breaks, ransom payments, and no environmental protections are transferring to society what are properly industrial production costs and banking those unpaid costs as profits.

While the buying power of the developed nations lasts, building industry in a low-wage country and selling to buyers in a high-wage society—while protecting that accumulated wealth through offshore front corporations—returns to the wealth-confiscation rates of a century ago, when labor had no power. Where the United States had a century of gaining rights and wealth, the past twenty-four years have, through the power of corporate mercantilism, seen a loss of rights for labor, and thus a loss of wealth for nonsupervisory labor.

To understand that this is a massive throwing away of wealth, one need only think in terms of ''units of production,'' such as a farm. No one would consider shutting down and abandoning a farm (a unit of production) and moving to an equally productive farm (an equal unit of production) on the other side of the world because labor is cheaper. Instead, the farm is sold to another farmer, the first farmer moves, and both units of production are kept producing, providing food for their regions and selling their surplus to the world. Idle land alongside of hungry people would be an oxymoron. Yet that is exactly what happens when industries are abandoned and rebuilt thousands of miles away.

Hunger while a region's most productive land is producing for export to the developed imperial centers of capital outlines the obvious: the developed world has firm control over the resources of its countryside, the impoverished Third World. Pick any consumer item—stoves, refrigerators, utensils, tractors, trucks, shoes, cloth, clothes, cars, or steel—virtually any item you think of is desired and typically badly needed by people in many parts of the world. If the previous perfectly good factory producing any one of those consumer items had continued producing instead of shutting down, the productive capacity of those ''units of capital'' would be double over today's subtly monopolized system and, through payment of adequate wages so labor could have buying power and the circulation of money within the local economy would produce more buying power, those new factories could be producing for the impoverished world.

The concepts that need reevaluation are: measurement of that wasted capital, rights of all people to their share, and the logic of increasing the buying power of needy people to expand the market to them rather than shutting down perfectly good factories (productive units), building others on the other side of the world, and shipping their production back around the world to the same consumers. The system, as structured, is designed to monopolize the tools of production, maintain the flow of resources to developed world industries at a fraction of their

value, and maintain the flow of manufactures to the same developed world consumers. This is identical to the monopolization of the tools of production and control of the countryside (control of industrial capital, resources, and trade) that took place when imperial centers of capital siphoned the wealth of the countryside centuries ago.

Although using the comparative advantages of soil and climate to trade bananas, grapes, wool, and cotton is fine, shipping manufactured products halfway around the world to another industrial society, when that region has the surplus resources and labor to produce its own, is economic (and ecological) insanity. There is no gain to the world in destroying an already efficiently operating factory and rebuilding an identical one elsewhere because the corporate mercantilists wish to move to areas without labor rights, environmental protection laws, or adequate taxes to build and maintain social infrastructure. Today's policies only look efficient because the primary measurement used is the corporate bottom line, which measures not only the corporate mecantilists' productivity, as they would have you believe, but also their excessive accumulation of wealth produced by, and siphoned from, others.

Notes

1. Richard Douthwaite, ''Community Money,'' *Yes* (Spring 1999), pp. 35–37.

2. John Ranelagh, *The Agency: The Rise and Decline of the CIA* (New York: Simon and Schuster, 1986), p. 120.

3. David C. Korten, *When Corporations Rule the World* (West Hartford, CT: Kumarian Press, San Francisco: Berrett-Koehler, 1995), pp. 174–75; Susan Strange, *The Retreat of the State: The Diffusion of Power in the Global Economy* (Cambridge, UK: Cambridge Studies in International Relations, number 49,

1998); Chakravarthi Raghavan, *Recolonization: GATT, the Uruguay Round & the Developing World* (London: Zed Books, 1990).

4. Korten, *When Corporations Rule,* p. 179; Kathy Collmer, ''Guess Who's Coming to Dinner?'' *Utne Reader* (July/August 1992), pp. 18–20.

5. Brian Burgoon, ''NAFTA Thoughts,'' *Dollars and Sense* (September/October 1995), pp. 10–14, 40.

6. Noam Chomsky, *The Prosperous Few and the Restless Many* (Berkeley: Odonian Press, 1993), p. 23.

7. Don Wiener, ''Will GATT Negotiators Trade Away the Future?'' *In These Times,* February 12–18, 1992, p. 7. See also Raghavan, *Recolonization.*

8. Korten, *When Corporations Rule,* pp. 174–77.

9. Noam Chomsky, *Year 501: The Conquest Continues* (Boston: South End Press, 1993), pp. 57–58; Andrew A. Reding, ''Bolstering Democracy in the Americas,'' *World Policy Journal* (Summer 1992); pp. 410; J.W. Smith, *The World's Wasted Wealth 2* (San Luis Obispo, CA: Institute for Economic Democracy, 1994), chapter 1.

10. Jean Zeagler, *Switzerland Exposed* (New York: Allison and Busby, 1981), p. 35, emphasis added.

11. Ingo Walter, *The Secret Money Market* (New York: HarperCollins, 1990), p. 187, chapter 8.

12. Jack Epstein, ''Dickens Revisited,'' *The Christian Science Monitor,* August 24, 1995, pp. 1, 8; Amy Kaslow, ''The Price of Low-Cost Clothes: U.S. Jobs,'' *The Christian Science Monitor,* August 20, 1995, p. 4; Christopher Scheer, ''Illegals Made Slaves to Fashion,'' *The Nation,* September 11, 1995, pp. 237–38.

13. John Stockwell, *The Praetorian Guard* (Boston: South End Press, 1991), p. 129.

14. Wlliam H. Kötke, *The Final Empire: The Collapse of Civilization and the Seed of the Future* (Portland, OR: Arrow Point Press, 1993).

12

World IMF/Bank/GATT/NAFTA/ WTO/MAI Structural Adjustments

Impoverishing Labor and, Eventually, Capital

A loss of buying power of nonsupervisory labor in the United States is occurring even as labor efficiency increases. Just as Britain, one hundred years ago, sold industrial technology to Germany, who then used it to take over profitable world markets (leading, of course, to the two world wars), U.S. labor has lost both industrial jobs and buying power through American technology and capital employing labor in other countries. The "miracle" of more Americans employed than ever before has been accomplished by reducing high-paying primary jobs and expanding lower-paying service jobs. In the process, the buying power of individual nonsupervisory U.S. labor declined 19 percent from 1973 to 1996, returning to the level of twenty-five years earlier. Before the 1996–98 increase in the minimum wage, the buying power of low-paid labor was declining at a rate exceeding 1 percent per year. In 1992 the drop was 2.7 percent and in the twelve months ending March 1995 it dropped another 2.3 percent.[1] Though the buying power of American labor initially rose when the Asian tigers and Russia underwent their 1997–98 financial meltdown, and the buying power of those who owned stocks rose sharply through the price spread between production costs on the periphery and sales prices in the center, the continued cheap imports (if permitted) will result in a quickening pay loss for European and American labor.

In 1987, it took only 40 percent as much labor to produce the same amount of goods as it did in 1973. During that time span, even as U.S. industrial productivity remained the highest in the world, the earnings of German and other European labor increased. The industrial wages of fourteen nations are now greater than the industrial wages in the United States. At twenty-three dollars an hour as opposed to fourteen dollars an hour, Germany's industrial labor is 64 percent ($17,000 dollars a year) better paid.[2] In 1979, a U.S. worker had to work twenty-three weeks to earn enough to buy an average-priced car. Having to work thirty-two weeks a decade later to buy the same quality car indicates labor has lost more buying power than the above-calculated 19 percent. However, this loss has not translated into political action. "Wall Street economists did not anticipate any great rebellion. *Wages have been falling for nearly two decades*, they noted, *and so far the American people have accepted it with patience and maturity.*"[3]

The world's workers should be aware what the Managers of State have in store for them. William Greider explains:

[O]rthodox economists routinely assume that the American wage decline must continue for at least another generation. . . . Wall Street economists, *without exception*, predicted further erosion for the next twenty to twenty-five years. Unfortunate but inevitable, they said, . . . wage patterns are moving toward equilibrium—a "harmonization" of labor costs among nations.[4]

While a bonanza for corporate mercantilists, that "harmonization of labor costs among nations" is, for the simple reason that its wages will continue to drop as prices continue to rise, a disaster for developed world labor. The story of the Jim Robbins Seat Belt Company illustrates the process. In 1972, it moved from Detroit, Michigan, to Knoxville, Tennessee, and reduced its labor costs from $5.04 an hour to $2.58 an hour. In 1980, the company started moving its operations to Alabama, where wages were about 60 percent those at Knoxville. Then in 1985 the factory was moved to Mexico, where wages were about thirty-seven cents per hour.[5]

The claims that labor is too small a share of production costs to influence major corporations to rebuild factories in low-wage countries is not valid. If labor costs of a runaway industry are 20 percent of production costs in the high-wage country, they will be only 5 percent in a country with one-quarter the wage rate. Add in tax savings, lack of pollution controls, cheap land, and cheap construction labor, and a former 10 percent profit rate becomes 25 to 40 percent. It is only in the markets of China and Southeast Asia, who had moved under the protection umbrella the United States placed over Japan, that wages had been consistently rising (until the 1997–98 financial meltdown). William Greider explains:

> On the streets of Juarez [Mexico], . . . [t]heir incomes are not rising, not in terms of purchasing power. They have been falling drastically for years. . . . In 1981, the industry association reported, the labor cost for a *Maquila* worker was $1.12 an hour. By the end of 1989, the real cost had fallen to 56 cents an hour.[6]

Before their approval, radio host Jim Hightower had been alerting America to the realities of the General Agreement on Trades and Tariffs (GATT, now superseded by the WTO/MAI) and its cousin, the North American Free Trade Agreement (NAFTA):

> No need to speculate on the impact of NAFTA. We can already *see* its future. Dozens of big-name U.S. corporations have already moved 500,000 jobs from our country to Mexico. . . . In 1985, Zenith employed 4,500 Americans making TV sets in Evansville, Indiana, and another 3,000 in Springfield, Missouri. Workers made about $9.60 an hour—hardly a fortune, but enough to raise a family. Today, all of Zenith's jobs are gone from Evansville, and only 400 remain in Springfield. No, Zenith hasn't gone out of business—it's gone to Mexico, where it pays Mexican workers only 64 to 84 cents an hour. . . . Consider this: The average manufacturing wage in Mexico is a buck eighty-five. The average wage U.S. companies pay down there is 63 cents—$29 a week. They're going to buy a Buick from us on that? Our companies aren't creating consumers in Mexico, they're creating serfs. . . . [Academics used by the government to promote NAFTA as a job creator] confessed that instead of a gain of 175,000 jobs for the United States—as they had claimed in their book . . . [it] would cause a job loss. . . . The real purpose behind NAFTA is not to help Mexican workers, but to use their low wages as a machete to whack down ours. "Take a paycut, or we'll take a hike," the companies say. The *Wall Street Journal* even found in a survey that *one-fourth* of the U.S. executives *admit* that this is what they've got in mind.[7]

There had been bloody battles in South Korea as workers there fought to increase their income. This power of workers to increase wages peaked and started declining in Western Europe, the United States, and Japan, while, until their 1997–98 financial meltdown, it was in the middle stages of increase in Taiwan and South Korea, and in the beginning stages in China, Malaysia, and Indonesia. Under free trade rules, and at the expense of developed world workers, wages of developed and developing countries will equalize and integrated economies will eventually balance but, unless the rights of labor and communities are reinstated, it will be at a low level:

> With the growth of worldwide sourcing, telecommunications, and money transfers, there is no pecuniary reason for U.S. firms to pay Americans to do what Mexicans or Koreans will do at a fraction of the cost. This is why "elite" U.S. working-class jobs are being sent abroad and "outsourcing" is the current rage in manufacturing. As a result, American multinationals remain highly competitive and their profits are booming, while the United States itself is becoming less and less competitive. In the 1980s, U.S. capital goods exports have collapsed while imports of both consumer and producer goods have surged, no doubt in part because U.S. firms are now importing these products from foreign lands. In other words, we once exported the capital goods used to manufacture our consumer imports; now we are also importing the capital goods to run what remains of our domestic industry. Even a growing percentage of output in "sunrise" industries like computers and telecommunications is moving offshore. At home, the result is downward pressure on wages and chronic job insecurity for the remaining manufacturing jobholders, who are more docile as a result. Meanwhile, the castoffs from manufacturing and mining plus new labor market participants flock to low-productivity jobs serving coffee, making hamburgers, and running copying machines. Barring protectionism or a decline in U.S. wages to Korean or Mexican levels, this situation will persist and, in fact, will probably get much worse.[8]

We should make no mistake about this: integrating a high-wage developed economy with a low-wage developing economy—without the protection of equalizing managed trade—will be traumatic. The developed society's labor income must take a severe cut and, without protection against even lower-paid labor, there is no assurance that developing world labor will see an increase. The balance—reached by equalization of labor costs—will not hold. The owners of capital will reach outside the newly balanced economies for even cheaper labor and the downward cycle will continue.

It is the inequalities between, and within, societies that permit evasion of social responsibilities. If all societies—and labor within each society—had achieved equality, the bottom line would still measure capital accumulation but it could be realized only by honest competition:

> Broadly speaking, employers can compete either by offering low wages and ignoring the need for effective environmental and other regulations or by achieving higher productivity and producing higher-quality goods. Without a social and environmental charter, a free-trade agreement will encourage competition of the first kind. If, on the other hand, such a charter is adopted, it will not only protect wider social interests but also encourage firms to seek comparative advantage by concentrating on innovative productivity-enhancing approaches. Equally important, a charter is necessary to ensure that workers share in the benefits of rising productivity, thus creating demand for the goods they produce. Simply put, if workers cannot buy the products they make, manufacturers cannot sell them—a point that Henry Ford stressed more than half a century ago.[9]

For decades, Sweden, Japan, and Germany successfully protected both their labor and capital, and their economies were the envy of the world.

But the loss of markets to cheaper producers is forcing those countries to abandon their protection of labor. Their capital is now fleeing and their wages are declining, albeit only slightly. This hollowing out of economies is due to the excessive rights of capital as they escape outside national boundaries (corporate imperialism). The loss of rights of labor as those industries flee is but the other side of the coin of the increased rights of property. A part of the earnings of labor has been transferred to the low-wage country and a part to increased corporate profits. In the Industrial Revolution, repressed skilled labor fled to the most productive centers of capital that were protected and firmly rooted within national boundaries. Today it is the reverse: capital is fleeing both national laws and labor.

The trauma to a country's finance structure and to workers within the countries whose economies are declining, and the almost certain restructuring of ideology and replacement of current leaders if that decline continues, are, of course, why countries go to war over trade. But corporate mercantilism provides a new international economic framework. If the economies of all nations are spiraling downward as capital parked outside national borders destroys capital protected within borders and various elements of this externally parked capital continue cannibalizing each other (capital destroying capital), it will be interesting to see who the Managers of State go to war with.

Financial Meltdown on the Periphery of Empire While the Center Holds

The 1997–98 financial meltdown of Southeast Asia with the simultaneous gain in health (likely temporary) of the economies of Europe and America requires analysis. We must remember that the world's Managers of State have been perfecting their system of laying claim to others' wealth and labor for centuries and surely have it down to a science. We know that most major wars, and especially the two world wars, were between white, Western, Christian, European-cultured nations battling over the world's wealth. We know that after the two world wars these white, Western, Christian, European-cultured nations agreed to protection for each other's economies (Friedrich List protection hiding under the flag of free trade). We know that the historic imperial centers of capital shared their technological monopoly, and thus shared their wealth, with Asia to stop fast-expanding socialism. We know that, with the collapse of the Soviet Union and China's acceptance of the West's model for world trade, there is no longer any powerful nation for other nations to ally with; thus there is no need to provide protection to anyone. Under that scenario, if the West's financial power is strong enough to keep the financial collapses offshore and its military strong enough to prevent other alliances, the world will again return to the white, Western, Christian, European-cultured nations maintaining a high living standard off the resources and labor of the rest of the world. This has all the appearances of the success of financial and economic warfare.

If the central bank or other agencies of an imperial nation subverted the value of other imperial nations' currencies and insisted they cut back on services to their citizens, this would be considered an act of war. It is just such attempts to control the economies and trade of other countries (called containment) so as to maintain control of industries, resources, and markets which caused World Wars I and II and most of the world's wars. Containing small countries, such as the current containment of Iraq and actual breakup of Yugoslavia, creates small wars in which the imperial center normally wins, while containing large countries creates major wars that decide which imperial center of capital shall dominate and who is powerful enough that they must be accepted as allies.

If the financial meltdown on the periphery of empire is kept outside and the center remains intact, this will be strong support for this analysis that financial warfare is waged simultaneously with covert and overt wars to win what are, upon final analysis, nothing but trade wars. The world is watching closely: Will the former economic tigers reenergize? Will the world return to the old balance of a wealthy center and poor, but functioning, periphery (successful financial warfare)? Or has control of technology and control of trade been lost, resulting in ultra-cheap manufactured products pouring into, and collapsing, the center (another great depression and failure of financial warfare)?

The financial collapse of the former Soviet Union, Mexico, Southeast Asia, and South America does not have to spread to the imperial nations. If banking and military monopolies are strong enough, the financial collapse of peripheral nations means lower import prices for the intact imperial centers of capital. There has been an $11 trillion increase in American stock market values between 1989 and 1999 plus large bond and real estate value increases, and over $200 billion was confiscated from the collapsing periphery through currency speculation in 1997–98. Over 50 percent of American heads of household own stock. If stockholders in the imperial centers stay broadly distributed, if speculations continue to lay claim to the wealth of the periphery, if profits increase even further due to higher profits from those lower import costs, if stock prices rise substantially due to money fleeing back to the security of America

and Europe being invested in those markets, and if those stockholders spend a substantial share of their increased wealth, the economies of the imperial centers can maintain their vigor.[10]

But we do not expect such an open monopolization of the world's wealth. Because it is difficult to take rights away once they have been given, strong efforts will be made, and are being made, to protect key South American countries and restart the Southeast Asian economies. However, this is being done under the rules of Adam Smith free trade, not Friedrich List protection under which those tiger economies first gained access to capital, technology, and markets.

Financial capital is safely banked in the currently intact imperial centers of capital and those collapsed economies on the periphery can restart only when finance capital flows back. If those economies are successfully restarted, finance capital monopolists of the imperial centers of capital will have, during the financial crisis on the periphery, bought title to many more industries and resources for a fraction of true value.

Under that scenario of successful financial warfare, economies on the periphery of empire will be restarted but not with the same vigor as before. Too much money will have been siphoned off by finance monopolists with their increased titles to others' wealth, money to fight a Cold War will no longer be flowing to the periphery, and there is massive excess capacity relative to the world's buying power. However, if the increased wealth flowing to the center of empire trickles down to the masses through both lower prices and buying power generated from stock market profits, it is possible for the center to be more vigorous than ever.

But a collapse of Western stock markets would eliminate the trickling down of wealth and reduce purchases. That reduction could multiply through the economy, and the recessions and depressions on the periphery will have come home to the imperial centers of capital. A substantial softening of European and American economies would blow back upon the already collapsed economies of Southeast Asia and put heavy pressure on the Chinese economy. If economies fall to that level, only relaxing the monopolization of finance capital and restructuring world trade (meaning equal rights, equal access to technology and capital, equal trade, etc., along the guidelines of Part III) can establish a *vigorous* world economy.

Corporate Welfare

As corporations and their Managers of State battle societies worldwide to maintain low import prices and high export prices for the imperial centers of capital, they simultaneously struggle with labor within the imperial centers. A key element of the struggle to maintain a pool of cheap reserve labor is painting union labor as featherbedders and those who receive unemployment or other government support as welfare queens.

But governments provide welfare to corporations to the tune of $125 billion a year, much to the wealthiest and most profitable corporations (collectively with $4.5 trillion in profits), while providing under $14.4 billion for welfare for the truly poor, of which a large share is consumed in administration and funds going to people not really in poverty. The equivalent of 4 percent of the wages of every working American subsidizes the wealthy while the equivalent of less than one-half of one percent of America's wages goes for welfare for the poor, and well over half of that goes to some who are not truly needy and to administrative costs.[11]

Federal corporate welfare takes the form of tax credits, tax exemptions, tax deferrals and deductions, a tax rate lower than others pay, price supports, funds to train workers, government-insured transactions of all kinds, government grants for research, government services (such as building logging roads for timber companies), outright subsidies, and lavish corporate lifestyles deducted from taxes.[12]

In attempts to attract industry to their communities, states and cities give corporate welfare in the form of forgiveness of local taxes for a number of years; low taxes; government and municipal bonds floated to build factories and infrastructure; outright grants of land; low-interest loans; free water, sewer, and garbage services due to those tax exemptions; and discounted utility bills. Thus Kentucky taxpayers paid $300 million (equal to the plant's wage bill for two to three years) for Toyota to build its automobile assembly plant there, Alabama paid Mercedes-Benz $253 million for the same purpose, Minneapolis $828 million, Illinois gave Sears $240 million worth of land as an incentive not to move, the Pentagon financed the Martin Marrietta/Lockheed merger to the tune of billions of dollars even as the two companies were making record profits, and the list goes on and on.[13]

Cities are bidding against other cities, states are bidding against other states, and nations are bidding against other nations. Those who bid the lowest taxes, least environmental protection costs, lowest wages, and highest subsidies get the corporate jobs.

> Externalizing environmental and social costs is one way to boost corporate profits. Paying child laborers slave wages in some countries may increase a U.S. firm's bottom line. It is a tragic lure that has its winners and losers determined before it even gets underway. Workers, consumers, and

communities in all the countries lose, short-term profits soar, and the corporation "wins."[14]

This is competition by bidding between societies, not competition by production and distribution efficiency. Most of these subsidies are done under the cover of producing jobs but careful analysis has determined that not only are jobs seldom produced, at times jobs are even lost.[15] A lay person can easily figure this out. There is a market for those products and, even if no subsidies were paid, those factories and jobs are going to be created somewhere by somebody. The job creations we hear so much about are only another imposed belief system to cover another transfer of wealth from the weak and poor to the powerful and wealthy. It is they who fund those think tanks which pour out this rhetoric which, in turn, is picked up by the corporate media and, unknowingly, even much of the small alternative media attempting to stem those massive corporate propaganda assaults.

Looking only at their bottom line, and listening to their own rhetoric, the managers of capital are unaware they are moving society back towards the wealth and rights discrepancies of the early Industrial Revolution. This return to quasi-aristocratic privileges is a recipe for eventual contraction of commerce, and destruction of their own wealth will likely come right behind the collapse of labor's buying power.

Notes

1. Lester Thurow, "Falling Wages, Failing Policy," *Dollars and Sense* (September/October 1996): p. 7; Mortimer B. Zuckerman, "Where Have the Good Jobs Gone," *U.S. News & World Report*, July 31, 1995, p. 68; Dean Baker, "Job Drain," *The Nation*, July 12, 1993, p. 68, addresses the 2.7 percent drop in 1992; Kevin Phillips, *Boiling Point: Democrats, Republicans, and the Decline of Middle Class Prosperity* (New York:

Random House, 1993), p. 24; Lester Thurow, "The Crusade That Is Killing Prosperity," *The American Prospect* (March/April 1996): pp. 54–59. The following sources were published before that year. Lester Thurow, *Head to Head: The Coming Economic Battle Among Japan, Europe, and America* (New York: William Morrow, 1992), p. 53; The *1980 Economic Report to the President* put the loss from 1973 to 1980 at 8 percent and that decline has continued even more rapidly; an editorial in *The Nation,* September 19, 1988, p. 187, puts the loss at 16 percent in weekly income and 11 percent in hourly earnings. Lester Thurow, "Investing in America's Future," Economic Policy Institute, C-Span Transcript, October 21, 1991, p. 9, puts the loss at 12 percent in hourly pay and 18 percent in weekly pay; Peter Drucker, *The New Realities* (New York: Harper and Row, 1989), p. 123.

2. Doug Henwood, "Clinton and the Austerity Cops," *The Nation,* November 23, 1992, p. 628. Colin Hines, Tim Lang, Jerry Mander and Edward Goldsmith, eds., *The Case Against the Global Economy and For a Turn Toward the Local* (San Francisco: Sierra Club, 1996), p. 487, cites $24.90 an hour for Germany, $16.40 for the U.S.

3. William Greider, *Who Will Tell the People?* (New York: Simon and Schuster, 1992), pp. 395–97, emphasis added; Jerry W. Sanders, "The Prospects for 'Democratic Engagement,'" *World Policy Journal* (Summer 1992), p. 375; Thurow, *Head to Head,* p. 163; Thurow, "The Crusade That is Killing Prosperity."

4. Greider, *Who Will Tell the People?* p. 396, emphasis added.

5. John Cavanagh, ed., *Trading Freedom* (San Francisco: The Institute for Food and Development Policy, 1992), pp. 19–23. Read also Jim Hightower, "NAFTA—We Don't Hafta," *Utne Reader* (July/August 1993); Donald L. Barlett and James B. Steele, *America: What Went Wrong?* (Kansas City: Andrews and McMeel, 1992), esp. p. 3.

6. Greider, *Who Will Tell the People?* pp. 381–82.

7. Jim Hightower, "NAFTA—We Don't Hafta," pp. 95–100.

8. Michael Moffitt, "Shocks, Deadlocks, and Scorched Earth," *World Policy Journal* (Fall 1987), pp. 359–60.

9. George E. Brown, Jr., J. William Goold, and John Cavanagh, "Making Trade Fair," *World Policy Journal* (Spring 1992), p. 313.

10. "The New 'Financial Architecture' Crumbles," *Economic Reform* (March 1999), pp. 10–11; "Marshall Plan for Creditors and Speculators," *Economic Reform* (January 1999), pp. 11, 14.

11. Laura Karmatz, Alisha Labi, and Joan Levinstein, Special Report, "States at War," *Time,* November 9, 1998, pp. 40–54; Donald L. Barlett and James B. Steele, "Fantasy Island and Other Perfectly Legal Ways That Big Companies Manage to Avoid Billions in Federal Taxes," *Time*, November 16, 1998, pp. 79–93; Donald L. Barlett and James B. Steele, "Paying a Price for Polluters," *Time,* November 23, 1998, pp. 72–82; Donald L. Barlett and James B. Steele, "The Empire of Pigs," *Time*, November 30, 1998, pp. 52–64; "Five Ways Out," *Time*, November 30, 1998, pp. 75–79; The Banneker Center's Corporate Welfare Shame Links, http://www.progress.org/banneker/cw.html. For funds not going to the really poor, read J. W. Smith, *The World's Wasted Wealth 2* (San Luis Obispo, CA: Institute for Economic Democracy, 1994), chapter 6.

12. See note 11.

13. See note 11.

14. Jerry Mander and Edward Goldsmith, *The Case Against the Global Economy* (San Francisco: Sierra Club Books, 1996), p. 106; Joanna Cagan and Neil DeMause, *Field of Schemes* (Monroe, ME: Common Courage Press, 1998); Susan Strange, *The Retreat of the State: The Diffusion of Power in the Global Economy* (Cambridge, UK: Cambridge Studies in International Relations, number 49, 1998); Joshua Karlinger, *The Corporate Planet: Ecology and Politics in the Age of Globalization* (San Francisco: Sierra Club, 1998); Edward Goldsmith, *The Future of Progress: Reflections on Environment and Development* (Berkeley: International Society for Ecology and Culture, 1995).

15. See note 11.

13

Unequal Trades in Agriculture

From the perspective of winning trade wars, the United States has an insurmountable advantage in agriculture. However, sales of most U.S. agricultural products are not only unnecessary, they are morally wrong. These exports destroy native agriculture in other countries by usurping their local markets. A smaller level of money circulates within the economies of these countries (the multiplier factor) as their money flows to the U.S. to pay for imported food. This limits the development of, or even destroys industries in, other sectors of the economy. Overseas markets are developed for U.S. farmers because they must sell, not because others must buy:

> A lot of attention is being paid these days to the developing world as a prime growth market for American farmers.... The United States has become more dependent on the developing world with more than 58 percent of total agricultural exports going to these countries in 1986–87.... Virtually every trade analysis by the USDA stresses the potential sales among developing nations in Latin America, Africa and Asia.... Agriculture Secretary Richard E. Lyng said he most wanted freedom for farmers "to produce what they want to produce" and that to accomplish that would involve solving international trade problems.... [James R. Donald, chairman of the department's World Agricultural Outlook Board, emphasized] "The developing countries likely will continue to increase global grain imports and could be a source of expansion for U.S. agricultural exports."[1]

One of the most sacred illusions of America is that its agriculture is above all reproach. Not only is the United States the "breadbasket of the world," but the developing world is somehow incapable of emulating America's productive farming methods. There is one thing Americans are sure about: without their food and generosity, much of the rest of the world would starve.

Yet 40 percent of the developing world that was once plagued by severe food shortages—China, Guinea-Bissau and, until impoverished by embargoes, Cuba and North Korea—produced and distributed the 2,300 to 2,400 calories per day required to sustain an adult. India has finally achieved and maintained self-sufficiency.[2] Angola, Mozambique, and Nicaragua had also achieved self-sufficiency, but their economic infrastructures were sabotaged by anti-government rebels who were organized, trained, and armed by the intelligence services of the industrialized world.

The countries that are newly self-sufficient in food production have far less cultivable land per person than most of the countries still suffering from chronic food shortages. China, for example, has only .13 hectares of arable land per person; the former North Vietnam had .10; and

North Korea (self-sufficient before the Korean War and the embargo) has .07. Despite having more arable land per person, their neighbors are unable to feed themselves. Pakistan has .40 cultivable hectares per person; Bangladesh has .16; and Indonesia has .15 hectares.[3]

The best-known example of a country that is continually faced with hunger is Bangladesh, where "two-thirds of the population suffers from protein and vitamin deficiencies." Yet the country exists on a fertile plain blessed with plenty of water and "grows enough in grain alone to provide everyone in the country with at least 2,600 calories a day."[4] Consider the bounty of vegetables and fruits grown in this rich soil and it is obvious that nature has provided this country with the ability to feed more than the present population.

The reasons for such anomalies become clearer when one studies Africa and South America, the two continents with the hungriest populations. The United Nations Food and Agriculture Organization estimates that only 60 percent of the world's arable land is farmed. In Africa and South America, the figure averages 20 percent, and their grain yields are only one-half those of industrialized countries. Brazil, for example, is burdened with a large hunger problem, but, even without the destruction of more rainforests, it has 2.3 cultivable acres per person. In Brazil, as well as most of South and Central America, one-half of the acres being farmed—invariably the best land—currently grow crops for feeding cattle or for export.[5] The masses are unable to feed themselves because their land is monopolized. Brazil has ranches with up to 250,000 head of cattle (that one owned by the Rockefellers) which monopolize land capable of feeding hundreds of millions of people.[6] Latin Americans and Africans, despite rampant hunger, consume only a small percentage of their land's agricultural potential while a substantial share is exported.

The remaining hungry areas, mostly in China and Southeast Asia, have such large populations that the land's capacity to feed the people entails a much smaller margin of safety. Yet, if they controlled their land, these nations could also produce an adequate supply of food. China, probably the best example of rational land reform, now adequately feeds 1.3 billion people. But when the population was one-third what it is today and the land was monopolized, there were massive famines.

Fifteen of the poorest countries in the world raise and export more agricultural products than they keep for their own use.[7] Some of these countries, the exported crops, and the percentage of farmland thus removed from local consumption include: Guadeloupe—sugar, cocoa, and bananas, 66 percent; Martinique—bananas, coffee, cocoa, and sugar, 70 percent; and Barbados—sugar cane, 77 percent. Guatemala plants cotton for export in blocks of 50,000 acres.[8]

These are all familiar developed world consumer items imported from these impoverished countries. In 1973, the United States imported 7 percent of its beef, much of it from the Dominican Republic and Central America. Costa Rica alone exported 60 million pounds to the United States in 1975, even though its own per capita beef consumption dropped from forty-nine pounds per year in 1950 to thirty-three pounds in 1971. If Costa Ricans had not exported this increased production, their per capita consumption would have been three times as high, or ninety-eight pounds per year.[9]

It is mind-boggling to discover that, while the United States imports all this beef, two-thirds of the grain it exports is used to feed livestock and much of the rest is distilled into liquors, both for elite consumption. In addition, it requires forty cents' worth of imported oil to produce and transport every dollar's worth of agricultural exports. "To produce and distribute 'just one can of corn containing 270 calories' consumes 2,790 calories of energy."[10]

During 1992, U.S. food imports are estimated to have been $22 billion and exports $40 billion.[11] Economists teach that there must be balanced trade and, from the perspective of maintaining the status quo, this may be true. However, the status quo reflects the unequal distribution of political and economic power in the world; the geography of world hunger is specifically the consequence of entire populations having lost control of their land and thus their destiny.

The impoverished countries do not need America's, or Europe's, surplus food. They only need the right to control their own land, the right to industrial capital, and the right to grow their own food. Given those rights, they will not generally be hungry. However, because only the affluent have money to purchase this production, monopolization of land diverts the production of social wealth to those already well-off. "The world can simply produce more than those who have money to pay for it can eat."[12] The results are small well-cared-for elite groups, primarily in the developed world, and hunger for the dispossessed.

Hunger: Is It Determined by Overpopulation or by Who Controls the Land?

The often-heard comment that "There are too many people in the world, and overpopulation is the cause of hunger" is the same myth that was expounded in sixteenth-century England, and this Social Control belief system has been

revived continuously since. Through repeated parliamentary acts of enclosure, the peasants were pushed off the land so that the gentry could raise more wool for the new and highly productive power looms. They could not have done this and allowed the peasants to retain their historical *entitlement* to a share of production from the land. Massive starvation was the inevitable result of this expropriation.

There were serious discussions in learned circles that decided peasant overpopulation was the cause of this poverty. This was the accepted reason because social and intellectual elites were doing the rationalizing and they controlled the educational institutions that studied the problem. Naturally the conclusions (at least those published) absolved the wealthy of any responsibility for the plight of the poor. The absurdity of suggesting that England was then overpopulated is clear when one realizes that "the total population of England in the sixteenth century was less than in any one of several present-day English cities."[13]

The hunger in undeveloped countries today is equally tragic and unnecessary. The European colonizers understood well that ownership of land gives the owners control over what a society produces. Military power has historically been the foundation of all law and the more powerful colonizers redistributed the valuable land titles to themselves, eradicating millennia-old traditions of common use. If shared ownership had ever been reestablished, the "rights" of the new owners would have been reduced. For this reason, much of the land was unused or underused until the new owners could use it profitably. Profits meant selling primarily to the developed world; the local populations, being far underpaid, had little money.

This pattern of land use characterizes most developing world countries today. External control guiding agricultural production to the wealthy developed world, instead of internal control managing production for indigenous use, is what causes hunger in this world. These conquered people are kept in a state of relative impoverishment. Permitting them any meaningful share of social wealth would negate the historical reason for conquest, which is ownership of that wealth.

The Market Economy, as Adam Smith Is Interpreted, Guides the World's Production to Imperial Centers of Capital

Currently the purchasing power of the poor keeps falling further and further behind that of the wealthy and powerful. André Gorz, in his book *Paths to Paradise,* explains why a market economy can work efficiently only when the purchasing power of the poor is increased:

> This is what we have to understand—growing soya for our [and other wealthy nations'] cows is more profitable for the big landowners of Brazil than growing black beans for the Brazilian masses. Because our cows' purchasing power has risen above that of the Brazilian poor, soya itself has got so expensive in Brazil that a third of the population can no longer afford to buy either its beans or oil. This clearly shows that it is not enough to ensure the developing world gets "a fair price" for its agricultural exports. The relatively high prices that we would guarantee might merely aggravate hunger in the developing world, by inciting the big landowners to evict their shareholders, buy agricultural machines, and produce for export only. Guaranteed high prices have positive effects only if they can be effectively used to raise the purchasing power of the poor.[14]

Thus the market guides the world's production to those with money. The defeated, dispos-

sessed, dependent, and impoverished have no money because their labor is far underpaid, and historically there has been no serious intent to let them have agricultural and industrial capital to produce their own wealth. The world's natural wealth automatically flows to the money-center countries where these basic commodities are processed into consumer products by highly paid industrial labor to produce the buying power which is the essence of a wealthy society.

The industrialized world is the prime beneficiary of this well-established system. Great universities search diligently for "the answer" to the problem of poverty and hunger. They invariably find it in "lack of motivation, inadequate or no education," or some other self-serving Social Control belief system. They look at everything except the cause: the powerful own the world's social wealth.

The major beneficiaries have much to gain by perpetuating the myths of overpopulation and cultural and racial inferiority. The real causes of poverty must be ignored; how else can this systematic siphoning away of others' wealth through inequality of trades be squared by what people are taught about democracy, rights, freedom, and justice?

If people had rights to their own land and the industrial capital to produce the tools to work it, every country in the world could feed itself. This access would have to be permanent and consistent. Any alienation of land rights, or underselling of regional agricultural production by cheap imports, disrupts food production, disrupts industrial development, and ensures hunger and poverty.

With capital and undisturbed access to their own land, the developing nations would have little need for the surplus food of the United States. Consequently, there would be no reason to plant the one-quarter of U.S. crops that are for export.[15] The current U.S. agricultural export multiplier of possibly $100 billion (60 percent of $50 billion in exports which go to the developing world times a multiplier of 3.5) would then be working its magic in developing countries as they produced, processed, and distributed their own food as well as other consumer products for which the increased buying power would create a market.

Stevia: Sweeter Than Sugar

Subsidies, acreage permits, and import restrictions to protect the developed world's beet and cane sugar industries are well-recorded history. But the Indians of South America know of the leaves of a plant, today called stevia, which is thirty times sweeter than sugar and which does not require expensive processing as do sugar beets and sugar cane.

Needing only harvesting, drying, and grinding into powder, stevia requires only minimal labor costs to raise and process it. Because possibly only one-thirtieth as much is required to sweeten foods, this natural sweetener would sell for a fraction of the cost of sugar. Scientifically tested for safety and used extensively in Japan, Brazil, and China, stevia is kept out of American markets by being classified and regulated as a herb.[16]

Whereas many monopolies are hard to bypass, the sugar monopoly is not. Besides the economic benefits to be gained through the elimination of substantial amounts of unnecessary labor spent producing sugar, there is the role sugar plays in health problems in the developed world. There would be a huge savings to the world's health care industry and a simultaneous increase in the quality of life if a shift were made to stevia, or a couple of other similarly sweet plants in Africa.

Beef: "A Protein Factory in Reverse"

In *Diet for a Small Planet,* Frances Moore Lappé teaches:

1. The human body can manufacture all but nine of the twenty-two amino acids that are the building blocks of protein—these nine are called the essential amino acids.
2. These nutrients are found in grains, vegetables, and fruits, but not all nine amino acids exist in any one non-meat food.
3. If any essential amino acid is missing or deficient in a person's diet, that sets the limit on the human body's ability to build protein; when consuming vegetables, grains, and fruits that include all nine essential amino acids in adequate amounts, the body builds its own protein; to fulfill the need for human protein, an amino acid is an amino acid whether it is in meat or vegetables.[17]
4. Chemically, an essential amino acid such as lysine is the same, whether the source is meat, vegetables, grains, or fruits.

Lappé points out that vegetables, grains, and fruits—properly balanced for amino acids—can provide more protein per acre than meat. Each sixteen pounds of perfectly edible human food in the form of grain fed to cattle produce only one pound of beef. This is "a protein factory in reverse."[18] Lappé's calculation is conservative; prime-fed cattle have 63 percent more fat than standard grade, and much of it is trimmed off, cooked away, or left on the plate. Even the fat that is eaten is usually not wanted. Subtracting that unwanted fat demonstrates that it requires much more than sixteen pounds of grain to produce one pound of meat actually consumed.

Cattle are ruminants with multiple stomachs, a digestive system designed by nature to efficiently convert roughage (grass) into muscle. But they are inefficient converters of grain to meat. Though they consume large amounts of this human food, the overwhelming share of grain is converted into worthless fat, bone, intestines, and manure. Grain fed to cattle, therefore, is subtracting from, not adding to, the world's already short supply of protein. If cattle were fed only roughage and the high-quality grains they now eat were consumed instead directly by the world's hungry human population, the available protein from those foods would increase by sixteen times, 1,600 percent. Hunger would be eliminated, while the pressure on the environment would be reduced. Professor David Pimentel of Cornell University estimates that the grain now fed to livestock worldwide would feed one billion people.[19]

If the developed world returned to the practice of growing cattle on roughage and feeding grain for only a short time before slaughter, the quality of the beef would be higher (measured by leanness, not by marbling) and the quantity available only slightly reduced. At 1991 prices, just eliminating the last two weeks of cattle feeding (finishing) would have saved American consumers at least forty cents per pound.[20]

Counting the grain required to produce the meat they eat, the consumption by the well-to-do of 8,000 to 10,000 calories per day is a major cause of world hunger.[21] Global production exceeds 3,000 calories of food per day for each person, while the daily need is only 2,300 to 2,400 calories, and the potential world calorie production could be raised much more by planting high-protein, high-calorie crops. On the average, the proper combination of leafy vegetables produces fifteen times more protein per acre than grain-fed beef, while peas, beans, and other legumes produce ten times more, and grain produces only five times more.[22]

When the multiplier factor is ignored, highly mechanized farms on large acreages can produce units of food more cheaply than even the poorest paid farmers of the developing world. When this cheap food is sold, or given, to the developing world, the local farm economy is destroyed.

If the poor and unemployed of the impoverished world were given access to land, access to industrial tools, and protection from cheap imports, they could plant high-protein, high-calorie crops and become self-sufficient in food. Consumers would buy their food from local producers, those farmers would spend that money in the community, the producers of those products and services would spend it on their needs. Thus purchasing local production multiplies by however many times that money circulates within an economy.

Although the multiplier factor varies, for simplicity, 350 percent is a good figure to use. Because the multiplier factor creates wealth, reclaiming their land and utilizing the unemployed would cost these societies almost nothing, feed them well, and save far more money than they now pay for the so-called "cheap" imported foods.

Conceptually Reversing the Process of Impoverishing Other Nations Through Selling Cheap Commodities

As addressed earlier, if American farmers were undersold by subsidized agricultural surpluses from another society or if imported food were given to American consumers this would subvert the historic rights to land. If that were to happen on a large scale, U.S. farmers would go bankrupt, the tractor and machinery companies would go bankrupt, the millions of people depending on these jobs would be without work, production of remaining industries would have to be sold to other societies to pay the import food bill, and America would quickly become impoverished.

Because they do not have industrial capital to produce manufactured wealth from their natural wealth, undeveloped countries have much bigger problems. Their natural resources must be sold to pay for "cheap" imported food and other consumer products from the industrialized world. Trade rules (structural adjustments) and debt traps have been put in place to maintain that dependency. Once those monopolies are in place, "free trade" is simply a method to siphon the wealth of the periphery, or even defeated powerful nations, to the victorious imperial centers of capital. This process is currently at work in Mexico. As its food imports rose to 60 percent of its needs, wages fell drastically, industrial production shrunk substantially, and debts increased dramatically.

Many believe that developing-world people "don't understand and will never change." But they do not consider what underselling of regional agricultural production does to already weak economies. Thus sincere, but misinformed, people go on producing for others what the others could produce for themselves if permitted the technology. And this is the process that siphons the wealth from the already poor and perpetuates their poverty.

The Periphery of Empire Functions as a Huge Plantation System Providing Food and Resources to the Imperial Center

That the periphery of empire functions as a huge plantation system providing agricultural products and resources to the imperial center can be determined by analyzing who consumes those exported agricultural products and resources. While Somoza was kept in power in Nicaragua by America, twenty-two times more farm land was utilized to produce crops for exports than was used for domestic consumption and 90 percent of all agricultural credits financed those agricultural exports.[23] Running the same statistical analysis on the agriculture of many countries on the periphery of empire will expose similarly high percentages of their land providing food for the imperial center. The same analysis on natural resources (timber, iron, copper, diamonds, etc.) on the periphery will show an even higher level of consumption by the imperial center and lower level of consumption by the periphery. (The earlier subchapter, "Producing for Local Consumption Is Not the Purpose of IMF/World Bank Loans to the Periphery of Empire," analyzes some of those statistics.)

Further analysis will conclude that the natural wealth of the periphery is being siphoned to the center of empire through monetary policies and unequal trades. Nations on the periphery simply are not paid enough for their resources and labor to earn the finance capital to build their own industry and social structure and utilize their own labor to transform their own resources into their own manufactured real wealth and capitalized financial wealth.

World hunger exists because: (1) Colonialism, mercantilism and neomercantilism (now transposed into corporate imperialism) dispossessed hundreds of millions of people from their land. The current owners are the new plantation managers producing for the mother countries; (2) the low-paid undeveloped countries sell to the highly paid developed countries because there is no local market—the defeated, dispossessed, and underpaid have no money; and, (3) cheap, subsidized agriculture exports from the wealthy world to the developing world are part of the process of stripping the natural wealth from the impoverished world to provide exotic foods, lumber, minerals, and—so long as the developed world financiers and intermediaries still maintain control of the direction of the flow of money—even manufactured products for the imperial center.

To eliminate hunger: (1) there must be equalizing managed trade to protect both the developing world and the developed world, so the dispossessed can reclaim use of their land; (2) the currently underfed people can then produce the more labor-intensive, high-protein, high-calorie crops that contain all nine essential amino acids; and (3) those societies must adapt dietary patterns so that vegetables, grains, and fruits are consumed in the proper amino acid combinations, with small amounts of meat or fish for protein and flavor. With similar dietary adjustments among the wealthy, there would be increased, improved, and adequate food for everyone.

Notes

1. Don Kendall, "U.S. Farmers Look to the Developing World," *The Spokesman-Review,* January 5, 1988, p. B5; Diane Johnstone, "GATTastrophe: Free-Trade Ideology Versus Planetary Survival," *In These Times,* December 19–25, 1990, pp. 12–13.

2. Frances Moore Lappé and Joseph Collins, *Food First: Beyond the Myth of Scarcity* (New York: Ballantine Books, 1979), p. 486; Susan George, *Ill Fares the Land* (Washington, DC: Institute for Policy Studies, 1984), pp. 8–9; Susan George, *How the Other Half Dies* (Montclair, NJ: Allen Osmun, 1977), p. 36; David Goodman, "Political Spy Trial in Pretoria," *In These Times,* September 19–25, 1984; "The Buffalo Battalion—South Africa's Black Mercenaries," *Covert Action Information Bulletin* (July/August 1981), p. 16; "Hunger as a Weapon," *Food First Action Alert* (San Francisco: Institute for Food and Development Policy), undated.

3. George, *How the Other Half Dies,* p. 36.

4. Lappé and Collins, *Food First,* p. 20.

5. Ibid., pp. 14–19, 48.

6. Gerard Colby and Charlotte Dennett, *Thy Will Be Done: The Conquest of the Amazon: Nelson Rockefeller and Evangelism in the Age of Oil* (New York: Harper Collins, 1995). Conversation with the authors shortly after their book was published.

7. Richard Barnet, *The Lean Years* (New York: Simon and Schuster, 1980), p. 153.

8. Lappé and Collins, *Food First,* pp. 42, 71.

9. Ibid., pp. 238–39, 289.

10. James Wessel and Mort Hartman, *Trading the Future* (San Francisco: Institute for Food and Policy Development, 1983), p. 4; Jeremy Rifkin, *Biosphere Politics* (San Francisco: HarperCollins, 1992), p. 83.

11. "Ag Export Value Projected to Climb," *Great Falls Tribune,* March 5, 1992, p. 6c.

12. Lester Thurow, *Head to Head: The Coming Economic Battle Among Japan, Europe, and America* (New York: William Morrow, 1992), p. 62.

13. Lappé and Collins, *Food First,* p. 27.

14. André Gorz, *Paths to Paradise: On the Liberation from Work* (Boston: South End Press, 1985), pp. 94–95.

15. *Statistical Abstract of the U.S., 1992,* charts 1094, 1112 (1990).

16. Linda Bonvie, Bill Bonvie, and Donna Gates, "Stevia: The Natural Sweetener That Frightens Nutrasweet," *Earth Island Journal* (Winter 1997–98), pp. 26–27.

17. Frances Moore Lappé, *Diet for a Small Planet* (New York: Ballantine Books, 1978), pp. 66–7. For the full story of how "The Great American Steak Religion" developed, read Jeremy Rifkin's *Beyond Beef* (New York: Dutton, 1992).

18. Lappé, *Diet for a Small Planet,* pp. 7, 17–18. Agricultural studies show that seven to nine pounds of grain produce one pound of meat. But that figure is for live weight and Lappé's is for dressed weight.

19. Jeremy Rifkin, "Beyond Beef," *Utne Reader* (March/April 1992), p. 97. This article consists of excerpts from his book of the same name.

20. Lappé, *Diet for a Small Planet,* pp. 17–18, roughly adjusted for 1991 beef prices; "Low Cholesterol Beef Produced on State Ranches," *The Missoulian,* October 15, 1986, p. 18.

21. Barnet, *Lean Years,* p. 151; George, *Ill Fares the Land,* p. 48.

22. Lappé, *Diet for a Small Planet,* p. 10.

23. Holly Sklar, *Washington's War on Nicaragua* (Boston: South End Press, 1988), p. 9.

14

Developing World Loans, Capital Flight, Debt Traps, and Forgiveness of Unjust Debt

Under present terms of international lending, a recipient of purchasing power abdicates its authority. The borrower [is] as firmly tied to the apron strings of the lender as he ever was by the chains of colonialization.

—CEO and author Alan F. Bartlett, *Machiavellian Economics*

Maintaining Control of the Puppets of the Imperial Centers of Capital

If one has any lingering doubts about corrupt leaders of nations on the periphery of empire being trapped puppets and even the honest leaders having limited options, consider this: large shares of the populations of oil-rich nations are poor, the elite are enormously wealthy, and that wealth is banked in Western banks. Not only are Western military forces guarding those resources for the West, so are Western banking institutions. Arab oil money or any other nation's accounts would be instantly frozen any time a puppet government declared its independence. Instead of building industry for Arabs or being used to build basic industry for the impoverished world which could then produce both more industry and consumer products, petrodollars not consumed by externally fomented wars were deposited in American and European banks and then lent to developing-world countries for nonproductive purposes:

> Banks everywhere, flush with petrodollars, had to struggle to find big customers to whom they could make big loans. Brazil, Mexico, Argentina, Nigeria, and others were wonderful customers, borrowing hundreds of billions worth of these "recycled petrodollars," as they were called. . . . Just moving that money out the door was an achievement because the sums were so vast. Bankers had to struggle to find clients. Never mind that at least $500 billion of those loans turned sour. Never mind that for a decade the biggest borrowers did not make a single payment. Nor, in all likelihood, will they ever.[1]

The banks ignored their responsibility to make sure their loans were used productively:

> [E]xternal loans were not used to finance large-scale industrial or other projects designed to improve the productivity of the national economy. The military dictatorships used them instead to open up domestic markets to imports in order to allow the middle classes a brief, and therefore all the more passionate, frenzy of consumption. . . . [Those debts] are still being paid for today with even greater poverty, unemployment and destitution for the majority of the population. Much of the contemporary wealth of such nations, including Argentina, can be found in numbered

Swiss bank accounts rather than between Tierra del Fuego and La Plata.[2]

Rectifying a Setback in Economic Warfare Through Financial Warfare

While bankers were busy converting those hundreds of billions of OPEC dollars into developing-world debt, top financial planners were studying how to reduce the financial claims the Arabs had against the industrialized world. Out of those studies came the financial warfare plans of the imperial centers of capital: debase their currencies.

> In the early 1970s, the United States and, to varying extents, the other OECD countries responded to OPEC's increases in oil prices by heavily expanding the money supply. The resulting inflation, together with the administered pricing policies in many basic U.S. industries, sharply increased the prices of U.S. exports and thus the cost of many imports to Third World countries. Such an inflationary policy enabled the OECD countries, as a group, to keep their current accounts in balance, despite the large oil prices. . . . In effect, the United States largely insulated itself from the oil price hikes by passing the burden on to the Third World, whose current accounts deficit mounted. The Third World in turn tried to ease this burden by borrowing heavily rather than by deflating.[3]

In short, those petrodollars were transferred to the developing world, then returned to the developed world through export purchases and capital flight; then dollars were printed to lower the value of Arab petrodollar deposits. If the petrodollars lent to the developing nations had been used to build industrial capital and agricultural self-sufficiency, inflating the dollar would have effectively reduced their debts along with the intended reduction of developed-world debts to the oil cartel.

But, as this money was spent on consumer goods (that properly should have been, on the average, produced by themselves) and funneled into personal bank accounts in the developed world, the developing world gained only the debt. The gains of the Arab cartel were largely erased as the value of its money was essentially halved and the developed nations retained their subtle monopolization of world capital in the form of a $1.7 trillion debt trap for the developing world (1998), which could only be paid off through sales of valuable resources.[4]

The World's Poor Are Subsidizing the Rich

Wealth that is skimmed off by the elite of developing countries and deposited in foreign banks is a large factor in the developing world's debt burden. Forty-seven percent of Argentina's and 50 percent of Mexico's borrowed funds have ended up in other countries via this route. The average loss of borrowed funds for eighteen of these impoverished countries was 44 percent. By 1985, according to economist Howard M. Wachtel, the total exceeded $200 billion. Susan George, in her 1992 book, *The Debt Boomerang: How Developing World Debt Harms Us All,* calculated that a net of $418 billion in borrowed funds flowed right back north between 1982 and 1990.[5] As of 1998, about half the debts of the southern nations are private deposits sitting in the accounts of northern banks through deposits in their subsidiaries in tax havens.

The net gain to the developed countries (loss to the underdeveloped) of $418 billion between 1982 and 1990 is more than what was spent to rebuild Europe after World War II. ''Capital flight from Mexico between 1979 and 1983 alone [was] $90 billion—an amount greater than the entire Mexican debt at that time.''[6]

> The big American banks . . . welcomed the money as savings, even though the lending officers in a different department had sent it to those same countries for supposedly productive uses . . . 40 percent of Mexico's borrowed money leaked away, 60 percent of Argentina's, and every penny of Venezuela's. Like alchemists, the Latin American elite converted the debt of the public at home into their private assets abroad. . . . About one dollar out of every three loaned to Latin America by banks between 1979 and 1983 made that round trip.[7]

Corporate mercantilist loans are almost invariably tied to purchases from the creditor nations. Over 80 percent of America's foreign aid returns immediately through exports tied to that aid.[8] Foreign aid of other nations carries the same self-repatriating provisions. In fact, aid money typically never leaves the donor country; it is credited to other institutions in the donor country to which money is owed. Commenting on such generosity, the prime minister of Malaysia pointed out that, ''Although Japan furnishes loans, it takes back with its other hand, as if by magic, almost twice the amount it provides.''[9]

As this book describes throughout, there are many more methods of claiming others' wealth than self-repatriating loans. Central American authorities estimated that by 1986 the wealth drained from Latin America was ''more than $70 billion in a single year in the form of money or merchandise for which [Latin America] didn't receive anything in exchange.''[10] The effect of this multifaceted assault on the wealth of the developing world is that real wages in Chile declined by 40 percent, in the decade of the 1980s in Mexico and Argentina by 50 percent, and in Peru by 70 percent.[11]

After recovering some, Mexican wages again dropped 40 percent (measured against the dollar) when the peso collapsed in 1995, and Mexico's economy went into a depression. Those wages dropped in half again in the 1997–98 currency collapses on the periphery of empire. Just as cheap imported agricultural products destroy an undeveloped country's agricultural economy and—through loss of the multiplier factor—preclude development of buying power, imported consumer goods forestall the building of industry to produce those products regionally and build an internal market economy.

If a loan is to be of lasting value to the country to which it is granted, it must be put to *productive,* not unnecessary, consumptive, or wasteful use. Equally important, if those loan funds were spent in the developing region instead of the loaning country as typically required, that money will be spent several times (the multiplier factor) and create buying power within that region. Producing a healthy economy in the industrial exporting nation through the multiplier factor is the reason most aid is tied to purchase of exports from the donor country. Continuation of that policy provides wealth for the nation exporting manufactured goods and poverty for the nation exporting raw produce and products produced with low-paid labor.

We must remember that the wages of labor define its ''entitlement'' to a share of social production. Only by paying labor equally and building tools of production (industry) instead of spending borrowed funds on consumption imports can a society become self-sufficient, build an internal market economy, gain equality in world trade, and eliminate poverty.

Building the Infrastructure to Mine and Harvest Resources and Transport This Natural Wealth to the Imperial Center

A 1987 *60 Minutes* documentary explained how billions of dollars were lent to Brazil to clear rain forest for homesteading. The World Bank's own agricultural experts testified that this plan was not feasible because, once cleared, the thin soil would be unable to sustain agriculture. The bank lent the money anyway and the result was just what the experts predicted and what slash and burn farmers have known for thousands of years.[12] Instead of using the rain forest for the sustainable production of medicines, rubber, timber, and even oxygen, it was clear-cut for about seven years of wasteful grazing, at the end of which time the nutrients were exhausted and the land became useless.

There were also loans for unsound and disastrous development projects in Kenya, Morocco, the Philippines, Tanzania, Togo, Zaire, Zambia, and other dependent countries, including Poland. The projects produced little or no income, and the loans had to be repaid by selling valuable resources and lowering the standard of living of already impoverished populations.[13]

A careful analysis will conclude that the purpose of many loans is to develop infrastructure to move the resources of the periphery to the imperial centers of capital. Much of the timber being cut from Brazil's rain forest ended up in the imperial centers of capital. A minimum infrastructure must be built to move those resources, which are then sold to fund a debt that, due to low prices for those exports and the expense of imported food and consumer products, proves unpayable and continues to grow.

Producing Debt Traps Through Loaning Excess Accumulations of Capital Back to the Producers of That Wealth

Third World development has not had serious consideration. Instead, vastly underpriced Third World natural resource commodities and underpaid labor (essentially dictated by IMF/World Bank/GATT/NAFTA/WTO/MAI structural adjustment policies and unequal currency values) and overpriced developed-world manufactures created excessive accumulations of capital in the already wealthy world, which were lent wastefully back to the developing world for purchase of developed-world exports (a major share being for arms). This forced the Third World to harvest ever more of its natural resources to pay that debt, which further increased surplus production, which lowered natural resource commodity prices still further, and the process keeps repeating itself. This is the little understood debt trap. Sooner or later the crunch of debt incurred under the massive assault of financial warfare will become unpayable:

> A debtor who repeatedly borrows more than the surplus his labor or business enterprise produces will fall further and further behind in his obligations until, sooner or later, the inexorable pressures of compound interest defeat him . . . interest [is] usurious when the borrower's rightful share of profit [is] confiscated by the lender. . . . The creative power of capital [is] reversed and the compounding interest [becomes] destructive.[14]

Professor Lester Thurow explains:

> The fundamental mathematics is clear. To run a trade deficit, a country must borrow from the rest of the world and accumulate international debt. Each year interest must be paid on this accumulated debt. Unless a country is running a trade surplus, it must borrow the funds necessary to

make interest payments. Thus the annual amount that must be borrowed gets larger and larger, even if the trade deficit itself does not expand. As debts grow, interest payments grow. As interest payments grow, debt grows. As time passes the rate of debt accumulation speeds up, even if the basic trade deficit remains constant.[15]

The size of a financial warfare debt trap can be controlled to claim all the surplus production of a society, and the magic of compound interest, to say nothing of the many forms of financial and economic warfare we have been describing, assures those unjust debts are unsustainable. One trillion dollars compounded at 10 percent per year will become $117 trillion in fifty years and $13.78 quadrillion in one hundred years, about $3.5 million for every man, woman, and child in the developing world. Developing world debt is almost twice this and has been compounding at twice that rate—over 20 percent per year between 1973 and 1999, from under $100 billion to $1.7 trillion.

Trading Debt for Equity

The trading of debt for equity so loudly touted as a success did not slow the loss of wealth of the impoverished world. On paper it may have lowered the debt but it essentially passed title of resources and industry from the impoverished world to the developed world and insured that the flow of wealth from the impoverished nations on the periphery to the wealthy imperial center would continue.

That debt increased from $1 trillion to $1.7 trillion even as those impoverished countries swapped debts for equity and even as public utilities and industries were sold to international investors. As the price of their export commodities reached a twenty-one-year low, the capitalized value of Third World industries also

went down, which means those countries went backwards much more than their $.7 trillion debt increase.

Buying Properties on the Periphery of Empire for Pennies on the Dollar

Due to structural adjustment loans forcing privatization, Third World resources and industries are being sold off to the powerful for pennies on the dollar, a massive overpayment for the powerful and underpayment for the weak in which the unpayable debts continue to climb ever faster.

As the massive funds floating around financial markets are used to buy resources and industries in the Third World and the collapsed former Soviet bloc for a fraction of real value, the wealth claimed by the wealthy world rapidly climbs, which can only mean that the wealth owned by the citizens of the defeated and oppressed nations rapidly declines.

Peonage Has Only Changed Its Name

Most of these debts are incurred without the recipient country receiving any lasting benefits. In fact, only about $400 billion of that $1.7 trillion debt was borrowed finance capital; the rest was runaway compound interest.[16] The situation is comparable to the loathsome form of slavery known as peonage:

> In classic peonage, workers, though nominally free and legally free, are held in servitude by the terms of their indenture to their masters. Because their wages are set too low to buy the necessities, the master grants credit but restricts the worker to buying overpriced goods from the master's own store. As a result, each month the peon goes deeper and deeper into debt. For as long as the arrangement lasts, the peon cannot pay off the

mounting debt and leave, and must keep on working for the master. Nigeria [and most other Third World countries] shares three crucial characteristics with a heroin-addicted debt-trap peon. First, both debts are unsecured consumer debts, made up of subsistence and spending-spree expenses, and with future income as the only collateral. Second, both loans are pure peonage loans, that is, loans made not because of the potential of the project the loan is to be used for, but simply in order to secure legal control over the economic and political behavior of the debtor. Third, the only way made available for getting out of both debts is by getting into more debt.[17]

Lending Responsibly Is a Well-recognized Tenet of Law

American citizens have won lawsuits against banks that foreclosed on their property for defaulted loans that were less blatantly irresponsible. Developed nations should cancel unjust and unpayable debts and start over, giving serious attention to plans that will eliminate waste, using the savings to capitalize impoverished countries, and developing true equality and balance of industry, agriculture, and trade.

The reason these sensible policies are not followed is that, under current corporate imperialist free trade policies, developing-world capitalization would be catastrophic for developed-world owners of capital. The development of productive capital with borrowed finance capital would produce profits, pay the debt, eliminate the need to borrow, eliminate dependency, and increase market competition to the detriment of the developed world and the gain of the impoverished dependent world.

With the productive use of export capital, interest rates (and the price of products) in both the former capital-accumulating country and the newly developed country must fall. In short, the productive use of borrowed capital would even-

tually eliminate the developed world's monopolization of the tools of production and markets and produce the level playing field that is continually touted but in reality greatly feared.

Canceling Unjustly Incurred Debts

There are compelling reasons for paying attention to this potential for catastrophe, as "every debt crisis in history since Solon of Athens has ended in inflation, bankruptcy or war, and there is no cause to believe we've solved this one, even if it has been postponed."[18]

As much of this imposed debt can never be paid back, most developing-world debt is severely discounted. As of June 1990, Argentina's debt traded at a low of 14.75 cents on the dollar while the average price of all developing-world debt was twenty-eight cents on the dollar.[19] Of course, although it is being traded at a 72 percent discount, the indebted countries must still pay full price. After the financial collapse on the periphery of empire seven years later, discounts for those debts can only trade at a sharply higher discount.

In the 1800s, the United States defaulted on much of its development debt, as did Latin America and others during the crisis of the Great Depression. American Managers of State knew their nation became wealthy due to avoiding the monopolization of their economy and their European cousins' eventual sharing of industrial capital and markets. America returned that favor by sharing its wealth after World War II to rebuild the ancestral home of its culture. There was no expectation of that shared wealth being repaid. The rational decision, and one that Professor Lester Thurow and others consider the developed world's only choice, would be to forgive the developing world's unjustly incurred and unpayable debts.[20] The precedent has been set by earlier defaults and by the quickness of decisions to protect trading allies. An honest accounting would find the developed world owing the developing world for the destruction of its social wealth, the earlier enslavement of its labor, and the long-term underpayment for its labor and resources.

Notes

1. Joel Kurtzman, *The Death of Money* (New York: Simon and Schuster, 1993), p. 72.

2. Elmar Altvater, Kurt Hubner, Jochen Lorentzen, and Raul Rojas, *The Poverty of Nations* (London: Zed Books, 1991) pp. 8–9.

3. Arjun Makhijani, *From Global Capitalism to Economic Justice* (New York: Apex Press, 1992), p. 159.

4. William Greider, *One World, Ready or Not* (New York: Simon and Schuster, 1997), p. 282.

5. Susan George, *The Debt Boomerang* (San Francisco: Westview Press, 1992), pp. xiv–xvi; Howard M. Wachtel, "The Global Funny Money Game," *The Nation,* December 26, 1987, p. 786; Fidel Castro, *Nothing Can Stop the Course of History* (New York: Pathfinder Press, 1986), p. 68; Howard M. Wachtel, *The Politics of International Money* (Amsterdam: TransNational Institute, 1987), p. 42; William Greider, *Secrets of the Temple* (New York: Simon and Schuster, 1987), p. 517. See also Susan George, *Fate Worse Than Debt* (New York: Grove Weidenfeld, 1990), especially pp. 16–34, 77–154; Philip Agee, "Tracking Covert Actions into the Future," *Covert Action Information Bulletin* (Fall 1992), p. 6.

6. George, *Fate Worse Than Debt,* pp. 20, 236, quoted by Agee, "Tracking Covert Actions," p. 6.

7. Lawrence Malkin, *The National Debt* (New York: Henry Holt, 1988), pp. 106–107; see also David Pauly, Rich Thomas, and Judith Evans, "The Dirty Little Debt Secret," *Newsweek,* April 17, 1989.

8. Dan Nadudere, *The Political Economy of Imperialism* (London: Zed Books, 1977), p. 219; Michael Moffitt, "Shocks, Deadlocks, and Scorched Earth: Reaganomics and the Decline of U.S. Hegemony," *World Policy Journal* (Fall 1987).

9. Ibid, p. 220.

10. Castro, *Nothing Can Stop the Course of History,* p. 69.

11. Duncan Green, *Silent Revolution* (London: Cassel, 1995), pp. 136–38; Kevin Danaher, ed., *50 Years Is Enough: The Case Against the World Bank and the International Monetary Fund* (Boston: South End Press, 1995), p. 26; James Petras, "Latin America's Free Market Paves the Road to Recession," *In These Times,* February 13–19, 1991, p. 17.

12. Danaher, *50 Years Is Enough,* chapter 8; *60 Minutes,* CBS, April 20, 1987; Bruce Rich, "Conservation Woes at the World Bank," *The Nation,* January 23, 1989, pp. 73, 88–91.

13. George, *Fate Worse Than Debt,* pp. 18, 19, 30–34, 50–57, 77–168.

14. Greider, *Secrets of the Temple,* pp. 707, 581–82; Susan George and Fabrizio Sabelli, *Faith and Credit* (San Francisco: Westview Press, 1994), pp. 80–84, 215.

15. Lester Thurow, *Head to Head: The Coming Economic Battle Among Japan, Europe, and America* (New York: William Morrow, 1992), p. 232.

16. Michael Barratt Brown, *Fair Trade* (London: Zed Books, 1993), pp. 43, 113.

17. Chinweiezu, "Debt Trap Peonage," *Monthly Review* (November 1985), p. 21–36.

18. George, *Fate Worse Than Debt,* p. 196.

19. *CNN News,* June 28, 1990; David Felix, "Latin America's Debt Crisis," *World Policy Journal* (Fall 1990), p. 734.

20. Thurow, *Head to Head,* p. 215.

15

Multiplier Factor

Accumulating Capital Through Capitalizing Values of Externally Produced Wealth

Although Social Control belief systems have always claimed otherwise, people throughout the world can, on the average, be trained to be equally productive. All it takes is an education and the opportunity. If adequate capital were equally distributed throughout the world, the reality that picking grapes is just as important to society as building automobiles would quickly become apparent.

The difference in skills hardly qualifies for the difference in pay. There are many grape pickers and other low-paid workers who are just as qualified as many production, construction, and transportation workers retiring today. Though not true of all, many high-paid workers learned on the job the same way those low-paid workers learned their skills and the work of a large share of well-paid labor is repetitive, just as simple, yet not as hard or dirty as the work of lower-paid labor.

Yet look at difference in capital accumulation through the discrepancy in pay as outlined in Chapter One: A ten times pay differential between equally productive labor results in a wealth accumulation advantage of 100 to one; to be paid twice as much for equally productive work is to accumulate four times as much wealth; and being paid 30 percent greater will still accumulate over twice as much wealth.

But the defeated, dependent world's loss of wealth is even greater than the above example. Besides the obvious loss of wealth through paying subsistence, or below subsistence, wages to produce export commodities, forcing these defeated dependent societies to import a product they do not need, or which they could produce themselves if permitted the requisite technology and capital, is a sale 100 percent overvalued. Actually, as those societies are also being denied the benefits of the multiple use of this money (the multiplier factor) as it moves through the economy and creates more commerce, this unneeded product is several hundred percent overvalued.

For example, if a society spends one hundred dollars to manufacture a product within its borders, the money that is used to pay for materials, labor, and other costs moves through the economy as each recipient spends it. Due to this multiplier effect, a hundred dollars' worth of primary production can add several hundred dollars to the Gross Domestic Product (GDP) of that country.[1] If money is spent in another country, circulation of that money, and thus the wealth generated, is within that exporting country.

If imports and exports are equal in labor input and produced by equally paid and equally productive labor, the trades will be equal. But they are not—they are unequal to the extreme. To understand that, we must understand not only multiplication of wealth through the horizontal flow of money (the economic multiplier) but the vertical expansion of wealth in an industrial economy as a society becomes wealthy through capitalizing values.

Friedrich List's Fundamental Thesis

The fundamental thesis of Friedrich List is: "Commerce emanates from manufactures and agriculture, and no nation which has not brought within its own borders both those main branches of production to a high state of development can attain... to any considerable amount of internal and external commerce."[2] Further challenging laissez-faire, List points out that governments should support and protect industry, which will utilize unused labor and resources to an ever higher level of production. The new manufacturing industries utilize otherwise wasted agriculture products and natural resources, producing valuable products to be marketed in trade for other products, preferably cheap natural resource commodities, to be again processed into finished manufactured goods.

List points out that such importation of natural resources and local manufacturing, as a national policy, would create a wealthy and powerful nation selling only what was surplus above the needs of the population, while nations allotted the role of providing those unprocessed natural resources and purchasing back their manufactured products would produce no surplus and would be poor.[3] Adam Smith's analysis is worth quoting a second time:

> A small quantity of manufactured produce purchases a great quantity of rude produce. A trading and manufacturing country, therefore, naturally purchases with a small part of its manufactured produce a great part of the rude produce of other countries; while, on the contrary, a country without trade and manufactures is generally obliged to purchase, at the expense of a great part of its rude produce, a very small part of the manufactured produce of other countries. The one exports what can subsist and accommodate but a very few, and imports the subsistence and accommodation of a great number. The other exports the accommodation and subsistence of a great number, and imports that of a very few only. The inhabitants of the one must always enjoy a much greater quantity of subsistence than what their own lands, in the actual state of their cultivation, could afford. The inhabitants of the other must always enjoy a much smaller quantity.... Few countries... produce much more rude produce than what is sufficient for the subsistence of their own inhabitants. To send abroad any great quantity of it, therefore, would be to send abroad a part of the necessary subsistence of the people. It is otherwise with the exportation of manufactures. The maintenance of the people employed in them is kept at home, and only the surplus part of their work is exported.... The commodities of Europe were almost all new to America, and many of those of America were new to Europe. A new set of exchanges, therefore, began to take place which had never been thought of before, and which should naturally have proved as advantageous to the new, as it certainly did to the old continent. The savage injustice of the Europeans rendered an event, which ought to have been beneficial to all, ruinous and destructive to several [most] of those unfortunate countries.[4]

Friedrich List's thesis, restructured as an international policy for all nations to have an equal share (which the highly respected President Franklin D. Roosevelt also suggested and President Kennedy hinted at just before his assassination), would create a peaceful and wealthy world. One hundred dollars paid to a community for what was once wasted resources and labor will create, through the multiplier factor, possibly $350 worth of economic activity within a community and thousands of dollars worth of capitalized values.

Producing Wealth Through Both the Vertical Building of Industrial Capital and the Horizontal Flow of Money

That $100 worth of formerly exported raw material can be processed ever finer and manufactured into ever more complicated products and services until the costs of the original raw materials are barely detectable in the product or service value (high-value-added products). Money spent building new industry to produce new products or services of continually higher values is continually spent horizontally for products and services that continually increase the economic activity of a newly industrializing nation. The high price received for that high-value-added product circulates within the economy and multiplies the economy to an ever-higher level.

It requires the proper balance of industry, resources, and agriculture to maintain those increased production values that in turn maintain land, industry, store, office, and home values. The resources necessary to maintain the economic balance of industrial nations are primarily in the undeveloped, impoverished world. Thus the centuries-long effort to control the countryside and maintain the flow of resources to developed world industries at a fraction of its value.

The industrial/agricultural ratio of a nation or region can vary greatly depending on the abundance or lack of natural resources. The scarce resources in wealthy, highly industrialized Japan and abundant resources in the poor nations cheaply providing Japan's factories with their raw materials dramatically outline the true cause of wealth in Japan and poverty in those who provide those resources. The poor nations provide the resources and purchase manufactured products. Japan buys the low-value resources and sells high-value manufactured products.

Because the developing world has little industry to utilize its labor and resources to produce high-value consumer products and it is paid a low price for its labor and resources, there is almost no vertical industrialization, little horizontal movement of money, and thus little wealth.

When one adds up both the vertical and horizontal multiplication of wealth in an industrialized country, one has to seriously question the advice given to developing nations by the imperial centers of capital that their successful future depends on continued mining and harvesting of raw material and forgoing manufacturing because that is their "comparative advantage."

The small savings on importing any item must be laid against the entire vertical and horizontal gain to the region when manufacturing its own consumer products. Industrial development multiplies consumer buying power, and profit from consumer spending further multiplies profits, which further multiply investments, further multiplying profit and consumer spending, and all continually multiplying capitalized values.

A new bloc of industrial nations producing for the current markets would become wealthy through the multiplier factor and, assuming the world's buying power had not expanded in step with productive power, the bloc of nations that lost that production would see its national wealth fall rapidly as the same multiplier factor worked in reverse in its economy.

This explains the demonization and containment of Iran, Libya, and Iraq. There is far more to the Iran/Iraq War and the Gulf War than we are told. Since they nationalized their oil, the Managers of State have been unable to find a faction to overthrow their current governments and Libyans and Iranians are refining much of their own oil and building other industries. Where the rest of the Middle East oil countries are firmly under the control of puppet governments and their oil wealth continues to flow to the developed world without industrial development of those countries, Iran, Libya, and Iraq are intent on maintaining control of government and resources and developing their nations.

Accumulation of Capital Through Creation of Scarcity

Besides wealth being accumulated by the powerful while the weak are impoverished through conquest and open confiscation of their wealth, loss of title to their lands, the abolition of their right to a voice in their own destiny, and then through enforced dependency and unequal trades, wealth can be accumulated by open destruction of a defeated nation's wealth to make a commodity scarce and the world dependent upon the monopolized source.

Adam Smith describes just such a destruction of a peaceful and happy society's wealth and its impoverishment for the accumulation of capital by a few. Spices and silk from the East brought overland comprised the majority of trade between Europe and the East for centuries, and efforts to control that trade resulted in many battles, large and small. Muslims shutting off the overland trade routes to the East forced the Europeans to search for a new route by sea.

Nutmeg and cloves grew wild and plentiful on the Molucca Islands; their profusion made them, like air, of high desirability but valueless.

Natives made an easy living picking the spicy blossoms, seeds, and leaves. If all traders had access to those spices, the European market (mostly nobles and wealthy traders, no commoners because they had no money) would become quickly flooded, and the price would collapse.

To create capitalized value for spice traders, it was necessary to monopolize those spice trees and keep spice prices high. So the Dutch burned every spice tree they could not control.[5] The other side of the coin of the immense wealth accumulated by a few Dutch traders through monopolization of the spice trade was the impoverishment and depopulation of the Molucca Islands.

The Molucca Island spice monopoly gives a quick lesson in how value is transferred from defeated nations to the powerful through capitalized value of entitled property. If those islanders had kept title to their islands and spice trees and a free market existed, it is they who eventually would have become wealthy through furnishing spices to the world. If all traders had access to those spices in those early years, there would have been much more, and cheaper, spice in the world, the islanders would have profited immensely, and they would have quickly learned the mechanics of gaining wealth through trade.

Creation of scarcity through open destruction of commodity production is a well-recognized principle of neoclassical economics. In America during the Great Depression, cattle and pigs were slaughtered and buried, and farmers being paid not to produce is standard practice yet today. Oil, coal, timber, and other natural resources are not openly destroyed to produce scarcity. But wasteful consumption of those resources when plentiful and cheap and their waste for war do produce scarcity. That contradiction of waste of plentiful resources can be accomplished only through a cooperative, coordinated social policy as addressed below.

Exclusive Property Titles Are the Foundation of All Capitalized Values

Titles can take many forms. Colonial conquest gained title to lands and the wealth it produced. The conquerors were "entitled" to do what they wished with their new property and, of course, they wished to transfer all wealth to themselves. Monopolization of natural wealth and the wealth-producing process through exclusive titles was specifically designed to claim the wealth produced. This subtle monopolization is exposed in Part IV by outlining the efficiency increases through *conditional title* to both land and technology as opposed to *exclusive* title.

Capitalizing Values by Underpaying the Weak on the Periphery of Empire

Slave labor was justified under the philosophical cover (a belief system) of describing natives on the periphery of empire as heathens, incompetent, and even not human because they had no souls. There were few limits to this assault on primitive societies all over the world as their labor and resources were reorganized to produce for the imperial center. The natives were decimated and the lands of the weakest (the Americas, Australia, parts of Africa, and many islands all over the world) were essentially depopulated.

Where the American Indians suffered the worst genocide in history and entire tribes and ethnic groups disappeared (by 1890, 97 to 98 percent of the Indian population of the Americas had been liquidated), the more developed, more heavily populated and stronger cultures (such as India and China) were not depopulated, but they are only now rebuilding their internal wealth.

As local workers are underpaid for equally productive labor, resources on the periphery are harvested and sold to the imperial centers for far less than full value. With that cheap labor, products are manufactured cheaply but primarily for export—those underpaid workers do not have the buying power to purchase what they produce. Lacking buying power, these nations do not develop industry and wholesale and retail infrastructure for local consumption.

Consumer products could be sold within the low-paid producing region if the value of both the industries and goods produced were priced relative to the wages paid to build the industry and manufacture the products. But high wages in the developed world channel those products to imperial centers. This is graphically demonstrated by current wages paid in the developing world being under 2 percent of a product's sales value in the developed world, even before the 1997–98 currency collapses on the periphery reduced those wages by half.[6]

Theoretically, over time, distribution within the developing world at low prices could develop. But the large buying power in the imperial center and the low buying power on the periphery dictate there will be a limited horizontal flow of money on the periphery and thus a limited development of a balanced regional economy outside the imperial centers of capital.

It is impossible for the developing nations to capitalize their wealth without owning their own resources, without owning and running their own factories, without being paid equally for equally productive labor, and without selling on established markets. Nor can they develop social capital without the broad-based local buying power that title to their own productive wealth and equally paid labor would create.

It is consumer purchasing power (adequate wages, adequate commodity prices, and profits from efficient industry and efficient traders) that determines who ends up with the world's products for a quality life. Consumer purchasing power and capitalized values are both derived from title to natural resources, title to industrial capital, title to distribution mechanisms, and adequately paid labor as well as efficient industries. High-capitalized values require mass markets and mass markets develop only from adequately paid labor.

The common thread of a society that is productive and profitable, with a high living standard, is sharing both work and wealth while using *and sharing* the increased efficiencies of technology. A truly wealthy society with equally paid labor and properly paid capital will have more real (consumer) wealth. Properly paid labor and capital mean elimination of monopolies, which means capitalized values will be far lower.

Multiplier Factor: Accumulating Capital Through Capitalized Values of Internally Produced Wealth

Although the above described accumulation of capital from the wealth of other nations through inequalities of external trade is little known, the accumulation of capital through appropriation of wealth produced by internal labor has been written about (and challenged) so many times that we will address it very briefly.

Capitalized values are largely appropriated labor values multiplied between ten and twenty times, depending on the current interest rate (current interest rates determine expected profit rates, which determine capitalized value).

There are other unacknowledged methods of wealth accumulation. Both the Japanese and Chinese governments own their cigarette industries and, to accumulate capital, are rapidly addicting their citizens to smoking through powerful ad programs. As a partial substitute for the slave labor and low-paid labor (appropriation of labor) that accumulated capital to build Western industries, this policy provides a part of the finance capital for Japan and China. Though a quick and politically painless way to accumulate capital, from the position of a socially efficient society it is social insanity at its finest.

Columbia, Peru, Thailand, Bolivia, Mexico, Afghanistan, Laos, the former Burma, and other countries producing, exporting, and distributing hundreds of billions of dollars in drugs to the developed world is a painful method (for the world) of accumulating capital. The interception of wealth through catering to people's vices, as opposed to production of wealth, is a time-honored way of accumulating wealth by both private citizens and governments.

The next chapter outlines Japan's methods of accumulation of capital.

Notes

1. In this process, the U.S. consumer expenditure multiplier may be about 3.5 but the industrial investment multiplier is just under six. In 1986 there were 108.5 million employed in the United States and 18.4 million of them were employed in basic industry, just under a multiplier of six (*Statistical Abstract of the U.S., 1990,* p. 734, chart 1295). Increased efficiencies should continually lower employment in basic industries and thus continually increase the industrial investment multiplier.

2. Friedrich List, *The National System of Political*

Economy (Fairfield, NJ: Augustus M. Kelley, 1977), p. 260.

3. List, *National System,* especially p. 260, chapter 19; see also chapters 12, 17, 20–25.

4. Adam Smith, *Wealth of Nations,* (New York: Random House, 1965), pp. 413, 426, 642.

5. Ibid., pp. 600–602.

6. Jack Epstein, "Dickens Revisited," *The Christian Science Monitor,* August 24, 1995, pp. 1, 8; Amy Kaslow, "The Price of Low-Cost Clothes: U.S. Jobs," *The Christian Science Monitor,* August 20, 1995, p. 4; Christopher Scheer, "Illegals Made Slaves to Fashion," *The Nation,* September 11, 1995, pp. 237–38.

16

Japan's Post–World War II Defensive Economic Warfare Plan

Few realize the desperation-bred cunning of Japan's post–World War II economic warfare. An American investment banker in Japan for fifteen years, R. Taggart Murphy had a catbird's view and wrote *The Weight of the Yen,* describing how, in an obvious effort to both survive and revenge the loss of World War II, Japan's postwar economy was structured under pure mercantilist principles to engender "the greatest transfer of wealth in history" from America to Japan.[1] Economist Joe Kurtzman's analysis of Japan's international trade is worth quoting at length. Japan has

> developed long-term strategies for entering existing markets and [has] composed detailed plans spanning twenty to fifty years for gaining a share of existing markets, usually by introducing new and highly refined versions of existing products and then slowly upgrading these products.... Beginning with crude copies of advanced German cameras like the Leica and the Rolliflex, the Japanese honed their skills by continually upgrading their entries into these markets until their level of quality and technology began to equal that of the Germans and then surpass it. In the span of less than twenty years, utilizing this long-range managerial approach, the Japanese were able to gain by far the largest share of the worldwide camera and optical goods market, thereby driving the previously dominant Germans to the sidelines. After the Japanese became the primary power in this huge market, they took aim at some

of the other existing markets in which they could use their advanced optical skills. Small copying machines, professional video recording devices, and computerized silicon chip etching equipment are markets that the Japanese went after and now dominate. But this time the firms bested by the Japanese were not German. They were American firms that failed to keep pace with the slow, steady unrelenting Japanese technological and managerial advance.... Planning twenty-four months ahead is considered long term by most U.S. companies, whereas the Japanese routinely look five, ten, and twenty years into the future when developing their approach to entering a market.... [O]ur companies tend to lose out to those Japanese and other foreign companies that take the long-term view and that have the backing of their governments.[2]

Under protection of the Western imperial centers of capital, and even as they "chanted the mantra of free trade and laissez-faire," Japan's Ministry of Finance (MOF) and Ministry of International Trade and Industry (MITI) controlled the government's budget; set monetary policy; collected taxes; supervised banks, brokers, and insurers; and established parameters for credit, asset values, capitalization, and lending.[3]

Japan's collapsed land and stock markets (down 70 percent and 75 percent respectively) are not the total failures they are loudly touted to be. The preceding bubble economy was specifically designed to create finance capital with which to build more industry. Earlier we described how Japan first industrialized in the nineteenth century through selling government-built industry to Japanese industrialists at 15 to 30 percent of construction costs. After World War II, the same rapid industrialization was accomplished through charging Japanese consumers three times the price for consumer products as the rest of the world. Those high prices were only a hidden tax that, along with other dictated policies and creative accounting, gave Japanese industry the same free finance capital as it received a hundred years earlier.

Japan's Post–World War II Mercantilist Economy

Understanding the economic multiplier, Japanese industry could actually sell to the world at what would be a loss for a free enterprise corporation and still keep running. Now that Japan has built the world's most modern industry and captured markets around the world, so long as the trade surpluses are maintained, losses can be absorbed, up to a point, by those high domestic prices taxing back a part of the economic multiplier gains.

Even as its industry is running at only 65 percent of capacity and its real estate and stock markets have collapsed, Japan's trade surpluses have been consistently in excess of $50 billion a year with the United States alone, and it is not about to release any markets it captured to anyone. All stops will be pulled out to prevent others from selling on its home market, and—with the exception that this accumulated wealth was invested in the world's most modern industry and Western financial instruments instead of gold, silver and jewels—that is pure mercantilism by anyone's definition.[4]

Even though it has the added features of planned industrial financing and good pay for Japanese labor so the economic multiplier will develop a strong economy, mercantilist scholars will easily recognize Japan's wealth-siphoning formula: Buy resources for industry cheaply, build and maintain the most efficient industry in the world, educate its citizens, pay Japanese labor well, charge Japanese citizens above that for the same exported product, price exports just under the products of other nations, and sell enough on the world markets to pay for it all with a substantial cushion to spare.

The American/Japanese Debt/Equity Embrace

Japan invested its accumulated surplus values (half the industrialized world's savings), above that needed for building industry, in U.S. treasury notes and other financial and real properties in the United States. This has locked both Japan and America into a debt/equity embrace that neither knows how to get out of.

Japan has only to drop those treasuries and other properties on the market and the U.S. dollar crashes. (Japan's continued purchase of those treasuries was an unwritten agreement between the two countries to maintain the health of both economies.)

The United States has the choice of doing what the entire industrialized world did when OPEC raised the price of oil: just print the money to cancel the debt. America's gain would be Japan's loss but there could be much worldwide distress from such an inflationary binge even if America won that financial warfare battle.

Americans would initially have all those TV sets, computers, recorders, and automobiles for the cost of printing the money. When Japan spent those devalued dollars Americans would have to work only a fraction of the time Japanese labor worked to produce the now inflation-valued products and services. Essentially, each has the other right by the throat and neither dares squeeze any harder and neither dares turn loose. Until the Soviet Union collapsed, each had to protect the other or Japan's economy would have collapsed and America's ability to finance the Cold War would have been severely weakened.

Care for Another's Economy Is Only Between Allies

Care for another nation's economy is between allied imperial centers of capital only. There is no such *sincere* concern over economic collapses in either a resource-providing or a competing country. Such collapses mean lower resource prices and higher profits for imperial centers of capital and are the primary policy of powerful developed nations even if unrealized by second-tier planners.

Except as an ally against China if it threatens to establish a competing trading empire, imperial centers of capital no longer need Japan. But letting it collapse would be seen as a failure of capitalism and loss of philosophical support for capitalism worldwide. So, unless again needed as an ally to contain China, the forecast is for a far less robust Japan but, so long as Europe and America avoid a financial meltdown, no total collapse.

Some grand strategists are discussing America, Japan, and China allying together to bring East Asia out of its financial and economic crisis. But 1.4 billion people will not accept a trade agreement in which they are denied equality in trade. Likewise, the United States is not going to be signatory to a trade agreement which

would result in China's, Japan's, and Southeast Asia's 1.6 billion people becoming equally powerful. Not only will Asia be the world's superpower long before that equality is reached, there are not enough world resources to support an American standard of living for that many people.

Japanese Industry Is Being Forced Offshore

Japan has reached the limits of taxing the public to finance industry (raising sales taxes in Japan the second quarter of 1997 shrank consumer purchases 2.5 percent), and the lower costs of offshore corporate mercantilism are forcing Japan's industry and its economic multiplier offshore. Because the multiplication of high wages paid labor for export production throughout the economy is the heart of Japan's economic planning,[5] this has a good chance of destabilizing Japan's already shaky house of cards. Japan's economy declined between 2 percent and 3 percent in 1998 and was still declining as this book goes to press.

It Is Far From Free Trade Wherever One Looks

All major powers, including the historically allied trading blocs and China, have Social Control belief systems to keep their own masses in line and a protective negotiating paradigm when dealing with the rest of the world. *The Weight of the Yen* is a textbook on how these Social Control belief systems work. The MOF and MITI present a protective belief system to the Japanese people, parroting Adam Smith free trade rhetoric back at the rest of the world, and all the time they are running a pure mercantilist operation.

Any Japanese industrialist who tries to function outside MOF/MITI rules instantly loses access to capital, resources, and markets. Any within the ruling structure who would expose to the Japanese people or the world that Japan is not following Adam Smith and that they operate on pure mercantilist trade policies suffers immediate loss of job, power, and friends, and the "internal embargoes" are so effective there is no recovery for either errant industry or official.[6]

The major powers, as a group, promote corporate imperialist "free trade" to the undeveloped world to maintain access to their valuable resources while, as we are outlining here with Japan, jockeying for advantage among themselves. If one looks deep enough, it is far from free trade or laissez-faire anywhere one looks. Virtually every imperial center of capital has massive subsidies for its industries and, as noted above, by 1998, seventy countries, 66 percent of the people on earth, were under some form of American embargo or sanction. The world needs others with catbird seats within the other six nations of the G7 countries and the IMF/World Bank/GATT/NAFTA/WTO/MAI, corporate-utopian, world-governing system to defect and tell the whole story. This is a rare occurrence because the primary Social Control belief system is so pervasive that defectors do not find an audience, they become instantly isolated, each person instinctively knows this, and peer pressure keeps them silent.

Mr. Murphy did not defect; he has an audience because Japan's mercantilist principles were so successful they were damaging other members of the G7 nations and the Japan/Taiwan/South Korea/Southeast Asia barrier was no longer necessary to contain fast-expanding socialism. In short, anyone who exposed Japan's mercantilist policies twenty years ago would have had no audience because Japan was crucial to the West's economic warfare defense strategy. Mr. Murphy's exposure of the same protectionist process today is welcomed with open arms because exposure of Japan's mercantilism is now crucial to protection of the historic imperial centers of capital.

Though he does not use those terms, Mr. Murphy has the best outline of Social Control belief systems we have seen.[7] Even if one is viewing the world through neoclassical lenses, few books could do more to alert one to what is really going on in this world as opposed to the rhetoric (elite-protective, social-control paradigms) we hear.

Notes

1. R. Taggart Murphy, *The Weight of the Yen* (New York: W.W. Norton, 1996), pp. 13, 109–10, 181, 184, 222, 278.

2. Joel Kurtzman, *The Decline and Crash of the American Economy* (New York: W.W. Norton, 1988), pp. 107–108.

3. Murphy, *Weight of the Yen,* pp. 29–30, 72, 77, 108, 185, 197–200, 206, 212–14, 218, 222, 231, 310.

4. Ibid., pp. 43, 48, 75–79, 93–99, 106–07, 126, 133, 184–85, 192–93, 195–202, 206, 212, 214, 218–19, 231, 244, 259–69, 279, 286–310, 303, 308.

5. Ibid.

6. Ibid., pp. 53–55, 72, 98–99, 118–19, 103, 255, 275, 281.

7. Ibid., pp. 118–19, 255, 275, 281.

17

Japanese/Chinese/Southeast Asian Post–World War II Development

An Accident of History and a Crisis for Western Imperial Centers of Capital

The current development of China and Southeast Asia due to being given access to technology and markets is accidental; they were only brought within the alliance of wealthy nations to prevent the further spread of socialism. Without a threat there is no basis in capitalism's free trade philosophy to give anything to anybody (and that is Adam Smith, not just neomercantilist interpretation). Instead, the stated tenet is pay the lowest possible price, charge all the market will bear, and give nothing to anybody: a great philosophy for power brokers with a monopoly on capital, technology, markets, and military might. That monopoly was broken only by the need for allies to contain the Soviet Union and suppress the world's break for economic freedom.

Once China and Southeast Asia are industrialized, considering that Japan was destroyed in World War II, this will be the first major accumulation of capital by cultures not tied ethnically and religiously to Europe. If this accident of history continues to succeed, and only war can prevent it, 40 percent of the world's population will be provided with adequate industrial capital, up from the traditional 15 percent.

If Asia successfully develops, over 60 per-

cent of the *developed world* (not the *entire world*) will then be other than descendants of European race and culture (85 percent, if India joins the club). Considering there have been none except white, Western, Christian, European-cultured descendants controlling the centers of imperial capital, this is a historic moment by any measure and Social Darwinists will take it as a very serious security threat.

That 25 percent of the world was rapidly industrializing under Friedrich List protection philosophy while the industrialized 15 percent, and much of the remaining world, was stagnating under neomercantilist free trade philosophy, and that those economic tigers collapsed when the Cold War was won and those protections withdrawn, suggests that free trade philosophies, as designed and promoted by the imperial centers of capital, are to maintain the dependency status of the periphery.

After World War II, the United States was the only remaining intact imperial center of capital. To contain socialism, this capital and the huge American market were shared with Western Europe, Japan, Taiwan, and South Korea, on the periphery of fast-expanding socialism. Thus, so long as the Cold War was being fought and those economies were being rebuilt, the entire Western bloc was effectively one imperial center of capital. While Germany and Japan were rebuilding their capital structures, U.S. aid and expenditures to fight the Cold War served to protect their industries. Once these industries matured, continued Cold War expenditures, consumer products sold on American markets, and neomercantilist protection of their markets effectively siphoned some of America's vast wealth to rebuild European and Japanese imperial centers of capital.

The post–World War II plan was for German economic power to be submerged in the European common market with its 350 million consumers. The neomercantilist threat of this historically powerful imperial center of capital was to be eliminated through the removal of all trade barriers between Europe, Japan, and the United States, essentially maintaining one imperial center of capital.

This was a sensible plan for the already developed world but unworkable as a development plan for developing nations. It was unworkable because the historic, and still operational, pattern of siphoning wealth from the weak to the strong dictates that there must be a countryside to furnish cheap commodities to the developed and developing imperial centers of capital.[1]

The Dilemma: Will Developing Nations Oppose, or Ally with, the Historic Imperial Centers of Capitals?

With the collapse of the Soviet center of capital, claims that the one worldwide imperial center of capital is now threatening to fragment into three imperial centers of capital are likely misplaced. After deadly wars over control of trade (e.g., between Britain and Holland, Britain and Spain, and Britain and the Allies against Germany and Japan) the record of neomercantilist countries has always been to avoid subsequent battles between themselves by sharing the monopolization of world trade and allying against other emerging centers of capital. For example, we see the worldwide developed world assaults against the emerging Soviet center of capital. After losing both armed struggles and trade battles, Portugal and Spain were left out of earlier sharing in world trade but are being brought into Europe's latest trade alliance.

Because a large bloc of industrial capital had been donated by the former Soviet Union, China had the basic industries with which to begin industrialization. Initially, corporate imperialists had no choice but to permit Southeast Asia and China to develop under that same protective umbrella spread over Japan, Taiwan, and South Korea. Having accommodated to that reality, Managers of State were unable to make a quick paradigm shift to contain China when the Soviet Union collapsed, nor could they control the capital now broadly diffused throughout the periphery of empire. However, with the Soviet collapse, there was now little need for allies to protect Southeast Asia's, or anyone else's, accumulations of capital or access to resources and markets.

But a quick paradigm shift to withdraw protection from China and Southeast Asia would have exposed the fiction of neomercantilist free trade, and there was now the problem of widely diffused capital fleeing high-priced labor, which would have made embargoing and containment of China a difficult task. As all nations of Southeast Asia were practicing Friedrich List protection rather than the free trade all were mouthing, they could have developed, and may still develop, into an opposing imperial center of capital with all the risks of trade wars and hot wars that entails. The nine-year recession in

Japan and the 1997–98 financial meltdown of Southeast Asia after protection was withdrawn have increased that potential.

Those countries are thinking about protecting their markets and currencies by forming a regional monetary fund. Grand Strategy philosophers are speaking of the yen as the primary currency. But true freedom can be only when each country ties its currency values to the value of a basket of commodities (as we will be addressing later). Once a region has a stable currency backed by commodities, the central bank of each nation will have the rights of creating money.

If economic collapse can be avoided and labor's race to the bottom (the law of wages) can be reversed, the equalization of labor values may eventually substantially expand rights and increase living standards. But there is no assurance that the race to the bottom can be halted. The world is yet locked within the jaws of that centuries-old policy of the countryside providing cheap resources and markets for developed imperial centers of capital. It remains to be seen whether the contradictions of lowering the buying power of labor in the developed world; the collapse of buying power on the periphery of empire due to the abandoning of supports (protections) for Southeast Asian countries; and the massive accumulations of capital cannibalizing each other will again create a worldwide economic crisis.

No matter how sincere Managers of State are, to negotiate honestly for world development is not possible under the current rules of neomercantilist free trade. Virtually every nation that developed did so while protecting its industries and internal markets. Trade between the developed world and the latest successfully developing countries was carefully managed, and to develop the remaining countries requires even more careful management. That, without massive economic restructuring within the developed world, is an extreme contradiction. Historically some societies had to provide those cheap resources. The one best hope for the world is to share those resources and the wealth produced through cooperative capitalism.

Notes

1. "Set in Concrete," *The Economist,* June 3, 1995, pp. 28–29.

18

Capital Destroying Capital

Factories moving offshore for low-paid labor develop little regional buying power in the undeveloped world, while the loss of those factories in the developed world reduces that region's buying power. The difference goes into corporate coffers to be distributed to owners of stock, corporate managers, and stock traders. As monopolized capital shuts down factories in the developed world and builds new industrial capacity in low-wage areas to produce products for high-paid workers in the developed world, the wealth of both the low-wage and high-wage regions is claimed by intermediaries and there is eventually insufficient market to absorb production fully. By expanding productive capacity without expanding equal buying power, capital destroys capital. (It is unrealistic to assume that this will be the first time in history those rising stock values that have been providing the consumer buying power will not turn around, go down, and collapse buying power.)

In 1987, "world overcapacity was estimated to be fifteen to twenty percent in automobile production, twenty percent in steel, twenty-five percent in semiconductors, and over twenty percent in petrochemicals."[1] From 1990 into 1999, Japan's industry was operating at only 65.5 percent of capacity while the world was producing at not over 75 percent of capacity. With such overcapacity in the developed world, and with the buying power—thus the only consumer market—being in the developed world, large sectors of the developing world cannot capitalize. The world's powerless cannot obtain their share of industrial capital and high-paying jobs that create buying power, profits, and capitalized values. Michael Moffitt quotes Stanley J. Mihelick, executive vice president for production at Goodyear:

"Until we get real wage levels down much closer to those of Brazil's and Korea's, we cannot pass along productivity gains to wages and still be competitive." With factory wages in Mexico and Korea averaging about $3 an hour, compared with U.S. wages of $14 or so, it looks as if we have a long way to go before U.S. wages will even be in the ball park with the competition. That the decline of U.S. industry is the natural and logical outcome of the evolution of the multinational corporate economy over the past twenty-five years has been a bitter pill to swallow and it will become increasingly distasteful as time goes on. *One consequence will be a nasty decline in the standard of living in the United States. . . .* [W]e have the outlines of a true vicious circle: the world economy is dependent on growth in the U.S. economy but the U.S. domestic economy is [now] skewed more towards consumption than production and investment, and this consumption is in turn sustained by borrowing—at home and abroad. . . . The deal with surplus countries essentially has been as follows: you can run a big trade surplus with us provided that you put the money back into our capital markets.[2]

The excessive accumulation of capital by stateless corporate imperialists, and the denial of capital to the world's powerless and their lack of prosperous internal market economies, are two sides of the same coin. There is too little buying power among the dispossessed to purchase all the production of industrial capital. When there is already a surplus, capital building more industry without developing more consumer buying power will destroy other capital:

> So long as global productive capacity exceeds global demand by such extravagant margins, somebody somewhere in the world has to keep closing factories, old and new. . . . South Korea will be losing jobs to cheap labor in Thailand and even China may someday lose factories to Bangladesh.[3]

In 1988, China offered to launch satellites at one-quarter the price charged by the United States. Under competition from such low-wage cartel-structured industries, even the huge U.S. industries that once dominated the satellite launching market could not survive. That threat to Western industry was eliminated by negotiation and Americans and Europeans still dominate the satellite launching industry (exposing the fictions of free trade and proving that China can be negotiated with rationally).

Currently one-third of the automobiles and 95 percent of the home electronics sold in the United States are imported, and 30 percent of *all* products purchased by the American people are manufactured overseas. In comparison, before the financial meltdown on the periphery of empire, the relatively small populations of Hong Kong, Singapore, South Korea, and Taiwan "account[ed] for ten percent of the world's

manufactured exports; the U.S. share [was] twelve percent.''[4]

If Korea, China, Malaysia, Thailand and other low-wage countries continue their economic development based on industrial cartels and protected home markets while selling to the developed Western markets under the fiction of free trade, industries in America, Europe, and Japan will be destroyed. The one who "distributes" (not necessarily produces) the cheapest and best product captures the market. Cheaper, however, normally means lower-paid labor, lax rules on pollution, and tax avoidance—not less labor expended or a better factory.

The elimination of more expensive manufacturers through free trade appears beneficial and, whenever an inefficient or shoddy producer is eliminated, it is. But many of the factories are closed not because of their low quality or inefficiency but because there are too many factories producing for the established market. The well-paid workers of the relatively developed countries are the logical losers and low-paid workers of fleeing industries will only gain a small part of what the former workers lost. When industrial capital is diverted to an undeveloped country to produce for a developed country, the advantage of the former's cheap labor destroys both the established industry and the consumer buying power of the developed country. William Greider explains:

> The world's existing structure of manufacturing facilities, constantly being expanded on cheap labor and new technologies, can now turn out far more goods than the world's consumers can afford to buy. . . . The auto industry is an uncomplicated example: Auto factories worldwide have the capacity to produce 45 million cars annually for a market that, in the best years, will buy no more than 35 million cars. . . . Somebody has to close his auto factory and stop producing.[5]

Capital Destroying Capital as Opposed to Expanding Buying Power to Keep Factories Running Is Economic Insanity

New industrial capital destroying both established equally productive industrial capital and the social capital built around that industry is economic insanity. Where industries and jobs disappear as capital destroys capital, both home and business values drop. Through neomercantilist free trade the developed nations are destroying each other's industries, while 70 percent of the world's population is desperately short of industrial capital. *There is currently no mechanism within the market system to build consumer buying power and implant this new technology where it is badly needed while keeping the already producing factories servicing the already established market.*

Industries Can Be Built Quickly But Markets Only Slowly

This vividly highlights the problems generated by monopolization of the tools of production. While industries can be built quickly, under neomercantilist free trade policies, markets can be developed only slowly. Instead of building market economies and developing consumers among the world's impoverished as the following chapters on external trade advocate, giant producers are busy competing with each other for control of current markets and destroying each other's capital in the process.

This cannibalization of each other's industries battling over the current developed markets is ultimately self-destructive. The destruction of industrial capital and social capital by wars is well-known. What is little known is that these struggles over limited purchasing power destroy perfectly good industrial capital, collapse the value of social capital (homes and businesses), and forgo the production of even more wealth; capital destroys capital.

Expanding Buying Power in Step with Increased Industrial Capacity

While nations scramble to build industries to sell to consumers in the imperial centers of capital, structural adjustment rules of subtly monopolized capital deny them the right to increase their buying power in step with that increased production. The immediate discounting of a nation's currency on the periphery of empire if it attempted to print money to generate buying power within its own economy exposes how control of trading currency monopolizes buying power for imperial centers of capital.

Only by creating money in step with, and in balance with, productive capacity will there be a market for the production from that easily built industrial capacity. As the productive combining of land (resources), labor, and capital (industrial technology) are the three requirements for a wealthy society, buying power is logically created by printing money to combine these economic factors and, so long as the money created is in balance with the wealth produced as addressed below, that new wealth will back that newly printed money as it circulates within the economy.

The Monopoly Hold on Technology and Markets Is Weakening

Even as capital is being indiscriminately destroyed, the world economic system keeps getting more efficient. "It took Britain and the United States fifty-eight and forty-seven years, respectively, to double their per capita output, but Japan did it in thirty-three years, Indonesia in seventeen, South Korea in eleven, and China in ten,"[6] and, if equal free trade under cooperative capitalism were economic policy instead of unequal free trade under corporate imperialism, the world could be industrialized to a sustainable level even more quickly.

What we are witnessing is the continued weakening hold of the monopolization of technology. Eliminate fully the control of markets through subtle monopolies and, as addressed below, the world economy would become so efficient that the world could be capitalized to a sustainable level and poverty largely eliminated in forty-five years.

The large profits being recorded by corporations and steadily increasing GNPs have been acclaimed by monopolists as proof that their theories are correct.[7] These profits show up in corporate expansions, foreign purchases of U.S. land and businesses, a climbing stock market, corporate takeovers, and the multiplication of billionaires, and, until the 1996–97 increase in the minimum wage, the 19 percent wage loss to nonsupervisory labor in the United States.[8]

Americans with no net share of the nation's wealth increased from 25 percent of the population in 1974 to 54 percent in 1988.[9] By 1996, virtually all statistics on income earned and wealth retained had increased broadly and rapidly for the wealthy, had lowered for the middle classes, and dropped substantially for the poor. While the earnings of nonsupervisory labor were dropping rapidly, CEO salaries climbed to 326 times a factory worker's pay (up from forty times twenty years earlier).

Elimination of Capital Destroying Capital Through Cooperative Capitalism Will Lower Prices and Raise Living Standards

Though some of the gains of the wealthy were taken directly from labor, that capital is destroying capital while profits are booming outlines the large overcharges required to pay for this continual cannibalism. The cost of moving factories, the cost of perfectly good factories destroyed, the loss of value of social infrastructure in abandoned communities, and the record profits are all part of the overcharge. So too is military expenditure for protection of this wealth-siphoning system also a loss to society. Both corporate and labor shares of taxes that go to produce arms are in those overcharges. And those losses could become even greater. With static, or even shrinking, world consumer buying power by the continued following of neoclassical economic theory, even more capital will be destroyed.

We see the dramatic forerunner of this in the long-running economic collapse in Japan, the 1997–98 financial meltdown in Southeast Asia, and the potential meltdown in Latin America. Even with an annual $50 billion trade surplus, the Japanese economy has been collapsing for ten years. Japan now has $11 trillion in savings, the trade surplus continues, massive funds are inserted into the economy to prevent a total collapse, and still (March 1999) the economy keeps dropping.

The fiction of $11 trillion in savings while Japan is in a depression will be exposed if the world crisis deepens. All that money is loaned out somewhere. If the equity values backing those loans drop far enough long enough, bankrupt banks will have to close and the money is gone. Those bad bank loans were estimated at $500 billion in 1997, increased to an estimated

$1.3 trillion in 1999, and could increase if property values continue to go down. However, if the Japanese and world economy turns around and those property values rise, the bad loans decline, and those savings become valid again. This hope is why Japan refuses to shut down those banks.

Underpaying for the raw material to feed those industries and the labor to operate them was a crucial element of the imbalance that created this crisis. The Third World, which furnished the raw material to feed East Asian and developed world industries, was not paid enough to purchase a balancing share of production, industries were built in cheap-labor countries to sell to consumers in the well-paid world, and their labor was not paid enough to buy their relative share of production. If a financial/Fascist fix cannot be put in place (a powerful imperial center siphoning the wealth of a powerless periphery), this threatens to pull down the whole world economy.

Conversely, restructuring to equal free trade (access to technology and markets and equal pay for equally productive work as opposed to unequal free trade) and establishing a just legal structure under cooperative capitalism would eliminate the cost of moving factories, the loss of destroyed industries, and the loss of value of abandoned communities. Those savings could then go towards industrializing the world within a sustainable level, protecting the environment, and reducing poverty.

This wasted industrial capital could just as well produce industrial tools for sale to the developing world. For that matter, why not return a share of this capital, as compensation, to those whose wealth has been confiscated through centuries of inequalities of trade? With the tools provided by that initial capital, and its own resources and labor, the developing world could build its regional economic infrastructure. As demonstrated below, cooperative capitalism would provide its tools for the impoverished world to build its own social capital (homes, roads, stores, etc.) to a sustainable level and eliminate most poverty in two generations.

Notes

1. Jeff Faux, "The Austerity Trap and the Growth Alternative," *World Policy Journal* (Summer 1988), p. 375.

2. Michael Moffitt, "Shocks, Deadlocks, and Scorched Earth," *World Policy Journal* (Fall 1987), pp. 560–61, 572–73 (emphasis added).

3. William Greider, *Who Will Tell the People?* (New York: Simon and Schuster, 1992), pp. 378–79, 399–400.

4. David C. Korten, *When Corporations Rule the World* (West Hartford, CT: Kumarian Press, 1995), p. 128; Steven Schlosstein, *Trade War* (New York: Congdon & Weed, 1984), chapter 28; Susan Dentzer, "The Coming Global Boom," *U.S. News & World Report,* July 16, 1990, pp. 22–28; Walter Russell Mead, "The Bush Administration and the New World Order," *World Policy Journal* (Summer 1991), p. 393.

5. Greider, *Who Will Tell the People?,* p. 399.

6. Samuel P. Huntington, *The Clash of Civilizations* (New York: Simon and Schuster, 1996), p. 103.

7. Karl Polanyi, *The Great Transformation* (Boston: Beacon Press, 1957), p. 29; Lester Thurow, *Head to Head: The Coming Economic Battle Among Japan, Europe, and America* (New York: William Morrow, 1992), p. 60.

8. Lester Thurow, "Falling Wages, Failing Policy," *Dollars and Sense* (September/October 1996), p. 7. There were over 140 billionaires worldwide in 1987, increasing to 358 in 1994. *Forbes Magazine* seems to have quit counting (check July issues each year). Lester Thurow, "The Crusade That Is Killing Prosperity," *The American Prospect* (March/April 1996), pp. 54–59.

9. Dean Baker, "Job Drain," *The Nation,* July 12, 1993, p. 68; Thurow, *Head to Head,* p. 53; Robert S. McIntyre, "The Populist Tax Act of 1989," *The Nation,* April 2, 1988, pp. 445, 462; Kevin Phillips, *The Politics of Rich and Poor* (New York: Random House,

1990), pp. 12, 14, 79, 164, 205. Phillips puts the gain of the top 1 percent from $174,498 in 1977 to $303,900 in 1988; Kevin Phillips, *Boiling Point* (New York: Random House, 1993), especially pp. 7, 24–25, 104, 108–109, 112; Gerald Epstein, "Mortgaging America," *World Policy Journal* (Winter 1990–91), pp. 31–32; Matthew Cooper and Dorian Freedman, "The Rich in America," *U.S. News & World Report,* November 18, 1991, p. 35; "Top 1% Own More Than Bottom 90%," *The Des Moines Register,* April 21, 1992, p. 4A; Hardy Green, "Income Erosion: Economic Landslides," *In These Times,* November 14–20, 1990, p. 18, taken from *Prosperity Lost,* by Philip Mattera; Lester C. Thurow, *Generating Inequality* (New York: Basic Books, 1975), p. 14; "Worker's State," *The Nation,* September 19, 1988, p. 187–88; Barry Bluestone and Irving Bluestone, *Negotiating the Future* (New York: Basic Books, 1992), p. 5.

19

A New Hope for the World

The least traumatic course may be to allow the labor costs between the trading countries to balance. But those economies will not retain that balance; capital will move to still cheaper labor. In 1988, China opened to outside investors coastal economic zones that encompass a population of 200 million cheap laborers. With the necessary political infrastructure in place to control labor and markets, leading-edge technology started flowing to China. Initially there were great profits for foreign investors as the latest technology, in tandem with China's cheap labor, took over others' markets.

However, most investment capital in China is internally generated (a fact that is studiously ignored) and, once she is developed and this labor force learns modern skills, the scene will change. Like Japan and South Korea while under Cold War protection, and before their financial meltdown when that protection was withdrawn, China (still financially sound, as of March 1999) will manage her economy to export a surplus. The price charged for products on world markets will drop to just below that of the competition, an ever-increasing amount of the world's consumer products will be produced by Chinese-owned industry, and an ever-increasing share of production costs will be paid to Chinese labor, which will, in turn, accumulate ever more capital in China. With that in-creased capital, China can produce more for export. If this process is allowed to reach its logical conclusion, much of the wealth of the United States, Japan, and other countries will then be siphoned to China. It will become the equivalent of ten Japans and Hong Kongs competing on world markets and other still lower wage countries will be entering the market.

If mainland China were to achieve the same per-capita surplus as Taiwan ($567), the United States would have an annual trade deficit of an obviously impossible $750 billion with China alone.[1] If India, Malaysia, South Korea, Pakistan, Bangladesh, and Indonesia were to achieve similar success, the U.S. trade deficit with Asia's NICs (Newly Industrializing Countries) would rise to something between an even more ridiculous $1.5 trillion and $2 trillion annually.

Before China agreed to limit increases to 3 percent per year (free trade is avoided when it becomes dangerous), its textile exports to the United States were climbing 19 percent a year. Its trade surplus with the United States climbed from $3 billion in 1989 to $33.8 billion in 1995 and to $60 billion in 1998.[2] We must analyze these figures with caution. Lost to history have been many gentle and just cultures that were overwhelmed and destroyed by unjust and violent ones (survival of the meanest). China claims for years it has followed positive and open trade policies, adhered to the trade principle of maintaining a basic balance between imports and exports, and sought to uphold that balance throughout its development. Apparently, the United States has seriously overstated the U.S. trade deficit, and the enormous unfavorable balance of the United States in its trade with China simply does not exist.[3]

China's minister of foreign trade, Wu Yi, has not addressed the wealth siphoned through unequal currency values we addressed in the Introduction. But she is backed by adequate statistics that the 1995 trade deficit of $33.8 billion claimed by the United States was actually $8.59 billion. Wu Yi points out that China exports primarily partially processed products and imports relatively finished products.

Such a natural resource and finished product trade imbalance unfavorable to China—as the wealthy world monetizes the natural wealth on the periphery of empire and transfers that wealth to itself through inequality of wages and prices in the manufacturing and trading process—would actually be transferring wealth to the United States even as America recorded a deficit. Partially finished products from China would be finished in America and Europe to further increase the wealth.

China has the resources, population, and internal cohesion to force honest trade upon the world by example if it so chooses. That same economic strength and cohesion will allow it to weather the economic storm that has arrived as the Cold War fades into history and corporate imperialism permits the "law of wages" to operate with full force and drive down the wages of both the developed and undeveloped worlds.

Three Powerful Economic Weapons Available for Developing World Use

There are three powerful economic weapons the impoverished developing nations can use: barter

their resources to the developed world in trade for technology, finance capital, and access to markets; create their own trading currencies; and manufacture their own consumer products for trade with each other. If the 1997–98 economic collapse continues, they will have idle resources, idle industry, and idle labor, and any coalition of trading nations can create their own trading currency. Trading currency is nothing more than the representation of wealth produced by combining land (resources), labor, and industrial capital. By combining their resources, the developing nations have all three foundations of wealth. If they create their own trading currencies and tie those currencies' values to a market basket of commodities as outlined below, the imperial centers of capital's financial warfare weapons will have been rendered harmless.

The developing-world countries can then trade with each other for the resources to keep their industries and their economies going and barter resources to the developed world in trade for the latest technology for those industries. Bartering avoids hard money monopolization and the resultant unequal trades between weak and strong nations. The developed world needs Third World resources just as badly as the Third World needs technology and finance capital. Except for the superior military power of the imperial centers of capital, the undeveloped world has the superior bargaining position. The imperial center's superior military forces maintaining firm control all over the world exposes military might as the final arbiter.

Barter was how Germany was breaking the financial blockade put in place to strangle it, and World Wars I and II settled that trade dispute. The imperial centers of capital own those factories and patents. If barter is again tried, then monopoly title to technology—and thus monopoly control of others' resources—

will be clearly visible. The efforts to prevent those barters will expose the monopolies even further and hopefully they can finally be bypassed.

Hope for the World Lies in Developing-world Regional Trading Blocs Attaining Equal Negotiating Power

If there is no ''countryside'' to maintain in dependency, there can be no imperial centers of capital enforcing unequal trades. The Soviet Union fought so long and so hard that after World War II America (the only remaining intact imperial center of capital) was forced to share its capital with Western Europe, Japan, Taiwan, and South Korea to retain them as loyal allies. Before the Soviets collapsed, while they were thus still a threat, China and Southeast Asia moved under that sharing protectionist umbrella and, until the Southeast Asia financial meltdown, were rapidly developing. A powerful and fast-developing China that does not fully incorporate the Western belief system is now the new threat to historic imperial centers of capital. So long as China can maintain its independence, industrial technology is now so diffuse that the monopoly power of capital has eroded.

Up until the economic and financial collapses on the periphery in 1997–98, Managers of State were losing control of technology (industrial capital). The next few years will tell us whether the financial power of the wealthy world has reinstated control (Mexico's, Southeast Asia's, and Russia's 1997–98 implosion); whether the attempt to reclaim control will collapse the world economy; whether fear of a flight from the old belief system will result in a central plan to recapitalize those collapsed emerging economies; or whether a Fascist combination of financial, political, and military power will organize and maintain firm control of the world economy. If China can maintain its independence, not only will it be impossible to embargo technology from it, but a new Social Control belief system, with a powerful China as the new enemy, will not work while China is rapidly developing and the rest of the world is stagnating. If China (or any other powerful trading bloc) retains the ideology of rights for all the world's people, if it is sincere in that belief (all nations, especially the imperial centers of capital, preach that philosophy but none follow it), if it is strong enough not to be subverted and too strong to be attacked, and if this blend of power and sincere caring for others results in all the world gaining access to technology and markets with equal pay for equally productive work, the world will then have the opportunity for the forty-five years of peace it would take to develop the world to a sustainable level and alleviate world poverty.

If China and Southeast Asia (25 percent of the world's population) successfully develop and the old empires (15 percent of the world's population) remain static, the balance of world power will shift to Asia. This is the fundamental reason for the continued rhetoric of Chinese human rights abuses. It is the threat that China will be successful and, in alliance with all Southeast Asia, emerge as a greater economic power than the old imperial centers of capital that worries the wealthy world's Managers of State.[4]

China could lead the way toward honest free trade. Once its satellite/fiber optic communication system is in place, China could bombard its citizens with a belief system for sustainable world development. Those promotions should outline the quality life that could be had for all if that were society's goal. One child per family would shrink a nation's population by 50 percent in three generations while doubling the amenities of life for each citizen. A steady increase in technological efficiency during the same time span could double the amenities of life again and all that gain would be without increasing the hours of labor, consumption of resources, or pollution of the environment. There are those who will decry such a policy as a denial of rights. But there are many kinds of rights. Not many serious philosophers will deny that a massive overpopulation collapsing the earth's ability to sustain its population will result in the most massive denial of the most basic rights the world has ever known.

We use China as an example because it has the necessary social cohesion. If China succeeds and the lowering of its population results in a rapid rise in its per capita living standards, others will take note, adopt the same policies, and their living standards will also rise rapidly.

Such a rapid expansion of rights will be a threat of the first order to the imperial nations. They know well that, once resources on the periphery are turned towards the care of its own impoverished, those resources will not be available for the high lifestyles in the imperial centers. The goal of the imperial center is to coopt the powerful within China so as not to be threatened by such expansions of rights, or to prevent such expansion of rights by containing China's access to technology and finance capital, which in turn will contain China's access to world re-sources and its economic development. Thus, reducing its population and rapidly increasing its per capita wealth without expansion of resource use is China's best hope for gaining economic freedom.

If corporate imperialists are able to coopt the newly wealthy of China and impose their monopoly competitive system of siphoning the wealth from the weak to the powerful upon that nation (as they have, at least temporarily, in the destabilized former Soviet Union), that hope will not be realized.

Notes

1. Walter Russell Mead, "The Bush Administration and the New World Order," *World Policy Journal* (Summer 1991), p. 404.

2. Wu Yi, "China-U.S. Trade Balances: An Objective Evaluation," *Beijing Review,* June 10–16, 1996, pp. 10–13; John Yochelson, "China's Boom Creates a U.S. Trade Dilemma," *The Christian Science Monitor,* March 1, 1994, p. 19; "China Maneuvering Around Quotas to Market Textiles to United States," *The Spokesman-Review,* January 10, 1989, p. B6; *CNN Headline News,* June, 28, 1990; Jim Mann, "China's Response to U.S.: Slow, Slow," *Los Angeles Times,* October 28, 1998, p. A5.

3. Wu Yi, "China-U.S. Trade Balances," pp. 10–13.

4. William Greider, *One World Ready or Not* (New York: Simon and Schuster, 1997), pp. 147–52, 166–70.

Part III

External Trade: Sharing Technology with the World Through Cooperative Capitalism: The Route to World Peace and Prosperity

20

The Earth's Capacity to Sustain Developed Economies

[The minerals in concentrated] deposits in the earth's crust, and the capacity of ecosystems to absorb large quantities of exotic qualities of waste materials and heat, set a limit on the number of person-years that can be lived in the "developed" state, as that term is understood today in the United States. How the limited number of person-years of "developed" living will be apportioned among nations, among social classes, and over generations will be the dominant economic and political issue for the future. World population has grown at around 2 percent annually, doubling every seventeen or eighteen years. . . . [For a sustainable, respectable world standard of living], births should equal deaths at low rather than high levels so that life expectancy is long rather than short. Similarly, new production of artifacts should equal depreciation at low levels so that durability or "longevity" of artifacts is high. New production implies increasing depletion of resources. Depreciation implies the creation of physical waste [and consumption of resources], which when returned to the environment, becomes pollution.[1]

Currently, the most effective way to control population is to raise a society's standard of living and provide access to family planning. To help feed, clothe, and house the family, and to care for parents in old age, impoverished people have many children. Successful social and family planning was demonstrated in Kerala, one of India's poorest regions, which has a birth rate half that of other low-income countries.[2]

Kerala's per capita income is only 60 percent that of India as a whole. Yet when it comes to meeting the needs of the people, Kerala is strikingly ahead of the rest of India. It has enforced progressive land reform and brought about major social benefits precisely for the most disadvantaged. Infant mortality in Kerala is twenty-seven per thousand, compared to eighty-six per thousand in other countries at the same income level. Life expectancy elsewhere in India is fifty-seven years, in Kerala sixty-eight. Elementary and secondary schools operate in practically every village, where one can also find health dispensaries, fair price shops, bus stops, all-weather roads—a far cry from village life in the rest of India.[3]

The developing countries of China, Sri Lanka, Colombia, Chile, Burma, and Cuba have a birthrate comparable to that of wealthy nations rather than the high rate of a subsistence economy.[4] With the biggest population problem, China first adopted a two-child policy, later reduced to one child, with a 10 percent salary cut for those who ignored those guidelines. Although still increasing at the rate of 17 million per year in 1990 (a combination of many young people and longer life spans), it is hoped that China's population will eventually stabilize, then, hopefully, shrink.

Each region should have its capacity to feed,

clothe, and house its population, while still protecting the world's ecosystem, mapped and statistically analyzed. People should be taught the limits of their country's capacity to sustain a population at a respectable standard of living while protecting resources and environment. To reach those goals, family planning information should be universally available. Since most people currently depend on their children in old age, family planning requires that all elderly be guaranteed adequate food, fiber, and shelter. *A reduction of one child per family will save a society far more than it will cost to maintain that family during retirement.*

It is not unreasonable to hypothesize that, if it were demonstrated that a lowering of population would give a sustainable secure lifestyle as opposed to poverty without it, individuals would restrict their birthrate to reach that goal. If a reduction of population can be obtained in those heavily populated areas while industrializing, the per capita living standard will increase dramatically and assure acceptance of that policy. A steady increase in technological efficiency during the same time span could double the amenities of life again and all without increasing consumption of resources or pollution of the environment. There will be great variation in potential depending on how high a living standard is used, what resources are used for housing (wood, soil, or salvage), what new technologies are developed, population increase or decrease, and so on. However, with those statistics common knowledge, goals can be set and reached.

Primary Concerns of World Industrialization

The hydrocarbons that produce much of the energy that fuels society were produced by hundreds of millions of years of plant life taking carbon dioxide out of the air and creating those carbon compounds. The amount of carbon dioxide in the atmosphere has increased 25 percent and it is estimated the world's temperature has risen one degree in this century. There is great concern that the burning of those fuels and the release of carbon dioxide and other gases back into the atmosphere will create a greenhouse effect and seriously disrupt the world's weather. (With eight of the last twelve years being the warmest in recorded history and the ozone layer rapidly thinning, this process may have started.) Scientists' primary concerns about world industrialization are the following:

1. "If the current trend of carbon dioxide, chlorofluorocarbon (CFC), nitrous oxide, and methane emissions continues into the next century, this could subject the entire globe to an increased temperature rise of four to nine degrees Fahrenheit or more in less than sixty years. . . . A global warming of [this magnitude] . . . would exceed the entire rise in global temperatures since the end of the last ice age. If the scientific projections are correct, the human species will experience the unfolding of an entire geological epoch in less than one lifetime."[5]

2. Of the estimated 10 million to 80 million animal and plant species on Earth (only 1.4 million of which have been scientifically identified), a minimum of 140 invertebrate species and one bird, mammal, or plant species are condemned to extinction each day. "Within [one] decade, we may lose nearly twenty percent of all the remaining species of life on earth." That is a rate thousands of times greater than the natural rate.[6]

3. Chlorofluorocarbons have been in use for about fifty years. It takes ten to fifteen years for one CFC molecule to work its way through the atmosphere to the ozone layer. Once there, those molecules survive for a century or more and, theoretically, each CFC molecule could destroy 100,000 ozone molecules. This 1974 theory of Professor Sherwood Rowland was given credence when a British research team discovered a huge seasonal thinning of the Antarctic ozone. Scientists calculated a 10 percent ozone depletion in the northern latitudes over a ten-year period but were astounded when that level was reached in only two years and another ozone hole opened in the north. The increased ultraviolet rays that would reach the Earth, if that thinning continues (which it is doing— by 1998 the first ozone hole was twice the size of the United States), are anticipated to cause cancers, harm to immune systems, destruction of some species of microorganisms, and thus, destruction of entire food chains.[7]

4. The human "species now consumes over forty percent of all the energy produced by photosynthesis on the planet, leaving only sixty percent for all other creatures. With the human population expected to double early in the next century [if limitations are not imposed], our species will be consuming eighty percent of the planet's photosynthetic energy, leaving little or nothing for millions of other species, and in the process we will be destroying the stable mix of gases in the atmosphere."[8]

5. If international consumption of oil continues to grow and even if new oil finds equal to four times the present reserves are discovered (which most experts consider unlikely), it will be only fifty years before the total exhaustion of all oil reserves.[9]

6. If 18 percent of the world adopted and attained the U.S. living standard of an automobile-throwaway society, it would consume all the annual resource production of the world, leaving nothing for the other 82 percent.[10]

7. The first law of thermodynamics says that "energy can be neither created nor destroyed, only transformed." The second law of thermodynamics says, "this energy can only be transformed one way, from usable to unusable." This means that, do what we may, it is only a matter of time until the world's resources are consumed. Albert Einstein pointed out that this law "is the only physical theory of universal content which I am convinced, that within the framework of applicability of its basic concepts, will not be overthrown."[11]

8. To prevent global warming, ozone depletion, and species extinction, there are limited logical choices. To avoid the greenhouse effect, the world must reduce the burning of fossil fuels, reforest the planet to absorb the increased carbon dioxide, and reduce the release of harmful pollutants into the atmosphere, water, and soils.[12]

Within the next twenty-five years, scientists should know if the well-documented trend towards global warming, ozone depletion, and species extinction is continuing and be able to estimate the damage. If the risk to life of burning fossil fuels, coupled with the destruction of forests needed to recycle carbon dioxide, proves threatening to human culture and survival, then, as addressed in chapters Twenty-Two and Twenty-Three, an ecological tax should be placed upon those fuels and the money generated used to develop and install ecologically safe technology such as solar energy.[13]

Civilizations Collapse When Soil Fertility Collapses

Since their origins in Central Asia and Northern China, the cultures of empire that term themselves civilized have collapsed their soils. One-half the area of present China was once covered with a vast temperate-zone forest. This forest was eliminated before recorded history by the expansion of the empires of China. For the thousands of years since, China has suffered some of the worst erosion in the world. The Yellow Sea is named for the surrounding land's eroding yellow loess soils carried into it by the rivers.[14]

The empires of Sumer and Babylon in the watershed of the Tigris-Euphrates River collapsed after irrigated agriculture and overgrazing by domesticated animals destroyed their land. Today, one-third of the arable land of Iraq cannot be used because it is still salinized by irrigation from 5,000 years ago. The mouth of the Tigris-Euphrates River has extended itself 185 miles into the Gulf as the fertility of that hapless land washed into the sea. Every empire has run, and still runs, a net deficit of the fertility of the earth in order to sustain the unnatural growth and material consumption of its population.[15] The cultural history of Babylon can be traced through time to the denuded Greece and to Rome, which denuded the ecology of that peninsula. Most of North Africa—which once had great forests, broad grassy plains, lions, tigers, and many other plants and animals—became a desert. Both the Greek and Roman empires used the then-healthy soils of

North Africa as their "breadbasket." Now cities that once were ports for shipping products to the old imperial centers are five and ten miles from water as the fertile soils that once produced those exports settled into the Mediterranean Ocean.[16] Before the rising Muslim societies cut Europe off from the light soils of their African breadbasket, there was one vast forest the width of Europe nourished by those heavy soils. That vast forest built ships, smelted ores, warmed homes, and was burned down so the land could be farmed.

The history of this culture can be traced through the deforested lands and exhausted soils of Europe, across North America, and now through the deforestation of the tropical forests of South America, Africa, and the Pacific islands. During the expansion of the American empire, the great forests that lay between the Allegheny Mountains and the Mississippi River (enough to have produced a set of fine hardwood furniture for every family then on earth) were burned to clear the land for farming. Soil scientists estimate that one-half the topsoil of the Great Plains has been exhausted since agriculture began there barely 150 years ago.[17]

Industrial agriculture has learned to create artificial fertilizer from petroleum feedstock so that it trades off biological energy for a finite amount of hydrocarbons. In many areas the soil is exhausted and without such inputs would grow nothing. Modern industrial agriculturists say this is no problem as all they need soil for now is to prop up the plants. Thus nearly half the population of the planet eat food produced with artificial fertilizer processed from petroleum.[18] The exponentially exploding population of civilization is out on the proverbial limb with a diet provided by a steadily declining, finite supply of petroleum.[19] Coal can provide those chemical fertilizers for a while longer but that too will eventually be exhausted and there are many minerals and other nutrients being lost that are not being replaced.

In addition to exhaustion of soil, half of all arable land on the planet is experiencing erosion over and above any soil buildup. Though the issue of soil fertility may have become a moot point, temporarily, with industrial agriculture, even that production method needs some soil to "prop up the plants." Erosion, desertification, toxification, and nonagricultural uses will consume one-fifth of the world's arable land as we begin the twenty-first century. Another one-fifth will go by 2025. These figures are for arable land only and do not include the general erosion and degradation of lands all over the earth from human activities such as deforestation, overgrazing, fire and other results of injudicious human occupancy.[20]

If democratic control of society can be accomplished and human society can be agile enough, this situation can be turned around. Permaculture, a complex method of edible landscape design with a wide variety of perennial plants, can rebuild soils and slowly restore ecosystems while growing more food per acre than modern industrial agriculture.[21]

Bio-intensive gardening, while not restoring ecosystems, can insure a food supply. Using the particular varieties of plants and the methods detailed by the Ecology Action Research Center at Willits, California, it is possible to feed one person on 1,000 square feet of soil in perpetuity without robbing any other ecosystem of humus. All composting material is grown on that thousand-square-foot plot. There are hundreds of permaculture projects around the world and groups have come from all corners of the world to learn these skills at workshops in Willits.[22]

Notes

1. Herman E. Daly, *Steady-State Economics* (San Francisco: W. H. Freeman, 1977), pp. 6, 7, 17.

2. Richard W. Franke and Barbara H. Chasin, "Power to the (Malayalee) People," *Z Magazine* (February 1998), pp. 16–20; Bill McKibben, "The Enigma of Kerala," *Utne Reader* (March/April 1996), pp. 103–112; Arjun Makhijani, *From Global Capitalism to Economic Justice* (New York: Apex Press, 1992), pp. 133–34.

3. Franke and Chasin, "Power to the (Malayalee) People," pp. 16–20; McKibben, "Enigma of Kerala," pp. 103–112; Harry Magdoff, "Are There Lessons To Be Learned?" *Monthly Review* (February 1991), pp. 12; Richard W. Franke and Barbara H. Chasin, "Kerala State, India; Radical Reform as Development," *Monthly Review* (January 1991), pp. 1–23.

4. Frances Moore Lappé and Rachel Schurman, *Taking Population Seriously* (San Francisco: Institute for Food and Development Policy, 1990), p. 55; James P. Grant, "Jumpstarting Development," *Foreign Policy* (Summer 1993), pp. 128–30.

5. Jeremy Rifkin, *Entropy: Into the Greenhouse World*, (New York: Bantam Books, 1989), pp. 8–9; Robert Goodland, Herman E. Daly, and Salah El Serafy, *Population, Technology, and Lifestyle* (Washington, DC: Island Press, 1992), pp. 8, 10–14.

6. Lester R. Brown, *State of the World, 1992* (New York: W. W. Norton, 1992), pp. 9–13; Goodland, Daly, and Serafy, *Population, Technology, and Lifestyle*, pp. 10–14.

7. Sandi Brockway, *Macrocosm USA* (Cambria, CA: Macrocosm USA, 1992), p. 3; Goodland, Daly, and Serafy, *Population, Technology, and Lifestyle*, pp. 8, 10–14; Christian Parenti, "NASA's Assault on the Ozone Layer," *Lies of Our Times* (September 1993), p. 22.

8. Jeremy Rifkin, *Biosphere Politics* (San Francisco: HarperCollins, 1992), pp. 73, 173.

9. Rifkin, *Entropy*, pp. 119–20, 226.

10. Ibid., p. 233.

11. Ibid., pp. 59, 80–81, 143, 273; Goodland, Daly, and Serafy, *Population, Technology, and Lifestyle*, 27–28.

12. Rifkin, *Entropy*, pp. 8–9, 59, 80–81, 119–20, 143, 233, 226, 273; *Biosphere Politics*, pp. 73, 173; Brown, *State of the World, 1992*, p. 9.

13. William Greider, *One World, Ready or Not* (New York: Simon and Schuster, 1997), pp. 460–62, 465–67. Ecological tax reform, pollution taxes, or resource depletion taxes are essentially the same thing see Lester R. Brown, Christopher Flavin, and Sandra Postel, *Saving the Planet*, New York: W.W. Norton, 1991, chapter 11. See also Barry Commoner, *Making Peace With the Planet* (New York: Pantheon, 1990), especially pp. 47, 97; Jack Weatherford, *Indian Givers* (New York: Fawcett Columbine, 1988), chapter 5.

14. George Börgstrom, *The Hungry Planet: The Modern World at the Edge of Famine* (New York: Collier Books, 1972), p. 106.

15. Erik P. Eckholm, *Losing Ground: Environmental Stress and World Food Prospects* (New York: W.W. Norton, 1976), p. 94.

16. Edward Hyams, *Soil and Civilization* (New York: Harper and Row, 1976), p. 69; David Attenborough, *The First Eden: The Mediterranean World and Man* (Boston: Little, Brown, 1987), p. 169; J. V. Thirgood, *Man and the Mediterranean Forest: A History of Resource Depletion* (New York: Academic Press, 1981), p. 62.

17. William L. Thomas Jr., ed., *Man's Role in Changing the Face of the Earth*, vol. 2 (Chicago: University of Chicago Press, 1956), p. 510; David Sheridan, *Desertification of the United States* (Washington, DC: U.S. Government Printing Office, #334–983: Council on Environmental Quality, 1981), p. 121.

18. Jonathan Turk, Janet T. Wittes, Robert Wittes, and Amos Turk, *Ecosystems, Energy, Population* (Toronto: W.B. Saunders, 1975), p. 123.

19. William Robert Catton, *Overshoot: The Ecological Basis of Revolutionary Change* (Champaign: University of Illinois Press, 1980).

20. Norman Myers, gen. ed., *Gaia: An Atlas of Planet Management* (Garden City, NY: Anchor Books, 1984), p. 40.

21. Bill Mollison, *Permaculture: A Designers' Manual* (Tyalgum, Australia: Tagari, 1988).

22. John Jeavons, *How to Grow More Vegetables than You Ever Thought Possible on Less Land than You Ever Imagined: A Primer on the Life Giving Biointensive Method of Organic Horticulture* (Berkeley: Ten Speed Press, 1991).

21

The Political Structure of Sustainable World Development

Every country is part of a natural, easily outlined region for production and distribution. Trade between economies on opposite sides of the earth, while they simultaneously deny the inclusion of close neighbors and ignore social scientists' demonstrations that every country in the world could feed itself, is economic insanity. This monstrous situation can be only because of politics, and bad politics at that. The world's engineers and progressive economists obviously were not consulted.

Integrating Regions for Adequate Resources and Markets for Efficient Economies

As a large population is essential for industries that require mass markets, progressive people have recognized and championed the integration and efficiency of large economic regions. These industries require a multitude of natural resources that are only available in specific regions of the earth. Engineers and economic planners can judge what countries form natural regional zones for efficient production and distribution.

Towards that goal, the Central American states formed the United Provinces on July 1, 1823, with a constitution based on that of the United States. This was only the first of over twenty-five such attempts at forming a viable united nation out of the fragmented Central American countries.[1] All Latin American countries could logically form one to three integrated regions that would support a balanced market economy. Similarly, though there are over a thousand languages throughout Africa, several efficient economic regions are conceivable. African nations have tried repeatedly to organize just such viable political and economic unions.[2]

The cultures of the Middle East have pride in centuries of grandeur under the Sumerian, Hittite, Phoenician, Assyrian, Egyptian, Babylonian, Mesopotamian, Persian, Islamic, and Ottoman empires. Time after time the social capital built by these great societies was destroyed as civilizations clashed. The rich cultural history, common language, and the bond of Islamic religion would be a solid foundation on which to build community identity and a regionally interdependent economic infrastructure. Muslims have tried to do this by forming a "Moslem Brotherhood" and an "Arab League" that reach across those artificial borders. They continue to speak of one Arab nation consisting of a number of Arab states.[3] Egypt, the Sudan, and Yemen formed the United Arab Republic in 1958, were joined by Syria and Iraq in 1963, but then fragmented back into previously dictated political boundaries.

Brunei, Indonesia, Malaysia, the Philippines, Singapore, and Thailand, with a market of 314 million consumers, have formed a regional bloc called ASEAN that, until the 1997–98 financial meltdown, was making rapid progress in developing their economies and markets.[4]

Small, fragmented, weak developing-world countries were created by imperial powers as extensions of the political divisions of Europe. Their small political groupings and small economies prevented their development of autonomous strength. While regional organization and development must have been the dream of progressive thinkers in every dependent country, the dismembering of these regions before they could become viable nations has been the policy of all empires.

Witness the response of President James Monroe's secretary of state, John Quincy Adams, to the previously described attempt to form the United Provinces in Central America:

> Adams and Congress stalled until it was too late for the two delegates to attend. Even if they had arrived in time, Adams had placed the two under strict instructions not to join any kind of alliance, not to assume that Latin Americans could ever form a union of states, and not to in any way compromise the right of the United States to act unilaterally in the hemisphere when it suited Washington officials.[5]

Once fragmented, and within the sphere of influence of an empire, these dependent countries develop their own selfish elite, protected and controlled (typically installed) by the dominant power. Together they control the wealth and the elite of those countries which gives them an incentive to avoid the formation of a regional democratic union. Whenever there is a potential federation, the outside powers use their influence to prevent it.

After World War II, the nations of Africa were not only breaking free, they were coalescing into cooperative blocs. Forty years of massive destabilizations shattered those merging countries and their hopes. After the Cold War they are again speaking of economic cooperation but it will be years before those once externally supported struggles play themselves out and stable governments emerge.

A Political Framework for Cooperative Capitalism

The political framework under which the necessary worldwide transfer of technology and tools can be carried out so that emerging nations can develop viable economies already exists within the United Nations.[6] This organization has long been working on these problems and has collected most of the necessary statistics. The representatives of many of these nations are already cooperating, and industrialization is their shared goal. If the decision were made to provide industrial tools to the developing world, an agreement could readily be made between most countries within a region. As the first capital would go only to those that are amenable to a just society, there is no need to obtain the consent of every country. Though actually propaganda for public consumption as the West mobilized to destabilize the Soviet Union, these were the stated rules under which the Marshall Plan rebuilt Europe.

> Our policy was "directed not against any country or doctrine but against hunger, poverty, desperation and chaos. Its purpose should be the revival of a working economy in the world so as to permit the emergence of political and social conditions in which free institutions can exist." Any government that was willing to assist in the task of recovery would find full cooperation, but any

government that maneuvered to block the recovery of others could not expect help from us. "Furthermore, governments, political parties, or groups which seek to perpetuate human misery in order to profit therefrom politically or otherwise will encounter the opposition of the United States."[7]

Europe has moved beyond that original rebuilding and is forming one cooperative unit of 350 million producers and consumers with one currency. With the proper support, instead of destabilizations, Africa or Latin America could form economic unions more easily as they industrialize, rather than after successful development individually.

Human Rights and Equality of Rights Are Necessary for Both Freedom and the Implementation of Economic Democracy

The developed world and Western cultures are far ahead of most (but not all) societies in human rights, equality of rights, rights for women, and separation of church and state necessary for a productive modern economy. But we must not forget that full rights include economic rights and the developed world is able to give its citizens many rights and a high standard of living because of the massive wealth siphoned from the weak undeveloped world to itself through inequalities of trade. Under these unequal trades, one society's good life and security is another society's impoverishment and insecurity.

As democracies of weak developing nations have been quickly and regularly overthrown by imperial centers of capital, the struggles to maintain control, or regain control, of the destinies of embattled societies have required authoritarian governments. When pushed to the wall, a society will collapse or it may maintain a semblance of control by retreating into the politically impenetrable fundamentalist beliefs of religion where equality and rights have little consideration.

All that would change if the pressures to maintain a region as a supplier of basic commodities were replaced by a sincere philosophy, and sincere effort, to support sustainable development. Few governments would endure for long if they rejected an offer to industrialize just because the conditions required a democratic government that recognized its citizens' full rights. Leaders who were reluctant to surrender their dictatorial powers would, under these conditions, risk almost certain revolution. In any case, these dictators would have disappeared long ago were they not put in power and kept in power through the external support of imperial powers.[8]

Since the goal would be to win hearts and minds through democracy and development, continuing to support reactionary regimes would be self-defeating. Most insurrections are attempts to regain control of a people's own resources and destiny—in short, to gain economic freedom. If these desires for justice and rights were supported by the powerful, instead of denied, the world would quickly abandon war.

These insurrections could all be stopped dead in their tracks by honestly and effectively promoting democracy and capitalizing underdeveloped countries in exchange for them giving up their weapons. This is what most are fighting for anyway. As production of armaments equaling several times the amount needed to produce industry for the world's impoverished would be eliminated, the cost would be nothing and there would be further substantial gains to the world in not having its social wealth destroyed by wars.

The United Nations overseeing peace in Namibia and Cambodia and the united military efforts to enforce a peace in Korea, Iraq, and the former Yugoslavia (even though they were actually reimposing control by allied trading blocs maintaining access to cheap resources and valuable markets) have established the principle of a world body ensuring world peace.

If there is consideration of everyone's rights instead of primarily the rights of those culturally, religiously, or economically tied to outside powers (the lack of which is a fatal flaw in most peace efforts), this principle needs to be expanded to all nations so they can industrialize, feed themselves, live a respectable life, and start rebuilding their soils and ecosystems devastated by years of war and exploitation.

Security Through Equality and Interdependence

Currently, no matter how loud the praises of free trade, every imperial center of capital fudges extensively on free trade rules. As these neomercantilist policies have been the cause of most wars, spheres of influence, power vacuums, balances of power, preponderances of power, containment, and realpolitiks (all functioning under each imperial center of capital's "Grand Strategy" in the "great game" of who will control the world's wealth) must be replaced by a guarantee of each society's security.

World trade should be restructured to provide *security through interdependence* as opposed to the current *insecurity through dependence*. Under guarantees of secure borders, the lower the level of weapons the more secure every nation will be. With all the world gaining rights and freedom, spheres of influence (which means little more than dominance over other societies) will disappear. Without dominant—and arbitrary—military power, there would then be no

power vacuums, balance of power, or containment struggles. As opposed to the current guarantees of war and oppression, realpolitiks, realist, and moralist statecraft theory will mean peace, freedom, justice, and rights for all instead of immediate insecurity for some and eventual insecurity for all. National security would then be obtained through world security. It would no longer be "international politics in the national interest but national politics in the international interest."[9]

These ideas are not new. In 1899, the recognition of the destructive power of modern weapons led to the formation of a "convention for the pacific settlement of disputes which was adopted by 24 major states." And, after the horrors of World War I, the General Treaty for the Renunciation of Wars was formulated and signed by some of the major powers on August 27, 1928.[10] When a retired American five-star general laid out a plan to eliminate all the world's nuclear weapons in late 1996, he was joined within six months by over twenty military leaders from virtually all the major industrial countries.

Turning Arms Factories into Producers of Consumer Products

Wars are now so destructive that they are counterproductive even for a dominant power. If the world's Managers of State were to abandon the interception of wealth through corporate mercantilist control of technology and trade, guarantee secure borders, industrialize impoverished societies, collect and destroy their weapons, and reduce the weapons of the superpowers in step with world disarmament, global peace could become a very real possibility.

If there were no arms among the disaffected, and an honest international body were overseeing peace, hostilities and minor clashes might develop, but wars would be impossible. With weapons adequate only for internal security, with borders guaranteed, and with honesty in sharing the fruits of nature and technology, societies would give up the losses from conflict for the gains from cooperation.

As stated previously, President Woodrow Wilson knew all this. His trusted political confidant, Edward Mandell House, studied the European secret agreements to divide the Ottoman Empire and

> was dismayed by their contents . . . [He told the British Foreign Secretary, Lord Balfour], "It is all bad. . . . They are making it a breeding place for future war." . . . [A]board ship enroute to the peace conference in 1919, [President] Wilson told his associates that "I am convinced that if this peace is not made on the highest principles of justice, it will be swept away by the peoples of the world in less than a generation. If it is any other sort of peace then I shall want to run away and hide . . . for there will follow not mere conflict but cataclysm."[11]

President Wilson fought for those goals even when he was severely ill with a stroke. But the political forces arrayed against him were too great and he failed to get the United States to join and lead the League of Nations in gaining and guaranteeing rights to all the world's people. President Franklin D. Roosevelt repeatedly tried to abandon the imposed inequalities of trade that created so much of the world's conflict. His "attempt to replace aggression with international understanding had failed in China and Spain. Undaunted, he wrote [Britain's] Prime Minister Neville Chamberlain proposing a great conference at which treaties would be altered without resorting to force and all nations assured access to raw materials. Chamberlain declined."[12]

Although he was at first carried along by the nation's cold warriors, President John F. Kennedy also spoke about peace and justice for the world. Just weeks before he was assassinated he spoke of a strategy for peace: "Not a *Pax Americana* enforced on the world by American weapons of war . . . not merely peace for Americans, but peace for all men; not merely in our time but peace for all time."[13]

Knowing that the enormous productivity of capital can produce a respectable lifestyle for all assures that most of the developing world will accept disarmament as the price of capitalization. Those elusive goals of capitalization and peace are what progressive developing world leaders have been fighting for anyway. In 1950, conservative Senators Brien McMahon and Millard Tydings "made dramatic speeches in the Senate . . . [about a] moral crusade for peace" and a fifty-billion-dollar ($300 billion 1990 dollars) "global Marshall Plan" financed by the United States and augmented by an undertaking by all nations to put two-thirds of their armament expenditures to "constructive ends."[14]

An Offer the Impoverished Nations Cannot Refuse: Turning the World's Arms Expenditures Toward Their Sustainable Development

In plain and unambiguous language, this should be the offer of the powerful industrialized nations to the world: the cancellation of all unjust debts; the conversion of industrial capital once producing arms to production of industrial tools for the Third World; the United Nations to oversee the balanced and peaceful capitalization of the Third World; the borders of all countries to be guaranteed; the United Nations given the authority, soldiers, and arms to back up that guarantee; and a worldwide embargo to go into effect automatically against any country that attacks or subverts another country.

Due to those major powers' addiction to living cheaply off other societies and the potential for cheating, perhaps earlier international efforts for sustained world peace were premature. However, with TV and radio soon to be present in most homes worldwide, it is possible for the entire world to have a basic understanding of the problems (of course, people must be told the problems honestly instead of propagandized) and satellites can spot any major arms production or troop movement anywhere in the world.

Assuming the collapsed former Soviet Union continues its rapid disarmament, and if the developing world accepted disarmament in exchange for capital, secure borders, and protection from internal destabilization, there would be few enemies, and no arms for those whose thoughts still turned to war. The major powers could then disarm in step with the disarmament of the world and could turn the industry currently wasted on arms production towards capitalizing the undeveloped world, rebuilding the world's soils, and protecting the ecosystem.

Until the openly declared policy of expanding NATO towards Russia's borders, the rapid demilitarization of the Commonwealth of Independent States had taken the lead in world disarmament. That eastward expansion of NATO is an eastward expansion of a trading bloc following the historical pattern of expanding empire and protection of markets and resources through military force.

The same expansion of industrial and trade rights to the entire world, as is intended to be extended only to allies within the current trading bloc, would eliminate the need for that military waste and free that productive capacity, resources, and labor for sustainable development of the world.

Whoever firmly establishes disarmament and expands it to developing world industrialization will go down in history as one of the world's greatest leaders, far exceeding the reputations of Presidents George Washington, Abraham Lincoln, and Franklin Roosevelt, Prime Minister Winston Churchill, or India's Mahatma Gandhi. Once other nations declare their willingness to disarm and place their security in the hands of the United Nations, the developed nations will be hard-pressed to find excuses not to utilize their surplus productive capacity to produce those all-important industrial tools.

Although it was not done to establish democracies, the pattern of openly deciding the future of another country has already been set by United Nations actions in the Korean and Persian Gulf wars, in the 1992–94 efforts to police the Cambodian and El Salvadorian peace processes, in embargoing Libya, Iran, Iraq, and various other countries from world trade, and (hopefully) in overseeing peace in the current break-up of Yugoslavia. The outstanding examples of interference to establish a democracy, as opposed to imposing the will of a powerful country, lay in overseeing Namibia's emergence as a free nation and the embargoing of South Africa to force the inclusion of blacks as citizens of their country. If the dominant powers sincerely chose demilitarization, peace, cooperation, and elimination of world poverty, they would not have to twist many arms.

Since most arms are normally used either to repress a country's own population or for external powers to provide support for a faction within a country, the foregoing guarantee should extend to the protection of existing democratic governments from internal overthrow by force. But that must also be matched by guarantees of freely elected, constitutional governments; freedom of speech; freedom of religion; and separation of church and state. Under the influence of the dominant powers, this world body should have the authority to oversee the disarming of belligerents, the establishment of democracies, and the holding of free elections in any country torn by revolution.

This does not mean governments and laws have to be patterned after those of the dominant powers or that religious and ethnic groups culturally tied to dominant powers must be imposed to govern. It means these people decide who governs (imperialists have always feared people democratically deciding their own destiny) and rights can be guaranteed minorities through the power to deny or permit access to capital and markets (embargoes), just as was accomplished in South Africa.

In Exchange for Sustainable Development, the World Can, and Will, Disarm

Under the guarantees against both internal and external aggression described, and with promises of capitalization and the sharing of markets and resources, the military weapons of developing states—above those needed for normal police duty—should be collected and destroyed.

Once the rest of the world is disarmed, and all are therefore safe from attack, the weapons of mass destruction can be destroyed and adequate conventional weapons can be transferred to a world body to oversee peace. With destruction of the weapons of war and equal rights to capital, resources, and trade, all societies could eventually produce for, and provide equal rights for, all their citizens.

As a condition of receiving capital, emerging nations would have to agree to permit inspection of any factory suspected of weapons production. With the current agreement to reduce the levels of superpower nuclear missiles—and with Iraq being forced to eliminate all arms of mass destruction, disarm to an acceptable level, and submit to inspection—this is a well-established principle.

The only way this can happen is if the dominant powers—and that now means only the United States and its allies—recognize the potential for peace and take the lead in disarming and capitalizing the world. The claim that one nation cannot abuse the sovereignty of another does not stand inspection. Intervention in others' affairs is the unacknowledged norm of all major imperial centers of capital, in fact, all empires throughout history.

By the open proclamations leading to the Korean, Vietnamese, Afghanistan, Grenadian, Panamanian, and Persian Gulf wars and by the tens of thousands of interventions (the majority covert) throughout history, the powerful nations have affirmed their right to interfere in the affairs of other nations. However, under the recommendations of this treatise, future interventions would carry the mantle of morality and justice and be carried out by the United Nations as opposed to the obvious injustice of destabilizations of other societies by individual nations.

Integrating Diverse Nationalities, Races, and Cultures

Countries with diverse nationalities, races, and cultures have special problems. Everyone should have equal access to jobs and capital and equal representation in government. Once the countries in a region are industrially integrated and markets are open to all, everyone's well-being will depend on cooperation. Such attainment of full rights, and the assurance of sanctions if war erupts, will eliminate most ethnic conflicts fought under religious banners, the example of Bosnia notwithstanding. That is an internal battle now but it developed from an external destabilization. As addressed above, these people were living cooperatively, peacefully, and broadly intermarrying until external powers allied with internal forces to expand their culture and wealth at the expense of Serbian Eastern Orthodox culture.[15]

Notes

1. Walter Lefeber, *Inevitable Revolutions* (New York: W.W. Norton, 1984), pp. 24–27.

2. Organizations formed to further African unity are: OAU (Organization of African Unity); OAAU (Organization for African American Unity (founded by Frantz Fanon); OCAM (Organization Commune Africaine et Malagache); OERS (Organization of States Bordering the Senegal River); UDEAC (Customs Union of Central African States); OERM (Economic Organization of North Africa); EACM (East African Community and Common Market); CEAO (West African Economic Community); CEDEAO (The Economic Community of West African States). Francois N. Muyumba and Esther Atcherson, *Pan-Africanism and Cross-Cultural Understanding: A Reader* (Needham Heights, MA: Ginn Press, 1993), chapter 3 by Andrew Conteh, chapter 15 by Edmond J. Keller, and chapter 19 by Bamidele A. Ojo; Cheikh Anta Diop, *Black Africa,* Harold J. Salemson, trans. (Westport, CT: Lawrence Hill, 1978), p. 1. For example, Mercosur (Southern Cone Common Market), and the Andean Pact.

3. Feroz Ahmad, "Arab Nationalism, Radicalism, and the Specter of Neocolonialism," *Monthly Review* (February 1991), p. 32.

4. *Depth News,* Manila, quoted by *World Press Review* (March 1991), p. 46.

5. Lefeber, *Inevitable Revolutions,* p. 24.

6. One is The United Nations Development Program (UNDP), 1 UN Plaza, New York, NY, 10017. *Human Development Report, 1991* (New York: Oxford University Press, 1991) addresses these needs and is only one of the UNDP's many publications.

7. D. F. Fleming, *The Cold War and Its Origins* (New York: Doubleday, 1961), p. 478; Walter Isaacson and Evan Thomas, *The Wise Men* (New York: Simon and Schuster, 1986), p. 414.

8. Sidney Lens, *Permanent War* (New York: Schocken Books, 1987), p. 27; John Stockwell, *The Praetorian Guard* (Boston: South End Press, 1991). See Chapter Seven of this work.

9. Anna Gyorgy, trans., *Ecological Economics* (London: Zed Books, 1991), p. 7; read between the lines of Robert J. Art and Kenneth N. Waltz's *The Use of Force: Military Power and International Politics* (New York: University Press of America, 1993) and read the treatises on diplomacy by authors listed therein.

10. William Preston Jr., Edward S. Herman, and Herbert I. Schiller, *Hope and Folly* (Minneapolis: University of Minnesota Press, 1989), p. ix.

11. David Fromkin, *A Peace to End All Peace* (New York: Avon Books, 1989), pp. 257, 262.

12. William Manchester, *The Glory and the Dream* (New York: Bantam Books, 1990), p. 178.

13. Ibid., pp. 989–90.

14. Dean Acheson, *Present at the Creation* (New York: W. W. Norton, 1987), p. 377.

15. Michel Chossudovsky, "Dismantling Yugoslavia, Colonizing Bosnia," *Covert Action Quarterly* (Spring 1996), pp. 31–37; Michael McClintock, *Instruments of Statecraft* (New York: Pantheon, 1992), pp. 71–82; Catherine Samaray, *Yugoslavia Dismembered* (New York: Monthly Review Press, 1995); Charles Lane, Theodore Stanger, and Tom Post, "The Ghosts of Serbia," *Newsweek,* April 19, 1993, pp. 30–31; Dusko Doder, "Yugoslavia: New War, Old Hatreds," *Foreign Policy* (Summer 1993), pp. 4, 9–11, 18–19; Sean Gervasi, "Germany, U.S., and the Yugoslavian Crisis," *Covert Action Quarterly* (Winter 1992–93), pp. 41–45, 64–66; Thomas Kielinger and Max Otte, "Germany: The Presumed Power," *Foreign Policy* (Summer 1993), p. 55.

22

Sustainable World Development

Equal Free Trade as Opposed to Unequal Free Trade

With today's educated populations and communication systems, it is possible to calculate the waste of past centuries and the current waste, calculate the earth's sustainable development level, educate the world's citizens to these realities, design a program for sustainable world development and elimination of poverty, and reach those goals.

Regional and Local Self-sufficiency

In a world that has not protected people's rights by eliminating subtle monopolization of land, technology, finance capital, and information, there must be rules to protect communities from the worldwide bidding wars that permit industry to flee, drive down the price of labor, reduce corporate taxes, subtly monopolize capital, waste resources, deplete the soils, and degrade the environment.

The developed and developing countries should be designed to be as regionally self-sufficient as possible in food and industry. The industries that require large-scale economies should be regionally planned and integrated with all countries within a balanced trading area.

Markets would be free within regions (both developed and developing), but with equalizing managed trade between these unequal regions, with protections to be lowered in step with the equalizing of industrial technology, capital accumulation, and labor skills. Thus the labor and industrial capital in wealthy countries would be protected from destruction by the low labor costs of impoverished countries, and the industries and markets of the undeveloped world would be protected from the cheap production costs of the developed world. This requires the development of balanced (yet competitive) economies within currently undeveloped regions. The necessary capital can come both from the equalizing surcharge and radically simplified and more equitable methods of capital accumulation.

If wages paid in basic industry are equal to wages paid by the consumer of those products (Adam Smith's concept of labor retaining the value of what it produces), this will create initial buying power, and the expenditure of those wages on consumer needs will produce more buying power (the economic multiplier and development of a market economy). Once the internal market economies of impoverished nations are developed and a skilled labor force trained, those countries should be integrated with, and enjoy free trade between, other developed regions using the maximum efficiencies (comparative advantage) of each region.

"What is needed is a global regulatory

framework for multinational corporations—a set of common standards for labor rights, tax and wage rates, and environmental protection—as well as the means, both national and international, to enforce them."[1] Instead of policies that bring well-paid labor down to the wages of the lowest paid, equalizing managed trade would be raising the wages of the poorly paid to those of the better paid.

Once control is wrenched from corporate imperialists, individual countries should allow access to their markets only to corporations that are good citizens working for the betterment of all societies. For the right to sell within that market and prevent tax and labor bidding wars between communities, a corporation can be required to meet basic standards of behavior:

> [The developed world] ought to reject any new trade agreements that do not include a meaningful social contract—rules that establish baseline standards for health, labor laws, working conditions, the environment, wages. The world economy needs a global minimum wage law—one that establishes a rising floor under the most impoverished workers in industrial employment.[2]

The Underpaid Developing Regions Should Be Trading with Each Other

Whenever possible, countries in the underpaid developing world should be trading with each other. If trading countries pay roughly equal wages for production of the products traded, neither confiscates the wealth of the other and the efficiencies of trade can function honestly.

By trading with each other while building industry, developing nations with low-paid labor can develop their economies much more rapidly than when trading with a nation with high-paid labor. If labor is idle and the treasury empty (it always is in the dependent trading nation—that

is the essence of a monopolized world economy), raw material or semi-processed goods can be bartered for industries (technology) as opposed to trading those resources for trinkets.

If the currently impoverished world industrialized, it would require few resources or finished products from the developed world. This would quickly reveal and eliminate the enormous confiscation of weak nations' wealth and just as quickly impoverish Europe, Japan, Taiwan, and South Korea (the United States, Canada, and Australia have adequate resources). Sharing industry and world resources equally between the resource-depleted old world or resource-deficient world and the resource-rich impoverished world would drastically reduce the current confiscation of weak nations and equalize world wealth. As they have depleted their resources or never had them in the first place, the currently powerful and wealthy nations of Europe and Japan, and other resource-poor countries, must be allotted a share of the natural wealth from the rest of the world.

Regional Trading Currencies

As we discuss later, money is only the representative value resulting from combining resources (land), labor, and industrial capital. By forming regional trading blocs, the Third World would have all three requirements for the production of wealth. The developing world need only form these regional trading blocs, manage its own trading currency, and utilize its money-printing power to build industries and develop an efficient economic infrastructure (roads, railroads, warehouses, etc). The building of the industries and economic infrastructure will provide buying power, and that buying power will be the engine to maintain economic development. By tying their currency values to a basket of commodities, all nations can gain the freedom and advantages that come when their central bank creates money. Once economic development is advancing rapidly, the proper share of development funds will come from money flowing within the economy.

Each undeveloped region of Asia, Africa, or Latin America has at least one country that is quite well developed (India, Brazil, Mexico, South Africa, South Korea, Taiwan, Japan, and China) that could serve as a center of development. China is large enough to develop industry and markets on its own. We noted above that a respected news weekly recognized that, ''Under the Bretton Woods system, the Federal Reserve acted as the world's central bank. This gave America enormous leverage over economic policies of its principal trading partners.'' No country is free when another country has such leverage over its banking system and its entire economy.

China and her neighbors should be organized as one production/distribution region and provided balanced industrial capital. With managed trade equalizing wage discrepancies as the world's natural resources are converted to consumer products and thus monetized, the employment of workers in balanced industries producing for their own societies will develop regional buying power and markets and capitalize those values in those regions. That region will then have both natural and capitalized wealth.

It must be emphasized that, when this capitalization is complete, each country will have equal rights (within its region) to resources, industrial capital, and markets. Those rights automatically translate into the ability of that nation's citizens to feed themselves and job rights that, in turn, translate into buying power and that society's share of social wealth.

Nations that are poorer in resources need to be assigned a higher level of industrial capital. But the regional average should still be that all-important ratio of approximately one unit of industrial capital to thirty units of social capital (see next chapter), and all capital should, on the average, be regionally and locally owned.

The Imperial Centers Understand Well the Importance of Equally Productive and Equally Paid Labor

To protect everybody's rights, it is imperative that industry and markets in the developed world be protected against the low-wage industry of the developing world. Profits would then be based on true efficiency, rather than corporate imperialists' power to lower a community's taxes, wage rates, or environmental quality.

The experienced imperial centers understand this well. When the relatively poor countries of Greece, Portugal, and Spain wanted to join the Common Market, the planners knew their low wages would drive down the wages of the rest of Europe, just as U.S. wages are being driven down at this time by the low wages of Mexico and the Pacific Rim. They therefore ''implemented a fifteen-year plan which included massive transfers of direct aid, designed to accelerate development, raise wages, regularize safety and environmental standards, and improve living conditions in the poorer nations.''[3]

The process of capitalizing poorer societies to develop internal market economies and integrate them into the society of developed nations, while protecting the living standards of the already developed nations, is well understood and practiced when it is in the interest of dominant imperial centers of capital. The American Revolution led this battle for world freedom:

The Declaration of Independence sounded the first global proclamation of the fundamental equality of human beings and their consequent entitlements to "inalienable rights." The Bill of Rights made many of those rights enforceable, especially for white men; yet it also acknowledged, in the Ninth Amendment, that the initial enumeration of rights was by no means comprehensive. A century later, the Reconstruction Amendments expanded coverage to all citizens regardless of race; and in 1920 the Nineteenth Amendment extended full citizenship to women. Following the atrocities of World War II, Presidents Franklin Roosevelt and Harry Truman sought to extend the concept of human rights worldwide. With Eleanor Roosevelt as chief U.S. negotiator, the Universal Declaration of Human Rights was adopted without a dissenting vote by the United Nations General Assembly in 1948.[4]

Those universal human rights include economic rights, which can only be obtained if the rights of labor are equal to the rights of capital:

[With] the mobility of capital threaten[ing] to ratchet down living standards for the great majority, what is needed is a regulatory framework for multinational corporations—a set of common standards for labor rights, tax and wage rates, and environmental protection. . . . [All societies] need to be able to exert greater control over multinational corporate activity so that the human and natural resources they possess are not merely exploited for the benefit of others. . . . The United States . . . could alter the terms of access to its markets that corporations (domestic and foreign) now enjoy. . . . In this way a more level playing field would emerge and multinational corporations would find it more difficult to ratchet down tax rates, public investment, wages, and environmental standards . . . corporations could be induced to help realize, rather than undermine, national and community goals. . . . In the early 1960s, for instance, auto manufacturers wishing to sell cars in California were required to meet tough emission standards adopted by the state.[5]

Returning Title to the World's Natural Wealth to Its Rightful Owners

Control at any one of several points (resources, technology, finance, markets, or figurehead governments) can give effective control of a society's wealth, which is a prerogative of ownership. Those mines, oil fields, forests, and fields could, through equalization surcharges, be returned to their rightful owners. The exposure of the current monopolies protected by the Adam Smith belief system and military force might explain why the IMF/World Bank/GATT/NAFTA/WTO/MAI/military colossus insists on destroying the power of governments and privatizing all social wealth. Only strong governments and firm policies can break the monopolies of the imperial centers of capital.

Tariffs Functioning to Collect Land Rents and Equalize Unequally Paid Labor

In neomercantilist world trade, one society's security is another society's insecurity. Where free trade as practiced by neomercantilists protected only the powerful wealthy world, the protection of both people and the environment starts with security for all people. Early tariffs were tolls for the right to cross or trade on land owned by lords and nobles. Such tariffs on exports confiscate a share of labor's wages and capital's profits in the exporting country, while tariffs on imports confiscate a share of the wages and profits of another country's labor and capital.

If the tariff is on imported oil or another commodity in which there is little labor or capital involved, that tariff is primarily a landrent tax (oil and other raw materials are land) confiscating the landrent of the exporting country. If the tariff is on a labor-intensive import item, that tariff is primarily confiscating labor values that properly belong to the exporting country. Landrent values and labor values of another society can be confiscated by importing undervalued commodities produced in dependent countries too weak to demand full landrent and labor values. That confiscation of weak societies' wealth can be eliminated by pricing raw materials relative to the cost of mining the world's poorer mineral deposits and harvesting from its poorer soils.

Pricing Commodities Relative to the Cost of Mining the World's Poorer Mineral Deposits and Harvesting Its Poorer Soils

Instead of mass privatizations that transfer title to corporate imperialists, commodities should be priced relative to the cost of mining and logging (or substitute commodities) in the resource-scarce developed world. Labor values should be calculated, equalizing surcharges collected, and these funds used to pay for the needed renewable energy capitalization for the undeveloped, commodity-exporting countries. Through such incentives and disincentives, resources will be conserved, pollution reduced, and the environment protected.

A part of the surcharge on exported commodities—rebalancing the unequal pay for equally productive labor and replacing the landrent historically going to the corrupt elite of impoverished nations—can be used to pay corporations (no longer corporate imperialists) for relinquishing monopolization of industrial technology. Fair value paid for developing world resources and labor will generate funds

to pay corporations for that industrial capital. There will be no debt trap. If industry and infrastructure are contracted to be built—as opposed to being funded by direct loans—there will be limited siphoning of wealth to Swiss bank accounts.

Currently the cost of minerals in the United States is only 1.7 percent of GNP and the cost of fuel only 2.0 percent.[6] This demonstrates that there is plenty of room to increase the price of minerals and carbon fuels to such a level that the lower-grade deposits in the developed world can be mined and renewable energy utilized. The recycling of minerals would then be profitable and renewable energy would be competitive.

With labor equally paid, initially through tariffs and resource depletion (landrent) surcharges balancing production costs, the world can then mine all deposits (rich and poor), maximize product life (because consumer products now appear expensive), and recycle (because they are actually now cheaper) the consumed minerals, paper, plastic, and other materials. Though developing-world resources may appear higher priced under these rules, they are really cheaper. Far more people will be provided with the amenities of life even as the world's resources and ecosystems are protected, which is the proper measure of cost.

Once resources are no longer wasted producing arms, and once social efficiencies—such as those outlined in the works of Thorstein Veblen, Stuart Chase, Ralph Borsodi, this author, and many others documenting the enormous wasted labor and resources—are instituted, the developed nations can afford to use their poorer deposits, develop new technology, or trade (equally now) with those who have rich deposits.

Equalizing Managed Trade for Balanced Integration of Industries and Markets

Regions must have balanced integration of their industries and markets. The European Economic Community provides the model and experience. Though against the rules of laissez-faire development, long before becoming serious about a common market, Western Europe integrated its production of steel and coal.[7] With their borders guaranteed and resources integrated, once-dependent countries can stop worrying about being attacked and can concentrate on building the industrial tools, infrastructure, and social structure for a productive regional economy.

To develop the impoverished world to a sustainable level, we need to apply Friedrich List's philosophies for the growth of powerful nations to the development of weak nations. If a country lacks natural resources, it should be permitted a higher level of industrial capital. This is what happened with the three miracle countries: Japan, Taiwan, and South Korea. With limited resources, they were given access to industrial technology, capital, and markets, they protected those industries and their home markets, and they became wealthy.

It is possible to turn "win-lose" or "lose-lose" trade wars into "win-win" equalizing managed trade. A wealthy importing country should pay an equalizing surcharge based upon equitable landrent and labor values on imports from the region which has lost title to its resources and whose labor is underpaid. Surcharges on trades between regions would be only relative to inequality of wage rates and to depletion of natural resources.

Those surcharges should not go directly to the typically corrupt Third World nation. They should go into a compensation/development/ecosystem protection fund to pay directly for developing Third World infrastructure, constructing Third World industries (industrial capital), developing environmentally sound products, designing and implementing ecologically sustainable lifestyles, rebuilding soils, and cleaning up and revitalizing the world's ecosystems. Those surcharges should be lowered in step with the industrialization and increase in wages of the developing nation. Once roughly equal in technology and labor equally paid, surcharges would be eliminated and honest free trade would flow between those regions.

But yet remaining should be a resource depletion tax to fund ecologically sustainable lifestyles for rebuilding the soils and cleaning up and revitalizing the world's ecosystems. Those regions would now have free trade and the world's ecosystems would be protected by what is essentially a worldwide landrent tax imposed upon depletable resources. As technological parity is reached, the surcharge protecting landrent and labor values would disappear but the ecosystem protection part of landrent charges would remain (it goes by many names, such as resource depletion tax and ecological tax, but they are all essentially a landrent tax).

Since—relative to its use-value—oil and coal production costs are so low, each country should place a landrent equalization surcharge on the oil and coal they consume at a level that makes renewable energy viable (in 1990, around thirty dollars per barrel of oil). The level of that surcharge (a landrent tax) should be lowered relative to the gains in efficiency of renewable energy technology.

With an equalization surcharge on fossil fuels financing world conversion to sustainable and nonpolluting energy while there is a relative surplus of oil and coal, both energy costs and environmental pollution will be far lower than if we wait for the exhaustion of fossil fuels. The funds generated should be used to develop solar and renewable energy technology and to industrialize—with relatively nonpolluting alternative energy technologies—currently impoverished societies that are not blessed with oil and coal. The consumption of the world's oil and coal will be slower, pollution pressures will be lower, and all countries will develop faster.

Under a world development plan that maintained regional competition between societies of roughly equal industrial development and wage rates, while managing trade between unequally developed societies, the destruction of viable industries and communities would cease even as competition within regions increased. With the social savings of capital protected from low-wage competition but maintaining efficient competition, prices would fall and living standards would rise dramatically.

Restoring the World's Soils and Ecosphere

Some scientists have concluded the only way to absorb increased carbon dioxide emissions, besides cutting back on fossil fuel burning, is to reforest the planet. In an experiment, a section of barren North Africa was fenced off from sheep and goats and planted to grass. That forage grew beautifully and stabilized the once-blowing sand. Grass grows in rich soils while, with even less rain, shrubs and trees grow in poor soils, so forests in suitable climates and soils will do well also. The Baltistan region of Pakistan went beyond those experiments and in parts of this desert region "there is a sea of green" where the local population has planted trees. If these impoverished people can be financed by a small Dutch aid program, the vast

oil wealth of the Arab world can finance the restoration of Middle Eastern soils. China, with its dense population and low per capita income, plans to reforest 20 percent "of the entire land mass of the country."[8]

A cooperative effort by a team of scientists, agronomists, engineers, and doctors in Gaviotas, Colombia, took title to 25,000 acres of that nation's worst soils and started rapid restoration of those desolate areas. To their surprise, in the shade of planted trees a part of the Amazon forest that had been destroyed so long ago it had disappeared from social memory started rapidly sprouting upon those barren *Los Llanos* plains.[9]

Once wars in a region are abandoned and industrial capital provides consumer products and tools, these people can replant their grasslands and forests. The initial grasses can be seeded to hold down the soil and then ecological restoration teams can begin locating the eliminated species of grasses, forbs, and shrubs to complete the restoration of a region's natural ecology.[10]

With care, local and regional ecosystems can be restored and grazing can continue. However, this cannot be done using the present corporate-controlled agricultural system. The many different species of grazing animals (deer, elk, bighorn sheep, pronghorn antelope, bison, etc.) consume different species of grasses, forbs, bushes, and even trees. Therefore, a natural ecosystem is cropped evenly, is not damaged, and can produce more meat per acre than a system of pasturing cattle. In a recent study on the African Serengeti plains, researchers found that "an untouched savanna is capable of an annual production of twenty-four to thirty-seven tons of meat per square kilometer in the form of wild animals while the best pasture-cattle system in Africa can yield only eight tons of beef per square kilometer per year."[11] Eliminating native species destroys the balanced ecology and pasturing only the cow leads to overgrazing of the grasses that are holding down the soil upon which the entire ecosystem depends.[12] If a preponderance of tree and shrub species has not become extinct, the complete ecosystem of forests can also be restored. Using the new science of ecoforestry, a new forest can be guided toward its maturation while being selectively harvested.[13]

With desertification threatening one-third of the planet and increasing global temperatures from increased carbon dioxide levels, forest restoration is of urgent concern.[14] Using local building materials for homes is actually much cheaper and more efficient than lumber, so timber cutting can be reduced to a sustainable level while those forests are rebuilding. Adobe, rammed earth, stone, straw bale, and even fired adobe with a ceramic interior have been demonstrated to equal or surpass wood frame buildings in cost, structural strength, warmth, and safety.[15] The second most intensive consumer of forests is paper. As we discuss below, society can be even better informed through electronic databases than through printed matter. Society can do away with disposable diapers and other timber-wasting social habits or it can produce such items from hemp and kenaf.[16]

There are great economic benefits from forest restoration: expensive hydroelectric reservoirs do not silt up as quickly; there is less need for expensive filtration plants; floods are reduced; forest soil holds the moisture and grows more timber and shrubs; long-dead springs come to life and currently dry stream beds run year round; fish return to those new streams; the retained water is expired back into the atmosphere and increases rainfall both upon that forest and on regions downwind; mushrooms, berries, medicinal herbs, and many other products and animals to enrich a society increase; and, of equal importance, a reforested earth, along with other conservation measures, could pull carbon dioxide out of the air to stave off the potential of the feared runaway greenhouse effect.

Extinction of plant and animal species in most areas makes it impossible to rebuild the original ecosystems that logging, grazing, and burning have destroyed. Soils that once grew a rich forest ecosystem and are now eroded to bedrock cannot be rebuilt within any useful time frame. Soils eroded to subsoil can be planted to shrubbery and a few hardy trees, but will take many centuries to rebuild topsoil that will support flora and fauna similar to what once grew there. Where there is still some topsoil left, grasses will take hold quickly, start holding onto the remaining topsoil, and—with controlled grazing—start the centuries-long job of rebuilding those soils. Replanting ponderosa pine forests where there is still topsoil will start rebuilding the soil immediately and they will mature enough in fifty to one hundred years for selective harvesting. Douglas fir, redwood forests, and equatorial rain forests will also start building soils immediately and can be harvested very selectively as they grow, but they will require three to five times longer to reach climax maturity.

Although the ecosystem rebuilding time frame must be measured in centuries, nature starts building topsoil and repairing the ecosystem damage done by 5,000 years of abuse as soon as people stop mining those soils through harvesting the covering flora and fauna. Where once roadway cuts stayed barren for decades when left for nature to heal, conservationists have learned how to quickly establish soil-building grasses and vegetation on those barren and rocky subsoils. So establishing a viable soil-building ecosystem on most eroded soils is very practical. Once that first soil-stabilizing vegetation is established, then ecoscientists can replant the plant species which once grew there and, so long as humans let that ecosystem rebuild, and once it has rebuilt do not overharvest, nature will do the rest.

The replanting of grasses and reforestation south of the Sahara would reverse the march of that desert, which is now moving south at the rate of ten miles per year. Only by such protection of the environment can the future of these indigenous people, and all the world's people, be protected. If those grasslands and forests are restored, this would soften regional temperatures and climates.

Conserving Hydrocarbon Fuels

Under an international program to conserve natural resources, promote the use of renewable fuels, and protect the ecosystem, the proper price of oil and coal should be assessed high enough to make wind, solar, and other renewable energy competitive and maintain the consumption rate of oil and coal at a level that would consume the world's oil and coal both in balance and within the ability of the earth to absorb the carbon dioxide and other pollutants produced. This can be accomplished through a resource depletion surcharge (note: oil, coal, minerals, forests—all natural resources—are land, and this is a landrent tax). Using up the world's oil in fifty years and moving to the coal fields when the oil fields are exhausted would only ensure waste of those precious fuels and create further unbalanced world economies as well as increase the threat of the greenhouse effect.

These hydrocarbons are so valuable for fabrics, plastics, medicines, smelting of ores, and powering ships and airplanes that—long before they are exhausted—their price should be held above that of other fuels both to limit pollution and to conserve them far into the future. With equalization surcharges going into a development and ecosystem protection fund, title to their own resources, rights to the latest industrial technology, and elimination of arms purchases and wars, the resource-rich—but impoverished—regions will have the necessary financial resources to pay for balanced industrialization, environmental cleanup, reforestation, replanting of grass, and other ecological protections.

The Middle East and the Caspian Basin have possibly 80 percent of the world's oil reserves, but that is expected to be depleted in fifty years. That is a very short time. Those desert regions have the advantage of solar energy being cheaper than in most other areas of the world, and it is imperative that they, along with the rest of the world, develop a sustainable energy policy.

The industrial nations should agree to provide industrial capital and technology to peaceful Middle East nations. If they were to give up their arms under guarantees of peace, inviolable borders, and access to capital and markets, they could no longer waste their wealth on wars, nor would they want to. Before these cheap hydrocarbon fuels became scarce, the world would be accustomed to less polluting solar, wind, tide, and geothermal energy. This would both protect the ecosystem and save those hydrocarbons for other much more valuable uses for future generations.

Even as light bulbs are being invented that require one-fourth the electricity—and similar efficiencies are being obtained for electric motors, refrigerators, and other equipment—electricity generated by windmills and solar energy through photovoltaic cells is becoming competitive with fossil-fuel-generated electricity. When a substantial share of electricity is generated by these relatively nonpolluting and limitless energy sources, the well-known efficiency gains of mass production will lower their costs, enabling society to make the decision to reduce consumption of fossil fuels radically. That decision can, and should, be made in the near future. Automakers plan to have cars fueled by hydrogen and oxygen that emit no pollution on the market in the first decade of the twenty-first century. As hydrogen and oxygen are two of the most plentiful elements on earth and mass produced fuel-cell-powered cars are expected to be priced competitively with gas-powered cars, the world does not have to abandon cars.

More Leisure Days than Working Days

In a modern technological society it is possible to have more leisure days than working days. Sweden and Germany require only half the energy for a standard of living roughly equal to that of the United States; Switzerland requires only one-third.[17] Instead of regions such as the San Joaquin Valley in California producing half the vegetables in the United States, it would be possible to use that free time raising vegetables and fruit in one's backyard and on farms close to population centers.

Life is but structuring time and much newly freed time would be available. If this time were so employed, the current seven to ten calories of fuel used to produce and distribute one calorie of food in the industrial world would drop to a fraction of current levels.[18] Though labor time might be higher, capital costs would—through the replacement of fossil fuels with human energy—be lower and actual costs far lower, because previously unpaid time and wasted human energy would be used. The de-

veloping world should utilize the efficiencies of both mechanized agriculture and local soils and labor while avoiding the inefficiencies of processed foods, grain-fed beef, and transport of foods over long distances.

Under the above policies, the world's resources would then be utilized by both the developed and developing world instead of the rich deposits producing only for the developed world, and when those are consumed, title to, and production from, the poorer deposits again going only to the wealthy.

A Modern Communication System to Educate the World

As they are in a race against the time when their populations will overwhelm them, all regions should be given the communications systems (radio and direct broadcast satellite TV) to reach all their people with the message of: (1) how to gain control of their land and grow and consume high-calorie crops with the proper proportions of the nine essential amino acids for the body to produce its own protein; (2) how to industrialize their regions, develop a balanced economy, and create buying power; (3) how to attain the population levels their resources will support while protecting the ecosystem; (4) how China, Sri Lanka, Colombia, Chile, Burma, Cuba, and the Indian state of Kerala slowed their population growths; (5) how they can achieve large gains from limiting, and especially reducing, their populations; and (6) how in all industrialized nations a rapid reduction in births took place automatically in step with the gains in quality of life and security.

It must be emphasized that, as addressed in the final two chapters, once this modern communications system is in place the developing nations can educate their citizens for from 5 to 15 percent of the cost in the imperial centers of capital. Simultaneously they can design their production/distribution systems for a sustainable lifestyle utilizing less than half the labor required in the custom-bound imperial centers. Remembering that we are considering only a sustainable lifestyle, it is possible these societies, properly designed, will require only a two-day workweek.

Lowering Populations Through Surplus Food Insuring the Elderly Against Hunger

So parents will not have to depend on their children in old age, the world's current surplus food production should go to insure those countries' elderly against hunger. But this should be only to the extent that a country is unable to produce its own food. The goal should be for an over-populated country to limit its birthrate to under two children per family until such time as its production and population balance with the region's sustainable resource capacity and the desired living standard.

Rapid sustainable development increasing a nation's standard of living by, say, 3 percent a year will lead to a 4 percent annual increase if the population is falling 1 percent a year. More important, resource limits and the limits on the ability of the biosphere, soil, and water to recycle wastes dictate that eventually the only way to achieve a higher standard of living will be through utilizing resources more efficiently or lowering the population. With a modern communications system educating the people to the great per-capita gains possible from a reduction in population, there will be political support for that reduction.

A Return to Using Durable, Regionally Produced Social Tools

Besides avoiding the insanity of automobiles from the United States destined for Japan passing automobiles in the middle of the Pacific Ocean coming from Japan, there could be large savings achieved by manufacturing longlasting products and keeping them repaired.

Remembering that equally productive developing world labor is paid only 20 percent that of the developed world (10 percent since the currency collapses on the periphery of empire), the reason products in the industrialized nations are cheap enough to throw away becomes clear; it is because labor in the developing world is underpaid:

> Goods manufactured with lowly paid labor are cheaper to throw away than to repair, since the relative wages for repair are higher. This not only affects the workers who are exploited, communities in all capitalist countries are awakening to the fact that the conveniences of high-resource consumption wind up in the local landfill, threatening their environment.[19]

Pay all equally productive labor equally well and the world will soon stop filling landfills with discarded products and tools.

Restructuring Patent Rights to Protect the Consumer, the Inventor, the Developing World, and the Developed World

Currently the developing world cannot use the latest patents without paying excessive royalties. This may appear to be a just right of property, but many critical early inventions were discovered by these now-dependent societies (writing, math, geometry, gunpowder—in fact most basic inventions; the Indians domesticated 60 percent of the plants used for human food and many pharmaceuticals).

Prosperous and inventive societies were overwhelmed by neomercantilist armed might, then denied the opportunity to work with modern tools and develop better tools (inventions). Once these societies were overwhelmed, control of their capital, resources, and markets—and unequal pay for equal labor—institutionalized their dependency in the world economy.

During their early industrialization, both the United States and Japan rejected the claims of others to intellectual property rights. If the developing world (with 70 percent of the world's population) had to pay corporate imperialists for the technology they have been denied, the cost to the defeated world and the gain to corporations would be enormous. The royalties due from the developing world were estimated in 1993 at $100 billion to $300 billion per year, not all collectable.[20] If the developing world were fully capitalized, the royalty claims would be $1 trillion a year or more, possibly seven times the annual capital required to industrialize the world over a forty-five-year period.

It was necessary for the development of the United States, Japan, and every other developed nation, and it is even more imperative for late-developing nations, to be given access to technology. Once a region is using the latest technology and creating its own inventions, it can then be integrated into a restructured world patent system as we will be addressing below.

For later developing societies to attain equality in industrial technology requires restructuring patent rights so all can use the latest technology by simply paying royalties. While these low-wage societies are developing and building buying power by raising the wages of equally productive labor to par with the industrialized world, equalizing managed trade will be required to protect the industries and markets of the developed societies while retaining competition internally within regions of both the developed and undeveloped worlds. To maintain its markets within those regions, and with the right to use any technology through payment of royalties, every business would be sure to use the latest technology and would study closely the technology of other regions and other companies to do so.

Assuming protection for both fledgling and developed economies through equalizing managed trade, and assuming buying power were developed in step with increased productive capacity, both labor and capital would be protected. And further assuming that the subtle monopolizations of patents were eliminated by giving everyone access to technology through payment of reasonable royalties, competition would be unhindered within a region and inventors would be adequately compensated. This would eliminate the abandonment of perfectly good factories and the collapse and impoverishment of communities caused by capital destroying capital.

Do Not Give the Needy Money: Build Them Industries Instead

With the record of corruption within impoverished countries, people will question giving them money. That can be handled by giving them the industry directly, not the money. To build a balanced economy, provide consumer buying power, and develop arteries of commerce that will absorb the production of these industries, contractors and labor in those countries should be used. Legitimacy and security of contracts is the basis of any sound economy. Engineers know what those costs should be and, if cost overruns start coming in, the contractor who has proven incapable should be replaced— just as any good contract would require.

Once the industry is built, shares should be issued to managers and workers. But that industrial capital is for the whole society so those shares should be paid for out of wages and profits and as that money is repaid it can be used for building social capital (homes, roads, libraries, etc.). The development of consumer buying power and arteries of commerce would require a protective period equalizing the pay of equally productive labor between regions. Once the region is economically viable, with adequate social capital and local buying power, the industry would then be on its own to sink or swim. With workers owning a share of the industry, the potential of gains through good management, the certainty of loss through poor management, the ability to regulate their own wages to stay competitive, and all this within an organized plan to develop a balanced economy, one can safely say most will succeed.[21] When provided the industry as opposed to the money to build industry, nations have physical capital. The only profits to be made then are in production; there is no development money to intercept and send to a Swiss bank account.

With care taken to organize homes and markets around jobs, and computers and modern communication permitting much work to be performed at home, the transportation needs of a well-planned, secure, well-cared-for society could be but a fraction of that currently seen as necessary in the developed world. A trend toward smaller homes—such as are the norm in Europe—could be fostered, consuming much less of the Earth's stored capital (timber, minerals, and fossil fuels).

Notes

1. Gerald Epstein, "Mortgaging America," *World Policy Journal* (Winter 1990–91), especially pp. 37, 53.

2. William Greider, *Who Will Tell the People?* (New York: Simon and Schuster, 1992), pp. 402–03.

3. AFL-CIO Task Force on Trade bulletin, 1992.

4. Andrew A. Reding, "Bolstering Democracy in the Americas," *World Policy Journal* (Summer 1992), p. 403.

5. Gerald Epstein, "Mortgaging America," pp. 52–56; see also p. 47.

6. Herman E. Daly, *Steady-State Economics* (San Francisco: W.H. Freeman, 1977), p. 109.

7. Dean Acheson, *Present at the Creation* (New York: W.W. Norton, 1987), pp. 382–84.

8. Lester Thurow, *Head to Head: The Coming Economic Battle Among Japan, Europe, and America* (New York: William Morrow, 1992), p. 223; Jeremy Rifkin, *Entropy: Into the Greenhouse World* (New York: Bantam Books, 1989), p. 220.

9. Alan Weisman, "Nothing Wasted, Everything Gained," *Mother Jones* (March/April 1998), pp. 56–59; Alan Weisman, "Colombia's Modern City," *In Context* 42 (1995), pp. 6–8.

10. Stephanie Mills, *In Service of the Wild: Restoring and Reinhabiting Damaged Land* (Boston: Beacon Press, 1995); John J. Berger, ed., *Environmental Restoration: Science and Strategies for Restoring the Earth* (Washington, DC: Island Press, 1990); William E. McClain, *Illinois Prairie: Past and Future: A Restoration Guide* (Springfield: Illinois Department of Conservation, 1986).

11. Jonathan Turk et al., *Ecosystems, Energy, Population* (Toronto: W.B. Saunders, 1975).

12. William Kötke, *The Final Empire* (Portland, OR: Arrow Point Press, 1993), p. 36.

13. Alan Dregson and Duncan Taylor, eds., *Ecoforestry: The Art and Science of Sustainable Forest Use* (Gabriola Island, BC: New Society, 1997); Michael Pilarski, *Restoration Forestry: An International Guide to Sustainable Forestry Practices* (Durango, CO: Kivaki Press, 1994).

14. A Report by The International Institute for Environment and Development and The World Resources Institute, *World Resources 1987: An Assessment of the Resource Base That Supports the Global Economy* (New York: Basic Books, 1987), p. 289.

15. Michael Potts, *The Independent Home: Living Well with Power from the Sun, Wind, and Water* (Post Mills, VT: Chelsea Green, 1993); Athena Swentzell, *The Straw Bale House* (White River Junction, VT: Chelsea Green, 1994).

16. Atossa Soltani and Penelope Whitney, eds., *Cut Waste, Not Trees* (San Francisco: Rainforest Action Network, 1995); United States Department of Agriculture, *First Conference on Kenaf for Pulp: Proceedings* (Peoria, IL: USDA, 1968).

17. Jeremy Rifkin, *Entropy,* pp. 117, 232.

18. Daly, *Steady-State Economics,* pp. 10–11.

19. Arjun Makhijani, *From Global Capitalism to Economic Justice* (New York: Apex Press, 1992), p. 89; see also pp. 121–27, 80–81, 159, 162–63.

20. Noam Chomsky, *Year 501: The Conquest Continues* (Boston: South End Press, 1993), pp. 115–16.

21. Roy Morrison, *We Build the Road as We Travel* (Philadelphia: New Society Publishers, 1991). Fawzy Mansour, Professor Emeritus of Political Economy at Ain Shams University, Cairo, Egypt, has a philosophy for Third World development quite similar to the one described in these last two chapters. Fawzy Mansour, "A Second Wave of National Liberation?" *Monthly Review* (February 1999), pp. 19–31.

Sharing Technology with the World Through Cooperative Capitalism

A Grand Strategy for World Peace and Prosperity

> To hell with the [peace] dividend. The Pentagon can keep it. We want the principal.
> —David McReynolds, "The Words and the Will to Talk about Change"

Since World War II, the military expenditures of NATO and Warsaw Pact nations have consumed and/or forgone production of about four times the value of everything manufactured and built in the United States (excluding clothes). Thus the wasted capital of the industrialized world during the Cold War is enough to have built homes, cars, and every other amenity of a modern country for 20 percent of the world or for 100 percent if a respectable, secure living were the goal as opposed to that of a throwaway society. Seymour Melman, professor of industrial engineering at Columbia University, has laboriously measured this waste:

> Without considering the full social cost to the American community, the combined Pentagon budgets of 1946–1981 represent a mass of resources equivalent to the cost of replacing just about all (ninety-four percent) of everything manmade in the United States [excluding the land but including every house, railroad, airplane, household appliance, etc.]. But when we take into account both the resources used by the military as well as the economic product forgone, then *we must appreciate the social cost of the military economy, 1946–1981, as amounting to about twice the "reproducible assets" of U.S. national wealth.* What has been forgone for American society is a quantity of material wealth sufficient to refurbish the United States, with an enormous surplus to spare.[1]

Almost $1 trillion a year was being spent on arms worldwide when the Soviets collapsed in 1990.[2] With the end of the Cold War, that annual cost dropped to $700 billion by 1998. The world has wasted $13 trillion building arms since Professor Melman made his calculations.

An economy structured to eliminate subtle monopolies siphoning wealth to the powerful and creating fictional values would provide these societies with a quality living standard with a fraction of the per capita resources, energy, and waste used in America. The two lifestyles are not even measurable. Some in the developed world have given up the "rat race," gone back to a quiet relaxed lifestyle, and prefer it. Depending on one's guidelines, the quality of life of a world society not based on an automobile/throwaway economy could exceed U.S. standards. Witness the Indian state of Kerala; it is one of the poorer regions of India but may have that nation's highest average quality of life.[3]

A more just paradigm for the world requires

a recognition of quiet days and evenings spent with the family watching TV, playing chess, and so forth, while working two days per week.[4] Many recognize this would be a far higher quality of life than driving $30,000 cars and piloting $100,000 boats to the detriment of the entire world. Experts in the field judge, by avoiding a throwaway economy, a secure, quality living can be attained while consuming roughly 20 percent per capita of what the United States currently consumes.[5]

Most developing world countries have the resources and labor to build their own social infrastructure. They lack only the tools of production (efficient industrial capital) and the training and experience to use them. These developing nations could, then, assuming they had fifty years of peace and cooperation (cooperative capitalism), produce their own social capital (homes, roads, bicycles, business, schools, libraries, recreation, etc.). The limits of the world's resources and the inability of the air, water, and soil to absorb wastes infinitely dictate that this development include few carbon-fuel-powered cars and other products of a throwaway society.

Compounding Sustainable Industrial Development

At the close of the Cold War, the United States had $21 trillion worth of reproducible social capital and $1 trillion worth of industrial capital (1990 dollars). Subtracting military and other wasted industry leaves a ratio of approximately one unit of civilian industrial capital to thirty units of social capital.[6] At that ratio, the developed world would have to provide to the developing nations only one-thirtieth of their needed wealth, those all-important industrial tools with which they would produce their social capital.

Since only 70 percent of U.S. industrial capacity is producing for consumer needs and the world sustainable development level is 20 percent that of the U.S. throwaway economy, rational planning would consider industrializing the developing world to 14 percent of the U.S. level. As in a balanced economy only 3.3 percent of a developed society's wealth is industrial capital producing for the civilian economy, the developing world would still have to build the remaining 96.7 percent of wealth that is social capital. The total world industrial capital in this development model equals the current world industrial level redistributed, but with the waste of trade wars and arms production eliminated, which testifies to the validity of this thesis.

That roughly 20 percent of the world's population (1996) has attained the living standard of America's throwaway economy and (considering the better-off within the developing world) another 40 percent the living standard of a bicycle/mass transit economy again testifies to the feasibility of this thesis. The wealthiest 60 percent of the world need only turn their minds to a nonthrowaway, but quality, lifestyle and the remaining 40 percent of the world needs only the industrial technology and training to produce that same quality lifestyle. Note: the math below allows for building industrial capital for 60 percent of the world's people so it is conservative. As unlikely a scenario as this is, the only other choices besides sustainable world development are the continued violence of Fascist control of world resources and war and the struggles of suppressed people to gain their economic freedom.

In these battles over the world's wealth, the

developing world and the developed world together have spent about $17 trillion on arms (converted to 1990 dollars) since World War II.[7] Without considering idle capital, capital supporting distribution through unnecessary labor (the thesis of this author's previous publication, *The World's Wasted Wealth 2*), capital destroying capital in trade wars, or capital destroyed in hot wars, that is *five times enough to have industrialized the developing world to a sustainable level over the past forty-five years.* The $3.15 trillion needed for developing world industries would have left $13.85 trillion to provide training to run the machines and society; to install initial communications infrastructure to reach the populations with that training (including population control); to guarantee food until a country was able to produce its own; to search for, catalog, and develop resources; and to protect the environment.

The loss to the world due to arms production is even greater than these statistics on arms costs indicate. There is the social capital destroyed by wars that were either openly or covertly financed by the superpowers—in Korea, Vietnam, Nigeria, Afghanistan, Iran, Iraq, Indonesia, El Salvador, Guatemala, Chile, Angola, Mozambique, Ethiopia, Somalia. Since World War II there have been 127 such wars with 21.8 million deaths, over half of which can easily be traced to superpower destabilizations and many of the rest under deep enough cover that they were undetected.

World Wars I and II each wasted several times enough wealth to have provided industrial tools (but not social capital) for the developing world—the territory, resources, and markets they were fighting over. World War II alone cost at least $10 trillion when measured in 1990 dollars and all combatants and destruction are

included, or three times enough to have industrialized the world at the current population level and six times enough at the prewar population level.[8] During World War II, the United States spent approximately $1.4 trillion, converted to 1990 dollars; some say almost double that. Counting the destruction of its social capital, the Soviet Union surely spent an equal amount. Germany, Britain, France, Italy, Japan, and the remaining countries together expended—or had destroyed—a similar amount.

Capitalizing the world would have been a much simpler job than waging all those wars, to say nothing of eliminating the reason for them. After all, under cooperative capitalism, as opposed to neomercantilist corporate imperialism, there would have been the cooperation of those societies instead of their battles attempting to gain or retain their economic freedom. With the developing nations using these industrial tools, and production compounding (this is what compounding interest is supposed to do), they could have built their own social capital. The history of the last seventy years could then have been one of world peace, prosperity, and care for the soil, water, and air, instead of intrigues, trade wars, covert wars, cold wars, hot wars, dispossessions, poverty, and ecological destruction.

Except for trying to protect its own, the regions of the former Soviet Union are now out of the battle over world resources. But the developed world has the excess productive capacity to *industrialize the world quickly using only a small part of the money currently wasted.* Roughly 20 percent of U.S. industry is wasted on arms (1982–91), possibly another 10 percent supports the distribution by unnecessary labor within the civilian economy. We do not measure the percent that is lost in trade wars as "capital destroys capital" but that is perhaps the greatest loss. Allowing for some overlap in the above figures, fully 30 percent of U.S. industrial capital is wasted, leaving only 70 percent producing for America's actual needs.

By Restructuring to Cooperative Capitalism, the World Can Be Developed to a Sustainable Level and Poverty Largely Eliminated in Forty-Five Years

We have calculated that a society can be well cared for at 20 percent of that consumption rate, or with as little as 14 percent of U.S. per capita industrial capacity at the peak of the Cold War. As of that date (1990), the value of industrial tools stood at about $5,600 per person in the United States. (Homes, cars, roads, bridges, electric power, water systems, sewers, etc., are social capital. Steel mills, factories, and so forth are industrial tools.) By the above calculation, one would consider 14 percent of that—or under $900 industrial capacity per person—as adequate for an efficient, peaceful society.[9] With approximately 3.5 billion people without modern tools, $3.15 trillion of industrial capital was needed at that time—or 18.5 percent the amount spent on arms by the world since World War II.[10]

Assuming it would require forty-five years for the developing world to be educated and to build social capital as it was being given industrial capital, and assuming a doubling of the developing world's population in that time span, it would require $6.3 trillion. That larger figure would be only $140 billion annually, or 14 percent of the $1 trillion spent on arms each year worldwide at the time of the Soviet collapse. Until that collapse, NATO and Warsaw Pact countries accounted for 86 percent of that expenditure, or about $860 billion (1990), and the Western alliance spent well over half of that.[11] *Thus it would require only 14 percent of the money habitually spent on arms by the world during the Cold War to industrialize the world.* As the Eastern bloc has collapsed, this leaves only the West, but the $140 billion a year needed to industrialize the world is only 28 percent of that spent by the West to win the Cold War (48 percent of that spent annually by the United States alone).[12]

Not only is this obvious in the slack world economy even as 25 percent of the world's population was rapidly industrializing (before their financial meltdown), any engineer can calculate it quickly. Modern industries can spit out industrial tools just as fast as they can cars, refrigerators, airplanes, tanks, guns, or warships. (In all those unneeded tanks, guns, and warships there is likely enough steel to produce the necessary industrial tools.) Since capital reproduces its value each year (actually every ten months), if one forty-fifth of the required industrial capital were installed each year and used by the developing world to build social capital, by the forty-fifth year of this mutual support policy of cooperative capitalism, the entire world would be industrially and socially capitalized to a level that would provide a secure lifestyle for most of the world's citizens and within the capacity of the earth's resources and its ability to absorb waste.

If It Is So Simple, Why Is It Not Done?

Why is this not done? Because profits are made by keeping capital scarce, scarce capital means relatively scarce consumer goods and high prices, and that translates into high profits. In short, the monopolization of the tools of production keeps these tools and the immense wealth they could produce out of the hands of the world's impoverished. The basic pattern of world trade was established centuries ago. So today's control of world trade is not a current conspiracy. It is the current structure of corporate imperialism monopolizing the tools of production, controlling trade, and enforcing inequalities of trade as established centuries ago.

Each imperial center of capital must defend its ownership of capital or lose the high profits and high wages with which it purchases cheaply the resources of those without capital, and with which it trades equally with allied imperial centers of capital. To share capital, technology, resources, and markets is to eliminate one's advantage.

Eliminate that waste of resources and labor outlined in this chapter, provide others with modern tools of production so they can produce for their needs, provide security through disarmament and security guarantees rather than arms, manage trade between regions, reduce those protections in step with increased industrial efficiency and labor skills, reduce populations to within the regional capacity for a sustainable quality lifestyle, and the world quality of life can rise rapidly.

Underdeveloped countries could not absorb those tools as fast as they could be built. Thus, we are considering using only roughly 28 percent of the West's industry formerly dedicated to arms production. This is, however, only a broad overview. It is not meant to outline either the exact methods or timetable for implementation. If engineers are authorized to proceed and are given access to productive capital, they can easily solve these problems. It is reasonable to assume that it is possible for the developing world to train workers, build the infrastructure (businesses, homes, roads, sewers, water, electricity, etc.), absorb this industrial capital, and produce the necessary social capital over a period of forty-five years.

Society Is a Machine Producing Its Needs

Industrial society is a machine; and every road, railroad, electric grid, water system, and sewer system makes this machine more efficient. Developing countries cannot compete in world trade until such time as their internal communication, production, and transportation systems (a major part of society's social capital) are equal to those of the developed nations. Even conservative economists have calculated that in the United States—with its highly developed, but deteriorating, infrastructure—returns on such "public core investment would average fifty to sixty percent per year."[13] Calculations have been made that the United States needs $4.5 trillion for infrastructure repairs and modernization of industry.[14] Such investment in the infrastructure of a relatively undeveloped country would see far greater increases in efficiency, thus far greater profits to that society.

We have not only China and Southeast Asia (before their financial meltdown) for a current example. The $170 billion (1990 dollars) Marshall Plan, with which the United States financed the reconstruction of Europe in five years, documents the plan's credibility.[15] It is supported also by the record of U.S. industrialization. I would quote again from the autobiography of one of America's premier Managers of State, Dean Acheson:

> Throughout the [ninteenth] century the flood of "foreign aid" grew and grew until in the half century preceding 1914 Western Europe, led by

Great Britain, "had invested abroad almost as much as the entire national wealth of Great Britain. . . . If the same proportion of American resources were devoted to foreign investment as Britain [then] devoted, . . . the flow of investment would require to be thirty times as great. The entire Marshall Plan would have to be carried out twice a year."[16]

If the United States shared its capital with the developing world at the same rate as Europe shared it with America, that would be $150 billion per year, or more than the $140 billion yearly industrial needs of the developing world. Of course there are still Western Europe, Japan, and the productive capacity in the former Soviet Union, as well as the industries in the developing world currently producing arms.

Any country which shouldered the bigger burden would, because internal distribution problems are resolved, find life easier in the short run. But when the need for producing industry for the developing world ends, the country providing this industry must lower its average workweek and share the remaining productive jobs. It must also reduce its regional industrial capital to that all-important ratio of one part industrial capital to thirty parts social capital.

Once Society Is Developed to a Sustainable Level, Industrial Production Can Be Cut Back

Let us assume a newly developing country produced a very good tractor and a full range of farm equipment. Because the useful life of most farm machinery is over twenty years, once its agriculture is capitalized less than 10 percent of normal production would provide replacements. There would be no place within its economy to sell 90 percent of what it could produce. If that production were exported, and assuming true free trade, this would destroy the machinery industry of another country. Capital will have destroyed capital.

The same principle holds true for capitalization of any economic sector of any society. When the home market is capitalized, the manufacturer must export or shut down much of the industry that produced those products. This is the primary reason capital looks for markets abroad. Certainly those industries can retool and enter another market, but their success in that market only means someone else must go out of business and again capital will have destroyed capital.

Cannibalization of capital by capital will be eliminated through cooperative capitalism and, with those enormous savings, the world can quickly be developed to a sustainable level. We now turn to the subtle monopolies within internal economies that must be removed before poverty can be eliminated.

Notes

1. Seymour Melman, *Profits Without Production* (New York: Alfred A. Knopf, 1983), p. 151, emphasis added.

2. Ruth Leger Sivard, *World Military and Social Expenditures* (Washington, DC: World Priorities).

3. Richard W. Franke and Barbara H. Chasin, "Power to the (Malayalee) People," *Z Magazine* (February 1998), pp. 16–20; Bill McKibben, "The Enigma of Kerala," *Utne Reader* (March/April 1996), pp. 103–112; Harry Magdoff, "Are There Lessons to Be Learned?" *Monthly Review* (February 1991), p. 12, analyzing Richard W. Franke and Barbara H. Chasin, "Kerala State, India: Radical Reform as Development," *Monthly Review* (January 1991), pp. 1–23.

4. J. W. Smith, *The World's Wasted Wealth 2* (San Luis Obispo, CA: Institute for Economic Democracy, 1994).

5. David C. Korten, *When Corporations Rule the World* (West Hartford, CT: Kumarian Press, 1995),

p. 35; Jeremy Rifkin, *Entropy: Into the Greenhouse World* (New York: Bantam Books, 1989), p. 233; Richard J. Barnet and John Cavanagh, *Global Dreams: Imperial Corporations and the New World Order* (New York: Simon and Schuster, 1994), pp. 177–178.

6. *Statistical Abstract of the U.S., 1990,* pp. 463, 734, charts 752, 1295 (check gross stock, total; value added by manufacture; gross book value of depreciable assets). These statistics demonstrate that each factory reproduces its value every ten months and that there is approximately $21 trillion worth of reproducible social capital and $1 trillion worth of industrial capital. Seymour Melman, probably the leading authority on military waste; Greg Bishak, of the National Commission for Economic Conversion and Disarmament; and William Greider, *Who Will Tell the People?* (New York: Simon and Schuster, 1992), p. 370, judge U.S. industry wasted on arms at roughly 20 percent.

7. Ibid.

8. Henry Wallace, *Towards World Peace* (Westport, CT: Greenwood Press, 1970), p. 12. Barry Bluestone and Irving Bluestone, *Negotiating the Future* (New York: Basic Books, 1992), pp. 33–34, 36.

9. That is about $3,600 worth of industrial capital per family and $100,000 worth of social capital.

10. Sivard, *World Military and Social Expenditures.*

11. *The Missoulian,* November 24, 1986, p. 7, obtained from Sivard's *World Military and Social Expenditures.*

12. When one includes the National Security Agency, the CIA, and weapons programs carried out under the umbrella of the Atomic Energy Commission and Energy Department, the military budget was at least $350 billion, as opposed to the $292 billion official military budget we are using. Between $4 trillion and $5 trillion was spent on nuclear arms alone, mostly under cover of the Energy Department, since 1945 (Jonathan S. Landay, "Study Reveals U.S. Has Spent $4 Trillion on Nukes Since '45," *The Christian Science Monitor,* July 12, 1995, p. 3. See also David Moberg, "Cutting the U.S. Military: How Low Can We Go?" *In These Times,* February 12–18, 1992, p. 3; "U.S. Becomes Biggest Dealer of Arms in Worldwide Market," *The Spokesman Review,* October 15, 1992, p. A2; William D. Hartung, "Why Sell Arms?" *World Policy Journal* (Spring 1993), p. 57.

13. David Moberg, "Can Public Spending Rescue the Infrastructure? A Tale of Three Deficits," *In These Times,* February 13–19, 1991, p. 11.

14. Joel Kurtzman, *The Decline and Crash of the American Economy* (New York: W.W. Norton, 1988), p. 149.

15. Lester Thurow, *Head to Head: The Coming Economic Battle Among Japan, Europe, and America* (New York: William Morrow, 1992), p. 94; Paul Kennedy, *The Rise and Fall of the Great Powers* (New York: Random House, 1987), p. 360; *ABC News* and *NBC News,* June 4, 1987; Michael Barrat Brown, in *Fair Trade* (London: Zed Books, 1993), p. 96, puts The Marshall Plan at $200 billion in 1987 dollars.

16. Dean Acheson, *Present at the Creation* (New York: W.W. Norton, 1987), p. 7, quoting A. K. Cairncross.

Part IV

Internal Trade: Economic Rights for All People Through Elimination of Subtle Monopolies

24

Subtly Monopolizing Land

Before the advent of title to social wealth through industrial capital and finance capital, all sustenance for life and thus all wealth came directly from land. Finance capital is the money symbol for industrial capital and these factories are only extremely efficient tools to process products from the land. So monopolization of finance capital and/or industrial capital is only an extension of land monopolization. When wealth began to be produced by capital as well as land, powerful people undertook to lay claim to these producers of wealth just as historically they had laid claim to land. The process of usurping rights through claiming society's wealth takes many generations and leads to great wealth for a relative few and dispossession and poverty for many. This has a long way to go in the United States but the well-documented trend suggests that fewer and fewer own more and more.

With wealth produced by labor and capital going primarily to title holders, the Federal Reserve calculated that 25 percent of U.S. citizens had no net assets in 1974; by 1988, this had increased to 54 percent.[1] As full rights include economic rights (actually primarily *are* economic rights), these people's rights are severely restricted. With the right to vote, and within the framework of America's ever-flexible Constitution, these rights can be reclaimed through re-

structuring law and custom; society should collect the landrent.[2]

Land is monopolized by the total tax structure of a nation. Before going on to a greater reward, almost every economist of high standing will say that Henry George's *Progress and Poverty,* describing the simplicity and justice of society collecting the landrent, outlines the most efficient and just tax structure. To eliminate monopolization, nothing is more important for establishing a productive society than society collecting the landrent.

Although this tax structure has been proposed by various philosophers for 300 years, America's preeminent economic philosopher Henry George is undoubtedly the master on the subject. The next few pages are his primary work—*Progress and Poverty*, published in 1879—condensed and simplified.[3]

The subtle monopolization of social wealth started centuries ago as the powerful structured superior rights into ownership of land. As British Prime Minister Winston Churchill said, land is "by far the greatest of monopolies—it is a perpetual monopoly, and it is the mother of all other forms of monopoly."[4] These excessive rights are now ingrained in law and custom. If you feel threatened by such a simple solution, keep in mind that when society collects its full due in a landrent tax, all use rights will be retained. Ownership of land for homes, businesses, and production will be both easier and cheaper. *Removal of subtle monopolization would not only increase your right to land and the profits from its productive use, it would ensure it.*

Land Is Social Wealth

If a person were born with fully developed intelligence, physical ability, and judgment—but without social conditioning—one of the first confusing realities he or she would face is that all land belongs to someone else. Before one could legally stand, sit, lie down, or sleep, he or she would have to pay whoever owned that piece of land. This can be shown to be absurd by reflecting on the obvious: land, air, and water nurture all life and each living thing requires, and is surely entitled to, living space on this earth. No person produced any part of it, it was here when each was born, and its bounty belongs to all.

By observing title claims in action, earlier economic philosophers were able to deduce that the essential factor in creation of wealth was the appropriation of a useful commodity by one person in unrestricted private title and its alienation from all others.[5] All materials to satisfy human needs come from the land. Over time, the alert realized that if they claimed a piece of land and defended that claim, others would have to ask permission and pay for its use:

> Wealth would be laid at one's feet and others were doing all the work. . . . The first man who, having enclosed a piece of ground, bethought himself as saying "this is mine," and found people simple enough to believe him, was the real founder of civil society. From how many crimes, wars, and murders, from how many horrors and misfortunes might not any one have saved mankind, by pulling up the stakes, or filling up the ditch, and crying to his fellows: "Beware of listening to this impostor; you are undone if you once forget that the fruits of the earth belong to us all, and the earth itself to nobody."[6]

Jean Jacques Rousseau, in *A Discourse on the Origins of Inequality,* was outlining the injustice of one person having *unrestricted* ownership of another's living space. This practice is only customary. It is part of the social conditioning (Social Control paradigms or belief systems) that all receive while growing up. Being thoroughly conditioned, and having never experienced or imagined anything else, few ever realize that under unrestricted private ownership of land they do not have all their rights. Instead, the possibility of *eventually owning* one's piece of land is viewed as evidence of full rights. Being conscious of the not-so-distant past when common people did not have even this right, citizens view and celebrate these limited rights as full rights.

Mark Twain recognized that appropriation of nature's gifts in unrestricted private title by one person means alienation and loss of rights for others. His article, "Archimedes," in Henry George's paper *The Standard,* July 27, 1889, describes how, if he owned all the world, all the wealth of the world would be his and all the world's citizens would be his slaves.[7]

While one's lack of full rights is difficult to visualize when a person is accustomed to unrestricted title to what nature provided free, it is easy to see if one uses a gift of nature, such as air, that has not yet been appropriated. Air is one of nature's gifts and if a group could claim title to it (when windmills were invented, such efforts were made to claim title to the wind), each person would have to pay for the right to breathe just as now they have to pay for the right for a place to live. Broadcast radio and TV bandwidths are just as much a gift of nature as air or the wind. Title to these has been claimed, society has been paid nothing for them, and the sums each citizen must pay, direct and indirect, to listen to a radio or watch TV add up to huge profits.

The enormous capitalized values of those bandwidths created by those huge profits is mute testimony that the airways are monopolized and the public (the proper owners of those bandwidths) are being grossly overcharged. Henry George pointed out that everyone would retain the right to land through a landrent tax covering normal costs of government. Radio and TV bandwidths are gifts of nature, unchanged by human labor, and society should receive those rental values and expend them on sustaining efficient social infrastructures such as communications, schools, and roads.

One notes that water was still free long after land was fully claimed. As population density increased and water became scarce, it became profitable to claim title to drinking water. Whenever those claims of ownership are encoded in law, water sources will develop high capitalized values and society will become accustomed to paying dearly for its drinking water. As one analyzes the primary monopolies of land, technology, money, and communications, it becomes apparent that all high capitalized values create a charge to the public for exclusive title to, or exclusive use of, a gift of nature. (Economists concerned with the question of how else one would accumulate capital should refer to the subchapters "Investment," "The Creation of Money," and especially "Accumulation of Capital through Cooperative Capitalism.")

Pride in Ownership Must be Maintained

Land is, unquestionably, social wealth. However, the right to one's space on this earth, the pride it returns to its owner, and the care normally given to one's personal property all are compelling reasons to keep most land under a *conditional* form of private ownership. If equal rights of all to a share of the production of land are acknowledged through society collecting the landrent, private ownership is socially efficient and fully justifiable. What is unjust is the unrestricted subtle monopolization of what nature freely produces on, above, and under this land. It is necessary to keep private ownership of land and its benefits while eliminating subtle land monopolization and its unavoidable inequities.

The Origins of Land Titles

Societies have battled for title to land for millennia. One society's violent claim to land is another society's violent loss. Today's landowners are the descendants of the winners of the latest clash of cultures.[8] After the collapse of the Roman Empire at the hands of the Germanic tribes, the common people regained their rights to the land, and the use of nature's wealth in common again developed a powerful following.[9] Their belief in freedom and natural rights resembles our allegiance to these principles today.

However, this reversion to social wealth in public ownership came under attack by powerful clans. Petr Kropotkin, that unique historian, describes the repression of these rights as the origin of the modern state: "Only wholesale massacres by the thousand could put a stop to this widely spread popular movement, and it was by the sword, the fire, and the rack that the young states secured their first and decisive victory over the masses of the people.''[10] They were struggling against imposition of a legal structure which protected private title to land previously owned by all.

As described by Kropotkin, the medieval roots of our culture grimly parallel the massive slaughter in many developing world countries today. People in these countries are fighting to retain, or reclaim, their right to a fair share of the earth's resources—resources now owned by the cultural descendants of earlier violent thefts. The resemblance here is not a coincidence; current struggles are a continuation of that medieval battle over who shall have rights to nature's wealth. However unjust, if a legal title to land or any other gift of nature (such as communication airways) can be established, the powerful can lay claim to the wealth produced by others.

In the fourteenth century, the sharing of social wealth was still practiced by local communities. But, tragically, that century saw the beginning of a 300-year effort by the aristocracy of Europe to erase all trace of communal rights. Kropotkin explains:

> The village communities were bereft of their folkmotes [community meetings], their courts and independent administration; their lands were confiscated. The guilds were spoilated of their possessions and liberties, and placed under the control, the fancy, and the bribery of the State's official. The cities were divested of their sovereignty, and the very springs of their inner life—the folkmote, the elected justices and administration, the sovereign parish and the sovereign guild—were annihilated; the State's functionary took possession of every link of what formerly was an organic whole. Under that fatal policy and the wars it engendered, whole regions, once populous and wealthy, were laid bare; rich cities became insignificant boroughs; the very roads which connected them with other cities became impracticable. Industry, art, and knowledge fell into decay.[11]

The efforts to alienate the individual from common use of the natural wealth of the land are documented in Britain by the nearly 4,000 enclosure acts passed between 1760 and 1844 that effectively gave legal sanction to this theft.[12] For the powerful to protect their title further, it was necessary to erase from social memory all traces of the earlier custom of social ownership of social wealth. Kropotkin points out that, ''It was taught in the universities and from the pulpit that the institutions in which men formerly used to embody their needs of mutual support could not be tolerated in a properly organized State.''[13] A Social Control belief system to protect a power structure had been designed and put into practice.

The classic descriptions of the evolution of capitalism explain how trade and industrial capital usurped the preeminent position of nobility with their historical title to all land. Yet in parts of Europe an elite social class still owns large tracts of land. As late as 1961, the Duke of Bedford, the Duke of Westminster, and the British Crown owned the most valuable sections of London, and large estates still abound throughout the countryside. In fact, at the turn of the twentieth century,

> the English upper class consisted ... of around ten thousand people drawn almost entirely from a core of 1,500 families.... The aristocracy owned great estates and houses and works of art—but, above all, they owned land. Well over ninety percent of the acreage of Britain was theirs.[14]

One can recognize the ongoing effort to prevent a rekindling of mutual support beliefs. Today we are taught, by those who parrot the original disinformation, that in an efficient economy virtually all property should be privately owned with each individual a "free" bargaining agent. Henry George's and our disagreement with this Social Control paradigm is that title to land, or any other gift of nature, should be conditional since no person built land and all are entitled to their share of nature's wealth.

Private Ownership of Social Wealth Moves to America

The powerful, aware that wealth comes from control of land, originally structured land ownership in America under the same rules as in Europe. The origins of "the manorial lords of the Hudson Valley" were huge landed estates "where the barons controlled completely the lives of their tenants." There were also huge estates in Virginia; one covered over 5 million acres and embraced twenty-one counties.[15] Such excessive greed contributed to the widespread dissatisfactions that fueled the American Revolution:

> Under Governor Benjamin Fletcher, three-quarters of the land in New York was granted to about thirty people. He gave a friend a half million acres for a token annual payment of 30 shillings. Under Lord Cornbury in the early 1700s one grant to a group of speculators was for two million acres. . . . In 1689, many of the grievances of the poor were mixed up in the farmers' revolt of Jacob Leisler and his group. Leisler was hanged, and the parceling out of huge estates continued.[16] [B]y 1698, New York had given thousands of acres to the Philipses, Van Cortlands, Van Rensselaers, Schuylers, Livingstons and Bayards; by 1754, Virginia had given almost three million acres to the Carters, Beverleys, and Pages—an early example of government "aid" to business men.[17]

Despite the egalitarian rhetoric of the American Revolution and an attempt to place a proclamation in the Constitution for a "common right of the whole nation to the whole of the land," the powerful looked out for their own interests by changing Locke's insightful phrase: "all men are entitled to life, liberty and land." This powerful statement that all could understand coming from a much-read and respected philosopher was a threat to the monopolizers of land, so they restructured those words to "life, liberty and [the meaningless phrase] pursuit of happiness." Knowledge of the substitution for phrases in America's Constitution which would protect every person's rights with phrases that protect only the rights of a few should alert one to check the meaning and purpose of all laws of all societies carefully.

Only portions of these huge estates described below were confiscated, and "speculation in western lands was one of the leading activities of capitalists in those days:"[18]

> Companies were formed in Europe and America to deal in Virginia lands, which were bought up in large tracts at the trifling cost of two cents per acre. This wholesale engrossment soon consumed practically all the most desirable lands and forced the home seeker to purchase from speculators or to settle as a squatter. [Moreover, observes Beard, as] the settler sought to escape the speculator by moving westward, the frontier line of speculation advanced.[19]

Some of America's famous leaders were deeply involved:

> In the Ohio Valley a number of rich Virginia planter families, amongst whom were counted both the Lees and the Washingtons, had formed a land company and this, the Ohio Company, founded in 1748, was given a crown grant of half

a million acres.[20] [And with] every member of the Georgia legislature but one [having] acquired a personal interest in the speculation schemes, [they sold thirty-five] million acres to three . . . land speculating companies for a total payment of less than $210,000.[21] [That is six-tenths of a cent per acre. Thus,] as the frontier was pushed back during the first half of the nineteenth century, land speculators working with banks stayed just ahead of new immigrants, buying up land cheap and then reselling it at high profits.[22]

While few who participated in these later land grabs were members of the old aristocracy, they knew well that the route to wealth lay in claiming land so that those who followed would have to buy it from them. Whether rented or sold at high capitalized values, a share of the wealth produced would be siphoned to the owners without expenditure of their labor.

Individuals became immensely wealthy, such as the butcher's son, John Jacob Astor, who had title to Manhattan Island. But Matthew Josephson, in *Robber Barons,* and Peter Lyon, in *To Hell in a Day Coach,* document the greatest land grab in history when the railroads, through control of state and federal governments, obtained deeds to 183 million acres of land (9.3 percent of the land in the United States). By the turn of the century this included "more than one-third of Florida, one-fourth of North Dakota, Minnesota, and Washington and substantial chunks of 25 other states":[23]

The state of Texas was the most generous of all: at one point they had actually given away about eight million more acres than they had in their power to bestow; as it finally turned out, they forked over to twelve railroad companies more than thirty-two million acres, which is more real estate than can be fitted inside the boundaries of the state of New York.[24]

Those to whom this land was parceled out had taken care to buy Congress and codify their title in legal statutes. The arrival of the railroads provided easy access to these lands and, as Henry George taught us, made them valuable. Every landless immigrant had a more just claim to that earth. Yet instead of immigrants being allowed to choose land on a first-come-first-served basis and using its rental value to develop social infrastructure, the land-hungry poor were forced to buy the land from these profiteers. Land sales by speculators were contracts that siphoned a part of the future labor of those who bought the land to the speculator. Any claim of need for that land by the powerful was dwarfed by the much greater needs of the poor.

America's celebrated Homestead Act of 1862 came after most of the choice land had already been claimed by speculators. Some 600,000 pioneers received 80 million acres under this act, but this was less than half that allotted to the railroad barons, who were only the latest in a long line of profiteers. These new lords of the land thoroughly understood the legal mechanics of siphoning wealth produced by others to themselves. They knew that all the surplus land had to be owned before their land could have significant value; thus the Homestead Act was vital to their plans of attaining great wealth.

Unrestricted Land Titles Permitted the Mobilization of Capital

Once land had been confiscated from the masses in the Middle Ages, it belonged permanently to the lord of that land and could only be lost through war. When English law changed to permit the sale of land, this created the foundation for modern capitalism. When an entrepreneur wished to speculate by building a factory or ship, land could be mortgaged for that venture.

This provided a broader base of wealth to loan against than loaning against potential profits from monopoly trade rights issued to favored friends by royalty.

The privatization of land and resultant mobilization of capital was a key stage in the development of capitalism that expanded rights to more people. However, full rights were not attained for all. Left in place were subtle forms of land, capital, and finance capital monopolizations that siphoned a large share of the wealth to those who escaped labor through unrestricted title to what is properly social wealth and title to what is properly the wealth of those whose labor produced it.

Slave labor has been a historic method to accumulate capital and pockets of slavery remain today. Export platforms in Third World countries that avoid taxes and pollution laws and pay thirteen cents to forty-three cents an hour for workers to produce items for sale in the developed world, where workers with the same qualifications are paid $6 to $10 an hour, are, as addressed in Chapter One, a simple capital accumulation scheme.

The forced acceptance of opium sales to China a century ago and the turnaround sales of drugs to the developed world today accumulate capital. The governments of Japan and China accumulate capital through monopolization of a milder drug, cigarettes. Charging Japan's well-paid citizens triple the price for Japanese manufactures as the same item would cost in Europe or America was a major capital accumulation scheme.

The "robber barons" of the late nineteenth and early twentieth century accumulated capital at an unnecessarily great cost to America. That enormous cost was neither visible nor acknowledged because, even with massive destruction of natural wealth (timber, topsoil), the remaining resources could still provide a good living for the relatively small population. The timber burned to clear the land could have provided a fine set of hardwood furniture for every family on earth. Likewise today, the powerful and greedy worldwide are, through enforced privatization by the IMF/World Bank (structural adjustment loans) and through confiscation of the social wealth of the impoverished world through unequal trades, accumulating enormous reserves of capital. Capital accumulations through land monopolization are more mundane. Through hard work, frugality and/or good fortune, a family owns a valuable piece of land. When the breadwinner's buying power decreases or ceases due to death, tracts of the land are sold off piecemeal to maintain the accustomed standard of living. All money from sales deposited within the banking system as savings becomes part of the nation's finance capital. Eventually all the tracts of land are sold, some of the money becomes accumulated capital, and the part spent to maintain the family, which also could have been accumulated capital, becomes consumed capital.

Those smaller tracts of land that were sold off continue to gain in value and continue to be split into smaller tracts. Each time those tracts are sold, capital is either accumulated or consumed. John Jacob Astor's exclusive title to, and piecemeal sale of, Manhattan Island is probably America's leading example of wealth accumulation through continued land monopolization as tracts of land become smaller and smaller and their use value becomes higher and higher. The enormous values (potential capital) lying untouched and capital wasted through high living of heirs tell us there are better ways to accumulate capital.

Accumulated capital is the engine of capitalism. An undeveloped society with excessive rights for a minority may well be forced to accept monopolization as the cheapest and quickest, if not the only, method of capital accumulation available to it. But an unrestricted monopoly is an excessive right that requires others to pay excessive charges.[25]

Once a society is developed it requires only a simple adjustment in the law to attain full rights, freedom, and justice for all: society collecting the landrent. All other monopolies will fall once the principle of full rights, requiring everyone to have equal rights to nature's wealth, is universally recognized and the "mother of all monopolies" (land) is eliminated. Once full freedom and rights have been attained through society collecting landrent, each member of society will retain rights to land and the wealth produced by land.

Profound Thinkers Who Believed in Society Collecting the Landrent

The French physiocrats were the originators of laissez-faire—the philosophy of little government interference. They held as a cornerstone of their philosophy (appropriated from the work of John Locke, William Penn, Baruch Spinoza, and Richard Cantillon fifty to one hundred years earlier) that society should collect the landrent. One of their most respected members, Mirabeau the Elder, held that this would increase social efficiency equal to the inventions of writing or money. This synthesis of Henry George's *Progress and Poverty* should convince one of the accuracy of that analysis.

David Ricardo formulated the law of rent, which supports the logic of Mirabeau's statement. Put in simple terms, Ricardo's law of rent means that all income above that necessary to sustain labor will be claimed by the owners of the land without the expenditure of their labor. A land monopolist retains ownership of land

until some innovative entrepreneur sees its potential for more productive use. The high price demanded effectively siphons a part of the wealth produced by that entrepreneur and society's labor to the previous owner, now holder of that mortgage and sales contract.

It was Henry George who most clearly understood how Ricardo's law of rent siphoned society's surplus wealth to the owners of land and how that monopoly maintained itself through the price of land. He outlined how wealth came directly from land and accrued to the owner; how all wealth above the survival needs of the hard-working people flowed to those with title to the land without expenditure of their labor; how these profits capitalized land values ever higher, perpetuating the flow of newly produced wealth to titleholders; how commercial successes were dependent on location and those profits too went largely to owners; and how new people were continually getting rich, accumulating their wealth through title to land and riding its value up to ever higher levels.

Adam Smith's statement that "every improvement in the circumstances of society raises rent" tells us he knew that title to land claims much of the wealth produced by the increased efficiencies of society.[26] The respected economist John Kenneth Galbraith, although questioning changing tax policy at this late date, accepted the justice of society collecting the landrent. In 1978, the conservative economist Milton Friedman stated, "In my opinion the least bad tax is the property tax on the unimproved value of land."[27]

Earlier philosophers who believed in the free enterprise philosophy of the physiocrat—"society collecting the landrent"—include Thomas Paine, who is credited with proposing much of the Bill of Rights; William Penn, the founder of Pennsylvania; Herbert Spencer, the noted philosopher, in his classic *Social Statics;* Thomas Sperry of the Newcastle Philosophical Society; and philosopher John Stuart Mill. These early economists were not radicals. They all "believed in the *sacredness* of private property, *particularly land.*"[28]

The Robert Schalkenbach Foundation lists over a hundred famous thinkers—including Confucius, Moses, Thomas Jefferson, Mark Twain, Henry Ford, John Maynard Keynes, Albert Einstein, President Eisenhower, and several popes—who recognized the principle that the natural product of the land belongs to all citizens, and lists various places in the modern world where these policies have been, at least in part, implemented.[29] In the early years of the twentieth century, Henry George's policies had substantial influence and candidates for public office were being advised to take a stand for a landrent tax.[30]

But those who owed their fortunes to the structure of property rights and taxes were too well entrenched to be dislodged. Their fear of Henry George's philosophy motivated the funding of neoclassical economics professors and politicians to prevent governments from adopting those policies, silenced the democratic dialogue begun by Henry George, and protected their vested monopoly interests.[31]

Just as corporations today fund professors and universities to produce studies that support their products or causes (believe it or not, one can find professors to produce studies to back up any cause), those who opposed Henry George's vision paid scholars to bend the truth and thus prevented people from insisting on their democratic rights.

Those corrupt scholars accomplished this feat, unwittingly aided by academics to this day, by corrupting economic language. Classic economics clearly points out there are three elements of production, land, labor, and capital.

Biased neoclassical economists combined land with capital, eliminating land as a separate factor, and left only capital and labor as elements of production. Those redefined terms created an economic jargon, confused the public debate, and prevented the spreading of Henry George's concepts.[32]

Mason Gaffney's and Fred Harrison's analysis of the working papers of these professors leaves no doubt that they were specifically designing their philosophy to eliminate the threat of Henry George. This is a replay of Kropotkin's statement, "It was taught in the universities and from the pulpit that the institutions in which men formerly used to embody their needs of mutual support could not be tolerated in a properly organized State."[33]

Commercial Land

Visualize a trade in a primitive society with someone standing by collecting tribute for trading on a particular piece of ground. The landowner does no productive labor—he only monopolizes that land. Of course, to avoid paying tribute, that early trader only needed to move to another piece of land. Today that nearby land would also be claimed.

Trading is one of the most valuable uses of land. As Henry George taught us, the closer one approaches the center of commerce, the higher the price of land. Every transit line from the suburbs to a commercial district will raise commercial land values a calculable amount. This high value represents the cheapness and the quantity of trades within any population center, and that saving (efficiency of trades) is recognized by the price business is willing to pay for that land.

Because rent lays claim to a large share of the wealth produced by commerce, the land values are very high in large population centers.

They gradually lower as the distance from the center of population becomes greater and the trades become less frequent and more expensive. But in the center, in a matter of minutes on that acre there would be millions of dollars' worth of trades in grain, diamonds, stocks, land, finance capital, or consumer products. A share of each trade is remitted to the landowner as rent: thus the high value of land within population centers.

It is not unusual for commercial land to be valued at three, four, or even ten times the value of the buildings placed upon it.[34] Probably the highest priced acre in the world was in the center of Tokyo, valued, before values dropped by 75 percent, at $1.5 billion. The space of one footprint in Tokyo was valued at $8,000. The land area of the twenty-three wards of Tokyo was equal in monetary value to the entire land area of the United States. The land upon which the emperor's palace sat was valued at the price of all the land in California. All the land in tiny Japan was worth four times as much as all the land in the huge United States. "In fact, the real estate value of Tokyo [in 1989] at $7.7 trillion [was] so high that, once collateralized and borrowed against (at 80 percent of [the then] current value), it could buy all the land in the United States for $3.7 trillion, and all the companies on the New York Stock Exchange, NASDAQ and several other exchanges for $2.6 trillion."[35] If it had held its value, that $1.5 billion acre in Tokyo earning 5 percent interest could have permanently retired 6,250 people from the labor force at $1,000 per month each. Three acres of farmland on the outskirts of that city at $3 million could have retired twelve. Thus, the relatively few total acres in and around Tokyo (or any population center) are capable of siphoning an enormous amount of unearned income to their owners, where as outside of a population center it requires a large amount of land to accumulate capital.

To their disadvantage, businesses join land monopolists in battling against increases in landrent taxes. If unnecessary government expenses were eliminated and landrent taxes were balanced to pay all government expenses, the cost of wages paid by business would lower by whatever amount of taxes was once paid by labor. Even more, there would be the additional savings of not having to keep track of sales, excise, and income taxes currently paid by both business and labor. Appropriate landrent taxes would roughly equal current interest or rent paid (or received) from land values and the current taxes paid on land.

Farm Land

David Ricardo makes the rather simple observation that the value of land will be lower as the quality lowers. (The quality of commercial land depends on population and accessibility for customers. The quality of farmland depends on rainfall, growing season, fertility, and accessibility to markets.) Once the quality is such that one can earn only the wages expended in production or distribution (at the margins), the land's value reaches zero. The economist's term "at the margins," then, represents the economic edge of profits. It also measures the edge of monopolies.

There is enough land in the United States to feed several times its current population. By exporting food to countries that—if their lands, resources, and trade were not monopolized— could just as well feed themselves, by converting grain into high-priced fat, and by farming the public treasury, agriculture in the United States has made handsome profits and evaded Ricardo's law of rent. Unearned income (rent) from the subtle monopoly created by those laws is capitalized into, and maintains the value of, land. Under Ricardo's law, but without sales to countries able to feed themselves or government supports ($31.2 billion average per year 1985–96[36]), the price of much of U.S. land would be zero while the use value of all the world's farmland would be greater than ever.

Home Sites

In smaller cities, a typical $84,500 house will be on a $20,000 lot. In major population centers, it is not uncommon for a house to cost double, triple, or even ten times that price. In Honolulu and parts of California, a comparable home would be $400,000 and in Washington, DC, it would be $800,000. As the labor and material prices of each of these homes are relatively equal, the price differential is the cost of land functioning under Ricardo's law of rent. The price of land accurately measures the monopolized landrent paid by those who were productive to owners who did no work.

For that matter, the high prices in population centers are traceable to the high price of land. Labor must be well paid to pay those high rents and taxes. A restaurant, or any other business, must charge high prices to pay those high wages and high rents. High prices from any form of monopolization (land, technology, or finance capital) are paid for through all consumer purchases.

The power brokers took from the physiocrats' free enterprise philosophy (or any other philosophy) only that which protected and further extended their wealth and power. As historically most members of legislative bodies were large landholders, naturally they did not accept that society should collect the landrent. If that were to happen, everyone would have

immediate rights to nature's wealth. The "divine rights" of private ownership of social wealth, which siphoned large amounts of wealth from those who produced to those who did not, would be converted to "conditional rights," where only those who produce are paid.

Take homes for an example: real estate taxes are currently levied mostly on the improvements and only in small part on the land. This tax structure is the key to subtle land monopolization. At 7 percent interest, the previously described $20,000 lot, if sold, would return $1,400 per year. Typically, the taxes on this typical home would also be $1,400. Removing all taxes on the house and placing them on the land (a combined total of $2,800), and collecting the same tax ($1,400) on all equally valued unused lots, would convert the current taxes to landrent taxes. This would reduce the land price to zero and eliminate the $1,400 interest (landrent) to the absentee landowner.

There would be no increase in costs for homeowners. The amount once paid annually in interest would now be paid annually in a landrent tax. Even though the monetized value of the land disappears, its use value actually increases. As land speculation would be eliminated, the purchase price would be only the value of labor and material that built the house. The initial capital required to purchase a home would drop to the cost of building the house or the depreciated value of an older home but the annual cost of owning that home would be only moderately less than under current rules. The former interest costs of a fully mortgaged home would be converted to landrent taxes to pay for essential social services.

With essential social services paid from a landrent tax, all other taxes and the accounting and collection costs incurred can be eliminated, providing great savings to most individuals and society. Occasionally city council persons will become aware of the social efficiency of taxing unused land within their jurisdiction (if idle land is properly taxed it will quickly be put to use). But these alert local officials quickly find that the power brokers, frightened by Henry George's exposure of their centuries-old land monopolization scheme, have inserted restrictions on local communities' ability to tax land into state constitutions and laws.

Interest on Mortgages Represents Landrent and Defines the Owners of Land

Mortgages define the primary owner of specific properties; the mortgage interest represents the rent. If that *rent* is not paid, the land will be repossessed. Whether renting or making house payments, people are paying both landrent and house rent. Interest currently paid on money borrowed to buy building lots or farms is privately collected landrent. Landrent is interest on the unearned monetary value of land. Savings on living costs from the homesite share of a paid-for home are landrent paid to oneself.

Society collecting the landrent eliminates monopolization. Owning land then requires only the investment capital to purchase or build the buildings upon it. Though capitalized value disappears, land's use value is the same or higher. Paying landrent encourages landowners to put idle land to productive use and restricts ownership to efficient producers. The immediate shifting of finance capital, once invested in land, to other investments that are both personally and socially profitable will create a burst in personal and social production.

Land held in unrestricted private ownership creates high capitalized land values. True free enterprise requires breaking that monopoly

through restricted ownership; society should collect the rent. Distribution of land by capitalized value (price) would then be replaced by distribution of land by rental value paid to society. The net cost to the homeowner would be slightly lower (much lower if Mason Gaffney and Fred Harrison's estimation of 35 percent of national income being landrent is correct[37]) but there would be no subtle monopoly intercepting others' labor through private collection of rent on what nature provided.

Whoever is the better producer and is willing to work the land can easily outbid the incompetent, lazy, or absentee landowners and, with tax advantages eliminated, can also outbid corporate agriculture. Thus those who use land for production or distribution will, almost universally, have secure ownership of their land. The landrent would go to society to replace all other taxes and cover the costs of public services, the interest to the owners of capital (improvements, machinery, livestock, or inventory), and wages to the farmer, business owner, or entrepreneur.

Oil, copper, iron ore, and the like, while still in the ground, are land and can very properly be privately owned so long as society is paid the landrent. The world has adequate reserves of most of these minerals. It is only richer deposits and cheaper labor in developing world countries that make their minerals more available. Under Adam Smith unequal free market philosophy, *the developed world's more expensive deposits are not mined until the undeveloped world's cheap deposits are exhausted.* Ecological taxes or surcharges on rich mineral deposits to equalize production costs between developed regions with their expensive mineral deposits and the developing world and their cheap minerals, as suggested in the previous two chapters, is really landrent.

Developing land—clearing, drainage projects, shaping the land, irrigation dams, canals, and so forth—involves capital expenditures requiring special consideration. As development is one of the most productive uses of land and labor, anyone who invests in such improvements should be well paid. However, unconditional title to land development is unconditional title to the land. Once the investor is well reimbursed, the value of land improvements (not buildings) should be incorporated into the landrent.

The market has measured the rent value of that land. The landrent collected by society should equal that which is now collected both publicly (taxes) and privately (interest). The price spread between the choice sites and lower-valued sites should still be maintained through the landrent tax imposed. To accomplish this, the current private land tax (interest) would be converted to a landrent tax that would be slightly lower than the former combination of taxes and land payments. With social costs covered by society collecting the landrent and with the former land monopolists now working productively for their living, all other taxes could be eliminated and the required working hours for all will be substantially reduced.

If Society Collected the Landrent, All Other Taxes Could Be Eliminated

Countries today are far different from when early philosophers concluded that society collecting landrent was the most efficient method of financing society. Roads, airports, and harbors are all added expenses. These, however, are directly provided services and their costs should be paid for through a user fee (tax) on gas, airplane tickets, harbor fees, and so on.

Except for schools and governing bodies, most public services authorized by law should not be supported by taxes. To cover those costs, a charge should be paid by those who use them, thus ensuring that equal labor is exchanged for providing those services. In this sense, a gas tax to cover highway costs is really a user's fee for the labor required to build and maintain roads. This principal is recognized and accepted in gas taxes and in water, electricity, natural gas, garbage, airport, and postal charges.

Social Security, Railroad Retirement, Federal Employees Retirement, unemployment insurance, Medicare, Medicaid, and other such programs, are—at this time—all improperly labeled as government expenses; they are actually insurance funds separate from expenses of running governments.[38] This is an accounting trick; President Lyndon Johnson added the retirement trust funds to the general budget to make the cost of the Vietnam War look smaller. According to Gore Vidal:

> In 1986 the gross revenue of the government was $794 billion. Of that amount, $294 billion was Social Security contributions, which should be subtracted from the National Security State. This leaves $500 billion. Of the $500 billion $286 billion went to defense; $12 billion to foreign arms to our client states; $8 billion to $9 billion to energy, which means, largely, nuclear weapons; $27 billion to veterans' benefits, the sad and constant reminder of the ongoing empire's recklessness; and finally, $142 billion to loans that were spent, over the past forty years, to keep the National Security State at war, hot or cold. So, of 1986's $500 billion in revenue, $475 billion was spent on National Security business. . . . Other Federal spending, incidentally, came to $177 billion . . . which is about the size of the deficit, since only $358 billion was collected in taxes.[39]

Landrent will not sustain government waste and corporations feeding at the federal trough but will easily finance proper government services.

In 1929, federal government expenditures were 1 percent of GNP—at the peak of the Cold War, they were approximately 24 percent.[40] David Stockman, a member of President Reagan's cabinet, calculated that after deducting bureaucratic waste and payments to

> law firms and lobbyists and trade associations in rows of shining office buildings along K Street in Washington; the consulting firms and contractors; the constituencies of special interests, from schoolteachers to construction workers, to failing businesses and multinational giants, all of whom came to Washington for money and legal protection against the perils of free competition, . . . that leaves seventeen cents for everything else that Washington does. The FBI and national parks, the county agents and the Foreign Service and the Weather Bureau—all the traditional operations of government—consumed only nine cents of each dollar. The remaining eight cents provided all the grants to state and local governments, for aiding handicapped children or building highways.[41]

The value of all land in the United States in 1990 was $3.7 trillion.[42] The current private tax (interest) at 6 percent converted to a landrent tax would bring in $222 billion. (Again, the cost would be well below that 6 percent if Gaffney and Harrison's estimation of 35 percent of national income being landrent is correct.) Former Budget Director David Stockman's calculation of only 9 percent of federal expenditure being for legitimate government business, applied to Gore Vidal's $500 billion in 1986 quoted above, leaves a proper cost of $45 billion to have run the federal government that year. Allowing $50 billion for a rational defense budget, as outlined in Chapter Twenty-Seven, and pointing all those feeding at the government trough back towards the free market that they

claim is their ideal, leaves $127 billion to return to state governments. Local governments already collect most of their expenses from property taxes. Removing all taxes from buildings and inventory and placing them upon the land would provide operating funds for local, state, and federal governments.

Serious Georgist scholars have calculated that in both the United States and Britain "the share of rent in the modern society, if the current system of taxation were abolished, would be [22 to 25 percent] of national income."[43] The waste of neomercantilist trade hiding under the banner of free trade (the primary thesis of this book) demonstrates that the cost of government in a true free enterprise, free market economy will be far below their estimate.

A Landrent Tax Is the Cheapest and Most Efficient Tax and It Cannot Be Evaded

A landrent tax is cash flow money. As all production and distribution requires land, socially collected landrent becomes part of the price structure. Through their purchases, and relative to the benefits they receive, all citizens would be paying these costs equally. Any proper expense not included in the above math can be calculated and included in the landrent tax.

Whether the final calculation exceeds current interest and tax charges against the land is immaterial. Those who own and till the land will simply be collecting this money, the same as today's sales taxes (or for that matter any tax), and delivering it to the government. This is the same service they previously provided to the land monopolist through the paying of rent or interest.

The accounting and collection costs of a

landrent tax would be but a tiny percentage of the cost of collecting sales taxes and, as all are paying landrent through the price of products, it will fall on each equally according to individual standard of living.

When necessary to regulate commerce, other taxes are proper but those funds should be returned to society through social services. For example, ecological taxes can support pollution-free energy development and resource conservation. The proper level of sin taxes (alcohol, tobacco, etc.) will lower disease through lowering consumption and the funds collected would offset health care costs incurred from such habits.

Because the purchase price of land is zero when society collects the landrent, accepting the job of the nation's tax collector would be a bargain to landowners. All farmers and business people know that machinery and inventory are relatively easy to obtain; it is the price of land that restricts ownership of farms and businesses. While land prices would drop to zero, use values would remain the same. Commerce would flourish as businesspeople, farmers, and other entrepreneurs—all true producers—would be able to start business with only the capital necessary to buy buildings, machinery, and inventory.

Landrent being paid to society out of cash flow means only hardworking and talented people would own farms and businesses. The mechanism whereby excessive rights of absentee or incompetent landowners intercept the labor of others through unrestricted ownership of land would be replaced by society receiving the earnings from that social wealth.

Where landrent taxes would be lower than current private taxes (land payments and interest are private taxes) and property taxes, labor costs would be reduced by whatever taxes labor previously paid. The elimination of sales taxes, income taxes, and a large share of accounting costs would make replacing all taxes with landrent taxes a bargain for any business.

Although society would be enormously richer, the land would not have monetized (capitalized) value. Through the community support structure of society collecting the landrent, the wealth it produced would be distributed relatively equally while retaining the efficiencies of private ownership. Society, not the landowners, put that value there by increased population, roads, water, electricity, and sewers. The wealth collected through landrent should then be returned to the people through social services—schools, parks, other public facilities, and government. It must be emphasized that the landowner would retain all rights to his or her land except the right to retain unearned landrent.

Land ownership has not changed much in the last 200 years. It has been estimated that over 85 percent of U.S. citizens are paying rent to fewer than 15 percent who really own the land (mortgage holders as well as title holders). The payment of interest in the form of rent to whoever bought that house (capital) is proper. The same is true of commercial rent. Interest should be paid to whoever produced, and thus owns, the machinery, buildings, improved livestock, fences, and so forth; the landrent properly belongs to society. Farmers and businesspeople in normal times (high land values occur in abnormal times) are not primarily collectors of rent. They are true producers.

An Opportunity to Restructure with Society Collecting the Landrent

Within the bounds of the American Constitution, and we would hope most others, it is possible to convert land taxes to a landrent tax by gradually increasing land taxes while simultaneously eliminating other taxes, including those on buildings.[44] China uses these tax principles extensively and continually updated literature from the Schalkenbach Foundation lists regions around the world where this tax reform has been substantially or partially instituted.[45] In 1995, the Henry George Foundation listed sixteen American cities partially restructuring to a landrent tax.[46] In western Pennsylvania, New Zealand, and Australia, taxes on land have been raised and those on buildings lowered, changing the customary one-to-one ratio of taxes on land to taxes on buildings to as high as five-to-one. Initial reactions were dramatic. McKeesport, Pennsylvania (population 31,000), which was on the verge of bankruptcy,

> raised taxes on land from 2.45 percent to 9 percent of assessed value, but cut taxes on existing buildings from 2.45 percent to 2 percent and granted a three-year tax exemption to all new construction. Neighboring Clairton (pop. 12,200) and Duquesne (pop. 10,100) where steel is also the main industry, left their 1-to-1 real estate tax alone. . . . The dollar value of construction in McKeesport rose by 38 percent in 1980–82, Clairton suffered a 28 percent decline, Duquesne a 22 percent decline.[47]

The social efficiency demonstrated by the lowering of other taxes while increasing that on land lends credence to the physiocrats' belief that society collecting the landrent would increase social efficiency equal to the invention of money or printing.

However, in spite of these highly successful experiments, the political barriers to this approach are normally unassailable—landowners have too much power in legislatures. But, just as Social Security, unemployment insurance,

Railroad Retirement, and banking reforms were all enacted into law under crisis, there will be an opportunity to restructure if the world economy should again collapse. Land values would return to zero, and the search for answers would be paramount.

The consumer price index rose a steady 1 or 2 percent annually from 1945 to 1966. True to Henry George's description of how land values rise to claim values from the increased efficiencies of capital and labor, land price increases compounded around 6 percent per year. After thirty years of a land boom, which created high land prices and their inevitable claim against labor, land prices have been collapsing. This caused farmland and some development land to lose value.

In a depression, characterized by inadequate income and collapsing values, ownership of bankrupt farms, homes, and businesses is normally relinquished to the counties in lieu of taxes. Almost all deposits and many loans are guaranteed by the U.S. government—meaning, while profits are privatized, risks are socialized. In a collapse, the public will own the loan institutions and through them much of the land and capital. Even now, taxes diverted to support unnecessary agricultural production are all that keep the value of most farmland above zero, to say nothing of the public funds spread all over the world to prevent the financial meltdown on the periphery of empire from imploding upon the center.

With such a collapse, and under Chapter Twelve of America's 1986 bankruptcy law, a farmer may erase all commercial debt above the value of his or her property.[48] In short, he or she may retain ownership and start over. This right, already in law for American farmers, should be extended to commercial property and homeowners. After all, the old values would no longer be there and all that can be reclaimed by the lender is current values. In fact, foreclosure, maintenance, and selling costs would cause lenders greater losses than accepting this new *real value*.

If ownership is relinquished to society in lieu of taxes or loan guarantees, whoever wishes to use that land could, just as now, purchase it by bid. The market value of the property would only be the value of the improvements. The land value would be zero but its use value would increase. Former owners would have the right to meet the high bid. The sale should be made with the understanding that the use rights to the land and the improvements were the owner's but all landrent (not rent on improvements) would be remitted to society in the form of a landrent tax. Both land and improvements could be bought and sold but only the improvements would have value. They are the only part of the farm that required compensated labor, so only they can be justly owned unconditionally.

Thus, even as society's rights are reclaimed, owners of mortgaged land have a better chance to attain and retain ownership of their land. The current land taxes, taxes on buildings and improvements, and interest payments (which are simply a private tax) on privately owned land would be converted to a landrent tax. With the elimination of waste, as outlined in this author's previous work,[49] the lowering of labor costs through the elimination of worker's income tax, business income taxes, sales taxes, and other regressive taxes, there will be a reduction in costs for all businesses.

Ten to 20 percent of all income illegally evades taxation; even more escapes taxation legally. With society collecting all taxes through landrent there would be no evasion of taxes. If landrent taxes were a part of the cost of every social transaction, those taxes would, on final analysis, be paid by all citizens and the costs of government would, through landrent taxes, be included in the cost of every product and service. This would be true equality in taxation— each person would be paying relative to the benefits received.

As values rise during a cyclical recovery or through an increase in population, the landrent tax should rise to absorb the increase in values. This would eliminate claiming others' labor through future increases in the value of land. The "divine right" of private ownership of social wealth will then have been converted to "conditional rights" that protect all society. Our calculation that the current level of formal land taxes and private land taxes (landrent or interest on land debt) is likely greater than the cost of proper social services indicates some value will remain in land. However, elimination of all monopolization would increase competition and there would be no monopoly profits. That can only mean lower prices. Society will be well paid for converting to Henry George's philosophy of society collecting the landrent.

There are many poor producers in farming and business who are there only through inheritances, economic windfalls, or through having bought land at depressed prices and having its value increase as society (not those landowners) increases in efficiency. With society collecting the landrent, those who produce from the land (be it farm, home, industry, or business) would be the owners. Interest income would go to capital (the owners of the buildings, machinery, livestock, or inventory), wages would go to those who worked (the farmer, industrialist, or businessperson), and landrent would go to society. Absentee ownership of land (but not capital) would disappear. Production is the basis of all wealth so there would be only productive, well-paid people producing on that land. This is the efficiency gain equaling the invention of money or writing that the French physiocrats recognized was possible if society collected the landrent.

A slow restructuring of tax policy to a land-rent tax, or a rapid restructuring during a severe economic crisis, would mean everybody's right to nature's bounty would be reclaimed without confiscating anyone's equity. Every tax restructuring that favors one group takes some wealth from another. Those carried out in the 1980s and 1990s in America and parts of Europe were of greater magnitude than these suggestions and drastically favored owners of wealth over the less fortunate. The elimination of subtle monop-olization of land would reclaim labor's rights and ensure all its proper share of society's bounty. Virtually every citizen would own, and be receiving, a share of the use value of the nation's land, although that land would now have no monetary value.

Notes

1. "Workers' State," *The Nation,* September 19, 1988, p. 187–88; Dean Baker, "Job Drain," *The Nation,* July 12, 1993, p. 68; Lester Thurow, *Head to Head: The Coming Economic Battle Among Japan, Europe, and America* (New York: William Morrow, 1992), p. 53; Robert S. McIntyre, "The Populist Tax Act of 1989," *The Nation,* April 2, 1988, pp. 445, 462; Kevin Phillips, *The Politics of Rich and Poor* (New York: Random House, 1990), pp. 12, 14, 79, 164, 205. Phillips puts the gain of the top 1 percent from $174,498 in 1977 to $303,900 in 1988; Kevin Phillips, *Boiling Point: Democrats, Republicans, and the Decline of Middle Class Prosperity* (New York: Random House, 1993), especially pp. 7, 24–25, 104, 108–109, 112; Gerald Epstein, "Mortgaging America," *World Policy Journal* (Winter 1990–91), pp. 31–32; Matthew Cooper and Dorian Freedman, "The Rich in America," *U.S. News & World Report,* November 18, 1991, p. 35; "Top 1% Own More Than Bottom 90%," *The Des Moines Register,* April 21, 1992, p. 4A; Hardy Green,

"Income Erosion: Economic Landslides," *In These Times,* November 14–20, 1990, p. 18; Lester C. Thurow, *Generating Inequality* (New York: Basic Books, 1975), p. 14. The hourly earning power of individual nonsupervisory labor has lowered over 22 percent from the 1973 level. With the 15 percent increase in hours worked, the average paycheck dropped 11 percent and, with an increase of 15 million in the labor force, average family income may have remained roughly the same (Barry Bluestone and Irving Bluestone, *Negotiating the Future* [New York: Basic Books, 1992], p. 5). To prevent the impoverishment of families to levels that could not be papered over, the earnings of labor have been quietly redistributed by employing more family members at lower wages.

2. "States' Right: Hawaii's Land Reform Upheld," *Time,* June 11, 1984, p. 27; "High Court: This Property Is Condemned," *Newsweek,* June 11, 1984, p. 69.

3. All works of Henry George and many authors writing on him are available from the Robert Schalkenbach Foundation, 41 East 72nd Street, New York, NY 10021 (212–988–1680), established for the purpose of keeping Henry George's philosophy alive.

4. Mason Gaffney and Fred Harrison, *The Corruption of Economics* (London: Shepheard-Walwyn, 1994), pp. 13, 193.

5. Gaffney and Harrison, *Corruption of Economics,* p. 48.

6. Michael Parenti, *Power and the Powerless* (New York: St. Martin's Press 1978), pp. 184–85, quoting Jean Jacques Rousseau, "A Discourse on the Origins of Inequality," in *The Social Contract and Discourses* (New York: Dutton, 1950), pp. 234–85.

7. Henry George School (New York) website: gopher://echonyc.com:70/11s/Cul/HGS.

8. Henry George, *Progress and Poverty* (New York: Robert Schalkenbach Foundation, 1981), p. 342.

9. Petr Kropotkin, *Mutual Aid* (Boston: Porter Sargent, 1914), p. 225.

10. Ibid.

11. Ibid., p. 226.

12. Ibid., pp. 234–35.

13. Ibid., p. 226. Read also George Renard's *Guilds in the Middle Ages* (New York: Augustus M. Kelley, 1968), Chapters 7, 8.

14. Lewis Mumford, *The City in History* (New York: Harcourt Brace Jovanovich, 1961), p. 264; An-

gela Lambert, *Unquiet Souls* (New York: Harper and Row, 1984), p. 6.

15. Charles A. Beard, *Economic Interpretation of the Constitution* (New York: Macmillan, 1941), p. 28; Howard Zinn, *A People's History of the United States* (New York: Harper Colophon Books, 1980), p. 48.

16. Zinn, *People's History,* p. 48. See also Howard Zinn, *The Politics of History* (Chicago: University of Chicago Press, 1990), pp. 61–68.

17. Herbert Aptheker, *The Colonial Era* (New York: International, 1966), pp. 37–38.

18. Zinn, *People's History,* p. 83; Herbert Aptheker, *The American Revolution* (New York: International, 1985), p. 264, quoted in Beard, *Economic Interpretation,* p. 23; Petr Kropotkin, *The Great French Revolution* (New York: Black Rose Books, 1989), p. 143.

19. Beard, *Economic Interpretation,* pp. 23, 27–28, quoting C. H. Ambler.

20. Olwen Hufton, *Europe: Privilege and Protest* (Ithaca, NY: Cornell University Press, 1980), p. 113.

21. Herbert Aptheker, *Early Years of the Republic* (New York: International, 1976), p. 125; Abraham Bishop, *Georgia Speculation Unveiled,* New Canaan, CT: Readex Microprint Corporation, 1966), in foreword.

22. James Wessel and Mort Hartman, *Trading the Future* (San Francisco: Institute for Food and Development Policy, 1983), p. 14.

23. Quoted by Peter Lyon, *To Hell in a Day Coach* (New York: J. B. Lippincott, 1968), p. 6. See also Edward Winslow Martin, *History of the Grange Movement* (New York: Burt Franklin, 1967); Joe E. Feagin, *The Urban Real-Estate Game* (Engelwood Cliffs, NJ: Prentice-Hall, 1983), pp. 57–58; speech by U.S. Representative Byron Dorgan, North Dakota, the statistics researched by his staff and quoted in *The North Dakota REC* (May 1984).

24. Lyon, *To Hell in a Day Coach,* p. 6.

25. "Mark Twain on Henry George," gopher:// echonyc.com:70/00/Cul/HGS/archimed; Bruno Heilig, "Why the German Republic Fell," gopher:// echonyc.com:70/00/Cul/HGS/germecon.

26. Adam Smith, *The Wealth of Nations* (New York: Random House, 1965), pp. 247, 647, 773–98.

27. *101 Famous Thinkers on Owning Earth* (New York: Robert Schalkenback Foundation); Durand Echeverria, *The Maupeou Revolution* (Baton Rouge: Louisiana University Press, 1985), p. 182; Guy Routh,

The Origin of Economic Ideas (Dobbs Ferry, NY: Sheridan House, 1989), p. 62; John Kenneth Galbraith, *Economics in Perspective* (New York: Houghton Mifflin, 1987), chapter 5, especially pp. 55, 168; Mark Blaug, *Great American Economists Before Keynes* (Atlantic Highlands, NJ: Humanities Press International, 1986), p. 86.

28. Herbert Spencer, *Social Statics* (New York: Robert Schalkenback Foundation, 1995); Dan Nadudere, *The Political Economy of Imperialism* (London: Zed Books, 1977), p. 186; Phil Grant, *The Wonderful Wealth Machine* (New York: Devon-Adair, 1953), pp. 416, 434–38; Hufton, *Privilege and Protest,* p. 113.

29. *101 Famous Thinkers.*

30. Eugene M. Tobin, *Organize or Perish* (New York: Greenwood Press, 1986), pp. 14, 21, 56.

31. Gaffney and Harrison, *Corruption of Economics.*

32. Ibid.

33. Kropotkin, *Mutual Aid,* p. 226; Renard's *Guilds in the Middle Ages,* chapters 7, 8.

34. Grant, *Wonderful Wealth Machine,* pp. 389–95.

35. Paul Zane Pilzer, *Unlimited Wealth* (New York: Crown, 1990), p. 169; *60 Minutes,* CBS, October 25, 1987; *World Monitor,* July 17, 1990; Jim Impoco, Jack Egan, and Douglas Pasternak, "The Tokyo Tidal Wave," *U.S. News and World Report,* September 17, 1990, p. 43; R. Taggart Murphy, *Weight of the Yen* (New York: W.W Norton, 1996), pp. 195–200, 206, 212, 214, 218–19, 231, 244, 259; Edward W. Desmond, "Japan's Trillion-Dollar Hole," *Time,* April 8, 1996, p. 46; Edward W. Desmond, "The Failed Miracle," *Time,* April 22, 1996, pp. 60–64. For a look at how these inflated land and stock prices intercept a nation's wealth, read Kevin Phillips, *Politics of Rich and Poor,* pp. xii, 118, 122, 144, 150, 118. There are other estimates of total values in the United States; *The Statistical Abstract of the U.S., 1990,* pp. 463, 734 (charts 752, 1295) claims $21 trillion in reproducible value. To that would have to be added capitalized values and land values. Including land, economist Robert Samuelson claims just under $29 trillion (Robert Samuelson, "The Great Global Debtor," *Newsweek,* July 22, 1991, p. 40).

36. Government Accounting Office, Letter Report, GAO/NSIAD–97–260, October 30, 1997.

37. Gaffney and Harrison, *Corruption of Economics,* p. 183.

38. Edward Boorstein, *What's Ahead? . . . The U.S. Economy* (New York: International, 1984), pp. 33–34.

39. Gore Vidal, "The National Security State: How to Take Back Our Country," *The Nation,* June 4, 1988, p. 782.

40. E.K. Hunt and Howard J. Sherman, *Economics* (New York: Harper and Row, 1990), p. 511.

41. William Greider, *The Education of David Stockman and Other Americans* (New York: New American Library, 1986), pp. 6, 17.

42. Samuelson, "Great Global Debtor," p. 40.

43. Gaffney and Harrison, *Corruption of Economics,* p. 183.

44. George, *Progress and Poverty,* Book VIII, chapter 2, also p. 437.

45. Geonomy Society, 30401 Navarro Ridge Road, Albion, CA 95410. See also the Henry George Foundation of America, 2000 Century Plaza, #238, Columbia, MD 21004; and the Robert Schalkenback Foundation, 41 E. 72nd Street, New York, NY 10021.

46. Henry George Foundation of America and the Robert Schalkenbach Foundation.

47. Gurney Breckenfield, "Higher Taxes That Promote Development," *Fortune,* August 8, 1983, p. 71.

48. Bert Caldwell, "Help for Farmers, Hurt for Lenders?", *The Spokesman-Review*, December 31, 1986, p. A12; Judy Tynan, "Farm Credit System's Transfers Face Trial," *The Spokesman-Review,* December 31, 1986, p. A9.

49. J.W. Smith, *The World's Wasted Wealth 2* (San Luis Obispo, CA: Institute for Economic Democracy, 1994).

25

Subtly Monopolizing Society's Tools (Technology) Through Stock Markets and Patents

For centuries, as modern economies developed, the hidden hands of the alert and powerful were busy structuring laws and property rights to gain, or retain, title to wealth-producing sectors of the economy. Stock markets, as well as patent laws, were being subtly structured to monopolize technology.

That stock markets are crucial to raising investment capital in a modern economy is a myth. Most stock traders have no contact with new issues of stock and those who do are primarily taking an already established private company public. Most corporate investment needs are financed from profits, liberal depreciation schedules, and borrowing. As currently structured, investing in stock markets is primarily a bet on which corporation will most successfully expand its share of national and world markets. These are not investments in production.

Expanding markets means increased profits capitalized into the value of a company's stock and those capitalized values are usually claimed before those profits are banked. "Behind the abstraction known as 'the markets' lurks a set of institutions designed to maximize the wealth and power of the most privileged group of people in the world, the creditor-rentier class of the first world and their junior partners in the third."[1]

Despite the centuries of carefully crafted laws to monopolize technology through the stock markets, a simple transfer tax (a Tobin Tax), at the proper level, on transfer of all financial instruments would quickly convert nonproducing speculators into productive savers and investors. Simultaneously restructuring patent laws so that any person may use a patent by simply paying a royalty will erase those centuries of carefully crafted monopoly laws.

Under those two simple legal changes, the inventors would be well paid for their inventions and the price of consumer products would drop precipitously. Combining those social savings with free trade between equally developed regions and with managed trade between unequally developed regions, and dropping those protections in step with increased technological development, would protect both labor and capital. The masochistic destruction of jobs and capital under the current economic structure would be eliminated.

Labor Should Employ Capital

That capital is properly owned and employed by labor is recognized by no less an authority than Adam Smith. We again repeat the quote from his bible of capitalism, *The Wealth of Nations*: "Produce is the natural wages of labor.

Originally the whole belonged to the labourer. If this had continued all things would have become cheaper, though in appearance many things might have become dearer.''[2] The ''appearance of becoming dearer'' is because each worker would have been fully paid. Things would have been cheaper because purchasing power would have been advancing in step with productive capacity and those who once made their living through claiming a share of others' labor would have to turn to productive labor. Those well-paid workers would have purchased more from other fully paid workers and with that increased buying power others would produce more to take advantage of that market.

In short, purchasing power—which is so hard to generate under current monopoly rules—would have developed in step with the producing power of industrial technology, which can be built quickly. If monopolization could have been avoided, labor would have been fully paid and the world could have developed far more rapidly and without destructive wars. To make the contradiction clear, let's assume that all industry suddenly increased 50 percent in efficiency. Half of the workforce would be unemployed and the owners of this new technology would rapidly claim all the production that was previously consumed or saved by those who were once employed. The wealth of the owners of technology—both actually and as a percentage of the nation's wealth—would increase dramatically, that of those still employed would remain the same, and those newly unemployed would be on welfare. It is only through steady expansion of distribution by unnecessary labor pulling a share of that siphoned wealth back as people search for a way to survive that society has avoided facing this reality.[3] An economy with 5 percent owners, 45 percent workers, and 50 percent welfare recipients is unthinkable in a country that claims equal rights for everybody.

If labor owned the capital it produced, then labor would employ—rather than be employed by—capital. Once monopolized by exclusive title, capital's use *can be denied* to labor at any time, and it *will be denied* if no profit is made. The natural order of labor employing tools (capital) is reversed. If land and capital were not subtly monopolized, land, labor, and capital could freely combine to produce social wealth, workers would receive their full wages from what they produced, and the owners of industry would receive full value for use of their capital. Thus, elimination of the monopolization of technology under current stock market and patent structures would also increase social efficiency equal to the invention of money or writing, as the French physiocrats recognized was possible by elimination of land monopolization.

Just as with land, we are accustomed to wealthy people claiming ownership of the nation's capital. We are taught that this is the proper and most efficient social arrangement. Therefore we do not recognize the obvious: capital is social wealth. It is composed of all tools of production, and all should be entitled to the opportunity of employing it, or being employed by it, and receiving a fair share of what is produced.

Capital, however, is often more productive under private ownership and, when this is so, private ownership is justified. In such cases, this capital could be properly bought from those who produced it by entrepreneurs whose special talents lead to increased production. These talents are productive labor, and a substantial share of society's capital has been thus justly claimed. Any ownership of capital that is obtained by means other than trading useful labor (physical, innovative, or special talent) is an unjust interception of the production of others.

That which is more efficient under social ownership belongs to all society, with all citizens receiving the profits. These profits are distributed silently. For example, no profits are directly distributed from the increased wealth produced by highways, airports, harbors, or post offices. But the wealth that society is able to produce and distribute due to these natural monopolies is many times more than a normal interest charge on their construction cost.

Social capital,* "real" private capital, and "fictitious" capital are all currently lumped together and collectively treated as private capital. Ownership of capital is considered proof that it was justly earned, and that the owner deserves compensation for its use. Below we are distinguishing between social, private, and fictitious capital. Once identified, the proper owners can claim their capital and the profits it produces. Fictitious capital can be eliminated altogether.

Efficient Socially Owned Capital

The basic difference between what is properly social capital and private capital is that social capital is used by everybody. It forms a natural monopoly, while proper private capital is used only to produce products or services for specific needs. Capital that is required for society's basic infrastructure (which is by its nature a monopoly and used by all citizens) cannot justly be bought and sold as private property. This includes not only highways, airports, harbors, and post offices, but also railroads, electric power

systems, community water systems, and banking and communications infrastructure. Most will recognize that these economic elements of infrastructure should belong to all society.

Although such facilities and services are publicly held in most Western nations, U.S. citizens are unaccustomed to railroads, electric power systems, banking, and communications being socially owned. These are nothing less than natural monopolies, and all claims of efficiency under private ownership are a rhetorical cover (a Social Control paradigm) to hide the siphoning of the fruits of others' labor to those who hold title to those economic crossroads.[4]

This siphoning of wealth is shown in the privately owned electric power monopolies. Almost 24 percent of the population is served by consumer-owned electric utilities (13.4 percent are publicly owned, 10.2 percent are rural cooperatives). Privately owned companies charge 42.5 percent more for electricity than those that are publicly owned. Yet, since they serve population centers with the highest density of customers per mile, their costs should be lower. The difference in electricity costs between privately owned and publicly owned electric companies is even greater than these statistics show. The publicly owned utilities provide enough profits for some of those communities to build swimming pools, stadiums, and parks.[5]

Matthew Josephson's classic *Robber Barons,* Peter Lyon's even more profound *To Hell in a Day Coach,* and Edward Winslow Martin's *History of the Grange Movement* cover how the American railroads were built at public expense. As much as half the funds collected for building them were pocketed and over 9 percent of the land in the United States was deeded to these railroads. The pocketing of those funds, claiming title to these natural monopolies, and being deeded that land were little more than thefts of

* "Social capital," as used here, refers to physical products of labor that benefit all, such as roads. The term is also used by some scholars to refer to the unquantified, but real, value of social interconnections that aid the functioning of society.

public wealth. Martin describes the building of the Union Pacific Railroad—perhaps the most flagrant example—but the pattern was typical:

> Who then was Crédit Mobilier? It was but another name for the Pacific Railroad ring. The members were in Congress; they were trustees for the bondholders; they were directors, they were stockholders, they were contractors; in Washington they voted subsidies, in New York they received them, upon the plains they expended them, and in the Crédit Mobilier they divided them. Ever-shifting characters, they were ubiquitous—now engineering a bill, and now a bridge—they received money into one hand as a corporation, and paid into the other as a contractor. As stockholders they owned the road, as mortgagees they had a lien upon it, as directors they contracted for its construction, and as members of Crédit Mobilier they built it. . . . reduced to plain English, the story of the Crédit Mobilier is simply this: The men entrusted with the management of the Pacific road made a bargain with themselves to build the road for a sum equal to about twice its actual cost, and pocketed the profits, which have been estimated at about thirty millions of dollars—this immense sum coming out of the taxpayers of the United States.[6]

"By 1870 the states alone had given $228,500,000 in cash, while another $300,000,000 had been paid over by counties and municipalities." Of course those millions of nineteenth-century dollars would be hundreds of billions in inflated twenty-first-century dollars. In the process of building those railroads, promoters skimmed off possibly one-half of this public investment and stockholders' capital, while simultaneously claiming 9.3 percent of the nation's land through land grants.[7] Josephson's description of them as robber barons is quite accurate.

With enforced privatizations through imposition of Reaganism/Thatcherism on the developing world and the collapsed former Soviet Union, social wealth was being placed under private title in the 1990s at a rate that makes America's robber barons of the late nineteenth and early twentieth century look like country bumpkins. Those defeated nations are being paid pennies on the dollar to give up title to their natural wealth, their banks, and their limited industrial capital. The masses, of course, have little to say. In many cases, if not most, one member of these less than honest groups (to put it mildly) was signing as government agent and another was the buyer.

Obviously there was, and is, no savings to society from the private ownership of a natural monopoly such as railroads. And, as shown in the following chapters, the true cost of banking and communications, when properly structured under a public authority, would be only pennies per dollar currently being charged.

Basic infrastructure (roads, water, electricity, etc.) is integral to a nation. *Society is a machine;* even though these basic facilities do not directly produce anything, an industrial society cannot function without them. They are an integral part of production and are just as important to social efficiency as modern factories.

To demonstrate this, compare the labor costs of a society with an undeveloped infrastructure to those of a society with a developed infrastructure. Vacation to any wilderness park, hike for a day, and calculate how efficient virtually any economic activity, such as sending and receiving mail, would be from that spot. In the eighteenth century, a letter traveling by U.S. mail from New York to Virginia (400 miles) took four to eight weeks and cost sixty cents a page.[8] Today it costs thirty-three cents (possibly equal to less then a penny 200 years ago) for several pages anywhere in the nation and that letter normally arrives in one to three days.

One can compare a society with a modern highway and railroad system with one that has dirt and gravel roads—the United States against the former Soviet Union, for example. The cost of transportation, and thus the cost of products transported, were far higher in the relatively undeveloped Soviet Union. When China built a road into once almost inaccessible Tibet, the price of a box of matches dropped from one sheep to two pounds of wool.[9]

Efficient Privately Owned Capital

Commercial activities other than building and operating basic infrastructure produce for variable individual needs rather than everybody's needs and are properly privately owned. As has been demonstrated in the former Soviet Union, the thousands of personal preferences (homes, clothes, furniture, jewelry, hobbies, recreational activities, etc.) cannot be provided efficiently by a public authority. Such personal needs can only be assessed by perceptive and talented individuals close enough to recognize and fulfill those needs. The capital to provide such services is more productive under private ownership. Unlike claiming the production of labor through subtle monopolization of land, capital, and finance capital, this increased productivity produces the wealth with which entrepreneurs pay the producers of that capital.

Most of the construction and production for basic social infrastructure operated under public authority is quite properly provided by thousands of privately owned industries. This free-enterprise, privately owned capital can, under contract, accommodate the needs of public institutions while also making available diverse consumer products and services. We see this every day in contracts to build roads, haul mail, and so on.

Fictitious Capital

Few economists agree on exactly what constitutes capital. Most include all wealth that produces a profit (titles, stocks, bonds, etc.). But, although the wealth this paper represents has a firm claim on part of society's income, much of it does not productively employ labor. It is properly defined as *fictitious capital*. Bonds used to construct harbors, deepen riverbeds, and build railroads represent true capital. The problem arises when part of this money is not productively employed.

In the previous example of building the Union Pacific Railroad, half the money was used to build; the other half was pocketed. The share of those certificates that was not productively used, yet had a claim on social production, was fraudulent. This fictitious capital may represent wealth to the owner, but it is not wealth to society. It is a certificate of ownership for capital that was paid for by others, that siphons wealth produced by others to an owner who has produced nothing.

The economically powerful issue these symbols of capital (stocks and bonds), but instead of employing these funds solely to build real capital for the purchasers of those securities, they use some to build capital as stated and pocket the rest to build capital in their name. The total capital underlying a debt instrument must pay profits to security holders at face value of those securities even though only a part of it actually built that industry. The share of those debt instruments that did not produce productive capital, social or private, is fictitious capital.

There are three physical foundations to production—land, labor, and capital. Land commands rent, labor is paid wages, and honest interest can only be for the use of true capital. Patent monopolies capitalize stock values far above tangible values and those high values demand profits. It is through those excess profits that the production of others' labor is siphoned from those who produce to those who produced nothing. All capital that demands payment greater than the labor value of services provided society is properly labeled *"fictitious capital."*

Invention: A Social Process

> There is no isolated, self-sufficing individual. All production is, in fact, a production in and by the help of the community, and all wealth is such only in society. Within the human period of the race development, it is safe to say, no individual has fallen into industrial isolation, so as to produce any one useful article by his own independent effort alone. Even where there is no mechanical co-operation, men are always guided by the experience of others.
>
> —Thorstein Veblen

These words from one of America's eminent philosophers are well spoken. The long march of technology leading up to the present sophisticated level is based upon thousands of earlier discoveries—fire, smelting, the wheel, lathe, and screw—and untold millions of improvements on those basic innovations.[10] Many primitive, but revolutionary, technologies were discovered by Asian and Arab societies. Greek, Roman, and other cultures improved upon these methods, which were, in turn, used by later Western cultures. Invention is a social process built upon the insights of others. Stuart Chase's list of such contributions of five thousand years ago barely touches the subject:

> The generic Egyptian of 3,000 B.C., though unacquainted with iron, was an expert metallurgist in the less refractory metals. He could smelt them, draw them into wire, beat them into sheets, cast them into molds, emboss, chase, engrave, inlay, and enamel them. He had invented the lathe and the potter's wheel and could glaze and enamel earthenware. He was an expert woodworker, joiner and carver. He was an admirable sculptor, draftsman and painter. He was, and is, the world's mightiest architect in stone. He made sea-going ships. He had devised the loom, and knew how to weave cotton to such a fineness that we can only distinguish it from silk by the microscope. His language was rich, and he engrossed it in the handsomest system of written characters ever produced. He made excellent paper, and upon it beautiful literature was written. . . . He had invented most of the hand tools now in existence. . . . He had worked out the rudiments of astronomy and mathematics.[11]

There were also wedges, drills, wheels, pulleys, and gears—all were necessary before modern machines were possible. There had to be countless earlier inventions, back to the control of fire, before the Egyptians could have reached even that level of technology.

Not only does every modern invention rest on millions of insights going back to antiquity, its development requires thousands of people with special talents. For example, penicillin, which has benefited almost every person in modern civilization, was discovered accidentally by a British scientist. More people worked to develop and produce this antibiotic for the wounded in World War II than worked on the atomic bomb, and they were all funded with public money. Yet the drug was patented by an American who recognized that, if he could obtain a patent, he would have a monopoly with a capitalized value that would siphon vast wealth to himself even though he had neither created nor produced anything.[12]

Every innovation is a part of nature. Just like land, oil, coal, iron ore, or any of nature's wealth, if something is to be discovered it had to have been there all the time. As technology is a part of nature, its fruits should be shared by everybody. Inventions not only use the insights of millions of people throughout history and prehistory, they require the support and skills of millions of present workers as well. Stuart Chase estimated that at least 5,000 people were involved in contributing data to the writing of his book and these had millions of others to thank for their knowledge.

These people provided tools, materials, and services: pencils, paper, graphite, rubber, lead, typewriters, telephones, cars, electricity, typing, printing presses, book distribution, banking, and so forth. The people directly involved in Chase's education required educators, authors of textbooks, and their educators, ad infinitum. Every one of these consumer items required the labor and skills of thousands of people, some in distant parts of the world (such as producers of rubber or tin). Though the labor charge of some of these is infinitesimal, each is real and definite. Collectively they accumulate a substantial, though incalculable, value.[13]

While the contribution of any one person to the pool of social knowledge is truly small, the wealth diverted to those who own the patents to social knowledge can be substantial. It has been estimated that, if the developing world were capitalized to the level of the developed world, the royalty claims, though many would be uncollectable, would be $1 trillion a year. These royalties would normally be going to people who "own" these efficient technologies but neither invented anything nor labored productively for this income. They are commercial chokepoints and the subtle monopolization of these tools of production (technology) permits huge overcharges that siphon an excessive share of the world's wealth to those who hold the patents.

Inventors rarely receive much reward or even

credit for their discoveries and innovations. The few who do receive but a small share of the tribute charged by those who own this social wealth. That a small number of powerful people monopolize the inventions of others—and ever afterwards siphon to themselves the wealth produced by others—defies both decency and justice. This was well known to prominent inventors and industrialists such as Thomas A. Edison and Henry Ford. Both "agreed that all patent laws should be repealed since they benefit the manufacturer and not the inventor."[14]

We disagree with patent laws being repealed. They should be redesigned so any person can use that technology by simply paying a royalty.

The Process of Capitalizing Actual and Fictitious Values

Inventions are a "more or less costless store of knowledge [that] is captured by monopoly capital and protected in order to make it secret and a 'rare and scarce commodity,' for sale at monopoly price[s]. So far as inventions are concerned a price is put on them not *because* they are scarce but *in order* to make them scarce to those who want to use them."[15]

The patent structure capitalizes value far above tangible values and, through those excess profits and without expenditure of real labor, intercepts wealth produced by others. Where inventions once went unchanged for decades or even centuries, many, if not most, patents are now obsolete before their seventeen-year life expires. By the time a key patent has run out, newer patents are able to boost efficiency yet more. As many of the earlier technologies are still essential to production, the owners of the latest patents control both the latest technologies and the support technologies developed by society decades earlier. Honda's exclusive ownership of patents on the stratified charge engine, even though the basic principles for this crucial technology were invented eighty years ago, makes this all quite evident.

Corporations are in such a powerful bargaining position that only occasionally will a new invention pose a threat to them. As corporate control of other critical patents limits the inventor's options, these patents are bought for a fraction of their true value, or they are patented around and the inventor receives nothing. Controlling markets is integral to controlling patents:

> Any move by the neo-colonial state to revoke the patent law as a defensive measure would have very limited results since the market belongs to the monopolies. This becomes quite clear when it is realized that the other markets to which such products would be exported would still have such legislation protecting the same patents, and the transnational corporation would be in a position to require compliance. The mere ownership without the actual know-how which is guarded by the monopoly at headquarters would be useless. This is the whole point about monopoly. The world imperialist monopoly market would not exist if such a system of market control were not in operation.[16]

We view the inventions of 400 to 1,100 years ago as primitive, yet in their time these simple inventions could produce—with less labor—both more and better products. Someone powerful enough to control these new techniques could trade one day's work for two, three, five, ten or as many days' production of other people's labor as the efficiency of his invention and political power allowed.

For example, the invention of the windmill was extremely valuable. If it could be monopolized, its owners could siphon to themselves the production of large amounts of others' labor. This potential created a dispute between the

nobles, priests, and emperor "as to which one the wind 'belonged.' "[17] A seventeenth-century French patent granted such a right to selected owners of windmills.[18]

However hard they tried, claiming ownership of the wind was quite difficult. But not so with other technology. The water mill, first used in Europe during the tenth century, permitted one worker to replace as many as ten others. A stone planer eliminated seven workers out of eight. One worker with an Owens bottle machine could do the work of eighteen hand blowers.[19] Modern technology has created even greater efficiency gains. Many credit the steam engine with the greatest single increase in productive efficiency, but Stuart Chase cites a study by C.M. Ripley of work costing $230 done by hand labor that would cost only $5 using electric power.[20] Modern electric furnaces and continuous casting have brought the direct labor expended in the steel industry down to only 1.8 hours per ton of steel produced.[21] So long as the production of others' labor could be claimed through a patent on any technology, that income potential is capitalized into the value of that industry.

The owner of that first water mill was able to trade his single day's work, grinding grain, for seven days' labor of a woodworker or blacksmith. In effect he was paid for seven days while working one. The owner of a patented stone planer would likely gain five days' value for only one of his own. Any person lucky enough to own a patented Owens bottle machine could probably have claimed twelve days' pay for each day's labor. If the manufacturer in Ripley's study had been able to patent that efficiency, he would have claimed title to the process. He could then have lowered his prices and still charged twenty to thirty times the labor value in his product. However, just like claiming ownership of the wind, it would be difficult to claim exclusive title to electricity, which accounts for the drop in costs in Ripley's study.

Royalty Rights Originated from Royalty Conferring Monopoly Trading Rights

That the owners of patents are entitled to *royalties* exposes the origin of the term. Patent rights to land and inventions were conferred upon favorites by kings and queens, with the understanding that the person so favored would share the earnings—royalties. In short, the origin of patents is indistinguishable from the paying of bribes for the privilege of doing business. Such bribes were the precursors of today's patent royalties.[22]

The Foundation of Law Is Military Power

The foundation of most law is power, largely expressed through military strength. Long before patents were protected by governments, they were protected by violence. "The struggle against rural trading and against rural handicrafts lasted at least seven or eight hundred years. . . . All through the fourteenth century regular armed expeditions were sent out against all the villages in the neighborhood and looms or fulling-vats were broken or carried away."[23] Those early claims to technology, enforced by violence, were the forerunners of today's industrial patents. Those who would control technology have just become more sophisticated. They encode these exclusive rights in legal titles. Today, being accustomed to it and unaware of society's loss, we accept this as normal.

The growing efficiency of textile machinery started the Industrial Revolution. Primitive looms were improved upon by inventions such as Kay's flying shuttle, Hargreaves's spinning jenny, Crompton's "mule," and the power loom. Between 1773 and 1795, the labor time to process 100 pounds of cotton went from 50,000 hours to 300 hours, an efficiency gain of 16,666 percent.[24] That efficiency gain within a timespan of only twenty-two years exposes how the owners of these technologies quickly dominated world trade. Quite simply, the technology was not shared. It was monopolized through the requirement of royalties.

The widespread use of machine weaving came about only because the technology was copied and the patents ignored. That 16,666 percent gain in twenty-two years is dwarfed by 150 power looms in Formosa weaving twenty-four hours a day under the watchful eyes of only one agile female operator on roller skates.[25] This is a gain of hundreds of thousands, if not millions, of times in efficiency. The labor component in the price of a yard of cloth produced by modern industry is small. This includes the labor to smelt the ore, fabricate the machines, produce raw materials, and so on, which is stored in that capital.

The economically powerful will say they are not claiming the production of anyone else's labor, as there is hardly any labor involved. But this is exactly how wealth is siphoned to those who monopolize the tools of production. The price charged for those products is far above the cost of production and others are forced to trade what required a large amount of labor to produce for what was produced with a small amount of labor.

All society is denied the full benefit of cheap industrial goods when labor is charged more than it is paid to produce that product. If a product requires one hour's labor to produce and distribute, and then sells for three hours' labor value, it effectively siphons away the value produced by two hours of labor. Standard economics and accounting do not measure this overcharge because it shows up in stock prices far beyond intrinsic value and in a market restricted to higher-priced labor. If that cloth were priced relative to the price paid labor to produce it (including fair interest for the stored labor value represented by that machinery), then it would be priced within reach of the world's low-paid labor.

A bushel of wheat required three hours to produce in 1830 but only ten minutes in 1900.[26] A call to Montana State University in Bozeman revealed that in 1986 it took only 3.2 minutes of labor to produce one bushel of dryland Montana wheat. Other crops have similar efficiency gains.

Railroad labor per ton-mile is roughly only 4 percent that required only forty years ago, and that 2,500 percent efficiency gain is dwarfed by the 4 million percent gain in transportation efficiency over the horse and wagon only 150 years ago. The steam engine increased the efficiency of industry more than any other invention. Thus, the owners of steam-powered railroads were chosen by Josephson as the archetypal example of the robber barons who laid claim to America's wealth.[27]

The public did receive a large share of the labor savings in textiles, agriculture, transportation, and other technologies. With the common people's newly won rights (the U.S. Constitution and Bill of Rights), and with the enormously wealthy and sparsely inhabited lands of the Americas, the gains were just too great for the powerful to claim them all. However, due to the failure to build the buying power of developing world labor in step with the productivity of capital, there is much more production forgone and wasted than that which society so gratefully receives.

The patent laws evolved specifically to claim title to the gains of technology. Patents are the power that separates an inventor from his or her rightful compensation and society from its rightful share of that efficiency gain. With multiple patents—occasionally with only one key patent and control of markets—the owners of technology siphon to themselves large amounts of the production of others' labor.

Ownership of a key technology, the telephone, was Bell Telephone's advantage when that monopoly was established. (Inventions not controlled by Bell, such as the dial phone, were suppressed.) The telegraph and telephone reduced communication costs by an amount comparable to the savings created by new technology in textiles and transportation. These efficiency gains of technology, protected by patents, produced the monopoly profits that established Bell Telephone, a corporation larger than any in textiles or transportation.

Henry Ford's assembly line was a milestone in industrial technology that rapidly picked up the pace of the Industrial Revolution:

> The factory is not a new tool but an organization of production that eliminates the periods of idleness in the use of tools, machines, and human beings that are characteristic of agrarian and artisan production. In the artisan's shop the saw, chisel, file, and so forth are idle while the hammer is being used. In the factory all the tools are simultaneously in use in the hands of specialized workers; production is "in line" rather than "in series." But production in line requires a large scale of total output before it becomes feasible. The division of labor is limited by the extent of the market, as Adam Smith told us. But transportation, urbanization, and international trade provided a market of sufficient scale.[28]

During 1913 alone, the time required to assemble an automobile dropped from 728 minutes to

93. Until that year, the wage rate averaged $2.50 for a ten-hour day. Ford doubled the daily wages of his workers and reduced their hours from ten to eight, all while lowering the price of his cars.[29] This was unheard of in those times and drew much criticism from business and the press.

What Ford knew, and others did not, was that the profits were so large that with that 800 percent efficiency gain the wages could have been increased to almost twenty dollars per day. Ford was strongly opposed by his managers and other investors. Had it not been for the influence of Emerson, it appears that the claim on others' wealth made possible through the innovation of the assembly line might have been much higher and lasted for a much longer time.

Attempts were made to monopolize the emerging auto industry. George Baldwin Seldon, a lawyer specializing in patents, understood that, as the law was structured, patents laid claim to wealth produced by others. In 1899,

> he set his mind to working out the precise legal definition and wording of a patent that would give him the sole right to license and charge royalties on future automobile development in America. . . . Seldon had gone into partnership with a group of Wall Street investors who saw their chance to cut themselves in on the profits of the growing American car industry.[30]

The near success of Seldon and his partners in patenting the automobile illustrates the basic injustice of the current patent structure. Neither Seldon nor these investors had anything to do with the invention of automobiles. The first ones had been built in Europe fourteen years earlier and virtually hundreds of auto companies were already in existence. Yet, if anyone had succeeded in patenting the process of building automobiles, every purchaser of an automobile would have had a part of the production of his or her labor siphoned to the owners of that patent.

Seldon's attempt at patenting the principle of the automobile is being successfully accomplished today in the patenting of processes. Corporations are being formed to patent embryo transfers, gene splicing, other advanced medical procedures, even title to human genes. Any doctor who wishes to use these new procedures has to obtain a special license and pay a royalty.[31]

This added tax, though common to medical equipment and drugs, has not, up to this time, been added to the cost of an operation. If ownership of procedures had been established years ago, every bill for an operation would have had royalties added. Only those licensed by the patent holder could perform operations and the added charges would siphon wealth to whoever owned the patent rights. Every future improvement in patented surgical procedures would also be patented; the patent holders' subtle monopoly would never run out. The cost to society can be imagined if each producer or service provider had to pay a patent holder for the use of fire, wheels, wedges, levers, and gears. Inversely, the savings are evident in their free use because they are not patented (subtly monopolized).

There is one recent and remarkable exception to this rule. In certain remote parts of Africa, "as many as sixty percent of the people over age fifty-five are partly or completely blind" from becoming infected with a parasitic worm. Possibly 18 million people are affected. The pharmaceutical corporation Merck and Company owned the patent on a drug (Ivermectin) used to kill worms in animals. In October 1987, Merck announced it would provide this drug free of charge for Africans afflicted with this parasite. The company chairman, Dr. P. Roy Vagelos, noted, "It became apparent that people in need were unable to purchase it."[32] Here the loss to society from exclusive title was so obvious and devastating that these corporate executives made a moral decision to save the sight of millions of people. The cost to them was negligible; the gain to society was beyond measure.

There is a loss to society from exclusive control of any technology, but it is usually not as obvious as in this dramatic example, where the patent rules of exclusive use were abandoned. This example demonstrates the original morality of the medical industry when *"to patent an essential medicine was considered morally indefensible."*[33] It is also morally indefensible for other inventions crucial to society. The previously mentioned Gaviotas community—which is regenerating the primeval Amazon forest of Colombia's barren Los Llanos plains while building a model community, using modern production methods to live off the land—does not believe in patenting technology. Its inventions—such as a cheap, one-hundred-pound, windmill-driven water pump and cost-free, maintenance-free air conditioning—are spreading throughout Latin America.[34]

Innovation and technology thus create large reductions in labor costs in all segments of the economy. Most are more modest than the previous examples, but reductions of 90 percent are common and "from 1945 to 1970, the average increase in output per hour was thirty-four to forty percent per decade."[35] Such savings do not exert the immediate shock to the economy that these numbers suggest. It takes time to retool industries, and these corporations are in no hurry to destroy the value of their old production and distribution complexes.

Such overcharges cannot exist if labor is fully paid for its work. It only appears proper because people are accustomed to a subsistence wage for most labor, equally accustomed to all increased profits going to owners and management, and unaware of how rapidly that technology would spread around the world if capital were accumulated along the guidelines in this treatise (technology shared, and labor fully paid). Under those restructured social rules, workers would have buying power, technology would be regionally available to produce desired products and, as we address below, the capital will have been accumulated to finance it all simply through creation of the money or through deposit of a part of all interest going into a socially owned capital accumulation fund.

A Nation's Wealth Is Measured By, and Siphoned to Titleholders Through, Capitalized Values

> Until late in the [19th] century, railroad securities were almost the only ones listed on the New York Stock Exchange. The man of speculative disposition was, perforce, limited in the play of his fancy.
>
> —Peter Lyon, *To Hell in a Day Coach*

There have been stock markets ever since there have been stock companies. However, those early investors were almost exclusively wealthy people investing to produce for other wealthy people. Fulfilling the needs of the masses was not a great concern of those times. Early owners of society's wealth normally held ownership of their profitable industries within a close-knit group. But today's basic industries, factories, and distribution systems are so expensive that few people have such financial resources.

Shares in corporations are sold with the price based on how profitable they are expected to be—their capitalized value. This idea proved to be a real bonanza. Where conservative business people typically estimated the capitalized value of the company at ten times the yearly profit, the stock markets—anticipating future increases in profits—capitalized these values far higher, frequently twenty to thirty times annual profits and occasionally even more. One Internet company with no profits went public in 1998 and its stock jumped 500 percent the first week. As these higher values claim a greater share of a nation's loans (created money), this is a capital accumulation bonanza. But the rapid movement of this accumulated capital from the hands of one speculator to another can do as much, or more, harm than it does good. Witness the current financial collapse of Southeast Asia, other such collapses throughout history, and the hot wars those financial struggles evolved into.

All in one stroke, an individual or group could lay claim to the efficiency of a technology through capitalizing its value and selling shares to other investors. This siphoning of the production of others' labor—through the mechanism of capitalized values—concentrated wealth in the hands of a few, accumulated capital, and gave capitalism its name.

Through carefully structured laws, the hidden hand of the wealthy kept claiming an ever-larger share of this wealth. Labor, just as naturally, tried to retain or reclaim what it produced. The rights gained in the American Revolution and enshrined in its Constitution, and the natural justice of those rights, eventually increased the power and income of labor. This and the expansion of unnecessary labor led to more people retaining a greater share of society's wealth.[36] With these savings more broadly distributed, there evolved the present diversified markets to sell shares in industry and concentrate money capital.

Most of the wealth measured by capitalized values is claimed by the primary subtle monopolizations of land, patents (technology), and finance capital. If these excessive rights of property were replaced by the right of society to collect the landrent and productive labor were fully paid, all society would be wealthier even though monetized (capitalized) wealth would be lower. The excessive charges of subtle monopolization create high capitalized values. By removing these subtle monopolizations and fully paying labor for what it produces (which would require sharing of those fully productive jobs and a radical reduction in the workweek), measured values would equal the value of the labor and capital (stored labor) that produced that wealth.

The Stock Market Is the Financial Structure to Harvest the Profits of Monopolized Patents

The battle for corporate ownership is centered in the stock market. Millions of hours are spent by speculators (they call themselves investors) trying to figure out which company is going to increase its capitalized value. The game is calculating profits that will translate into capitalized value. It is viewed as a simple method of keeping score. But claiming the production of others' labor—through profits from shares in the nation's industry as technology continually replaces labor—is the underlying theme. Values that were once claimed by labor are now claimed by the shareowners of the new industrial technology.

Innovators, investors, and underwriters of hot new companies will print enough stock to absorb any foreseeable fictitious value. (Market psychology and speculation may inflate these values higher yet, and the lucky or astute small investor may gain wealth.) This process takes place in all companies where the owners become aware of the potential of capitalization to produce instant wealth. The alert tap into the wealth-siphoning process that their predecessors encoded into law.

Securities analyst and investment fund manager George J.W. Goodman, under the pseudonym Adam Smith, outlined the magic of capitalizing this unearned income. He christened this stock, and titled his book, *Supermoney*. He proves that this stock is in reality a "Supercurrency":

> In 1972 we have a good example of Supercurrency. The Levitz brothers . . . were furniture retailers whose company netted $60,000 or so a year. Then the company noticed that sales were terrific when they ran the year-end clearance sale from the warehouse: furniture right in the carton, cash on the barrelhead, 20 percent off. The idea was successful, they added more warehouses, and the company went public—in fact, superpublic. At one point, it was selling for seventeen times its book value. . . . [They] banked $33 million of public money for their stock, and still held $300 million worth. . . . Now when they want to pay grocery bills [buy a boat, a summer home, travel abroad or whatever], they peel off some of the [$333 million], as much as the market can stand. They have moved into the Supercurrency class.[37]

Goodman's example of "Supercurrency" is just another way of describing capitalization of fictitious values. There are the successful company, the underwriters, the innovation of a cheaper production or distribution system, and investors clamoring for shares in this innovative company, and—at seventeen times tangible assets—94 percent of the stock value is a fictitious monopolized value. The stock market abounds in examples of much higher fictitious capitalized values. The 1998–99 Internet stocks that have never turned a profit yet are valued at hundreds of billions of dollars are recent examples. The overcharge to maintain that assumed value is the interception of the production of others' labor. If that illusory value cannot be sustained, then the wealth of the purchaser of that stock at that illusory value will disappear. While these fortunes were made through title claims to technology (those values are based on efficiencies of technology), the Federal Reserve calculated that 25 percent of U.S. citizens in 1974, increasing to 54 percent in 1988, had no net assets.[38] Lester Thurow explains that this impoverishment of many while wealth is accumulated by a lucky few is due to "the process of capitalizing disequilibrium" (distortions of trade" and thus distortions of values—either internal or external) and that "patient savings and reinvestment has little or nothing" to do with generating large fortunes.[39] Thurow concludes that

> at any moment in time, the highly skewed distribution of wealth is the product of two approximately equal factors—instant fortunes and inherited wealth. Inherited fortunes, however, were themselves created in a process of instant wealth in an earlier generation. *These instant fortunes occur because new long-term disequilibriums in the real capital market are capitalized in the financial markets.* . . . Those who are lucky and end up owning the stocks that are capitalized at high multiples win large fortunes in the random walk. Once fortunes are created, they are husbanded, augmented, and passed on, not because "homo economicus" [economic man] desires to store up future consumption but because of desires for power within the family, economy, or society.[40]

Of course, the small fortunes accumulated by the upper middle class are from these same disequilibriums in the value of land and capital. Except by violence or trickery, how else can wealth beyond what one produces be accumulated? The income demanded by these fictitious values is a private tax upon the rest of society, and quite accurately labeled *air*. "By reducing air to vendability, scarcity could be capitalized. Business would be richer—and every man, woman and child in the country would be poorer."[41]

A study of the market over a full boom and bust cycle will find these fictitious values developing in most stocks. The reasons given may be many but the underlying cause is clear: the steady rise in the nation's efficiency is captured by, and mirrored in, stock and land values. Every speculator dreams of owning some of these stocks or land and becoming wealthy. The powerful and cunning, with better than even odds, buy and sell in rhythm with the inflation and deflation of stock and land prices to lay claim to much of this new wealth.

Those who win the gamble on who will own the world's land and industrial and distributive technology are freed from the necessity of laboring for their living. This is not a contradiction. Their speculative efforts are certainly labor. However, when unnecessary, that labor is fictitious, and such earnings are winnings of bets.

Capitalizing values is necessary to decide the sale price of a business. However, not only should everyone involved receive proper compensation for his or her labor, innovations, and risk; society should receive its share. Society not only provided tens of thousands of necessary preceding innovations; it also provided the schools, skills, tools, labor, markets, and infrastructure. Nature provided the resources, including the inventions that were waiting to be discovered. To monopolize technology subtly is to deny others full rights to its use even when independently invented.

There is a necessity for a stock market. It has, however, gone far beyond its proper function of providing capital to industries through the sale of stock. That the stock market's primary purpose today is financing the nation's business is pure fiction; trades in the stock market have little to do with capital investment:

> Buying a stock from a broker does not add one red cent to the corporate treasury and provides no investment capital except if the stock is newly issued. But new issues by major corporations are fairly rare because issuing new stock dilutes equity and depresses stock prices. As a result, the bulk of shares now traded on the stock markets were issued twenty or fifty years ago. Since then the shares have passed through many hands, and their prices have fluctuated over a wide range. Yet all these transactions have been strictly between the buyers and sellers of stocks, aided and abetted by stockbrokers trying to eke out a modest living. . . . [S]peculators are not really interested in the company whose stock they temporarily own. They want to take their profits and get out. They are not investing in the proper sense of the word; they are simply gambling. Ownership of corporations has become largely a game of chance in which the individual players try to guess what the other players will do.[42]

Market Bubbles and Crashes

Speculators are unaware that their gains are unearned. If the market wipes them out, they feel they have lost earnings when actually it was just the odds of the gamble and their turn to lose. Like the casinos they are, the stock markets are primarily a mechanism for the redistribution of wealth, not its production. It is a gambling game in which the rest of society's members are spectators—spectators who continually have their share of the nation's increased wealth thrown on the table of a game of chance they are not playing.

The danger of gambling with the nation's wealth was addressed by *Business Week*'s 1987 cover story, "Playing With Fire":

> By stoking a persuasive desire to beat the game, innovation and deregulation have tilted the axis of the financial system away from investment toward speculation. The U.S. has evolved into what Lord Keynes might have called a "casino society"—a nation obsessively devoted to high-stakes financial maneuvering as a shortcut to wealth. . . . "Speculators may do no harm as bubbles on a steady stream of enterprise. But the position is serious when enterprise becomes the bubble on a whirlpool of speculation. When the capital development of a country becomes a by-product of the activities of a casino, the job is likely to be ill-done."[43]

What is normally spoken of as a market "bubble" is only the claiming of wealth produced by others through rights of ownership that have gotten out of hand. Thus, in a market boom, the price of stocks tends to have no relation to either the value of the actual capital or its capitalized, fictitious value. History is replete with examples. Charles Mackay, in *Extraordinary Popular Delusions and the Madness of Crowds,* describes the tulip craze that broke out in Europe in the seventeenth century. Before that particular insanity dissipated, one particular tulip bulb cost "two lasts of wheat, four lasts of rye, four fat oxen, eight fat swine, twelve fat sheep, two hogsheads of wine, four tuns of butter, one thousand lbs. of cheese, a complete bed, a suit of clothes and a silver drinking cup."[44]

One wonders at the variety of commodities traded for that one flower bulb, but their total value of 2,500 florins serves as a guideline to the money value paid for other bulbs. During this period, prices ranged from 2,000 florins for an inferior bulb to 5,500 florins for the choicest varieties. "Many persons were known to invest a fortune of 100,000 florins in the purchase of 40 roots."[45] Although tulips are not stocks, the principle is the same.

At the turn of the eighteenth century, John Law implemented a plan to sell stock in enterprises in the Mississippi wilderness to pay off the huge debt of the French government. Though this scheme was seriously flawed, Law's banking reforms were quite sound, and the French economy prospered. The plan went awry when the money rolled in. Those selling paper were so busy getting rich they neglected to invest in production anywhere; they merely reinvested in more paper. In a speculative frenzy, fortunes changed hands as people sold, and then rebought, nothing but paper.

The stock in this Mississippi scheme had no value because there was no investment and thus no production. But Law's scheme seemed like such an effortless way to get rich that it caught the attention of cunning financiers in England. (Of course, the English also had to do something to protect their capital. It was fleeing to France to buy into Law's Mississippi scheme.) Although Spain controlled most of South America, and the English had limited trade rights within it, stock companies were set up to trade within this territory. Visions of wealth stirred up a speculative fever, and companies were formed for very unlikely endeavors. Soon, so many joined the game that it got out of hand and the government had to call a halt to new issues. The intention of most of these promoters can be summed up by one audacious proposal. This promoter touted "a company for carrying on an undertaking of great advantage, but nobody to know what it is."[46]

Since the organizers of these companies had no intention of producing anything, their capital was 100 percent fictitious. Proof that this capital was not real was given when the speculative bubble collapsed. There was no production to cover either expenses or profits; there was only the transferring of wealth from the naive to the cunning or lucky.

When wild speculation breaks loose, there is no relationship between value and price. Even when the stock market behaves normally, there are always stocks whose prices defy logic. This activity can only be attributed to crowd psychology, as described by Mackay, although sly promoters pull strings at every opportunity.

When the psychology of the market is understood, it is possible to intercept others' wealth using almost entirely fictitious capital. The psychology of crowds and peer pressure create loyalty to brand names and the desire to possess what one's peers own. This is accounted for on corporate ledgers as goodwill and creating this fictitious value is the cornerstone of advertising. For example, Levi jeans, once used as everyday work clothes, suddenly became the rage as society sought to adopt the Western look. The retail price of Levi's jumped from four dollars to twenty dollars, and the value of Levi Strauss stock can only have multiplied as they capitalized these fictitious values. Likewise, before the 1997–98 tobacco settlement, "the Marlboro man himself had a 'goodwill' value of $10 billion even as he drastically lowered the quality of life of millions drawn to his image."[47]

Options, Futures, and Other Derivatives Are Gambling Chips in a Worldwide Casino

Computer and communications technologies have created a fundamental change in world markets. The markets for stocks, bonds, commodities, futures, options, currencies, mortgages, money markets, in fact virtually every exchange market anywhere in the world, are now one huge market.

The stock market is mostly a gambling spree. Options or futures, for example, are only the buyer betting the stock will go up and the seller that it will go down; neither has a stake in that stock beyond the gamble. Options and futures may appear to have a legitimate purpose in takeover schemes, but when purchased by those attempting the takeover, they are not even gambles. The psychology of the market almost guarantees that the stock price will rise. This increase in wealth and the target company's own assets provide the money for takeovers.

The historic speculations in options, futures, and other simple bets is dwarfed by the derivative markets of the late twentieth century, which evolved both to reduce risk and to bypass the market's margin limitations. Long-Term Capital Management's bankruptcy crisis in 1998 uncovered the unsettling reality that this small hedge fund with a capital base of only $2 billion had over $1 trillion in bets in the derivatives markets. This was a margin of only 0.02 percent and many of the estimated 400 other hedge funds would have similar slim margins.

"Corporations have become chips in a casino game, played for high stakes by people who produce nothing, invent nothing, grow nothing and service nothing. The market is now a game in itself."[48] Capitalized fictitious values are also like chips on a poker table; they finance the game. But, unlike chips, when the game is over these deflated stocks cannot be traded in for full value.

The markets are a high stakes, *low risk* (except at the peak of a bubble) gambling casino where these overcapitalized values are distributed. Everyone recognizes the high stakes. The unacknowledged low risk is due to the constantly increasing value of the nation's capital accruing to stock owners. This increase in value is due to the capitalized value of the production of labor claimed by the owners of increasingly efficient technology. Due to exposés of fraud in the commodities and futures markets, farmers became aware of this fact and some have clamored for the closing down of the nonproductive futures markets.[49]

Just as selling short and other trading practices developed in the early established markets as a form of harvesting profits, sharp traders have leveraged world markets with stock and currency options, futures on options (options on options), futures on interest rates, warrants (a form of option), and thousands of other similar subdivisions of value called "derivatives":[50]

> Futures contracts on interest rates did not exist in 1971.... Today there are outstanding contracts for $3 trillion worth of them, a little more than half of the gross national product of the United States.... The market for tradable options has grown from essentially zero in 1973—the year the Chicago Board Options Exchange opened for the first time—to a market where more than $170 billion changes hands each day. One hundred and seventy billion is enough money to build 1.7 million average homes.... Eight hundred billion dollars ... is exchanged each day in the world's currency markets.... Every three days a sum of money passes through the fiber-optic network under the pitted streets of New York equal to the total output for one year of all of America's companies and all its workforce. And every two weeks the annual product of the world passes through the network of New York.... Sums of similar magnitude pass through the streets of Tokyo, London, Frankfurt, Chicago, and Hong Kong.... [This] "financial economy" is somewhere between twenty and fifty times larger than the real economy. It is not the economy of trade but of speculation. Its commerce is in financial instruments [paper].[51]

Strip away all the hype and derivatives are simply bets on the direction of a particular market.

With personal computers able to track stocks, bonds, commodities, futures, options, and so on in virtually any of these markets worldwide, there are massive gyrations of values as speculators buy and sell these packaged paper symbols of wealth.[52] Just as the formation of the stock market and the manipulation of stock values became the primary mechanism through which robber barons appropriated the industrial wealth of America and laid the base for America's financial aristocracy, a new breed of robber barons are harvesting fortunes running the markets of the world up and down. A fresh crop of bright people have placed themselves between the world's savers and its producers and consumers to intercept the new wealth produced by the increased efficiencies of technology. As these speculators produced nothing, thus had nothing to trade of value, that wealth can only have come from true producers.

While the world economy staggered and labor's share of wealth declined, the world market in paper symbols of wealth missed a few beats: the U.S. stock market collapse of October 19, 1987 (from which it recovered to go to new highs), the savings and loan and banking crisis in the United States in 1990 (now recovered),[53] the collapse of the Tokyo stock and land markets (from which they have not yet recovered), and the 1997–98 financial meltdown of 40 percent of the world, all on the periphery of imperial centers of capital (which has not yet turned around as this book goes to press). Insecurity forced capital to flee back to its imperial centers, forcing those markets to new highs, then new lows, and they continued rising and falling as speculators jockeyed for position and/ or fled for safer havens.

We have yet to see if the enormous sums of accumulated capital in the imperial centers of capital will bid the limited available stocks to atmospheric heights and then crash, whether they will be used to build even more industrial capacity to service a shrunken world consumer market and crash from that excess capacity, whether a Fascist financial and military fix will protect the current monopolizers of capital, or whether the tigers on the periphery can be restarted. Though those tigers may rise above their current lows, that they can regain their previous vigor is doubtful. The intense competition of surplus productive capacity that goes with a reduction in world buying power makes capital accumulation very difficult.

Bringing the World's Markets Under Control

Buying and selling investments is the legitimate purpose of stock markets; any activity beyond that is gambling. A particularly simple method of reining in all stock, commodities, and currency speculations would be a small transfer tax (Tobin Tax) on short-term purchases. That law would be a good start but in the subchapter "Inflation, Deflation, and Constant Value: Creating Honest Money" Chapter 26, we demonstrate how easy it would be to stabilize commodity prices by tying currency values to commodity values. Stable prices would eliminate all need for derivatives and all purpose of market speculation. Once the markets were stabilized by tying the world's money to commodity markets as outlined, speculation in commodities and markets would disappear. Those of speculative nature would now invest in the beating heart of capitalism, entrepreneurial speculation.

Restructuring Patent Laws

> I know of no orginal product invention, not even electric shavers or heating pads, made by any of the giant laboratories or corporations, with the possible exception of the household garbage grinder.... The record of the giants is one of moving in, buying out and absorbing the smaller creators.
> —T.K. Quinn, *Giant Business: Threat to Democracy*

Quinn was later informed that the garbage disposal was also an appropriated idea.[54]

The knowledge and skills of labor are now divided into minute segments of the production process. How a society retains that knowledge and those skills has become as important as an inventor's creative ability. The collection, organization, and monopolization of these critical elements of production are managed by the use of patents.

Currently, the incentive to preserve and use this knowledge lies in the amount of other people's labor that can be claimed under the heading of profits. These claims are made through investments in shares of industrial technology in the stock market. This system appears efficient because most of the calculations are in terms of profit; there is no calculation of the lost potential described throughout this treatise. A tracking system accounting for all the potential efficiencies of technology and quality of life would lead to far different conclusions.

Inventions and innovations are the cornerstones of prosperity. To establish them in social memory and reward the inventors and innovators, those technologies must be used and those inventors and innovators must be well paid.[55] It is necessary to reward both those who had the original innovative ideas and those who put those ideas to work.

The present policy of restricting access to technology should be changed to allow easy access with proper compensation for inventors, developers, and producers while returning the maximum savings to society. Old patents should be left intact. New patents should be available for all to use with but one stipulation:

"royalties will be paid to the patent holder." This does not reduce anyone's rights. Many holders of older patents will see financial advantages to the new system and will transfer to the new patent structure. After seventeen years, the last of the older patents will have expired and the subtle monopolization of technology, and its overcharge to society, will disappear.

All patents should be required to be recorded in simple, easily understood language. People with knowledge of production and distribution needs could then browse through these patents and spot those that might be useful. (Many patents are now filed in deliberately obscure language to delay any possible use by competitors.[56]) To analyze and catalog these inventions and innovations would require an extensive "national network of regional assistance centers" for the orderly registration of patents.[57]

Many innovations are never patented; they survive only as closely held trade secrets. The law should protect these secrets only as long as is reasonably required to perfect their innovation. Patentable ideas that are now protected as trade secrets should then be registered and made available for the entire world to use. The present holders of these trade secrets would not lose proper compensation—upon recording their patent, they would be entitled to royalties.[58] Failure to record the innovation would risk someone else recording the patent.

The expense and risk involved in product development and market penetration are far greater than those associated with invention; these efforts should receive the largest share of the patent royalties. Once a product is brought to market, a *development patent* would be established by filing with the regional patent office. Development patent holders would be entitled to royalties, but all would be free to use the innovation after filing notice of their use.

Under this mutual support structure, new inventions would be available for all to use. The inventors, developers, and producers would be adequately paid for their ideas, capital, labor, and risk. Society would be paid through low-priced products and services. This is all within the framework of the American Constitution, and most others; each person's labor and property are fully protected and no one's rightful wealth is confiscated.

With everybody having the right to use these innovations, the overcharges for fictitious capital and fictitious wages of the present patent system would be eliminated. This would do away with the current policy of industries buying up and shelving patents that threaten to destroy the value of obsolete industrial capital. Every producer would have a right to their use:

> There are countless numbers of patents which, if in operation, would much cheapen the articles they could produce, but they are intentionally shelved to prevent competition. Concerns operating under old inventions for which they have expended great sums to erect plants buy up these new and cheaper methods to prevent competitors from getting hold of them. They then tuck them away in their safes never to be used.[59]

"Technical knowledge in a functional society would be free." Without it,

> new inventions may not only be suppressed, they may be pre-suppressed. A concern may get patents on a whole series of processes in order to tie up the field for the next generation or more. . . . If scientific advance could be kept free and accessible, with proper reward for the inventor duly secured—a large amount of labor power which now trades on the processes of patenting and mystification—lawyers, "fixers," patent clerks and the like, would be released to useful service, a large amount of duplicated scientific research would be saved, and above all the way

cleared to let society benefit at once and directly in the new discovery.[60]

Producers would register all patents used in their production process. This registration would include where patented technology is being used and the gross sales of products or services using this technology. Royalties, predetermined by volume on a sliding scale, would then be distributed to the patent holders.

Full Rights to Use of Any Technology Are More Efficient and Pay Inventors Better

However, the patent system could be far simpler and administration costs lowered to almost nothing by evaluating a patent, paying inventors and developers its capitalized value, and placing their innovations in the public domain. The inventor and/or developer would have instant wealth with which to develop more inventions, all would be free to use the inventions, and there would be no cost for accounting or for disbursing royalties. The value would be instantly capitalized with the inventor the gainer, instead of the current complex process of capitalization through the stock market. There can be little doubt that most inventors would opt for that instant cash and free use by all. Inventions not recognized as valuable, a frequent occurrence, would be proved by developers who would then file development patents.

The greatest gain from having unrestricted access to patents is that industry would no longer be so vulnerable to destruction through trade wars. A producer need only stay alert and incorporate every useful patent into his or her product. Because producers can use the most efficient technology to remain competitive,

businesses and communities would no longer have to shut down because their market was overwhelmed by a competitor with a patent monopoly (capital destroying capital). Under the current patent structure, entire communities (industry, businesses, and homes) can become almost valueless if they lose out in battles for market shares. Under this recommended patent structure, the world's communities and businesses would be quite secure even as they, and all society, gained the maximum benefits from the newest technologies.

Competitive Monopolies, Developmentally Mature Technology, and Standardization

A vast range of intellectual pursuits is required to develop the tens of thousands of inventions involved in the manufacture of most consumer products. The most efficient way to develop new inventions or techniques is through competition. Inventors must be free to invent and develop products as they see fit. There is, however, a time when a technology becomes developmentally mature. At that time, society should consider standardization, a common practice in industry.

Once standardized, development and production costs will drop to a fraction of those for competitive monopolies. Automobiles are a good example. There were at least 502 automobile companies formed in the United States between 1900 and 1908. There has been a great rationalization of this industry and only three U.S. manufacturers are left.

Labor expended in production and distribution of automobiles could be reduced even further through more standardization. In early November 1998, airline companies had concluded they could reduce costs 20 percent through standardizing passenger jets. Carrying this rationalization of production to its unavoidable conclusion would create a corporate, centrally planned, privately owned economy.

The cost of research and development for the first color TV was $125 million. The development of high-definition TV will require several billions. A new generation of computers in 1985 required $750 million. The development of these many incompatible computer systems was necessary to sort out which technology would be the most efficient. But there comes a time when a decision must be made as to when society will be served by standardizing technology. The cost of research, development, manufacturing, consumer education, and distribution of several incompatible technologies is roughly the cost of one multiplied by the number of incompatible technologies.

For example: To duplicated development costs of incompatible computers would be added the loss of social efficiency resulting from their inability to communicate with each other, the complicated software necessary to write around already patented software, the smaller number of citizens who could afford them, the increased time and effort spent learning to operate them, and finally the greater number of trained technicians required to train and support the unsophisticated public.

The moment society decided to develop one primary computer hardware/software technology and language, it would be impossible to bring to market an incompatible computer. All producers would then expend their efforts on developing and producing compatible hardware and software. The cost of computers and communications would drop precipitously and their uses expand exponentially. Every major computer user is frustrated by the many incompatible languages and software. If most keystrokes or symbols were standardized to mean the same

thing in all software, education time would drop even as proficiency increased.

Once the affected industries made the decision to standardize, innovators would need only to develop hardware and software products in a compatible form and register the patent. Each additional innovation would be welcomed into an already functioning and efficient system. The savings on labor and capital should properly accrue to all society in the form of lower costs. These savings would permit generous compensation to the nation's creative talent and risk-takers.

The relatively few people who produced these products would be well rewarded, while the cost, as a percentage of the consumer price, would be negligible. Detractors will claim that standardizing products would stagnate innovation, but efficiency in any product has required some level of standardization—for example, threaded bolts in industry, compatible telephone equipment, interchangeable railroad equipment. Just as no one would abandon the efficiencies of these standardizations, computers, software, and other technologies would produce better products and increase social efficiency, and all at lower costs. Experts feel the computer industry should have been standardized from the beginning:

> The computer industry is tackling this problem decades later than it should have—after selling 50 million computers that work pretty much alone, much like isolated islands with little or no connection to the outside world. Just the opposite happened with telephones. There the standards—established in 1885—came first. Every country in the world adopted them. That's why you can pick up the phone and call anywhere in the world—and why manufacturers of telephones, answering machines and fax machines can build their products to plug directly into the phone network and go right to work. "The world's 600

million phones are interconnected,'' says Doehler [executive director of Siemens AG]. ''Computers should be too.'' . . . Computers from all vendors will [then] be able to exchange information easily. The ''global village'' envisioned by Marshall McLuhan in the 60's finally will become a reality. You'll be able to sit down at any computer terminal anywhere on the globe, and send a message or electronic file to any computer, regardless of its make.[61]

The efficiencies of computer/software compatibility will be here shortly and then a further market shakeout will come with a few large producers and distributors remaining. In fact, the monopolizers of computer technology should be looking closely at the operating system available for free on the Internet that is capturing 11 percent of the market and growing. Once enough free software has been created to work with it, the developing world will surely use that operating system. It could then swiftly take over and wipe out the entire developed-world software market.

There is a need for stock and commodities markets. The countless opportunities to use industry and technology to fulfill social needs can hardly be taken care of by a central authority. When a producer or entrepreneur sees such an opportunity he or she must have access to capital, but it is important that pure speculation be discouraged. We next address how to increase access to finance capital for talented and motivated citizens.

Notes

1. Doug Henwood, *Wall Street* (New York: Verso, 1997), p. 7.

2. Adam Smith, *The Wealth of Nations* (New York: Random House, 1965), p. 64.

3. J.W. Smith, *The World's Wasted Wealth 2* (San Luis Obispo, CA: Institute for Economic Democracy, 1994).

4. John D. Donahue, *The Privatization Decision: Public Ends and Private Means* (New York: Basic Books, 1989).

5. *Public Power Directory and Statistics for 1983* (Washington, DC: American Public Power Association, 1983); Jeanie Kilmer, ''Public Power Costs Less,'' *Public Power Magazine* (May/June 1985), pp. 28–31; Lee Metcalf and Vic Reinemer, *Overcharge* (New York: David McKay, 1967).

6. Edward Winslow Martin, *History of the Grange Movement* (New York: Burt Franklin, 1967), pp. 62, 70.

7. Matthew Josephson, *Robber Barons* (New York: Harcourt Brace Jovanovich, 1962), p. 92; Joe E. Feagin, *The Urban Real Estate Game* (Englewood Cliffs, NJ: Prentice-Hall, 1983), pp. 57–58; Peter Lyon, *To Hell in a Day Coach* (New York: J. B. Lippincott, 1968), p. 6; see also Martin, *Grange Movement*.

8. Wilfred Owen, *Strategy for Mobility* (Westport, CT: Greenwood Press, 1978), p. 23.

9. John Prados, *The Presidents' Secret Wars* (New York: William Morrow, 1986), p. 152.

10. Lewis Mumford, *Pentagon of Power* (New York: Harcourt Brace Jovanovich, 1964), pp. 134, 139; Stuart Chase, *Men and Machines* (New York: Macmillan, 1929), chapters 3–4.

11. Chase, *Men and Machines*, pp. 42–43.

12. PBS, *Nova*, September 2, 1986.

13. Stuart Chase, *The Economy of Abundance* (New York: Macmillan, 1934), chapter 8.

14. Phil Grant, *The Wonderful Wealth Machine* (New York: Devon-Adair, 1953), pp. 301–306.

15. Dan Nadudere, *The Political Economy of Imperialism* (London: Zed Books, 1977), p. 251, quoting in part from E. Penrose, *The International Patent System*, 1951, p. 29.

16. Ibid., pp. 186, 255.

17. Karl Marx, *Capital* (New York: International, 1967), vol. 1, p. 375, footnote 2.

18. Nadudere, *Political Economy of Imperialism*, p. 38, quoting Leo Huberman, *Man's Worldly Goods*, pp. 128–29.

19. Lewis Mumford, *Technics and Civilization* (New York: Harcourt Brace Jovanovich, 1963), pp. 227–28, 438. Read also Nadudere, *Political Economy of Imperialism*, pp. 51–55.

20. Chase, *Economy of Abundance*, p. 166.

21. Lester Thurow, *Head to Head: The Coming*

Economic Battle Among Japan, Europe, and America (New York: William Morrow, 1992), p. 187.

22. Grant, *Wonderful Wealth Machine*, pp. 301–306.

23. Karl Polanyi, *The Great Transformation* (Boston: Beacon Press, 1957), p. 277, quoting from Pirenne, *Medieval Cities*, p. 211.

24. Marx, *Capital*, vol. 1, pp. 372–74, 428, 435, 562; Eric R. Wolf, *Europe and the People Without History* (Berkeley: University of California Press, 1982), pp. 273–74, 279.

25. Richard Barnet, *The Lean Years* (New York: Simon and Schuster, 1980), p. 260. Besides the ownership of patents, Third World development requires the control of resources and markets as outlined in Part 2.

26. Howard Zinn, *A People's History of the United States* (New York: Harper Colophon Books, 1980), p. 277.

27. Josephson, *Robber Barons*, p. 258.

28. Herman E. Daly and John B. Cobb Jr., *For the Common Good* (Boston: Beacon Press, 1989), p. 11.

29. Robert Lacey, *Ford* (New York: Ballantine Books, 1986), pp. 118–40; also Juliet Schor, *The Overworked American* (New York: Basic Books, 1991), p. 61.

30. Lacey, *Ford*, pp. 105–06.

31. Stanley Wohl, *Medical-Industrial Complex* (New York: Harmony Books, 1984), pp. 69–71; Ivan Illich, *Medical Nemesis* (New York: Bantam Books, 1979), p. 245.

32. Stephen Budiansky, "An Act of Vision for the Developing World," *U.S. News and World Report*, November 2, 1987, p. 14.

33. Jean-Pierre Berlan, "The Commodification of Life," *Monthly Review* (December 1989), p. 24 (emphasis added).

34. Alan Weisman, "Columbia's Modern City," *In Context* 42 (1995), pp. 6–8.

35. E.K. Hunt and Howard Sherman, *Economics* (New York: Harper and Row, 1990), p. 166.

36. Smith, *World's Wasted Wealth 2*.

37. "Adam Smith" (George J.W. Goodman), *Supermoney* (New York: Random House, 1972), pp. 21–22.

38. Lester C. Thurow, *Generating Inequality* (New York: Basic Books, 1975), p. 14; "Worker's State," *The Nation*, September 19, 1988, pp. 187–88.

39. Thurow, *Generating Inequality*, p. 149.

40. Ibid., p. 154 (emphasis added).

41. Chase, *Economy of Abundance*, p. 165.

42. Rolf H. Wild, *Management by Compulsion* (Boston: Houghton Mifflin, 1978), pp. 92, 94–95.

43. Anthony Banco, "Playing With Fire," *Business Week*, September 16, 1987, p. 78, quoting Keynes.

44. Charles Mackay, *Extraordinary Popular Delusions and the Madness of Crowds* (New York: Farrar, Straus and Giroux, 1932), p. 91.

45. Ibid., p. 90; John Train, *Famous Financial Fiascoes* (New York: Clarkson N. Potter, 1985), pp. 33–41, 108–89.

46. Mackay, *Delusions*, p. 55; see also Train, *Fiascoes*, pp. 88–95; Charles P. Kindleberger, *Manias, Panics, and Crashes* (New York: Basic Books, 1978), pp. 220–21.

47. Richard J. Barnet and John Cavanagh, *Global Dreams: Imperial Corporations and the New World Order* (New York: Simon and Schuster, 1994), p. 188.

48. " 'Teflon' 80s Bear Striking Resemblance to 'Giddy' 20s," *The Missoulian*, March 25, 1987, reprinted from the *Washington Post*.

49. Paul Richter, "Commodity Marts Face Fraud Fallout," *Los Angeles Times*, quoted in *The Missoulian*, July 4, 1989, p. A2.

50. Joel Kurtzman, *The Death of Money* (New York: Simon and Schuster, 1993), pp. 18–19, 67, 101, 128, 142–43.

51. Kurtzman, *Death of Money*, pp. 12, 17, 77, 128; see also pp. 39, 64–65, 236.

52. What Joel Kurtzman, economist and business editor for *The New York Times*, calls "images of labor, wisdom, and wealth" (Kurtzman, *Death of Money*, p. 161).

53. Kurtzman, *Death of Money*, pp. 73, 96, 99, 113, 117, 120–21, 196, 228.

54. Paul A. Baran and Paul M. Sweezy, *Monopoly Capital* (New York: Monthly Review Press, 1968), p. 49, quoted from T.K. Quinn, *Giant Business: Threat to Democracy* (New York: Exposition Press, 1954), p. 117.

55. Society can forget. Assuming this is not one of history's frauds, a copresenter from China told us at a conference of a 3,000-year-old stainless steel sword found in China with virtually no rust on it. The Chinese protected their technology by passing the knowledge from father to son and it only required an unexpected death for society to lose that knowledge.

56. Michael Goldhaber, *Reinventing Technology* (New York: Routledge & Kegan Paul, 1986), p. 185.

57. Ibid., pp. 185, 197.

58. This very sensible approach was, in part, suggested by Goldhaber, *Reinventing Technology*, pp. 98, 184–87, 189, 198.

59. Stuart Chase, *The Tragedy of Waste* (New York: Macmillan, 1925), pp. 204–205.

60. Ibid.

61. John Hillkirk, "Users' Aim: 1 Language in All Computers," *USA Today*, June 7, 1988, p. B1.

26

Subtly Monopolizing Money

Money is the mirror image of a modern economy and many people instinctively point to financiers as the source of society's problems. Yet one has to research deeply to get beneath the Social Control belief systems which protect the subtle monopolization of money and finance capital.[1]

From Barter to Commodity Money

Before the widespread use of money, trading involved the simplest form of commercial transaction, barter. Barter is the exchange of two or more products of roughly equal value. This limits most trading to persons possessing equally valuable items. Eventually cattle, tobacco, salt, tea, blankets, skins, and other items were used as a form of money. Such commodities were the most desirable because they were durable, portable, readily exchangeable, and had the most recognizable common measure of value.

Products intended for consumption typically have one or two owners on their way from producer to consumer. Those that are used as money may have dozens or even hundreds of owners. Whether a product is used for exchange or consumption distinguishes it as money or a commodity. The products listed above were imperfect as a medium of exchange, and their limited usefulness limited trade. They created problems of storage, transportation, and protection, and not everyone could use these commodities.

From Commodity Money to Coins of Precious Metal

Only highly desirable, useful items could become money. No one would accept a piece of paper, brass, or copper in trade for what he or she had worked so hard to produce. Such a trade would effectively rob one of hard-earned wealth.

Gold and silver have been highly esteemed and accepted as money in most cultures. The first known coin, the shekel, was minted in "the temples of Sumer about 5,000 years ago," and coins of measured value have been routinely minted from precious metals ever since.[2] Except for scarcity values, the labor required to produce a given amount of gold, silver, or precious stones was roughly equal to the labor required to produce any other item that this treasure could buy. As accustomed as we are to viewing gold as money, it is still commodity money: desirable, useful, and requiring roughly equal labor to produce.

Inequality of money values is only inequality of exchanged labor values. Often when rulers became strapped for cash (usually because of war), they resorted to debasing their currency by lowering the gold or silver content and replacing it with inexpensive metals such as copper. The labor value represented by these debased coins was less than the labor value of the items purchased. Assuming the labor cost of gold was 300 times that of copper, each day's production of copper substituted and traded as gold would confiscate the value of 300 days of labor spent producing useful items. It was the universally recognized value of pure precious metals that became the first readily acceptable money.[3]

With gold (or any precious metal) divisible into units of measurable value, a trade could be made for any product. This convenience fueled world trade, for it was only with handy universally accepted money that commerce could flourish. However, as these precious metals had to be located, mined, delivered, stored, and protected before society could have money, trades were still clumsy.

From Gold, to Gold-Backed Paper Money, to Paper Money

The use of gold as money was handicapped by its weight, bulk, and the need for protection against debasement. These problems were eventually eliminated by printing paper money that could be redeemed for a stated amount of gold or silver (the gold standard). As this paper money was backed by gold, there remained the complication of finding, mining, smelting, and storing this valuable commodity.

The next step in the evolution of money was the use of pure paper money. (Paper money was almost universally resorted to in revolutions, although it usually had little value once the banking systems returned to the gold standard.) Benjamin Franklin had proposed paper money, and, while it was used less successfully in the New England colonies, it was used productively in the middle colonies in promoting production and commerce while controlling deflation. The powerful of Britain recognized the threat to their control of trade and outlawed the printing of money in the colonies. This effectively dictated control of commerce and who would profit, and was a contributory cause of the American Revolution.[4]

World Wars I and II weakened the old imperial nations, eroding the subtle monopoly of the gold standard.[5] As most of their gold had been traded for war materiel, these countries had to keep printing money to rebuild their shattered cities and industrial plants. To return to money backed by gold would have been to leave their economies at the mercy of U.S. bankers. Thus the subtle monopoly of the gold standard was partially broken in these countries. The arms race that followed World War II almost totally eliminated gold-backed money as nations continued to print money wastefully for war.

Once freed from its bondage to gold, paper money *represented* rather than possessed value. Printed at little cost, it could be traded for as much wealth as its stated value. Society now required only one finished product to make a trade. Those who sold their labor in the form of these products received in return the paper symbols of value and needed only save this money until they wished to buy products produced by others. Paper money, used productively and not backed by gold, was true money.

From Paper Money, to Checkbook Money, to Money as a Blip on a Computer Screen

As simple and light as paper money was, it was still too clumsy for most trades. Most of these units of value called money were deposited in a bank (just as gold had been) and trades were then consummated with checks. These were more efficient than cash, because each check was a symbol that the signer had produced, saved, or borrowed that much wealth, and that its money form, safely deposited in the bank, was now being traded for equal value in other products or services. Most family, business, corporate, and international trades are done with these symbols of deposited savings—checks, drafts, notes, bills of exchange, and the like.

Commodity money (hides, tobacco, etc.) had dozens, possibly hundreds, of owners before this trading medium returned to its status as a commodity to be consumed. Gold (still commodity money) retained the status of money much longer and had thousands of owners. Gold-backed paper money traded more conveniently and had many more owners. Reserve deposit money, traded by check—via bank debits and credits—can have an endless number of owners, as this representation of value keeps moving from owner to owner. Modern computer money (still reserve deposit money) is but a blip on magnetic tape or disk that can be instantly debited from one account and credited to another. Though still tied closely to checkbook money, this is the ultimate in efficient money.

Paper money and checks are familiar to everybody. Even a child learns quickly what they are and how to use them. When most of the historical and ideological mystique is eliminated, money is easy to understand. The banking system collects all production (symbolized by money), completes society's trades through debits and credits, lends the surplus production (savings) to those who—at any particular moment—have capital or consumer needs greater than their savings, and—through borrowing from the Federal Reserve to expand their reserves and increase their loan capacity—creates more money for an expanding economy. Money is no more complicated than this.

What makes money appear mysterious is that the powerful have always controlled it. Its secrets are protected by governments, bankers, and subtle finance monopolists of every shade trying to siphon to themselves others' wealth. The process is quite simple. In a trade, symbolized by money, the actual value of products or services, bought or sold, could be higher or lower than its actual labor value (higher priced or lower priced). The production of labor may be claimed either by underpaying for labor, by overcharging for products or services, or both. To make this clear, we will quote our own words from our opening chapter:

> In direct trades between individuals or countries, wealth accumulation potential compounds in step with the pay differential for equally productive labor. If the pay differential is five, the difference in wealth accumulation potential is twenty-five to one. If the pay differential is ten, the wealth accumulation advantage is one hundred to one. If the pay differential is twenty, the wealth accumulation advantage is 400 to one. If the pay differential is forty, the wealth accumulation advantage is 1,600 to one. If the pay differential is sixty (the pay differential between the defeated Russia and the victorious America [twenty-three cents an hour against $14 an hour]), the wealth accumulation advantage is 3,600 to one.

Credit or Trust Money

People accept money because they trust that the value represented can be replaced by equal value in another commodity or service. Credit (pure trust) is both the oldest and most modern currency. When credit is given, nothing is received for the item of value except a promise. Each month, families and businesses are provided with products or services (value) and then billed. This is a procedure based on trust. Cash money is also based on the trust that it can be redeemed for equal value.

If money is controlled with equality and honesty, there is trust. Money then exchanges freely and is easily understood. We are describing money and banking in the everyday language that would apply if the remaining flaws in money's creation and control were eliminated.

The Different Meanings of Money

Money is correctly referred to as a unit of accounting, savings, stored value, a measure of value, a standard of value, a receipt for value, a system of accounting, a deferred payment, a transferable claim, a lien against future production, an IOU, and an information medium. At a fundamental level, money represents the value of the final product of combining the elements of production—land, capital, and labor. In a properly structured society, money represents the value of labor, profits on stored labor (capital), and a share of the costs of running society represented by landrent being paid to society as outlined in the above chapter on land.

To the layperson, money is normally explained as a medium of exchange. This is true. However, a medium of exchange implies equality and, as demonstrated throughout this treatise, it is precisely the *inequality of exchanges* that is the greatest problem. To understand these inequalities, we must have a better explanation of money.

Money Is a Contract Against Another Person's Labor

Money is, first and foremost, a contract against another person's labor. Except for land or art, value is properly a measure of the time and quality of labor spent producing a product or service. If the difference between the payment received for productive labor and the price paid by the consumer for a product or service is greater than fair value for expediting that trade, either the producer was underpaid, the final consumer was overcharged, or both. When intermediaries underpay producers or overcharge consumers, they are siphoning away the production of the labors of one or the other, or both. This process is seen in the notorious and once common practice of forced shopping at the company store. The underpaid workers' meager wages were further reduced by their compulsory purchase of overpriced merchandise.[6]

Savings implies that something has been produced and not consumed. But even if a commodity is produced for consumption, it is properly understood as capital until sold to the final consumer. It then becomes his or her wealth for consumption (some commodities, such as a meal, are consumed in minutes and some, such as homes, are consumed in decades or even centuries) and is no longer capital. Products are sold, production expenses are paid, any surplus is deposited in a bank, and that deposit is credited at the Federal Reserve, which expands that bank's reserves. Banks lend these reserves to others for investment or consumption. The savings (stored labor) has become money capital. The parties who labored to create or distribute these products are only lending their surplus production in its money form with the promise to be paid interest for what their stored labor produced. Interest is the money form of wealth produced by that stored labor (capital).

Money Productively Contracting Labor

Because money is always controlled by those who rule, revolutionaries always resort to printing money to finance their insurrections. As opposed to wars to control trade, successful revolutionary wars, like those of the United States, France, the Soviet Union, and China, are fought for freedom, are productive expenditures of labor, and are fought with paper money.[7] Every battle for freedom requires large expenditures. Most labor is donated by those directly involved, but much of the weaponry, clothing, food, and medicine must be paid for with money. Money is thus a tool for mobilizing society's labor to produce great things—in this case freedom.

Examples of money properly employing labor are seen every day in farming, in the creation of consumer products, and in the building of homes, roads, schools, shopping centers, and factories. The rebuilding of Europe after World War II was a productive use of labor employed by U.S. capital, as was the industrialization of Japan, Taiwan, and South Korea. However, as most of this book exposes, the politics of their capital development would point more to the powerful protecting their interests than to meeting humanitarian needs.

Money Unproductively Contracting Labor

To use one's own *earned* money for speculation is properly one's privilege. But, as addressed in the previous chapter, borrowing society's money capital for speculating on land, gold, silver, commodities, or already issued stock is an attempt to intercept social production by speculating with society's savings; there is no intent to produce. The use of society's savings for corporate takeovers usually is a battle between the powerful for control. Whether the takeover is successful or not, these unproductive uses of social capital continually milk money from the economy. All this unnecessary activity diverts money capital from its true purpose, production

and distribution. More appropriately, it is an exercise in social insanity. By taking the easy way out, society is being irresponsible.

An even more nonproductive use of money occurs when labor is contracted to destroy others' capital (war), or to work at endeavors from which neither the present generation nor its descendants will benefit (waste). In 1800, Robert Owen, manager of a family textile mill in Scotland, began his famous social experiment of paying workers well, giving them decent housing, educating their children, and doing all this profitably. He calculated that this community of 2,500 persons (workers and families) was producing as much as a community of 600,000 did less than fifty years before.

Owen wondered where the wealth from such a large increase in efficiency was going. He studied the problem and concluded it was being consumed by the petty wars continually fought by aristocracy.[8] (The same wars fought by a financial aristocracy are wasting today's wealth.) The mill workers were being underpaid for their work, the customers were being overcharged for their cloth, and the production of their labor, in its money form, was being siphoned away and used to contract material and labor for war. Labor was being paid to fight because this generated the greatest rewards for those who controlled the use of money. This was wasteful to the rest of society; nothing useful was produced when that confiscated wealth was spent, and much of what existed was destroyed.

In the sixteenth century, "about seventy percent of Spanish revenues and around two-thirds of the revenues of other European countries" were employed in these wars.[9] Most of this revenue was siphoned away from a country's own citizens. The treasure pillaged from the Americas was but a small share of the wealth destroyed in European wars:

Until the flow of American silver brought massive additional revenues to the Spanish crown (roughly from the 1560s to the late 1630s), the Habsburg war effort principally rested upon the backs of Castilian peasants and merchants; and even at its height, the royal income from sources in the New World was only about one-quarter to one-third of that derived from Castile and its six million inhabitants.[10]

Throughout this treatise we are documenting how the powerful are wasting massive wealth battling over the world's wealth, identical to Robert Owen's analysis 200 years ago.

There Must Be Money Before Wealth

In a modern economy, credit money (trust) must be available. People would not produce beyond their immediate needs unless they knew they could safely lend that production (savings) and reclaim it when needed. Just like a powerful train or modern roads, money expedites the transfer of commodities between producers and consumers. Because it represents a set value of labor, a person can trade that value for equal value of any of the millions of items or services produced by other people.

If there are not enough savings to fully employ the resources, labor, and capital, it is a simple matter to create more money. This is the enormous power of money. So long as money contracts labor to produce needed products, the value represented by that money (the item or service produced) is real. First printed to contract labor for increased production of wealth, this money continues through the economy employing more labor for the needs of whoever passes it along the economic chain, or it is lent to others to finance their needs. Once an economy is fully employed and in balance, there is a continual circulation of these contracts against

labor we call money, and there is no need to print more. It is worth noting that the Federal Reserve does expand the money supply, supposedly for the reasons suggested.[11] It is, however, usually done for the wrong reasons—arming for and fighting wars, sustaining (rather than productively employing) those on welfare, and paying interest on America's own internal "debt trap."[12]

If there is to be trust in money, and if the financial machinery of a society is to function smoothly, there must be fair pay for productive labor. But with land, industrial capital (technology), and money capital subtly monopolized, it is not surprising that labor is underpaid. Much money is spent on siphoning more wealth away from the weak, graft spent for that same purpose, extravagant lifestyles, and wars to protect it all.

Allowing for protection of the environment and conservation of resources, if the best possible living standard for every person were society's goal, resources, labor, and industrial capital would be used to capacity through efficient contracting of all labor for true production. As technology improves and social efficiency increases, the decision will eventually have to be made that living standards are adequate at the current production level or that resources are inadequate to employ more labor. Working hours should then be reduced in step with that gain in efficiency without lowering living standards.

Here subtle monopolization becomes highly visible. Let us assume that society wrenched control of government from the powerful. Society could then print the necessary money to employ the idle labor and resources to produce the amenities of life many people are currently unable to obtain. Those who control land, capital, money capital, and fictitious capital would immediately protest that they have the capacity to produce for these needs. This would be true. However—within the American economy—unearned rent, unearned profits, and the fictitious wages of wasted labor siphon away at least 60 percent of productive labor's efforts without having produced anything of value to trade.[13] This creates unnecessarily high costs, leaves the underpaid and unemployed with insufficient money to contract for their needs, and assures that industrial capital will produce at some small fraction of capacity. If each person were productively employed, the average hours worked per week would shrink by half or more.

For those who look at every progressive recommendation as communist, remember that communism had as one of its specific goals the elimination of money. The philosophy suggested here considers money an indispensable tool for modern society. It only seeks to maximize money's efficiency, as any businessperson would his or her tools.

Learning the Secret of Bank-created Money

The secret of creating money was first learned by goldsmiths. Others' gold was deposited with them for safekeeping. Over time, goldsmiths learned that deposits were usually left for a substantial period, and they could safely make loans in the form of receipts for gold. These receipts circulated as money with the gold remaining on deposit. On balance, loans were paid off faster than the gold was reclaimed. Therefore, loans could be issued for several times the amount on deposit, and loans of several times the value of the deposited gold became "created" money.[14]

Whenever Rothschilds or other early bankers loaned ten certificates of gold at 10 percent interest, for every unit of gold they owned or held for safekeeping, each year their personal net worth would increase equal to all gold on deposit. When a banking system used gold or gold-backed currency as money, its creation of money was identical to that of the goldsmiths.

One hundred years ago, a prudent bank with $1 million in gold that decided to maintain its reserves at 10 percent could print $10 million in banknotes and loan them all that same day and $9 million of that would be bank-created money. A bank today with $1 million in reserves and a 10 percent reserve requirement could initially make only $900,000 in loans. But, as the money kept circulating back, it could loan 90 percent of each new reserve deposit and eventually would loan out $10 million, the same as the prudent banker 100 years ago. Assuming a sound economy and *prudent bankers,* the money created in a modern economy is backed by the wealth produced.

The thirteen American colonies printed money to fight the Revolutionary War but this power of government to create money was not used by the United States again in any great measure until President Lincoln printed greenbacks to finance the Civil War. As soon as the Civil War was over, the U.S. government ceased creating money and started pulling those greenbacks out of the economy. This destruction of money caused bankruptcies to soar for the first ten postwar years as wealth was again consolidated within the hands of entrenched wealth.[15] There was no need for those bankruptcies. If those greenbacks had been allowed to stand, and so long as there were unemployed resources and labor and consumer needs, that money would have continued to circulate freely within the economy, combining labor and industrial capital with America's immense natural wealth, and creating even more wealth.

While conservative banks were reining in loans, a post–Civil War level of $33.60 of gold or gold-backed currency in reserve for every

$100 on deposit dropping to $1 for each created dollar (as it was gold-backed, it was bank-created money) by 1913 hid the fact that greedy bankers loaned twenty to fifty times their reserves or even more. Banks pooled funds to cover runs on banks but runs on weak banks would spill over into runs on strong banks. With their depositors' money loaned out operating the economy, and thus not immediately collectable (illiquid), perfectly sound banks would go under and bankrupt many farms and businesses with them.

Primary Created Money and Circulation-created Money

Bankers substantially resolved their liquidity problems in 1913 through the establishment of the Federal Reserve System.[16] Since the Federal Reserve Act of 1913, U.S. banks that were members of the Federal Reserve System could not loan above a set multiple of their reserves. The reserve requirement of state chartered non-member banks varied for the next sixty-seven years, some requiring no reserves. In 1980, all U.S. banks were brought under the Federal Reserve System and, ever since, creation of money has been regulated by the Federal Reserve, not private banks.

Ever since all banks were brought under the Federal Reserve, it has been the circulation of money proper that creates money, not the banks themselves. Money already created by the U.S. Treasury or the Federal Reserve is only assisted by banks in its circulation and creation of more money, just as every other person through whose hands that money passes assists in money circulation and money creation. A bank cannot credit a customer's account unless that bank is already credited with those funds in its account at the Federal Reserve. In short, the first, or primary, money in the historic circulation of money is first created by the Federal Reserve or Treasury (government) through crediting a bank's reserves without debiting anyone's funds. When those credited reserves (primary created money) are loaned out, spent, and returned to a bank to be credited to their reserves and again loaned out, that is circulation-created money.

If a bank credits a borrower's account with $10,000, we are taught this is the creation of money by private banks. But that is not so. That bank must have 110 percent that much money credited to it in its reserve account at the Fed before that loan could be made. Not one cent will have been created except to the extent the borrower—and others into whose hands the money circulates—spends that money.

At any point in the circulation of that money, if the receiver puts it under the mattress instead of depositing it into a reserve account, no money has been created. But as soon as that person spends that money or deposits it into a reserve account, the money continues to circulate and create more money each time it changes hands.

So each person spending money is every bit as important in the creation of circulation money as the banks which credit their borrowers' accounts with 90 percent of their reserves. In fact, one could argue that the spenders of that money are more important. That money could be spent several times as cash, be counted each time, and, until someone deposits it in a bank from which it is loaned, there is no need to deduct any part for reserves.

The Fed's Open Market Operations Hide the Simplicity of Money Creation

To maintain the mystery of how simple money creation really could be, bankers conceived the devious Open Market Operations of the Fed. The interest on Treasury securities owned by the Fed was returned to the U.S. Treasury, leaving no other conclusion than that this money was surreptitiously created under cover of the Fed. By investors purchasing treasury notes, an original pool of U.S. treasuries was established. A part of the increase in reserves (primary created money) is from the U.S. Treasury selling bonds to the Fed and the Treasury essentially "printing" the money for the Fed to buy those bonds. The Treasury was thus spending what appeared to be money borrowed from the Fed but was actually money it had printed itself.[17]

The same applies to any treasuries purchased by the Fed to expand the money supply. Even if treasuries were originally purchased with private funds, that money has been spent and is now circulating within the economy as a part of the current money supply. When all the books are balanced, money used to purchase treasuries on the open market by the Fed can only be Treasury-created money. Any money printed and spent for government purposes or used to purchase treasuries on the open market, both expanding the money supply and neither debited from another account, is primary created money.

Money printed and spent by the U.S. Treasury and that used to purchase treasuries on the open market ends up in private bank reserve accounts from which, under current reserve requirements, 90 percent can be loaned out. Private borrowers would spend that loaned to them, and those borrowed and spent moneys would circulate within the economy and be deposited back into some bank's reserve account. Those increased reserves permit more loans, which are again spent within the economy, eventually returning to the banks to increase reserves again, to be loaned out again. Due to one bank's reserves being debited as another's are credited, there is no increase in reserves from

the circulation of money. But each time the Fed transfers reserves from one bank's reserve account to another bank's reserve account (via cashed checks), 90 percent of those transferred reserves can be loaned out. While there is no increase in reserves, there is an increase in loans (to a maximum multiple of ten times the original primary created money under today's 10 percent reserve requirements). Once the limit of money creation through circulation of money is reached, any further increase in the money supply requires either the Treasury openly printing more money for government expenditures, private banks borrowing from the Federal Reserve to increase their reserves (which is identical to openly printed money), or the Federal Reserve creating money through purchasing bonds in the market (which is again identical to openly printed money).[18]

The purchasing of treasury bonds on the open market is the Fed's primary money creation tool but, when one analyzes that the final owner of those treasuries, or goods and services from that created money, is the American people, all three methods of creating money function the same. The Fed's check is cashed, the banking system returns the check to the Fed for clearing. The Fed credits the bank in which that check was deposited with an increase in reserves equal to the face value of the check. However, no account is debited as it is with private checks presented to the Federal Reserve for clearance; it is all primary created money of which currently (1999) 90 percent can be loaned out. The loaned money is spent and is deposited back into some bank's reserves, 90 percent of those reserves are again loaned out, and this circulation continues until the money is too small an amount to consider.

At the current 10 percent reserve requirement, the banking system can loan out ten times the original primary created money. At a 5 percent reserve requirement, twenty times the original government-created money can be loaned out. It must be noted that before the Fed was established in the United States there were both government-created money and bank-created money, and bank-created money was primary. Currently there is only money printed by the Treasury under the cover of money being created by the Fed through purchase of T-bills on the open market. On balance, all other money is created from the circulation of this primary created money through the economy. (The Canadian banking system has had no reserve requirement for several years, so Canadian banks do create money.)

The interest paid by the U.S. Treasury on Fed-purchased T-bills goes to the Fed, which annually returns all that plus a part of other profits (currency trading, priced services to banks, etc.) to the Treasury. Thus in 1994 the Fed received $19.247 billion from the U.S. Treasury in interest on bonds and paid to the Treasury $20.470 billion, $1.223 billion more than it received in interest.

That the Fed is creating this money is all a shell game. The unpaid principal and interest on those Fed-purchased, and thus government-owned, bonds are simply credits and debits on the Fed's and Treasury's books. Both are government agencies and when interest is paid to the Fed by the Treasury it is promptly returned to the Treasury, thus proving there never was a debt to the Fed. Those Fed-held Treasury bonds are a charade. The Treasury could have openly created that money and bought back those treasuries, just as was done surreptitiously by the Fed. But this would have made the simplicity of non-debt-created money visible to all and maintaining that secret is the whole purpose of the charade.

Many will disagree with our statement, "both are government agencies." But the Fed is only technically owned by its member banks. If they really owned it, they would be receiving the interest on bonds owned by the Fed. In 1994, as discussed above, member banks received $212 million in dividends and $283 million for their mysterious "surplus fund," which only means the government should have received $20.965 billion instead of $20.470 billion.

Those Fed buildings were built with created money, operation costs are paid for by charges to banks, the Fed reports to Congress, and the payment of 97 percent of the profits of the Fed to the Treasury is proof that bankers know well that the Fed is an appendage to the Treasury and thus an arm of the federal government.

Under the fiction of ownership, bankers do control Fed policy. They do not have the courage to distribute amongst themselves the profits from those Fed-owned bonds, which proves they know themselves they do not own the Fed. The one-fifteenth of the federal debt owed by the Fed to the Treasury can be eliminated by simply writing it off. After all, one cannot owe money to oneself.

A growing economy requires more money, which banks obtain by selling government bonds to the Federal Reserve.[19] To pay for these bonds, when the Fed's check comes back to itself for clearing, the Fed simply credits the selling bank with that number of dollars without debiting from any account; it is primary created money. That primary created money is deposited into some bank's reserves and that bank can now make new loans at whatever multiple is dictated by reserve requirements; that is circulation-created money.

When loans are being made faster than they are being repaid, a multiple of the increase in loans is circulation-created money. When loans are being repaid faster than money is borrowed, the money disappears from an economy by that same multiple. It has been consumed or converted to real wealth owned by those who produced more than they consumed.

In a steady state economy, money is being destroyed (by consumption and depreciation) as fast as it is created or, if you prefer, created as fast as it is destroyed. To put it another way, consumption and production are in balance. The Treasury, rather than the Fed, could openly purchase bonds to increase the money supply and sell bonds to decrease the money supply. But this acknowledgement that the Fed is a public institution fronting for the Treasury would obligate private bankers to relinquish control of the Federal Reserve.

Whether used for fighting wars, building social infrastructure, expanding industry, or providing services, primary created money is continually circulating. Each time this money changes hands between a depositor in a reserve account and a borrower from those reserve accounts, it is used either to create value or purchase value. Each change of hands between saver and borrower is counted. This, we are taught, is the classic creation of money by banks. However, when checks are presented to a bank for deposit into one reserve account or for payment of that loan, the funds are deducted from another reserve account. The primary created monies, the reserve accounts, do not increase as money circulates.

So a bank making a loan based on reserves does not create money. Money circulation itself creates money. For the first loan of a classical circulation of money to have been made from a reserve account, the primary funds had to have been created by government printing money for social infrastructure or services, or by the Fed printing money through purchasing treasuries. A lowering of reserve requirements creates money but that is only an expansion of use of the originally created money.

If an economy is stable, savings within the circulation of money, in the form of continual crediting and debiting of reserve deposits, will continue to operate the economy. Although the speed of circulation has some bearing on quantity of money, an expansion of an economy typically will require the creation of more money.

Money is destroyed when it is deposited in a bank and not loaned back out. Pay off all debts and all that is left is circulating currency. When reserve deposit money quits circulating, money disappears from the economy even if vast pools of reserve deposits (potential circulating money) have built up. The moribund Japanese economy with $11 trillion in savings on the books (1998), as addressed above, is a prime example. If equity prices in Japan continue to fall, the fiction of $11 trillion on the books will be exposed. If the economy turns around and those equities rise, those savings will be valid.

It is a matter of semantics. One can claim the money creation process starts at any point. A person is creating money by writing a check without funds in the bank and then earning that money (we assume honestly through productive labor) and depositing it in the bank before the check comes in. The bank only balances the reserve deposits and loans. Assuming the earnings from that productive labor are in cash, no bank has made any loan and no one's reserve deposits are lowered, but money has been created.

All borrowers (consumers of the moment) are borrowing the deposits of all producers (savers of the moment). One may be borrowing from oneself, either from a checking account or out of pocket, and expecting to replenish the bank account or pocket change (savings).

The banking system keeps an account of these trades between people. Many are equal trades—in a month or year, most people earn roughly what they spend—but the unequal trades (more produced—earned—than spent, or more consumed—spent—than earned) are balanced by lending and borrowing deposited savings residing in banks' reserve accounts.

Some believe that it is by producing value that money is created. Commodities are produced and offered for sale, money is borrowed to buy them, and—on balance—the money received by the producer goes right back to the bank and essentially finances the sale of what was produced. Others hold that it is the offering of money that motivates production of wealth. The first argument is more accurate in describing the early use of money and the second is more typical of a modern economy.

As described throughout this author's *The World's Wasted Wealth 2* and the classics of Veblen, Chase, Borsodi, and others, it is possible to be paid but not produce value. If the purchasers think they are receiving value, in the current monetary system that is tantamount to real value. However, if money contracted only productive labor and full value were paid for that labor, then money would represent a more realistic value and would become a symbol of actual wealth. Money would then be only a tool, a symbol for the trade of productive labor.

Under conditions of equal rights (when each person is fairly paid for his or her genuinely productive work), money lent combines land, labor, and capital to produce full value in needed goods and services. A society can be fully productive only if each of its citizens is fully productive. Neither money nor the economy can become truly efficient until all nonproductive siphoning of wealth through unequal trades in value, as opposed to producing and trading equal value, is eliminated. Likewise, every contracting of labor for nonproductive use must, on final analysis, be paid for by others' loss of the fruits of their productive labor.

A Banking System Structured to Protect the Rights of All

People unproductively attached to the arteries of commerce, either for making a living or making fortunes, see only their momentary self-interest and will not permit the necessary changes. Because of the Social Control belief systems perpetuated through the university system and the media (see Part I), only under extreme crisis can change be imposed upon them. For the sake of precision and clarity, and recognizing that only small changes are likely and then only under severe crisis, we will be outlining a fully reconstructed banking system.

Let's assume that an economically viable, highly educated population emigrates and starts up a brand-new economy in virgin territory and is planning to manage it honestly, equally, and efficiently. There are no labor-created values in this virgin territory but this population brings with them basic industrial tools and have the knowledge to run an economy and create a new nation. These modern Pilgrims arrive with the papers already prepared to establish a Treasury to create money, a Federal Reserve to keep account of this new nation's trades through debiting and crediting between bank reserves, and private bankers to provide a place to deposit savings and from these bank reserves to provide loans for both production and consumption.

The Treasury is empowered to create money for combining their industrial tools (capital) and labor with the plentiful resources to produce the necessities of life, basic infrastructure, and more industrial tools. The primary created money that created that wealth is deposited into reserve deposits where 90 percent is loaned out, circulated within the community, returned as new reserve deposits, and is continually loaned out again.

This primary created money, and the circulation of that money, finances cutting and sawing timber, mining ore, smelting ore, producing machine tools, building shoe and textile factories, building factories to produce consumer durables, building retail outlets, and so forth. Of course, to make the function of money and banking visible, we have theoretically shrunk two generations of building industrial and social capital into a few cycles of the creation and circulation of money.

So long as there is surplus labor, unused resources, and a social need not cared for through the current circulation of money, a nation's treasury can properly create (print) primary money. A society can design the proper balance between money creation and money destruction. The proper balance between wealth creation and wealth destruction (consumption) will mirror that proper money balance.

Efficient money will be so productive it will quickly strip the earth's resources. Thus the creation of money must be planned within the earth's resource capacity and its ability to absorb society's wastes without ecological destruction. In a nation's early development stage—so long as there are surplus labor, resources, and industry—primary money can be created to build schools, roads, railroads, electric power, sanitation, and post offices. Such infrastructure makes society far more efficient and the wealth created backs the new money. This productive wealth provides the backing for the money created to produce it and the commodities and services produced are the wealth that both backs and absorbs the circulating money operating those industries and services.

When primary created money is spent for de-velopment, society owns what is built with it. When primary created money is spent as a subsidy to capital, it becomes a part of capitalists' capital. If it is spent as a subsidy to labor, this primary created money becomes circulation money and, depending on how profitable the economy is, the share retained by capital may be more or less than the original primary created money.

To the extent an economy needs an increase in the money supply, federal, state, and local needs and basic infrastructure (roads, railroads, schools, etc.) could be financed by Treasury-created money and there would be no debt. To the extent there are unemployed workers, unused resources, unused industrial capital, and unmet human needs—and taking into consideration the capacity of the earth to recycle wastes to protect resources, ecology, and environment for future generations—it is only necessary for a nation's treasury to create the money to employ those labor and resources and meet those needs.

Instead of almost exclusively lending against equity, bankers would need to be knowledgeable about community needs and lend appropriately for those needs. Each region and each community should have equal rights to a nation's (or the world's) savings and equal rights to created money.

So long as an economy is expanding productively, and providing value to be purchased by this newly created money, there is no need to tax the public for constructing public buildings or providing services. However, if there are not the idle resources or labor to expand wealth production, creation of money will create inflation. If there is not to be an expansion of wealth production, public construction and operation of governments must come out of taxes.

Through a ''Revolving Reserve Account,'' total deposits and loans of each individual bank should be accounted for just as they are now through banks debiting and crediting customer accounts and the Fed debiting and crediting bank reserves. Reserve requirements should be regulated just as now. Banks should be collectors and loaners of the nation's savings, just as now. All loan institutions should be brought under reserve requirements. All money loaned above the revolving reserves would be created by the Treasury Department (which is just as now except the accounting of Treasury-created money is buried in a fictional debt of the Treasury to the Fed).[20]

The Fed can lower margin requirements where loan needs are high (poorer regions which need development, regions of natural disaster, etc.) and raise margin requirements in booming sectors of the economy. (That would be primarily the "paper" sector—stocks, derivatives, currency speculations, commodities, and bonds, which each should have the purely speculative aspect, but not the entrepreneurial speculative aspect, eliminated.) The affluent sectors of the economy awash in funds are thus rebalanced with the undeveloped sectors deprived of finance capital.

There should be *local rights to finance capital*. Each region and each bank should have "rights" to, and pay interest on, its share of created money and savings, but only the national treasury should create primary money. The creation of money would be by a formula established by law and, adjustable to the needs or surpluses of a region, automatically distributed. There would be neither control by an elite nor control by politics. It would be a formula of regional, local, and individual rights to created money and savings. The sucking of regional money to money center banks to be used for speculation would disappear.

The success of local currencies proves that regions, localities, and individuals are denied

their full rights to finance capital. But local scrip is not legal tender, not universally accepted, and thus limited in circulation. With banks attuned to take care of those needs, each locality would, in the form of rights to finance capital, effectively have its local currency and, because it is legal tender and can be spent anywhere, it would be much more efficient than current local currency schemes.

The Populists of the late nineteenth century studied banking reform. We will repeat William Greider's description of their conclusions. Their agenda

> became a sourcebook for political reforms spanning the next fifty years: a progressive income tax; federal regulation of railroads, communications, and other corporations; legal rights for labor unions; government price stabilization and credit programs for farmers.... The populist plan would essentially employ the full faith and credit of the United States government directly to assist the "producing classes" who needed financing for their enterprises. In effect, the government would *circumvent the bankers and provide credit straight to the users.... The government would provide "money at cost," instead of money lent by merchants and bankers at thirty-five or fifty or a hundred per cent interest.*[21]

There have been many reforms since those days of blatant extortion by the owners of finance capital, but "the money-creation system that Congress adopted in 1913 [and reformed during the Great Depression] ... preserved the private banking system as the intermediary that controlled the distribution of new money and credit."[22]

That current exorbitant interest rates are unnecessary was demonstrated by early Scottish bankers, whose thrift is so well known that even today a person careful with his or her money is called "Scotch." In the nineteenth century, the universal practice of Scottish banks was to set interest on loans between 1 and 2 percent above that paid depositors. Their innovative practices are still considered a model of banking stability.[23] With the proper banking service charge having been well established at 1 to 2 percent for small-volume banking using expensive hand accounting, 1 percent would be a proper service charge for large-volume banking using inexpensive computerized accounting.

During the stable years following World War II, the real rate of interest in the United States (allowing for inflation) hovered between that 1 and 2 percent. Previously, the normal world rate had been 2 to 3 percent.[24] Although the real rate of interest in the United States during what were considered the best years the world economy has ever known was under 2 percent, we will allow the highest long-term average real rate of interest, 3 percent, as a fair rate. With subtle monopolization and the waste it engenders eliminated, with labor fully paid for its fully productive labor, and with true interest at the high end of historical norms, both capital (stored labor) and current labor would be well paid. People would save, and those savings would be available for productive investments.

There need be nothing more than checking accounts paying, by law, 3 percent interest. Each person's checking and savings would be the same account. Interest rate controls would eliminate money market instruments and the attendant wasted labor competing for deposits. Detractors may decry this as a loss of their rights. But the only right lost is that of the powerful to intercept the production of others' labor, especially those pure gamblers whose wagers in the world market casinos amount to at least fifty times the investment, labor, commodity, bond, and loan activity in the real economy.

In every banking system, total debits and credits will balance (withdrawals equaling deposits). With a fully integrated banking system, any deviation from that balance could be quickly corrected by loan policy. The visible flow of funds would be the economic pulse of the nation. Any unexplained deficit in one bank could be immediately looked into while normal deficits are balanced by others' normal surpluses. The economy would be easily balanced by increasing or decreasing the interest rate for consumer credit and/or decreasing or increasing it for investment in productive capital

As a tool under a banking authority (under community control), money can fine-tune an economy to the maximum capacity of resources and labor. It must be emphasized that such a truly efficient society could quickly consume the world's resources and pollute the environment. The needs of a society must be balanced with conservation of these resources and protection of the environment. As Part IV demonstrates, this can be done only with social policy firmly under social control—not under corporate, finance monopoly control.

To provide an adequate living standard for all people and still protect the world's resources and environment, a balance between a respectable living standard and the capacity of the earth's resources and ecosystem would have to be reached. Assuming centers of capital could no longer siphon the world's wealth to themselves and then waste it battling over that wealth as we have suggested, societies could then progress calmly. To prevent inflation, an empowered Treasury/Federal Reserve could both restrict creation of money and/or increase interest rates. Energy taxes (really landrent taxes) can be quickly raised to pull surplus money out of an economy or lowered to put more money into the economy. To prevent inflation, interest and/or energy taxes flowing to the Treasury could be increased where that money would be destroyed by virtue of not loaning it back out. To prevent deflation, an empowered Treasury need only lower interest rates and/or create more money.

The opportunity to restructure could happen by default. In all banking crises in all countries, massive public funds are infused into the banking system to stabilize it. Under the rules of capitalism, those whose money is invested own, and make decisions on, that property.[25]

As Eastern Europe and the former Soviet Union have demonstrated, restructuring any society is painful. But restructuring to honest banking after a financial crisis will stabilize, not destabilize, an economy. As one integrated banking system, all loan institutions, including money markets, should be subject to reserve requirements and regulated interest. The regulated interest rate on savings should be a real rate of 3 percent, which, as typically the bank rate paid on savings is less than the rate of inflation, is much more than most of the world's banks are now paying.

Even with a nation's Treasury Department as the only creator of money, countries cannot control their finance markets except by coordinated action of the major currency nations. To prevent flight of capital, all major countries would have to act simultaneously to bring money markets under control.

Most countries' banks are publicly owned and currencies in the world banking system cannot escape even from a private banking system such as in America. Whenever a serious policy dispute erupts between any country (Iran, Iraq, Cuba, North Korea) and the United States, their dollar accounts throughout the world are frozen. Every trade financed by money capital of any currency just creates a change in bank reserves at the central bank for that currency. If that central bank does not honor a transaction in its currency, no money can change hands. The U.S. central bank (the Federal Reserve) can control dollars anywhere in the world. Theoretically other countries can control their currencies but this is true only of countries that are economically powerful. The power to discount currencies of weak nations gives powerful nations effective control over other nations' currency values.

With coordinated action to bring the world's money markets within a banking system with required reserves and regulated interest, bidding for a nation's savings—and all other subtle methods of finance monopolization—can be eliminated. Nothing is more important to a nation than productive use of its investment funds, and nothing is more important to the world than the stability of currency and commodity markets. We next discuss how to control these volatile markets while creating honest money for the world. This too must happen before an honest world banking system can be established.

Inflation, Deflation, and Constant Value: Creating Honest Money

Eliminating inflation and deflation and maintaining a constant-value currency while expanding the money supply to finance true production and distribution are as simple as, and an extension of, the obsolete gold standard. A banking authority need only tie its money to the value of ''a basket of thirty or more of the most commonly used commodities—gold, wheat, soybeans, rice, steel, copper, etc.''[26] The uncontrolled money markets can be brought within the banking system by law and required to deposit reserves with the Federal Reserve. To establish this stable-value money, a nation's treasury/central reserve could use a part of the reserves to buy commodity contracts and would be the official arbitrageur for those contracts. As this use only replaces previous users of these same reserves, this does not reduce the money supply (reserves) operating the economy. Ralph Borsodi, economist and lifetime promoter of a banking authority issuing money backed by a broad base of commodities, sums it up:

> The essential difference [between speculation and arbitrage in commodity and currency markets] is that the arbitrageur buys and sells [contracts of different maturity dates] simultaneously [on different markets] while the speculator buys and sells at different times. The effect of arbitrage on price movements is to stabilize them; the effect of speculation is to intensify them. If arbitrage were to be conducted on a large enough and wide enough scale, speculation would become less and less enticing. But perhaps even more than this, if it were to be promoted and practiced by an independent international agency such as the bank-of-issue I am calling for on the magnitude this would make possible, it would stabilize prices to such a degree that stabilization as a serious problem would disappear. Stabilization would make speculation peripheral instead of central in the determination of the prices of basic commodities of the world.[27]

It is not necessary to wait for a nation to establish honest money. Any international bank could do so by establishing a commodity market database, updating it continuously by computer, and agreeing to debit and credit trades in a constant value backed by this "basket of commodities." In the currency markets, with the value of this new money indexed to, and backed by, those commodities, other currencies would adjust their value to this constant value and those currency values too would be updated continuously. With the risk of loss eliminated, the contracts of international traders would be tied to constant-value accounts and they would accept payments and make payments at that constant value. Commodity-basket contracts would be purchased with these reserve deposits. When a demand was made on that account, they would convert the money to the currency demanded using its commodity basket value, pay the demand, and debit the account. The natural function of the market pays owners of those contracts and, rather than interest on loans, normal holding profits would be made on commodity contracts. As currently commodity contracts require funding, there would be no increase in demand for finance capital. Financing would only shift from speculation financing to stability financing.

Once enough constant-value accounts were established, incoming and outgoing money would roughly balance. As the purpose is to maintain the broad average of values, the bank commodities traders would do no speculating. They would be selling contracts approaching their delivery dates and buying new ones of later delivery dates. The security provided by this constant-value money would be so attractive that it would drain money from other banks and money markets, which would have to follow suit or lose deposits. "We will have Gresham's law operating in reverse; good money will be driving bad money out of circulation."[28]

With the pattern established, commodity markets could also establish contracts for this basket of commodities and update its value continuously. It would be most economical to include the maximum amount of commodities in one basket, and all countries, banks, and markets could index their money to this same standard. If done properly, there would be one international currency. Any bank in any country could then buy these commodity-basket contracts to back constant-value reserve deposits and sell them to debit demands against those reserve deposits.

In the currency markets, the value of any currency relative to that stable money would be available to everyone at all times. The more banks and countries that backed their money with these commodity-basket contracts, the fewer funds they would need to keep in reserve to protect their money. If all countries tied their currencies to these stable values and speculation were eliminated, world trades would match currency transfers and all would have a secure international currency that could be redeemed by simply spending it in the marketplace. The "national character of currencies would be of no consequence, since they would be but different tokens representing the same commodities."[29] Their value could be realized simply by being spent.

With speculation eliminated, the value of all contracts, and thus the money required to fund them, would equal the value of all commodities in transit and storage. So long as the elimination of market speculation was maintained, all money would retain its value relative to those commodity contracts.

If producers and buyers organized into respective trade associations that continually analyzed world supply and demand, this would not eliminate the producers' opportunity as sellers to maximize their prices or as buyers the right to minimize prices.[30] That would still be subject to supply and demand.

Because banks could not protect against counterfeiting, they would issue credits but could not print currency. But with computers to verify a customer through thumb prints, infrared thermogram images of palm, artery, vein, eye pattern, and signature scanning (procedures now being market tested), a check on a constant-value account would be equal to currency. This would attract world traders looking for secure currency and other countries would have to follow suit or lose finance capital. As it can protect against counterfeiting, any nation that desired stable money values could print a constant-value currency and protect it with commodity-basket contracts. This would be of high value to world travelers desiring constant-value currency.

Money "cannot be stabilized unless trade is stable."[31] Assuming the shenanigans—selling short, futures on options, and other "derivative products" designed within the worldwide market casino to accelerate the siphoning of wealth from the weak and innocent to the powerful and clever—were eliminated, each country would produce commodities equal to the contracts sold by its firms and industries. The more waste that is eliminated and replaced by true production and efficient distribution, the more commodity contracts a country can sell, the more of others' commodities they can buy, and the wealthier it will be. Assuming subtle monopolizations were eliminated, all had access to capital and markets, and these newly capitalized countries formed trade associations to sell their commodities and labor at fair market prices (meaning elimination of the massive wage differentials between equally productive labor worldwide), each currency would be valued and backed by its nation's production. Understanding and implementing this process would be the best method of minimizing waste, maximizing production, protecting a nation's wealth, and organizing a peaceful, wealthy world.

To depositors who kept an adequate bank balance, credit cards could be issued in this constant-value money. A part of these funds would be invested in constant-value commodity-basket contracts. Once constant-value money was widely used, countries could no longer debase their currency by printing money for non-productive purposes. It would be immediately discounted in the markets, citizens would flock to the constant-value money, and nothing would be gained (meaning their citizens' wealth could not be arbitrarily siphoned away by inflation induced by their government). Neither could external powers siphon away their wealth through discounting their currency and thus deflating its value.

With stable constant values, individuals not using those commodities or currencies in their businesses would no longer borrow society's finance capital to speculate in commodity markets, nor would they do so with their own cash. Protected by constant-value money backed by the world's commodities, true producers would not need to speculate. Speculation in commodity and currency markets would cease and the funds of both speculators and true producers would be available for true investment.[32] Commodity prices would decrease by whatever amount was once siphoned away by these gamblers and confidence in constant-value money would increase efficiencies in international trade, creating even more values. Individual commodities could suffer temporary losses in value but average values would remain stable and those stabilized values would virtually eliminate world economic collapses.

During the adjustment to a balanced economy with honest money, losses by one group and gains by another through inflation or deflation could be eliminated by indexing reserve deposits and loans to commodity-basket values. Of course, by that indexing (assuming wages were included), a country would be placing its

currency on a commodity-basket standard and responsible law would require that the printing of money could not exceed any increase in a nation's commodity or service production.[33]

Any printing of money for nonproductive purposes would be offset by corresponding changes in currency values. Once all commodity contracts were owned by the world's treasuries/central reserves, with banks backing reserve deposits and businesses dealing in those commodities, the world would have achieved honest money. Therefore, if ever commodity-basket backed money were started anyplace, it could eventually force honest money on the world.

Accumulation of Capital Through Cooperative Capitalism

Powerful bankers thousands of miles away have no concept of local needs and no loyalty to local people. Farmers, homeowners, and small businesses are strapped for finance capital with their locally produced wealth siphoned thousands of miles away and lent to stock speculators, merger and takeover artists, currency speculators, and other gamblers in the worldwide market casino.

It will be a simple matter to calculate finance capital needs and assign a loan surcharge to all loans to go into a socially owned capital accumulation fund kept in, and loaned from, local banks. Capital needs of each region, state, county, and community could be calculated. So long as there are surplus labor and resources and real value is to be produced, finance capital can be obtained through printing money (primary created money). But once the capital accumulation fund is established, it will largely replenish itself through loan repayments. Once fully funded, a capital accumulation loan surcharge need be only enough to cover economic expansion and loan losses.

A quick analysis of the simplicity of a socially owned capital accumulation fund makes it clear that capital accumulated in the past through monopolization has gone for many other things besides society's finance capital needs, primarily for extravagant living without reciprocally expended productive labor and for wild, not entrepreneurial, speculation.

Every alert entrepreneur knows that the big profits end up with those who call the tune with their money. With a socially owned capital accumulation fund, instead of capital accumulation through monopolies (as addressed in Part IV), citizens with sound ideas, but no capital, would have the opportunity to realize the profits from their abilities and accumulate capital in their own names. Wealth, now accumulated by true producers, would quickly diffuse itself broadly and relatively equally throughout the population.

Just as each individual has rights, regions and communities should have rights to their share of a nation's finance capital. By outlawing the borrowing of social funds for speculation in the worldwide gambling casino (but not borrowing for new speculative enterprises), and giving each community or region rights to capital, a national banking authority could guide lending into productive channels throughout the nation. An international authority could guide capital to productive channels worldwide. Regional authorities could lend productively within their region, and local authorities within their locality. A nation's banking system would then be structured for the maximum support of all its citizens, and the needs of other countries would be receiving attention. Society could set a minimum housing standard and eventually reach that goal; innovative businesses should have high priority, but a society could give equal priority to ecological protection, farms, homes, schools, roads, parks, public buildings, or whatever investment would maximize that society's well-being.

Assuming they had access to voters through reserved TV channels as advocated in the final chapter and were elected to a single ten- to twelve-year term, regional directors could be freed of political pressures. These directors could oversee their region's financial rights, with directors to oversee state, county, and community funding rights. A national director should be little more than an umpire overseeing the equitable sharing of the nation's finance capital as outlined in law or, better yet, the Constitution. If those rights of access to capital were coupled with the elimination of unnecessary labor, with the remaining productive jobs shared, and if equally productive work were equally paid, there would be equality relative to one's ability and energy expended.

Consumer credit (within limits) should be a right instantly available, just as it has been pioneered by computerized credit cards. Risks would be minimal once the technology was in place to confirm identity (many such procedures are now being market tested). Each person's right to credit would be tempered by being subject to standards much as they are now, and the local credit union—now an integrated member of the banking system—would be in a position to know a member's creditworthiness. Local bankers should best know the needs of society and the creditworthiness of those who borrow to build and produce for that society. If not, they should not be bankers.

The American economy has been dynamic

due to the hopes and dreams of its citizens. These hopes are the motivation for the millions of small businesses springing up. The economic health of a nation requires that those with ideas, talents, and energy have access to finance capital. With rights to credit, a nation's talented can bring together land, labor, capital, and technology at the right time and in the right place to fulfill society's needs. If there is a shortage of finance capital for productive use, and the resources are available and can be used without destroying the environment, a nation's treasury can quickly create the money to increase the reserves of the private banking system.

Only individuals operating under free enterprise and competition can develop the millions of ideas necessary for the progress of science, industry, and society. In order for citizens to fulfill these visions and provide their special expertise, it is necessary that they have access to credit. With entrepreneurs having rights to finance capital and banking personnel trained to be generous, yet careful, innovation in production by business and industry (productive speculation) would be unhampered.

Credit is now rationed by the simple method of checking track records and lending up to a certain percentage of the borrower's equity—a great rule for monopolists. "Loans are made in a very impersonal way—everything depends on 'track record,' and if you don't have a 'track record' [or equity], as most young people do not—you can forget it."[34] Access to investment capital should be a right based on productive merit as well as collateralized equity. Thus credit for productive people in their first ventures would be easier to obtain. With employees of the banking authority trained to be alert to productive investment requests, these loans would be quite simple. When a loan request was

received, an evaluation would be made of its potential productive and financial success. If it looked reasonable, the loan would be approved. This is precisely how loans were made for the first fifteen to twenty years after World War II. It was only after wealth started becoming reentrenched that banking reverted to primarily loans against equity.

With the elimination of capitalized values in land, monopolized capital, and "fictitious capital," there will not be these artificial values against which to lend. But neither will money capital be needed to purchase these fictitious values. Smaller loans will be backed by a smaller, but more secure, true value. A loan would, of course, require financial accountability by the borrower just as it does now.

With initial capital promised from the regional capital accumulation fund, an entrepreneur could issue stock for the rest of his or her financial needs and this primary bank loan would be secure. With elimination of subtle communication monopolies (addressed next), those who buy this stock will be investing risk capital directly into production rather than having to go through finance monopolies that will claim most of the physical and intellectual labors involved in the endeavor.

It is not necessary to lend strictly to owners who would then hire workers. Those with insight need only prepare a prospectus describing the product or service, market potential, profit expected, financial requirement, and labor needs. The loan institution would study the proposal and—assuming the ideas were sound and beneficial to the community—would approve the loan. Workers would study the prospectus, and agree to 10 to 20 percent of their wages being deducted to buy 60 to 80 percent of the stock.

With workers owning a share of an industry

and a share of their wages being used to pay off the loan as we have suggested earlier, the owners of this capital would be true producers. Society would be receiving useful products or services. It would receive landrent from the increased economic activity. And the nation's savers and national treasury would be fully paid for providing finance capital.

With these triple benefits to society, bankers should be taught to pay close attention to requests for investment credits; they are the sinews of capitalism. Most workers would stay on the job, but, once the new business was secure and their new stock had capitalized value, the talented ones would search out another prospectus, help develop another business, train more workers, gain more capitalized value, and move on again. Labor would be both mobile and highly productive just as capital is now and the most productive of those workers would be the accumulators of capital. This would be mobilization of labor without the dispossession that has been so typical of past capitalization processes. Labor would have the same rights to gains in efficiencies of technology as investors now have. The talented would be in high demand by the developers of industry.

Besides collateral protection, there are three flows of money that make those loans secure— landrent, profits, and a share of wages. Society's collection of landrent could, and should, permit it to accept a larger share of the risks of new entrepreneurs. Every success increases the use value, and thus the rental value, of that land. The risk of uncollateralized investment loans could also be offset by a higher interest charge to go into an insurance fund. With these restructured borrowing rights, many more people would qualify for investment capital than under equity loans. If entrepreneurs were successful,

they and their workers, through the shares purchased, would own that capital honestly, as opposed to the current custom of capitalizing values through subtle monopolization of social wealth.

Those searching for a higher return—and confident they have found good investments— could directly employ their capital. Those who wished to, and who could find the opportunity to lend their savings at a higher rate, would be free to do so. But they could no longer obtain high profits by simple tribute for the use of subtly monopolized capital. Those who once bid for money market funds would now have to compete for loans on their projects' productive merits. This would eliminate pure speculation with social funds while retaining that right with personal funds.

Once restructured, a society will have to address the increased efficiencies and technology's massive reduction of labor needs. They must then reduce labor time and share the productive jobs. If this is not done, new monopolizers will be created.

A socially owned capital accumulation fund will eliminate the centers of power created through monopoly capital accumulation that have historically controlled governments and maintained the wealth-siphoning system and its inevitable wars.

As we discussed above, Japan operated just such a capital accumulation fund and utilized it with a vengeance to reach its current position in world trade. As other nations have to survive, we do not suggest a nation's international trade capital accumulation fund be that aggressive, but it would be great protection against predatory trade practices.

(The subchapters ''If Society Collected Landrent, All Other Taxes Could Be Eliminated,'' ''Creation of Money'' and ''Investment'' are extensions of this subchapter.)

Negative Interest

Throughout the expansion and stable stages of business cycles, most property and business owners clearly recognized that a steady inflation rate increased their property values faster than interest on money borrowed. Entrepreneurs recognized that this negative interest carried them through the early tough years until their business matured and this had a lot to do with establishing a productive economy.

Where slightly negative interest rates were the rule during the early and middle stages of an economic cycle, supernegative interest rates were the rule in bubble phases of economic cycles. When those bubbles collapsed, loans then carried superpositive interest rates with all the destructive forces a theoretician would expect.

Negative interest can function well on the investment side of the ledger of an economy but not on the savings side. Money saved is properly only a symbol for produced wealth. In a modern economy, where capital accumulation depends upon the individual savings of millions of people, there would be inadequate investment money if savings decreased in value each year.

Money: A Measure of Productive Labor Value

Citizens judge the value of most commodities by imperfect memory and comparison. Witness our exposure in the next chapter of unnecessary costs built into the price of products and services. Our earlier research, documenting distribution through unnecessary labor, outlines even greater unnecessary costs.[35] Using money to contract only for productive employment would give a true measure of labor value to every product and service. It is the responsibility of the leaders of society to maintain an honest relationship between the compensation paid capital and labor to produce and distribute commodities and services, and the price charged the consumer.

This philosophy—first proposed by the founders of free-enterprise philosophy, the French physiocrats—can become reality only by eliminating the unearned share of income from landrent, monopolized capital, fictitious capital, and fictitious wages. All inflate costs and siphon to nonproducers the wealth created by truly productive labor. This does not limit a person's right to contract out his or her labor, or to contract for others' labor. It eliminates the nonproductive element of contracts siphoning away the labor of others. If the labor value of wealth is protected from inflated fictional values, the value of the symbol of wealth (money) will be stable. The public will then much more accurately judge values and society will function efficiently and equitably.

With proper control of society's money we could have full employment, stable prices, low interest rates, and stable exchange rates. If this could be managed, there would be no inflation, deflation, recessions, or depressions (except from natural disasters or war). How to achieve a peaceful and just society is no secret; what is required just conflicts with the privileges of powerful people.

Notes

1. William F. Hixson, *It's Your Money* (Toronto: COMER, 1997); T.R. Thoren and R.F. Warner, *The Truth in Money Book* (Chagrin Falls, Ohio: Truth in Money, 1994).

2. Joel Kurtzman, *The Death of Money* (New York: Simon and Schuster, 1993), p. 11.

3. William Greider, *Secrets of the Temple* (New York: Simon and Schuster, 1987), p. 335.

4. John Kenneth Galbraith, *Money* (Boston: Houghton Mifflin, 1976), pp. 62–70.

5. Ibid., pp. 167–78; Greider, *Secrets of the Temple*, pp. 228, 282.

6. Philip S. Foner, *From Colonial Times to the Founding of the American Federation of Labor* (New York: International, 1947), p. 67.

7. S.P. Breckinridge, *Legal Tender* (New York: Greenwood Press, 1969), chapter 7; Galbraith, *Money*, pp. 72–75.

8. Carl Cohen, ed., *Communism, Fascism, Democracy* (New York: Random House, 1962), pp. 13–14; Paul Kennedy, *The Rise and Fall of the Great Powers* (New York: Random House, 1987), p. 53.

9. Galbraith, *Money*, pp. 18–19.

10. Kennedy, *Rise and Fall of the Great Powers*, p. 53.

11. Marcia Stigum, *Money Markets* (Homewood, IL: Dow Jones-Irwin, 1978), p. 18.

12. Donald L. Barlett and James B. Steele, *America: What Went Wrong?* (Kansas City: Andrews and McMeel), 1992, p. 51.

13. J.W. Smith, *The World's Wasted Wealth 2* (San Luis Obispo, CA: Institute for Economic Democracy, 1994).

14. E.K. Hunt and Howard J. Sherman, *Economics* (New York: Harper and Row, 1990), pp. 491–93, 505–508.

15. Thoren and Warner, *Truth in Money*, pp. 120–24.

16. William F. Hixson, *Triumph of the Bankers: Money and Banking in the Eighteenth and Nineteenth Centuries* (Westport, CT: Praeger, 1993), chapter 23; Hixson, *It's Your Money*, chapter 7.

17. Hixon, *It's Your Money*, chapters 5, 6.

18. Ibid.

19. Greider, *Secrets of the Temple*, pp. 61–62.

20. Hixson, *It's Your Money*, chapters 5, 6.

21. Greider, "Annals of Finance," *The New Yorker*, November 16, 1987, pp. 72, 78, emphasis added.

22. Ibid.

23. George Tucker, *The Theory of Money and Banks Investigated* (New York: Greenwood Press, 1968), pp. 219, 255.

24. Michael Moffitt, *The World's Money* (New York: Simon and Schuster, 1983) p. 197; John H. Makin, *The Global Debt Crisis* (New York: Basic Books, 1984), p. 162.

25. Greider, *Secrets of the Temple*, p. 630; Christian Miller, "Wall Street's Fondest Dream: The Insanity of Privatizing Social Security," *Dollars and Sense* (November/December 1998), pp. 30–35; Edward S. Herman, "The Assault on Social Security," *Z Magazine* (November 1995), pp. 30–35; Merton C. Bernstein and Joan Brodshaug Bernstein, *Social Security: The System That Works* (New York: Basic Books, 1988).

26. Ralph Borsodi, *Inflation* (Great Barrington, MA: E.F. Schumacher Society, 1989). See also Irving Fisher's work in the 1930s; Arjun Makhijani, *From Global Capitalism to Economic Justice* (New York: Apex Press, 1992), pp. 121–27, appendix; Michael Barratt Brown, *Fair Trade* (London: Zed Books, 1993), especially pp. 53–63, 150; Kurtzman, *Death of Money*, p. 236.

27. Borsodi, *Inflation*, p. 73.

28. Ibid., p. 8.

29. Ibid.

30. Brown, *Fair Trade*, especially pp. 53–63, 150.

31. William Greider, "The Money Question," *World Policy Journal* (Fall 1988), p. 608.

32. Only if there are substantial price movements will speculators be interested. "When for a time in the 1970s the price of copper was held fairly steady many dealers went out of business. There was nothing to speculate on in that market (Brown, *Fair Trade*, p. 56).

33. Julian Schuman, *China: An Uncensored Look* (Sagaponack, NY: Second Chance Press, 1979), pp. 49–50, 160.

34. Robert Swann, *The Need for Local Currencies* (Great Barrington, MA: E.F. Schumacher Society, 1990), p. 6.

35. Smith, *The World's Wasted Wealth 2*.

27

Subtly Monopolizing Information

The technology is at hand to educate a population for as little as 5 to 15 percent of what is considered normal today. Here the developing world has the opportunity to make an end run around the developed world. Restructuring in the developed world is prevented because information is monopolized by the financial power of the three primary monopolies, land, technology, and finance capital. To open the channels of communication to the masses as suggested herein is to lose control of those monopolies.

Control of information controls people (albeit without their realization), which in turn protects these subtle monopolies. This process ensures that the distribution of wealth will remain in the same channels going to approximately the same people. Wealth will circulate among a predetermined group of people as they each intercept a part of social production. These Social Control belief systems are kept firmly in place through subtle monopolization of the communications industry. And it requires no conspiracy. Each one does just what you or I would do: they protect the source of their livelihood and wealth.

The Television Industry's Capitalized Value

Commercial television makes so much money doing its worst, it can't afford to do its best.
—Harry F. Waters and Janet Huck,
"The Future of Television"

Communication is considered cheap. Yet it is possible to make long-distance contacts for a fraction of current costs. By 1967, scientists had determined they could build a satellite powerful enough to broadcast directly to home television sets. This satellite would simultaneously handle transoceanic phone calls for about a penny a minute (about ten cents in 1998 dollars) and phone call charges would easily cover the cost of TV transponders included in the satellites.[1] However, *U.S. News & World Report* predicted at the time that, "The big decision will be made by statesmen and politicians, not by scientists."[2]

With hundreds of TV channels available to every home piggybacking on telephone satellites, and assuming those small costs were paid for by all society (pennies per person), monopolization of the TV broadcast spectra would have been eliminated. Of course, democratic access to the masses over cheap airways for any group who could build a broadcasting station (at a cost of a few hundred thousand dollars thirty years ago) was not acceptable to the powerful who controlled the communications airways. Those few hundred thousand dollars in tangible construction costs per station would be converted to hundreds of millions of dollars of capitalized value if monopolized.

Politicians were influenced not only by owners of regional broadcasting and cable television stations, but by major corporations who wanted to manipulate consumers' buying choices. These interests were so successfully protected that cheap direct broadcast never became a reality until the signal scrambling/unscrambling technology maintaining a monopoly was developed. The primary reason for strictly controlling television channels is to concentrate the audience for advertisers. Corporations will not pay premium rates if TV broadcasting is so cheap that several hundred program choices are available at any one moment. The audience would be so fragmented that any one channel would reach only limited numbers of consumers.[3]

In 1973, "television stations in major markets earn[ed] 90- to 100-percent return[s] on tangible investments annually."[4] A TV station in Tampa, Florida, which had been bought in 1979 for an already inflated $17.6 million, sold six years later for $197.5 million. The average price of all TV stations doubled between 1982 and 1984, yet one year later they were still earning 40 to 60 percent profits. In major markets, a typical station and license worth $10 million in 1959 was worth $400 to $500 million by 1987.[5]

The true dimension of this interception of wealth through not-so-subtly monopolized technology can be gauged by "one major-market PBS broadcasting station . . . cost[ing] $1.5 million" in 1987.[6] That $1.5 million actual construction cost as opposed to the $400 million to $500 million capitalized value the market placed on these stations accurately measures the fictitious capital and its interception of the production of others' labor. The conservative periodical *U.S. News & World Report* recognized this when it headlined:

> Who Will Control TV? This Battle Has It All—
> Power, Money, Politics. On the Outcome Rides

the Future of America's Most Pervasive Medium and the Programs It Brings into Homes. . . . Wall Street has discovered that ownership of TV stations is tantamount to running a money machine that churns out profits in good times and bad.[7]

The Public Paid for Satellite Development

The American public paid for satellite development, and corporate ownership of this technology is corporate socialism at its best. During the 1950s and 1960s, the U.S. public paid $24 billion (about $160 billion in inflated 1989 dollars) to develop satellite communications.[8] The cost of building and launching the first satellites was less than $100 million each, or under $1.9 billion for the nineteen satellites in use in 1989. There were then about 900 television stations in the United States. Given that $1.5 million would establish a PBS station in a metropolitan area, and allowing a generous initial cost of $5 million per station, the total actual cost of the 900 TV stations then in use would be $4.5 billion. The entire system in use in 1989 could have been constructed for $6.4 billion. That is about $52 per U.S. family, a 3 percent addition to the $160 billion they had already paid.

For an understanding of the U.S. communication overcapacity, consider the Syncom satellite, designed by Hughes Aircraft Company in 1961, which alone could "handle twenty-two times the [then] existing volume of long-distance telephone service in the United States."[9] By 1998, far more powerful multipurpose satellites with total capacity of many times any anticipated use were being launched, several hundred commercial communications satellites were in orbit, and 1,554 commercial and educational TV stations were licensed for use.

The rapid increase in technological efficiency multiplied the capacity of the communications systems. The changeover from analog to digital signals multiplied communications capacity several times over with relatively little investment.[10] Then technological breakthroughs squeezed a further ten times the original signals into the bandwidths used by these communications satellites. This was the foundation of the much-discussed gift when these added spectra were essentially given to communication corporations in 1998. Not only were there far more bands available than needed, but each TV station was now able to split its assigned spectrum into six channels.

Thus, with minimal investment, technological breakthroughs provided a capacity gain of one hundred times or more on the already orbiting satellites. The latest fiber-optic lines have a capacity 4 million times the old copper lines. If there were enough traffic to use this capacity, the value of those systems would be multiplied many times their already obscene capitalized values with almost no investment. Communication charges are dropping rapidly but it is paying for that overcapacity that prevents those charges from dropping even further. It is actually possible for a nation, or the world, to establish a communications system where everyone can talk to anyone anywhere in the world for pennies.

A Totally Integrated Communications System

The technology is here to communicate across the country or around the world as cheaply as we now telephone a neighboring town. Using local computerized switching terminals, each servicing several city blocks, these fiber-optic lines are capable of transmitting those hundreds of TV channels described above to every properly wired home. Where homes are widely separated, those same channels can be received by direct broadcast. Upon electronic command from a home TV set, any channel on any satellite can be instantly routed to that home.

It is anticipated that replacing the present copper lines and switching equipment to fiber-optic lines and computerized switching systems will cost about $1,000 per business and home. The United States will require about 100 million of these consumer communications terminals to replace telephones, at a cost of about $120 billion.[11] The immense capacity of satellite communication for long-distance, point-to-point, and point-to-multipoint communications, and the equally large capacity of fiber-optics for point-to-point and local service (under 400 miles), can be combined with compatible computerized telephones, personal computers, software, database supercomputers, laser recorders, and high-resolution picture tubes to form a totally integrated communications system.

With this technology, communication would be practically instantaneous. Information would be stored in a databank computer, and when specific information was requested, it would be sent out with an automatically encoded route code. This "packet switch" (the almost instantaneously transmitted information signal) would find its way in split seconds through many switching terminals, satellites, and trunk lines to the requesting communications terminal, there to be stored in an electronic buffer of a computerized telephone, laser recorder, or computer.

With fully compatible computers and software and all producers having access to technology, the above home equipment and databanks should cost the United States possibly another $250 billion. A totally integrated communications system could thus cost Americans about $370 billion while, in the battle for market share, several times this amount will be spent.

Though this equipment may be expensive initially, it has such a large capacity that even long distance will be inexpensive per unit of information transferred. This will create great savings in other segments of the economy—predominantly in distribution, as here the major costs are in obtaining information. Only if this technology is monopolized will it be beyond the reach of the ordinary person.

A communications system designed to care for all citizens' needs and operated by a publicly mandated authority would be even more accessible than highways. Such easily accessible communications lines would permit consumers to bypass the intermediaries currently claiming the production of their labors. But those people must live too. The only way economies can avoid enormous waste in distribution (or an economic collapse) is to share the remaining productive jobs.

Communication Eliminates Intermediaries and Reduces Trading Costs

Thorstein Veblen's and Stuart Chase's estimation that labor in the retail industry in the 1920s could be reduced over 50 percent[12] is being proven by Wal-Mart Stores. It is establishing superstores ten to thirty miles apart, buying directly from manufacturers, and distributing directly to those superstores. As Wal-Mart sells consumer products for less than individual stores can purchase them, small-town retail stores are closing down all over America.[13] As efficient as Wal-Mart appears, using modern communications technology to purchase directly from the producer and bypass retailers altogether offers even greater savings.

The difference between manufacturing cost and the consumer price measures the major cost of most products—distribution. Typically, manufacturing costs are under 20 percent of the final selling price of a consumer product.[14] With mail-order shipping charges from 2 to 5 percent, no one would pay intermediaries three to five times the production cost if it were feasible to study the products on the Internet, contact the producer, buy the item, and have it shipped directly.

With today's communications system, one need only transport oneself to and from one's job (or perform that job right at home using modern communications) to produce one's share of the nation's wealth, and then search for and order electronically one's share of what others produce. This would substantially reduce the 1.9 people distributing for every one currently producing.

Shopping requires information and middlemen are primarily in the information business. With an integrated communications system employing the latest technology, it would be possible for producers and consumers to trade directly and cheaply again, just as those first traders did thousands of years ago. The monopolization of distribution, now exploited by an army of intermediaries, would be largely eliminated.

Dell Computers pioneered this sales technique for computers and is forcing others to do the same. Trades over the Internet directly between the manufacturer and consumer had been increasing 80 percent a year, and actually tripled in 1998 to 3 percent of total retail sales. Those sales increases will continue to compound and direct trades will be the norm early in the twenty-first century.

Currently America has ten square feet of retail floor space for each shopper and, with four stores being established for each one being closed, the figure approaches twelve square feet. For comparison, Britain has only two square feet per shopper. That surplus retail floor space can only mean higher costs even as Internet shopping is rapidly lowering costs to a fraction of the current costs. A great shakeout of the retail industry will take place.

The savings to the developing world through establishing direct trades between consumer and producer will be enormous. The buildings and support infrastructure for possibly 30 percent of what the developed world considers necessary businesses do not have to be built.

Bill Gates, who accumulated $60 billion (April 1999) because he understood communications technology better than most, said, ''The information highway isn't quite right. A metaphor that comes closer to describing a lot of the activities that will take place is the ultimate market.''[15] This chapter is an outline of that ''ultimate market.''

Big-ticket, Infrequently Purchased Items

Autos, appliances, furniture, farm equipment, industrial equipment, and major tools are all big-ticket, infrequently purchased items whose buying requires accurate information but not the promotional, persuasive advertising that hammers at us incessantly. We trust and get information from direct experience and we make the most important decisions by observing products in daily use. Early in the twenty-first century, customers will make purchase decisions by dialing an index of different manufacturers of the particular product in which they are interested.

This index would have basic information about all manufactures of that product required to make an informed decision: energy efficiency, noise level, hours of useful life, price,

and other features. (Note the pressure this would put on manufacturers to make the most efficient products and stand out in this all-important master index.) From this master index, the consumer would choose brands and models for visual inspection. The precoded computerized telephone would dial the product databank, request the information, and receive it in an audio-video electronic buffer, laser recorder, or computer—all in seconds.

Buyers would, at their leisure, study engineering specifications and styling on their television or computer. Once a decision was made, they would need only to punch in the code for the desired order—model, color, and accessories—and a databank computer would instantly note the closest distribution point where that item was available. If one was not available at a distribution center close by, buyers would choose delivery from the factory.

The bank account number, thumbprint, and/or signature of an Internet shopper would be verified by a master computer and that account instantly debited. If a credit line had been established at the local credit union or bank and recorded in an integrated computer, credit needs would be handled simultaneously. The entire process need not involve advertising, sales, or banking labor, and would greatly reduce storage and transportation labor (remember, capital costs are stored labor).

Product guarantees would be handled much as they are now, while maintenance and repairs would be taken care of by local private enterprise under standardized guarantees. The secret of successful direct trades between manufacturer and consumer over the Internet, and the resultant elimination of distribution intermediaries, will be high-quality products and full guarantees.

From the initial information request to the

completion of a trade, the communication arteries would only be in use for a few seconds. There would be tens of thousands of simultaneous communications. Both seller and buyer would save time and labor, as verbal explanations and mailing of information are largely eliminated. The current time-consuming exchange of information would be handled in split seconds.

This automatic and instantaneous transfer of massive amounts of information would mean an infinitesimal labor and capital cost per communication. This would conserve millions of acres of trees and eliminate thousands of jobs currently manufacturing paper, producing brochures, and distributing that information, including salespersons and all labor servicing and maintaining retail establishments.

Monopolization of information would be eliminated. Every qualified producer would enjoy the right to place his or her product or service in the databank and pay the charges (a percentage of gross sales) out of cash flow. In place of millions of dollars up front to advertise through the present openly monopolized newspaper, radio, and TV system, there would be only a small charge for entering the product information in a retail database computer. To eliminate clogging the databanks with useless information of producers no longer in business, regular payments would be required to retain the privilege of selling through this integrated communications network.

This would break the monopolization of our production and distribution system by wealthy corporations. Currently only those with large financial backing can pay the monopoly charges of the media and gain access to the public; all others are financially excluded. Starting up a truly productive industry would become quite simple. A new company's advertising would

have full billing alongside that of major entrenched producers. A few wealthy corporations would no longer decide, through promotional persuasive advertising, what the public wants or what is good for them. Consumers would have easy access to all choices.

In the late 1980s, several large corporations began establishing just such databanks. They are, however, individual databanks for each corporation without that all-important master index and thus are an extension of monopolization.[16] Without that master index, individual databases will be relatively hard to find and that one crucial aspect, the ability to compare, would be lost.

Inexpensive, Small, Frequently Traded Items

The markup on perishable groceries is about 100 percent while the markup on small nonperishable consumer durables is several hundred percent. There is a competitive sales monopoly at work in the latter. Taking full advantage of modern communications would remove all purchases above an intermediate price range out of the wasteful, duplicated retail outlets. Simultaneously, the consumers' choices would be increased by access to these products through databanks.

On trades directly between distant producers and consumers, individual shipping and handling costs would be too high for most small, frequently purchased items. Thus groceries, household supplies, cosmetics, knickknacks and most small, inexpensive consumer items would be most efficiently distributed through the present retail outlets. The breakeven point would be in the lower range of the intermediate-priced occasionally purchased items.

But even now companies in Japan are attempting to establish cheaper computer grocery shopping. "A housewife can switch on her personal computer and scan the list of goods available for sale. . . . The order will be delivered strictly on time."[17]

With high-capacity communications, plans are under way for offices at home. These plans would reduce traffic congestion and require fewer expensive buildings on valuable land. Such plans are in line with our suggestions and the savings are quite apparent.

Wholesalers of small-ticket consumer items would keep the quality and price of all products posted in a databank computer. Purchasing agents would periodically analyze this information. Once initial trust had been established, a retailer would check those updated bulletin boards for the best buys. This would eliminate the need for many jobbers and other salespeople.

Shopping as a Social Event Entails a Cost

Shopping is recreation for many people and a status symbol for others. Direct communication between producers and consumers might change society's psychological profile. If enough people decided they wished to do their shopping socially and expensively, that would be their choice. They would have no trouble finding merchants to accommodate them. To compensate for the additional labor, the products would cost more. The added unit costs would be properly accounted for under socializing and recreation (like Tupperware or Avon), or social status (like Tiffany's). The majority of shoppers, however, would surely choose to save their money by using the most direct and least labor-intensive (cheapest) method of completing a trade. As direct trades would be only for

intermediate to big-ticket items, this would in no way impinge on local coffeehouse-type trades where socializing is the primary activity.

Modern Communications Doubling Distribution Efficiency

When a manufacturer produces a product, it is normally ready to use, and customers already understand the use for which it was designed. All that is missing for potential consumers is complete information on where the best quality product is available at the lowest possible price. In the United States, once direct contact is established between producer and consumer, it would only require roughly 100,000 railroaders, possibly one million truckers (down from 1991's 1.3 million), and a system of organized freight terminals to distribute the nation's production. It would be quite simply a freight postal system: the item would be delivered just as United Parcel Service delivers Christmas packages today or consumers would receive notices of the arrivals of their purchases and pick them up at the local freight terminal.

As it requires a central dispatching office, most truck freight is handled by moderate to large trucking companies. They may either own all their trucks or sublease from independent truckers who own and drive their own rigs. There are normally several trucking companies in any moderate-size city, each complete with loading docks, storage capacity, dispatching equipment, and staff.

If a society chose to be efficient and the communications systems were in place, the following scene would be possible: (1) shippers would punch into their communications terminal the information on loads to be shipped; (2) an independent trucker with a laptop computer would dial a computer programmed for dispatching all loads; (3) the trucker would punch in current location, freight preferences, and preferred destination for delivery of the next load; (4) the computer would tell instantly where the loads were, the type of freight, the required pickup and delivery times, the rate per mile, etc.; (5) the trucker would choose a load, inform the computer, and record an identification number; (6) the computer would record the acceptance, remove that load from the databank, provide a contract number to the trucker, and inform the shipper.

The minimal dispatching costs would be included in the freight charge. Recording and billing would be handled automatically by computer. Only a few intermediaries would be necessary. There would be no need for duplicated dispatching services, loading docks, storage facilities, equipment, and personnel. This system would not restrict any trucker or company from signing contracts outside the national computerized dispatching system. It would, however, break the competitive monopoly created by the minimum capital requirements for a trucking company. Each independent trucker would be on an equal footing with corporate trucking companies.

When producers and consumers trade directly over communications arteries operated by public authority, just as they now transport over publicly maintained transportation arteries, costs will drop precipitously. The competitive monopolies of retail outlets for intermediate- to high-priced products will be eliminated. The nation's freight will quickly settle into flow patterns and be moved as regularly as mail by the cheapest combination of rail, truck, ship, and plane.

It might take consumers from one day (small items) to a week (large items) to receive a purchase, but, at possibly one-half the price, they would be well paid for this wait. The actual transit time of products between producer and consumer would be a fraction of that currently taken through jobbers, wholesalers, and retailers.

This efficient distribution system would eliminate most wholesale storage and retail buildings, as well as use of heat, electricity, inventory, stocking clerks, sales clerks, maintenance workers, building repairs, security, and so on. Those who formerly bought, stored, and sold these products would be available to engage in productive labor. Society would attain an undreamed-of efficiency. Over 50 percent of these intermediaries between producer and consumer would be eliminated and, assuming society was alert and restructured labor's working hours, all would be free to share the remaining productive work. Sharing the remaining productive jobs would create a corresponding increase in free time for everybody.

The present communications infrastructure is already capable of handling this long-distance information transmission, and the distribution efficiency we are discussing requires only the establishment of databanks for public use, just as we now use highways. The only way this can happen without a total collapse of economies (such as the Asian tigers and the former Soviet Union experienced) is if fully productive jobs are shared equally to expand buying power in step with increased productive capacity. Sharing those jobs equally would lower paid working time to less than twenty hours per week.

If the world's citizens had equality and opportunity instead of daily battles for survival feeding on the fringes of these massive subtle monopolies, family trauma would decline rapidly, fewer children would be abused and neglected, prisons would shrink, more than 80 percent of the insurance industry would disappear even as society was better insured, the medical and law industries would shrink to a fraction of their present size even as those needs were better cared for, other nations would produce their own food and developed world agriculture would shrink accordingly even as the world's citizens were more secure, equities markets would shrink to a tiny fraction of today's trades, the arms industry would disappear, and on and on. The world is far richer than we realize; much of that wealth is wasted.

Once those productive jobs were shared, the average workweek reduced, and labor fully paid, the small amount of time necessary to labor for one's share of the nation's wealth would be the proper measure of the price of products and services. Our previous research concluded that an efficient economy using modern technology of production and distribution could reduce its labor time by well over 70 percent.[18] That potential reduction in costs through elimination of unnecessary labor and fully paying labor is the meaning of Adam Smith's little-noticed insightful statement, "If produce had remained the natural wages of labor, all things would have become cheaper, though in appearance many things might have become dearer."

Trades Should Still Pay for "Free" TV

Paying full programming and transmission costs on a voluntary basis (cable and other pay TV) excludes large segments of the population. TV programming therefore should not be financed through direct viewer financing or tax revenues, which are too visible and arbitrary. As most families watch TV and all purchase products, the fairest source of funds is to collect them through consumer purchases, just as advertisers do now. Companies would pay a fee for advertising products or services through paying for

listing on indexes and databases within society's integrated communications system. These companies would recover both their costs and television programming and broadcasting charges from the consumer just as now advertising costs and sales taxes are priced in, or added onto the price of, products sold.

Producers using this service need only calculate the price markup necessary to cover a communications surcharge on gross revenues. There is such a surplus of communication channels to carry TV and phone conversations simultaneously that there would be little need for additional equipment. With the elimination of monopolization of the airwaves as described above, the TV transmission charges would be minimal, and most of the funds collected would go toward programming and entertainers. All producers would have access to every consumer. Impulse buying would be greatly reduced, creating more savings for society. When people wanted or needed something, they would buy it without being pressured.

Reserving TV Time for Totally New Products

While innovations on a familiar product would be readily presented to the public through a databank, totally new products are expensive to market. Innovators would require special access to the public. To complement other methods of familiarization, some TV channels should be specifically reserved to promote such innovations. Novelty buffs comprise a large segment of the population, and there are few of us who do not have some interest. A program demonstrating these creations would be quite popular.

An undeveloped society needs promotional, persuasive advertising to alert a population to the standard of living possible with developed capital. There must be demand before the industries and distribution arteries can be established. However, once the production/distribution infrastructure is in place with society energized to produce and accustomed to that standard of living, promotional, persuasive advertising becomes wasteful. Rather than titillate the consumer with thousands of toys to be played with and discarded, it would be much more socially efficient to abandon promotional, persuasive advertising and permit people to advance to a higher intellectual and social level.

The low cost of reaching the shopper through a databank gives society this opportunity. The maximum average living standard within the capabilities of the earth's resources and ecosystem can be calculated. Society could, and should, use those proven promotional, persuasive methods to educate people about the waste of that lifestyle. Within those guidelines, shoppers would decide what products they want by observing them in use or scanning the databanks. Any item that is truly useful will become a common household item. There would be fewer nonessential products sold and those resources currently wasted on titillating toys would be diverted to producing for the world's needy. In short, just as many in the developed world have already abandoned the "conspicuous consumption" lifestyle, a rational lifestyle would be made popular. Once a rational lifestyle was established, peer pressure would tend to encourage it.

If people are so dull that a society with a respectable living standard cannot function without promotional, persuasive advertising (which we do not believe), society would analyze advertising for essential and nonessential products for the desired standard of living. After all, many items (cigarettes, alcohol, and chemical-laden processed foods) lower the qual-

ity of life, and spending social funds on their promotion is economic insanity. Even when spent by private industry, advertising for cigarettes and alcohol is still social funds. Those costs are recovered in the sales price. The public pays the bill for the debasement of their life.

The same holds true for nonessential, resource-consuming, and environment-polluting lifestyles. Driving a $60,000 automobile while others are driving $15,000 cars may draw admiration today, but if society were taught that this was at the expense of humankind's survival it would incur broad disapproval. The resources saved and pollution prevented by that refocused social mindset would be substantial, and essential to the survival of thousands of species, to humankind's quality of life, and most probably to our survival.

Like television thirty years later, when radio first came on the scene its most prominent use was for public education programs. When cable television arrived with its potential for hundreds of channels, idealistic planners again tried to establish an education medium. In each case powerful interests subverted the public interest and monopolized these valuable media for commercial interests. The chance for society to become truly informed was lost. Communication corporations are fully aware of society's potential savings because it is their potential loss of the ability to siphon wealth from the masses. When CBS's brilliant scientist, Peter Karl Goldmark, was proposing just such uses for TV as we are outlining, CBS was so worried about his plan that it offered him $75,000 a year (which he turned down) to do nothing.[19]

Rather than being radical, the following suggestions are similar to the original plans for radio and cable television and are only one of the many ways these hundreds of TV channels could be organized. Possibly 20 percent of the current satellite channels would be more than adequate if organized along the lines suggested in the following subchapters.

Music, Sports, Movies, and Game Shows

Music, sports, movies, and game shows have an established market and draw large audiences. Fifteen to twenty channels should be reserved for each of these program areas. Only pennies per viewer, paid painlessly through consumer purchases, would bring in millions per broadcast to the investors, stars, directors, managers, and support labor. There would be adequate channels to guarantee all promising entertainers the opportunity to present their shows for a probationary period. If successful, as shown by automatic computer recording of viewer interest, their shows would be made permanent.

With communication channels now open there would no longer be monopolization through high-priced promotion. With these equal rights, it would be talent that counted. There would be many more able people investing, designing, producing, and starring in many more shows. Along with more time to enjoy TV, viewer choices would rise, and the truly talented artists would be well paid for their efforts. All would have a reasonable opportunity to prove their abilities.

A formula of gradually reduced pay per million viewing hours as a show increased in popularity would compensate performers relative to their popularity, which would be little different from the way it is now. If the industry were designed for access to the public for new performers, monopoly control of entertainment industries would disappear, along with the interception of others' labor that their substantial income represents.

Investment

The subchapters "Creation of Money" and "Accumulation of Capital through Cooperative Capitalism" (Chapter 26) are an integral part of this subchapter.

Several TV channels should be reserved for direct communication between those offering investment opportunities and investors looking for those opportunities. As everyone with savings would have access to this investment information stored in databanks, the subtle money monopolists would be totally bypassed. Individual investors would put their risk capital in innovations that went unrecognized by regular loan institutions. If the entrepreneurs' insights and talents were truly productive, investors would receive much higher than average returns. However, if their claims to insight were not valid, they would not be able to hide behind the protective shield of subtle monopolization.

An entrepreneur who had obtained community approval and initial investment capital from the bank (nothing new: entrepreneurs need both these now) would deposit a prospectus in a databank. Investors would study the various investment plans, buy shares in the most promising ventures, and have their accounts automatically debited—all without intermediaries.

Talented workers would look over prospectuses, which would include labor needs and incentives, and, if they saw where their talents would be used productively and profitably (and assuming they had fulfilled their contract to train a replacement), they could transfer to that new job. Labor would be mobile and free (not dispossessed as in a reserve labor force), with rights to its share of the efficiency gains of technology. (Remember, in a modern industrial society, each worker could work less than two days per week. See the work of Charles

Fourier 180 years ago and Thorstein Veblen, Bertrand Russell, Lewis Mumford, Stuart Chase, Upton Sinclair, and Ralph Borsodi in the first half of the twentieth century. Late-twentieth-century writers describing the same phenomenon are Juliet Schor, Seymour Melman, Samuel Bowles, David Gordon, Thomas Weiskopf, Jeremy Rifkin, Andre Gorz, numerous European authors, and this author's *The World's Wasted Wealth 2.*)

If a replacement were not immediately available, other workers at the factory could double their pay by working four days a week, or triple it by working six days. Strict rules, however, would have to be followed here. To permit doubling up on established jobs would subvert the entire economy. Those workers will have appropriated the labor rights of others. The unemployed would be denied their rights to a share of social production while those working excessive hours would have more than their share.

For their risk, the original innovators and investors would receive the initial higher profits plus royalties. Through sharing in the profits, workers and management who bought stock through deductions of 10 to 20 percent of their wages would be well compensated. The profit potential would maximize their desire to maximize efficiency and provide incentive to look for new industries to develop and again share in the profits.

Assuming society had eliminated subtle patent monopolies as discussed in the previous chapter, others would quickly analyze and duplicate the innovative production or distribution process; prices would fall to just that required to compensate the innovators, labor, and capital. Through those low prices, society would be well compensated.

If communications technology reduced pro-duction and distribution costs 60 percent, and adequate compensation to the innovators was 10 percent, the public would quickly benefit by a 50 percent reduction in costs, realized through reduced working hours. This chapter alone outlines just such a potential labor savings through the use of modern communication technology. Societies which decided to forego a throwaway society and opt for fuel cell car/bicycle economy and other efficient production technologies would provide a quality lifestyle with even less labor.

Education

Since the desire to emulate is the basis of all learning, educating children can be quite simple. Children imitate their elders and their peers. They want the approval of their parents, love to excel, and desire equality with their peers. They are curious and, if not discouraged, love to learn. The present educational system puts too many barriers in their way. At present "half of all gifted children float through school with average or worse grades, never realizing their potential . . . [while] almost 20 percent will drop out."[20]

There are many reasons for this: a child may be timid and terrified of school, an inferiority complex may prevent a student from functioning, or excessive pressure to do well may be daunting. The school district may have obsolete books and teaching aids; the school may be understaffed so students don't get the individual attention they need. Local peer groups (gangs) may replace parents and teachers as role models. Parents may not be involved enough in their child's learning. Or the curriculum may be so slow it is boring. With elimination of these and other barriers, many students with low grades might well blossom right along with their peers.

With forty to sixty TV channels reserved for education, every subject now taught at elementary, secondary, college, and university level would reach every home free of charge.[21] Logically, each subject would have several teachers and be broadcast at various hours of the day. The competition would be intense for the teaching positions on such programs and, once picked, these best educators in the nation would be well paid. Each taped course would be edited for maximum clarity, simplicity, and comprehension. Reasoning is quite natural and nothing can beat a good educator whose taped lectures anticipate, and are carefully structured to answer, most questions. With all society having access, the fictions and omissions of history (especially omissions) would be challenged, researched, and corrected.

With their lessons on tape, these high-quality educators would be spending less time teaching than any one of the tens of thousands of teachers they replaced. They would concentrate on studying their own and others' lectures for ways to improve. Modeling is the most potent teacher of all and these great teachers would be great role models.

The minimum equipment required for each student would be a TV set, while the local education system would provide workbooks to match the TV lessons. As these lessons should be in a databank and accessible through the integrated communications system, a VCR would be desirable. With recorders and societal incentives, students would tape the lessons and study when they had the free time and were emotionally ready. They could replay the lessons as many times as necessary for maximum comprehension.

So long as a student maintained an adequate grade average, a share of the money society saved on maintaining the present school system could be paid to each child's family. Allowing, of course, for each child's ability, it would be logical to pay this incentive for each subject and on an average of all subjects. This would be high motivation for families to restructure their time for home education. With spending money earned for each subject, motivated students would zip through many subjects. Since developing nations do not have to deconstruct an entrenched, expensive educational system, and their motivation for education is high, they have no need for incentive pay. But they would have high incentive to utilize current classrooms as administrative and testing stations and educate their populations, children and adults, through satellite television.

With the two-day workweek possible in a developed country, there would be adequate time for parents to stay home and monitor their children's learning. With rapport between parent and child, intelligent children would cover a current year's education in as little as four months. The potential is unlimited. The most intelligent and motivated would have the knowledge of Ph.D.s at the age when today's students are in middle to upper university classes—which, incidentally, would break another monopoly.

Actually those students would have a much broader education than most Ph.D.s. Most doctoral studies are very narrow in focus. Thus the famous dictum: "Professors are learning more and more about less and less." Without that breadth of education, the answers to the world's problems will not be found. Conversely, if universities emphasized graduate degrees that covered a broad spectrum of disciplines instead of narrow fields, answers would be found relatively quickly. Through free TV studies, students would have that broad education.

Students would not be pressured to follow

the teaching of any one professor. Other professors might have a different view on history or society, and really interested students would listen to many views. Students would make judgments while still young and idealistic. All this would be gained while parent and child enjoyed irreplaceable quality time together. Some talented students who do not have parental support would, by immersing themselves in education, find a surrogate family.

Private or public day-care education centers would be operated for the few who could not function under, or who were unable to arrange for, home self-education. Those who were intellectually capable but who failed to maintain a minimum average would lose their incentive funds and would be required to attend these specially structured classes.

The compensations and identity received by siblings and friends for successful home schooling would be noticed by younger children, which would provide motivation to avoid the formal school setting. With motivation for home education high, most students would easily see the advantage.

This plan is actually quite conservative. A first-grader would be proud to go shopping with earnings and it is hard to visualize many children being irresponsible toward their education if it meant losing both their freedom of choice and their spending money. They would quickly learn responsibility when it meant both financial and emotional rewards. Once in operation, society would quickly become accustomed to such a system and the need for formal schools would be minimal.

Children can be just as easily culturally trained to quality as they can to trash. All society would gain from more positive cultural training, so it would be logical to eliminate the senseless violence in today's children's programs. At the least, quality children's programs could be assigned a block of channels so conscientious parents could maximize their children's intellectual and moral growth.

Incentive funds, as a right, would in no way impinge on others' rights. Those rights could only be exercised by obtaining a set grade average. Citizens without children already pay taxes to support schools and home education would save society more than the cost of these incentive funds. In fact, those funds cost nothing; they go right back to the people from whom they came. Over time, society would become accustomed to this system, and such incentives would be considered as normal as wages earned from a job. This arrangement would go a long way towards balancing per capita earnings between families with children and those without.

Older students would soon learn to structure their flexible education time around their job. There need not be a sharp cutoff between school years and entering the workforce. The options of both pursuing education for a career and earning one's living would be increased. Instead of a division between students and workers, the two would overlap until the young adults opted for a career.

Motivated children, youths, young adults, and adults would obtain most of their education at home and at their own pace. Curious children with a desire to learn—which is most of them—would find the field wide open. Left to their own devices, they would quickly learn that it was their time and labor that were being conserved by dedication and attention to the subjects being taught.

Many talented children's potential, now lost through boredom and diversion to socially undesirable activities, would be salvaged. The brightest would probably attain a twelfth-grade education in less than eight years, the middle level in ten or less, and with these motivations even the slower group, which currently sets the pace of a classroom, would learn more quickly. There would be adequate resources and time to give special support to those who are unable to cope for various reasons. This would not only conserve society's labor, it would economize students' energy and time. This potential was shown by an experiment with interactive videos that reduced learning time while increasing comprehension 30 percent.[22]

Having watched great videos on The Learning Channel, The History Channel, The Arts and Entertainment Channel, The Discovery Channel, public broadcasting channels, CNN, and an occasional program on other stations, we conclude that the statement "A picture is worth a thousand words" should be changed to "One documentary is worth a million words." The best of those documentaries combine the wisdom of many researchers developed by many lifetimes of study. That knowledge will be absorbed at some level by all viewers. Avid reading will seldom bring one close to the understanding gained from a well-researched one-hour documentary. The gain for the slower and less avid readers could only be of much greater dimension. As opposed to being bored and discouraged, students will enjoy their education.

A central testing facility would be maintained that would issue scholastic level certificates and incentive funds. These achievement tests would be designed to evaluate the students' ability to compete with the best in the world. This would quickly equip all nations to compete in world trade.[23] Since credentials are crucial to obtaining good jobs, all students would have access to their scores, the right to analyze their wrong answers, and the right to retake tests.

Classes that require hands-on learning would

be held in a classroom setting just as now, along with supporting taped programs. The savings to society would be substantial, and the increase in the nation's educational level would be equally dramatic. Millions who dreamed of additional education would find it freely available in what was previously their idle time.

As no one's knowledge is complete, every curriculum would be subject to review and correction. The Great Saint-Mihiel battle of World War I that never happened (see final chapter) and other such examples of improperly or incompletely recorded history addressed throughout this book are not exceptions. They are the norm and such failures to tell the full truth seriously retard democratic development. Correct and full knowledge of such events is critical to society planning its future.

There have been possibly over 1,000 sensationalist and inaccurate books written on the assassination of President John F. Kennedy.[24] With the Warren Commission report obviously a cover-up, a sincere academic 200 years from now searching for the truth would have a difficult job. Good documentaries produced today can reach the truth of that traumatic period in U.S. history as well as many more deeply buried secrets of the Cold War of which the public is only dimly aware.

Learning is fundamental to everyday life. Every day we learn something new or reinforce what we already know. To waste huge amounts of resources and to inflict enormous violence, injustice, and poverty as we have been documenting—while continually affirming nice-sounding slogans about efficiency, justice, and compassion—seriously limit true knowledge. Redesigning society to produce and distribute efficiently would give children a better cultural education. Likewise with the centuries of protomercantilism, mercantilism, neomercantilism, and corporate imperialism—and the wars they engendered as societies battled over the world's wealth—as we have addressed in depth: an education fully exposing the causes of this waste and violence would provide a much firmer foundation for the further evolution of society towards its stated goals of peace, justice, and freedom from want.

Though a society can be guided towards a sustainable lifestyle, it is not possible and probably is not desirable to get every student to enjoy learning for its own sake. After all, given a choice, most people would choose to do things that best support their need for identity and security, which for many is often satisfied in work, sports, and hobbies rather than in intellectual pursuits. There will be those who, though unable to compete across the board scholastically, will take great interest and do well in one field. These suggestions would eliminate all barriers and give the maximum incentive to learn in the fields of one's choice.

Schools, as now structured, do perform a babysitting function. But, if that is the criterion, society should be aware that the potential of many children is lost and that babysitting is what they are paying for, not education. One must also be aware that early industrialists hoped that "the elementary school could be used to break the labouring classes into those habits of work discipline now necessary for factory production. . . ." Putting little children to work at school for very long hours at very dull subjects was seen as a positive virtue, for it made them "habituated, not to say naturalized, to labour and fatigue."[25]

Inspired Teachers for Every Student

People feel insecure at any suggestion of fundamental change in their social institutions and most are closely attached to the institutions of education. But, in the current school structure,

where is that all-important role model if the student has a poor, mediocre, or burned-out teacher? Under the system proposed here there would be many great teachers, each teaching his or her deepest beliefs, and their videotaped lectures would be freely available for all.

Students watching those videotaped lectures would judge for themselves what was closest to the truth. By eliminating the current monopoly on education (in the soft sciences—economics, political science, some social studies, and, believe it or not, history—what passes for education is really programming [propaganda]), production of low-quality lectures would be the exception.

Certainly, good hands-on teachers are wonderful, but how can they hold enthusiasm with twenty-five or thirty children to teach? Is not honest interaction quite impossible with even half that number? Would not the best possible teacher, backed up by professional graphics, be able to put on an enthusiastic performance and that enthusiasm captured forever on videotape? Hands-on teachers are limited by the speed of the slower students. With an inspired teacher and professional graphics, even a slow student could learn more than in a crowded and socially isolated classroom. And why slow the others? A slow or timid student, not having to compete directly with others, would avoid discouraging feelings of inferiority and thus do better.

Parents Interacting Closely with Their Children's Education

With their increased free time, motivated parents would enjoy watching their children learn and answering their questions. Children would ask an interested parent many more questions than they would a teacher. Motivated parents would go into deeper detail than the teacher who has so little time to spare for individual attention. Students too timid to function freely in class would function better in a home setting. In the upper grades, motivated parents would share the experience and learn with their children.

Better Institutions for Socialization

Socialization is of high importance but the elimination of this function of schools would free both timid and slower students for concentration on their studies. Youth social clubs would spring up and children would sign up voluntarily, as opposed to the requirement to attend school. When children join a social club by choice, they would be bound by the rules of social courtesy, not classroom discipline, and would mix, relate, and learn social graces at a faster pace than in a school setting. Parents would automatically seek such groups to replace the babysitting function of schools.

Maintaining Curiosity, Creativity, and Love of Learning

Education freely available to all in their free time would bypass that greatest of all destroyers of curiosity and creativity, the straitjacketing of children into conformity. Many parents have the misfortune of a poor teacher for their children. We cannot count on a great teacher in every classroom. We cannot count on even half being good. Witness Massachusetts, a state with much higher quality schools than the average, where in 1998 over half the teachers failed state qualification tests. There are over 15,000 educational experiments yearly. Some show dramatic improvements in education scores. Yet the overall average of scores does not improve. Either these better teaching methods are not spreading to other schools or those schools do not have

motivated teachers. Why not combine modern technology with the students' abilities and desires and trade the constraints of the current system for the opportunity of a full education?[26]

Certainly one can point to great teachers and the gains for their lucky students. But there would be no loss to those children in this proposed educational structure. Instead, the number of children educated to their maximum potential would increase by a factor of two or three, or maybe more. What about all the adults who would gain an education? What about those who have a burning desire for another profession but who, under the stress of their job, limited finances, and the present educational structure cannot gain the credentials for their desired career? What about potentially great artists who have no opportunity even to discover their talents—painters, poets, writers, singers, sculptors, ad infinitum?

There are undoubtedly many latent Einsteins currently spending their lives in drudgery who would educate themselves and have their genius suddenly blossom for all the world to see and enjoy in the form of a book, a song, a new theory, an invention. A large percentage of the population educating itself to a much higher level would develop an even more efficient and productive society while protecting the environment and natural resources.

Students Who Were once Borderline Teachable Graduating at the Top of Their Class

Inspirational teachers and programs have proven they can parent impoverished children with damaged psyches into becoming successful citizens. One such teacher is Ms. Marva Collins in Chicago. She worked among her students, rather than from her desk. Each time one did well she would put her hand under the child's chin, lift the child's eyes to hers, and say, "You are brilliant," or give some other sincere compliment. Minority children in her class deemed borderline teachable graduated from the university at the top of their class, and went on to become professors, lawyers, and other successful professionals. Failures were almost nonexistent.

Charles Murray, in his infamous book *The Bell Curve,* cited Ms. Collins' program specifically, pointing out that such programs could not possibly improve academic achievement or cognitive functioning. Having documented Ms. Collins' successes twenty years earlier, *60 Minutes* went back after Murray's book came out and checked on those thirty-three children.[27] Those students were the roaring successes described above and thoroughly proved Murray's thesis was racist nonsense.

While restructuring to a just society, such programs would be used to salvage such at-risk children. But, once all people have equal access to a society's benefits and opportunities, most will be good parents and, through modern technology, most children can be well educated.

Culture and Recreational Learning

Fine arts and recreational learning programs, such as are produced by public broadcasting stations (and increasingly by for-profit shows), are enjoyable to people and add to their knowledge. Fifteen to twenty TV channels would be blocked out and reserved for these high-quality shows. The social benefits of learning while relaxing are self-evident. Popular educational talk shows and good recreational, educational TV command a loyal audience.

Most of these shows, however, are on public broadcasting stations outside the system of col-

lecting costs through advertising. They depend on grants and donations. One live commercial show can easily exceed one PBS station's yearly cost for all of its taped shows.[28] With their fair share of TV funds coming to them through a restructured advertising medium still financed by sales as described above, the present financial struggles of those who broadcast quality programs would be eliminated. This income would permit expansion of these stations as the rental costs of their taped shows would be minuscule compared to the original productions.

New methods of distribution and governing skills that contribute to social efficiency are as much a matter of invention as mechanical devices. Among the cultural and educational programs would be one or more channels reserved for introducing and demonstrating innovations and inventions. Alert, imaginative minds would relate their special expertise to other machines, production processes, distribution methods, and social policies, and along with new products would devise simpler methods of manufacturing, distributing, and governing.

Minority Cultures

Five to ten TV channels would be reserved for ethnic minorities. They are now inadequately represented and participate in national culture only to a limited extent. With these new rights, they would quickly develop outstanding media and political personalities to articulate essential issues and challenge the Social Control belief systems that protect power structures and keep them in bondage. With their own communications channels, equal access to land and jobs, and the right to retain what their labors produce, members of minorities would share the nation's work and its wealth and participate in national decision making. Every citizen might at last attain and exercise the full rights of equal citizenship.

Foreign Cultures

Guaranteeing representation of their views should apply also to foreign cultures. When the vulnerable are not present to defend themselves, Managers of State, seeking followers for aggressive intent, can portray them as enemies. Eight to twelve channels would be reserved for their views. With all sides presenting their views, society would be hard-pressed to falsely accuse others. It would be equally difficult for Managers of State to hide their aggressive intentions.

By mutual agreement there should be reciprocal presentations of cultural programs between countries to provide cross-cultural information. Broadcast standards would limit propaganda. Beamed to every home, programs would show people throughout the world at work and at play. People would begin to appreciate—and thus respect—both what we have in common and what is distinctly different. There would be intense popular pressure to extend full rights globally once the impoverished of the world had access to a world audience. Their representatives would be able to explain how they are kept in poverty by the siphoning of their wealth to centers of capital. The careful documenting of the waste and inefficiencies of corporate mercantilism would result in laws that would quickly rein in its excess power.

Local Television

Most local TV stations now pick up national programs from satellites and rebroadcast them to local viewers. Though their primary purpose is to transmit local shows and events, with a totally integrated system, these stations would broadcast nationally when a local event was of national interest. Local stations would be a source of community information and culture—ideally a medium for citizens to share ideas and experiences with each other. Local elections and community development would have complete coverage. There would be adequate time to broadcast local sports, concerts, plays, parades, and community information forums on a broad range of issues. Meetings of governing bodies, normally open to the public by law, would be beamed over local TV.

The rights to a share of the TV fund would provide adequate income for coverage of popular local events. Having already paid their share through consumer purchases, all could watch for free in the comfort of their living rooms. Talented local people would have their chance at national exposure without the time, expense, and risk of leaving their local area and the security it provides.

Elections

Many leaders are so busy leading their constituents down the path of confiscation of the wealth of the weak that they have, or take, little time for a sincere research of innovative ideas. In fact, politics as now contrived is hardly amenable to new ideas. As explained in Chapter Nine, "Suppressing the Freedom of Others Under the Flag of Freedom," society is kept to the right of the political spectrum. Self-protective Social Control belief systems keep political rhetoric within those permitted parameters of debate. To move outside these parameters is political and social suicide.

To break that control of information by the powerful, ten to twenty reserved TV channels would be needed for serious leaders to present their views. Please consider the final chapter "Media to Empower the Powerless" as an integral part of this chapter. There we describe how to break the chains placed upon the minds of the masses. Once those chains are removed, leaders sincerely promoting the rights of all people can come to the fore.

With politicians having access to the public through reserved TV channels, there would be no need to spend private funds for elections. Such money makes the recipient beholden to that supporter. Private funding should be prohibited by law. Massive numbers of unused channels are available. Putting them to use by law would cost almost nothing. With those running for office having free access to the public and elections becoming commonsense debates of the issues, the advantage would be with those who were most knowledgeable and articulate.

Without a crisis, few of the above reforms can become social policy. However, knowing these reforms are possible, progressive citizens and politicians may insist on them. Power may eventually shift to permit the claiming of these rights. Facing a crisis such as the Great Depression, everyone would be looking for answers and the masses can reclaim their rights to communication channels and with those rights more rights will be reclaimed. Past social-control rhetoric will then be exposed.

Homes as Low-Budget TV Stations

New communications technology is being invented so fast and becoming so cheap that the economically powerful are having a hard time controlling it. Local TV stations can now be almost as cheap as their radio counterparts. Low-power TV transmitters (LPTV) that can transmit up to fifteen miles are available. As of 1989 there were over 500 licensed in the United States and as the new millennium rolls in there will be over 2,000. The government pays about 75 percent of the roughly $90,000 start-up costs for each station:[29]

> The FCC awarded the first 23 licenses for LPTV stations in September 1983 by drawing the names of applicants from the same plexiglass barrel used by Selective Service officials to pick draft registration numbers during the Vietnam War. One can only hope that the second drawing bodes better for activists than the first. Chances are that it will. Eight of the first 23 licenses went to minority firms. Both the lottery method and the sheer number of potential stations seem to favor greater access by radicals and reformers to LPTV than to standard TV, where the purchase price of a station in a major metropolitan area can run into tens of millions of dollars. Low-power television should increase access to the airwaves by minorities, women, political activists, environmentalists, workers, and other elements of the broad, loose coalition of the disenfranchised that has, of necessity, invented alternative media.[30]

These stations should be established with by-laws limiting them to ownership and control by the community. If not, whenever they develop an audience, monopolists would offer such a price for them that few would survive to provide alternative information to the nation.

Corporations have discovered they can target specialty markets with radio ads and, as the profits climb, the price of radio stations soars.[31] There are no more channels available and low-income groups have lost many opportunities for inexpensive communication:

> Doing without information is tantamount to being excluded from the democratic process. Still it is this principle that now is being introduced across the informational spectrum—from pay TV, to "deregulated" telephone services, to charges for

on-line data bank services, to the disappearance of modestly priced government and academic information. . . . The *kind and character* of the information that will be sought, produced and disseminated will be determined, if the market criteria prevail, by the most powerful bidders in the information market place—the conglomerates and the transnational companies. . . . [In this process] Americans are forever being congratulated by their leaders for being the beneficiaries of the most technologically advanced, complex, expensive, and adaptable communications facilities and processes in the world. This notwithstanding, and this is the paradox, people in the United States may be amongst the globe's least knowledgeable in comprehending the sentiments and changes of recent decades in the international arena. Despite thousands of daily newspapers, hundreds of magazines, innumerable television channels, omnipresent radio, and instantaneous information delivery systems, Americans are sealed off surprisingly well from divergent outside (or even domestic) opinion. . . . There is a demonstrable inability to recognize, but much less empathize with, a huge have-not world.[32]

Professor Herbert Schiller explains how Americans are "sealed off" from the realities of the have-not world:

> How many movies did [corporate America] make about the labor movement? After all, America is made up of people who work. Where is the history of these people? Where's the day-in day-out history of the African American population? Where's the day-in and day-out history of women? Not just one program. Where's the whole history of the people? Where's the history of protest movements in America? Can you imagine the kind of material that could come from American protest movements? The entertainment people are always saying that they don't have enough dramatic material. Who are they kidding?[33]

As the laws controlling the communications media are now structured, the rights of corpo-

rate imperialists to decide the world's future are firmly in place. We can only hope that communication becomes just like the windmill, steam engine, and electricity—so cheap that the powerful will lose control. It is then that the weak may claim their full rights.

This may happen. In Springfield, Illinois, a blind thirty-one-year-old black man, M'Banna Kantako, became fed up because nothing in the media addressed the problems of blacks. He set up a one-watt radio transmitter the size of a toaster that covers a diameter of two miles. Just as government attacks on George Seldes's weekly *In Fact* were ignored forty years ago, local media ignore the Federal Communication Commission (FCC) attempts to shut Kantako's station down. "Not one has defended Kantako's right of access to the airwaves. Not one has defended the right to the free flow of information that we selectively demand of certain other countries. . . . Not one has mentioned the pro-democracy potentials of Kantako's model."[34]

There is also a little-known "deep dish" TV network in operation providing alternative news. It has aired programs on the Persian Gulf War. It has beamed a program called "Behind Censorship" directly to individual PBS stations and individuals with dish antennas. Its views are so at odds with the rhetoric pouring out of the media that some felt the Public Broadcasting System would be forced to censor these documentaries.[35] It is important to note that, if one has read deeply enough, many documentaries are addressing in a low key some of the frauds of the Cold War. Assassinations are being lightly addressed: one actually pointed out that, after the assassination of Trotsky, the Soviet Union established a policy of no assassinations outside its borders. Covert actions are heavily sanitized but they are covered. One documentary actually discussed that Soviet archives demonstrate the Soviet Union did not exercise monolithic control over other nations within its sphere of influence, but instead was frustrated at times by the policies of its satellites.

The format proposed here—each interest group presenting its views within the same forum—would avoid fragmentation or control by powerful groups. When on the same platform with those who were emotionally well-balanced and conceptually sound, those with far-out concepts would be recognized for the demagogues they are and would be ignored by most. It is to the benefit of all to restructure to a socially managed communications system that maximizes individuality rather than letting society fragment into ideological segments.

Notes

1. Joseph C. Goulden, *Monopoly* (New York: Pocket Books, 1970), p. 96; Robert McChesney, ed., *Capitalism and the Information Age: The Political Economy of the Global Communication Revolution* (New York: Monthly Review Press, 1998); Robert McChesney, *Corporate Media and the Threat to Democracy* (New York: Seven Stories Press, 1997).

2. Robert McChesney and Edward S. Herman, *The Global Media: The Missionaries of Global Capitalism* (Washington, DC: Cassell, 1997).

3. Ben Bagdikian, *Media Monopoly* (Boston: Beacon Press, 1987), pp. 138–40, 148, 229. Herman, McChesney, and Herman, *The Global Media.*

4. Mark Green, *The Other Government* (New York: W.W. Norton, 1978), p. 222.

5. Bernard D. Nossiter, "The F.C.C.'s Big Giveaway Show," *The Nation,* October 26, 1985, p. 403; PBS, *McNeil/Lehrer News Hour,* March 21, 1987; Alvin P. Sanoff et al., "Who Will Control TV," *U.S. News and World Report,* May 13, 1985, p. 60; the 40 to 60 percent profits were reported on *CBS News,* March 25, 1985.

6. John Stromnes, "Rural Montana Gets Taste of Public TV," *The Missoulian,* October 8, 1987, p. 9. Stromnes's source is Dan Tone from the University of Nevada at Reno.

7. Sanoff, "Who Will Control TV," p. 60.

8. Goulden, *Monopoly,* p. 110.

9. Ibid., p. 104.

10. "Firm Claims Breakthrough in High-Definition Television," *The Spokesman-Review,* July 13, 1989, p. A9.

11. Bill Gates, "The Road Ahead," *Newsweek,* November 27, 1995, p. 61.

12. Thorstein Veblen, *Engineers and the Price System* (New York: B.W. Huebsch, 1921), p. 110; Stuart Chase, *The Tragedy of Waste* (New York: Macmillan, 1925), p. 222, quoting Thorstein Veblen; Lester Thurow, *Head to Head: The Coming Economic Battle Among Japan, Europe, and America* (New York: William Morrow, 1992), p. 49.

13. Veblen, *Engineers and the Price System,* p. 110; Chase, *Tragedy of Waste,* p. 222; Thurow, *Head to Head,* p. 49; CBS, *60 Minutes,* September 2, 1995.

14. Paul Zane Pilzer, *Unlimited Wealth* (New York: Crown, 1990), p. 44.

15. Steven Levy, "Bill's New Vision," *Newsweek,* November 27, 1995, p. 68.

16. William J. Cook, "Reach Out and Touch Everyone," *U.S. News and World Report,* October 10, 1988, pp. 49–50.

17. Ivan Ladanov and Vladimar Pronnikov, "Craftsmen and Electronics," *New Times* 47 (November 1988), pp. 24–25.

18. J. W. Smith, *The World's Wasted Wealth 2* (San Luis Obispo, CA: Institute for Economic Democracy, 1994).

19. Bagdikian, *Media Monopoly,* 1987, pp. 138–40, 148, 229; William Manchester, *The Glory and the Dream* (New York: Bantam Books, 1988), p. 975.

20. Anne Windishar, "Expert: 20% of Gifted Kids Drop Out," *Spokane Chronicle,* January 7, 1988, p. B7.

21. Representative Ron Wyden of Oregon and Senator Edward Kennedy introduced bills which "would require the dedication of an entire channel on the new public-TV satellite to instructional shows aimed at preschoolers and elementary-school children" (Miriam Horn, "Can the Boob Tube Finally Get Serious," *U.S. News & World Report,* August 24, 1992, p. 61).

22. *CNN News,* May 24, 1988.

23. Thurow, *Head to Head,* pp. 273–79, especially p. 278.

24. Four books written by people who were in the right place at the right time to know key facts, and who

have dedicated their lives to seeing that history is recorded correctly, are: Robert J. Groden and Harrison Edward Livingstone, *High Treason: The Assassination of President John F. Kennedy and the New Evidence of Conspiracy* (San Francisco: Berkeley Books, 1990); Jim Garrison, *On the Trail of the Assassins* (New York: Sheridan Square Press, 1988); Anthony Summers, *Conspiracy* (New York: Paragon House, 1989); Jim Marrs, *Crossfire: The Plot That Killed Kennedy* (New York: Carroll and Graf, 1989). Those books and a documentary, "The Men Who Killed Kennedy," made in Britain for release on the twenty-fifth anniversary of Kennedy's assassination, but not shown in the U.S. until eleven years later, leave little doubt it was a political assassination.

25. Juliet B. Schor, *The Overworked American* (New York: Basic Books, 1991), p. 61.

26. Thurow, *Head to Head,* pp. 261–62.

27. Richard J. Herrnstein and Charles Murray, *The Bell Curve* (New York: Free Press, 1994), p. 399; *60 Minutes*, CBS, September 24, 1995.

28. According to Salt Lake City's PBS station, $1 million per year rented all its tapes.

29. *Broadcasting and Cablecasting Yearbook;* Stromnes, p. 9.

30. David Armstrong, *Trumpet to Arms* (Boston: South End Press, 1981), p. 340.

31. "The Rush to Gulp US Radio Stations," *The Christian Science Monitor,* May 7, 1996, p. 18. The title of this article says it well.

32. Herbert I. Schiller, *Information and the Crisis Economy* (Boston: Oxford University Press, 1986), pp. 109, 122.

33. Herbert Schiller (interview), "The Information Highway: Paving Over the Public," *Z Magazine* (March 1994), pp. 46–50. See also Peggy Norton, "Independent Radio's Problems and Prospects," *Z Magazine* (March 1990), pp. 51–57.

34. Mike Townsend, "Microwatt Revolution," *Lies of Our Times* (January 1991).

35. Dan Cohen, "Deep Dish: Outsiders on Public TV," *The Guardian,* May 6, 1992, p. 19.

28

Media to Empower the Powerless

Society is controlled for the benefit of the powerful through a variety of methods: simultaneous massive funding by foundations, corporations, and the intelligence service of think tanks, biased professors, and universities—most not realizing their own biases (those tens of thousands of fraudulent articles planted around the world and those twenty-five to thirty CIA-funded fraudulent books published per year, with the intelligence agencies of other nations doing the same); covert establishment of supportive (hard right) media with public (intelligence service) funds; every world event being run through intelligence services' wordsmiths who restructure the event to the desired view of the world. If a country needs to be brought under control (Iran, Libya, Cuba, etc.—countries which have killed very few of their citizens), there will be loud rhetoric about human rights abuses, state terrorism, or a particularly vicious dictator. When a country's leader is needed as an ally (Syngman Rhee in South Korea, Suharto in Indonesia, and Somoza in Nicaragua, all of whom killed tens of thousands of peaceful and productive citizens), one will hear only a rhetoric of authoritative governments.

These created views of the world are put out while massive slaughters by covertly supported dictators are totally ignored, downgraded, or blamed on others. Thus the public is not aware that many violent events—planned, financed, armed, and guided by their nation's intelligence services—even happened.

Sincere but unwitting professors and equally sincere and unaware writers and reporters, not realizing how this massive fraudulent information was planted, have put out articles and books by the thousands based on this badly tainted and frequently totally false information, and continue to do so. Thousands of novels produced to entertain the masses are also based on this created view of the world, and all are making a lot of money producing this propaganda nonsense for the already propagandized masses as both serious education and entertainment.

Some Frauds of History

The battle of Saint-Mihiel is recorded in virtually every history book as the turning point of World War I. Five hundred and fifty thousand Allied troops were supposedly involved and tens of thousands of Germans captured. Yet no such battle occurred. "There was not one German soldier or one German gun within forty or fifty miles." One "blundering war correspondent," as George Seldes called himself, and "two United States Army artists 'captured' the town," hours before the Allied army arrived.[1]

What became written history was the timed press releases the army had prepared in advance—a clear example of the creation of a Social Control belief system. As addressed earlier, the same was true of much of the Korean War. It was a war of U.S. military press releases.

Certainly there were some hard battles in the Korean War. But, as we documented above, many battles describing "hordes of Chinese" never happened, and horrendous naval and aerial assaults against defenseless North Korean civilians designed to prevent the North Koreans from accepting a peace settlement were excluded from the news and from history.[2] (Western leaders were programming the world so they could arm and fight covert wars, overt wars, and their Cold War.) The same is true of much else in history.

The turning over of many European governments to fascism during the Great Depression when the entrenched power structures were threatened with the loss of that power through the vote (known only to a few in-depth researchers) is one example of history that needs to be addressed in popular literature.[3] With the masses unaware of how democratic solutions were avoided in that crisis, the potential for a replay is high.

The improperly named Spanish Civil War took place in the one country in which the powerful did permit the vote and the alliance of aristocracy and wealth lost control of the government. The fascists used foreign military power to take back the government. Analyzing that history makes it evident that fascism is an arm of the world's wealthy power brokers and the wars they start are either to protect their monopoly powers or to decide among themselves who will establish the rules of unequal trade (World Wars I and II). The false histories currently recorded retard the evolution of democracy and need to be corrected.

With government information services, intelligence services, and think tank press releases; with foundation, corporate, and intelligence service funding of the propaganda process; and with negligible resources among the impoverished and politically weak, the belief systems of the world stay to the right of the political spectrum. There is no left and no functioning middle. There is only a right and an extreme right, which are viewed by the people as a political right and a political left.

Restructuring the Media to Cover the Full Political Spectrum

Instead of only the agenda of the Managers of State and the powerful being supported and promoted by these carefully crafted interpretations of national and international events, newspapers, magazines, TV, and radio should provide the spokespeople for the groups or societies under assault (the true middle and the true left) with equal space and time to present their side. It does not even have to be done by law. One conscientious publisher or broadcaster can do it.

60 Minutes is the most popular news documentary on TV, even if it does not present with balance the controversial views of the world we are describing. If similar newspapers, news magazines, TV programs, or radio stations expanded the horizons of their audiences by laying the carefully crafted, propagandized view of events side by side with articulate spokespersons for peace, freedom, justice, rights, and majority rule for all in the world, they would soon be in high demand nationwide, especially if they simultaneously explained the propaganda process that has historically kept the masses under control.

The rules would be very basic: all exposures of human rights abuses would be encouraged but no one would be permitted to put out propaganda or promote hatred of another group or society. Of course this would mean that the State Department, intelligence agencies, and their spokespersons (ambassadors and other government agencies) would have to abandon their propaganda. No public institution or policy can stand after it has been exposed to the public and they reject it.

Now that the Cold War is over, the media could, by simple one-liners, quickly alert the public to suppressed history without losing their audience and, in most cases, without losing their advertisers. For example, a news report on Iranian terrorism followed by the sentence, ''The Iranians are angry over America's Operation Ajax, which overthrew their democracy and reestablished the dictatorship of the Shah,'' would be very informative.

Subtle, but Explosive, One-Liners Would Alert the Masses

Concerning politics, economics, and history—all soft disciplines—the developed world is primarily programmed, not educated. What we are addressing is available in select classes in the university system but in very narrow fields attended by a very small percentage of students. The proof can be found by simply talking to people. Not only are few aware of the distortions of reality by Managers of State that this book has addressed in depth, they will be upset at any suggestion they were not fully informed.

Occasionally a one-line snapshot of true history is shown, but not with a big enough picture to alert the masses. A vitriolic report on Russia's Boris Yeltsin's statement addressed earlier that ''They (Russia) may have American prisoners over there yet'' was followed by such a one-sentence statement: ''There were over 730 American airmen shot down over the Soviet

Union during the Cold War.'' Those vitriolic statements were meaningless; the real story was that last sentence. If analyzed, that sentence would blow away the fog created by the propaganda of the Cold War.

Another example: Whenever discussing the dictator Suharto of Indonesia it would only be necessary to add, ''Indonesia's democratically elected Sukarno was overthrown on the second attempt by the CIA, which resulted in the slaughter of between 500,000 and 1 million civilians.'' The public would be instantly alerted and demand to know the facts, and such covert actions would cease. Especially if that sentence was followed by a second: ''Between 12 million and 15 million people have been violently slaughtered by such covert and overt actions; the United States has been the primary promoter and supporter of such destabilizations.'' Instead, the masses hear volumes of injustices done by others. These injustices are primarily manufactured by the CIA, or other intelligence agencies, and described in government press releases as reality.

Roughly 500 of Argentina's disappeared were pregnant women who were imprisoned to term, gave birth by cesarean section, were drugged and loaded on a nightly flight of death to be dropped into the Atlantic Ocean and their babies were adopted into military families. This slaughter of mostly innocents was well known to the government and, through their confessions to their priests, the church. We say mostly innocents because most of those drugged and dropped into the Atlantic under cover of darkness were only speaking up for their rights and were totally nonviolent.

Not only would this largely unknown horror never have happened, neither would the other thousands of state-sponsored terrors (which included so-called insurgency wars) adding up to 12 to 15 million violently killed.

The media, like most people, are conscientious and if they knew how the news was controlled, and if they knew the true history, they would keep slipping in those little one-liners that would expose the propaganda. Whenever a news release comes over the wire about slaughter in Latin America by insurgents such as in the 1970s and 1980s, almost certainly intelligence service and/or State Department press releases, the local reporter needs only to add one line: "U.S. intelligence established and supported death squads during the Cold War that killed between 150,000 and 300,000 peaceful prospective leaders (the potential Gandhis and Martin Luther Kings) of those countries." Sources should be given so the reader can quickly check on these facts. This would quickly alert the masses to the reality that these were suppressions of the same freedoms Americans fought for in 1776 and the War of 1812.

Putting the West's state-sponsored terrorism alongside any other terrorism or human rights abuses would quickly demonstrate who has created the most terror and insecurity throughout the world. Once alerted by the exposure of how propaganda works in a "free" society, the people would easily spot these intelligence agency creations and, because it would mean defeat at election time, propaganda would cease. Their integrity at stake, universities would weed out compliant professors who take intelligence service or corporate money to produce fraudulent research and the news media would become much more responsible.

The Developing World Can Leapfrog Decades in the Development Process

For the cost of producing the documentaries, establishing the satellite TV system, providing the TV sets and workbooks, and establishing testing stations, all Third World children of all ages would have access to all grades of education, including a master's or doctorate, for a fraction of the cost in the developed world.

Education would start on any subject as soon as the education documentaries were filmed. Students or communities able to finance TVs, work tables, notebooks, slates, and soon would start their formal education immediately. Those with access to a TV but too poor to afford the other basics would develop keen enough memories to pass tests, just as their ancestors handed down the wisdom of the ages by memorized stories.

This new system will be an advantage over the developed world. Developed-world education bureaucracies are locked into the current expensive structure so thoroughly that it will be impossible to uproot them. Not only can the Third World be educated for from 5 percent to 15 percent the cost of the developed world, it could, if it can avoid those imposed belief systems, be much better educated.

Although all societies resort to programming to control their populations, think what the Third World could do if it could avoid propaganda masquerading as an honest education, which is the reason the developed world will go to any length to prevent the dependent world from gaining control of its information systems. To lose control of the world's information systems is to lose control of the imposed belief systems that in turn would eliminate control of the periphery of empire, which would reduce the inequality of trades, which all translates into eliminating much of the inequalities of wealth.

Politicians Speaking to, and Listening to, the People, Not Just Corporations

The purpose of McCarthyism was to lock academics, the media, and all opinion makers inside the permitted parameters of debate of the

Cold War. Although it destroyed the lives of thousands of conscientious people, it worked brilliantly and is still a powerful force today. It is only because we are so totally immersed in it, and thus consider it customary and normal, that we are unaware of the true hold of this massive Social Control belief system.

William Greider, in *Who Will Tell the People?*, explains how the big guns of those Social Control belief systems work. The leaders of Congress know well the rough outline of most laws that will be passed. What the public hears is a thunderous rhetoric within narrow parameters at the right of the political spectrum, jockeying for position with the voters. Except for corporations which fund the elections, the public is essentially unrepresented and decisions are made far from the public arena.

Politics, as now contrived, is hardly amenable to new ideas. Society is kept at the right of the political spectrum and Social Control belief systems keep political rhetoric within those permitted parameters of debate. To move outside these parameters is political and social suicide.

Assuming there is no crisis, an ideologically programmed population is guaranteed to vote in support of the social policy the current power structure shrilly promotes; there are no choices outside those parameters. To move to what is a true middle position is to be instantly attacked as liberal, socialist, heretical, un-American, or even communist—the reductionist clichés of the Social Control paradigm, the Cold War, in effect since 1946. Therefore, few knowledgeable leaders can freely say what they believe. They avoid all in-depth analysis and commitments.

These politicians should not be too heavily criticized for their evasions. To admit openly that the Soviet military threat was not real, to recognize that mercantilist principles still dominate world trade, to acknowledge the ongoing suppressions (political, financial, economic, diplomatic, and military) of developing nations' attempts to gain control over their governments and economies after World War II, or to promote truly progressive social policies would cost them their political life.

If they suggested even moderate plans to restructure any of the wasteful segments of the economy we have been outlining, the big guns of the many subtle monopolies would, through cranking up the rhetoric of the operative Social Control belief system, collectively and immediately sink their political ships.

Ten to twenty reserved TV channels would be needed for serious leaders to present their views. Serious, in this instance, means having a substantial segment of the population to represent—corporations, business people, farmers, labor, women, minorities, the poor, conservationists, peace groups, and so forth.

If there is anywhere politicians must be, it is in the spotlight. Those not attending these indepth background discussions would be relinquishing their claim to leadership. With authorities such as those cited throughout this book invited to these forums, it would be difficult to duck the issues. There would just be too many questions.

Here is where the elimination of monopolization of information is of the highest importance. Only when all have the opportunity to present their views and thus deny the opportunity of social-control rhetoric, or even make it counterproductive, can there be true democracy. Those who presented a consistent and accurate view of reality, and promoted a policy for the maximum good of the people, would gather a loyal following.

Most of the public would not watch these indepth discussions, but those who did would gain from the knowledge of these experts. Interested people would make value judgments on the history leading to the present problems, study the different solutions that were presented, and analyze the intelligence and integrity of the leaders proposing these solutions. It is these interested people and their opinions that guide the thinking of the nation.

These opinion makers (intellectuals, leaders, and the news media) would watch the information forums to inform themselves and, in turn, inform the public. To do less would leave one uninformed and lose one's followers. With elections structured for candidates to prove their mettle—like the famous Lincoln-Douglas debates—the now-informed citizens would be enabled to make responsible voting decisions.

Notes

1. George Seldes, *Even The Gods Can't Change History* (Secaucus, NJ: Lyle Stuart, 1976), p. 16.

2. I.F. Stone, *The Hidden History of the Korean War* (Boston: Little Brown, 1952). See Chapter Six in this work for a synopsis.

3. Karl Polanyi, *The Great Transformation* (Boston: Beacon Press, 1957), chapter 20, especially p. 38.

Conclusion

A Grand Strategy for Cooperative Capitalism in the Twenty-first Century

It is a recognized tenet of philosophy that no society dare tell the truth about itself until centuries later when it has supposedly become more civilized and democratic. It can then refer to the violence it imposed upon others in earlier history as something that would not happen in its present restructured, benevolent, gentle, and democratic culture. If violence, wars, and poverty are to be addressed sincerely, we must look at reality today, not a hundred years later. Now that the Cold War is over, an occasional honest analysis appears that gives tantalizing glimpses of the Grand Strategies used by imperial centers of capital for protecting their wealth and power.[1] By describing those Grand Strategies in a language all can understand, as opposed to diplomatic language designed to conceal, we are putting in print for serious study what would normally not be openly acknowledged in official history books until generations later. If the violence of the past is not to be repeated over and over, we must understand the Grand Strategies that produced our violent history.

The Grand Strategy for Colonial Imperialism Summarized

During the time of classical colonial imperialism, human rights and democracy were not yet the norm. The early ruling of colonies under trading companies (East India Company, Africa Company, Hudson Bay Company, etc.) was quite straightforward: Demonize those targeted for dispossession of their land and resources (or even their life); defeat those weak, primitive, and typically gentle cultures; push those too weak to defend themselves off their land or off the face of the earth (North America, some of Latin America, Australia, New Zealand, Hawaii); and establish colonial governments to dictate policy over more culturally advanced and denser populations (India, China, Egypt, Algeria, the Middle East). The rest of the colonial world (most of Africa, much of Latin America) simply involved too large a territory and too many people, and there was not enough time, for European settlers to dispossess them of their land.

The Grand Strategies for Corporate Imperialism of the Last Half of the Twentieth Century Summarized

Human rights and democracy were forced upon the power structures of the imperial nations through the American Revolution, the revolt of the masses in the French, Russian, and Chinese revolutions, Mahatma Gandhi's passive and peaceful revolution, and thousands of smaller struggles against both external and internal dictatorships. While the claiming of democracy and rights within the imperial centers was substantial, even if incomplete, the reforms on the periphery were minimal. Of course this is another tenet of philosophy, "The more things change, the more they stay the same." Peace, freedom, justice, rights, and majority rule have made substantial advances within centers of empires, but as soon as one includes the rights and destiny of those on the periphery, those words have little meaning. The essential power relationships have not changed. The wealth of the periphery is still transferred to the center, the already poor remain impoverished, they have few tangible rights, they do not have economic freedom, many do not know peace, and that certainly is not justice. The options, and thus the quality of life, on the periphery under corporate imperialism are little better than under colonial imperialism. This did not just happen by chance; maintaining control of the periphery while expounding on human rights required planning and management. This book is a study of the colonial Grand Strategies of the Managers of State revised for corporate imperialism.

Under the rhetoric of democracy, citizens have the right to change their leaders by the vote. This constitutional right requires that power brokers inculcate their citizens (voters) with the belief that their system of government, law, and rights are superior to all others; that this is the source of their wealth and high standard of living; and that others have only to emulate the imperial center to become wealthy. Societies on the periphery, which are the real source of that wealth and who were once dismissed as uncivilized (to pick the softest cliché), now had to be at least spoken of sympathetically, while at the same time it was essential to continue demonizing competing powerful centers of capital and nations that

were demanding more freedom. Thus various imperial centers of capital were demonizing each other, leading to World Wars I and II; the West and the East were demonizing each other during the Cold War; human rights abuse rhetoric is constantly thrown against the remaining threatening center of capital, China; and nations that do not passively accept others controlling their destiny (Cuba, Iran, Iraq, Libya, etc.) are continually demonized as terrorists. Likewise, if there is resistance to expansions of the imperial center, those resisters must be demonized (the breakup of Yugoslavia to push the line between the Western Christian center of capital and Eastern Orthodox Christianity's collapsing center of capital further East).

For the imperial centers to maintain control while sermonizing on democracy and while the periphery was simultaneously clamoring for freedom required replacement of colonial governments with puppet governments. Maintaining a fragmented political structure on the periphery required covertly destabilizing governments which could not be controlled. A powerful military had to be maintained to bring into line nations that could not be subverted and were in danger of breaking out of the imposed belief system and legal structure. As control of others was antithetical to democracy as taught throughout the world—as well as to the conventional rhetoric of peace, freedom, justice, rights, and majority rule—this external governance had to be kept secret from voters of the imperial center and elections on the periphery had to be monitored carefully and covertly controlled. The imperial centers concealed in nearly total secrecy the fact that they were behind most of the destabilizations on the periphery, the CIA's "Mighty Wurlitzer"—mentioned throughout this thesis—hid these covert actions under a blanket of misinformation and plausible denial, and that distorted history is now recorded in history books as reality. The Cold War was only an especially intense period of empires doing what they have always done to protect their wealth and power: impose belief systems upon the masses of both the center and, through those puppet governments, the periphery. Hand in hand with those belief systems, laws are put in place to protect monopolization of finance capital, monopolization of technology (industry), and monopoly titles to nature's gifts to everybody, those precious natural resources

All other choices for the periphery had been discredited by the almost 100 percent failure rate for those attempting to gain control of their destiny. No choice was left but to accept the fiction that the imperial center was functioning under free trade and that they too must accept the belief system and rules of trade of the imperial center. Of course, those failures were guaranteed by the 100 to 200 major and thousands of minor covert destabilizations that we have addressed in depth. While a few people on the periphery may be aware and violent and angry, the majority are unaware and attempt to accommodate to the reality that there are no other options, accepting the structural adjustments being forced upon them. That acceptance opens up their resources, labor, and markets for continued exploitation by the same corporate imperialists who designed the GATT/NAFTA/WTO/MAI unequal rules of trade.

Under those structural adjustment rules, the pay differential between the imperial center and the periphery for equally productive work widens. As the wages on the periphery collapse, the wealth accumulated by the imperial center increases exponentially. When equally productive labor on the periphery is paid 20 percent that of equally productive labor in the imperial center, the wealth accumulation advantage of the imperial center is twenty-five to one (high pay divided by the low pay, squared, as we learned in Chapter One). The doubling of the pay differential for equally productive labor to ten to one from the currency meltdowns increased the wealth accumulation advantage of the still stable imperial center to one hundred to one. In short, assuming the Managers of State avoid a collapse of the center, the wealth accumulation power of the imperial center trading with the collapsed periphery quadrupled as the wealth accumulation power of that periphery collapsed by a similar amount. So long as the buying power holds, the wealth will now flow to the imperial centers faster than ever. The slogans of peace, freedom, justice, rights, and majority rule appear very valid to populations of the imperial center living well off that wealth pouring in from the periphery. But as soon as one steps into the shoes of those on the periphery, it is anything but peace, freedom, justice, rights, or majority rule.

A New Grand Strategy for Sustainable Development and Alleviation of World Poverty

This is an opportune moment to stake a claim to the moral high ground, share the enormous productivity of technology, eliminate most poverty, protect the world's ecosystems, and gain the respect and loyalty of the world. Any nation, or group of nations, which leads the world down that path to world peace and prosperity will go down in history as the most moral and conscientious society.

The route to alleviation of world poverty is, of course, reversing the policies that impoverished naturally wealthy nations in the first place. Destabilizations and fragmentation must be abandoned and true democracy, including economic democracy, must be embraced. Sustainable development and guarantees of borders should be offered in trade for regional disarmament. The factories, labor, and resources now producing arms should be turned to producing industries for sustainable development of large regions of producers and consumers constitutionally organized for human rights, equal rights, and economic rights. If the world can build a trillion dollars' worth of military hardware every year, it can certainly build $140 billion worth of productive tools per year and loan (or give) them to needy societies. Tools lent for productive purposes can be repaid from the wealth generated; tools for war—when built—subtract from the world's potential wealth, and—when used—destroy already produced wealth.[2]

These same reorganized industries of the developed world and the new industries in the developing world should produce a modern communications system for the world's poor. With direct TV and radio, those regions can educate their populations at a cost of 5 to 15 percent of the cost of the classroom-based education systems of the developed world. That education should include outlining a Grand Strategy for sustainable development to leapfrog the culturally bound imperial centers and become fully developed to a sustainable level in forty-five years. This will be a true informed democracy promoting regional integration and cooperation, the exact opposite of competing nations creating enemy belief systems as, for their very survival, they gird for either aggression or defense.

A crucial part of that Grand Strategy will be informing the people of three foundation principles of imperial centers of capital: (1) Every nation which became wealthy under capitalism developed under the principles of Friedrich List protection philosophy; none developed under Adam Smith free trade philosophy. (2) To maintain their access to the cheap natural resources and labor on the periphery, imperial centers supported destabilizing factions to prevent the political and economic consolidation of emerging countries. (3) Once an emerging region has a trained labor force, a modern industry, and a developed economic infrastructure, then those protections must be dropped and they must compete on the world markets. Armed with that knowledge, a population would look closely at all who aspire to power for any evidence that they were supported by external powers and turn on any who would destabilize their government and derail their sustainable development plans.

That same Grand Strategy requires the population to understand three foundation principles of a truly efficient economy: (1) Henry George's system of private ownership and utilization of land, with society collecting the landrent, is crucial for a maximally efficient economy.[3] (2) Development of the impoverished former periphery can only be through restructured patent laws which permit use of any technology by any company by simply paying a modest royalty for products sold internally and a normal royalty on products exported.[4] (3) Providing equal rights to finance capital as per the subchapters "Accumulation of Capital Through Cooperative Capitalism" (subchapter of Chapter 26), and "Investment" (subchapter of Chapter 27), will easily replace the finance capital formerly accumulated through the monopolization of land, technology, and finance capital.

These low-paid emerging regions should

trade equally with each other. With an understanding of how capital accumulates exponentially with the increased differential in pay for equally productive labor,[5] tariffs, resource depletion taxes, ecological taxes (all actually land-rent taxes) should be used to price commodities equal with the cost of mining and harvesting the world's poorer deposits and soils. Funds from those equalization taxes should be used for repayment for industrial and finance capital and for development of nonpolluting energy and a competitive technological base.[6]

The regional resource capacity should be studied to ascertain what level of sustainable lifestyle it will support. If the people wish a higher lifestyle, they must understand that others are entitled to their share of the world's resources and that population control is the only choice to reach those living standards rapidly without imposing upon the rights of others. Essential for any lifestyle decided upon will be life-sustaining fertile soils. Futuristic planners are researching rebuilding the ecosystem on Mars. We are advocating the same thoughtful care for the Earth's soils and ecosystems.

With the replacement of corporate imperialism with cooperative capitalism and the development of modern industries in the emerging world, leisure days can exceed working days in both the former developed world and the newly developed world.[7] This leisure time can allow the creation of a gardening culture that allows society to take back and ensure the safety of its food supply. Industrial agriculture requires massive acreage for row crops and mass production machinery. This is extremely energy- and capital-intensive. In place of corporate agriculture, each region developing a modified permaculture using tree crops, interplanted with perennial bush and vine crops that are themselves interplanted with annual crops, can increase the production per acre far beyond current soil-depleting monoculture farming while simultaneously protecting and rebuilding the soil.[8]

Developing societies through rational planning—and following the principles of peace, compassion, and social justice—will create a world that is immensely richer than one based on the monopolization of the tools of production and unequal trades. Once societies within balanced regional economies are developed, each with its proper and balanced share of world industrial capital, with society collecting the landrent, with any industry able to use any patent through simply paying a reasonable royalty, and with equally productive labor equally paid, then—and only then—will the efficiencies of free enterprise and free trade function for the benefit of all.

Compassion, good judgment, and very possibly even the survival of humankind require that the world trading system be restructured from the current corporate imperialism, with its violence, poverty, and despoiling of environments, to a caring cooperative capitalism with a minimum level of violence and poverty and a rebuilding of the ecosystems so crucial for the survival of all life. In the words of John Maynard Keynes, "Ultimately, mankind would be freed of the morbid love of money to confront the deeper questions of human existence—how to live wisely and agreeably and well."[9]

Notes

1. Christopher Layne, "Rethinking American Grand Strategy," *World Policy Journal* (Summer 1998): pp. 8–28.
2. Chapter 23.
3. Chapter 24.

4. Chapter 25.

5. Chapter 1.

6. Chapters 22 and 23.

7. J.W. Smith, *The World's Wasted Wealth 2* (San Luis Obispo, CA: Institute for Economic Democracy, 1994), chapters 1–6.

8. William H. Kötke, *The Final Empire: The Collapse of Civilization and the Seed of the Future* (Portland, OR: Arrow Point Press, 1993).

9. William Greider, *Secrets of the Temple* (New York: Simon and Schuster, 1987), pp. 173–74.

Bibliography

Acheson, Dean. *Present at the Creation.* New York: W.W. Norton, 1987.

Ackland, L. *Credibility Gap: A Digest Of The Pentagon Papers.* Philadelphia, PA: The National Literature Service, 1972.

Adams, J. *Secret Armies.* New York: The Atlantic Monthly Press, 1987.

Addison, Charles G. *The Knights Templar.* London: Longman, Brown, Green, and Longman, 1842.

AFL-CIO Task Force on Trade bulletin, 1992.

"Ag Export Value Projected to Climb." *Great Falls Tribune* (March 5, 1992).

Agee, Philip. "Tracking Covert Actions into the Future." *Covert Action Information Bulletin* (Fall 1992).

———. *Inside the Company: CIA Diary.* New York: Bantam Books, 1975.

———. Louis Wolf, *Dirty Work.* London: Zed Books, 1978.

"Ag Exports Projected to Climb." *AP, Great Falls Tribune* (March 5, 1992).

Ahmad, Feroz. "Arab Nationalism, Radicalism, and the Specter of Neocolonialism." *Monthly Review* (February 1991).

Allen, Terry. "In GATT They Trust." *Covert Action Information Bulletin* 40 (Spring, 1992).

Altvater, Elmar, Kurt Hubner, Jochen Lorentzen, Raul Rojas. *The Poverty of Nations.* New Jersey: Zed Books, 1991.

Ambrose, S.E. *Ike's Spies.* Garden City, New York: Doubleday, 1981.

Ameringer, C.D. *U.S. Foreign Intelligence.* Lexington, MA: Lexington Books, 1990.

Andrew, C. *For the President's Eyes Only: Secret Intelligence and the American Presidency From Washington To Bush.* New York: HarperCollins Publishers, 1995.

Anta Diop, Cheikh. *Black Africa.* Translated by Harold J. Salemson. Westport, CT: Lawrence Hill, 1978.

Aptheker, Herbert. *The American Revolution.* New York: International Publishers, 1985.

———. *The Colonial Era.* second ed. New York: International Publishers, 1966.

———. *Early Years of the Republic.* New York: International Publishers, 1976.

Arévalo, Juan José. *Anti-Kommunism in Latin America.* New York: Lyle Stuart, 1963.

Armstrong, David. *Trumpet to Arms.* Boston: South End Press, 1981.

Art, Robert J., Kenneth N. Waltz. *The Use of Force: Military Power and International Politics.* New York: University Press of America, 1993.

Attenborough, David. *The First Eden: The Mediterranean World and Man.* Boston: Little, Brown, 1987.

Avirgan, Tony, M. Honey, editors, *Lapenca: On Trial in Costa Rica.* San Jose, CA: Editorial Porvenir, 1987.

Bagdikian, Ben. *Media Monopoly.* Boston: Beacon Press, 1987.

Baker, Dean. "Job Drain." *The Nation* (July 12, 1993).

Banco, Anthony. "Playing With Fire." *Business Week* (September 16, 1987).

The Banneker Center's Corporate Welfare Shame Links. Http://www.progress.org/banneker/cw.html.

Baran, Paul A., Paul M. Sweezy. *Monopoly Capital.* London: Monthly Review Press, 1968.

Barnet, Richard. *The Lean Years.* New York: Simon and Schuster, 1980.

———. *The Alliance.* New York: Simon and Schuster, 1983.

———. *The Rockets' Red Glare: War, Politics and American Presidency.* New York: Simon and Schuster, 1983.

———. "Lords of the Global Economy." *The Nation* (December 19, 1994).

———. John Cavanagh. *Global Dreams: Imperial Corporations and the New World Order.* New York: Simon and Schuster, 1994.

Barr, Cameron W. "Making the Financial Architecture More Crisis Proof." *The Christian Science Monitor* (March 3, 1999).

Bartlett, Alan F. *Machiavellian Economics.* England: Schumacher, 1987.

Barlett, Donald L., James B. Steele. *America: What Went Wrong?* Kansas City: Andrews and McMeel, 1992.

———. "Fantasy Island and Other Perfectly Legal Ways that Big companies Manage to Avoid Billions in Federal Taxes," *Time* (November 16, 1998).

———. "Paying a Price for Polluters," *Time* (November 23, 1998).

———. "The Empire of Pigs," *Time* (November 30, 1998).

Beard, Charles A. *An Economic Interpretation of the Constitution.* New York: Macmillan Publishing Co, 1941.

Beaud, Michel. *A History of Capitalism, 1500 to 1980.* New York: Monthly Review Press, 1983.

Beeching, Jack. *The Chinese Opium Wars.* New York: Harcourt Brace Jovanovich, 1975.

Bello, W. *U.S. Sponsored Low Intensity Conflict in the Philippines.* San Francisco: Institute for Food and Development Policy (December, 1987).

Bemis, Samuel Flagg. *A Diplomatic History of the United States.* New York: Henry Holt, 1936.

Bennet, David H. *The Party of Fear.* Chapel Hill: University of North Carolina Press, 1988.

Bentley, Michael. *Politics Without Democracy.* London: Fontana Paperbacks, 1984.

Berger, John J., editor. *Environmental Restoration: Science and Strategies for Restoring the Earth.* Washington, DC: Island Press, 1990

Børgstrom, T George. *The Hungry Planet: The Modern World at the Edge of Famine.* New York: Collier Books, 1972.

Berlan, Jean-Pierre. "The Commodification of Life." *Monthly Review* (December 1989).

Bernstein, Carl. "The Holy Alliance." *Time Magazine* (February 24, 1992).

Bernstein, Merton C., Joan Brodshaug Bernstein. *Social Security: The System That Works.* New York: Basic Books, 1988.

Bishop, Abraham. *Georgia Speculation Unveiled.* Readex Microprint Corporation, 1966.

Blackstock, Nelson. *Cointelpro: The FBI's Secret War on Political Freedom.* New York: Anchor Foundation, 1988.

Blaufarb, D.S. *The Counterinsurgency Era: U.S. Doctrine and Performance 1950 To Present.* New York: The Free Press, 1977.

Blaug, Mark. *Great American Economists Before Keynes.* Atlantic Highlands, NJ: Humanities Press International, 1986.

Bluestone, Barry, Irving Bluestone. *Negotiating the Future.* New York: Basic Books, 1992.

Blum, William. *The CIA: A Forgotten History.* New Jersey: Zed Books Ltd., 1986.

———. *Killing Hope: U.S. Military Interventions Since World War II.* Monroe, ME: Common Courage Press, 1995.

Bond, Gordon C. *The Grand Expedition.* Athens: University of Georgia Press, 1979.

Bonner, R. *Waltzing With A Dictator.* New York: Times Books, 1987.

Bonvie, Linda, Bill Bonvie, Donna Gates. "Stevia: The Natural Sweetener That Frightens Nutrasweet." *Earth Island Journal* (Winter 1997–98).

"Bookworld," *Washington Post* (April 14, 1994, from McGehee CIABASE, Box 5022, Herndon, VA 22070, http://come.to/CIABASE/.

Boorstein, Edward. *What's Ahead?—––The U.S. Economy.* New York: International Publishers, 1984.

Boorstin, Daniel J. "History's Hidden Turning Points." *U.S. News & World Report* (April 22, 1991).

Börgstrom, George. *The Hungry Planet: The Modern World at the Edge of Famine.* New York: Collier Books, 1972,

Borosage, R.L., Marks, J. editors. *The CIA File.* New York: Grossman Publishers, 1976.

Borsodi, Ralph. *Inflation.* Great Barrington, MA: E.F. Schumacher Society, 1989.

Bortzutzky, Silvia. "The Chicago Boys, Social Security and Welfare in Chile", *The Radical Right and the Welfare State: An International Assessment of International Social Policy and Welfare,* Howard Glennerster, James Midgley, ed. Lanham, MD: Barnes and Noble, 1991.

Breckenfield, Gurney. "Higher Taxes That Promote Development." *Fortune* (August 8, 1983).

Breckinridge, S. P. *Legal Tender.* New York: Greenwood Press, 1969.

Bridge, F.R., *The Habsburg Monarchy.* New York: St. Martin's Press, 1990.

Broadcasting and Cablecasting Yearbook.

Brockway, Sandi. *Macrocosm USA.* Cambria, CA: Macrocosm USA, Inc., 1992.

Brody, Reed. *Contra Terror in Nicaragua: Report of a Fact Finding Mission: September 1984-January 1985.* Boston: South End Press, 1985.

Brown, George E. Jr., William J. Goold, John Cavanagh. "Making Trade Fair." *World Policy Journal* (Spring, 1992).

Brown, Lester R. *State of the World.* New York: W.W. Norton, 1998.

———. Christopher Flavin, Sandra Postel. *Saving the Planet.* New York: W.W. Norton, 1991.

Brown, Michael Barratt. *Fair Trade.* London: Zed Books, 1993.

Browne, Lewis. *Stranger Than Fiction: A Short History of the Jews.* New York: Macmillan, 1925.

Budiansky, Stephen. "An Act of Vision for the Third World." *U.S. News & World Report* (November 2, 1987).

"Buffalo Battalion—South Africa's Black Mercenaries." *Covert Action Information Bulletin* (July/August 1981).

Bulletin from the AFL-CIO Task Force on Trade (1992).

Bulletin Of Concerned Asian Scholars. Boulder, CO.

Burgoon, Brian. "NAFTA Thoughts." *Dollars and Sense.* (September/October 1995).

Burman, Edward. *The Inquisition: Hammer of Heresy.* New York: Dorset Press, 1992.

Burnes, James. *The Knights Templar.* London: Paybe and Foss, 1840.

Buzgalin, Alexander, Andrei Kolganov. *Bloody October in Moscow: Political Repression in the Name of Reform.* New York: Monthly Review Press, 1994.

Cagan, Joanna, Neil DeMause. *Field of Schemes.* Monroe, ME: Common Courage Press, 1998.

Caldwell, M., ed. Ten Years Military Terror Indonesia. Nottingham: Spokesmen Books, no date.

Calloni, Stella. "The Horror Archives of Operation Condor." *Covert Action Quarterly* 50 (Fall 1994).

Carsten, F. L. *Britain and the Weimar Republic.* New York: Schocken Books, 1984.

———. *The Rise of Fascism.* Berkeley: University of California Press, 1982.

Castro, Fidel. *Nothing Can Stop the Course of History.* New York: Pathfinder Press, 1986.

Catton, William Robert. *Overshoot: The Ecological Basis of Revolutionary Change.* Champaign, IL: University of Illinois Press, 1980.

Caute, David. *The Great Fear.* New York: Simon and Schuster, 1978.

Cavanagh, John. "Review of *The Rise and Fall of Economic Liberalism: The Making of the Economic Gulag.*" *Monthly Review* (May 1997).

———, ed. *Trading Freedom.* San Francisco: The Institute for Food and Development Policy, 1992.

CBS News

Chamberlain, E. R. *The Fall of the House of Borgia.* New York: Dorset Press, 1987.

Chamorro, E., "Packaging the Contras: A case of CIA Disinformation." *Monograph Series Number 2.* New York: Institute For Media Analysis, 1987.

"Change." *Railway Age* (November 1984).

Chase, Stuart. *The Economy of Abundance.* New York: The Macmillan Company, 1934.

———. *Men and Machines.* New York: The Macmillan Company, 1929.

———. *The Tragedy of Waste.* New York: The Macmillan Company, 1925.

Chavkin, Samuel. *The Murder of Chile.* New York: Everest House, 1982.

Chester, E.T. *Covert Network: Progressives, the International Rescue Committee, and the CIA.* Armonk: M.E. Sharpe, 1995.

Chien, Arnold J. "Tanzanian Tales." *Lies of Our Times* (January 1991).

"China Maneuvering Around Quotas to Market Textiles to United States." *The Spokesman-Review* (January 10, 1989).

Chinweiezu. "Debt Trap Peonage." *Monthly Review* (November 1985).

Chomsky, Noam. "Enduring Truths: Changing Markets." *Covert Action Quarterly* (Spring 1996).

———. *The Culture of Terrorism.* Boston: South End Press, 1988.

————. *Deterring Democracy.* New York: Verso, 1992.

————. *Year 501: The Conquest Continues.* Boston: South End Press, 1993.

————. *The Prosprous Few and the Restless Many.* Berkeley: Odonian Press, 1993.

Chossudovsky, Michel. "*Dismantling Yugoslavia, Colonizing Bosnia.*" *Covert Action Quarterly* (Spring, 1996).

————. *The Globalization of Poverty: Impacts of IMF and World Bank Reforms.* London: Zed Books, 1997.

Choucri, Nazli, Robert C. North. *Nations in Conflict.* San Francisco: W. H. Freeman, 1974.

Church Committee Report. Congressional Record. 1975–76.

Churchhill, Ward. *Cointelpro Papers : Documents from the FBI's Secret Wars Against Domestic Dissent.* South End Press, 1990.

————. *Agents of Repression : The FBI's Secret Wars Against the Black Panther Party and the American Indian Movement.* Boston: South End Press, 1989.

The Christian Science Monitor (December 4, 1997).

Clairmont, Frederic F. *The Rise and Fall of Economic Liberalism.* Goa, India: The Other India Press, 1996.

Clarridge, Duane R. *A Spy for all Seasons: My Life in the CIA..* New York: Scribner, 1997.

Cline, R.S. *Secrets, Spies, and Scholars.* Washington, DC: Acropolis Books, 1976.

CNN Frontline (November 18, 1991).

CNN Headline News (June 28, 1990).

Cockburn, Alexander. "Beat the Devil." *The Nation* (March 6, 1989).

Codevilla, Angelo. *Informing Statecraft.* New York: The Free Press, 1992.

Cohen, Carl, ed. *Communism, Fascism, Democracy.* New York: Random House, 1962.

Cohen, Dan. "Deep Dish: Outsiders on Public TV." *The Guardian* (May 6, 1992).

Colby, Gerard, Charlotte Dennett. *Thy Will Be Done: The Conquest of the Amazon: Nelson Rockefeller and Evangelism in the Age of Oil.* New York: Harper Collins, 1995.

Colby, Gerard. *Du Pont: Behind the Nylon Curtain.* Englewood Cliffs, N.J.: Prentice-Hall, 1974.

Colby, William. *Honorable Men.* New York: Simon and Schuster, 1978.

Coleman, Peter. *Liberal Conspiracy.* London: Collier Macmillan, 1989.

Collmer, Kathy. "Guess Who's Coming to Dinner?" *Utne Reader* (July/August, 1992).

Committee of Concerned Asian Scholars, *The Indochina Story: A Fully Documented Account.* New York: Pantheon Books, 1970.

Commoner, Barry. *Making Peace With the Planet.* New York: Pantheon, 1990.

Commons, John R. *Legal Foundations of Capitalism.* London: Transaction Publishers, 1995.

————. *Institutional Economics.* London: Transaction Publishers, 1995.

Conboy, K., J. Morrison. *Shadow War: The CIA's Secret War in Laos.* Bolder, CO: Paladin Press, 1995.

Condliffe, J. B. *The Commerce of Nations.* New York: Norton, 1950.

Constantino, R., L.R. Constantino. *The Philippines: The Continuing Past.* Quezon City, Philippines: The Foundation for Nationalist Studies, 1978.

Cook, B. *The Declassified Eisenhower.* Garden City, NY: Doubleday, 1981.

Cook, Don. *Forging the Alliance.* London: Seeker and Warburg, 1989.

Cook, William J. "Reach Out and Touch Everyone." *U.S. News & World Report* (October 10, 1988).

Cooper, Mathew, Dorian Friedman. "The Rich in America." *U.S. News & World Report* (November 18, 1991).

Cooper, Mathew. "Give Trade a Chance." *U.S. News & World Report* (February 14, 1994).

Copeland, M. *Beyond Cloak and Dagger.* New York: Pinnacle Books, 1975.

Cordovez, D, S.S. Harrison, *Out of Afghanistan: The Inside Story of the Soviet Withdrawal.* New York: Oxford University Press, 1995.

Corn, D. *Blond Ghost: Ted Shackley and the CIA's Crusades.* New York: Simon and Schuster, 1994.

Corn, David, Jefferson Morley. "Beltway Bandits." *The Nation* (April 9, 1988).

Corwin, Julie, Douglas Stranglin, Suzanne Possehl, Jeff Trimble. "The Looting of Russia." *U.S. News & World Report* (March 7, 1994).

"The Costs of War." *The Nation* (December 24, 1990).

Counterspy (all issues).

Covert Action Quarterly (all issues).

Covington, Sally. "Right Thinking, Big Grants, and

Long Term Strategy: How Conservative Philanthropies and Think Tanks Transform U.S. Policy.'' *Covert Action Quarterly* (Winter 1998).

Currey, C.B. *Edward Lansdale: The Unquiet American.* Boston: Houghton Mifflin Company, 1988.

Daly, Herman E. *Steady-State Economics.* San Francisco: W.H. Freeman 1977.

———. John B. Cobb Jr. *For the Common Good.* Boston: Beacon Press, 1989.

———. Salah El Serafy, editors. *Population, Technology, and Lifestyle.* Washington, DC: Island Press, 1992.

Danaher, Kevin, Editor. *50 Years Is Enough: The Case Against the World Bank and the International Monetary Fund.* Boston: South End Press, 1995.

Daraul, Arkon. *A History of Secret Societies.* Secaucus, NJ: Citadel Press, 1961.

David, Arie E. *The Strategy of Treaty Termination.* New Haven: Yale University Press, 1975.

DeForest, O., Chanoff, D. *Slow Burn.* New York: Simon and Schuster, 1990.

Dentzer, Susan. ''The Coming Global Boom.'' *U.S. News & World Report* (July 16, 1990).

Depth News, Manila, Quoted by *World Press Review* (March 1991).

De Rosa, Peter. *Vicars of Christ: The Dark Side of the Papacy.* New York: Crown Publishers, 1988.

Desmond, Edward W. ''Japan's Trillion-Dollar Hole.'' *Time* (April 8, 1996).

———. ''The Failed Miracle.'' *Time* (April 22, 1996).

Dinges, John, Saul Landau. *Assassination on Embassy Row.* New York: Pantheon Books, 1980.

Dobbowski, Michael N., Isodor Wallimann. *Radical Perspectives on the Rise of Fascism in Germany.* New York: Monthly Review Press, 1989.

Doder, Dusko. ''Yugoslavia: New War, Old Hatreds.'' *Foreign Policy* (Summer 1993).

Donahue, John D. *The Privatization Decision: Public Ends and Private Means.* New York: Basic Books, 1989.

Donner, Frank J. *The Age of Surveillance: The Aims and Methods of America's Political Intelligence System.* New York: Random House, 1981.

Dorgan, Byron, Senator. *The North Dakota REC* (May 1984).

Douglas-Hamilton, James. *Motive For a Mission: The Story Behind Rudolf Hess's Flight to Britain.* New York: Paragon House, 1979.

Douthwaite, Richard. ''Community Money.'' *Yes* (Spring 1999).

Dregson, Alan, Duncan Taylor, Editors. *Ecoforestry: The Art and Science of Sustainable Forest Use.* Gabriola Island, BC: New Society Publishers, 1997

Drucker, Peter. *The New Realities.* New York: Harper & Row, 1989.

Echeverria, Durand. *The Maupeou Revolution: A Study in the History of Libertarianism.* Baton Rouge: Lousiana State University Press, 1985.

Eckholm, Erik P. *Losing Ground: Environmental Stress and World Food Prospects.* New York: W.W. Norton, 1976.

Emerson, S. *Secret Warriors.* New York: G.P. Putnam, 1988.

Epstein, Gerald. ''Mortgaging America.'' *World Policy Journal* (Winter 1990–91).

Epstein, Jack. ''Dickens Revisited,'' *The Christian Science Monitor* (August 24, 1995).

Erdman, Andrew. ''The Billionaires.'' *Fortune* (September 10, 1990).

Erickson, J. *The Road to Berlin.* New Haven: Yale University Press, 1983.

Etzold, Thomas H., John Lewis Gaddis. *Containment: Documents On American Policy and Strategy, 1945–50.* New York: Columbia University Press, 1978.

Fallows, James. ''How the World Works.'' *The Atlantic Monthly* (December 1993).

Faux, Jeff. ''The Austerity Trap and the Growth Alternative.'' *World Policy Journal* (Summer 1988).

Feagin, Joe E. *The Urban Real Estate Game.* Engelewood Cliffs, NJ: Prentice-Hall, 1983.

Feffer, John. ''The Browning of Russia.'' *Covert Action Quarterly* (Spring 1996).

Felix, David. ''Latin America's Debt Crisis.'' *World Policy Journal* (Fall 1990).

''Firm Claims Breakthrough in High-Definition Television.'' *The Spokesman-Review* (July 13, 1989).

Fisher, Fritz. *Germany's Aims in the First World War.* New York: W. W. Norton, 1967.

''Five Ways Out,'' *Time* (November 30, 1998).

Flaherty, Patrick. ''Behind Shatalinomics: Politics of Privatization,'' *Guardian* (October 10, 1990).

Fleming, D. F. *The Cold War and Its Origins.* 2 vol. New York: Doubleday, 1961.

Foner, Philip S. *Labor and World War I.* New York: International Publishers, 1987.

————. *Abraham Lincoln: Selections From His Writings.* New York: International Publishers, 1944.

————. *From Colonial Times to the Founding of the American Federation of Labor.* New York: International Publishers, 1947.

————. *From the Founding of the A.F. of L. to the Emergence of American Imperialism.* New York: International Publishers, 1982.

Francis, David R. "Debt-Riddled Russia to Ask for Forgiveness." *The Christian Science Monitor* (April 5, 1999).

Franke, Richard W., Barbara H. Chasin. "Power to the Malayalee People." *Z Magazine* (February 1998).

————. "Kerala State, India: Radical Reform as Development." *Monthly Review* (January 1991).

Frazer, Phillip. "Dirty Tricks Down Under." *Mother Jones* (February/March 1984).

Frazier, H., ed. *Uncloaking the CIA.* New York: The Free Press, 1978.

Freemantle, B. *CIA.* New York: Stein and Day, 1983.

Fromkin, David. *A Peace To End All Peace.* New York: Avon Books, 1989.

Gaffney, Mason, Fred Harrison. *The Corruption of Economics: With The Development of Democracy, Mind Control Became the Urgent Need: Neo-Classical Economics Was the Tool.* London: Shepheard-Walwyn, 1994.

Galbraith, John Kenneth. *Economics in Perspective.* New York: Houghton Mifflin, 1987.

————. *Money.* New York: Houghton Mifflin, 1976.

————. "Which Capitalism for Eastern Europe." *Harpers* (April 1990).

————, Stanislav Menshikov. *Capitalism, Communism, and Coexistence.* Boston: Houghton Mifflin Company, 1988.

Galeano, Eduardo. *Guatemala: Occupied Country.* New York: Monthly Review Press, 1969.

Gardner, Lloyd C. *Safe for Democracy.* New York: Oxford University Press, 1984.

Garrison, Jim. *On the Trail of the Assassins.* New York: Sheridan Square Press, 1988.

Garvin, G. *Everybody Has His Own Gringo: The CIA and the Contras.* New York: Brassey's, 1992.

Garwood, Darrell. *Under Cover: Thirty-Five Years of CIA Deception.* New York: Grove Press, 1985.

Gates, Bill. "The Road Ahead." *Newsweek* (November 27, 1995).

Geonomy Society, 30401 Navarro Ridge Rd, Albion, CA 95410 .

George, Henry. *Progress and Poverty.* New York: Robert Schalkenbach Foundation,1981.

George, Susan. *Ill Fares the Land.* Washington, DC: Institute for Policy Studies, 1984.

————. *A Fate Worse Than Debt.* Rev. New York: Grove Weidenfeld, 1990.

————. *How the Other Half Dies.* Montclair, NJ: Allen Osmun, 1977.

————. *The Debt Boomerang.* San Francisco: Westview Press, 1992.

————. Fabrizio Sabelli. *Faith and Credit.* San Francisco: Westview Press, 1994.

Gervasi, Sean. "Germany, U.S., and the Yugoslavian Crisis." *Covert Action Quarterly* (Winter 1992–93).

Gervasi, S., Wong, S. *"The Reagan Doctrine and The Destabilization Of Southern Africa"* April 1990. Unpublished paper from McGehee Gettleman, M., J. Franklin, M. Young, B. Franklin, *Vietnam and America: The Most Comprehensive Documented History Of The Vietnam War.* New York: Grove Press, 1995.

Gibbs, D., *The Political Economy of Third World Intervention: Mines, Money and U.S. Policy in the Congo Crisis* Chicago, IL: The University of Chicago Press, 1991.

Gill, Stephen. The Geopolitics of the Asian Crisis." *Monthly Review* (March 1999).

Gleijeses, P. *Shattered Hope: The Guatemalan Revolution and the United States,* 1944–1954. Princeton, NJ: Princeton University Press, 1991.

Goldhaber, Michael. *Reinventing Technology.* New York: Routledge & Kegan Paul, 1986.

Goldsmith, Edward. *The Future of Progress: Reflections on Environment and Development.* Berkeley: International Society for Ecology and Culture, 1995.

Goodland, Robert, Herman E. Daly, Salah El Serafy, editors. *Population, Technology, and Lifestyle.* Washington, DC: Island Press, 1992.

Goodman, David. "Political Spy Trial in Pretoria." *In These Times* (September 19–25, 1984).

Goodspeed, D. J. *The German Wars.* New York: Bonanza Books, 1985.

Gorbachev, Mikhail. *Perestroika.* New York: Harper & Row, 1987.

Gorz, André. *Ecology as Politics*. Boston: South End Press, 1980.

———. *Paths to Paradise: On the Liberation From Work*. Boston: South End Press, 1985.

Goulden, Joseph C. *Monopoly*. New York: Pocket Books, 1970.

Government Accounting office, Letter Report, GAO/NSIAD-97-260. (October, 30, 1997).

Gowan, Peter. "Old Medicine in New Bottles." *World Policy Journal* (Winter 1991–92).

Grant, James P. "Jumpstarting Development." *Foreign Policy* (Summer 1993).

Grant, Phil. *The Wonderful Wealth Machine*. New York: Devon-Adair, 1953.

Green, Duncan. *Silent Revolution*. London: Cassel, 1995.

Green, Hardy. "Income Erosion: Economic Landslides." *In These Times* (November 14–20, 1990).

Green, Larry. "Subsidies: Half of '87 Farm Income to Come from Government." *Los Angeles Times,* reprinted in *The Missoulian* (October 25, 1987).

Green, Mark. *The Other Government*. Rev. New York: W.W. Norton, Inc., 1978.

Greenberg, Michael. *British Trade and the Opening of China 1800–1842*. New York: Monthly Review Press, reprint of 1951 edition.

Greider, William. *One World Ready or Not*. New York: Simon and Schuster, 1997.

———."Annals of Finance." *The New Yorker,* (November 9, 1987; Nov. 16, 1987; November 23, 1987).

———. *The Education of David Stockman and Other Americans*. New York: New American Library, 1986.

———. "The Money Question." *World Policy Journal* (Fall 1988).

———. *Secrets of the Temple*. New York: Simon and Schuster, 1987.

———. *Who Will Tell the People*? New York: Simon and Schuster, 1992.

Groden Robert J., Harrison Edward Livingstone. *High Treason: The Assassination of President John F. Kennedy and New Evidence of Conspiracy*. New York: Berkeley Books, 1990.

Grose, Peter. *Gentleman Spy : The Life of Allen Dulles*. Boston: University of Massachusetts Press, 1996.

Gross, Bertram. "Rethinking Full Employment." *The Nation* (January 17, 1987).

Grosser, Paul E., Edwin G. Halperin, *Anti-Semitism: Causes and Effects*. New York: Philosophical Library, 1983.

Grun, Bernard. *Timetables of American History*. New York: Simon and Schuster, 1979.

Guma, Greg. "Cracks in the Covert Iceberg." *Toward Freedom* (May 1998).

Gunson, P., A. Thompson, G. Chamberlain. *The Dictionary of Contemporary Politics of South America*. New York: Routledge, 1989.

Gyorgy, Anna, trans. *Practical Programme for Global Reform*. London: Atlantic Highlands, N.J.: Zed Books, 1992

———. *Ecological Economics*. London: Zed Books, 1991.

Hahnel, Robin. "Capitalist Globalism in Crisis." *Z Magazine* (March 1999).

Hancock, Graham. *Lords of Poverty*. New York: Atlantic Monthly Press, 1989.

Hartmann, Betsy, James K. Boyce. *Needless Hunger: Voices from a Bangladesh Village*. Rev. San Francisco, CA: Institute for Food and Development Policy, 1982.

Hartung, William D. "Why Sell Arms?" *World Policy Journal* (Spring 1993).

Hatal, William H. Richard J. Verey. "Recognizing the 'Third Way.' *The Christian Science Monitor* (March 3, 1999).

Heckscher, Eli F. *Mercantilism,* 2 vol. New York: The Macmillan Company, 1955.

Heidenry, D. *Theirs Was the Kingdom: Lila and Dewitt Wallace the Story of the Reader's Digest*. New York: W.W. Norton, 1993.

Heilig, Bruno. *"Why The German Republic Fell:"* gopher://echonyc.com:70/00/Cul/HGS/germecon.

Henry George Foundation of America, 2000 Century Plaza, #238, Columbia, MD, 21004

Henry George School. New York: gopher://echonyc.com:70/11s/Cul/HGS.

Henwood, Doug. *Wall Street*. New York: Verso, 1997.

———. "Clinton and the Austerity Cops." *The Nation* (November 23, 1992).

———. "The U.S. Economy: The Enemy Within." *Covert Action* (Summer 1992).

Herman, Edward S. *The Real Terror Network*. Boston: South End Press, 1982.

———. "The Assault on Social Security." *Z Magazine* (November 1995).

————, F. Broadhead. *Demonstration Elections: U.S. Staged Elections in the Dominican Republic, Vietnam, and El Salvador,* Boston: South End Press, 1984 .

————. Gerry O'Sullivan. *The Terrorism Industry.* New York: Pantheon Books, 1989.

Herrnstein, Richard J., Charles Murray. *The Bell Curve: Intelligence and Class Structure in American Life.* New York: Free Press, 1994.

Hersh, Burton. *The Old Boys: The American Elite and the Origins of the CIA.* New York: Charles Scribner's Sons, 1992.

Heuvel, Katrina vanden. Editorial, *The Nation* (August 10–17, 1998).

"High Court: This Property Is Condemned," *Newsweek* (June 11, 1984).

Hightower, Jim. "NAFTA, We Don't Hafta." *Utne Reader* (July/August 1993).

Hillkirk, John. "Users' Aim: 1 Language in All Computers." *USA Today* (June 7, 1988).

Hinckle, Warren, William Turner. *The Fish Is Red: The Story of the Secret War Against Castro.* New York: Harper & Row, 1981.

————. *Deadly Secrets: The CIA-Mafia War Against Castro and The Assassination of J.F.K.* New York: Thunder Mouth Press, 1992.

Hines, Colin, Tim Lang, Jerry Mander, Edward Goldsmith, eds. *The Case Against the Global Economy and For A Turn Toward the Local.* San Francisco: Sierra Club, 1996.

Hixson, William F. *It's Your Money.* Toronto, Canada: Comer Publications, 1997.

————. *Triumph of the Bankers: Money and Banking in the Eighteenth and Nineteenth Centuries.* Westport, CT: Praeger, 1993.

Hizak, Shlomo. *Building or Breaking: What Does a Jew Think When A Christian Says "I Love You"?* San Diego: Jerusalem Center for Biblical Studies and Research, 1985.

Hofstadter, Richard. *The Paranoid Style in American Politics.* Chicago: University of Chicago Press, 1979.

Horn, Miriam. "Can the Boob Tube Finally Get Serious." *U.S. News & World Report* (August 24, 1992).

Howarth, Stephen. *Knights Templar.* New York: Dorset Press, 1982.

Hufton, Olwen. *Europe: Privilege and Protest.* Ithaca, NY: Cornell University Press, 1980.

Human Development Report, 1991. New York: Oxford University Press, 1991.

"Hunger as a Weapon." *Food First Action Alert.* Institute for Food and Development Policy, undated.

Hunt, E. K., Howard J. Sherman. *Economics.* New York: Harper & Row, 1990.

Hunt, H.J. *Undercover: Memoirs of an American Secret Agent.* New York: Berkeley Publishing, 1974.

Huntington, Samuel P. *The Clash of Civilizations.* New York: Simon and Schuster, 1996.

Hyam, Ronald. *Britain's Imperial Century, 1815—1914: A Study of Empire and Expansion.* London: B. T. Batsford, 1976.

Hyams, Edward. *Soil and Civilization.* New York: Harper & Row, 1976.

Impoco, Jim, Jack Egan, Douglas Pasternak. "The Tokyo Tidal Wave." *U.S. News & World Report* (September 17, 1990).

"In Fact." *The Nation,* (March 25, 1996).

Isaacson, Walter, Evan Thomas. *The Wise Men.* New York: Simon and Schuster, 1986.

Jacobs, Dan. *The Brutality of Nations.* New York: Alfred A. Knopf, 1987.

Jayko, Margaret. *FBI on Trial: The Victory in the Socialist Workers Party Suit against Government Spying.* New York: Pathfinder Press, 1989.

Jeavons, John. *How to Grow More Vegetables Than You Ever Thought Possible On Less Land Than You Ever Imagined: A Primer On The Life Giving Biointensive Method Of Organic Horticulture.* Berkeley, CA: Ten Speed Press, 1991.

Jeffreys-Jones, R. *The CIA & American Democracy.* New Haven, CT: Yale University Press, 1989.

Johnson, Haynes. "Teflon 80s Bear Striking Resemblance to 'Giddy' 20s." *The Missoulian* (March 25, 1987).

Johnson, Loch .K. *America's Secret Power.* New York: Oxford University Press, 1989.

Johnstone, Diane. "GATTastrophe: Free-Trade Ideology Versus Planetary Survival." *In These Times.* (December 19–25, 1990).

Jonas, Susanne. *The Battle for Guatemala: Rebels, Death Squads, and U.S. Power.* San Francisco: Westview Press, 1991.

Josephson, Matthew. *Robber Barons.* New York: Harcourt Brace Jovanovich, 1962.

Joynt, Carey B., Percy E. Corbett. *Theory and Re-*

ality in World Politics. Pittsburgh: University of Pittsburgh Press, 1978.

Jukes, Jeffrey. *Stalingrad at the Turning Point.* New York: Ballantine Books, 1968.

Kadane, Kathy. *States News Service* and Ralph McGehee's http://come.to/CIABASE/.

Kagarlitsky, Boris. *Square Wheels: How Russian Democracy Got Derailed.* New York: Monthly Review Press, 1994.

Kahin, G.M., J.W. Lewis, *United States in Vietnam.* New York: Dell Publishing Company. 1969.

Kahin, McT. *Subversion as Foreign Policy: The Secret Eisenhower and Dulles Debacle in Indonesia.* New York: New Press, 1995.

Kaplan, D. *Fires of the Dragon: Politics, Murder and the Kuomintang.* New York: Atheneum, 1992.

Karmatz, Laura, Alisha Labi, Joan Levinstein, Special Report, "States at War," *Time* (November 9, 1998).

Karnow, S. *In Our Image: America's Empire In The Philippines.* New York: Random House, 1989.

Kaslow, Amy. "The Price of Low-Cost Clothes: US Jobs." *The Christian Science Monitor* (August 20, 1995).

Kelley, Sean. *America's Tyrant: The CIA and Mobutu of Zaire.* (Washington, DC: American University Press, 1993),

Kendall, Don. "Meat-eaters Consuming Less Fat." *The Missoulian* (February 4, 1987).

———. "U.S Farmers Look to the Developing World." *The Spokesman-Review* (January 5, 1988).

Kennedy, Paul. *The Rise and Fall of the Great Powers.* New York: Random House, 1987.

Kernaghan, Charles. "Sweatshop Blues." *Dollars and Sense* (March/April, 1999).

Kessler, R. *Inside The CIA: Revealing The Secrets Of The World's Most Powerful Spy Agency.* New York: Pocket Books, 1992.

Kettle, Michael. *The Allies and the Russian Collapse.* Minneapolis: University of Minnesota Press, 1981.

Khan, Sadruddin Aga, Editor. *Policing the Global Economy: Why, How and for Whom.* Cameron Bay Publishers, 1998.

Kielinger, Thomas, Max Otte. "Germany: The Presumed Power." *Foreign Policy* (Summer 1993).

Kindleberger, Charles P. *Manias, Panics, and Crashes.* New York: Basic Books, Inc., 1978.

King, Martin Luther, Junior, *The Black Panthers Speak.* Da Capo Press, 1995.

Klare, Michael T., P. Kornbluh. *Low Intensity Warfare.* New York: Pantheon Books, 1988.

Knightley, Philip. *The First Casualty.* New York: Harcourt Brace Jovanovich, 1975.

Kolko, Gabriel. *The Politics of War.* New York: Pantheon, 1990.

Komisar, Lucy. "Documented Complicity: Newly Released Files Set the Record Straight on U.S. Support for Pinochet." *The Progressive* (September, 1999).

Kornblush, Peter. *Nicaragua, The Price of Intervention: Reagan's War Against the Sandinistas.* Washington DC: Institute for Policy Studies, 1987.

Kornblush, P., M. Byrne. *The Iran-Contra Scandal: The Declassified History.* New York: A National Security Archive Documents Reader, The New Press. 1993.

Korten, David. *When Corporations Rule the World.* West Hartford, CT: Kumarian Press and San Francisco: Berret-Koehler, 1995

Kötke, William H. *The Final Empire: The Collapse of Civilization and the Seed of the Future.* Portland, OR: Arrow Point Press, 1993.

Kotz, David. "Russia in Shock: How Capitalist 'Shock Therapy' is Destroying Russia's Economy." *Dollars and Sense* (June 1993).

Kropotkin, Petr. *Mutual Aid.* Boston: Porter Sargent Publishers Inc., 1914.

———. *The Great French Revolution.* New York: Black Rose Books, 1989.

———. *The State.* London: Freedom Press, 1987.

Kurtzman, Joel. *The Death of Money.* New York: Simon and Schuster, 1993.

———. *The Decline and Crash of the American Economy.* New York: W.W. Norton, 1988.

Kwitny, Jonathan. *The Crimes of Patriots.* New York: W.W. Norton, 1987.

———. *Endless Enemies: The Making of an Unfriendly World.* New York: Congdon & Weed, 1984.

Lacey, Robert. *Ford.* New York: Ballantine Books, 1986.

Ladanov, Ivan, Vladimar Pronnikov. "Craftsmen and Electronics." *New Times* 47 (November 1988).

Lambert, Angela. *Unquiet Souls.* New York: Harper & Row, 1984.

Landau, Saul, Sarah Anderson. "Autumn of the Autocrat." *Covert Action Quarterly* 64 (Spring 1998).

————. "Moscow Rules Moss's Mind." *Covert Action Quarterly* 16 (Summer 1985).

————. "Opus Die: Secret Order Vies for Power." *Covert Action Quarterly* 18 (Winter 1983).

Landay, Jonathan S. "Study Reveals U.S. Has Spent $4 Trillion on Nukes Since '45." *The Christian Science Monitor* (July 12, 1995).

Landis, F.S. *Psychological Warfare and Media Operations in Chile* 1970–1973. Doctoral dissertation, University of Illinois, 1975.

Lane, Charles, Theodore Stanger, Tom Post. "The Ghosts of Serbia." *Newsweek* (April 19, 1993).

Lansdale, E.G. *In the Midst of Wars*. New York: Harper & Row, 1972.

Lappé, Frances Moore. *Diet for a Small Planet*. Rev. New York: Ballantine Books, 1978.

————. Joseph Collins. *Food First: Beyond the Myth of Scarcity*. Rev. New York: Ballantine Books, 1979.

————. Rachel Schurman. *Taking Population Seriously*. San Francisco: Institute for Food and Development Policy, 1990.

Layne, Christopher. "Rethinking American Grand Strategy." *World Policy Journal* (Summer 1998).

Lea, Henry Charles. *The Inquisition of the Middle Ages*. New York: Citidel Press, 1954.

Lee, Dwight E. *Europe's Crucial Years*. Hanover, NH: Clark University Press, 1974.

Lefeber, Walter. *Inevitable Revolutions*. New York: W.W. Norton, 1984.

Leigh, David. *The Wilson Plot*. New York: Pantheon, 1988.

Lens, Sidney. *Permanent War*. New York: Schocken Books, 1987.

Levant, V. *Quiet Complicity: Canadian Involvement In The Vietnam War*. Toronto, Canada: Between the Lines, 1986.

Levy, Steven. "Bills New Vision." *Newsweek* (November 27, 1995).

Lewis, Hunter, Donald Allison. *The Real Cold War*. New York: Coward, McCann, and Geoghegan, 1982.

Lilliston, Ben. "Shredding the Ecologist." *The Progressive* (February 1999).

Lindsey, Hal. *The Road to the Holocaust*. New York: Bantam Books, 1989.

List, Friedrich. *The National System of Political Economy*. Fairfield, NJ: Augustus M. Kelley, 1977.

Litvinoff, Barnet. *The Burning Bush*. New York: E.P. Dutton, 1988.

Loftus, John. *The Belarus Secret*. New York: Alfred A. Knopf, 1982.

Lohbeck, K. *Holy War, Unholy Victory: Eyewitness to the CIA's Secret War in Afghanistan*. Washington DC: Regnery Gateway, 1993,

"Low Cholesterol Beef Produced on State Ranches." *The Missoulian* (October 15, 1986).

Lyon, Peter. *To Hell in a Day Coach*. New York: J. B. Lippincott Company, 1968.

Mackay, Charles. *Extraordinary Delusions and Madness of Crowds*. second ed. New York: Farrar Straus and Giroux, 1932.

MacKenzie, Angus, David Weir, *Secrets: The CIA's War at Home*. Berkeley: University of California Press, 1997.

Madsen, Wayne. "Crypto Ag: The NSA's Trojan Whore?" *Covert Action Quarterly* (Winter 1998).

Magdoff, Harry. "A Note on the Communist Manifesto." *Monthly Review,* (May 1998).

————. "Are There Lessons To Be Learned?" *Monthly Review* (February 1991).

————. Paul M. Sweezy. *Stagnation and the Financial Explosion*. New York: Monthly Review Press (1987).

Makhijani, Arjun. *From Global Capitalism to Economic Justice*. New York: Apex Press, 1992.

Makin, John H. *The Global Debt Crisis*. New York: Basic Books, 1984.

Malkin, Lawrence. *The National Debt*. New York: Henry Holt, 1988.

Manchester, William. *The Glory and The Dream*. New York: Bantam Books, 1988.

Mander, Jerry, Edward Goldsmith. *The Case Against the Global Economy*. San Francisco: Sierra Club Books, 1996.

Mann, Jim. "China's Response to U.S.: Slow, Slow." *Los Angeles Times* (October 28, 1998).

Mansour, Fawzy "A Second Wave of National Liberation?" *Monthly Review* (February 1999).

Manz, Beatriz. *Refugees of A Hidden War: The Aftermath of Counterinsurgency in Guatemala*. New York: State University of New York, 1988.

Marchetti, Victor, John D. Marks. *The CIA and the Cult of Intelligence*. New York: Knopf 1974; Dell Publishing, 1980.

Marcuse, Peter. "Letter from the German Democratic Republic." *Monthly Review* (July/August 1990).

"Mark Twain on Henry George" at gopher://echonyc.com:70/00/Cul/HGS/archimed

Marrs, Jim. *Crossfire: The Plot That Killed Kennedy.* New York: Carroll and Graf, 1989.

Marshall, J., P.D. Scott, J. Hunter. *The Iran-Contra Connection.* Boston, MA: South End Press, 1987.

"Marshall Plan for Creditors and Speculators." *Economic Reform"* (January 1999).

Martin, D. *Wilderness of Mirrors.* New York: Harper and Row, 1980.

Martin, Edward Winslow. *History of the Grange Movement.* New York: Burt Franklin, 1967.

Martin, Hans-Peter, Harald Schuman. *The Global Trap: Globalization & the Assault on Democracy and Prosperity.* London: Zed Books, 1997.

Marton, Kati. *The Polk Conspiracy: Murder and Cover Up in the Case of CBS News Correspondent George Polk.* New York: Farrar, Staus & Giroux, 1990.

Marx, Karl. *Capital,* 3 vols. edited by Frederick Douglas. New York: International Publishers, 1967.

Mayer, Milton. *They Thought They Were Free.* Chicago: University of Chicago Press, 1955.

Mayers, David. *George Kennan.* New York: Oxford University Press, 1988.

McCann, T. *An American Company: The Tragedy of United Fruit.* New York: Crown Publishers, 1976.

McChesney, Robert. *Corporate Media and the Threat to Democracy.* New York: Seven Stories Press, 1997.

———. ed. *Capitalism and the Information Age: The Political Economy of the Global Communication Revolution.* New York: Monthly Review Press, 1998.

———. Edward S. Herman. *The Global Media: The Missionaries of Global Capitalism.* Washington, D. C.: Cassell, 1997.

McClain, William E. *Illinois Prairie: Past and Future: A Restoration Guide.* Springfield, IL: Illinois Department of Conservation, 1986.

McClintock, Michael. *Instruments of Statecraft: U.S. Guerrilla Warfare, Counter Insurgency, and Counter Terrorism* 1940–1990. New York: Pantheon, 1992.

———. *The American Connection: State Terror and Popular Resistance in Guatemala.* London: Zed Books, 1985.

———. *The American Connection: State Terror and Popular Resistance in El Salvador.* London: Zed Books, 1985.

McGehee, Ralph W. *Deadly Deceits.* New York: Sheridan Square Press, 1983.

———. CIABASE, Box 5022, Herndon, VA 22070; http://come.to/CIABASE/.

McIntyre, Robert S. "The Populist Tax Act of 1989." *The Nation* (April 2, 1988).

McKibben, Bill. "The Enigma of Kerala." *Utne Reader* (Mar/April 1996).

McNeill, William H. *The Pursuit of Power.* Chicago: University of Chicago Press, 1982.

McReynolds, David. "The Words and the Will to Talk About Change." *The Progressive* (March 28, 1991).

Mead, Walter Russell. "After Hegemony." *New Perspective Quarterly,* (1987).

———. "American Economic Policy in the Antemillenial Era." *World Policy Journal,* (Summer 1989).

———. "The Bush Administration and the New World Order." *World Policy Journal* (Summer 1991).

———. *Mortal Splendor.* Boston: Houghton Mifflin Company, 1987.

———. "Saul Among the Prophets." *World Policy Journal,* (Summer 1991).

Medvedev, Roy. "Parallels Inappropriate." *New Times* (July 1989).

Melman, Seymour. *Profits Without Production.* New York: Alfred A. Knopf, 1983.

Metcalf, Lee, Vic Reinemer. *Overcharge.* New York: David McKay, 1967.

Miller, Christian, "Wall Street's Fondest Dream: The Insanity of Privatizing Social Security," *Dollars and Sense* (November/December 1998).

Miller, N. *Spying for America.* New York: Paragon House, 1989.

Mills, Stephanie. *In Service of the Wild: Restoring and Reinhabiting Damaged Land.* Boston: Beacon Press, 1995.

Minnick, Wendell. *Spies and Provocateurs: A Worldwide Encyclopedia of Persons Conducting Espionage and Covert Action, 1946–1991.* Jefferson, North Carolina: McFarland,1992.

Minter, W. *Apartheid's Contras: An Inquiry into the Roots of War in Angola and Mozambique.* London: ZED Books, 1994.

Mirow, Kurt Rudolph, Harry Maurer. *Webs of Power.* Boston: Houghton Mifflin Company, 1982.

Moberg, David. "Cutting the U.S. Military: How Low Can We Go?" *In These Times* (February 12–18, 1992).

———. "Can Public Spending Rescue the Infrastructure: A Tale of Three Deficits." *In These Times* (February 13–19, 1991).

Moffitt, Michael. "Shocks, Deadlocks, and Scorched Earth: Reaganomics and the Decline of U.S. Hegemony." *World Policy Journal* (Fall 1987).

———. *The World's Money*. New York: Simon and Schuster, 1983.

Mohammad, Yousai, M. Adkin. *The Beartrap: Afghanistan's Untold Story*. London, England: Leo Cooper, 1992.

Mollison, Bill. *Permaculture: A Designers' Manual*. Tyalgum, Australia: Tagari Pub., 1988.

Morrison, Roy. *We Build the Road as We Travel*. Philadelphia: New Society Publishers, 1991.

Mumford, Lewis. *The City in History*. New York: Harcourt Brace Jovanovich, 1961.

———. *Pentagon of Power*. New York: Harcourt Brace Jovanovich, 1964, 1970.

———. *Technics and Civilization*. New York: Harcourt Brace Jovanovich, 1963.

———. *Technics and Human Development*. New York: Harcourt Brace Jovanovich, 1967.

Murphy, R. Taggart. *The Weight of The Yen*. New York: W.W. Norton, 1996.

Muyumba, Francois N., Esther Atcherson. *Pan-Africanism and Cross-Cultural Understanding: A Reader*. Needham Heights, MA: Ginn Press, 1993.

Myers, Norman, General Editor. *Gaia: An Atlas of Planet Management*. Garden City, New York: Anchor Books, 1984.

Nadudere, Dan. *The Political Economy of Imperialism*. London: Zed Books, 1977.

Nair, K. Devil and His Dart: How the CIA is Plotting in The Third World. New Delhi: Sterling Publishers, 1986.

Narton, Kati. *The Polk Conspiracy: Murder and Cover-up in the case of Correspondent George Polk*. New York: Farrar, Straus, and Giroux, 1990.

National Endowment for Democracy, Annual Report.

National Geographic TV (August 23, 1987).

Neilson, Francis. *How Diplomats Make War*. New York: Robert Schalkenbach Foundation, 1984.

"New Financial Architecture Crumbles." *Economic Reform* (March 1999).

Newman, Richard J. "A Kosovo Numbers Game," *U.S. News & World Report* (July 12, 1999).

Noakes, J., G. Pridham, editors. *Nazism 1919–1945*. 2 vols. New York: Schocken Books, 1988.

Norton, Peggy. "Independent Radio's Problems and Prospects." *Z Magazine* (March, 1990).

Nossiter, Bernard D. "The F.C.C.'s Big Giveaway Show." *The Nation* (October 26, 1985).

Nova. PBS (September 2, 1986).

Oberman, Heiko A. *The Roots of Anti-Semitism*. Philadelphia: Fortress Press, 1984.

Omestat, Thomas. "Addicted to Sanctions." *U.S. News & World Report* (June 15, 1998).

101 Famous Thinkers on Owning Earth, New York: Robert Schalkenback Foundation, no date.

O'Toole, G.J.A. *Honorable Treachery*. New York: Atlantic Monthly Press, 1991.

Owen, Wilfred. *Strategy for Mobility*. Westport, CT: Greenwood Press, 1978.

Parakal, P.V. *Secret Wars Of CIA*. New Delhi: Sterling Publishers Private Limited, 1984.

Parenti, Christian. "Nasa's Assault on the Ozone Layer." *Lies of Our Times* (September 1993).

Parenti, Michael. *Power and the Powerless*. New York: St. Martin's Press, 1978.

Parnas, David Lorge. "Con: Dayton's a Step Back—Way Back," *Peace* (March/April 1996).

Patterson, Charles. *Anti-Semitism: The Road to the Holocaust and Beyond*. New York: Walker, 1982.

Pauly, David, Rich Thomas, Judith Evans,. "The Dirty Little Debt Secret." *Newsweek* (April 17, 1989).

Pearson, Hugh. *The Shadow of the Panther: Huey Newton and the Price of Black Power in America*. Perseus Press, 1995.

Pentagon Papers: The Defense Department History of United States Decision Making on Vietnam, Senator Mike Gravel Ed. Boston: Beacon Press, 1971.

Peterzell, J. *Reagan's Secret Wars*, CNSS Report 108. Washington, DC: Center for National Security Studies, 1984.

Petras, James. "Latin America's Free Market Paves the Road to Recession." *In These Times* (February 13–19).

———. Henry Veltmeyer, "Latin America at the End of the Millennium," *Monthly Review* (July/August 1999).

Phillips, D.A. *The Night Watch.* New York: Atheneum, 1977.

Phillips, Kevin. *Boiling Point: Democrats, Republicans, and the Decline of Middle Class Prosperity.* New York: Random House, 1993.

————. *The Politics of Rich and Poor.* New York: Random House, 1990.

Pilarski, Michael. *Restoration Forestry: An International Guide to Sustainable Forestry Practices.* Durango, CO: Kivaki Press, 1994.

Pilzer, Paul Zane. *Unlimited Wealth.* New York: Crown Publishing, 1990.

Pirenne, Henri. *Economic and Social History of Medieval Europe.* New York: Harcourt, Brace, 1937.

Pike Committee Report. Congressional Record (1975–76)

Polanyi, Karl. *The Great Transformation.* Boston: Beacon Press, 1957.

Poole, Fred, Max Vanzi. *Revolution in the Philippines: The United States in A Hall of Cracked Mirrors.* New York: McGraw-Hill, 1984.

Pool, James, Suzanne Pool. *Who Financed Hitler?* New York: The Dial Press, 1978.

Porter, G. "The Politics of Counterinsurgency in the Philippines: Military and Political Options." Philippine Studies Occasional Paper No. 9. Honolulu: University of Hawaii, Center for Philippine Studies (1987).

Potts, Michael. *The Independent Home: Living Well with Power from the Sun, Wind, and Water.* Post Mills, VT: Chelsea Green Pub. Co., 1993.

Powers, T. *The Man Who Kept The Secrets.* New York: Alfred A. Knopf, 1979.

Prados, John. *The Presidents' Secret Wars.* New York: William Morrow, 1986.

————. *The Presidents Secret Wars,* revised. Chicago: Ivan R. Dee, 1996.

————. *Keepers Of The Keys: A History Of The National Security Council From Truman To Bush.* New York: William Morrow, 1991.

Prager, Dennis. *Why the Jews: The Reason for Antisemitism.* New York: Simon and Schuster, 1983.

Preston, William, Jr., Edward S. Herman, Herbert I. Schiller. *Hope and Folly.* Minneapolis: University of Minnesota Press, 1989.

"Proud Russia on Its Knees." *U.S. News & World Report* (February 8, 1999).

Prouty, L.F. *JFK: The CIA, Vietnam, and the Plot to Assassinate John F. Kennedy.* New York: Birch Lane Press, 1992.

————. *The Secret Team.* Englewood Cliffs, NJ: Prentice-Hall, 1973.

Public Power Directory and Statistics for 1983. Washington, DC: American Public Power Association, 1983.

Quinn, T. K. *Giant Business: Threat to Democracy.* third ed. New York: Exposition Press, 1954.

Raghavan, Chakravarthi. *Recolonization: GATT, the Uruguay Round & the Developing World.* London: Zed Books, 1990.

Ranelagh, John. *The Agency: The Rise and Decline of the CIA.* New York: Simon and Schuster, 1986.

Ratner Michael. "The Pinochet Principle: Who's Next?" *Covert Action Quarterly* 66 (Winter 1999)

Rayack, Elton. *Not So Free to Choose: The Political Economy of Milton Friedman and Ronald Reagan.* Westport, Conn: Praeger, 1986.

Re Latin America Magazine, August, 1974,

Reding, Andrew A. "Bolstering Democracy in The Americas." *World Policy Journal* (Summer 1992).

Reed, John. *The Education of John Reed.* New York: International Publishers, 1955.

Renard, George. *Guilds of the Middle Ages.* New York: Augustus M. Kelly, 1968.

A Report by The International Institute for Environment and Development and The World Resources Institute. *World Resources* (1987): *An Assessment of the Resource Base That Supports the Global Economy.* New York: Basic Books, 1987.

Rich, Bruce. "Conservation Woes at the World Bank." *The Nation* (January 23, 1989).

Richelson, J. *American Espionage and The Soviet Target.* New York: William Morrow, 1987.

————. *The U.S. Intelligence Community.* Cambridge, MA: Ballinger Publishing Company, 1985.

Richter, Paul. "Commodity Marts Face Fraud Fallout." *Los Angeles Times,* Quoted in the *Missoulian* (July 4, 1987).

Ridenour, R. *Back Fire: The CIA's Biggest Burn.* Havana, Cuba: José Marti Publishing House, 1991.

Rifkin, Jeremy. *Beyond Beef.* New York: Dutton, 1992.

————. "Beyond Beef." *Utne Reader* (March/April 1992).

————. *Biosphere Politics.* San Francisco: HarperCollins, 1992.

———. *Entropy: Into the Greenhouse World.* Rev. ed. New York: Bantam Books, 1989.

Robert Schalkenbach Foundation, 41 E. 72nd Streets, New York, NY 10021.

Roberts, J.M. *The Triumph of the West.* London: British Broadcasting Company, 1985.

Robbins, C. *The Ravens: The Men Who Flew In America's Secret War.* New York: Crown Publishers, 1987.

Robinson, Linda. "What Didn't We Do to Get Rid of Castro." *U.S. News & World Report* (October 26, 98).

Robinson, William I. *A Faustian Bargain: U.S. Intervention in the Nicaraguan Elections and American Foreign Policy in the Post-Cold War Era.* Boulder, CO: Westview Press, 1992.

Rodman, Peter. *More Precious Than Peace.* New York: Charles Scribner & Sons, 1994.

Rojas, Raul. *The Poverty of Nations.* New Jersey: Zed Books, 1991.

Roosevelt, Kermit. *Countercoup: The Struggle for the Control Of Iran.* New York: McGraw-Hill, 1979.

Rositzke, H. *The CIA's Secret Operations.* New York: Thomas Y. Crowell Company, 1977.

Ross, Michael. "Yeltsin: POWs 'Summarily Executed.' " *The Spokesman Review* (November 12, 1992).

Rousseau, Jean Jacques. "A Discourse on the Origins of Inequality." *The Social Contract and Discourses.* New York: Dutton, 1950.

Routh, Guy. *The Origin of Economic Ideas.* Dobbs Ferry, NY: Sheridan House, 1989.

Rubenstein, Richard L. *Approaches to Auschwitz: The Holocaust and Its Legacy.* Atlanta: John Knox Press, 1987.

———. *The Age of Triage.* Boston: Beacon Press, 1983.

Ruether, Rosemary. *Faith and Fratricide: The Theological Roots of Anti-Semitism* New York: Seabury Press, 1974.

"Rural Montana Gets Taste of Public TV." *The Missoulian* (October 8, 1987).

"The Rush To Gulp US Radio Stations." *The Christian Science Monitor* (May 7, 1996).

Rzheshevsky, Oleg. *World War II: Myths and the Realities.* Moscow, USSR: Progress Publishers, 1984.

Sachar, Abram L. *A History of the Jews.* New York: Knopf, 1965.

Samaray, Catherine. *Yugoslavia Dismembered.* New York: Monthly Review Press, 1995.

Sampson, Anthony. *The Midas Touch.* New York: Truman Talley Books/Plume, 1991.

———. *The Money Lenders.* New York: Penguin Books, 1981.

Samuelson, Robert. "The Great Global Debtor." *Newsweek* (July 22, 1991).

Sanders, Jerry W. "The Prospects for 'Democratic Engagement'." *World Policy Journal* (Summer 1992).

Sandford, R.R. *The Murder of Allende.* A. Conrad, translator, New York: Harper & Row, 1975.

Sanoff, Alvin P., et al. "Who Will Control TV." *U.S. News & World Report* (May 13, 1985).

Scheer, Christopher. "Illegals Made Slaves to Fashion." *The Nation* (September 11, 1995).

Schiller, Herbert I. *Information and the Crisis Economy.* Boston: Oxford University Press, 1986.

———. *Communications and Cultural Domination.* White Plains, NY: M.E. Sharp, Inc., 1976.

———. "The Information Superhighway: Paving over the Public." *Z Magazine* (March 1994).

———. *Mind Managers.* Boston: Beacon Press, 1973.

Schirmer, Daniel B., Stephen Rosskamm Shalom. *The Philippines Reader: A History of Colonialism, Dictatorship, and Resistance.* Boston: South End Press, 1987.

Schlesinger, Stephen. "The CIA Censor's History." *The Nation* (September 7, 1997).

———, Stephen Kinzer. *Bitter Fruit.* New York: Anchor Press/Doubleday, 1984.

Schlosstein, Steven. *Trade War.* New York: Congdon and Weed, 1984.

Schor, Juliet B. "Workers of the World Unwind." *Technology Review* (November/December 1991).

———. *The Overworked American.* New York: Basic Books, 1991.

Schrecker, Ellen. *No Ivory Tower: McCarthyism in the Universities.* New York: Oxford University Press, 1986.

Schuman, Julian. *China: An Uncensored Look.* Sagaponack, NY: Second Chance Press, 1979.

Scott, P.D. "Exporting military-economic development: America and the overthrow of Sukarno, 1965–67." In M. Caldwell, editor. *Ten Years Military Terror Indonesia.* Nottingham: Spokesmen Books.

Seldes, George. *Even the Gods Can't Change History.* Secaucus, NJ: Lyle Stuart, Inc., 1976.

———. *Never Tire of Protesting.* New York: Lyle Stuart, 1968.

———. "The Roman Church and Franco." *The Human Quest* (March/April 1994).

Seneker, Harold. "The World's Billionaires." *Forbes* (October 5, 1987).

Sergeyev, F.F. *Chile: CIA Big Business,* L. Bobrov, translator. Moscow, USSR: Progress Publishers, 1981.

"Set in Concrete." *The Economist.* (June 3, 1995).

Shalom, Stephan Rosskamm. "Bullets, Gas, and The Bomb." *Z Magazine* (February 1991).

———. *Imperial Alibis.* Boston: South End Press, 1993.

Sheehan, N. *A Bright Shining Lie.* New York: Random House, 1988.

Sheridan, David. *Desertification of the United States.* Washington DC: U.S. Government Printing Office, #334-983: Council on Environmental Quality, 1981.

Shoup, L., W. Minter *Imperial Brain Trust: The Council on Foreign Relations & United States Foreign Policy.* New York: Monthly Review Press, 1977.

Simon, Jean-Marie. *Guatemala: Eternal Spring Eternal Tyranny.* New York: W.W. Norton, 1988.

Simpson, Christopher. *Blowback.* New York: Weidenfeld & Nicolson, 1988.

Sipols, Vilnis. *The Road to Great Victory.* Moscow, USSR: Progress Publishers, 1985.

Sivard, Ruth Leger. *World Military and Social Expenditures.* Washington, DC: World Priorities, published annually, all issues.

60 Minutes (CBS). April 20, 1987; October 25, 1987; September 2, 1995; May 19, 1996.

Skidmore, Thomas, Peter Smith, *"The Pinochet Regime", In Modern Latin America,* second ed.. New York: Oxford University Press, 1989.

Sklar, Holly, *Washington's War On Nicaragua.* Boston: South End Press, 1988.

Smith, Adam. *The Wealth of Nations.* New York: Random House, 1965.

"Smith, Adam" (George J.W. Goodman). *Supermoney.* New York: Random House, 1972.

———. *Nightly Business Report, PBS* (June 17, 1987).

Smith, J. Allen. *The Spirit of American Government: A Study of the Constitution: Its Origin, Influence and Relation to Democracy,* New York: Macmillan, 1907.

Smith, J.W. *The World's Wasted Wealth 2.* San Luis Obispo, CA: The Institute For Economic Democracy, 1994.

Snepp, Frank. *Decent Interval.* New York: Random House, 1977.

Soltani, Atossa, Penelope Whitney, Editors. *Cut Waste, Not Trees.* San Francisco,CA: Rainforest Action Network, 1995.

Spencer, Herbert. *Social Statics.* Robert Schalkenback Foundation, 1850 unabridged ed.

"States' Right: Hawaii's Land Reform Upheld." *Time* (June 11, 1984).

Statistical Abstract of the United States. Washington, DC: U.S. Government Printing Office, 1990, 1992.

Stigum, Marcia. *Money Markets.* Homewood, IL: Dow Jones-Irwin, 1978.

Stockwell, John. *In Search of Enemies.* New York: W. W. Norton, 1978.

———. *The Praetorian Guard.* Boston: South End Press, 1991.

Stone, I.F. *The Hidden History of the Korean War.* Boston: Little, Brown, 1952.

———. *Polemics and Prophecy.* Boston: Little Brown, 1970.

Strange, Susan. *The Retreat of the State: The Diffusion of Power in the Global Economy,* Cambridge, UK: Cambridge Studies in International Relations number 49, 1998.

Stromnes, John. "Rural Montana Gets Taste of Public TV." *The Missoulian* (October 8, 1987).

Summers, Anthony. *Conspiracy.* New York: Paragon House, 1989.

Swann, Robert. *The Need for Local Currencies.* Great Barrington, MA: E.F. Schumacher Society, 1990.

Swearingen, M. Wesley. *FBI Secrets : An Agent's Exposé.* Boston: South End Press, 1995.

Swentzell, Athena. *The Straw Bale House.* White River Junction,VT: Chelsea Green Pub. Co., 1994..

Synan, Edward A. *The Pope and the Jews in the Middle Ages.* New York: Macmillan, 1965.

Taheri, Amir. *Nest of Spies: America's Journey to Disaster in Iran.* New York: Pantheon Books, 1988.

Taylor, Edmond. *The Fall of the Dynasties: The Fall of the Old Order, 1905–1922.* New York: Dorset Press, 1989.

Thirgood, J.V. *Man and the Mediterranean Forest: A*

History of Resource Depletion. New York: Academic Press, 1981.

Thomas, E. *The Very Best Men: Four Who Dared: The Early Years of the CIA.* New York: Simon & Schuster, 1995.

Thomas, Rich. "From Russia, With Chips," *Newsweek* (August 1990).

Thomas, William L. Jr., Ed. *Man's Role In Changing The Face Of The Earth,* 2 vols. Chicago, Ill: University of Chicago Press, 1956.

Thomas, Rich. "From Russia, with Chips," *Newsweek* (August 6, 1990).

Thompson, D., R. Larson. *Where Were You Brother?* London: War on Want Publishers, 1978.

Thompson, E. P., Dan Smith. *Protest and Survive.* New York: Monthly Review Press, 1981.

Thoren, Theodore R., Richard F. Warner. *The Truth in Money.* Chagrin Falls, Ohio: Truth in Money Publishers, 1994.

"Three Musketeers, The." *Time.* (February 15, 1996).

Thurow, Lester C. *Head to Head: The Coming Economic Battle Among Japan, Europe, and America.* New York: William Morrow, 1992.

———. "Falling Wages, Failing Policy." *Dollars and Sense* (September/October 1996).

———. "The Crusade That is Killing Prosperity." *The American Prospect* (March/April 1996).

———. *Dangerous Currents.* New York: Random House, 1983.

———. *Generating Inequality.* New York: Basic Books, 1975.

———. "Investing in America's Future." Economic Policy Institute, C-Span Transcript. (October 21, 1991).

Tobin, Eugene M. *Organize or Perish.* New York: Greenwood Press, 1986.

"Top 1% Own More Than Bottom 90%," *The Des Moines Register* (April 21, 1992)

Townsend, Mike. "Microwatt Revolution." *Lies of Our Times* (January 1991).

Train, John. *Famous Financial Fiascoes.* New York: Clarkson N. Potter, 1985.

Treverton, G. *Covert Action: The Limits of Intervention in the Post-War World.* New York: Basic Books, 1987.

Tuchman, Barbara. *The March of Folly.* New York: Alfred A. Knopf, 1984.

Tucker, George. *The Theory of Money and Banks Investigated.* New York: Greenwood Press, 1968.

Tucker, Robert W. "The Triumph of Wilsonianism." *World Policy Journal* (Winter 1993/94).

Turk, Jonathan, Janet T. Wittes, Robert Wittes, Amos Turk. *Ecosystems, Energy, Population.* Toronto: W.B. Saunders Co., 1975.

Turner, Stansfield. *Secrecy and Democracy: The CIA in Transition.* Boston: Houghton Mifflin Company, 1985.

"TV Direct From Satellite to Your Home—It Could Be Soon." *U.S. News & World Report* (June 26, 1967).

Twentieth Century Fund. *The Need to Know: The Report of The Twentieth Century Fund Task Force on Covert Action and American Democracy.* New York: The Twentieth Century Fund Press, 1992.

United Nations Commission on the Truth in El Salvador. *From Madness To Hope: The 12-Year War In El Salvado*r. U.N. Security Council (1993).

United Nations Human Development Report. 1991, 1998.

United Nations Truth Commission on Guatemala. U.N Security Council (1995, 1999).

"U.S. Becomes Biggest Dealer of Arms in Worldwide Market." *The Spokesman Review* (October 15, 1992).

United States Department of Agriculture, *First Conference on Kenaf for Pulp: Proceedings.* Peoria, IL: USDA, 1968.

Uribe, A. *The Black Book of American Intervention in Chile.* Boston, MA: Beacon Press, 1975.

Tynan, Judy. "Farm Credit System's Transfers Face Trial." *The Spokesman-Review* (December 31, 1986).

Valentine, Douglas. *The Phoenix Program.* New York: William Morrow, 1990.

Veblen, Thorstein. *Engineers and the Price System.* New York: B. W. Huebsch, Inc., 1921.

———. *Essays in Our Changing Order.* New York: The Viking Press, 1934.

———. *The Vested Interests.* New York: B.W. Huebsch Inc., 1919.

Vidal, Gore. "The National Security State: How To Take Back Our Country." *The Nation* (June 4, 1988).

Volkman, Ernest, Blaine Baggett. *Secret Intelligence.* New York: Doubleday, 1989.

Volman, Dennis. "Salvador Death Squads: A CIA Connection?" *The Christian Science Monitor* (May 8, 1984).

Wachtel, Howard M. "Labor's Stake in WTO." *The American Prospect* (March/April 1998).

———. "The Global Funny Money Game." *The Nation* (December 26, 1987).

———. *Money Mandarins.* New York: Pantheon Books, 1986.

———. *The Politics of International Money.* Amsterdam: Transnational Institute, 1987.

Wallace, Henry. *Towards World Peace.* Westport, CT: Greenwood Press, 1970.

Wallerstein, Immanuel. *The Origin of the Modern World System.* 2 vol. New York: Academic Press, 1974.

Walter, Ingo. *The Secret Money Market.* New York: HarperCollins, 1990.

Waters, Mary-Alice. *The Rise and Fall of the Nicaraguan Revolution.* New York: New International, 1994.

Watson, B., S. Watson, G. Hopple. *United States Intelligence: An Encyclopedia.* New York: Garland Publishing, 1990.

Watt, Donald Cameron. *How War Came: The Immediate Origins of the Second World War.* New York: Pantheon Books, 1989.

Weatherford, Jack. *Indian Givers.* New York: Fawcett Columbine, 1988.

Wedel, Janine R. "The Harvard Boys Do Russia," *The Nation.* (June 1, 1998).

Weiner, T. *Blank Check*: The Pentagon's Black Budget. New York: Warners Books, 1990.

Weir Fred. "Brain Drain." *In These Times* (December 14, 1992).

———. "Interview: Fred Weir in Russia." *Covert Action Quarterly* (Summer 1993).

Weisman, Alan. "Columbia's Modern City." *In Context* 42 (1995).

———. "Nothing Wasted, Everything Gained." *Mother Jones* (March/April, 1998).

Weissman, Steve. *The Trojan Horse.* Rev. ed. Palo Alto: Ramparts Press, 1975.

Wessel, James, Mort Hartman. *Trading the Future.* San Francisco: Institute for Food and Policy Development, 1983.

West, Nigel. *Games of Intelligence.* New York: Crown Publishers, 1989.

Westerfield, H. B. editor. *Inside CIA's Private World: Declassified Articles from the Agency's Internal Journal 1955–1992.* New Haven, CT: Yale University Press, 1995.

Wiener, Don. "Will GATT Negotiators Trade Away the Future." *In These Times* (February 12–18, 1992).

Wild, Rolf H. *Management by Compulsion.* Boston: Houghton Mifflin Company, 1978.

Willan, P. *Puppetmasters: The Political Use of Terrorism in Italy.* London: Constable, 1991.

Williams, Eric. *From Columbus to Castro.* New York: Vintage Books, 1984.

Williams, William Applemam. *The Contours of American History.* New York: W.W. Norton, 1988.

———. *Empire as a Way of Life.* Oxford: Oxford University Press, 1972.

———. *The Tragedy of American Diplomacy.* New York: W. W. Norton, 1988.

Williamson, Samuel Jr. *The Politics of Grand Strategy.* London: Ashfield Press, 1969.

Willis, Henry Parker, B.H. Beckhart. *Foreign Banking Systems.* New York: Henry Holt, 1929.

Wilson, Edward O. *Life On Earth.* Stamford, CT: Sinauer Associates, 1973.

———. *Life: Cells, Organisms, Populations.* Sunderland, MA: Sinauer Associates, 1977.

———. *In Search of Nature.* Washington, DC: Island Press, 1996.

Wilson, Edward O., Charles J. Lumsden. *Genes, Mind, and Culture: The Coevolutionary Process.* Cambridge, MA: Harvard University Press, 1981.

———. *Promethean Fire: Reflections On the Origin of Mind.* Cambridge, MA: Harvard University Press, 1983.

Wilson, Edward O., Robert H. MacArthur. *The Theory of Island Biogeography.* Princeton, NJ: Princeton University Press, 1967.

Windishar, Anne. "Expert: 20% of Gifted Kids Drop Out." *Spokane Chronicle* (January 7, 1988).

Winks, Robin W. *Cloak & Gown: Scholars in the Secret War, 1939–1961.* New York: Quill, 1987.

Wise, David, Thomas B. Ross. *The Espionage Establishment.* New York: Bantam Books, 1978.

Wittner, Lawrence. *American Intervention in Greece.* New York: Columbia University Press, 1982.

Wolf, Eric R. *Europe and the People Without History.* Berkeley: University of California Press, 1982.

Wolf, Louis. "Inaccuracy in Media: Accuracy in Media Rewrites the News and History. *Covert Action Quarterly* 21 (Spring 1984).

Woodhouse, C.M. *The Rise and Fall of the Greek Colonels.* New York: Franklin Watts, 1985.

"Workers' State." Editorial in *The Nation* (September 19, 1988).

World Monitor. July 17, 1990.

World Resources. Report by the International Institute for Environment and Development and The World Resources Institute (1987).

Wu, Harry. "A Prisoner's Journey." *Newsweek* (September 23, 1991).

Wu Yi, "China-US Trade Balances: An Objective Evaluation." *Beijing Review* (June 10–16, 1996).

Wyden, P. *Bay Of Pigs: The Untold Story.* New York: Simon and Schuster, 1979.

Yallop, David A., *In God's Name.* New York: Bantam Books, 1984.

Yochelson, John. "China's Boom Creates a U.S. Trade Dilemma." *The Christian Science Monitor* (March 1, 1994).

Young, M. *The Vietnam Wars* 1945–1990. New York: HarperCollins, 1991.

Zeagler, Jean. *Switzerland Exposed.* New York: Allison & Busby, 1981.

Zinn, Howard. *A People's History of the United States.* New York: Harper Colophon Books, 1980.

———. *The Politics of History.* Chicago: University of Illinois Press, 1990.

———. *The Twentieth Century.* New York: Harper & Row, 1984.

Zuckerman, Mortimer B. "Where Have the Good Jobs Gone" *U.S. News & World Report* (July 31, 1995).

Index

Acheson, Dean, 65, 66, 151–52
Afghanistan, 103
Africa, 166, 167
Agricultural trade, 166–73
  Africa, 166, 167
  Angola, 166
  Bangladesh, 167
  beef industry, 170–71
  belief systems and, 43
  Brazil, 167
  China, 166–67
  Costa Rica, 167
  Cuba, 166
  Indonesia, 167
  inequality reversal, 172
  market economy and, 169–70
  Mexico, 172
  Mozambique, 166
  Nicaragua, 166
  North Korea, 166, 167
  North Vietnam, 167
  Pakistan, 167
  plantation system, 172–73
  South America, 166, 167
  stevia industry, 170
  sugar industry, 170
  United States, 166, 167–68, 169–70, 172
  world hunger and, 168–69, 173
Allende, Salvador, 100–1
American Revolution, 118, 123
Angola
  agriculture, 166
  CIA operations, 103–4

Arbenz, Jacobo, 99–100
Argentina
  labor value, 28
  loans, 176, 177, 180
Armaments
  disarmament, 218–21
  expenditure for, 237, 239, 240
    arms race, 73–74, 75–76, 89–90
Asian Monetary Fund (AMF), 46–47

Bangladesh, 167
Banking system, 303–14
  capital accumulation and, 311, 313–14
  constant money value, 308, 309–10
  cooperative capitalism and, 310–14
  credit, 311–13
  deflation, 308
  honest money, 308–10
  inflation, 308
  interest rates, 306, 307, 314
  labor value and, 314–15
  local rights, 305
  natural resources and, 306–7
  revolving reserve account, 305
  See also Loans; Money
Barter system
  evolution of, 292
  natural resources, 203–4
Bay of Pigs (Cuba), 135
Beef industry, 170–71
Belief systems
  Central Intelligence Agency (CIA)
    Angola, 103–4

Belief systems, Central Intelligence Agency *(continued)*
  Chile, 100–1
  corporate mercantilism, 128, 135–36
  death squads, 106–7
  economic freedom and, 94–95, 96, 97–98, 99–101,
      103–4, 108–9
  Guatemala, 99–100
  Indonesia, 98
  information control, 8–10, 12–14, 107–8
  Iran, 97–98
  leadership control, 107
  "Mighty Wurlitzer" campaign, 6–14
  Nicaragua, 102–3
conscientious intellectuals, 5–6, 96–97, 127
Federal Bureau of Investigation (FBI), 12–13
historically
  agricultural production, 43
  American Revolution, 118, 123
  Asian Monetary Fund (AMF), 46–47
  Bavarian Illuminati, 118–19
  Bolshevik Revolution, 120–21
  Cold War, 6–14
  Continental System (France), 41, 43, 45
  corporate control, 128–30
  enemy belief systems, 114–23
  equal trade, 45–46
  Fascism, 121–22, 133–34
  French Revolution, 118–19
  Germany, 45–46, 121–22, 133–34
  Grand Strategy, 45, 126, 131
  Great Britain, 41–46
  Holocaust, 119–20
  imperialism alliance, 46–47
  imperialism protection, 41–43, 46–48,
      125–27
  industrialization, 45–46
  Inquisitions, 114–18
  International Monetary Fund (IMF), 46
  Jewish persecution, 119–20, 122
  Knights Templar, 116–17
  Korean War, 68–70
  leadership for, 134–36
  Marshall Plan, 46, 47, 216–17
  McCarthyism, 7–8, 122, 130–32
  media libel, 127–28
  media propaganda, 79–80, 86,
      87–89, 96–98, 100, 105–6, 127, 132–33
  media suppression, 136–39
  mercantilism, 35, 41–43, 47–48, 125–26
  Middle Ages, 114–18

Belief systems, historically *(continued)*
  national interests, 36–37, 126
  Palmer Raids (U.S.), 120
  religious control, 80, 114–18, 119–20, 122
  secondary nation development, 48–49
  socialism, 133–34
  Spanish Inquisition, 115–16
  United States, 44–49
  See also Cooperative capitalism; World development
Bolshevik Revolution, 120–21
Bonner, Ray, 138
Bosnia, 78
Boston Tea Party, 44
Brazil
  agriculture, 167
  loans, 178
Bretton Woods agreement, 150–51
Brzezinski, Zbigniew, 103
Bush, George, 144
Butler, Smedley, 95–96

Canada, 153
Capital accumulation
  belief systems and, 29–30
  capital destruction by, 196–200
    cooperative capitalism and, 199–200
    currency and, 198
    foreign labor and, 196–97
    income distribution, 199
    industrial capital, 198
    Japan, 196, 199–200
    overproduction and, 196–97
    purchasing power and, 196–97, 198
    social capital, 198
    technological monopolization, 198–99
    United States, 196–97, 199
    wage rates and, 196
  debt trap, 30
  imperialist control, 23–24, 26, 28–29, 30–31
  labor ownership of, 23
  labor value and, 23–28
    Argentina, 28
    currency values, 24, 26–28, 30–31
    Germany, 24–25
    Indonesia, 27
    Mexico, 28
    Peru, 28
    Purchasing Power Parity (PPP), 27–28
    Russia, 24–25
    Southeast Asia, 27, 29

Capital accumulation, labor value and *(continued)*
  South Korea, 27
  sweatshop exploitation, 27
  technological monopolization, 24–25, 30–31
  unnecessary labor, 31
  wage differentials, 23–26, 28–29
  wage equality, 25–26, 28
  land monopolization and, 252–54
  multiplier factor, 182–87
    external trade, 182–87
    industry capital, 184–85
    internal trade, 187
    natural resources, 183–84, 186
    production values, 182–84
    property entitlement, 186
    scarcity creation, 185–86
    wage rates, 182, 186–87
  natural resources and, 24, 29, 30–31, 183–84, 186
  purchasing power and, 23, 27–28
Casey, William, 94–95, 108, 135
Ceku, Agim, 78
Central Intelligence Agency (CIA)
  Angola, 103–4
  Chile, 100–2, 107, 108
  corporate mercantilism and, 128, 135–36
  death squads, 106–7
  economic freedom and, 94–95, 96, 97–98, 99–101, 103–4, 108–9
  Guatemala, 99–100, 108
  Indonesia, 98
  information control, 8–10, 12–14, 107–8
  Iran, 97–98
  leadership control, 107
  "Mighty Wurlitzer" campaign, 6–14
  Nicaragua, 102–3
Chammoro, Violeta, 103
Chiang Kai-shek, 67
Chile
  CIA operations, 100–2, 107, 108
  loans, 177
China
  agriculture, 166–67
  British control of, 55–56
  democratic freedom, 63, 64
  economic threat of, 193–95, 202–5
  environmental quality, 209, 212
  world development and
    population control, 205, 209
    soil fertility, 212
    trade equality, 202–3, 204–5

Chlorofluorocarbons, 210–11
Chou En Lai, 107
Codex Alimentarius Commission, 152
Colbert, Jean Baptiste, 51
Communication systems. *See* Information monopolization;
    Media
Continental System (France), 41, 43, 45
Cooperative capitalism
  armament expenditure, 237, 239, 240
  banking system and, 310–14
  capital destruction and, 199–200
  Grand Strategies revealed, 345–49
    colonial imperialism, 345
    corporate imperialism, 345–47
    sustainable development, 16, 347–49
  industrial development, 238–39, 241–42
  political structure for, 216–17
  throwaway society, 237–38
  vs. corporate mercantilism, 155–56, 195
  vs. profitability, 240–41
  world sustainability rate, 240
  See also World development
Coordination Committee for Multilateral Export Controls, 76
Corporate mercantilism, 150–56
  belief systems, 128–30
  Bretton Woods agreement, 150–51
  Canada, 153
  capital monopolization, 151
  CIA operations and, 128, 135–36
  Codex Alimentarius Commission, 152
  Dunkel Plan, 152–53
  Fascism and, 151
  General Agreement on Tariffs and Trade (GATT), 151, 152–53
  International Monetary Fund (IMF), 151
  labor and, 152–53, 154–55
  legal structure for, 15–16, 151–55
  military enforcement, 151
  Multilateral Agreement on Investment (MAI), 151, 152
  North American Free Trade Agreement (NAFTA), 151, 152
  price control, 154
  tax havens, 154
  technology and, 150
  vs. cooperative capitalism, 155–56
  World Bank, 151
  World Trade Organization (WTO), 151, 152–53
Corporate welfare, 163–64
Costa Rica, 167

Credit system
    bank restructuring and, 311–13
    evolution of, 294–95
Cuba
    agriculture, 166
    Bay of Pigs (1961), 135
    economic freedom, 105–6
Currency. *See* Banking system; Money
Czechoslovakia, 63

Dayton Accords (1995), 78
Debt
    cancellation of, 180–81
    debt traps
        capital accumulation and, 30
        world trade organizations and, 143, 145–46,
            178–79
    vs. equity, 179
Democratic freedom
    arms race, 73–74, 75–76, 89–90
    Bosnia, 78
    capital containment, 64–65
    China, 63, 64
    Czechoslovakia, 63
    Dayton Accords (1995), 78
    Eastern Europe destabilization, 76–85
    enemy belief system, 68–70
    European Community (EC), 76–77
    France, 63, 64
    Germany, 63, 64
    Greece, 63
    Herzegovinia, 78
    Hungary, 63
    India, 63, 64
    International Monetary Fund (IMF),
        76–77
    Italy, 63, 64
    Japan, 63, 64
    Korean War, 66–70
    Kosovo, 78–80
    media propaganda, 79–80, 86, 87–89
    National Security Council
        Directive 54, 77
        Directive 68, 10–11, 65–66
        Directive 133, 77
    natural resource control, 64–66, 80–81, 82
    overproduction crisis, 65–66
    religious control, 80
    South Korea, 63
    Soviet Union

Democratic freedom, Soviet Union *(continued)*
        competence threat, 90
        containment of, 70–72
        corruption of, 82–85
        German relations, 71–72, 86–87
        industrialization errors, 75
        natural resources, 74–75
        war consequences, 72–73, 85–87
    Taiwan, 63
    threat of, 63–64
    war fabrication, 68
    Yugoslavia, 77–82
    See also World development
Dulles, Allen, 99–100, 135–36
Dulles, John Foster, 99–100, 135
Dunkel Plan, 152–53

El Salvador, 102, 108
English Enclosure Acts, 38
Environmental quality, 209–13
    carbon dioxide, 210
    China, 209, 212
    chlorofluorocarbons, 210–11
    global warming, 211
    industrialization, 210–12
    Iraq, 212
    oil reserves, 211, 228–29, 231–32
    photosynthesis, 211
    population control, 209–10, 233
    reforestation, 229–31
    soil fertility, 212–13, 230–31
    species extinction, 210
    taxation for, 211–12, 228–29
European Community (EC), 76–77

Fallows, James, 138
Famine, 168–69, 173
Fascism
    as belief system, 121–22, 133–34
    corporate mercantilism and, 151
    media propaganda and, 340
Federal Bureau of Investigation (FBI), 12–13
Federal Reserve System, 295, 297
    money creation, 299–303
France
    British defeat of, 51–52
    British dependency, 51
    Continental System, 41, 43, 45, 51–52
    democratic freedom, 63, 64
    Edict of Nantes, 51

France *(continued)*
    French Revolution, 118–19
    industrial independence, 51

General Agreement on Tariffs and Trade (GATT)
    corporate mercantilism, 151, 152–53
    structural adjustment rules, 143, 144, 145, 146, 148
    See also World trade organizations
Genocide, 55, 186
Genscher, Hans Dietrich, 77
George, Henry, 247
Germany
    belief systems, 45–46, 119–20, 121–22,
        133–34
    democratic freedom, 63, 64
    Fascism, 121–22, 133–34
    Holocaust, 119–20
    Jewish persecution, 119–20, 122
    labor value, 24–25, 158, 161
    war relations
        Great Britain, 57–60
        Japan, 60–61
        Soviet Union, 71–72, 86–87
        United States, 59–60, 61
    world trade organizations and, 143–44, 145
Global warming, 211
Goodman, George J. W., 280
Great Britain
    belief systems, 41–46
    China control, 55–56
    economic warfare, 38–39
    English Enclosure Acts, 38
    French defeat, 51–52
    genocide, 55
    German war relations, 57–60
    Holland and, 38
    India control, 53–55
    Japan control, 55
    Methuen Treaty, 38, 51
    Middle Ages, 38–39
    Navigation Acts, 38
    opium trade, 55–56
    Spain and, 38–39
    Staple Act, 38
    technological control, 38
    trade control, 38–39
Greece, 63
Greenspan, Alan, 46
Guatemala, 99–100, 108

Hanseatic League, 37
Harriman, Averell, 151–52
Herzegovinia, 78
Hess, Rudolf, 71
Heydrich, Reinhard, 88
Hidden History of the Korean War, The (Stone), 66–67
Historical context
    belief systems
        agricultural production, 43
        American Revolution, 118, 123
        Asian Monetary Fund (AMF), 46–47
        Bavarian Illuminati, 118–19
        Bolshevik Revolution, 120–21
        Continental System (France), 41, 43, 45
        corporate control, 128–30
        enemy belief systems, 114–23
        equal trade, 45–46
        Fascism, 121–22, 133–34
        French Revolution, 118–19
        Germany, 45–46, 119–20, 121–22, 133–34
        Grand Strategy, 45, 126, 131
        Great Britain, 41–46
        Holocaust, 119–20
        imperialism alliance, 46–47
        imperialism protection, 41–43, 46–48, 125–27
        industrialization, 45–46
        Inquisitions, 114–18
        International Monetary Fund (IMF), 46
        Jewish persecution, 119–20, 122
        Knights Templar, 116–17
        Korean War, 68–70
        leadership for, 134–36
        Marshall Plan, 46, 47, 216–17
        McCarthyism, 122, 130–32
        media libel, 127–28
        media propaganda, 79–80, 86, 87–89, 96–98, 100,
            105–6, 127, 132–33
        media suppression, 136–39
        mercantilism, 35, 41–43, 47–48, 125–26
        Middle Ages, 114–18
        national interests, 36–37, 126
        Palmer Raids (U.S.), 120
        religious control, 80, 114–18, 119–20, 122
        secondary nation development, 48–49
        socialism suppression, 133–34
        Spanish Inquisition, 115–6
        United States, 44–49
    China
        British control of, 55–56
        democratic freedom, 63, 64

Historical context *(continued)*
  democratic freedom
    arms race, 73–74, 75–76, 89–90
    Bosnia, 78
    capital containment, 64–65
    China, 63, 64
    Czechoslovakia, 63
    Dayton Accords (1995), 78
    Eastern Europe destabilization, 76–85
    enemy belief system, 68–70
    European Community (EC), 76–77
    France, 63, 64
    Germany, 63, 64
    Greece, 63
    Herzegovinia, 78
    Hungary, 63
    India, 63, 64
    International Monetary Fund (IMF),
        76–77
    Italy, 63, 64
    Japan, 63, 64
    Korean War, 66–70
    Kosovo, 78–80
    media propaganda, 79–80, 86, 87–89
    National Security Council Directive 10-11, 54,
        65–66, 68, 77, 133
    natural resource control, 64–66, 80–81, 82
    overproduction crisis, 65–66
    religious control, 80
    South Korea, 63
    Taiwan, 63
    threat of, 63–64
    USSR competence threat, 90
    USSR containment, 70–72
    USSR corruption, 82–85
    USSR/German relations, 71–72, 86–87
    USSR industrialization errors, 75
    USSR natural resources, 74–75
    USSR war consequences, 72–73, 85–87
    war fabrication, 68
    Yugoslavia, 77–82
  France
    British defeat of, 51–52
    British dependency, 51
    Continental System, 41, 43, 45, 51–52
    democratic freedom, 63, 64
    Edict of Nantes, 51
    French Revolution, 118–19
    industrial independence, 51
  Germany

Historical context, Germany *(continued)*
    belief systems, 45–46, 119–20, 121–22, 133–34
    British war relations, 57–60
    democratic freedom, 63, 64
    Fascism, 121–22, 133–34
    Holocaust, 119–20
    Japanese war relations, 60–61
    Jewish persecution, 119–20, 122
    U.S. war relations, 59–60, 61
    USSR war relations, 71–72, 86–87
    war relations, 57–61, 71–72
  Great Britain
    belief systems, 41–46
    China control, 55–56
    economic warfare, 38–39
    English Enclosure Acts, 38
    French defeat, 51–52
    genocide, 55
    German war relations, 57–60
    Holland and, 38
    India control, 53–55
    Japan control, 55
    Methuen Treaty, 38, 51
    Middle Ages, 38–39
    Navigation Acts, 38
    opium trade, 55–56
    Spain and, 38–39
    Staple Act, 38
    technological control, 38
    trade control, 38–39
  India
    British control of, 53–55
    democratic freedom, 63, 64
  Japan
    British control of, 55
    democratic freedom, 63, 64
    German war relations, 60–61
  Middle Ages, 33–39, 114–18
    current monopolization and, 33, 34–35, 36–37
    economic community, 36–37
    economic warfare, 33–35
    enemy belief system, 114–18
    Great Britain, 38–39
    Hanseatic League, 37
    Holland, 37–38
    Inquisitions, 114–18
    mercantilism, 35
    monopolization and, 33, 34
    national interests, 36–37
    natural resources, 34–35

Historical context, Middle Ages *(continued)*
    production tools, 34, 35
    property rights, 34
    trade control, 35
    water routes, 37–38
  natural resources
    democratic freedom and, 64–66, 80–81, 82
    Middle Ages, 34–35
    Soviet Union, 74–75
    U.S. economic suppression and, 95–96, 97, 98, 99,
      101–2, 104–5
  Soviet Union
    arms race, 73–74, 75–76, 89–90
    Bolshevik Revolution, 120–21
    competence threat, 90
    containment of, 70–72
    corruption in, 82–85
    German war relations, 71–72, 86–87
    industrialization errors, 75
    market economy, 85
    media propaganda, 86, 87–89
    natural resources, 74–75
    WW II consequences, 72–73
  United States
    American Revolution, 118, 123
    belief systems, 44–49
    Boston Tea Party, 44
    Eastern Europe destabilization, 77–78
    enemy belief system, 68–70
    German war relations, 59–60, 61
    Grand Strategy, 45, 126, 131
    imperialism alliance, 46–47
    industrialization, 45–46
    Korean War, 66–70
    Marshall Plan, 46, 47, 216–17
    McCarthyism, 122, 130–32
    National Security Council Directive, 10–11, 54,
      65–66, 68, 77, 133
    Palmer Raids, 120
    post-war imperialism, 61
    USSR arms race, 73–74, 75–76, 89–90
    USSR war relations, 72–73, 85–86
    war fabrication, 68
    War of 1812, 44–45
  U.S. economic suppression
    Afghanistan, 103
    Angola, 103–4
    Chile, 100–2, 107, 108
    CIA operations, 94–95, 96, 97, 98, 99–101, 102,
      103–4, 106–9, 128, 135–36

Historical context, U.S. economic suppression *(continued)*
    Cuba, 105–6
    death squads, 106–7
    El Salvador, 102, 108
    Guatemala, 99–100, 108
    Indonesia, 98
    Iran, 97–98
    leadership control, 107
    Libya, 104–5
    media propaganda, 96–98, 100, 105–6
    Mexican-American War (1848), 95
    Mozambique, 104
    natural resource control, 95–96, 97, 98, 99, 101–2,
      104–5
    Nicaragua, 102–3
    Nigeria, 98
    Philippines, 95
    record erasure, 107–8
    strategy for, 96
    Vietnam, 99
    Zaire, 104
    See also War
Ho Chi Minh, 99
Holland, 37–38
Holocaust, 119–20
Hungary, 63

Illuminati (Bavaria), 118–19
Income distribution
  capital destruction and, 199
  world trade organizations and, 144, 145
India
  British control of, 53–55
  democratic freedom, 63, 64
Indonesia
  agriculture, 167
  CIA operations, 98
  labor value, 27
Inflation, 176, 308
Information monopolization
  communications integration, 318–19
  retail industry effects, 319–24
    distribution, 322–24
    major purchases, 320–21
    minor purchases, 321–22
    recreational shopping, 322
  television industry
    cultural promotion, 333–34
    educational promotion, 232–33, 316, 327–33
    foreign cultures, 334

Information monopolization, television industry *(continued)*
    home stations, 335–37
    innovation promotion, 324–26
    investment opportunities, 326–27
    local events, 334
    minorities, 333–34
    public expenditure for, 317–18, 324
    recreational shows, 326
    satellite development, 317–18
    socialization promotion, 332
    value capitalization, 316–17
  See also Media
Inquisitions, 114–18
Interest rates
  banking, 306, 307, 314
  mortgage, 258–59
International Monetary Fund (IMF), 46, 76–77
  corporate mercantilism, 151
  structural adjustment rules, 143, 144, 145, 146, 148
  See also World trade organizations
Inventions, 272–75
  automobiles, 276–77
  communications, 276
  patents, 272, 273–74, 275, 276, 277, 285, 286
  pharmaceuticals, 277–78
  public domain, 287
  royalties, 273, 275, 277, 287
  value capitalization, 273–75
Iran, 97–98
Iraq, 97–98
  environmental quality, 212
Italy, 63, 64

Japan
  British control of, 55
  capital destruction and, 196, 199–200
  democratic freedom, 63, 64
  economic warfare, 189–92
    belief systems, 191–92
    debt/equity position, 190–91
    German relations, 189
    imperialist alliance, 191
    industry, 189–90, 191
    mercantilism, 190, 191–92
    U.S. relations, 189, 190–91
  German war relations, 60–61
  world trade organizations and, 143–44
Jewish persecution, 119–20, 122
Kennedy, John F., 135–36
Kissinger, Henry, 103

Kistiakowsky, George, 73
Knights Templar, 116–17
Korean War, 68–70
Kosovo, 78–80
Labor impoverishment, 158–64
  Asia, 159, 160, 161
  corporate mercantilism, 152–53, 154–55
  corporate welfare, 163–64
  financial imperialism, 161–63
  foreign labor, 158, 159
  Germany, 158, 161
  Mexico, 159–60
  North American Free Trade Agreement (NAFTA), 159–60
  purchasing power, 158
  Sweden, 161
  technology and, 158
  wage rates, 158–61
Labor value
  capital accumulation and, 23–28
    Argentina, 28
    currency values, 24, 26–28, 30–31
    Germany, 24–25
    Indonesia, 27
    Mexico, 28
    Peru, 28
    Purchasing Power Parity (PPP), 27–28
    Russia, 24–25
    Southeast Asia, 27, 29
    South Korea, 27
    sweatshop exploitation, 27
    technological monopolization, 24–25, 30–31
    unnecessary labor, 31
    wage differentials, 23–26, 28–29
    wage equality, 25–26, 28
  money and, 24, 26–28, 30–31, 294
    bank restructuring, 314–15
    contract labor, 295–97
    productive labor, 295–96
    unproductive labor, 296–97
  See also Wage rates
Land monopolization
  capital accumulation and, 252–54
  collective ownership, 254–55
  evolution of, 249–54
    Great Britain, 250, 252–53
    Middle Ages, 250, 252
    slave labor, 253
    United States, 247, 251–52, 253
  landrent taxation
    commercial land, 255–56

Land monopolization, land rent taxation *(continued)*
  economic restructuring with, 261–64
  efficiency of, 260–61
  evasion of, 260–61
  farm land, 256–57
  home sites, 257–58
  mortgage interest and, 258–59
  societal collection of, 254–55, 259–60, 261–64
  taxation elimination and, 259–60
 land rights, 248–49, 250–51
 private ownership, 249
 social wealth and, 247–49
 water rights, 249
Libel law, 127–28
Libya, 104–5
List, Friedrich, 14–15, 42–43, 45–46, 47, 183–84
Loans, 175–81
 Argentina, 176, 177, 180
 Brazil, 178
 Chile, 177
 debt cancellation, 180–81
 debt traps, 30, 143, 145–46, 178–79
 debt vs. equity, 179
 developed nation subsidization, 176–78
 foreign aid, 177
 foreign currency value, 176
 inflationary policy, 176
 Mexico, 176, 177
 natural resources and, 178
 oil industry, 175–76
 peonage, 179–80
 Peru, 177
 property values, 179
 responsible lending, 175–76, 178, 180
 United States, 180
 wage rates and, 177–78
 world trade organizations and, 143, 144, 145–46, 178
Lumumba, Patrice, 104

MacArthur, Douglas, 67
Marshall, George, 151–52
Marshall Plan, 46, 47, 216–17
McCarthyism, 7–8, 122, 130–32
McCloy, John J., 100
Media
 libel law, 127–28
 propaganda by, 127, 132–33, 339
  Cuba, 105–6
  economic freedom and, 96–98, 100
  Fascism, 340

Media, propaganda by, *(continued)*
  Korean War, 340
  Soviet Union, 86, 87–89
  Spanish Civil War, 340
  World War I, 339–40
  Yugoslavia, 79–80
 restructuring of, 340–44
  belief systems, 343–44
  one-liners for, 341–42
  Third World education, 342–43
 suppression of, 136–39
 See also Information monopolization
Mercantilism, 35, 41–43, 47–48, 125–26
Methuen Treaty (Great Britain), 38, 51
Mexican-American War (1848), 95
Mexico
 agriculture, 172
 labor value, 28
 loans, 176, 177
 NAFTA, 159–60
Middle Ages, 33–39, 114–18
 current monopolization and, 33, 34–35, 36–37
 economic community, 36–37
 economic warfare, 33–35
 enemy belief system, 114–18
 Great Britain, 38–39
 Hanseatic League, 37
 Holland, 37–38
 Inquisitions, 114–18
 mercantilism, 35
 monopolization and, 33, 34
 national interests, 36–37
 natural resources, 34–35
 production tools, 34, 35
 property rights, 34
 trade control, 35
 water routes, 37–38
Military. *See* Armaments; War
Mobutu, Joseph, 104
Molluca Islands, 185
Money
 bank restructuring, 303–14
  capital accumulation, 311, 313–14
  constant value, 308, 309–10
  cooperative capitalism, 310–14
  credit, 311–13
  deflation, 308
  honest money, 308–10
  inflation, 308
  interest rates, 306, 307, 314

money, bank restructuring and *(continued)*
 labor value, 314–15
 local rights, 305
 natural resources and, 306–7
 revolving reserve account, 305
 capital and
  accumulation of, 311, 313–14
  destruction of, 198
 creation of
  bank-created, 298–99, 301
  circulation-created, 299–300, 302
  Federal Reserve System, 299–303
  open market system, 300–303
  primary-created, 299–302, 304
 credit system
  bank restructuring and, 311–13
  evolution of, 294–95
 defined, 295
 evolution of
  barter system, 292
  checkbook money, 293–94
  credit system, 294–95
  paper money, 293, 294
  precious metal, 292–93, 294
  representational value, 293
  trust and, 294–95
 Federal Reserve System, 295, 297
  money creation, 299–303
 foreign loans and, 176
 labor value and, 24, 26–28, 30–31, 294
  bank restructuring, 314–15
  contract labor, 295–97
  productive, 295–96
  unproductive, 296–97
 monopolization of, 294, 295, 297–98, 307, 312
 trade equality and, 224–25, 309–10
 wealth and, 297–98
 See also Loans
Monsanto, 128
Mossadeq, Mohammad, 97
Mozambique, 104
 agriculture, 166
Multilateral Agreement on Investment (MAI)
 corporate mercantilism, 151, 152
 structural adjustment rules, 143, 144, 146, 148
 See also World trade organizations
Murphy, R. Taggart, 189, 191, 192

Napoleon, 41, 42–43, 45, 51–52, 119
National interest, 3–5, 36–37, 126

National Security Council Directive, 10–11, 54, 65–66, 68, 77, 133
National System of Political Economy, The (List), 15, 42, 45
National Union for Total Independence of Angola (UNITA), 103
Natural resources
 capital accumulation and, 24, 29, 30–31, 183–84, 186
 democratic freedom and, 64–66, 80–81, 82
 loans and, 178
 Middle Ages, 34–35
 Soviet Union, 74–75
 trade equality and, 224, 226, 227–28
 U.S. economic suppression and, 95–96, 97, 98, 99, 101–2, 104–5
 world trade organizations and, 145–48
Navigation Acts (Great Britain), 38
Nicaragua
 agriculture, 166
 CIA operations, 102–3
Nigeria, 98
North American Free Trade Agreement (NAFTA)
 corporate mercantilism, 151, 152
 labor impoverishment, 159–60
 structural adjustment rules, 143, 144, 145, 146, 148
 See also World trade organizations
North Korea
 agriculture, 166, 167
 Korean War, 66–70
North Vietnam, 167

Oil industry
 imperialism and, 175–76, 184–85
 trade equality, 211, 228–29, 231–32
Opium trade, 55–56
Origin of the Modern World System, The (Wallerstein), 34
Overproduction, 65–66, 196–97

Pakistan, 167
Palmer Raids (U.S.), 120
Parry, Robert, 138
Patent rights
 inventions, 272, 273–74, 275, 276, 277, 285, 286
 public domain, 287
 restructuring of, 267, 285–87
 royalties, 273, 275, 277, 287
 trade equality and, 234
Peru
 labor value, 28
 loans, 177
Philippines, 95

Popular Movement for the Liberation of Angola (MPLA), 103–4
Population control
    China, 205, 209
    environmental quality and, 209–10, 233
    India, 209
Price control, 154
Progress and Poverty (George), 247
Property
    capital accumulation and, 186
    loans and, 179
    Middle Ages, 34
    See also Land monopolization
Protocols of the Learned Elders of Zion, The, 119
Prouty, L. Fletcher, 108–9
Purchasing power
    capital accumulation and, 196–97, 198
    labor impoverishment and, 158
    world trade organizations and, 158
Purchasing Power Parity (PPP), 27–28

Reagan, Ronald, 144
Reforestation, 229–31
Religious control, 80, 114–18, 119–20, 122
Rhee, Syngman, 63, 67
Ricardo, David, 254
Rubin, Robert, 46
Russia. *See* Soviet Union

Sachs, Jeffrey, 83
Savimbi, Jonas, 104
Smith, Adam, 14–15
    capital accumulation, 23
    labor value, 267–68
    mercantilism, 35, 41–43, 47–48
Smith, Walter Bedell, 99–100, 135
Socialism, 133–34
Soil fertility, 212–13, 230–31
South America, 166, 167
    See also specific countries
Southeast Asia
    economic threat of, 193–95
    labor value, 27, 29
    See also specific countries
South Korea, 63
    Korean War, 68–70
    labor value, 27
Soviet Union
    arms race, 73–74, 75–76, 89–90
    Bolshevik Revolution, 120–21

Soviet Union *(continued)*
    competence threat, 90
    containment of, 70–72
    corruption in, 82–85
    German war relations, 71–72, 86–87
    industrialization errors, 75
    labor value, 24–25
    market economy, 85
    media propaganda, 86, 87–89
    natural resources, 74–75
    World War II consequences, 72–73
Spain, 38–39
Spanish Inquisition, 115–6
Species extinction, 210
Staple Act (Great Britain), 38
Stevia, 170
Stock markets
    bubbles/crashes, 281–83
    options/futures, 283–85
    Tobin Tax, 267, 285
    value capitalization, 267, 278–81
Stockwell, John, 103, 107
Stone, I. F., 66–67
Subsidization, 144
Sugar industry, 170
Summers, Larry, 46
Supermoney (Goodman), 280
Sweatshop exploitation, 27
Sweden, 161

Taiwan, 63
Taxation
    corporate tax havens, 154
    for environmental quality, 211–12, 228–29
    landrent
        commercial land, 255–56
        economic restructuring with, 261–64
        efficiency of, 260–61
        evasion of, 260–61
        farm land, 256–57
        home sites, 257–58
        mortgage interest and, 258–59
        societal collection of, 254–55, 259–60, 261–64
        taxation elimination and, 259–60
    stock markets, 267, 285
    trade equality and, 226–27
Technological monopolization
    capital destruction, 198–99
    competition, 287–88
    corporate mercantilism, 150

Technological monopolization *(continued)*
    fictitious capital, 269
    Great Britain, 38
    infrastructure
        private capital and, 269
        social capital and, 270–71
    inventions, 272–75
        automobiles, 276–77
        communications, 276
        patents and, 272, 273–74, 275, 276, 277, 285,
            286
        pharmaceuticals, 277–78
        public domain and, 287
        royalties and, 273, 275, 277, 287
        value capitalization and, 273–75
    labor and
        capital ownership, 267–69
        impoverishment of, 158
        value of, 24–25, 30–31, 158, 267–68, 278
    patent rights
        inventions, 272, 273–74, 275, 276, 277, 285, 286
        public domain, 287
        restructuring of, 267, 285–87
        royalties, 273, 275, 277, 287
        trade equality and, 234
    power and, 275–78
    private capital and, 269
    social capital and, 269–71
        electric power, 269
        infrastructure, 270–71
        railroads, 269–70
    Soviet Union, 271
    standardization and, 287–89
    stock markets
        bubbles/crashes, 281–83
        options/futures, 283–85
        Tobin Tax, 267, 285
        value capitalization, 267, 278–81
    value capitalization and
        inventions, 273–75
        stock markets, 267, 278–79
Television industry. *See* Information monopolization
Tobin Tax, 267, 285
Truman, Harry, 66

United Fruit Company, 99–100, 135
United States
    agriculture, 166, 167–68, 169–70, 172
    capital destruction and, 196–97, 199

United States *(continued)*
    economic suppression
        Afghanistan, 103
        Angola, 103–4
        Chile, 100–2, 107, 108
        Cuba, 105–6
        death squads, 106–7
        El Salvador, 102, 108
        Guatemala, 99–100, 108
        Indonesia, 98
        Iran, 97–98
        leadership control, 107
        Libya, 104–5
        media propaganda, 96–98, 100,
            105–6
        Mexican-American War (1848), 95
        Mozambique, 104
        natural resource control, 95–96, 97, 98, 99,
            101–2, 104–5
        Nicaragua, 102–3
        Nigeria, 98
        Philippines, 95
        record erasure, 107–8
        strategy for, 96
        Vietnam, 99
        Zaire, 104
    historically
        American Revolution, 118, 123
        Boston Tea Party, 44
        enemy belief system, 68–70
        German war relations, 59–60, 61
        Grand Strategy, 45, 126, 131
        imperialism alliance, 46–47
        industrialization, 45–46
        Korean War, 66–70
        Marshall Plan, 46, 47, 216–17
        McCarthyism, 122, 130–32
        National Security Council Directive, 10–11, 54,
            65–66, 68, 77, 133
        Palmer Raids, 120
        post-war imperialism, 61
        USSR arms race, 73–74, 75–76, 89–90
        USSR war relations, 72–73, 85–86
        war fabrication, 68
        War of 1812, 44–45
    Japan relations, 189, 190–91
    land monopolization, 247, 251–52, 253
    loans, 180
    See also Central Intelligence Agency (CIA)

Vietnam, 99, 167

Wage rates
    capital and
        accumulation of, 182, 186–87
        destruction of, 196, 199
    income distribution
        capital destruction and, 199
        world trade organizations and, 144, 145
    labor and
        impoverishment of, 158–61
        value of, 3, 23–26, 28–29
    loans and, 177–78
    trade equality and, 225–26
Wallerstein, Immanuel, 34
War
    economic warfare
        Great Britain, 38–39
        Japan, 189–92
        Middle Ages, 33–35
    Germany
        Great Britain and, 57–60
        Japan and, 60–61
        Soviet Union and, 71–72, 86–87
        United States and, 59–60, 61
    Great Britain
        economic warfare, 38–39
        France and, 51–52
        Germany and, 57–60
    Iran-Iraq War, 97–98
    Korean War, 68–70
    Mexican-American War, 95
    Soviet Union
        arms race, 73–74, 75–76, 89–90
        Germany and, 71–72, 86–87
        WW II consequences, 72–73
    Spanish Civil War, 340
    United States
        Germany and, 59–60, 61
        Iran-Iraq War, 97–98
        Korean War, 66–70
        Mexican-American War, 95
        post-war imperialism, 61
        USSR arms race, 73–74, 75–76,
            89–90
        USSR war relations, 72–73, 85–86
        war fabrication, 68
        War of 1812, 44–45
    world wars, 57–61

Wealth of Nations, The (Smith), 15, 35, 41, 43,
    267–68
Webb, Gary, 138
Weight of the Yen, The (Murphy), 189, 191, 192
World Bank
    corporate mercantilism, 151
    progressive philosophy of, 16–17
    structural adjustment rules, 143, 144, 145, 146, 148
    See also World trade organizations
World development
    China
        population control, 205, 209
        soil fertility, 212
        trade equality, 202–3, 204–5
    cooperative capitalism
        armament expenditure, 237, 239, 240
        banking system and, 310–14
        capital destruction and, 199–200
        Grand Strategies revealed, 345–49
        industrial development, 238–39, 241–42
        political structure for, 216–17
        throwaway society, 237–38
        vs. corporate mercantilism, 155–56, 195
        vs. profitability, 240–41
        world sustainability rate, 240
    environmental quality, 209–13
        carbon dioxide, 210
        China, 209, 212
        chlorofluorocarbons, 210–11
        global warming, 211
        industrialization, 210–12
        Iraq, 212
        oil reserves, 211, 228–29, 231–32
        photosynthesis, 211
        population control, 209–10, 233
        reforestation, 229–31
        soil fertility, 212–13, 230–31
        species extinction, 210
        taxation for, 211–12, 228–29
    political structure, 215–22
        Asia, 216
        Central America, 215, 216
        cooperative capitalism, 216–17
        disarmament, 218–21
        ethnic conflicts, 221–22
        human rights, 217–18
        Middle East, 215
        regional integration, 215–16
        world security, 218

World development *(continued)*
  population control
    China, 205, 209
    environmental quality and, 209–10, 233
    India, 209
  resource barter, 203–4
  trade equality, 223–35
    China, 202–3, 204–5
    communication systems, 232–33
    corporate regulations, 224
    environmental quality, 229–31
    equalized management of, 228–29
    industry development, 235
    interregional, 224
    leisure time, 232
    mineral resources, 227–28
    natural resource control, 224, 226, 227–28
    oil reserves, 228–29, 231–32
    patent rights, 234
    population control, 233
    product durability, 233
    regional currency, 224–25
    regional self-sufficiency, 223–24
    tariffs, 226–27
    wage rates, 225–26
World trade organizations
  corporate mercantilism, 150–56
    Bretton Woods agreement, 150–51
    Canada, 153
    capital monopolization, 151
    Codex Alimentarius Commission, 152
    Dunkel Plan, 152–53
    Fascism and, 151
    labor and, 152–53, 154–55
    legal structure for, 15–16, 151–55
    military enforcement, 151
    price control, 154
    tax havens, 154
    technology and, 150
    vs. cooperative capitalism, 155–56
  General Agreement on Tariffs and Trade (GATT)
    corporate mercantilism, 151, 152–53
    structural adjustment rules, 143, 144, 145, 146, 148
  International Monetary Fund (IMF), 46, 76–77
    corporate mercantilism, 151

World trade organizations, IMF *(continued)*
    structural adjustment rules, 143, 144, 145, 146, 148
    labor impoverishment, 158–64
      Asia, 159, 160, 161
      corporate welfare, 163–64
      financial imperialism, 161–63
      foreign labor, 158, 159
      Germany, 158, 161
      Mexico, 159–60
      purchasing power, 158
      Sweden, 161
      technology and, 158
      wage rates, 158–61
    loans, 143, 144, 145–46, 178
  Multilateral Agreement on Investment (MAI)
    corporate mercantilism, 151, 152
    structural adjustment rules, 143, 144, 146, 148
  North American Free Trade Agreement (NAFTA)
    corporate mercantilism, 151, 152
    labor impoverishment, 159–60
    structural adjustment rules, 143, 144, 145, 146, 148
  structural adjustment rules, 143–48
    debt traps, 143, 145–46
    developed vs. undeveloped nations, 148
    developing world effects, 143–45
    enforced dependency, 145
    Germany, 143–44, 145
    income distribution, 144, 145
    Japan, 143–44
    loans, 144, 145–46
    local consumption production, 145–48
    mercantilism, 145
    natural resource control, 145–48
    Republican administrations, 144
    subsidization, 144
  World Bank
    corporate mercantilism, 151
    progressive philosophy of, 16–17
    structural adjustment rules, 143, 144, 145, 146, 148
  World Trade Organization (WTO)
    corporate mercantilism, 151, 152–53
    structural adjustment rules, 143, 144, 145

Yugoslavia, 77–82

Zaire, 104

About the Author

J.W. Smith earned his PhD in environmental and political economics from the Union Institute in Cincinnati, Ohio. He is the author of *The World's Wasted Wealth: The Political Economy of Waste* and *The World's Wasted Wealth 2: Save our Wealth, Save our Environment.* Dr. Smith is the founder of the Institute for Economic Democracy, a nonprofit, educational foundation devoted to research on sustainable development. The Institute's website may be found at: http://www.slonet.org/~ied/, and Dr. Smith may be reached directly by e-mail at: jwsmith@slonet org.

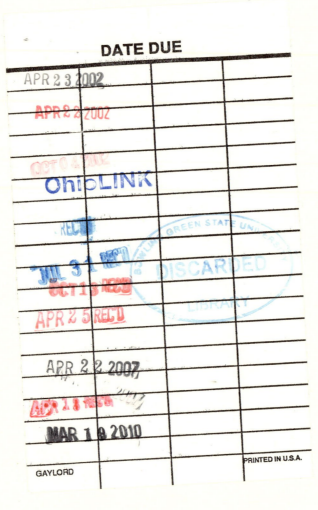